THE PSYCH SOLUTION

Every 4LTR Press solution includes:

Visually Engaging Textbook + **Online Study Tools** + **Tear-out Review Cards** + **Interactive eBook**

Heading Numbers Connect Print & eBook

STUDENT RESOURCES:
- Interactive eBook
- Auto-Graded Quizzes
- Flashcards
- Interactive Practice
- Games
- Videos
- Review Cards

INSTRUCTOR RESOURCES:
- All Student Resources
- Engagement Tracker
- First Day of Class Instructions
- LMS Integration
- Instructor's Manual
- Test Bank
- PowerPoint® Slides
- Instructor Prep Cards

Students sign in at **www.cengagebrain.com**

Instructors sign in at **www.cengage.com/login**

"The prose in **PSYCH** is cleverly and enticingly written, which makes a three chapter assignment more enjoyable. Additionally, the tear-out cards at the end of each book are great study guides." — **Diego**, Student, *Santa Ana College*

JULY 2010
4LTR Press adds eBooks in response to a 10% uptick in digital learning preferences.

Engagement Tracker launches, giving faculty a window into student usage of digital tools.

AUGUST 2010
1 out of every 3 (1,400) schools has adopted a 4LTR Press solution.

NOVEMBER 2010
750,000 students are IN.

Third party research confirms that 4LTR Press digital solutions improve retention and outcomes.

CourseMate
Students access the 4LTR Press website at 4x's the industry average.

IN 2011
60 unique solutions across multiple course areas validates the 4LTR Press concept.

IN 2011
2,000

APRIL 2011
1 out of every 2 (2,000) schools has a 4LTR Press adoption.

AUGUST 2011
Over 1 million students are IN.

2012 AND BEYOND
We're always evolving. Join the 4LTR Press In-Crowd on Facebook at www.facebook.com/4ltrpress

WADSWORTH
CENGAGE Learning·

PSYCH, **Third Edition**
Spencer A. Rathus

Editor in Chief: Linda Ganster

Publisher: Jon-David Hague

Senior Acquisitions Editor: Jaime Perkins

Developmental Editors: Linda Stewart and Shannon LeMay-Finn

Assistant Editor: Jessica Alderman

Editorial Assistant: T. Christian Holland

Media Editor: Mary Noel

Marketing Manager: Jessica Egbert

Executive Marketing Communications Manager: Talia Wise

Product Development Manager, 4LTR Press: Steven E. Joos

Senior Content Project Manager: Michelle Clark

Art Director: Pamela Galbreath

Manufacturing Planner: Karen Hunt

Image and Text Rights Acquisitions Specialist: Don Schlotman

Production Service/Project Manager: Graphic World Inc./Cassie Carey

Photo Researcher: Bill Smith Group

Text Researcher: Bill Smith Group

Interior Designer: Trish Knapke

Cover Designer: Trish Knapke

Cover Image: Masterfile Royalty Free

Compositor: Graphic World Inc.

For product information and technology assistance, contact us at **Cengage Learning Customer & Sales Support, 1-800-354-9706.**

For permission to use material from this text or product, submit all requests online at **www.cengage.com/permissions.**

Further permissions questions can be e-mailed to **permissionrequest@cengage.com.**

Library of Congress Control Number: 2012942035

Student Edition:

ISBN-13: 978-1-133-96080-5

ISBN-10: 1-133-96080-4

Wadsworth
20 Davis Drive
Belmont, CA 94002-3098
USA

Cengage Learning is a leading provider of customized learning solutions with office locations around the globe, including Singapore, the United Kingdom, Australia, Mexico, Brazil, and Japan. Locate your local office at **www.cengage.com/global.**

Cengage Learning products are represented in Canada by Nelson Education, Ltd.

To learn more about Wadsworth, visit **www.cengage.com/Wadsworth**

Purchase any of our products at your local college store or at our preferred online store **www.CengageBrain.com.**

Ad images:
Inside front cover
© iStockphoto.com/sdominick
© iStockphoto.com/A-Digit
© iStockphoto.com/alexsl

Page i
© iStockphoto.com/CostinT
© iStockphoto.com/photovideostock
© iStockphoto.com/Leontura

Inside back cover
© Cengage Learning

Printed in the United States of America
3 4 5 6 7 16 15 14 13

PSYCH BRIEF CONTENTS

PSYCH

CONTENTS

Image Source Photography/Veer

© Bruce Coleman Inc./Alamy

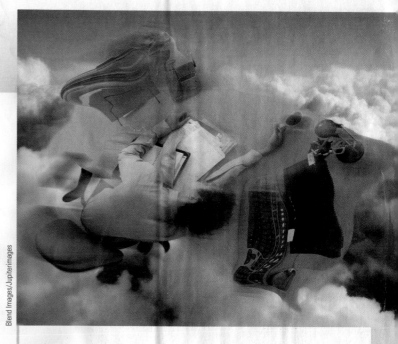

Blend Images/Jupiterimages

Rubberball/Mike Kemp/
Jupiterimages

© Ocean/Corbis

© Michael Newman/Photo Edit

Susan Kuklin/Photo Researchers, Inc.

©C Squared Studio/Getty Images

Oliver Rossi/Photographer's Choice RF/Getty Images

Workbook Stock/Jupiterimages/Getty Images

12 PSYCHOLOGICAL DISORDERS 284

13 METHODS OF THERAPY 308

14 SOCIAL PSYCHOLOGY 330

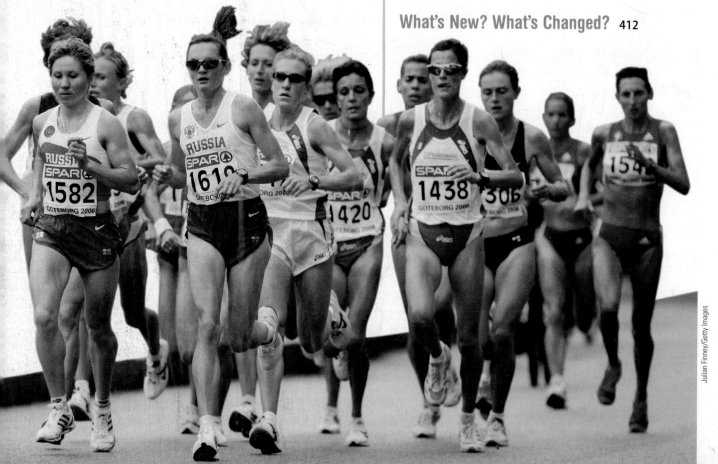

Julian Finney/Getty Images

THE

CROWD

IN-

Share your 4LTR Press story on Facebook at
www.facebook.com/4ltrpress for a chance to win.

To learn more about the In-Crowd opportunity 'like' us on Facebook.

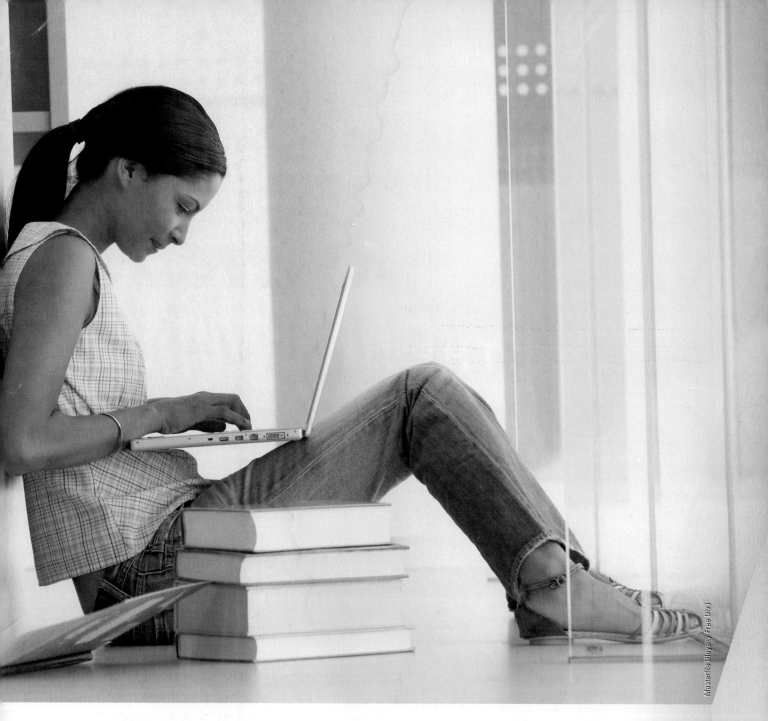

Masterfile (Royalty-Free Div.)

LEARNING OUTCOMES

1-1 Define psychology

1-2 Describe the various fields of psychology

1-3 Describe the origins of psychology and identify people who made significant contributions to the field

1-4 Identify the theoretical perspectives from which today's psychologists view behavior and mental processes

1-5 Explain how psychologists study behavior and mental processes, focusing on critical thinking, research methods, and ethical considerations

 STUDY TOOLS

After you read the chapter, go to the Study Tools at the end of the chapter, page 23.

CHAPTER 1

What Is PSYCHOLOGY?

My favorite place: The checkout counter of the supermarket. After being buffeted about by the crowds in the aisles and trying to convince myself that I really will survive until the people in line ahead of me are checked out, I am rewarded by the display of all the supermarket tabloids. The headlines cry out. Each week, there are 10 new sightings of Elvis and 10 new encounters with extraterrestrials. There are 10 new "absolutely proven effective" ways to take off weight and 10 new ways to conquer stress and depression. There are 10 new ways to tell if your partner has been cheating and, of course, 10 new predictions by astrologers and psychics.

Extraterrestrials regularly kidnap us Earthlings. Although they possess the technology to leap between the stars, the aliens must apparently prod and poke us to figure out how we work. Although we update our iPhones with the latest apps and music, and download the latest ringtones, tabloid drawings suggest that the aliens have been flying the same-model flying saucer for decades. Their sense of style is nothing to text home about.

Although we can find some humor in tales of abduction by aliens, psychologists and other scientists are interested in the questions these tales raise about human nature and the distinction between sensationalism and science. What do we know about people who claim to have been abducted by aliens? How can we sort truth from fiction and decide whether we will believe the "kidnap victims"?

Psychologists who have studied reported alien kidnappings conclude that the kidnappings never occurred. However, the people making the claims are not necessarily mentally ill, nor are they even lying (Clancy et al., 2002). By and large, these are people who have "remembered" their "experiences" while undergoing therapy, often under hypnosis. Tales of alien abduction are widely known throughout our culture, so it is not at all surprising that the "memories" of these "kidnap" victims would tend to coincide (Meyersburg et al., 2009; Swami et al., 2009).

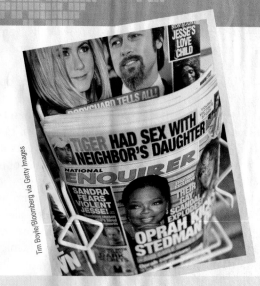

Tim Boyle/Bloomberg via Getty Images

WHAT DO YOU THINK? FOLKLORE, COMMON SENSE, OR NONSENSE? CIRCLE THE T FOR "TRUTH" OR THE F FOR "FICTION," AND CHECK THE ACCURACY OF YOUR ANSWERS AS YOU READ THROUGH THE CHAPTER.

T	F	MORE THAN 2,000 YEARS AGO, ARISTOTLE WROTE A BOOK ON PSYCHOLOGY WITH CONTENTS SIMILAR TO THE BOOK YOU ARE NOW HOLDING.
T	F	THE ANCIENT GREEK PHILOSOPHER SOCRATES SUGGESTED A RESEARCH METHOD THAT IS STILL USED IN PSYCHOLOGY.
T	F	MEN RECEIVE THE MAJORITY OF DOCTORAL DEGREES IN PSYCHOLOGY.
T	F	EVEN THOUGH SHE HAD WORKED TO COMPLETE ALL THE DEGREE REQUIREMENTS, THE FIRST FEMALE PRESIDENT OF THE AMERICAN PSYCHOLOGICAL ASSOCIATION TURNED DOWN THE DOCTORAL DEGREE THAT WAS OFFERED TO HER.
T	F	YOU COULD SURVEY MILLIONS OF VOTERS AND STILL NOT ACCURATELY PREDICT THE OUTCOME OF A PRESIDENTIAL ELECTION.
T	F	IN MANY EXPERIMENTS, NEITHER THE PARTICIPANTS NOR THE RESEARCHERS KNOW WHO IS RECEIVING THE REAL TREATMENT AND WHO IS NOT.

psychology
the science that studies behavior and mental processes

theory
A set of hypothesized statements about the relationships among events

"Abductees" generally claim that they are awakened in their sleep by the aliens and unable to move. Psychologists know that many of our voluntary muscles—the ones involved in movement—are "paralyzed" when we sleep, which is why we usually don't thrash about (and assault our bed partners) when we dream (Clancy, 2008; Forrest, 2008). *Hallucinations*—that is, seeing and hearing things that are not really there—are quite common as we are waking from a sleep-paralyzed state, and it seems that the reported experiences of "abductees" fit the pattern.

Psychologists also know that people are quite open to suggestion (Bernstein & Loftus, 2009; Clark & Loftus, 1996). Memories are not perfect snapshots. When trial witnesses are asked leading questions—that is, questions that might encourage them to recall events in a certain way—the opposing attorney will usually object ("Leading the witness, your Honor"). Sometimes, the person interviewing the supposed kidnap victim asks leading questions, looking for experiences with aliens.

All in all, "UFO memories may be constructed from bits and pieces of sleep-related hallucinations, nightmares, and media attention and fixed solidly into place with the suggestion of hypnosis and the validation of support groups" (Clark & Loftus, 1996, p. 294). "Abductees" may also be trying to escape, temporarily, from their humdrum lives—as might be buyers of supermarket tabloids (Clancy et al., 2002).

Psychologists have thus worked to "explain" how it can be that many people report being abducted by aliens and being subjected to tests by them. But is there *scientific evidence* that people have been abducted by aliens? In sum, when we subject the stories in the supermarket tabloids to scientific analysis, we usually find that they fall short of any reasonable requirements of evidence.

This book will take you on a journey. It's not a journey into outer space. It's a journey into the inner space of thinking critically about the world around you, about stories and arguments made by other people, about human behavior and mental processes. In our overview of reported alien abductions, we touched on people's memories, the state of consciousness known as sleep, hallucinations, hypnosis, the search for stimulating events, social influences on witnesses, and the effects of social support and the media. All these, and much, much more, lie within the science of psychology. We will see who psychologists are, what they do, what they have learned, and perhaps most important, how they

sort out truth from fiction. Let us begin by asking, *What is psychology?*

1-1 Psychology as a Science

Psychology is the scientific study of behavior and mental processes. Topics of interest to psychologists include the nervous system, sensation and perception, learning and memory, intelligence, language, thought, growth and development, personality, stress and health, psychological disorders, ways of treating those disorders, sexual behavior, and the behavior of people in social settings such as groups and organizations.

Sciences have certain goals. Psychology, like other sciences, seeks to describe, explain, predict, and control the events it studies. Psychology thus seeks to describe, explain, predict, and control *behavior and mental processes*. Note that the goal of *controlling* behavior and mental processes doesn't mean that psychologists seek ways to make people do their bidding, like puppets on strings. Rather, psychologists seek to understand the factors that influence behavior and apply this knowledge for the public good—for example, to help individuals cope with problems such as anxiety and depression.

When possible, descriptive terms and concepts—such as anxiety and depression—are interwoven into **theories**. Theories propose reasons for relationships among events, as in perception of a threat can arouse feelings of anxiety. They allow us to derive explanations and predictions. Many psychological theories combine statements about behavior (such as eating or aggression), mental processes (such as attitudes and mental images), and biological processes. For instance, many of our responses to drugs such as alcohol and marijuana can be measured as overt behavior, and they are presumed to reflect our (mental) expectations of the drugs and the biological effects of the drugs themselves.

A satisfactory psychological theory allows us to predict behavior. For instance, a theory of hunger should allow us to predict when people will or will not eat. If our observations cannot be adequately explained by, or predicted from, a given theory, we should consider revising or replacing it.

The remainder of this chapter presents an overview of psychology as a science. You will see that psychologists have diverse interests and fields of specialization. We discuss the history of psychology and the major perspectives from which today's psychologists view behavior. Finally, we consider the research methods psychologists use to study behavior and mental processes.

What Psychologists Do

pure research
research conducted without concern for immediate applications

applied research
research conducted in an effort to find solutions to particular problems

Psychologists share a keen interest in behavior, but they may differ markedly in other ways. Psychologists engage in research, practice, and teaching. Some researchers engage primarily in basic, or pure, research. **Pure research** is undertaken because the researcher is interested in the research topic. Pure research has no *immediate* application to personal or social problems and has therefore been characterized as research for its own sake. However, although pure research is sparked by curiosity and the desire to know and understand, today's pure research frequently enhances tomorrow's way of life. For example, pure research on learning and motivation in pigeons, rats, and monkeys done early in the 20th century has found applications in today's school systems. It has shown, for example, that learning often takes time and repetition and also profits from "booster shots" (repetition after the learning goal has been reached). Pure research into the workings of the nervous system has enhanced knowledge of disorders such as epilepsy, Parkinson's disease, and Alzheimer's disease. Other psychologists engage in **applied research**, which is designed to find solutions to specific personal or social problems.

Many psychologists do not conduct research. Instead, they *practice* psychology by applying psychological knowledge to help individuals change their behavior so that they can meet their own goals more effectively. Still other psychologists primarily teach. They share psychological knowledge in classrooms, seminars, and workshops. Psychologists may also engage in all three: research, practice, and teaching.

1-2a FIELDS OF PSYCHOLOGY

Psychologists are found in a number of specialties. Although some psychologists wear more than one hat, most carry out their functions in the following fields.

Clinical psychologists help people with psychological disorders adjust to the demands of life. Clinical psychologists evaluate problems such as anxiety and depression through interviews and psychological tests. They help clients resolve problems and change self-defeating behavior. For example, they may help clients face "threats," such as public speaking, by exposing them gradually to situations in which they make presentations to actual or virtual groups (see virtual therapy in Chapter 13). Clinical psychologists are the largest subgroup of psychologists (see Figure 1.1). *Counseling psychologists*, like clinical psychologists, use interviews and tests to define their clients' problems. Their clients typically have adjustment problems but not serious psychological disorders. For example, clients may have trouble making academic or vocational decisions or making friends in college.

School psychologists are employed by school systems to identify and assist students who have problems that interfere with learning. They help schools make decisions about the placement of students in special classes. *Educational psychologists*, like school psychologists, attempt to facilitate learning, but they usually focus on course planning and instructional methods for a school system rather than on individual children. Educational psychologists research issues such as how learning is affected by psychological factors such as motivation and intelligence, sociocultural factors such as poverty and acculturation, and teachers.

Developmental psychologists study the changes—physical, cognitive, social, and emotional—that occur throughout the life span. They attempt to sort out the influences of heredity and the environment on development.

Personality psychologists identify and measure human traits and determine influences on human thought processes, feelings, and behavior. They are particularly concerned with issues such as anxiety, aggression, and gender roles. *Social psychologists* are concerned with the nature and causes of individuals' thoughts, feelings, and behavior in social situations. Whereas personality psychologists tend to look within the person to explain behavior, social psychologists tend to focus on social influences.

Environmental psychologists study the ways that people and the environment—the natural environment and the human-made environment—influence one another. For example, we know that extremes of temperature and loud noises interfere with learning in school. Environmental psychologists study ways to encourage people to recycle and to preserve bastions of wilderness.

Psychologists in all specialties may conduct experiments. However, those called *experimental psychologists* specialize in basic processes such as the nervous system, sensation and perception, learning and memory, thought, motivation, and emotion. For example, experimental psychologists have studied what areas of the brain are involved in processing math problems or listening to music. They use people or animals such as pigeons and rats to study learning.

Industrial psychologists focus on the relationships between people and work. *Organizational psycholo-*

FIGURE 1.1

New Doctorates in Psychology (median age = 32)

DEMOGRAPHIC FACTORS	
Women	78.1%
Men	21.7%
Asian American/Pacific Islander	4.8%
African American	5.6%
Latin American	6.3%
Native American	<1.0%
European American	76.4%
TYPE OF DEGREE	
Ph.D.	52.9%
Psy.D.	47.1%
WORK SETTING	
Academia	20.2%
Hospitals	19.6%
Other Human Service	16.0%
Independent Practice	13.7%
Business/Government	13.5%
Schools/Educational	7.8%
Managed Care	7.3%
Other	1.9%
SUBFIELDS	
Clinical Psychology	62.0%
Counseling Psychology	11.1%
School Psychology	9.5%
Clinical Child Psychology	6.4%
Other	10.7%

Source: Adapted from the American Psychological Association (2009). *Doctoral Psychology Workforce Fast Facts*. Health Service Provider Subfields. Center for Workforce Studies. http://research.apa.org/fastfacts-09.pdf. © Copyright 2009 APA Center for Workforce Studies. Washington, DC.

gists study the behavior of people in organizations such as businesses. *Human factors psychologists* make technical systems such as automobile dashboards and computer keyboards more user-friendly. *Consumer psychologists* study the behavior of shoppers in an effort to predict and influence their behavior. They advise store managers on how to lay out the aisles of a supermarket in ways that boost impulse buying, how to arrange window displays to attract customers, and how to make newspaper ads and TV commercials more persuasive.

Health psychologists study the effects of stress on health problems such as headaches, cardiovascular disease, and cancer. Health psychologists also guide clients toward healthier behavior patterns, such as exercising and quitting smoking.

Forensic psychologists apply psychology to the criminal justice system. They deal with legal matters such as whether a defendant was sane when he or she committed a crime. Forensic psychologists may also treat psychologically ill offenders, consult with attorneys on matters such as picking a jury, and analyze offenders' behavior and mental processes. They may conduct research on matters ranging from evaluation of eyewitness testimony to methods of interrogation (Crighton & Towl, 2010).

Sport psychologists help athletes concentrate on their performance and not on the crowd, use cognitive strategies such as positive visualization (imagining themselves making the right moves) to enhance performance, and avoid choking under pressure.

Why are people so fascinated by crime, and by psychopaths such as the one played by Javier Bardem in the film *No Country for Old Men*? Forensic psychologists and personality psychologists investigate the personalities of criminals and also bring psychological expertise to hostage negotiations, threat assessment, the decision to use deadly force, and the interrogation of offenders and witnesses to crime.

ARISTOTLE

How do we number Aristotle's contributions to psychology?

1 He argued that science could rationally treat only information gathered by the senses.

2 He numbered the so-called five senses of vision, hearing, smell, taste, and touch.

3 He explored the nature of cause and effect.

4 He pointed out that people differ from other living things in their capacity for rational thought.

5 He outlined laws of *associationism* that have lain at the heart of learning theory for more than 2,000 years.

6 He also declared that people are more motivated to seek pleasure and avoid pain—a view that remains as current today as it was in ancient Greece.

1-3 Where Psychology Comes From: A History

Have you heard the expression "Know thyself"? It was proposed by the ancient Greek philosopher Socrates more than 2,000 years ago. Psychology, which is in large part the endeavor to know ourselves, is as old as history and as modern as today. Knowledge of the history of psychology allows us to appreciate its theoretical conflicts, its place among the sciences, the evolution of its methods, and its social and political roles.

Another ancient contributor to psychology was the Greek philosopher Aristotle (384–322 BCE). Aristotle argued that human behavior, like the movements of the stars and the seas, is subject to rules and laws. Then he delved into his subject matter topic by topic:

TRUTH ARISTOTLE WROTE A BOOK ON PSYCHOLOGY WITH CONTENTS SIMILAR TO THE BOOK YOU ARE NOW HOLDING MORE THAN 2,000 YEARS AGO. IN FACT, THE OUTLINE FOR THIS BOOK COULD HAVE BEEN WRITTEN BY ARISTOTLE. HIS *PERI PSYCHES* BEGINS WITH A HISTORY OF PSYCHOLOGICAL THOUGHT AND HISTORICAL PERSPECTIVES ON THE NATURE OF THE MIND AND BEHAVIOR.

personality, sensation and perception, thought, intelligence, needs and motives, feelings and emotion, and memory.

Other ancient Greek philosophers also contributed to psychology. Around 400 BCE, Democritus suggested that we could think of behavior in terms of a body and a mind. (Contemporary psychologists still talk about the interaction of biological and mental processes.) He pointed out that our behavior is influenced by external stimulation. Democritus was one of the first to raise the question of whether there is free will or choice. Putting it another way, where do the influences of others end and our "real selves" begin?

Socrates suggested that we should rely on rational thought and **introspection**—careful examination of one's own thoughts and emotions—to gain self-knowledge. He also pointed out that people are social creatures who influence one another.

Had we room enough and time, we could trace psychology's roots to thinkers farther back in time than the ancient Greeks, and we could trace its development through the great thinkers of the Renaissance. As it is, we must move on to the development of psychology as a laboratory science during the second half of the 19th century. Some historians set the marker date at 1860. It was then that Gustav Theodor Fechner (1801–1887) published his landmark book *Elements of Psychophysics*, which showed how physical events (such as lights and sounds) are related to psychological sensation and perception. Fechner also showed how we can scientifically measure the effect of these events. Most historians set the debut of modern psychology as a laboratory science in the year 1879, when Wilhelm Wundt established the first psychological laboratory in Leipzig, Germany.

introspection
deliberate looking into one's own cognitive processes to examine one's thoughts and feelings

 TRUTH SOCRATES SUGGESTED A RESEARCH METHOD THAT IS STILL USED IN PSYCHOLOGY—INTROSPECTION, WHICH IS BASED ON SOCRATES' ADVICE TO "KNOW THYSELF," WHICH HAS REMAINED A MOTTO OF PSYCHOLOGY EVER SINCE.

1-3a STRUCTURALISM

The German psychologist Wilhelm Wundt (1832–1920) looked as if he were going to be a problem child. He did poorly in elementary school—his mind would wander—and he had to repeat a grade. Eventually he attended medical school because he wanted to earn a good living.

structuralism
the school of psychology that argues that the mind consists of three basic elements—sensations, feelings, and images—that combine to form experience

functionalism
the school of psychology that emphasizes the uses or functions of the mind rather than the elements of experience

But he did not like working with patients and dedicated himself to philosophy and psychology.

Like Aristotle, Wundt saw the mind as a natural event that could be studied scientifically, like light, heat, and the flow of blood. Wundt used introspection to try to discover the basic elements of experience.

Wundt and his students founded the school of psychology called *structuralism*. **Structuralism** attempted to break conscious experience down into *objective* sensations, such as sight or taste, and *subjective* feelings, such as emotional responses, and mental images such as memories or dreams. Structuralists believed that the mind functions by combining objective and subjective elements of experience.

WILHELM WUNDT

© Everett Collection Inc/Alamy

1-3b FUNCTIONALISM

Toward the end of the 19th century, psychologist William James (1842–1910) became a major figure in the development of psychology in the United States. He focused on the relation between conscious experience and behavior. He argued, for example, that the stream of consciousness is fluid and continuous. Introspection convinced him that experience cannot be broken down into objective sensations and subjective feelings as the structuralists maintained.

James was a founder of the school of **functionalism**, which focused on behavior as well as the mind or consciousness. Functionalists looked at how our experience helps us function more adaptively in our environments—for example, how habits help us cope with common situations. (When eating with a spoon, we do not create an individual plan to bring each morsel of food to our mouths.) They also turned to the laboratory for direct observations as a way to supplement introspection. Structuralists tended to ask, "What are the pieces that make up thinking and experi-

"I wished, by treating Psychology like a natural science, to help her become one."
—WILLIAM JAMES

ence?" In contrast, functionalists tended to ask, "How do behavior and mental processes help people adapt to the requirements of their lives?"

James was also influenced by Charles Darwin's (1809–1882) theory of evolution. Earlier in the 19th century, the British naturalist Darwin had argued that organisms with adaptive features—that is, the "fittest"—survive and reproduce. Functionalists adapted Darwin's theory and proposed that adaptive behavior patterns are learned and maintained. Maladaptive behavior patterns tend to drop out, and only the fittest behavior patterns survive. These adaptive actions tend to be repeated and become habits. James wrote that "habit is the enormous flywheel of society." Habit keeps the engine of civilization running.

1-3c BEHAVIORISM

Imagine you have placed a hungry rat in a maze. It meanders down a pathway that ends in a T. It can then turn left or right. If you consistently reward the rat with food for turning right at this point, it will learn to turn right when it arrives there, at least when it is hungry. But what does the rat *think* when it is learning to turn right?

Does it seem absurd to try to place yourself in the "mind" of a rat? So it seemed to John Broadus Watson (1878–1958), the founder of American behaviorism. Watson was asked to consider the contents of a rat's "mind" as one of the requirements for his doctoral degree, which he received from the University of Chicago in 1903. Functionalism was the dominant view of psychology at the University of Chicago, and functionalists were concerned with the stream of consciousness as well as observable behavior. But Watson (1913) believed that if psychology was to be a natural science, like physics or chemistry, it must limit itself to observable, measurable events—that is, to behavior alone—hence the term *behaviorism*.

© Mary Evans Picture Library/Alamy

FIGURE 1.2 | The Power of Reinforcement

In the photo we see a feathered friend that has learned to drop shapes into their proper places through reinforcement. Behaviorists teach animals complex behaviors such as this by first reinforcing approximations to the goal (or target behavior). As time progresses, closer approximations are demanded before reinforcement is given.

Tom McHugh/Photo Researchers, Inc.

Behaviorism is the school of psychology that focuses on learning observable behavior. The term *observable* refers to behaviors that are observable by means of specialized instruments, such as heart rate, blood pressure, and brain waves. These behaviors are *public*—they can be measured easily and different observers would agree about their existence and features. Given their focus on behavior, behaviorists define psychology as the scientific study of *behavior*, not of *behavior and mental processes.*

B. F. Skinner (1904–1990) also contributed to behaviorism. He believed that organisms learn to behave in certain ways because they have been **reinforced** for doing so—that is, their behavior has a positive outcome. He demonstrated that laboratory animals can be trained to carry out behaviors through strategic use of reinforcers, such as food. He trained rats to turn in circles, climb ladders, and push toys across the floor.

Because Skinner demonstrated that remarkable combinations of behaviors could be taught by means of reinforcement, many psychologists adopted the view that, in principle, one could explain complex human behavior in terms of thousands of instances of learning through reinforcement (see Figure 1.2).

1-3d GESTALT PSYCHOLOGY

In the 1920s, another school of psychology—**Gestalt psychology**—was prominent in Germany. In the 1930s, the three founders of the school—Max Wertheimer (1880–1943), Kurt Koffka (1886–1941), and Wolfgang Köhler (1887–1967)—left Europe to escape the Nazi threat. They carried on their work in the United States, giving further impetus to the growing American ascendance in psychology.

Gestalt psychologists focused on perception and how perception influences thinking and problem solving. The German word *Gestalt* translates roughly to "pattern" or "organized whole." In contrast to behaviorists, Gestalt psychologists argued that we cannot hope to understand human nature by focusing only on overt behavior. In contrast to structuralists, they claimed that we cannot explain human perceptions, emotions, or thought processes in terms of basic units. Perceptions are *more* than the sums of their parts: Gestalt psychologists saw our perceptions as wholes that give meaning to parts, as we see in Figure 1.3.

Gestalt psychologists showed that we tend to perceive separate pieces of information as integrated wholes depending on the contexts in which they occur. In Figure 1.3A, the dots in the centers of the con-

behaviorism
the school of psychology that defines psychology as the study of observable behavior and studies relationships between stimuli and responses

reinforcement
a stimulus that follows a response and increases the frequency of the response

Gestalt psychology
the school of psychology that emphasizes the tendency to organize perceptions into wholes and to integrate separate stimuli into meaningful patterns

FIGURE 1.3 | The Importance of Context

A. Are the dots in the center of the configurations the same size? Why not take a ruler and measure them?

B. Is the second symbol in each line the letter *B* or the number *13*?

C. Which of the gray squares is brighter?

figurations are the same size, yet we may perceive them as being different in size because of their surroundings. The second symbol in each line in part B is identical, but in the top row we may perceive it as a B and in the bottom row as the number 13. The symbol has not changed, but its context has. The inner squares in part C are equally bright, but they do not appear so because of their contrasting backgrounds.

Gestalt psychologists believed that learning could be active and purposeful, not merely responsive and mechanical as in Watson's and Skinner's experiments. They demonstrated that much learning, especially in problem solving, is accomplished by *insight*, not by mechanical repetition.

Consider Köhler's research with chimpanzees, as shown in Figure 1.4. At first, the chimp is unsuccessful in reaching bananas suspended from the ceiling. Then he suddenly stacks the boxes and climbs up to reach the bananas. It seems the chimp has experienced a sudden reorganization of the mental elements of the problem—that is, he has had a "flash of insight." Köhler's findings suggest that we often manipulate the elements of problems until we group them in such a way that we can reach a goal. The manipulations may take quite some time as mental trial and error proceeds. But once the proper grouping has been found, we seem to perceive it all of a sudden.

1-3e PSYCHOANALYSIS

Psychoanalysis is the name of both the theory of personality and the method of psychotherapy developed by Sigmund Freud (1856–1939). As a theory of person-

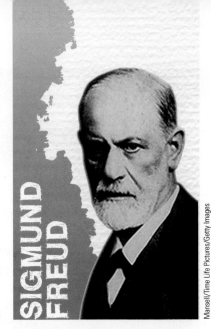

Mansell/Time Life Pictures/Getty Images

SIGMUND FREUD

ality, psychoanalysis proposes that much of our lives is governed by unconscious ideas and impulses that originate in childhood conflicts. As a method of psychotherapy, psychoanalysis aims to help patients gain insight into their conflicts and to find socially acceptable ways of expressing wishes and gratifying needs. We'll discuss psychoanalysis in more depth in Chapter 10.

1-4 How Today's Psychologists View Behavior and Mental Processes

Today, we no longer find psychologists who describe themselves as structuralists or functionalists. Although the school of Gestalt psychology gave birth to current research approaches in perception and problem solving, few would label themselves Gestalt psychologists. But we do find Gestalt *therapists* who focus on helping clients integrate conflicting parts of their personality (making themselves "whole"). The numbers of orthodox behaviorists and psychoanalysts have been declining (Robins et al., 1999). Many con-

FIGURE 1.4 | Some Insight into Insight

At first, the chimpanzee cannot reach the bananas hanging from the ceiling. After some time has passed, the chimp has an apparent "flash of insight" and piles the boxes on top of one another to reach the fruit.

© Cengage Learning 2012

temporary psychologists in the behaviorist tradition look on themselves as social-cognitive theorists.

The history of psychological thought has taken many turns, and contemporary psychologists differ in their approaches. Today, there are several broad, influential perspectives in psychology: biological, cognitive, humanistic–existential, psychodynamic, learning, and sociocultural. Each approaches its topics in its own way.

1-4a THE BIOLOGICAL PERSPECTIVE

Psychologists with a **biological perspective** seek the relationships between the brain, hormones, heredity, and evolution, on the one hand, and behavior and mental processes on the other. Psychologists assume that thoughts, fantasies, and dreams—and the inborn or instinctive behavior patterns of various species—are made possible by the nervous system and especially by the brain.

Biologically oriented psychologists also study the role of heredity in behavior and mental processes such as psychological disorders, criminal behavior, and thinking. Generally speaking, our heredity provides a broad range of behavioral and mental possibilities. Environmental factors interact with inherited factors to determine specific behavior and mental processes.

Biologically oriented psychologists focus on the evolution of behavior and mental processes as well. Charles Darwin argued that in the age-old struggle for existence, only the fittest (most adaptive) organisms manage to reach maturity and reproduce. For example, fish that swim faster or people who are naturally immune to certain diseases are more likely to survive and transmit their genes to future generations. Therefore, species tend to evolve in adaptive directions. Evolutionary psychologists suggest that much human social behavior, such as aggressive behavior and mate selection, has a hereditary basis. People may be influenced by social rules, cultural factors, and personal choice, but evolutionary psychologists believe that inherited tendencies sort of whisper in people's ears and tend to move them in certain directions.

Mary Evans/Photo Researchers, Inc.

CHARLES DARWIN

1-4b THE COGNITIVE PERSPECTIVE

Psychologists with a **cognitive** perspective venture into the realm of mental processes to understand human nature. They investigate the ways we perceive and mentally represent the world, how we learn, remember the past, plan for the future, solve problems, form judgments, make decisions, and use language. Cognitive psychologists, in short, study those things we refer to as the *mind*.

The cognitive tradition has roots in Socrates' advice to "Know thyself" and in his suggested method of introspection. We also find cognitive psychology's roots in structuralism, functionalism, and Gestalt psychology, each of which, in its own way, addressed issues that are of interest to cognitive psychologists.

1-4c THE HUMANISTIC–EXISTENTIAL PERSPECTIVE

The humanistic–existential perspective is cognitive in flavor, yet it emphasizes the role of subjective (personal) experience. Let's consider each of the parts of this perspective: *humanism* and *existentialism*.

Humanism stresses the human capacity for self-fulfillment and the central roles of consciousness, self-awareness, and decision making. Humanists believe that self-awareness, experience, and choice permit us, to a large extent, to "invent ourselves" and our ways of relating to the world as we progress through life. Consciousness—our sense of being in the world—is seen as the force that unifies our personalities. *Existentialism* views people as free to choose and as being responsible for choosing ethical conduct. Grounded in the work of Carl Rogers (1951) and Abraham Maslow (1970), the humanistic–existential perspective has many contemporary adherents (Elkins, 2009).

1-4d THE PSYCHODYNAMIC PERSPECTIVE

In the 1940s and 1950s, psychodynamic theory dominated the practice of psychotherapy and was influential in scientific psychology and the arts. Most psychotherapists were psychodynamically oriented. Many renowned artists and writers consulted psychodynamic therapists as a way to liberate the expression of their unconscious ideas. Today, Freud's influence continues to be felt, although it no longer dominates psychotherapy. Contemporary psychologists who follow theories derived from Freud are likely to call themselves *neoanalysts*. Famous neoanalysts such as Karen Horney (1885–1952) and Erik Erikson (1902–1994) focused less on unconscious processes and more on conscious choice and self-direction.

1-4e PERSPECTIVES ON LEARNING

Many contemporary psychologists study the effects of experience on behavior. Learning, to them, is the essential factor in describing, explaining, predicting, and controlling behavior. The term *learning* has different meanings to psychologists of different persuasions, however. Some students of learning find roles for consciousness and insight. Others do not. This distinction is found today among those who adhere to the behavioral and social-cognitive perspectives.

Early proponents of behaviorism, like John B. Watson, viewed people as doing things because of their learning histories, their situations, and rewards, not because of conscious choice. Like Watson, contemporary behaviorists emphasize environmental influences and the learning of habits through repetition and reinforcement. **Social-cognitive theorists**, in contrast, suggest that people can modify and create their environments. They also grant *cognition* a key role. They note that people engage in intentional learning by observing others. Since the 1960s, social-cognitive theorists have gained influence in the areas of personality development, psychological disorders, and psychotherapy.

1-4f THE SOCIOCULTURAL PERSPECTIVE

The profession of psychology focuses mainly on the individual and is committed to the dignity of the individual. However, many psychologists believe we cannot understand people's behavior and mental processes without reference to their diversity (Alarcón et al., 2009).

The **sociocultural perspective** addresses many of the ways that people differ from one another. It studies the influences of ethnicity, gender, culture, and socioeconomic status on behavior and mental processes (Sanchez et al., 2009; Vodosek, 2009). For example,

David Buffington/PhotoDisc/Jupiterimages

what is often seen as healthful, self-assertive, outspoken behavior by most U.S. women may be interpreted as brazen behavior in Latin American or Asian American communities.

Ethnicity

One kind of diversity involves ethnicity. Members of an *ethnic group* share their cultural heritage, race, language, or history. The experiences of various ethnic groups in the United States highlight the impact of social, political, and economic factors on human behavior and development (Phinney & Ong, 2007).

In the 1940s, Kenneth Bancroft Clark (1914–2005) and Mamie Phipps Clark (1917–1983) conducted research that showed the negative effects of school segregation on African American children. In one such study, African American children were shown white and brown dolls and asked to "Give me the pretty doll," or "Give me the doll that looks bad." Most children's choices showed that they preferred the white dolls over the brown ones. The Clarks concluded that the children had swallowed the larger society's prejudiced views that favored European Americans. The Clark's research was cited by the Supreme Court in 1954 when it overturned the "separate but equal" schools doctrine that had allowed inequalities in school services for various ethnic groups.

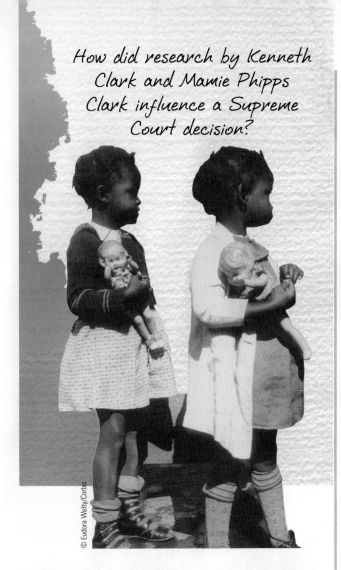

How did research by Kenneth Clark and Mamie Phipps Clark influence a Supreme Court decision?

© Eudora Welty/Corbis

Latin American and Asian American psychologists have also made their mark. Jorge Sanchez was among the first to show how intelligence tests are culturally biased—to the disadvantage of Mexican American children. Latina American psychologist Lillian Comas-Diaz (e.g., 2008) has edited a journal on multicultural mental health. Asian American psychologist Richard M. Suinn (e.g., 2001) studies mental health and the development of identity among Asians and Asian Americans.

Gender

Gender refers to the culturally defined concepts of *masculinity* and *femininity*. Gender is not fully defined by anatomic sex. It involves a complex web of cultural expectations and social roles that affect people's self-concepts and hopes and dreams as well as their behavior.

iStockphoto.com/desuza communications

FICTION IT IS NOT TRUE THAT MEN RECEIVE THE MAJORITY OF DOCTORAL DEGREES IN PSYCHOLOGY. WOMEN DO.

gender
the culturally defined concepts of *masculinity* and *femininity*

Just as members of ethnic minority groups have experienced prejudice, so too have women.

Although American women have attended college only since 1833, when Oberlin College opened its doors to women, most American college students today are in fact women. Women now receive the majority of undergraduate degrees in psychology and, as shown in Figure 1.1 (refer back to page 4), some 78% of the doctoral degrees (American Psychological Association, 2009).

TRUTH THE FIRST FEMALE PRESIDENT OF THE AMERICAN PSYCHOLOGICAL ASSOCIATION, MARY WHITON CALKINS, DID TURN DOWN THE DOCTORAL DEGREE THAT WAS OFFERED TO HER FROM RADCLIFFE.

Women have made indispensable contributions to psychology. Mary Whiton Calkins (1863–1930) introduced the method of paired associates to study memory (see Chapter 7), discovered the primacy and recency effects, and engaged in research into the role of the frequency of repetition in the vividness of memories. Calkins had studied psychology at Harvard University, which she had to attend as a "guest student," because

© Archives of the History of American Psychology. The Center for the History of Psychology—The University of Akron

At a time when men dominated the discipline of psychology, Mary Whiton Calkins was one of the pioneers who fought the male-centered bias and encouraged psychology to incorporate the values of the "new woman" (D. Rogers, 2009). She pioneered research in memory at Wellesley College, where she founded a psychology laboratory in 1891. She introduced the method of paired associates, discovered the primacy and recency effects, and engaged in research into the role of the frequency of repetition in the vividness of memories.

critical thinking
a way of evaluating the claims and comments of other people that involves skepticism and examination of evidence

Harvard was not yet admitting women. When she completed her Ph.D. requirements, Harvard would not award her the degree because of her sex. Instead, Harvard offered to grant her a doctorate from its sister school, Radcliffe. As a form of protest, Calkins declined the offer. Even without the Ph.D., Calkins went on to become president of the American Psychological Association.

In more recent years, Mary Salter Ainsworth (1913–1999) revolutionized our understanding of attachment between parents and children by means of her cross-cultural studies. Elizabeth Loftus (e.g., Laney & Loftus, 2009) has shown that our memories are not snapshots of the past. Instead, they often consist of something old (what actually happened), something new (that is, influenced by more recent events), something borrowed (for example, further shaped by our biases and prejudices), and something blue (altered by tinges of color or emotion).

The contributions of members of diverse ethnic groups and women have broadened our understanding of the influences of ethnicity and gender on behavior and mental processes. They have also increased our knowledge of differences among Europeans. For example, Southern European singles (from Italy, Greece, and Portugal, for example) are more likely than Northern European singles (from the United Kingdom, France, Germany, and Scandinavia) to live with their parents until they get married (Giuliano, 2007). The researcher suggests that the family ties of Southern Europeans seem to be relatively stronger.

1-5 How Psychologists Study Behavior and Mental Processes

Does alcohol cause aggression? Does watching violence on TV cause children to be violent? Why do some people hardly ever think of food, whereas others are obsessed with it and snack all day? Why do some unhappy people attempt suicide, whereas others don't? How does having people of different ethnic backgrounds collaborate in their work affect feelings of prejudice?

Many of us have expressed opinions—maybe strong opinions—on questions like these. But as we saw in our discussion of people who claim to be abducted by aliens from outer space, scientists insist on evidence.

Psychologists, like other scientists, use careful means to observe and measure behavior and the factors that influence behavior.

The need for evidence is one of the keys to critical thinking. Critical thinking is a life tool for all of us as well as a pathway toward scientific knowledge.

1-5a CRITICAL THINKING

Psychologists are guided by scientific principles, and one hallmark of science is critical thinking. **Critical thinking** has many meanings. On one level, it means taking nothing for granted—not believing things just because they are in print or because they were uttered by authority figures or celebrities. On another level, critical thinking refers to a process of thoughtfully analyzing and probing the questions, statements, and arguments of others.

Principles of Critical Thinking

1. *Be skeptical:* Keep an open mind. Politicians and advertisers try to persuade you. Are some of your attitudes and beliefs superficial or unfounded? Accept nothing as the truth until you have examined the evidence.

2. *Insist on evidence:* It is not sufficient that an opinion is traditional, that it appears in print or on the Internet, or that it is expressed by a doctor or a lawyer. Ask for evidence.

3. *Examine definitions of terms:* Some statements are true when a term is defined in one way but not when it is defined in another way. Consider the statement, "Head Start programs have raised children's IQs." The correctness of the statement depends on the definition of IQ. (You will see later in the text that *IQ* is not the same thing as *intelligence*.)

4. *Examine the assumptions or premises of arguments:* Consider the statement that one cannot learn about human beings by engaging in research with animals. One premise in the statement seems to be that human beings are not animals. We are, of course.

5. *Be cautious in drawing conclusions from evidence:* For many years, studies had shown that most clients who receive psychotherapy improve. It was therefore generally assumed that psychotherapy worked. Some 40 years ago, however, psychologist Hans Eysenck pointed out that most psychologically troubled people who did *not* receive psychotherapy also improved. The question thus becomes whether people receiving psychotherapy are *more* likely to improve than those who do not. Current research on the effectiveness of psychotherapy therefore compares the bene-

fits of therapy techniques to the benefits of other techniques or no treatment at all. Be especially skeptical of anecdotes. When you hear "I know someone who . . . ," ask yourself whether this person's reported experience is satisfactory as evidence.

6. *Consider alternative interpretations of research evidence:* Does alcohol cause aggression? Later in the chapter we report evidence that there is a *connection,* or *correlation,* between alcohol and aggression. But does the evidence show that drinking *causes* aggression? Might other factors, such as gender, age, or willingness to take risks, account for both drinking and aggressive behavior?

7. *Do not oversimplify:* Most human behavior involves complex interactions of genetic and environmental influences. For example, consider the issue of whether psychotherapy helps people with psychological problems. A broad answer to this question—a simple yes or no—might be oversimplifying. It is more worthwhile to ask: What *type* of psychotherapy, practiced by *whom,* is most helpful for *what kind of problem?*

8. *Do not overgeneralize:* Again, consider the statement that one cannot learn about humans by engaging in research with animals. Is the truth of the matter an all-or-nothing issue? Are there certain kinds of information we can obtain about people from research with animals? What kinds of things are you likely to learn only through research with people?

9. *Apply critical thinking to all areas of life.*

1-5b THE SCIENTIFIC METHOD

The **scientific method** is an organized way of using experience and testing ideas to expand and refine knowledge. Psychologists do not necessarily follow the steps of the scientific method as we might follow a recipe in a cookbook, but research is guided by certain principles.

Psychologists usually begin by *formulating a research question.* Research questions can have many sources. Our daily experiences, psychological theory, and even folklore all help generate questions for research. Daily experience in using day-care centers may motivate us to conduct research on whether day care affects the development of social skills or the bonds of attachment between children and their parents. Social-cognitive principles of observational learning may prompt research on the effects of TV violence. Research questions may also arise from common knowledge. Consider familiar adages such as "misery loves company" and "opposites attract." Psychologists

may ask: *Does* misery love company? *Do* opposites attract?

A research question may be studied as a question or reworded as a *hypothesis* (see Figure 1.5). A **hypothesis** is a statement about behavior or mental processes that is testable through research. A hypothesis about day care might be that preschoolers who are placed in day care will acquire greater social skills in relating to peers than preschoolers who are cared for in the home.

Psychologists next examine the research question or *test the hypothesis* through controlled methods such as the experiment. For example, we could take a group of preschoolers who attend day care and another group who do not and introduce each to a new child in a con-

scientific method
an organized way of using experience and testing ideas to expand and refine knowledge

hypothesis
in psychology, a specific statement about behavior or mental processes that is tested through research

FIGURE 1.5 | The Scientific Method

The scientific method is a systematic way of organizing and expanding scientific knowledge.

© Cengage Learning 2012

correlation
an association or relationship among variables, as we might find between height and weight or between study habits and school grades

selection factor
a source of bias that may occur in research findings when participants are allowed to choose for themselves a certain treatment in a scientific study

sample
part of a population

population
a complete group of interest to researchers, from which a sample is drawn

trolled setting such as a child-research center. We could then observe how children in each group interact with the new acquaintance.

Psychologists draw conclusions about their research questions or the accuracy of their hypotheses on the basis of their observations or findings. When their observations do not bear out their hypotheses, they may modify the theories from which the hypotheses were derived. Research findings often suggest refinements to psychological theories and new avenues of research. In our research on day care, we might find that children in day care show greater social skills than children who are cared for in the home (Belsky et al., 2001).

As psychologists draw conclusions from research evidence, they are guided by principles of critical thinking. For example, they try not to confuse **correlations**—or associations—between findings with cause and effect. Although more aggressive children apparently spend more time watching violent TV shows, it may be erroneous to conclude from this kind of evidence that TV violence *causes* aggressive behavior. A **selection factor** may be at work because the children being studied choose (select) for themselves what they will watch. Perhaps more aggressive children are more likely than less aggressive children to tune in to violent TV shows.

TRUTH IT IS TRUE THAT YOU COULD SURVEY MILLIONS OF VOTERS AND STILL NOT PREDICT THE OUTCOME OF A PRESIDENTIAL ELECTION.

Does this telephone make me look rich?

H. Armstrong Roberts/Getty Images

1-5c SAMPLES AND POPULATIONS

Consider a piece of history that never quite happened: The Republican candidate Alf Landon defeated the incumbent president, Franklin D. Roosevelt, in 1936. Or at least Landon did so in a poll conducted by a popular magazine of the day, the *Literary Digest.* In the actual election, however, Roosevelt routed Landon by a landslide. In effect, the *Digest* accomplished something like this when they predicted a Landon victory. How was so great a discrepancy possible?

The *Digest,* you see, had surveyed voters by phone. Today, telephone sampling is still widely practiced, but the *Digest* poll was taken during the Great Depression, when people who had telephones were much wealthier than those who did not. People at higher income levels are also more likely to vote Republican, in this case, for Landon. Question: Is telephone sampling valid if it omits people—like many college students!—whose only telephone is a cellphone?

The *Digest* poll failed because of its method of sampling. A **sample** is a segment of a **population** that must be drawn so that it accurately *represents* that population. Only representative samples allow us to *generalize*—or *extend*—our findings from research samples to target populations, such as U.S. voters, and not subgroups such as southern Californians or European American members of the middle class.

1-5d PROBLEMS IN GENERALIZING FROM PSYCHOLOGICAL RESEARCH

Many factors must be considered when interpreting the accuracy of the results of scientific research. One is the nature of the research sample. Later in the chapter, we consider research in which the participants were drawn from a population of college men who were social drinkers. That is, they tended to drink at social gatherings but not when alone. Whom do college men represent other than themselves? To whom can we extend, or generalize, the results? For one thing, they do not extend to college women, who, as we see in Chapter 4, are affected more quickly than men are by alcohol.

Also, compared to the general adult male population, college men are younger and score higher on intelligence tests. Social drinkers may also differ biologically and psychologically from alcoholics, who have difficulty controlling their drinking.

By and large, we must also question whether findings of research with men can be generalized to women, and

Observers use unobtrusive measures to avoid interfering with the behaviors they are observing. For example, Jane Goodall has observed the behavior of chimpanzees in their natural environment to learn about their social behavior, sexual behavior, use of tools, and other facts of chimp life (Peterson, 2006; Pusey et al., 2008). Her observations have shown us that (a) we were incorrect to think that only humans use tools and (b) kissing on the lips, as a greeting, is used by chimps as well as humans.

1-5f CORRELATION

Are people with higher intelligence more likely to do well in school? Are people with a stronger need for achievement likely to climb higher up the corporate ladder? What is the relationship between stress and health?

Such questions are often answered by means of the **correlational method**. Correlation follows observation. By using the correlational method, psychologists investigate whether observed behavior or a measured trait is related to, or correlated with, another. Consider the variables of intelligence and academic performance. These variables are assigned numbers such as intelligence test scores and academic averages. Then the numbers are mathematically related and expressed as a **correlation coefficient** (r). A correlation coefficient is a number that varies from $r = +1.00$ to $r = -1.00$.

Studies report *positive correlations* between intelligence test scores and academic achievement, as measured, for example, by grade point averages. That is, the higher people score on intelligence tests, the better their academic performance is likely to be. Intelligence test scores tend to be positively correlated (about $r = +0.30$ to $r = +0.60$) with academic achievement (see Figure 1.6). But factors *other* than performance on intelligence tests also contribute to academic success. These include desire to get ahead, self-discipline, ability to manage stress, and belief in one's ability to succeed (Duckworth & Seligman, 2005; Jennings et al., 2009; Thomas, 2008).

Many correlations are *negative correlations*; that is, as one variable increases, the other variable decreases. For example, there is a negative correlation between

correlational method a mathematical method of determining whether one variable increases or decreases as another variable increases or decreases

correlation coefficient a number between +1.00 and −1.00 that expresses the strength and direction (positive or negative) of the relationship between two variables

FIGURE 1.6 | Positive and Negative Correlations

When there is a positive correlation between variables, as there is between intelligence and achievement, one increases as the other increases. By and large, the higher people score on intelligence tests, the better their academic performance is likely to be, as in the diagram on the left. (Each dot represents an individual's intelligence test score and grade point average.) But there is a negative correlation between stress and health. As the amount of stress we experience increases, the functioning of our immune system tends to decrease.

Positive correlation, as found between intelligence and academic achievement

Negative correlation, as found between stress and functioning of the immune system

© Cengage Learning 2012

What kind of correlation would you expect between teenagers' grades in school and their numbers of delinquent acts? Why?

liquidlibrary/Jupiterimages

experiment

a scientific method that seeks to confirm cause-and-effect relationships by introducing independent variables and observing their effects on dependent variables

independent variable

a condition in a scientific study that is manipulated so that its effects may be observed

dependent variable

a measure of an assumed effect of an independent variable

experimental groups

in experiments, groups whose members obtain the treatment

control groups

in experiments, groups whose members do not obtain the treatment, while other conditions are held constant

stress and health. As the amount of stress affecting us increases, the functioning of our immune system decreases. Under high levels of stress, many people show poorer health.

What kinds of correlations (positive or negative) would you expect to find among behavior patterns such as the following: Churchgoing and crime? Language ability and musical ability? Grades in school and delinquency? Why?

Correlational research may suggest, but does not prove, cause and effect. For example, it may seem logical to assume that high intelligence makes it possible for children to profit from education. However, research has also shown that education contributes to higher scores on intelligence tests (Nisbett, 2009). Preschoolers who are placed in stimulating Head Start programs later attain higher scores on intelligence tests than age-mates who did not have this experience. What of the link between stress and health? Does stress impair health, or is it possible that people in poorer health encounter more stress?

1-5g THE EXPERIMENTAL METHOD

The preferred method for answering questions about cause and effect is the experiment. In an **experiment**, a group of participants obtains a treatment, such as a dose of alcohol, a change in room temperature, or perhaps an injection of a drug. The participants are then observed to determine whether the treatment makes a difference in their behavior. Does alcohol alter the ability to take tests, for example? What are the effects of differences in room temperatures and the level of background noise?

Experiments allow psychologists to control the experiences of participants and draw conclusions about cause and effect (Roediger & McCabe, 2007). A psychologist may theorize that alcohol leads to aggression because it reduces fear of consequences or because it energizes the activity levels of drinkers (Sayette et al., 2009). She or he may then hypothesize that a treatment in which participants receive a specified dosage of alcohol will lead to increases in aggression. Let's follow the example of the effects of alcohol on aggression to further our understanding of the experimental method.

Independent and Dependent Variables

In an experiment to determine whether alcohol causes aggression, participants are given an amount of alcohol and its effects are measured. In this case, alcohol is an **independent variable**. The presence of an independent variable is manipulated by the experimenters so that its effects may be determined. The independent variable of alcohol may be administered at different levels, or doses, from none or very little to enough to cause intoxication or drunkenness.

The measured results, or outcomes, in an experiment are called **dependent variables**. The presence of dependent variables presumably depends on the independent variables. In an experiment to determine whether alcohol influences aggression, aggressive behavior would be a dependent variable. Other dependent variables of interest might include sexual arousal, visual-motor coordination, and performance on cognitive tasks such as math problems.

In an experiment on the relationships between temperature and aggression, temperature would be an independent variable and aggressive behavior would be a dependent variable. We could set temperatures from below freezing to blistering hot and study its effects on aggression. We could also use a second independent variable such as social provocation; we could insult some participants but not others and see whether insults affect their level of aggression. This method would allow us to study how two independent variables—temperature and social provocation—affect aggression, by themselves and together.

Experimental and Control Groups

Ideal experiments use experimental groups and control groups. Participants in **experimental groups** obtain the treatment. Members of **control groups** do not. Every effort is made to ensure that all other conditions are held constant for both groups. This method enhances the researchers' confidence that the outcomes of the experiment are caused by the treatments and not by chance factors or chance fluctuations in behavior.

For example, in an experiment on the effects of alcohol on aggression, members of the experimental group would ingest alcohol, and members of the control group would not (Eriksson, 2008). The researcher would then measure how much aggression was shown by each group.

Blinds and Double Blinds

One experiment on the effects of alcohol on aggression (Boyatzis, 1974) reported that men at parties where beer and liquor were served acted more aggressively than men at parties where only soft drinks were served. But participants in the experimental group knew they had drunk alcohol, and those in the control group knew they had not. Aggression that appeared to result from alcohol might not have reflected drinking per se. Instead, it might have reflected the participants' expectations about the effects of alcohol. People tend to act in stereotypical ways when they believe they have been drinking alcohol (Eriksson, 2008). For instance, men tend to become less anxious in social situations, more aggressive, and more sexually aroused. To what extent do these behavior patterns reflect the direct effects of alcohol on the body, and to what extent do they affect people's *beliefs* about the effects of alcohol?

In medicine, physicians sometimes give patients **placebos** (a fake treatment, such as sugar pills, that appears to be genuine) when the patient insists on having a medical cure but the physician does not believe that medicine is necessary. When patients report that placebos have helped them, it is because they expected the pills to be of help and not because of the biochemical effects of the pills. Placebos are not limited to sugar pills. Interestingly, the taste of vodka and tonic water is almost impossible to distinguish from tonic water alone. Therefore, tonic water can be used as a placebo in experiments on the effects of alcohol. Moreover, if participants believe they have drunk alcohol but have actually been given tonic water only, we may conclude that changes in their behavior result from their beliefs about the effects of alcohol and not from alcohol itself.

Well-designed experiments control for the effects of expectations by creating conditions under which participants are unaware of, or **blind** to, the treatment. Placebos are one way of keeping participants blind as to whether they have received a particular treatment. Yet researchers may also have expectations. They may be "rooting for" a certain treatment outcome, a phenomenon known as *experimenter bias*. For instance, tobacco company executives may wish to show that cigarette smoking is harmless. In such cases, it is useful if the people measuring the experimental outcomes are unaware of which participants have received the treatment. Studies in which neither the participants nor the experimenters know who has obtained the treatment are called **double-blind studies**.

Neither the participants nor the researchers know who is receiving the real treatment in many experiments. For example, the Food and Drug Administration requires double-blind studies before it allows the marketing of new drugs. The drug and the placebo look and taste alike. Experimenters assign the drug or placebo to participants at random. Neither the participants nor the observers know who is taking the drug and who is taking the placebo. After the final measurements have been made, a neutral panel (a group of people who have no personal stake in the outcome of the study) judges whether the effects of the drug differed from those of the placebo.

TRUTH IT IS TRUE THAT NEITHER THE PARTICIPANTS NOR THE RESEARCHERS KNOW WHO IS RECEIVING THE REAL TREATMENT IN MANY EXPERIMENTS.

In one double-blind study on the effects of alcohol on aggression, Alan Lang and his colleagues (1975) pretested a highball of vodka and tonic water to determine that it could not be discriminated by taste from tonic water alone. They then recruited college men who described themselves as "social drinkers" to participate in the study. Some of the men drank vodka and tonic water. Others drank tonic water only. Of the men who drank vodka, half were misled into believing they had drunk tonic water only (see Figure 1.7). Of those who drank tonic water only, half were misled into believing their drink contained vodka. Thus, half the participants were blind to their treatment. Experimenters defined aggression as pressing a lever that participants believed would deliver an electric shock to another person. The researchers who measured the men's aggressive responses were also blind concerning which participants had drunk vodka.

The research team found that men who believed that they had drunk vodka responded more aggressively (selected a higher level of shock) in response to a provocation than men who believed that they had drunk tonic water only. The actual content of the drink was immaterial. That is, the men's *belief* about what

placebo
a bogus treatment that has the appearance of being genuine

blind
in experimental terminology, unaware of whether or not one has received a treatment

double-blind study
a study in which neither the subjects nor the observers know who has received the treatment

informed consent
a participant's agreement to participate in research after receiving information about the purposes of the study and the nature of the treatments

they drank affected their behavior more than what they actually consumed. The results of the Lang study differ dramatically from those reported by Boyatzis, perhaps because the Boyatzis study did not control for the effects of expectations or beliefs about alcohol.

1-5h ETHICS OF RESEARCH WITH HUMANS

If the Lang group were running their experiment today rather than in the 1970s, they would probably have been denied permission to do so by a university ethics review committee. Why? Because the researchers gave some participants alcohol to drink—a potentially harmful treatment, especially to participants who might have drinking problems—and deceived the entire group about the purposes and methods of the study. Was their method ethical?

Psychologists adhere to a number of ethical standards that are intended to promote individual dignity, human welfare, and scientific integrity. The standards are also intended to ensure that psychologists do not undertake research methods or treatments that are harmful. In virtually all institutional settings, including colleges, hospitals, and research foundations, ethics review committees help researchers consider the potential harm of their methods and review proposed studies according to ethical guidelines. When such committees find that proposed research might be unacceptably harmful to participants, they may withhold approval until the proposal has been modified. Ethics review committees also weigh the potential benefits of research against the potential harm.

Today, individuals must provide **informed consent** before they participate in research (Knaus et al., 2012). Having a general overview of the research and the opportunity to choose not to participate apparently give them a sense of control and decrease the stress of participating (Fisher, 2009). Is there a way in which participants in the Lang study could have provided informed consent? What do you think?

Psychologists keep the records of research participants and clients confidential because they respect people's privacy and because people are more likely to express their true thoughts and feelings when researchers or therapists keep their disclosures confidential (Fisher, 2009). Sometimes, conflicts of interest arise, as

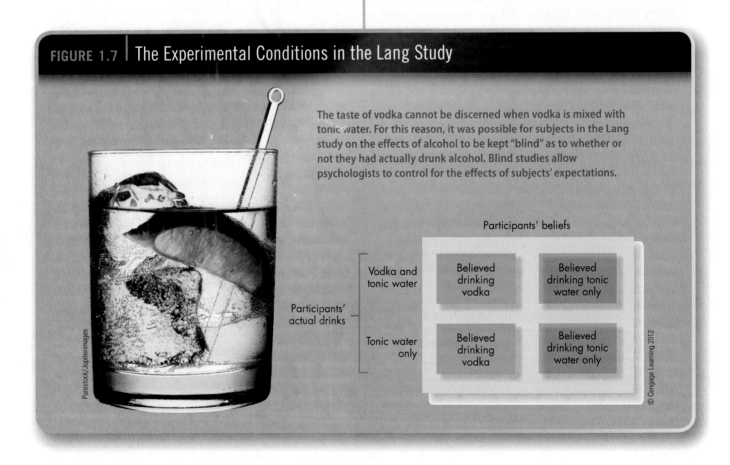

FIGURE 1.7 | The Experimental Conditions in the Lang Study

The taste of vodka cannot be discerned when vodka is mixed with tonic water. For this reason, it was possible for subjects in the Lang study on the effects of alcohol to be kept "blind" as to whether or not they had actually drunk alcohol. Blind studies allow psychologists to control for the effects of subjects' expectations.

Participants' beliefs

	Believed drinking vodka	Believed drinking tonic water only
Vodka and tonic water		
Tonic water only	Believed drinking vodka	Believed drinking tonic water only

Participants' actual drinks

Purestock/Jupiterimages

© Cengage Learning 2012

when a client threatens to harm someone, and the psychologist feels an obligation to warn the victim (Knaus et al., 2012).

Some studies could not be conducted if participants know what the researchers were trying to learn or which treatment they had received (for example, a new drug or a sugar pill). According to the American Psychological Association's *Handbooks of Ethics in Psychology* (Knaus et al., 2012), psychologists may use deception only when they believe the benefits of the research outweigh its potential harm, when they believe the individuals might have been willing to participate if they had understood the benefits of the research, and when participants are **debriefed** afterward—that is, the purposes and methods of the research are explained.

Participants in the Lang study on alcohol and aggression were deceived in two ways. The researchers (a) misinformed them about what they were drinking and (b) told them they were shocking other participants when they were actually only pressing switches on an unconnected control board. (*Aggression* was defined for purposes of the study as pressing these switches.) The study could not have been run without deception, but the ethics of deceiving research participants remains debated.

1-5i ETHICS OF RESEARCH WITH ANIMALS

Psychologists and other scientists frequently use animals to conduct research that cannot be carried out with humans. For example, experiments on the effects of early separation from the mother have been done with monkeys and other animals. Such research has helped psychologists investigate the formation of parent–child bonds of attachment.

Experiments with infant monkeys highlight some of the ethical issues faced by psychologists and other scientists who contemplate potentially harmful research. Psychologists and biologists who study the workings of the brain destroy sections of the brains of laboratory animals to learn how they influence be-

> "An act has no ethical quality whatever unless it be chosen out of several all equally possible."
> —WILLIAM JAMES

havior. For instance, a lesion in one part of a brain structure causes a rat to overeat. A lesion elsewhere causes the rat to go on a crash diet. Psychologists generalize to humans from experiments such as these in the hope of finding solutions to problems such as eating disorders (Mehta & Gosling, 2008). Proponents of the use of animals in research argue that major advances in medicine and psychology could not have taken place without them (Ringach & Jentsch, 2009). For example, we would know much less about how experimental drugs affect cancerous growths and the brain.

According to the ethical guidelines of the American Psychological Association, animals may be harmed only when there is no alternative and when researchers believe that the benefits of the research justify the harm (American Psychological Association, 2002; Fisher, 2009).

Now that we have an overview of psychology as a science, we will move on to the connections between psychology and biology in Chapter 2. Psychologists assume that our behaviors and our mental processes are related to biological events. In Chapter 2 we consider the evidence for this assumption.

debrief to explain the purposes and methods of a completed procedure to a participant

Percent of new doctoral degrees in psychology earned by women

78

1879 Year that Wilhelm Wundt established the first psych lab

+1.00 to -1.00

Range of possible correlation coefficients

0

As a correlation coefficient, means that there is no linear relationship between the variables

iStockphoto.com/AnsonLu

STUDY TOOLS ▶ 1

Ready to study? In the book, you can:

- ● Review what you've read with Fill-Ins and Multiple Choice quizzes (below).
- ● Rip out Chapter Review card (in the back).

Or you can go online to CourseMate at www.cengagebrain.com for these resources:

- ● Complete Practices Quizzes to prepare for tests.
- ● Review Key Terms Flash Cards (online or print).
- ● Play games to master concepts.

FILL-INS

Answers can be found in the back of the book, starting on page 368.

1. Psychology is defined as the study of _____ and mental processes.

2. _____ psychologists evaluate problems such as anxiety and depression through interviews and psychological tests.

3. _____ founded the school of structuralism.

4. _____ psychologists saw our perceptions as wholes that give meaning to parts.

5. _____ psychologists note that only the fittest organisms reach maturity and reproduce, thereby transmitting their genes to future generations and causing species to evolve in adaptive directions.

6. Kenneth and Mamie Phipps _____ conducted research that influenced a Supreme Court decision on segregated schools.

7. Samples must accurately represent the target _____.

8. In the _____, a large sample of people answer questions about their attitudes or behavior.

9. Ideal experiments use experimental and _____ groups.

10. Psychologists adhere to _____ standards that help promote the dignity of the individual, maintain scientific integrity, and protect research participants and clinical clients from harm.

1. Psychology is defined as the scientific study of
   a. behavior and mental processes.
   b. diagnosis and treatment of behavioral disorders.
   c. conscious and unconscious mental processes.
   d. the mind.

2. School psychologists are employed by school districts to
   a. develop achievement and aptitude tests.
   b. identify and assist students who have problems that interfere with their learning.
   c. assess the development of children in the school system.
   d. develop curriculum for teachers to deliver.

3. What distinguished Wilhelm Wundt's contribution from other contributions to psychology?
   a. He wrote the first textbook of psychology.
   b. He defined psychology as the science of behavior.
   c. He established psychology as a laboratory science.
   d. He studied insight in lower animals.

4. The school of psychology that places unconscious impulses and desires at the center of human behavior is
   a. psychoanalysis.
   b. humanism-existentialism.
   c. functionalism.
   d. Gestalt psychology.

5. The first female president of the American Psychological Association was
   a. Mary Ainsworth.   c. Karen Horney.
   b. Elizabeth Loftus.   d. Mary Whiton Calkins.

6. A(n) _____ is a specific statement about behavior or mental processes that is tested through research.
   a. observation   c. theory
   b. scientific method   d. hypothesis

7. In a _____, each member of a population has an equal chance of being selected to participate.
   a. random sample
   b. selection sample
   c. stratified sample
   d. free sample

8. A disadvantage of survey research is _____. For example, people tend to overrate behaviors like church attendance and proper hygiene.
   a. inaccurate self-report
   b. too much detail
   c. that people are too honest
   d. too few survey companies

9. You design a test of intelligence. On the theory that intelligence is related to academic performance, you use _____ to test the relationship between performance on your new test and grades in school.
   a. an experimental method
   b. a test-retest method
   c. the correlational method
   d. naturalistic observation

10. Dr. Liu was interested in testing the effects of violent television on six-year-old children. She showed one group a particularly violent episode of *Power Rangers* and another group watched a short nonviolent episode of an old Bill Cosby show. She then observed the groups in the playground and measured their behaviors. What is the dependent variable in this study?
    a. Bill Cosby and his family
    b. Violent or nonviolent TV show
    c. The behavior on the playground
    d. The amount of time watching TV

USE THE TOOLS.

• Rip out the Review Cards in the back of your book to study.

Or Visit CourseMate to:

• Read, search, highlight, and take notes in the Interactive eBook

• Review Flashcards (Print or Online) to master key terms

• Test yourself with Auto-Graded Quizzes

• Bring concepts to life with Games, Videos, and Animations!

Go to CourseMate for PSYCH3 to begin using these tools.
Access at **www.cengagebrain.com**

Complete the Speak Up survey in CourseMate at **www.cengagebrain.com**

Follow us at **www.facebook.com/4ltrpress**

©iStockphoto.com/A-Digit | © Cengage Learning 2011

Colin Anderson/Getty Images

LEARNING OUTCOMES

2-1 Describe the nervous system, including neurons, neural impulses, and neurotransmitters

2-2 List the structures of the brain and their functions

2-3 Explain the role of the endocrine system and list the endocrine glands

2-4 Describe evolutionary psychology and the connections between heredity, behavior, and mental processes

 STUDY TOOLS ▶

After you read the chapter, go to the Study Tools at the end of the chapter, page 54.

CHAPTER 2

Biology and PSYCHOLOGY

"**G**age is no longer Gage," said those who had known him before the accident.

There are many key characters in the history of psychology, and some of them did not arrive there intentionally. One of these was a promising railroad worker who was helping our young nation stretch from coast to coast. His name was Phineas Gage. Gage was highly admired by his friends and coworkers. But all that changed one day in 1848. While he was tamping down the blasting powder for a dynamite charge, Gage accidentally set the powder off. The inch-thick metal tamping rod shot upward through his cheek and brain and out the top of his head.

If the trajectory of the rod had been slightly different, Gage would have died. Although Gage fell back in a heap, he was miraculously alive. His coworkers watched in shock as he stood up a few moments later and spoke. While the local doctor marveled at the hole through Gage's head, Gage asked when he'd be able to return to work. Two months later, Gage's external wounds had healed, but the psychological aspects of the wound were now obvious. His former employer, who had regarded him as "the most efficient and capable foreman in their employ previous to his injury" (Harlow, 1868), refused to rehire him because he had changed so much:

> The equilibrium or balance, so to speak, between his intellectual faculties and animal propensities, seems to have been destroyed. He is ... irreverent, indulging at times in the grossest profanity (which was not previously his custom). [He showed little consideration for other people, was] impatient of restraint or advice when it conflicts with his desires ... obstinate, yet capricious and vacillating, devising many plans of future operation, which are no sooner arranged than they are abandoned in turn for others ... But all had not been lost in Gage's brain. In fact, many of his intellectual skills were just fine, apparently untouched.

Generations of researchers—psychologists, physicians, biologists, neuroscientists—have wondered how the changes in Gage's personality might have been caused by the damage to his brain. Perhaps the trajec-

> "Gage is no longer Gage."

 TRUTH OR **FICTION**

WHAT DO YOU THINK? FOLKLORE, COMMON SENSE, OR NONSENSE? CIRCLE THE T FOR "TRUTH" OR THE F FOR "FICTION," AND CHECK THE ACCURACY OF YOUR ANSWERS AS YOU READ THROUGH THE CHAPTER.

T	F	A SINGLE CELL CAN STRETCH ALL THE WAY FROM YOUR SPINE TO YOUR TOE.
T	F	MESSAGES TRAVEL IN THE BRAIN BY MEANS OF ELECTRICITY.
T	F	A BRAIN CELL CAN SEND OUT HUNDREDS OF MESSAGES EACH SECOND—AND MANAGE TO CATCH SOME REST IN BETWEEN.
T	F	FEAR CAN GIVE YOU INDIGESTION.
T	F	THE HUMAN BRAIN IS LARGER THAN THAT OF ANY OTHER ANIMAL.
T	F	IF A SURGEON WERE TO STIMULATE A CERTAIN PART OF YOUR BRAIN ELECTRICALLY, YOU MIGHT SWEAR THAT SOMEONE HAD STROKED YOUR LEG.
T	F	CHARLES DARWIN WAS NEARLY EXCLUDED FROM THE VOYAGE THAT LED TO THE DEVELOPMENT OF HIS THEORY OF EVOLUTION BECAUSE THE CAPTAIN OF THE SHIP DID NOT LIKE THE SHAPE OF HIS NOSE.

neuron

a specialized cell of the nervous system that receives and transmits messages

glial cells

cells that remove dead neurons and waste products from the nervous system, nourish and insulate neurons, form myelin, and play a role in neural transmission of messages

tory of the rod spared parts of the frontal lobes that are involved in language and movement but damaged areas connected with personality and emotional response (Damasio, 2000; Wagar & Thagard, 2004). In this chapter, we will learn about the frontal lobes of the brain and much more. We will travel from the small to the large—from the microscopic brain cells that hold and transmit information, to the visible structures that provide the basis for functions such as memory, speech, sensation, thought, planning, and voluntary movement.

2-1 The Nervous System: On Being Wired

The nervous system is a system of nerves involved in thought processes, heartbeat, visual–motor coordination, and so on. The nervous system contains the brain, the spinal cord, and other parts that make it possible for us to receive information from the world outside and to act on that world.

The nervous system is composed of cells, most of which are *neurons*, which is where we will begin our study of the nervous system.

2-1a NEURONS: INTO THE FABULOUS FOREST

Within our brains lies a fabulous forest of nerve cells, or neurons. **Neurons** are specialized cells of the nervous system that conduct impulses. Neurons can be visualized as having branches, trunks, and roots—something like trees. As we voyage through this forest, we see that many nerve cells lie alongside one another like a thicket of trees. But neurons can also lie end to end, with their "roots" intertwined with the "branches" of the neurons that lie below. Neurons receive "messages" from a number of sources such as light, other neurons, and pressure on the skin, and they can pass these messages along in a complex biological dance. We are born with more than 100 billion neurons. Most of them are found in the brain.

The nervous system also contains **glial cells**. Glial cells remove dead neurons and waste products from the nervous system; nourish and insulate neurons; form a fatty, insulating substance called *myelin*; and play a role in neural transmission of messages. But neurons occupy center stage in the nervous system. The messages transmitted by neurons somehow account for phenomena ranging from the perception of an itch from a mosquito bite to the coordination of a

KuS/plainpicture

FIGURE 2.1 | The Anatomy of a Neuron

SENDING NEURON   **RECEIVING NEURON**

Neural impulse

Axon

Axon terminals

Dendrites

Nucleus

Cell body (soma)

Myelin sheath

Closeup of axon terminal button and synapse

Neurotransmitters

Synaptic cleft   Receptor sites

"Messages" enter neurons through dendrites, are transmitted along the trunklike axon, and then are sent from axon terminal buttons to muscles, glands, and other neurons. Axon terminal buttons contain sacs of chemicals called *neurotransmitters*. Neurotransmitters are released into the *synaptic cleft*, where many of them bind to *receptor sites* on the dendrites of the receiving neuron.

© Cengage Learning 2010

skier's vision and muscles to the composition of a concerto to the solution of an algebraic equation.

Neurons vary according to their functions and their location. Neurons in the brain may be only a fraction of an inch in length, whereas others in the legs are several feet long. Most neurons include a cell body, dendrites, and an axon (see Figure 2.1). The cell body contains the core or *nucleus* of the cell. The nucleus uses oxygen and nutrients to generate the energy needed to carry out the work of the cell. Anywhere from a few to several hundred short fibers, or **dendrites**, extend like roots from the cell body to receive incoming messages from thousands of adjoining neurons.

Each neuron has an **axon** that extends like a trunk from the cell body. Axons are very thin, but those that carry messages from the toes to the spinal cord extend several feet. Like tree trunks, axons can branch off in different directions. Axons end in small, bulb-shaped structures called *axon terminals* or *terminal buttons*. Neurons carry messages in one direction only: from the dendrites or cell body through the axon to the axon terminals. The messages are then transmitted from the terminal buttons to other neurons, muscles, or glands.

As a child matures, the axons of neurons become longer and the dendrites and terminals proliferate, creating vast interconnected networks for the transmission of complex messages. The number of glial cells also increases as the nervous system develops, contributing to its dense appearance.

Myelin

The axons of many neurons are wrapped tightly with white, fatty **myelin** that makes them look like strings of sausages under the microscope (Figure 2.1). The fat insulates the axon from electrically charged atoms, or *ions*, found in the fluids that surround the nervous system. The myelin sheath minimizes leakage of the electrical current being carried along the axon, thereby allowing messages to be conducted more efficiently.

Myelination is part of the maturation process that leads to a child's ability to crawl and walk during the first year. Infants are not physiologically "ready" to engage in visual–motor coordination and other activities until the coating process reaches certain levels. In people with the disease multiple sclerosis, myelin is replaced with a hard fibrous tissue that throws off the timing of nerve impulses and disrupts muscular control.

Afferent and Efferent Neurons

If someone steps on your toes, the sensation is registered by receptors or sensory neurons near the surface of your skin. Then it is transmitted to the spinal cord and brain through *sensory neurons*, or **afferent neurons**, which can be as long as 2 to 3 feet in length. In the brain, subsequent messages might be conveyed by associative neurons that are only a few thousandths of an inch long. You experience the pain through this process and perhaps entertain some rather nasty thoughts about the perpetrator, who is now apologizing and begging for understanding.

Long before you arrive at any logical conclusions, however, *motor neurons*, or **efferent neurons**, send messages to your foot so that you withdraw it and begin an impressive hopping routine. Efferent neurons transmit messages from the brain or spinal cord to muscles and glands. Other efferent neurons stimulate glands so that your heart is beating more rapidly, you are sweating, and the hair on the back of your arms has become erect! Being a good sport, you say, "Oh, it's nothing." But considering all the neurons involved, it really is something, isn't it?

TRUTH IT IS TRUE THAT A SINGLE CELL CAN STRETCH ALL THE WAY FROM YOUR SPINE TO YOUR TOE.

In case you think that afferent and efferent neurons will be hard to distinguish because they sound pretty much the SAME to you, remember that they *are* the "SAME." That is, Sensory Afferent, and Motor Efferent.

2-1b THE NEURAL IMPULSE: "THE BODY ELECTRIC"[1]

In the 18th century, the Italian physiologist Luigi Galvani (1737–1798) conducted a shocking experiment in a rainstorm. While his neighbors had the sense to remain indoors, Galvani and his wife were out on the porch connecting lightning rods to the heads of dissected frogs whose legs were connected by wires to a well of water. When lightning blazed above, the frogs' muscles

---

dendrites
rootlike structures, attached to the cell body of a neuron, that receive impulses, or incoming messages, from other neurons

axon
a long, thin part of a neuron that transmits impulses to other neurons from bulb-shaped structures called *axon terminals or terminal buttons*

myelin
a fatty substance that encases and insulates axons, facilitating transmission of neural impulses

afferent neurons
neurons that transmit messages from sensory receptors to the spinal cord and brain; also called *sensory neurons*

efferent neurons
neurons that transmit messages from the brain or spinal cord to muscles and glands; also called *motor neurons*

---

[1] From Walt Whitman's *Leaves of Grass*.

neural impulse
the electrochemical discharge of a nerve cell, or neuron

polarize
to ready a neuron for firing by creating an internal negative charge in relation to the body fluid outside the cell membrane

resting potential
the electrical potential across the neural membrane when it is not responding to other neurons

depolarize
to reduce the resting potential of a cell membrane from about 70 millivolts toward zero

action potential
the electrical impulse that provides the basis for the conduction of a neural impulse along an axon of a neuron

contracted. Galvani was demonstrating that the messages—or **neural impulses**—that travel along neurons are electrochemical in nature.

Neural impulses are messages that travel within neurons at somewhere between two (in nonmyelinated neurons) and 225 miles an hour (in myelinated neurons). This speed is not impressive when compared with that of an electrical current in a toaster oven or a lamp, which can travel at close to the speed of light—over 186,000 miles per second. Distances in the body are short, however, and a message will travel from a toe to the brain in perhaps 1/50th of a second.

An Electrochemical Voyage

The process by which neural impulses travel is electrochemical. Chemical changes take place within neurons that cause an electrical charge to be transmitted along their lengths. Neurons and body fluids contain *ions*—positively or negatively charged atoms. In a resting state—that is, when a neuron is not being stimulated by its neighbors—negatively charged chloride (Cl^-)

ions are plentiful within the neuron, contributing to an overall negative charge in relation to the outside. The difference in electrical charge readies, or **polarizes**, a neuron for firing by creating an internal negative charge in relation to the body fluid outside the cell membrane. The electrical potential across the neural membrane when it is not responding to other neurons—its **resting potential**—is about −70 millivolts in relation to the body fluid outside the cell membrane.

When an area on the surface of the resting neuron is adequately stimulated by other neurons, the cell membrane in the area changes its permeability to allow positively charged sodium ions to enter. Thus the area of entry becomes positively charged, or **depolarized**, with respect to the outside (see Figure 2.2A). The permeability of the cell membrane then changes again, allowing no more sodium ions to enter (see Figure 2.2B).

The electrical impulse that provides the basis for the conduction of a neural impulse along an axon of a neuron is termed its **action potential**. The inside of the cell axon at the disturbed area has an action potential of 110 millivolts. This action potential, added to the −70 millivolts that characterizes the resting potential, brings the membrane voltage to a positive charge of about +30 to +40 millivolts (see Figure 2.3). This inner change causes the next section of the cell to become

---

FIGURE 2.2 | Changes in Electrical Charges as a Neural Impulse Is Transmitted Along the Length of an Axon

Electrical charges inside and outside axons are measured by microscopic glass tubes placed inside and outside the cell membranes of axons. As shown in part A, when an axon is at rest, it has a negative charge of about −70 millivolts. But when sodium ions enter and the area of entry is depolarized, as shown in part B, the charge in that part of the axon rises to +30 to +40 millivolts. The change causes the next part of the cell membrane to become permeable to sodium ions, continuing the transmission of the neural impulse along the axon.

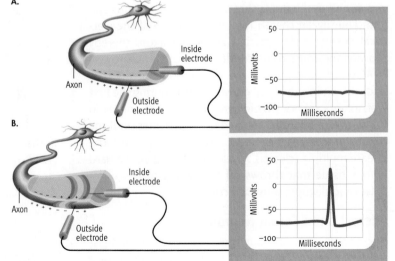

permeable to sodium ions. At the same time, other positively charged (potassium) ions are being pumped out of the area of the cell that was previously affected, which returns the area to its resting potential. In this way, the neural impulse is transmitted continuously along an axon. Because the impulse is created anew as it progresses, its strength does not change.

Firing: How Messages Voyage from Neuron to Neuron

The conduction of the neural impulse along the length of a neuron is what is meant by *firing*. When a rifle fires, it sends a bullet speeding through its barrel and discharges it at more than 1,000 feet per second. Neurons also fire, but instead of a barrel, a neuron has an axon. Instead of discharging a bullet, it releases *neurotransmitters*.

Some neurons fire in less than 1/1,000th of a second. When they fire, neurons transmit messages to other neurons, muscles, or glands. However, neurons will not fire unless the incoming messages combine to reach a certain strength, which is defined as the *threshold* at which a neuron will fire. A weak message may cause a temporary shift in electrical charge at some point along the cell membrane, but this charge will dissipate if the neuron is not stimulated to its threshold.

Every time a neuron fires, it transmits an impulse of the same strength. This occurrence is known as the **all-or-none principle.** That is, either a neuron fires or it doesn't. Neurons fire more often when they have been stimulated by larger numbers of other neurons. Stronger stimuli cause more frequent firing, but again, the strength of each firing remains the same.

TRUTH MESSAGES WITHIN NEURONS *DO* TRAVEL BY MEANS OF ELECTRICITY. HOWEVER, COMMUNICATION *BETWEEN* NEURONS IS CARRIED OUT DIFFERENTLY.

For a few thousandths of a second after firing, a neuron is in a **refractory period**; that is, it is insensitive to messages from other neurons and will not fire. This period is a time of recovery during which sodium is prevented from passing through the neuronal membrane. Because such periods of "recovery" might occur hundreds of times per second, it seems a rapid recovery and a short rest indeed.

The Synapse: On Being Well-Connected

A neuron relays its message to another neuron across a junction called a **synapse**. A synapse consists of an axon terminal from the transmitting neuron, a dendrite, or the body of a receiving neuron, and a fluid-filled gap

TRUTH IT IS TRUE THAT NEURONS IN THE BRAIN CAN SEND OUT HUNDREDS OF MESSAGES EACH SECOND—AND MANAGE TO CATCH SOME REST IN BETWEEN. THAT "REST" IS TERMED THE *REFRACTORY PERIOD*.

all-or-none principle the fact that a neuron fires an impulse of the same strength whenever its action potential is triggered

refractory period a phase following firing during which a neuron is less sensitive to messages from other neurons and will not fire

synapse a junction between the axon terminals of one neuron and the dendrites or cell body of another neuron

---

FIGURE 2.3 | Changes in Electrical Charges as a Neural Impulse Is Transmitted Across an Axon

The resting potential of a segment of a cell axon is about −70 millivolts. But the inside of the cell axon at the disturbed area has an action potential of about 110 millivolts. When we add this figure to the −70 millivolts that characterize the resting potential, we bring the membrane voltage to a positive charge of about +30 to +40 millivolts. The inner change causes the next section of the cell to become permeable to sodium ions. In this way, the neural impulse is transmitted continuously along an axon.

© Cengage Learning 2012

neurotransmitters
chemical substances involved in the transmission of neural impulses from one neuron to another

receptor site
a location on a dendrite of a receiving neuron tailored to receive a neurotransmitter

acetylcholine (ACh)
a neurotransmitter that controls muscle contractions

hippocampus
a structure of the brain that is involved in memory formation

dopamine
a neurotransmitter that affects the ability to perceive pleasure, voluntary movement, and learning and memory; it is involved in Parkinson's disease and appears to play a role in schizophrenia

between the two that is called the *synaptic cleft* (see Figure 2.1). Although the neural impulse is electrical, it does not jump across the synaptic cleft like a spark. Instead, when a nerve impulse reaches a synapse, axon terminals release chemicals into the synaptic cleft like myriad ships being cast into the sea. Scientists have identified a few dozen of these chemicals to date. Let's consider a few that are usually of the greatest interest to psychologists.

2-1c
NEUROTRANSMITTERS: THE CHEMICAL KEYS TO COMMUNICATION

Sacs called *synaptic vesicles* in the axon terminals contain **neurotransmitters**—the chemical keys to communication (see Figure 2.1). When a neural impulse (action potential) reaches the axon terminal, the vesicles release varying amounts of neurotransmitters into the synaptic cleft. From there, they influence the receiving neuron.

Each kind of neurotransmitter has a unique chemical structure, and each can fit into a specifically tailored harbor, or **receptor site**, on the receiving cell (see Figure 2.1). The analogy of a key fitting into a lock is often used to describe this process. Once released, not all molecules of a neurotransmitter find their way into receptor sites of other neurons. "Loose" neurotransmitters are usually either broken down or reabsorbed by the axon terminal (a process called *reuptake*).

Some neurotransmitters act to *excite* other neurons—that is, to cause other neurons to fire. Other neurotransmitters *inhibit* receiving neurons. That is, they prevent the neurons from firing. The sum of the stimulation—excitatory and inhibitory—determines whether a neuron will fire.

Neurotransmitters are involved in physical processes such as muscle contraction and psychological processes such as thoughts and emotions. Excesses or deficiencies of neurotransmitters have been linked to psychological disorders such as depression and schizophrenia. Let's consider the effects of some neurotransmitters that are of interest to psychologists: acetylcholine (ACh), dopamine, norepinephrine, serotonin, GABA, and endorphins.

Acetylcholine (ACh) is a neurotransmitter that controls muscle contractions. It is excitatory at synapses between nerves and muscles that involve voluntary movement but inhibitory at the heart and some other locations. The effects of *curare* highlight the functioning of ACh. The poison curare is extracted from plants by South American indigenous people and used in hunting. If an arrow tipped with curare pierces the skin and the poison enters the body, it prevents ACh from binding to the receptor sites on neurons. Because ACh helps muscles move, curare causes paralysis. The victim is prevented from contracting the muscles used in breathing and dies from suffocation. Botulism, a disease that stems from food poisoning, prevents the release of ACh and has the same effect as curare.

ACh is normally prevalent in a part of the brain called the **hippocampus**, a structure involved in the formation of memories (Louie & Wilson, 2001). When the amount of ACh available to the brain decreases, as in Alzheimer's disease, memory formation is impaired (Packard, 2009). In one experiment, researchers decreased the ACh available to the hippocampus of laboratory rats. As a result, the rats were incapable of learning their way through a maze, apparently because they could not remember which way to turn at various choice points (Egawa et al., 2002).

Dopamine is a neurotransmitter that acts in the brain and affects the ability to perceive pleasure, voluntary movement, and learning and memory. Nicotine, alcohol, and many other drugs are pleasurable because they heighten levels of dopamine. Deficiencies of dopamine are linked to Parkinson's disease, in which people progressively lose control over their muscles (Fuentes et al., 2009). They develop muscle tremors and jerky, uncoordinated movements.

The psychological disorder *schizophrenia* is characterized by confusion and false perceptions, and it has been linked to dopamine. People with schizophrenia may have more receptor sites for dopamine in an area of the brain that is involved in emotional responding. For this reason, they may "overutilize" the dopamine available in the brain (Neve, 2009; Roth et al., 2009). Overutilization is connected with hallucinations and disturbances of thought and emotion. The phenothiazines, a group of drugs used in the treatment of schizophrenia, inhibit the action of dopamine by blocking some dopamine receptors (Neve, 2009). Because of their action, phenothiazines may have Parkinson's-like side effects, which are usually treated by lowering the dosage or prescribing other drugs that lessen the Parkinson-like effects.

The boxer Muhammad Ali and actor Michael J. Fox are two of the better-known individuals who are afflicted with Parkinson's disease.

©Stephen Jaffe/AFP/Getty Images

Norepinephrine is produced largely by neurons in the brain stem and acts both as a neurotransmitter and as a hormone. It is an excitatory neurotransmitter that speeds up the heartbeat and other body processes and is involved in general arousal, learning and memory, and eating. Excesses and deficiencies of norepinephrine have been linked to mood disorders. Deficiencies of both ACh and norepinephrine particularly impair memory formation (Qi & Gold, 2009).

The stimulants cocaine and amphetamine ("speed") boost norepinephrine (as well as dopamine) production, increasing the firing of neurons and leading to persistent arousal. Amphetamines both facilitate the release of these neurotransmitters and prevent their reuptake. Cocaine also blocks reuptake.

Serotonin is a neurotransmitter that is involved in emotional arousal and sleep. Deficiencies of serotonin have been linked to eating disorders, alcoholism, depression, aggression, and insomnia (Polina et al., 2009; Risch et al., 2009). The drug LSD decreases the action of serotonin and is also believed to increase the utilization of dopamine, which may be the mechanism by which it produces hallucinations.

Gamma-aminobutyric acid (GABA) is another neurotransmitter of great interest to psychologists. One reason is that GABA is an inhibitory neurotransmitter that may help calm anxiety reactions (Cunningham et al., 2009). Tranquilizers and alcohol may quell anxiety by binding with GABA receptors and amplifying its effects. One class of antianxiety drug may also increase the sensitivity of receptor sites to GABA. Other studies link deficiencies of GABA to depression (Karolewicz et al., 2009).

Endorphins are inhibitory neurotransmitters. The word *endorphin* is the contraction of *endogenous morphine*. *Endogenous* means "developing from within." Endorphins occur naturally in the brain and in the bloodstream and are similar to the narcotic morphine in their functions and effects. They lock into receptor sites for chemicals that transmit pain messages to the brain. Once the endorphin "key" is in the "lock," the pain-causing chemicals are locked out. Endorphins may also increase our sense of competence, enhance the functioning of the immune system, and be connected with the pleasurable "runner's high" reported by many long-distance runners (Shah et al., 2009).

There you have it—a fabulous forest of neurons in which billions upon billions of axon terminals are pouring armadas of neurotransmitters into synaptic clefts at any given time. The combined activity of all these neurotransmitters determines which messages will be transmitted and which ones will not. You experience your sensations, your thoughts, and your control over your body as psychological events, but the psychological events come from billions upon billions of electrochemical events.

We can think of neurons as the microscopic building blocks of the nervous system. Millions upon millions of these neurons gather together to form larger, visible structures that we think of as the parts of the nervous system. We discuss those parts next.

2-1d THE PARTS OF THE NERVOUS SYSTEM

The nervous system consists of the brain, the spinal cord, and the **nerves** linking them to the sensory organs, muscles, and glands. As shown in Figure 2.4, the

norepinephrine
a neurotransmitter whose action is similar to that of the hormone epinephrine and that may play a role in depression

serotonin
a neurotransmitter involved in emotional arousal and sleep; deficiencies of serotonin have been linked to eating disorders, alcoholism, depression, aggression, and insomnia

gamma-aminobutyric acid (GABA)
an inhibitory neurotransmitter that apparently helps calm anxiety

endorphins
inhibitory neurotransmitters that occur naturally in the brain and in the bloodstream and are similar to the narcotic morphine in their functions and effects

nerve
a bundle of axons from many neurons

central nervous system
the brain and spinal cord

peripheral nervous system
the part of the nervous system consisting of the somatic nervous system and the autonomic nervous system

somatic nervous system
the division of the peripheral nervous system that connects the central nervous system with sensory receptors, skeletal muscles, and the surface of the body

autonomic nervous system (ANS)
the division of the peripheral nervous system that regulates glands and activities such as heartbeat, respiration, digestion, and dilation of the pupils

brain and the spinal cord make up the **central nervous system**. If you compare your nervous system to a computer, your central nervous system would be your central processing unit (CPU).

The sensory (afferent) neurons, which receive and transmit messages to the brain and spinal cord, and the motor (efferent) neurons, which transmit messages from the brain or spinal cord to the muscles and glands, make up the peripheral nervous system. In the comparison of the nervous system to a computer, the **peripheral nervous system** makes up the nervous system's peripheral devices—keyboard, mouse, DVD drive, and so on. You would not be able to feed information to your computer's central processing unit without these *peripheral* devices. Other peripheral devices, such as your monitor and printer, allow you to follow what is happening inside your CPU and see what it has done.

The Peripheral Nervous System: The Body's Peripheral Devices

The peripheral nervous system consists of sensory and motor neurons that transmit messages to and from the central nervous system. Without the peripheral nervous system, our brains would be like isolated CPUs. There would be no keyboards, mouses, DVDs, or other ways of inputting information. There would be no monitors, printers, modems, or other ways of displaying or transmitting information. We would be detached from the world. We would not be able to perceive it; we would not be able to act on it. The two main divisions of the peripheral nervous system are the *somatic nervous system* and the *autonomic nervous system*.

The **somatic nervous system** contains sensory (afferent) and motor (efferent) neurons. It transmits messages about sights, sounds, smells, temperature, body positions, and so on, to the central nervous system. Messages transmitted from the brain and spinal cord to the somatic nervous system control purposeful body movements such as raising a hand, winking, or running, as well as the tiny, almost imperceptible movements that maintain our balance and posture.

The **autonomic nervous system (ANS)** also has afferent and efferent neurons and regulates the glands and the muscles of internal organs. Thus, the ANS controls activities such as heartbeat, respiration, digestion, and dilation of the pupils. These activities can occur automatically, while we are asleep. But some of them can be overridden by conscious control. You can breathe at a purposeful pace, for example. Methods like biofeedback and yoga also help people gain voluntary control of functions such as heart rate and blood pressure.

The ANS also has two branches, or divisions: *sympathetic* and *parasympathetic*. These branches have largely opposing effects. Many organs and glands are stimu-

---

FIGURE 2.4 | The Divisions of the Nervous System

The nervous system contains two main divisions: the central nervous system and the peripheral nervous system. The central nervous system consists of the brain and spinal cord. The peripheral nervous system contains the somatic and autonomic systems. In turn, the autonomic nervous system has sympathetic and parasympathetic divisions.

© Cengage Learning 2012

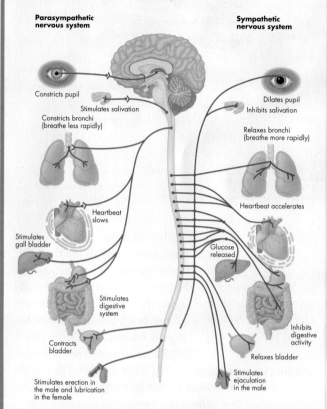

FIGURE 2.5 | The Branches of the Autonomic Nervous System (ANS)

Parasympathetic nervous system

Constricts pupil

Stimulates salivation

Constricts bronchi (breathe less rapidly)

Heartbeat slows

Stimulates gall bladder

Stimulates digestive system

Contracts bladder

Stimulates erection in the male and lubrication in the female

Sympathetic nervous system

Dilates pupil
Inhibits salivation

Relaxes bronchi (breathe more rapidly)

Heartbeat accelerates

Glucose released

Inhibits digestive activity

Relaxes bladder

Stimulates ejaculation in the male

The parasympathetic branch of the AMS generally acts to replenish stores of energy in the body. The sympathetic branch is most active during activities that expend energy. The two branches of the ANS frequently have antagonistic effects on the organs they service.

Weiten W. *Psychology*, 8e. Copyright © 2010. Cengage Learning.

lated by both branches of the ANS (see Figure 2.5). When organs and glands are simultaneously stimulated by both divisions, their effects can average out to some degree. In general, the **sympathetic division** is most active during processes that involve spending body energy from stored reserves, such as a fight-or-flight response to a predator or when you find out that your rent is going to be raised. The **parasympathetic division** is most active during processes that replenish reserves of energy, such as eating. When we are afraid, the sympathetic division of the ANS accelerates the heart rate. When we relax, the parasympathetic division decelerates the heart rate. The parasympathetic division stimulates digestive processes, but the sympathetic branch, which can be activated by fear, inhibits diges-

TRUTH FEAR CAN INDEED GIVE YOU INDIGESTION.

tion. Thus fear can give you indigestion. The ANS is of particular interest to psychologists because its activities are linked to various emotions such as anxiety and love.

The Central Nervous System: The Body's Central Processing Unit

The central nervous system consists of the spinal cord and the brain. The **spinal cord** is a true "information superhighway"—a column of nerves as thick as a thumb. It transmits messages from sensory receptors to the brain and from the brain to muscles and glands throughout the body. The spinal cord also carries out some "local government." That is, it responds to some sources of external stimulation through spinal reflexes. A **spinal reflex** is an unlearned response to a stimulus that may require only two neurons—a sensory neuron and a motor neuron (see Figure 2.6). In some reflexes, a third neuron, called an *interneuron*, transmits the neural impulse from the sensory neuron through the spinal cord to the motor neuron.

The spinal cord and brain contain gray matter and white matter. **Gray matter** consists of nonmyelinated neurons. Some of these are involved in spinal reflexes. Others send their axons to the brain. **White matter** is composed of bundles of longer, myelinated (and thus whitish) axons that carry messages to and from the brain. A cross-section of the spinal cord shows that the gray matter, which includes cell bodies, is distributed in a butterfly pattern (see Figure 2.6).

The spinal cord is also involved in reflexes. We blink in response to a puff of air in our faces. We swallow when food accumulates in the mouth. A physician may tap below the knee to elicit the knee-jerk reflex, a sign that the nervous system is operating adequately. Sexual response involves many reflexes. Urinating and defecating are reflexes that occur in response to pressure in the bladder and the rectum. It is your central nervous system that makes you so special. Other

sympathetic division
the branch of the ANS that is most active during emotional responses, such as fear and anxiety, that spend the body's reserves of energy

parasympathetic division
the branch of the ANS that is most active during processes (such as digestion) that restore the body's reserves of energy

spinal cord
a column of nerves within the spine that transmits messages from sensory receptors to the brain and from the brain to muscles and glands throughout the body

spinal reflex
a simple, unlearned response to a stimulus that may involve only two neurons

gray matter
the grayish neurons and neural segments that are involved in spinal reflexes

white matter
axon bundles that carry messages to and from the brain

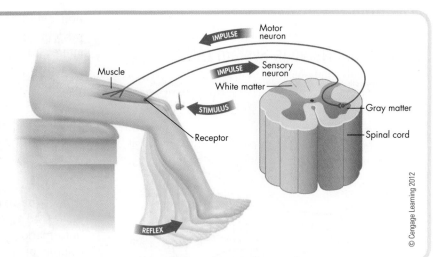

FIGURE 2.6 | The Reflex Arc

Reflexes are inborn, stereotyped behavior patterns that have apparently evolved because they help individuals adapt to the environment even before they can understand and purposefully manipulate the environment. Here we see a cross-section of the spinal cord, highlighting a sensory neuron and a motor neuron, which are involved in the knee-jerk reflex. In some reflexes, interneurons link sensory and motor neurons.

species see more sharply, smell more keenly, and hear more acutely. Other species run faster, or fly through the air, or swim underwater, without the benefit of artificial devices such as airplanes and submarines. But it is your central nervous system that enables you to use symbols and language, the abilities that allow people not only to adapt to their environment but also to create new environments and give them names (Bandura, 1999).

FICTION IT IS NOT TRUE THAT THE HUMAN BRAIN IS LARGER THAN THAT OF ANY OTHER ANIMAL. HOWEVER, OUR BRAINS ACCOUNT FOR A LARGER PERCENTAGE OF OUR BODY WEIGHT THAN DO THE BRAINS OF ELEPHANTS OR WHALES.

2-2 The Brain: Wider Than the Sky

When I was a child, I was told that the human nervous system is more complex than that of any other animal and that our brains are larger than those of any other animal. Now, this last piece of business is not quite true. A human brain weighs about 3 pounds, but the brains of elephants and whales may be four times as heavy. Still, our brains account for a greater part of our body weight than do those of elephants or whales. Our brains weigh about 1/60th of our body weight. Elephant brains weigh about 1/1,000th of their total weight, and whale brains are a paltry 1/10,000th of their weight.

"The Brain—is wider than the Sky—
For—put them side by side—
The one the other will contain
With ease—and you—beside—"
—EMILY DICKINSON

Philosophers and scientists have wondered about the functions of the brain throughout history. Scientists today generally agree that the mind is a function of the brain (American Psychological Association, 2008; Block, 2009). Some engage in research that attempts to pinpoint exactly what happens in certain parts of the brain when we are listening to music or trying to remember someone's face. At other times—as in the case of Phineas Gage—knowledge has almost literally fallen into their laps. From injuries to the head—some of them minimal, some horrendous—we have learned that brain damage can impair consciousness, perception, memory, and abilities to make plans and decisions. In some cases, the loss of large portions of the brain may result in little loss of function. But the loss of smaller portions in certain locations can cause language problems, memory loss, or death. It has been known for about two centuries that damage to the left side of the brain is connected with loss of sensation or movement on the right side of the body, and vice versa. Thus it has been assumed that the brain's control mechanisms cross over from right to left, and vice versa, as they descend into the body.

Accidents provide unplanned—and uncontrolled—opportunities of studying the brain. Still, scientists learn more about the brain through methods like experimentation, electroencephalography, and brain scans.

2-2a EXPERIMENTING WITH THE BRAIN

The results of disease and accidents (as in the case of Phineas Gage) have shown us that brain injuries can be connected with changes in behavior and mental processes. Scientists have also purposefully damaged part of the brain in laboratory animals to observe the results. For example, damaging one part of the brain region called the *hypothalamus* causes rats to overeat. Damaging another part of the hypothalamus causes them to stop eating. It is as if parts of the brain contain on–off switches for certain kinds of behavior, at least in lower animals.

Because the brain has no receptors for pain, surgeon Wilder Penfield (1969) was able to stimulate parts of human brains with electrical probes. As a result, his patients reported perceiving certain memories. Electrical stimulation of the brain has also shown that parts of the brain are connected with specific kinds of sensations (as of light or sound) or motor activities (such as movement of an arm or leg).

The Electroencephalograph

Penfield stimulated parts of the brain with an electrical current and asked people to report what they experienced. Researchers have also used the **electroencephalograph (EEG)** to record the natural electrical activity of the brain. The EEG (see Figure 2.7) detects minute amounts of electrical activity—called *brain waves*—that pass between the electrodes. Certain brain waves are associated with feelings of relaxation, with various stages of sleep, and with neurological problems such as epilepsy.

Brain-Imaging Techniques

When Phineas Gage had his fabled accident, the only ways to look into the brain were to drill holes or crack it open, neither of which would have contributed to the well-being of the subject. But in the latter years of the 20th century, researchers developed imaging techniques that use the computer's ability to generate images of the parts of the brain from sources of radiation.

Computerized axial tomography (CAT or CT scan), shown in Figure 2.8A, passes X-rays through the head and measures the structures that reflect the beams from various angles, generating a three-dimensional image. The CAT scan reveals deformities in shape and structure that are connected with blood clots, tumors, and other health problems.

A second method, **positron emission tomography (PET scan)**, shown in Figure 2.8B, forms a computer-generated image of the activity of parts of the brain by tracing the amount of glucose used (or metabolized) by these parts. More glucose is metabolized in more active parts of the brain. To trace the metabolism of glucose, a harmless amount of a radioactive compound, called a *tracer*, is mixed with glucose and injected into the bloodstream. When the glucose reaches the brain, the patterns of activity are revealed by measurement of the positrons—positively charged particles—that are given off by the tracer.

electroencephalograph (EEG) a method of detecting brain waves by means of measuring the current between electrodes placed on the scalp

computerized axial tomography (CAT or CT scan) a method of brain imaging that passes a narrow X-ray beam through the head and measures the structures that reflect the beams from various angles, enabling a computer to generate a three-dimensional image

positron emission tomography (PET scan) a method of brain imaging that injects a radioactive tracer into the bloodstream and assesses activity of parts of the brain according to the amount of glucose they metabolize

FIGURE 2.7 | The Electroencephalograph (EEG)

The EEG detects brain waves that pass between electrodes that are attached to the scalp. It has been used to reveal electrical activity associated with relaxation and the stages of sleep.

© Richard T. Nowitz/Corbis

A third imaging technique is **magnetic resonance imaging (MRI)**, which is shown in Figure 2.8C. In MRI, the person lies in a powerful magnetic field and is exposed to radio waves that cause parts of the brain to emit signals, which are measured from multiple angles. MRI relies on subtle shifts in blood flow. (More blood flows to more active parts of the brain, supplying them with oxygen.) **Functional MRI (fMRI)** provides a more rapid picture and therefore enables researchers to observe the brain "while it works" by taking repeated scans while subjects engage in activities such as mental processes and voluntary movements. fMRI can be used to show which parts of the brain are active when we are, say, listening to music, using language, or playing chess (Krueger et al., 2008; Newman et al., 2009; Stocco & Anderson, 2008).

Some researchers consider the prefrontal cortex to be the "executive center" of the brain, where decisions are made to keep information in working memory and to solve problems. The prefrontal cortex is the part of the frontal lobe (see Figure 2.11 on page 41) that is closest to the front of the brain. Research with the PET scan and MRI supports the view that the prefrontal cortex is where we process much of the information involved in making plans and solving problems (Gilbert et al., 2008; Wang et al., 2008).

2-2b A VOYAGE THROUGH THE BRAIN

Let's begin our tour of the brain with the *hindbrain*, where the spinal cord rises to meet the brain (see Figure 2.9). Here we find three major structures: the *medulla*, the *pons*, and the *cerebellum*. Many pathways pass through the **medulla** to connect the spinal cord to higher levels of the brain. The medulla regulates basic

---

FIGURE 2.8 | Brain Imaging Techniques

Part A shows a CAT scan, part B shows a PET scan, and part C shows an MRI.

A. Computerized axial tomography (the CAT scan) passes a narrow X-ray beam through the head and measures structures that reflect the rays from various angles, enabling a computer to generate a three-dimensional image.

B. Positron emission tomography (the PET scan) injects a radioactive tracer into the bloodstream and assesses activity of parts of the brain according to the amount of glucose they metabolize.

C. Magnetic resonance imaging (MRI) places a person in a magnetic field and uses radio waves to cause the brain to emit signals which reveal shifts in the flow of blood which, in turn, indicate brain activity.

A. CAT scan

B. PET scan

C. MRI

functions such as heart rate, blood pressure, and respiration. (In fact, Gage survived his accident because his medulla escaped injury.) The medulla also plays roles in sleeping, sneezing, and coughing. The **pons** is a bulge in the hindbrain that lies forward of the medulla. *Pons* is the Latin word for "bridge"; the pons is so named because of the bundles of nerves that pass through it. The pons transmits information about body movement and is involved in functions related to attention, sleep and arousal, and respiration.

Behind the pons lies the **cerebellum** ("little brain" in Latin). The cerebellum has two hemispheres that are involved in maintaining balance and in controlling motor (muscle) behavior. You may send a command from your forebrain to get up and walk to the refrigerator, but your cerebellum is key to organizing the information that enables you to engage in these movements. The cerebellum allows you to place one leg in front of the other and reach your destination without tipping over. Injury to

> **"The brain is a wonderful organ; it starts working the moment you get up in the morning and does not stop until you get into the office."**
>
> —ROBERT FROST

iStockphoto.com/Fotografia/Basica

the cerebellum may impair motor coordination and cause stumbling and loss of muscle tone.

As we tour the hindbrain, we also find the lower part of the **reticular formation**. That is where the reticular formation begins, but it ascends through the midbrain into the lower part of the forebrain. The reticular formation is vital in the functions of attention, sleep, and arousal. Injury to the reticular formation may result in a coma. Stimulation of the reticular formation causes it to send messages to the cerebral cortex (the large wrinkled mass that you think of as your brain), making us more alert to sensory information. In classic neurological research, Giuseppe Moruzzi and Horace Magoun (1949) discov-

pons
a structure of the hindbrain involved in respiration, attention, and sleep and arousal

cerebellum
a part of the hindbrain involved in muscle coordination and balance

reticular formation
a part of the brain involved in attention, sleep, and arousal

---

FIGURE 2.9 | The Parts of the Brain

This view of the brain, split top to bottom, shows some of the most important structures. Note how close the hypothalamus is to the pituitary gland. The proximity allows the hypothalamus to readily influence the pituitary gland. The "valleys" in the cerebrum are called *fissures*.

Corpus callosum
Thick bundle of axons that serves as a bridge between the two cerebral hemispheres

Cerebrum
Center of thinking and language; prefrontal area contains "executive center" of brain

Thalamus
Relay station for sensory information

Hypothalamus
Secretes hormones that stimulate secretion of hormones by the pituitary gland; involved in basic drives such as hunger, sex, and aggression

Pituitary gland
Secretes hormones that regulate many body functions, including secretion of hormones from other glands; sometimes referred to as the "master gland"

Cerebellum
Essential to balance and coordination

Reticular formation
Involved in regulation of sleep and waking; stimulation of reticular formation increases arousal

Pons
Involved in regulation of movement, sleep and arousal, respiration

Medulla
Involved in regulation of heart rate, blood pressure, respiration, circulation

© Cengage Learning 2013

thalamus

an area near the center of the brain involved in the relay of sensory information to the cortex and in the functions of sleep and attention

hypothalamus

a bundle of nuclei below the thalamus involved in body temperature, motivation, and emotion

limbic system

a group of structures involved in memory, motivation, and emotion that forms a fringe along the inner edge of the cerebrum

amygdala

a part of the limbic system that apparently facilitates stereotypical aggressive responses

ered that electrical stimulation of the reticular formation of a sleeping cat caused it to awaken at once. But when the reticular formation was severed from higher parts of the brain, the cat fell into a coma from which it would not awaken. Drugs known as central nervous system depressants, such as alcohol, are thought to work, in part, by lowering the activity of the reticular formation.

Key areas of the forwardmost part of the brain, or forebrain, are the *thalamus*, the *hypothalamus*, the *limbic system*, and the *cerebrum* (see Figure 2.10). The **thalamus** is located near the center of the brain and could be said to lie between the forebrain and the midbrain. It consists of two joined egg-shaped structures. The thalamus serves as a relay station for sensory stimulation. Nerve fibers from sensory systems enter from below; their information is then transmitted to the cerebral cortex by fibers that exit from above. For example, the thalamus relays sensory input from the eyes to the visual areas of the cerebral cortex. The thalamus also regulates sleep and attention in coordination with other brain structures, including the reticular formation.

The **hypothalamus** lies beneath the thalamus and above the pituitary gland. It weighs only four grams, yet it is vital in the regulation of body temperature, concentration of fluids, storage of nutrients, and motivation and emotion. Experimenters learn many of the functions of the hypothalamus by implanting electrodes in parts of it and observing the effects of electrical stimulation. They have found that the hypothalamus is involved in hunger, thirst, sexual behavior, caring for offspring, and aggression. Among lower animals, stimulation of various areas of the hypothalamus can trigger instinctual behaviors such as fighting, mating, or nest building.

Canadian psychologists James Olds and Peter Milner (1954) made a splendid mistake in the 1950s. They were attempting to implant an electrode in a rat's reticular formation to see how stimulation of the area might affect learning. Olds, however, was primarily a social psychologist and not a biological psychologist. He missed his target and found a part of the animal's hypothalamus instead. Olds and Milner dubbed this area the "pleasure center" because the animal would repeat whatever it was doing when it was stimulated. The term *pleasure center* is not used frequently because it appears to attribute human emotions to rats. Yet the "pleasure centers" must be doing something right, because rats stimulate themselves in these centers by pressing a pedal several thousand times an hour, until they are exhausted (Olds, 1969).

The hypothalamus is important to humans as well as to lower animals. Unfortunately (or fortunately), our "pleasure centers" are not as clearly defined as those of the rat. Then, too, our responses to messages from the hypothalamus are less automatic and relatively more influenced by higher brain functions—that is, cognitive factors such as thought, choice, and value systems.

The **limbic system** forms a fringe along the inner edge of the cerebrum and is fully evolved only in mammals (see Figure 2.10). It is made up of several structures, including the amygdala, hippocampus, and parts of the hypothalamus. It is involved in memory and emotion and in the drives of hunger, sex, and aggression. People with hippocampal damage can retrieve old memories but cannot permanently store new information. As a result, they may reread the same newspaper day in and day out without recalling that they read it before. Or they may have to be perpetually reintroduced to people they have met just hours earlier (Squire, 2004).

The **amygdala** is near the bottom of the limbic system and looks like two little almonds. Studies using lesioning and electrical stimulation show that the amygdala is connected with aggressive behavior in monkeys, cats, and other animals. Early in the 20th century, Heinrich Klüver and Paul Bucy (1939) lesioned part of the amygdala of a rhesus monkey. Rhesus monkeys are normally a scrappy lot and try to bite or grab at intruders, but de-

---

FIGURE 2.10 | The Limbic System

The limbic system is made up of structures that include the amygdala, the hippocampus, and parts of the hypothalamus. It is evolved fully only in mammals and forms a fringe along the inner edge of the cerebrum. The limbic system is involved in memory and emotion, and in the drives of hunger, sex, and aggression.

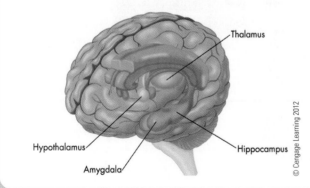

© Cengage Learning 2012

struction of this animal's amygdala made it docile. No longer did it react aggressively to people. It even allowed people to poke and pinch it. Electrical stimulation of the part of the amygdala that Klüver and Bucy had destroyed, however, triggers a "rage response." For example, it causes a cat to hiss and arch its back in preparation to attack. The amygdala is also connected with a fear response (Ahs et al., 2009; Feinstein et al., 2010). If you electrically stimulate another part of the amygdala, the cat cringes in fear when you cage it with a mouse.

The amygdala is also connected with vigilance. It is involved in emotions, learning, and memory, and it behaves something like a spotlight, focusing attention on matters that are novel and important to know more about.

Only in humans does the **cerebrum** make up such a large part of the brain (refer back to Figure 2.9). The cerebrum is responsible for thinking and language. The surface of the cerebrum—the **cerebral cortex**—is wrinkled, or convoluted, with ridges and valleys. The convolutions allow a great deal of surface area to be packed into the brain—and surface area is apparently connected with cognitive ability. Valleys in the cortex are called *fissures*. A key fissure almost divides the cerebrum in half, creating two hemispheres with something of the shape of a walnut. The hemispheres are connected by the **corpus callosum** (Latin for "hard body"), a bundle of some 200 million nerve fibers (refer back to Figure 2.9).

2-2c THE CEREBRAL CORTEX

The cerebral cortex is the part of the brain that you usually think of as your brain. *Cortex* is a Latin word meaning "bark," as in the bark of a tree. Just as the bark is the outer coating of a tree, the cerebral cortex is the outer coating of the cerebrum. Despite its extreme importance and its creation of a world of civilization and culture, it is only about 1/8″ thick.

The cerebral cortex is involved in almost every bodily activity, includ-

ing most sensations and responses. It is also the part of the brain that frees people from the tyranny of genetic dictates and instinct. It is the seat of thinking and language, and it enables humans to think deeply about the world outside and to make decisions.

The cerebral cortex has two hemispheres, left and right. Each of the hemispheres is divided into four lobes, as shown in Figure 2.11. The *frontal lobe* lies in front of the central fissure and the *parietal lobe* behind it.

cerebrum
the large mass of the forebrain, which consists of two hemispheres

cerebral cortex
the wrinkled surface area (gray matter) of the cerebrum

corpus callosum
a thick fiber bundle that connects the hemispheres of the cortex

FIGURE 2.11 | The Geography of the Cerebral Cortex

The cortex has four lobes: frontal, parietal, temporal, and occipital. The visual area of the cortex is in the occipital lobe. The hearing or auditory cortex lies in the temporal lobe. The motor and somatosensory areas—shown below—face each other across the central fissure. Note that the face and the hands are "super-sized" in the motor and somatosensory areas. Why do you think this is so?

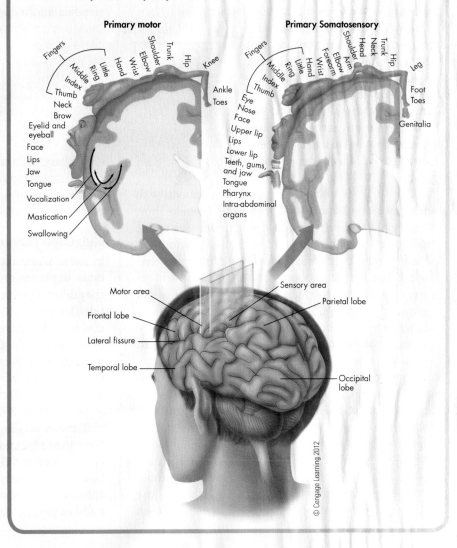

© Cengage Learning 2012

somatosensory cortex
the section of cortex in which sensory stimulation is projected. It lies just behind the central fissure in the parietal lobe

motor cortex
the section of cortex that lies in the frontal lobe, just across the central fissure from the sensory cortex; neural impulses in the motor cortex are linked to muscular responses throughout the body

aphasia
a disruption in the ability to understand or produce language

The *temporal lobe* lies below the side, or lateral, fissure—across from the frontal and parietal lobes. The *occipital lobe* lies behind the temporal lobe and behind and below the parietal lobe.

When light strikes the eyes, neurons in the occipital lobe fire, and as a result, we "see" (that is, the image is projected in the brain). Direct artificial stimulation of the occipital lobe also produces visual sensations. If neurons in the occipital region of the cortex were stimulated with electricity, you would "see" flashes of light even if it were pitch-black or your eyes were covered. The hearing or auditory area of the cortex lies in the temporal lobe along the lateral fissure. Sounds cause structures in the ear to vibrate. Messages are relayed from those structures to the auditory area of the cortex; when you hear a noise, neurons in this area are firing.

Just behind the central fissure in the parietal lobe lies a sensory area called the **somatosensory cortex**, which receives messages from skin senses all over the body. These sensations include warmth and cold, touch, pain, and movement. Neurons in different parts of the sensory cortex fire, depending on whether you wiggle your finger or raise your leg.

Many years ago it was discovered that patients with injuries to one hemisphere of the brain would show sensory or motor deficits on the opposite side of the body below the head. This led to the recognition that sensory and motor nerves cross in the brain and elsewhere. The left hemisphere controls, acts on, and receives inputs from the right side of the body. The right hemisphere controls, acts on, and receives inputs from the left side of the body. The motor area of the cerebral cortex, or **motor cortex**, lies in the frontal lobe, just across the valley of the central fissure from the somatosensory cortex. Neurons firing in the motor cortex cause parts of our body to move. More than 100 years ago, German scientists electrically stimulated the motor cortex in dogs and observed that muscles contracted in response (Fritsch & Hitzig, 1870/1960). Since then, neuroscientists have mapped the motor cortex in people and lower animals by inserting electrical probes and seeing which muscles contract. For example, José Delgado (1969) caused one patient to make a fist even

though he tried to prevent his hand from closing. The patient said, "I guess, doctor, that your electricity is stronger than my will" (Delgado, 1969, p. 114).

Thinking, Language, and the Cortex

Areas of the cerebral cortex that are not primarily involved in sensation or motor activity are called *association areas*. They make possible the breadth and depth of human learning, thought, memory, and language. The association areas in the *prefrontal* region of the brain—that is, in the frontal lobes, near the forehead—are the brain's executive center. It appears to be where we solve problems and make plans and decisions.

Executive functions like problem solving also require memory, like the memory in your computer. Association areas also provide the core of your working memory (Rawley & Constantinidis, 2008). They are connected with various sensory areas in the brain and can tap whatever sensory information is needed or desired. The prefrontal region thus retrieves visual, auditory, and other memories and manipulates them; similarly, a computer retrieves information from files in storage and manipulates it in working memory.

Certain neurons in the visual area of the occipital lobe fire in response to the visual presentation of vertical lines. Others fire in response to presentation of horizontal lines. Although one group of cells may respond to one aspect of the visual field and another group of cells may respond to another, association areas put it all together. As a result, we see a box or an automobile or a road map and not a confusing array of verticals and horizontals.

Language Functions

In some ways, the left and right hemispheres of the brain duplicate each other's functions. In other ways, they differ. The left hemisphere contains language functions for nearly all right-handed people and for two out of three left-handed people (Pinker, 2007). However, the brain remains "plastic," or changeable, through about the age of 13. As a result, children who lose the left hemisphere of the brain because of medical problems may transfer speech functions to the right hemisphere (Mbwana et al., 2008; Mercado, 2008).

Two key language areas lie within the hemisphere of the cortex that contains language functions (usually the left hemisphere): Broca's area and Wernicke's area (see Figure 2.12). Damage to either area is likely to cause an **aphasia**—that is, a disruption of the ability to understand or produce language.

TRUTH IT IS TRUE THAT IF AN AREA OF YOUR SOMATOSENSORY CORTEX IS STIMULATED WITH AN ELECTRICAL PROBE, IT MIGHT SEEM TO YOU AS IF SOMEONE IS TOUCHING YOUR ARM OR LEG.

FIGURE 2.12 | Broca's and Wernicke's Areas of the Cerebral Cortex

The areas that are most involved in speech are Broca's area and Wernicke's area. Damage to either area can produce an aphasia—a disruption of the ability to understand or produce language.

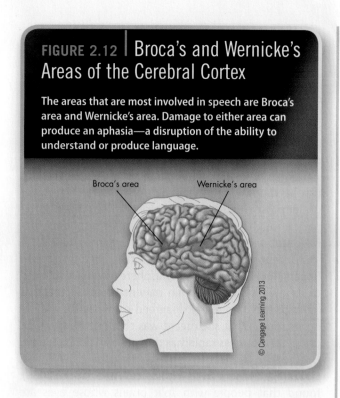

Broca's area　　Wernicke's area

© Cengage Learning 2013

may laboriously say "walk dog." The phrase can have various meanings, such as "I want to take the dog for a walk" or "Take the dog out for a walk."

A part of the brain called the *angular gyrus* lies between the visual cortex and Wernicke's area. The angular gyrus "translates" visual information, as in perceiving written words, into auditory information (sounds) and sends it on to Wernicke's area. Brain imaging suggests that problems in the angular gyrus can seriously impair reading ability because it becomes difficult for the reader to segment words into sounds (Milne et al., 2002).

2-2d LEFT BRAIN, RIGHT BRAIN?

You may have heard that some people are "left-brained," whereas others are "right-brained." The notion is that the hemispheres of the brain are involved in very different kinds of intellectual and emotional functions and responses. According to this view, left-brained people would be primarily logical and intellectual. Right-brained people would be intuitive, creative, and emotional. Those of us who are fortunate enough to have our brains "in balance" would presumably have the best of it—the capacity for logic combined with emotional richness.

Like many other popular ideas, the left-brain–right-brain notion is exaggerated. Research does suggest that in right-handed individuals, the left hemisphere is relatively more involved in intellectual undertakings that require logical analysis and problem solving, language, and mathematical computation (Corballis, 2009). The other hemisphere (typically the right hemisphere) is usually superior in visual–spatial functions (it's better at putting puzzles together), recognition of faces, discrimination of colors, aesthetic and emotional responses, understanding metaphors, and creative mathematical reasoning. Despite these differences, the hemispheres of the brain do not act independently such that some people are truly left-brained and others are right-brained (American Psychological Association, 2008). The functions of the left and right hemispheres overlap to some degree, and they tend to respond simultaneously as we focus our attention on one thing or another.

Whether we are talking about language functions or being "left-brained" or "right-brained," we are talking about people whose hemispheres of the cerebral cortex communicate back and forth.

Wernicke's area lies in the temporal lobe near the auditory cortex. It responds mainly to auditory information (sounds). As you are reading this page, however, the visual information is registered in the visual cortex of your occipital lobe. It is then recoded as auditory information as it travels to Wernicke's area. Broca's area is located in the frontal lobe, near the section of the motor cortex that controls the muscles of the tongue, throat, and other areas of the face used when speaking. Broca's area processes the information and relays it to the motor cortex. The motor cortex sends the signals that cause muscles in your throat and mouth to contract. If you are "subvocalizing"—saying what you are reading "under your breath"—that is because Wernicke's area transmits information to Broca's area via nerve fibers.

People with damage to Wernicke's area may show **Wernicke's aphasia**, which impairs their abilities to comprehend speech and to think of the proper words to express their own thoughts. Ironically, they usually speak freely and with proper syntax. Wernicke's area is essential to understanding the relationships between words and their meanings. When Broca's area is damaged, people usually understand language well enough but speak slowly and laboriously, in simple sentences. This pattern is termed **Broca's aphasia**.

Some people with Broca's aphasia utter short, meaningful phrases that omit small but important grammatical words such as *is*, *and*, and *the*. Such an individual

2-2e HANDEDNESS

Being left-handed was once seen as a deficiency. Left-handed students were made to learn to write with their right hands. We are usually labeled right-handed or left-handed on the basis of our handwriting preferences, yet some people write with one hand and pass a football with the other.

Being left-handed appears to provide a somewhat-greater-than-average probability of language problems, such as dyslexia and stuttering, and health problems such as migraine headaches and allergies (Fasmer et al., 2008; Goez & Zelnik, 2008; Lengen et al., 2008). But there may also be advantages to being left-handed. Left-handed people are more likely than right-handed people to be numbered among the ranks of gifted artists, musicians, and mathematicians (Preti & Vallante, 2007).

The origins of handedness may have a genetic component. In the English royal family, Queen Elizabeth II and Princes Charles and William are all left-handed, as was Queen Elizabeth's mother. On the other hand, a recent study of more than 27,000 Dutch and Australian twin families found that heritability makes only about a 24% contribution to the likelihood of being right- or left-handed (Medland et al., 2008).

2-2f SPLIT-BRAIN EXPERIMENTS

A number of people with severe cases of **epilepsy** have split-brain operations in which much of the corpus callosum is severed (refer back to Figure 2.9). The purpose of the operation is to confine seizures to one hemisphere of the cerebral cortex rather than allowing a neural tempest to reverberate. Split-brain operations do seem to help people with epilepsy.

People who have undergone split-brain operations can be thought of as winding up with two brains, yet under most circumstances their behavior remains ordinary enough. Still, some aspects of hemispheres that have stopped talking to each other are intriguing.

As reported by pioneering brain surgeon Joseph Bogen (1969, 2000), each hemisphere may have a "mind of its own." One split-brain patient reported that her hemispheres frequently disagreed on what she should be wearing. What she meant was that one hand might undo her blouse as rapidly as the other was buttoning it.

Another pioneer of split-brain research, Michael Gazzaniga (American Psychological Association, 2008), found that people with split brains whose eyes are closed may be able to verbally describe an object such as a key when they hold it in one hand, but not when they hold it in the other hand. If a person with a split brain handles a key with his left hand behind a screen,

FIGURE 2.13 | A Divided-Brain Experiment

In the drawing on the left, we see that visual sensations in the left visual field are projected in the occipital cortex of the right hemisphere. Visual sensations from the right visual field are projected in the occipital cortex in the left hemisphere. In the divided-brain experiment diagrammed on the right, a person with a severed corpus callosum handles a key with his left hand and perceives the written word *key* in his left visual field. The word "key" is projected in the right hemisphere. Speech, however, is usually a function of the left hemisphere. The written word "ring," perceived by the right visual field, is projected in the left hemisphere. So, when asked what he is handling, the divided-brain subject reports "ring," not "key."

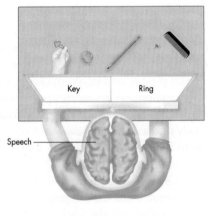

© Cengage Learning 2012

tactile impressions of the key are projected into the right hemisphere, which has little or no language ability (see Figure 2.13). Thus, he will not be able to describe the key. If he holds it in his right hand, he will have no trouble describing it because sensory impressions are projected into the left hemisphere of the cortex, which contains language functions. To further confound matters, if the word *ring* is projected into the left hemisphere while the person is asked what he is handling, he will say "ring," not "key."

This discrepancy between what is felt and what is said occurs only in people with split brains. Even so, people who have undergone split-brain operations tend to lead largely normal lives. And for the rest of us, the two hemispheres work together most of the time, such as when we are playing the piano or solving math problems.

(2-3) The Endocrine System

The body has two types of **glands**: glands with ducts and glands without ducts. A *duct* is a passageway that carries substances to specific locations. Saliva, sweat, tears, and breast milk all reach their destinations through ducts. A number of substances secreted by *ductless* glands have effects on behavior and mental processes.

FIGURE 2.14 | The Endocrine Glands

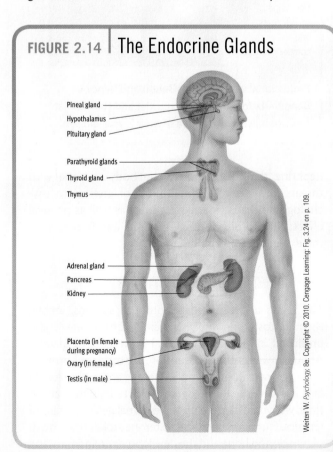

Pineal gland
Hypothalamus
Pituitary gland
Parathyroid glands
Thyroid gland
Thymus
Adrenal gland
Pancreas
Kidney
Placenta (in female during pregnancy)
Ovary (in female)
Testis (in male)

Weiten W. *Psychology*, 8e. Copyright © 2010. Cengage Learning: Fig. 3.24 on p. 109.

The ductless glands make up the **endocrine system** (see Figure 2.14), and they release **hormones** into the bloodstream. Hormones are then picked up by specific receptor sites and regulate growth, metabolism, and some forms of behavior. That is, they act only on receptors in certain locations.

Much hormonal action helps the body maintain steady states—fluid levels, blood sugar levels, and so on. Bodily mechanisms measure current levels; when these levels deviate from optimal, they signal glands to release hormones. The maintenance of steady states requires feedback of bodily information to glands. This type of system is referred to as a *negative feedback loop*. When enough of a hormone has been secreted, the gland is signaled to stop.

2-3a THE PITUITARY AND THE HYPOTHALAMUS

The pituitary gland and the hypothalamus work in close cooperation. The **pituitary gland** lies below the hypothalamus. Although the pituitary is only about the size of a pea, it is so central to the body's functioning that it has been dubbed the "master gland."

The anterior (front) and posterior (back) lobes of the pituitary gland secrete hormones that regulate the functioning of many other glands. *Growth hormone* regulates the growth of muscles, bones, and glands. Children whose growth patterns are abnormally slow may catch up to their age-mates when they obtain growth hormone. *Prolactin* regulates maternal behavior in lower mammals such as rats and stimulates production of milk in women. As a water conservation measure, *vasopressin* (also called *antidiuretic hormone*) inhibits production of urine when the body's fluid levels are low. Vasopressin is also connected with stereotypical paternal behavior in some mammals. *Oxytocin* stimulates labor in pregnant women and is connected with maternal behavior (cuddling and caring for young) in some mammals (Champagne et al., 2009). Obstetricians can induce labor by injecting pregnant women with oxytocin. During nursing, stimulation of the nerve endings of the nipples signals the brain to secrete oxytocin, which then causes the breasts to eject milk.

Although the pituitary gland may be the "master gland," the master has a "commander": the hypothalamus. We know today that the hypothalamus regulates much pituitary activity. The hypothalamus secretes a number of releasing hormones, or "factors," that stimulate the pituitary gland to secrete related hormones. For example, growth hormone releasing factor (hGRF) causes the pituitary to produce growth hormone. Blood vessels between the hypothalamus and the pituitary gland provide a direct route for these factors.

2-3b THE PINEAL GLAND

The pineal gland secretes the hormone *melatonin*, which helps regulate the sleep–wake cycle and may affect the onset of puberty. Melatonin may also be connected with aging. In addition, it appears that melatonin is a mild sedative, and some people use it as a sleeping pill (Ismail & Mowafi, 2009). Melatonin may be used to help people adjust to jet lag (Arendt, 2009).

2-3c THE THYROID GLAND

The thyroid gland could be considered the body's accelerator. It produces *thyroxin*, which affects the body's *metabolism*—the rate at which the body uses oxygen and produces energy. Some people are overweight because of *hypothyroidism*, a condition that results from too little thyroxin. Thyroxin deficiency in children can lead to *cretinism*, a condition characterized by stunted growth and mental retardation. Adults who secrete too little thyroxin may feel tired and sluggish and may put on weight. People who produce too much thyroxin may develop *hyperthyroidism*, which is characterized by excitability, insomnia, and weight loss.

2-3d THE ADRENAL GLANDS

The adrenal glands, located above the kidneys, have an outer layer, or cortex, and an inner core, or medulla. The adrenal cortex is regulated by the pituitary hormone ACTH (adrenocorticotrophic hormone). The adrenal cortex secretes hormones known as *corticosteroids*, or cortical steroids. These hormones regulate the heartbeat, increase resistance to stress, promote muscle development, and cause the liver to release stored sugar, making more energy available in emergencies, such as when you see another car veering toward your own. Epinephrine and norepinephrine are secreted by the adrenal medulla. *Epinephrine*, also known as adrenaline, is manufactured exclusively by the adrenal glands, but norepinephrine (noradrenaline) is also produced elsewhere in the body. (Norepinephrine acts as a neurotransmitter in the brain.) The sympathetic branch of the autonomic nervous system causes the adrenal medulla to release a mixture of epinephrine and norepi-

✳ Steroids, Behavior, and Mental Processes

Steroids increase muscle mass, heighten resistance to stress, and increase the body's energy supply by signaling the liver to release glucose into the bloodstream. The steroid testosterone is connected with the sex drive in both males and females (females secrete some testosterone in the adrenal glands). Anabolic steroids (synthetic versions of the male sex hormone testosterone) have been used, sometimes in tandem with growth hormone, to enhance athletic prowess. Not only do these steroids enhance athletic prowess, but they are also connected with self-confidence and aggressiveness. Anabolic steroids are generally outlawed in sports; however, many athletes, such as professional wrestler Chris Benoit, have used them. Benoit, sadly, may be best known for murdering his wife and his son before taking his own life. Benoit had had a number of explosive outbursts, and it has been suggested that he might have been experiencing "roid rage" due to his use of anabolic steroids to pump up his muscle mass and his competitiveness.

George Napolitano/FilmMagic/Getty Images

Professional wrestler Chris Benoit and Nancy Benoit—before his double murder and suicide that took their lives and the life of their 7-year-old son.

nephrine that helps arouse the body to cope with threats and stress. Epinephrine is of interest to psychologists because it has emotional as well as physical effects. It intensifies most emotions and is central to the experience of fear and anxiety.

2-3e THE TESTES AND THE OVARIES

The testes and ovaries also produce steroids, among them testosterone and estrogen. (Testosterone is also produced in smaller amounts by the adrenal glands.) About six weeks after conception, the male sex hormone testosterone causes the male's sex organs to develop. In fact, if it were not for the secretion of testosterone at this time, we would all develop the external genital organs of females. During puberty, testosterone stokes the growth of muscle and bone and the development of primary and secondary sex characteristics. *Primary sex characteristics* are directly involved in reproduction and include the increased size of the penis and the sperm-producing ability of the testes. *Secondary sex characteristics,* such as the presence of a beard and a deeper voice, differentiate males from females but are not directly involved in reproduction.

The ovaries produce *estrogen* and *progesterone* as well as small amounts of testosterone. (Estrogen is also produced in smaller amounts by the adrenal glands.) Estrogen fosters female reproductive capacity and secondary sex characteristics such as accumulation of fatty tissue in the breasts and hips. Progesterone stimulates growth of the female reproductive organs and prepares the uterus to maintain pregnancy. Estrogen and testosterone have psychological effects as well as biological effects, which we will explore further in Chapter 9.

"My nose had spoken falsely."
—CHARLES DARWIN

2-4 | Evolution and Heredity

Charles Darwin almost missed the boat. Literally. Darwin had volunteered to serve on an expeditionary voyage on the *H.M.S. Beagle.* However, he was nearly prevented from undertaking his historic voyage due to the shape of his nose. The captain of the ship, Robert Fitz-Roy, believed that you could judge a person's character by the outline of his facial features, and Darwin's nose didn't fit the . . . bill. But Fitz-Roy relented, and in the 1830s, Darwin undertook the historic voyage to the Galápagos Islands that led to the development of his theory of evolution.

In 1871 Darwin published *The Descent of Man,* which made the case that humans, like other species, were a product of evolution. He argued that the great apes (chimpanzees, gorillas, and so on) and humans were related and shared a common primate ancestor (see Figure 2.15). Evidence from fossil remains suggests that such a common ancestor might have lived about 13 million years ago (Moyà-Solà et al., 2004). Many people ridiculed Darwin's views because they were displeased with the notion that they

TRUTH IT IS TRUE THAT DARWIN WAS ALMOST PREVENTED FROM UNDERTAKING HIS HISTORIC VOYAGE BECAUSE THE SHIP CAPTAIN DID NOT LIKE THE SHAPE OF HIS NOSE.

FIGURE 2.15 | The Human Skeleton and the Skeletons of Some Relatives

The idea that humans were genetically related to monkeys and other animals was so divergent from other 19th-century views of our species that Darwin was initially reluctant to discuss his theory of evolution. *The Descent of Man,* published in 1871, made the case that humans, like other species, were a product of evolution. Darwin believed that the great apes (chimpanzees, gorillas, and so on) shared a common primate ancestor. We did not descend from Neanderthals, but we coexisted with them for thousands of years. Neanderthals became extinct some 35,000 years ago.

Broad funnel-shaped chest
Long, narrow pelvis
Long, robust, curved fingers
Small, low braincase
Thick-walled limbs
Opposable big toe

CHIMPANZEE
Pan troglodytes

High, rounded braincase
Barrel-shaped chest
Short, wide pelvis
Slender fingers
Thin-walled bones
Big toe in line with foot

HUMAN
Homo sapiens

Long, low braincase
Funnel-shaped chest
Short, wide pelvis
Robust fingers
Thick-built bones & joints
Big toe in line with foot

NEANDERTHAL
Homo neanderthalensis

© American Museum of Natural History

natural selection
the concept that holds that adaptive genetic variations among members of a species enable individuals with those variations to survive and reproduce

mutation
a sudden variation in an inheritable characteristic, as distinguished from a variation that results from generations of gradual selection

evolutionary psychology
the branch of psychology that studies the ways in which adaptation and natural selection are connected with mental processes and behavior

instinct
a stereotyped pattern of behavior that is triggered by a particular stimulus and nearly identical among members of a species, even when they are reared in isolation

might share ancestry with apes. Others argued that Darwin's theory contradicted the Bible's book of Genesis, which stated that humans had been created in one day in the image of God.

The concept of a *struggle for existence* lies at the core of Darwin's theory of evolution. At the Galápagos Islands, Darwin found himself immersed in the unfolding of a huge game of "Survivor," with animals and plants competing for food, water, territory, even light. But here the game was for real, and the rewards had nothing to do with fame or fortune. The rewards were reaching sexual maturity and transmitting one's genes into subsequent generations.

As described by evolutionary theory, some creatures have adapted successfully to these challenges, and their numbers have increased. Others have not met the challenges and have fallen back into the distant mists of time. Evidence suggests that 99.99% of all species that ever existed are now extinct (Gould, 2002). Which species prosper and which fade away are determined by **natural selection**; that is, species that are better adapted to their environment are more likely to survive and reproduce.

When we humans first appeared on Earth, our survival required a different sort of struggle than it does today. We fought or fled from predators such as leopards. We foraged across parched lands for food. But because of the evolution of our intellect, we prevailed. Our numbers have increased. We continue to transmit the traits that led to our selection down through the generations by means of genetic material whose chemical codes are only now being cracked.

Just what is handed down through the generations? The answer is biological, or physiological, structures and processes. Our biology serves as the material base for our behaviors, emotions, and cognitions (our thoughts, images, and plans). Biology somehow gives rise to specific behavioral tendencies in some organisms, such as the chick's instinctive fear of the shadow of the hawk. But the behavior of many species, especially higher species such as humans, is flexible and affected by experience and choice, as well as by heredity.

According to the theory of evolution, species and individuals compete for the same resources. Natural variations from individual to individual, along with sudden changes in genes called **mutations**, lead to differences among individuals, differences which affect the ability to adapt to change. Those individuals whose traits are better adapted are more likely to survive (that is, to be "naturally selected"). Survival permits them to reach sexual maturity, to reproduce, and to transmit their features or traits to the next generation. What began as chance variation becomes embedded over the generations—if it fosters survival. Chance variations that hinder survival are likely to disappear from the gene pool.

2-4a EVOLUTIONARY PSYCHOLOGY: DOING WHAT COMES NATURALLY

These same concepts of *adaptation* and *natural selection* have also been applied to psychological traits and are key concepts in **evolutionary psychology**. Evolutionary psychology studies the ways in which adaptation and natural selection are connected with mental processes and behavior (Buss, 2009a). Over the eons, evolution has provided organisms with advantages such as stronger fins and wings, sharper claws, and camouflage. Human evolution has given rise to various physical traits and also to such diverse activities as language, art, committed relationships, and warfare.

One of the concepts of evolutionary psychology is that not only physical traits but also many patterns of behavior, including social behavior, evolve and can be transmitted genetically from generation to generation. Behavior patterns that help an organism to survive and reproduce may be transmitted to the next generation. Such behaviors are believed to include aggression, strategies of mate selection, even altruism (that is, self-sacrifice of the individual to help perpetuate the family grouping) (Buss, 2009b; Lukaszewski & Roney, 2009). Such behavior patterns are termed *instinctive* or *species-specific* because they evolved within certain species.

An **instinct** is a stereotyped pattern of behavior that is triggered in a specific situation. Instinctive behavior is nearly identical among the members of the species in which it appears. It tends to resist modification, even when it serves no purpose (as in the interminable barking of some breeds of dogs) or results in punishment. Instinctive behavior also appears when the individual is reared in isolation from others of its kind and thus cannot learn the behavior from experience.

Consider some examples of instinctive behavior. If you place an egg from the nest of a goose a few inches in front of her, she will roll it back to the nest with her beak. However, she won't retrieve it if it's farther away—in the "not my egg" zone. If you rear a white-crowned sparrow in isolation from other sparrows, it will still sing a recognizable species-specific song when it matures. The male stickleback fish instinctively attacks fish (or pieces of painted wood) with the kinds of red bellies that are characteristic of other male sticklebacks. Many psychologists consider language to be "instinctive" among humans. Psychologists are trying to determine what other kinds of human behavior may be instinctive. However, even instinctive behavior can be modified to some degree by learning, and most psychologists agree that the richness and complexity of human behavior are made possible by learning.

2-4b HEREDITY, GENETICS, AND BEHAVIORAL GENETICS

Heredity defines one's *nature*, which is based on biological structures and processes. Heredity refers to the biological transmission of traits that have evolved from generation to generation. Fish are limited in other ways by their natural traits. Chimpanzees and gorillas can understand many spoken words and express some concepts through nonverbal symbol systems such as American Sign Language. Apes cannot speak, however, apparently because of limitations in the speech areas of the brain.

The subfield of biology that studies heredity is called **genetics**. The field of genetics looks at both species-specific behavior patterns (instincts) and individual differences among the members of a species. *Behavioral genetics* focuses on the contribution of genes to behavior.

Behavioral genetics bridges the sciences of psychology and biology. It is concerned with the genetic transmission of traits that give rise to patterns of behavior. Psychologists are thinking in terms of behavioral genetics when they ask about the inborn reasons why individuals may differ in their behavior and mental processes. For example, some children learn language more quickly than others. Part of the reason may lie in behavioral genetics—their heredity. But some children also experience a richer exposure to language at early ages.

Heredity appears to be a factor in almost all aspects of human behavior, personality, and mental processes (Plomin & Asbury, 2005; Plomin & Haworth, 2009). Examples include sociability, shyness, social dominance, aggressiveness, leadership, thrill seeking, effectiveness as a parent or a therapist, happiness, even interest in arts and crafts (Blum et al., 2009; Ebstein et al., 2010; Leonardo & Hen, 2006).

Heredity is apparently involved in psychological disorders ranging from anxiety and depression to schizophrenia, bipolar disorder, alcoholism, and personality disorders (Dworzynski et al., 2009; Farmer et al., 2007; Hill et al., 2007; Metzger et al., 2007). These disorders are discussed in Chapter 12, but here we can note that a study of 794 pairs of female twins by Kendler and his colleagues (2000) found six aspects of psychological health that were connected with genetic factors: feelings of physical well-being, social relationships, anxiety and depression, substance abuse, use of social support, and self-esteem.

The Kendler group also found, however, that the family environment contributed strongly to social relationships, substance abuse, and social support. Although psychological health is influenced by environmental factors, our understanding of the role of heredity continues to expand. Unlocking these mysteries depends on how well we understand genes and chromosomes.

2-4c GENES AND CHROMOSOMES

Genes are the most basic building blocks of heredity. Genes regulate the development of specific traits. Some traits, such as blood type, are controlled by a single pair of genes. (One gene is derived from each parent.) Other traits are determined by combinations of genes. The inherited component of complex psychological traits, such as intelligence, is believed to be determined by combinations of genes. It is estimated that the cells within your body contain 20,000 to 25,000 genes (International Human Genome Sequencing Consortium, 2004).

Genes are segments of **chromosomes**. That is, chromosomes are made up of strings of genes. Each cell in the body contains 46 chromosomes arranged in 23 pairs. Chromosomes are large complex molecules of **DNA** (short for *deoxyribonucleic acid*), which has sev-

heredity
the transmission of traits from parent to offspring by means of genes

genetics
the area of biology that focuses on heredity

gene
a basic unit of heredity, which is found at a specific point on a chromosome

chromosome
a microscopic rod-shaped body in the cell nucleus carrying genes that transmit hereditary traits from generation to generation; humans normally have 46 chromosomes

DNA
acronym for deoxyribonucleic acid, the substance that forms the basic material of chromosomes; it takes the form of a double helix and contains the genetic code

polygenic
referring to traits that are influenced by combinations of genes

genotype
one's genetic makeup, based on the sequencing of the nucleotides we term A, C, G, and T

eral chemical components. The tightly wound structure of DNA was first demonstrated in the 1950s by James Watson and Francis Crick. DNA takes the form of a double helix—a twisting molecular ladder (see Figure 2.16). The "rungs" of the ladder are made up of chemicals whose names are abbreviated as A, T, C, and G. A always links up with T to complete a rung, and C always combines with G. Therefore, you can describe the *genetic code* in terms of the nucleotides you find along just one of the rungs—CTGAGTCAC and so on. A single gene can contain hundreds of thousands of base pairs. So if you think of a gene as a word, it can be a few hundred thousand letters long and completely unpronounceable.

A group of scientists working together around the globe—referred to as the Human Genome Project—has learned that the sequencing of your DNA consists of about 3 billion DNA sequences spread throughout your chromosomes (Plomin & Schalkwyk, 2007). These sequences—the order of the chemicals we call A, T, C, and G—caused you to grow arms and not wings, and skin

FIGURE 2.16 | Cells, Chromosomes, and DNA

A. The nuclei of cells contain chromosomes. B. Chromosomes are made up of DNA. C. Segments of DNA are made up of genes. The genetic code—that is, the order of A, G, T, and C—determines your species and all those traits that can be inherited, from the color of your eyes to predispositions toward many psychological traits and abilities, including sociability and musical talent.

Cell   Nucleus

A.

Chromosomes

B.

DNA

C.

Weiten W. *Psychology*, 8e. Copyright © 2010. Cengage Learning.

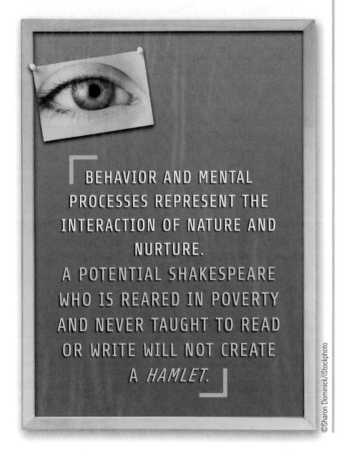

BEHAVIOR AND MENTAL PROCESSES REPRESENT THE INTERACTION OF NATURE AND NURTURE.
A POTENTIAL SHAKESPEARE WHO IS REARED IN POVERTY AND NEVER TAUGHT TO READ OR WRITE WILL NOT CREATE A *HAMLET*.

©Sharon Dominick/iStockphoto

rather than scales. Psychologists debate the extent to which genes influence complex psychological traits such as intelligence, aggressiveness, and happiness, and the appearance of psychological disorders such as schizophrenia. Some traits, such as eye color, are determined by a single pair of genes. Other traits, especially complex psychological traits such as sociability and aggressiveness, are thought to be **polygenic**—that is, influenced by combinations of genes.

Your genetic code provides your **genotype**—that is, your full genetic potential, as determined by the sequencing of the chemicals in your DNA. But the person you see in the mirror was also influenced by your early experiences in the home, injuries, adequacy of nourishment, educational experiences, and numerous other environmental influences. Therefore, you see the outer appearance of your phenotype, including the hairstyles of the day. Your **phenotype** is the manner in which your genetic code manifests itself because of your experiences and environmental circumstances. Your genotype enables you to acquire language. Your phenotype reveals that you are likely to be speaking English if you were reared in the United States or Spanish if you were reared in Mexico (or both, if you are Mexican American).

Your genotype provides what psychologists refer to as your **nature**. Your phenotype represents the interaction of your nature (heredity) and your **nurture** (environmental influences) in the origins of your behavior and mental processes. Psychologists are especially interested in the roles of nature and nurture in intelligence and psychological disorders. Our genotypes provide us with physical traits that set the stage for certain behaviors. But none of us is the result of heredity alone. Environmental factors such as nutrition, learning opportunities, cultural influences, exercise, and (unfortunately) accident and illness also determine our phenotypes and

Down syndrome is caused by an extra chromosome on the 21st pair and becomes more likely to occur as the mother's age at the time of pregnancy increases. Persons with Down syndrome have characteristic facial features including downward-sloping folds of skin at the inner corners of the eyes, are intellectually deficient, and usually have health problems that lead to death by middle age.

Michael Greenlar/The Image Works

whether genetically possible behaviors will be displayed. Behavior and mental processes represent the interaction of nature and nurture. A potential Shakespeare who is reared in poverty and never taught to read or write will not create a *Hamlet*.

We normally receive 23 chromosomes from our father's sperm cell and 23 chromosomes from our mother's egg cell (ovum). When a sperm cell fertilizes an ovum, the chromosomes form 23 pairs. The 23rd pair consists of **sex chromosomes**, which determine whether we are female or male. We all receive an X sex chromosome (so called because of the X shape) from our mother. If we also receive an X sex chromosome from our father, we develop into a female. If we receive a Y sex chromosome (named after the Y shape) from our father, we develop into a male.

When people do not have the normal number of 46 chromosomes (23 pairs), physical and behavioral abnormalities may result. Most persons with **Down syndrome**, for example, have an extra, or third, chromosome on the 21st pair. Persons with Down syndrome have a downward-sloping fold of skin at the inner corners of the eyes, a round face, a protruding tongue, and a broad, flat nose. They are cognitively impaired and usually have physical problems that cause death by middle age.

2-4d KINSHIP STUDIES

Kinship studies are ways in which psychologists compare the presence of traits and behavior patterns in people who are biologically related or unrelated to help determine the role of genetic factors in their occurrence. The more *closely* people are related, the more *genes* they have in common. Identical twins share 100% of their genes. Parents and children have 50% of their genes in common, as do siblings (brothers and sisters). Aunts and uncles related by blood have a 25% overlap with nieces and nephews. First cousins share 12.5% of their genes. If genes are involved in a trait or behavior pattern, people who are more closely related should be more likely to show similar traits or behavior. Psychologists and behavioral geneticists are especially interested

phenotype
one's actual development and appearance, as based on one's genotype and environmental influences

nature
the inborn, innate character of an organism

nurture
the sum total of the environmental factors that affect an organism from conception onward

sex chromosomes
the 23rd pair of chromosomes, whose genetic material determines the sex of the individual

Down syndrome
a condition caused by an extra chromosome on the 21st pair and characterized by mental deficiency, a broad face, and slanting eyes

in running kinship studies with twins and adopted individuals (Plomin & Haworth, 2009).

Twin Studies

The fertilized egg cell (ovum) that carries genetic messages from both parents is called a *zygote*. Now and then, a zygote divides into two cells that separate, so that instead of developing into a single person, it develops into two people with the same genetic makeup. Such people are identical, or **monozygotic (MZ), twins**. If the woman releases two ova in the same month and they are both fertilized, they develop into fraternal, or **dizygotic (DZ), twins**. DZ twins, like other siblings, share 50% of their genes. MZ twins are important in the study of the relative influences of nature (heredity) and nurture (the environment) because differences between MZ twins are the result of nurture. (They do not differ in their heredity—that is, their nature—because their genetic makeup is the same.)

Twin studies compare the presence of traits and behavior patterns in MZ twins, DZ twins, and other people to help determine the role of genetic factors in their occurrence. If MZ twins show greater similarity on a trait or behavior pattern than DZ twins, a genetic basis for the trait or behavior is suggested.

Twin studies show how strongly genetic factors influence physical features. MZ twins are more likely to look alike and to be similar in height, even to have more similar cholesterol levels than DZ twins (Souren et al., 2007). MZ twins also resemble one another more strongly than DZ twins in intelligence and personality traits like sociability, anxiety, friendliness, and conformity, even happiness (Lykken, 2007; McCrae et al., 2000; Veselka et al., 2009). Monozygotic twins are more likely than dizygotic twins to share psychological disorders such as autism, depression, schizophrenia, and vulnerability to alcoholism (Dworzynski et al., 2009; Plomin, 2000; Veenstra-Vanderweele & Cook, 2003). Research also shows that MZ twins are more alike than DZ twins in their blood pressure, brain wave patterns, even in their speech patterns, gestures, and mannerisms (Ambrosius et al., 2008; Lykken, 2007; Wessel et al., 2007).

Of course, twin studies are not perfect. MZ twins may resemble each other more closely than DZ twins partly because they are treated more similarly. MZ twins frequently are dressed identically, and parents sometimes have difficulty telling them apart. One way

Monozygotic twins share 100% of their genes, whereas dizygotic share 50% of their genes.

TWINS

Image Source Photography/Veer

to get around this difficulty is to find and compare MZ twins who were reared in different homes. Then, any similarities between MZ twins reared apart could not be explained by a shared home environment and would appear to be largely a result of heredity. In the fascinating Minnesota Study of Twins Reared Apart (Lykken, 2007), researchers have been measuring the physiological and psychological characteristics of 56 sets of MZ adult twins who were separated in infancy and reared in different homes.

In sum, MZ twins reared apart are about as similar as MZ twins reared together on a variety of measures of intelligence, personality, temperament, occupational and leisure-time interests, and social attitudes. These traits thus would appear to have a genetic underpinning.

Adoption Studies

The results of kinship studies can be confused when relatives share similar environments as well as genes. *Adoption studies* overcome some of this problem by comparing children who have been separated from their parents at an early age (or in which identical twins are separated at an early age) and reared in different environments. Psychologists look for similarities between children and their adoptive and natural parents. When children reared by adoptive parents are more similar to their natural parents in a particular trait, strong evidence exists for a genetic role in the development of that trait.

In later chapters we will see that psychologists have been particularly interested in the use of adoption studies to sort out the effects of nature and nurture in the development of personality traits, intelligence, and various psychological disorders. Such traits and disorders apparently represent the interaction of complex groupings of genes as well as environmental influences.

By the Numbers

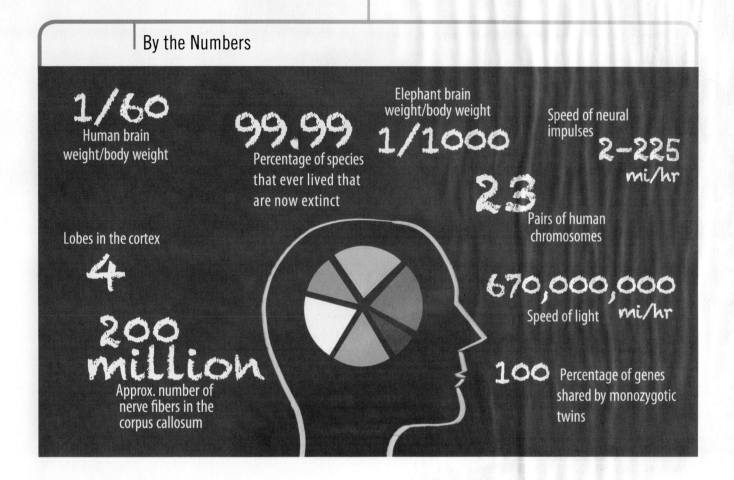

1/60 Human brain weight/body weight

99.99 Percentage of species that ever lived that are now extinct

Elephant brain weight/body weight **1/1000**

Speed of neural impulses **2-225 mi/hr**

23 Pairs of human chromosomes

Lobes in the cortex **4**

200 million Approx. number of nerve fibers in the corpus callosum

670,000,000 mi/hr Speed of light

100 Percentage of genes shared by monozygotic twins

STUDY TOOLS ▶ 2

Ready to study? In the book, you can:

➊ Review what you've read with Fill-Ins and Multiple Choice quizzes (below).

➊ Rip out Chapter Review card (in the back).

Or you can go online to CourseMate at www.cengagebrain.com for these resources:

➊ Complete Practices Quizzes to prepare for tests.

➊ Review Key Terms Flash Cards (online or print).

➊ Play games to master concepts.

FILL-INS

Answers can be found in the back of the book, starting on page 368.

1. Neurons transmit messages to other neurons by means of chemical substances called _____.

2. Neurons have a cell body, or soma; dendrites, which receive "messages"; and a(n) _____, which extends from the cell body and transmits messages.

3. The axons of many neurons have a fatty insulating sheath called _____.

4. It is theorized that people with the psychological disorder called _____ apparently overutilize the neurotransmitter dopamine.

5. The _____ nervous system regulates the glands and involuntary activities such as heartbeat and digestion.

6. The brain structure called the _____ is involved in balance and coordination.

7. The concept of a struggle for _____ lies at the core of the theory of evolution.

8. Stereotypical behavior patterns that have evolved within a species are called _____.

9. People with _____ syndrome have an extra chromosome on the 21st pair.

10. The behavior of _____ twins is of special interest to psychologists because their genetic endowment is the same.

1. An axon's length can range from a few millimeters to
   a. 1 inch.
   c. several feet.
   b. 12 inches.
   d. up to a mile.

2. A neuron can fire up to a limit of about _____ times per second.
   a. 40
   c. 4,000
   b. 400
   d. 40,000

3. If someone steps on your toes, resulting in pain and the movement of your foot, which of the following describes this process?
   a. Afferent neurons transmit the sensation of pain to the spinal cord and to the brain followed by efferent neurons sending the message to your foot to move.
   b. Efferent neurons transmit the sensation of pain to the spinal cord and to the brain followed by afferent neurons sending the message to your foot to move.
   c. Efferent neurons transmit the sensation of pain to the spinal cord and to the brain followed by efferent neurons sending the message to your foot to move.
   d. Afferent neurons transmit the sensation of pain to the spinal cord and to the brain followed by afferent neurons sending the message to your foot to move.

4. When Charlotte hears something embarrassing, she blushes. Being a student of psychology, she knows that this condition is controlled by the
   a. motor cortex.
   b. autonomic nervous system.
   c. somatosensory cortex.
   d. motor nervous system.

5. Wernicke's aphasia causes
   a. impairment of one's ability to comprehend speech and to think of the proper words to express his or her own thoughts.
   b. one to speak slowly and laboriously in simple sentences.
   c. serious impairment in reading.
   d. an inability to segment words in sounds while reading.

6. An editor gets so upset that she is late in working on a manuscript that she throws up her lunch. This probably occurred because of activity of the
   a. longest neurons in her body.
   b. corpus callosum.
   c. parasympathetic division of her autonomic nervous system.
   d. sympathetic division of her autonomic nervous system.

7. Ellen loses weight and becomes somewhat agitated. Her doctor is most likely to theorize that she is suffering from a deficiency of
   a. epinephrine.
   b. dopamine.
   c. cortisol.
   d. thyroxin.

8. _____ are the most basic building blocks of heredity.
   a. Genes
   b. Hormones
   c. Neurons
   d. Neurotransmitters

9. Dizygotic twins
   a. develop when two ova are fertilized.
   b. share 100% of their genes.
   c. are referred to as identical twins.
   d. demonstrate differences that are the result of nurture.

10. "Messages" travel within neurons by means of _____ and from neuron to neuron by means of _____.
    a. electricity, electricity
    b. neurotransmitters, neurotransmitters
    c. neurotransmitters, electricity
    d. electricity, neurotransmitters

Chung Sung-Jun/Getty Images

LEARNING OUTCOMES

3-1 Define and differentiate between sensation and perception

3-2 Identify the parts of the eye; explain the properties of light and the theories of color vision

3-3 Describe the organization of visual perceptions

3-4 Identify the parts of the ear; describe the sense of hearing

3-5 Describe the chemical senses

3-6 Explain the properties of the skin senses and theoretical explanations for pain

3-7 Describe the kinesthetic and vestibular senses

3-8 Explain why psychologists are skeptical about extrasensory perception

 STUDY TOOLS ▶ After you read the chapter, go to the Study Tools at the end of the chapter, page 82.

CHAPTER 3

Sensation and PERCEPTION

The tsunami that hit the coast of southern Asia in 2004 killed as many as a quarter of a million people. The people were caught off guard, but not the animals.

Along the western coast of Thailand, elephants giving rides to tourists began to trumpet agitatedly hours before the tsunami, just about when the earthquake that fractured the ocean floor sent the big waves rushing toward the shore. An hour before the waves slammed into the area, the elephants began wailing. Before the waves struck, they trooped off to higher ground. Elephants, tigers, leopards, deer, wild boar, water buffalo, monkeys, and reptiles in Sri Lanka's Yala National Park escaped the tsunami unharmed.

People have noticed that animals appear to detect earthquakes, hurricanes, volcanic eruptions, and tsunamis before the earth starts shaking. Some animals are apparently supersensitive to sound, others to temperature, touch, or vibration, which gives them advance warning.

Elephants are particularly sensitive to ground vibrations and probably sensed the earthquake that caused the tsunami in their feet and trunks. Some birds, dogs, tigers, and elephants can sense sound waves whose frequencies are too low for humans to hear. Dogs' superior sense of smell might detect subtle chemical changes in the air that warn them of calamities.

Different animals, then, have different sensory apparatuses, and many of them sense things that people cannot sense. Just how do humans sense the world around them?

3-1　Sensation and Perception

Sensation is the stimulation of sensory receptors and the transmission of sensory information to the central nervous system (the spinal cord or brain). Sensory receptors are located in sensory organs such as the eyes and ears, the skin, and elsewhere in the body. Stimulation of the senses is an automatic process. It results from sources of energy, like

Ben Cranke/The Image Bank/Getty Images

Elephants detected the tsunami before the earth started shaking.

TRUTH OR *FICTION*

WHAT DO YOU THINK? FOLKLORE, COMMON SENSE, OR NONSENSE? CIRCLE THE T FOR "TRUTH" OR THE F FOR "FICTION," AND CHECK THE ACCURACY OF YOUR ANSWERS AS YOU READ THROUGH THE CHAPTER.

T	F	PEOPLE HAVE ONLY FIVE SENSES.
T	F	IF WE COULD SEE WAVES OF LIGHT WITH SLIGHTLY LONGER WAVELENGTHS, WARM-BLOODED ANIMALS WOULD GLOW IN THE DARK.
T	F	PEOPLE SOMETIMES HEAR WHAT THEY WANT TO HEAR.
T	F	WHEN WE MIX BLUE LIGHT AND YELLOW LIGHT, WE OBTAIN GREEN LIGHT.
T	F	MANY PEOPLE EXPERIENCE PAIN "IN" LIMBS THAT HAVE BEEN AMPUTATED.
T	F	SOME PEOPLE CAN READ OTHER PEOPLE'S MINDS.

sensation
the stimulation of sensory receptors and the transmission of sensory information to the central nervous system

perception
the process by which sensations are organized into an inner representation of the world

absolute threshold
the minimal amount of energy that can produce a sensation

pitch
the highness or lowness of a sound, as determined by the frequency of the sound waves

light and sound, or from the presence of chemicals, as in smell and taste.

Perception is not mechanical. Perception is an *active* process in which sensations are organized and interpreted to form an inner representation of the world (Hafemeister et al., 2010; Rouder & Morey, 2009). Perception may begin with sensation, but it also reflects our experiences and expectations as it makes sense of sensory stimuli. A person standing 15 feet away and a 12-inch-tall doll right next to you may cast similar-sized images on the back of your eye, but whether you interpret the size to be a foot-long doll or a full-grown person 15 feet away is a matter of perception that depends on your experience with dolls, people, and distance.

In this chapter you will see that your perception of the world of changing sights, sounds, and other sources of sensory input depends largely on the so-called five senses: vision, hearing, smell, taste, and touch. But touch is just one of several "skin senses," which also include pressure, warmth, cold, and pain. There are also senses that alert you to your own body position without your having to watch every step you take. As we explore each of these senses, we will find that similar sensations may lead to different perceptions in different people—or to different situations in the same person.

Before we begin our voyage through the senses, let's consider a number of concepts that we use to talk about the relationships between sensations and perceptions: *absolute threshold, subliminal stimulation, difference threshold, signal-detection theory, feature detectors,* and *sensory adaptation.* In doing so, we will learn why we can dim the lights gradually to near darkness without anyone noticing. We will also learn why

"The great art of life is sensation, to feel that we exist, even in pain."

—LORD BYRON

we might become indifferent to the savory aromas of delightful dinners.

3-1a ABSOLUTE THRESHOLD

Nineteenth-century German psychologist Gustav Fechner used the term **absolute threshold** to refer to the weakest level of a stimulus that is necessary to produce a sensation. For example, the absolute threshold for light would be the minimum brightness (physical energy) required to activate the visual sensory system.

Psychophysicists look for the absolute thresholds of the senses by exposing individuals to progressively stronger stimuli until they find the minimum stimuli that the person can detect 50% of the time. These absolute thresholds are not all that absolute, however. Some people are more sensitive than others, and even the same person might have a slightly different response at different times (Rouder & Morey, 2009). Nevertheless, under ideal conditions, our ability to detect stimuli is quite sensitive. (See the box feature, this page.)

How different our lives would be if the absolute thresholds for the human senses differed! If your ears were sensitive to sounds that are lower in **pitch**, you might hear the collisions among molecules of air. If you

✳ Absolute Thresholds of the Senses

The following are measures of the absolute thresholds for the human senses of vision, hearing, taste, smell, and touch:

- *Vision:* a candle flame viewed from about 30 miles on a clear, dark night.
- *Hearing:* a watch ticking from about 20 feet away in a quiet room.
- *Taste:* 1 teaspoon of sugar dissolved in 2 gallons of water.
- *Smell:* about one drop of perfume diffused throughout a small house (1 part in 500 million).
- *Touch:* the pressure of the wing of a fly falling on a cheek from a distance of about 0.4 inch

Thinkstock/Jupiterimages

FICTION IT IS NOT TRUE THAT PEOPLE HAVE ONLY FIVE SENSES. PEOPLE ACTUALLY HAVE MANY MORE THAN FIVE SENSES.

could see light with slightly longer wavelengths, you would see infrared light waves and people and other animals would glow in the dark. Your world would be transformed because heat generates infrared light.

3-1b SUBLIMINAL STIMULATION

Do TV commercials contain words or sexual images that are flashed so briefly on the screen that we do not become conscious of them, but they still influence us? Behaviorist John B. Watson was a pioneer in associating appealing stimuli with products, as auto ads frequently associate attractive women with cars. But most ads make the associations openly.

Sensory stimulation that is below a person's absolute threshold for conscious perception is termed **subliminal stimulation**—and its perception is called *subliminal perception*. Visual stimuli can be flashed too briefly to enable us to process them. Auditory stimuli can be played at a volume too low to consciously hear or can be played backward.

In one experiment, Johan Karremans and his colleagues (2006) repeatedly flashed "Lipton Ice" for about 1/50th of a second—too briefly to be consciously recognized—on a computer screen that was viewed by a group of participants. They flashed a message without a brand name to a control group. Afterward, thirsty participants in the first group showed a preference for Lipton Ice.

3-1c DIFFERENCE THRESHOLD

How much of a difference in intensity between two lights is required before you will detect one as being brighter than the other? The minimum difference in *magnitude* of two stimuli required to tell them apart is their **difference threshold**. As with the absolute threshold, psychologists agree to the standard of a difference in strength that can be detected 50% of the time.

Psychophysicist Ernst Weber discovered through laboratory research that the threshold for perceiving differences in the intensity of light is about 2% (actually closer to 1/60th) of their intensity. This fraction, 1/60th, is known as **Weber's constant** for light. A related concept is the **just noticeable difference (jnd)**—the minimum difference in stimuli that a person can detect. For example, at least 50% of the time, most people can tell if a light becomes just 1/60th brighter or dimmer. Weber's constant for light holds whether we are comparing moderately bright lights or moderately dull lights. But it becomes inaccurate when

TRUTH IT IS TRUE THAT PEOPLE AND OTHER ANIMALS WOULD GLOW IN THE DARK IF YOU COULD SEE LIGHT WITH SLIGHTLY LONGER WAVELENGTHS.

we compare extremely bright or extremely dull lights.

Weber's constant for noticing differences in lifted weight is 1/53rd. (Round it off to 1/50th, or 2%.) That means if you are strong enough to heft a 100-pound barbell, you would not notice that it was heavier until about 2 pounds were added. Yet if you are a runner who carries 1-pound dumbbells, you would definitely notice if someone slipped you dumbbells even a pound heavier because the increase would be 100%.

What about sound? People are most sensitive to changes in the pitch (frequency) of sounds. The Weber constant for pitch is 1/333, meaning that on average, people can tell when a tone rises or falls in pitch by an extremely small one-third of 1%. (Even a small error in pitch makes singers sound sharp or flat.) Remember this when friends criticize your singing.

The sense of taste is much less sensitive. On average, people cannot detect differences in saltiness of less than 20%. That is why "low-salt" chips that have 15% less salt than your favorite chips do not taste so bad.

3-1d SIGNAL-DETECTION THEORY

From the discussion so far, it might seem that people are simply switched on by certain amounts of stimulation. This is not quite so. People are also influenced by psychological factors. **Signal-detection theory** considers these factors.

According to signal-detection theory, the relationship between a physical stimulus and a sensory response is not fully mechanical (Gigerenzer, 2010). People's ability to detect stimuli such as blips on a radar screen depends not only on the intensity of the blips but also on their training (learning), motivation (desire to perceive blips), and psychological states such as fatigue or alertness (Rouder & Morey, 2009).

The intensity of the signal is one factor that determines whether people will perceive sensory stimuli (signals) or a difference between signals. Another is the

subliminal stimulation
sensory stimulation below a person's absolute threshold for conscious perception

difference threshold
the minimal difference in intensity required between two sources of energy so that they will be perceived as being different

Weber's constant
the fraction of the intensity by which a source of physical energy must be increased or decreased so that a difference in intensity will be perceived

just noticeable difference (jnd)
the minimal amount by which a source of energy must be increased or decreased so that a difference in intensity will be perceived

signal-detection theory
the view that the perception of sensory stimuli involves the interaction of physical, biological, and psychological factors

feature detectors

neurons in the sensory cortex that fire in response to specific features of sensory information such as lines or edges of objects

sensory adaptation

the processes by which organisms become more sensitive to stimuli that are low in magnitude and less sensitive to stimuli that are constant or ongoing in magnitude

sensitization

the type of sensory adaptation in which we become more sensitive to stimuli that are low in magnitude. Also called *positive adaptation*

desensitization

the type of sensory adaptation in which we become less sensitive to constant stimuli. Also called *negative adaptation*

degree to which the signal can be distinguished from background noise. It is easier to hear a friend speaking in a quiet room than in a room in which people are singing and clinking glasses. The sharpness of a person's biological sensory system is still another factor. Is sensory capacity fully developed? Is it diminished by age?

TRUTH PEOPLE DO SOMETIMES HEAR WHAT THEY WANT TO HEAR BECAUSE THAT IS WHAT THEY PAY ATTENTION TO.

We also tend to detect stimuli we are searching for. People sometimes hear what they want to hear. The place in which you are reading this book may be abuzz with signals. If you are focusing your attention on this page, the other signals recede into the background. One psychological factor in signal detection is focusing on signals one considers important.

3-1e FEATURE DETECTORS IN THE BRAIN

Imagine you are standing by the curb of a busy street as a bus approaches. When neurons in your sensory organs—in this case, your eyes—are stimulated by the approach of the bus, they relay information to the sensory cortex in the brain. Nobel Prize winners David Hubel and Torsten Wiesel (1979) discovered that various neurons in the visual cortex of the brain fire in response to particular features of the visual input. Many cells in the brain detect (i.e., fire in response to) lines

I think I can hear a watch ticking on an earlier page.

© Michael Haegele/Corbis

presented at various angles—vertical, horizontal, and in between. Other cells fire in response to specific colors. Because they respond to different aspects or features of a scene, these brain cells are termed **feature detectors**. In the example of the bus, visual feature detectors respond to the bus's edges, depth, contours, textures, shadows, speed, and kinds of motion (up, down, forward, and back). There are also feature detectors for other senses. Auditory feature detectors, for example, respond to the pitch, loudness, and other aspects of the sounds of the bus.

3-1f SENSORY ADAPTATION

Our sensory systems are admirably suited to a changing environment. **Sensory adaptation** refers to the processes by which we become more sensitive to stimuli of low magnitude and less sensitive to stimuli that remain the same, such as the background noises outside the window (Lawless & Heymann, 2010).

Consider how the visual sense adapts to lower intensities of light. When we first walk into a darkened movie theater, we see little but the images on the screen. As we search for our seats, however, we become increasingly sensitive to the faces around us and to the features of the theater. The process of becoming more sensitive to stimulation is referred to as **sensitization**, or *positive adaptation*.

But we become less sensitive to constant stimulation. When we live in a city, for example, we become desensitized to sounds of traffic except, perhaps, for the occasional backfire or siren. The process of becoming less sensitive to stimulation is referred to as **desensitization**, or *negative adaptation*.

Our sensitivities to stimulation provide our brains with information that we use to understand and influence the world outside. Therefore, it is not surprising that psychologists study the ways in which we sense and perceive this information—through vision, hearing, the chemical senses, and still other senses, as we see throughout the remainder of the chapter.

3-2 Vision

Our eyes are literally our "windows on the world." Because vision is our dominant sense, blindness is considered by many to be the most debilitating sensory loss. To understand vision, let's first "look" at light.

3-2a LIGHT

Light is fascinating stuff. It radiates. It illuminates. It dazzles. In almost all cultures, light is a symbol of goodness and knowledge. We speak of genius as "brilliance." People who aren't in the know are said to be "in the dark."

It is **visible light** that triggers visual sensations. Yet visible light is just one small part of a spectrum of electromagnetic energy that surrounds us (see Figure 3.1). All forms of electromagnetic energy move in waves, and different kinds of electromagnetic energy have signature wavelengths:

- *Cosmic rays:* The wavelengths of these rays from outer space are only a few *trillionths* of an inch long.
- *Radio waves:* Some radio signals extend for miles.
- *Visible light:* Roses are red, and violets are blue. Why? Different colors have different wavelengths, with violet the shortest at about 400 *billionths* of a meter in length and red the longest at 700 billionths of a meter.

"IT IS A TERRIBLE THING TO SEE AND HAVE NO VISION."
—HELEN KELLER

Sir Isaac Newton, the British scientist, discovered that sunlight could be broken down into different colors by means of a triangular solid of glass called a *prism* (see Figure 3.1). You can remember the colors of the spectrum, from longest to shortest wavelengths, by using the mnemonic device *Roy G. Biv* (red, orange, yellow, green, blue, indigo, violet). The wavelength of visible light determines its color, or **hue**. The wavelength for red is longer than the wavelength for orange, and so on through the spectrum.

3-2b THE EYE

Consider the major parts of the eye, as shown in Figure 3.2. As with a camera, light enters through a narrow opening and is projected onto a sensitive surface. Light

visible light
the part of the electromagnetic spectrum that stimulates the eye and produces visual sensations

hue
the color of light, as determined by its wavelength

FIGURE 3.1 | The Visible Spectrum

By passing a source of white light, such as sunlight, through a prism, we break it down into the colors of the visible spectrum. The visible spectrum is just a narrow segment of the electromagnetic spectrum. The electromagnetic spectrum also includes radio waves, microwaves, X-rays, cosmic rays, and many others. Different forms of electromagnetic energy have wavelengths that vary from a few trillionths of a meter to thousands of miles. Visible light varies in wavelength from about 400 to 700 *billionths* of a meter. (One meter = 39.37 inches.)

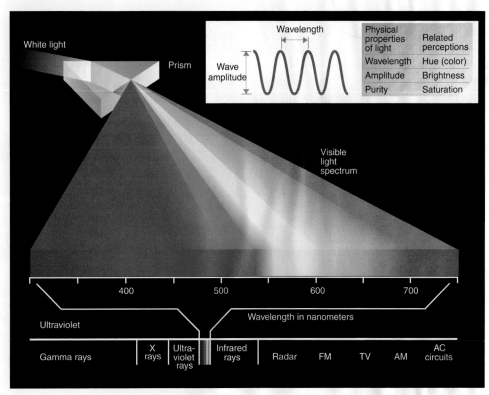

cornea
transparent tissue forming the outer surface of the eyeball

iris
a muscular membrane whose dilation regulates the amount of light that enters the eye

pupil
the black-looking opening in the center of the iris, through which light enters the eye

lens
a transparent body behind the iris that focuses an image on the retina

first passes through the transparent **cornea**, which covers the front of the eye's surface. (The "white" of the eye, or *sclera*, is composed of hard protective tissue.) The amount of light that passes through the cornea is determined by the size of the opening of the muscle called the **iris**, which is the colored part of the eye. The opening in the iris is the **pupil**. The size of the pupil adjusts automatically to the amount of light present. Therefore, you do not have to purposely open your eyes wider to see better in low lighting—the more intense the light, the smaller the opening. Pupil size is also sensitive to your emotions: We can be truly "wide-eyed with fear."

Once light passes through the iris, it encounters the **lens**. The lens adjusts or accommodates to the image by changing its thickness. Changes in thickness permit a clear image of the object to be projected onto the retina. These changes focus the light according to the distance of the object from the viewer. If you hold a finger at arm's length and slowly bring it toward your nose, you will feel tension in the eye as the thickness of the lens accommodates to keep the retinal image in focus. When people squint to bring an object into focus, they are adjusting the thickness of the lens.

FIGURE 3.2 | The Human Eye

In both the eye and a camera, light enters through a narrow opening and is projected onto a sensitive surface. In the eye, the photosensitive surface is called the retina, and information concerning the changing images on the retina is transmitted to the brain. The retina contains photoreceptors called rods and cones. Rods and cones transmit sensory input back through the bipolar neurons to the ganglion neurons. The axons of the ganglion neurons form the optic nerve, which transmits sensory stimulation through the brain to the visual cortex of the occipital lobe.

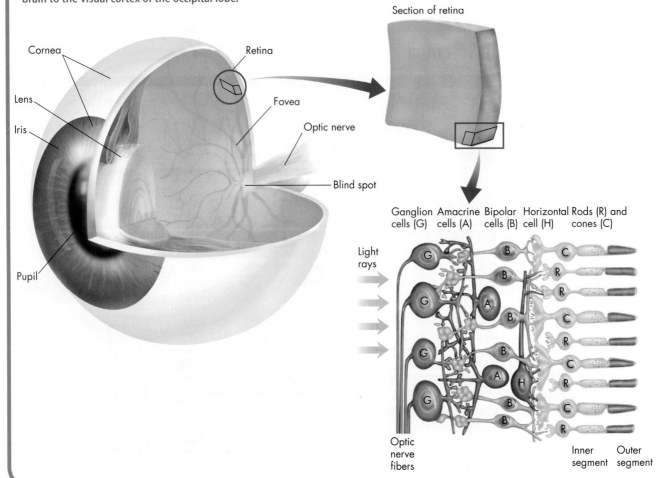

© Cengage Learning 2013

The **retina** consists of cells called **photoreceptors** that are sensitive to light (photosensitive). There are two types of photoreceptors: *rods* and *cones*. The retina (see Figure 3.2) contains several layers of cells: the rods and cones, **bipolar cells**, and **ganglion cells**. All of these cells are neurons. The rods and cones respond to light with chemical changes that create neural impulses that are picked up by the bipolar cells. These then activate the ganglion cells. The axons of the million or so ganglion cells in our retina converge to form the **optic nerve**. The optic nerve conducts sensory input to the brain, where it is relayed to the visual area of the occipital lobe.

As if this were not enough, the eye has additional neurons to enhance this process. Amacrine cells and horizontal cells make sideways connections at a level near the rods and cones and at another level near the ganglion cells. As a result, single bipolar cells can pick up signals from many rods and cones, and, in turn, a single ganglion cell is able to funnel information from multiple bipolar cells. In fact, rods and cones outnumber ganglion cells by more than 100 to 1.

Rods and Cones

Rods and **cones** are the photoreceptors in the retina (see Figure 3.2). About 125 million rods and 6.4 million cones are distributed across the retina. The cones are most densely packed in a small spot at the center of the retina called the **fovea** (see Figure 3.2). Visual acuity (sharpness and detail) is greatest at this spot. The fovea is composed almost exclusively of cones. Rods are most dense just outside the fovea and thin out toward the periphery of the retina.

Rods allow us to see in black and white. Cones provide color vision. Rods are more sensitive to dim light than cones are. Therefore, as light grows dim during the evening hours, objects appear to lose their color before their outlines fade from view.

In contrast to the visual acuity of the fovea is the **blind spot**, which is insensitive to visual stimulation. It is the part of the retina where the axons of the ganglion cells converge to form the optic nerve (see Figure 3.2).

Figure 3.3 will help you "view" your blind spot.

Visual acuity (sharpness of vision) is connected with the shape of the eye. People who have to be unusually close to an object to discriminate its details are *nearsighted*. People who see distant objects unusually clearly but have difficulty focusing on nearby objects are *farsighted*. Nearsightedness can result when the eyeball is elongated such that the images of distant objects are focused in front of the retina. When the eyeball is too short, the images of nearby objects are focused behind the retina, causing farsightedness. Eyeglasses or contact lenses help nearsighted people focus distant objects on their retinas. Laser surgery can correct vision by changing the shape of the cornea. Farsighted people usually see well enough without eyeglasses until they reach their middle years, when they may need glasses for reading.

Beginning in their late 30s to the mid-40s, people's lenses start to grow brittle, making it more difficult to accommodate to, or

retina
the area of the inner surface of the eye that contains rods and cones

photoreceptors
cells that respond to light

bipolar cells
neurons that conduct neural impulses from rods and cones to ganglion cells

ganglion cells
neurons whose axons form the optic nerve

optic nerve
the nerve that transmits sensory information from the eye to the brain

rods
rod-shaped photoreceptors that are sensitive only to the intensity of light

cones
cone-shaped photoreceptors that transmit sensations of color

fovea
an area near the center of the retina that is dense with cones and where vision is consequently most acute

blind spot
the area of the retina where axons from ganglion cells meet to form the optic nerve

visual acuity
sharpness of vision

FIGURE 3.3 | The Blind Spot

To try a "disappearing act," close your left eye, hold the book close to your face, and look at the boy with your right eye. Slowly move the book away until the pie disappears. The pie disappears because it is being projected onto the blind spot of your retina, the point at which the axons of ganglion neurons collect to form the optic nerve. Note that when the pie disappears, your brain "fills in" the missing checkerboard pattern, which is one reason that you're not usually aware that you have blind spots.

© Cengage Learning 2012

focus on, objects. This condition is called **presbyopia**, from the Greek words for "old man" and "eyes." Presbyopia makes it difficult to perceive nearby visual stimuli. People who had normal visual acuity in their youth often require corrective lenses to read in middle adulthood.

Light Adaptation

When we walk out onto a dark street, we may at first not be able to see people, trees, and cars clearly. But as time goes on, we are better able to discriminate the features of people and objects. The process of adjusting to lower lighting is called **dark adaptation**.

The amount of light needed for detection is a function of the amount of time spent in the dark. The cones and rods adapt at different rates. The cones, which permit perception of color, reach their maximum adaptation to darkness in about 10 minutes. The rods, which allow perception of light and dark only, are more sensitive to dim light and continue to adapt for 45 minutes or so.

Adaptation to brighter lighting conditions takes place more rapidly. For instance, when you emerge from the theater into the brilliance of the afternoon, you may at first be painfully surprised by the featureless blaze around you. But within a minute or so of entering the street, the brightness of the scene dims and objects regain their edges.

3-2c COLOR VISION

For most of us, the world is a place of brilliant colors. Color is an emotional and aesthetic part of our everyday lives. In this section, we explore some of the dimensions of color and then examine theories about how we manage to convert different wavelengths of light into perceptions of color. The perceptual dimensions of color include *hue*, *value*, and *saturation*.

The wavelength of light determines its color, or *hue*. The *value* of a color is its degree of brightness or darkness. The *saturation* refers to how intense a color appears to us. A fire-engine red is more saturated than a pale pinkish-red.

Colors also have psychological associations within various cultural settings. For example, in the United States a bride may be dressed in white

FICTION ACTUALLY, WHEN WE MIX BLUE *LIGHT* AND YELLOW *LIGHT*, WE GET GRAY, NOT GREEN LIGHT. WE GET GREEN BY MIXING BLUE AND YELLOW *PIGMENTS*, NOT LIGHTS.

as a sign of purity. In traditional India, the guests would be shocked, because white is the color for funerals. Here we mourn in black.

Warm and Cool Colors

If we bend the colors of the spectrum into a circle, we create a color wheel, as shown in Figure 3.4. Psychologically, the colors on the green–blue side of the color wheel are considered to be cool in temperature. Those colors on the yellow–orange–red side are considered to be warm.

Complementary Colors

The colors across from one another on the color wheel are labeled **complementary**. Red–green and blue–yellow are the major complementary pairs. If we mix complementary colors together, they dissolve into gray.

"But wait!" you say. "Blue and yellow cannot be complementary because by mixing pigments of blue and yellow we create green, not gray." True enough, but we have been talking about mixing *lights*, not *pigments*. Light is the source of all color. Pigments reflect and absorb different wavelengths of light selectively. The mixture of lights is an *additive* process. The mixture of pigments is *subtractive*. Figure 3.5 shows mixtures of lights and pigments of various colors.

Pigments gain their colors by absorbing light from certain segments of the spectrum and reflecting the

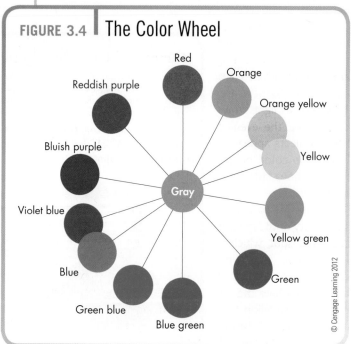

FIGURE 3.4 The Color Wheel

Red
Orange
Reddish purple
Orange yellow
Yellow
Bluish purple
Gray
Violet blue
Yellow green
Blue
Green
Green blue
Blue green
Green

© Cengage Learning 2012

FIGURE 3.5

The mixture of lights is an *additive* process. The mixture of pigments is *subtractive*.

Fritz Goro/Time Life Pictures/Getty Images

rest. For example, we see most plant life as green because the pigment in chlorophyll absorbs most of the red, blue, and violet wavelengths of light. The remaining green is reflected. A red pigment absorbs most of the spectrum but reflects red. White pigments reflect all colors equally. Black pigments reflect very little light.

Afterimages

Try this experiment: Look at the strangely colored American flag on the next page for at least half a minute. Try not to blink as you are doing so. Then look at a sheet of white or light-gray paper. What has happened to the flag? If your color vision is working properly, and if you looked at the miscolored flag long enough, you should see a flag composed of the familiar red, white, and blue. The flag you perceive on the white sheet of paper is an **afterimage** of the first. (If you didn't look at the green, black, and

yellow flag long enough the first time, try it again.) In afterimages, persistent sensations of color are followed by perception of the complementary color when the first color is removed. The same holds true for black and white. Staring at one will create an afterimage of the other. The phenomenon of afterimages has contributed to one of the theories of color vision, as we will see.

3-2d THEORIES OF COLOR VISION

Adults with normal color vision can discriminate thousands of colors across the visible spectrum. Different colors have different wavelengths. Although we can vary the physical wavelengths of light in a continuous manner from shorter to longer, many changes in color are discontinuous. Our perception of a color shifts suddenly from blue to green, even though the change in wavelength may be smaller than that between two blues.

Our perception of color depends on the physical properties of an object and on the eye's transmission of different messages to the brain when lights with different wavelengths stimulate the cones in the retina. There are two main theories of color vision: the *trichromatic theory* and the *opponent-process theory* (Gegenfurtner & Kiper, 2003).

Trichromatic theory is based on an experiment conducted by the British scientist Thomas Young in the early 1800s. As in Figure 3.5, Young projected red, green, and blue-violet lights onto a screen so that they partly overlapped. He found that he could create any color in the visible spectrum by varying the intensities of the three lights. When all three lights fell on the same spot, they created white light, or the appearance of no color at all.

The German physiologist Hermann von Helmholtz saw in Young's discovery an explanation of color vision. Helmholtz suggested that the retina in the eye must have three different types of color photoreceptors or cones. Some cones must be sensitive to red light, some to green, and some to blue. We see other colors when various color receptors are stimulated simultaneously. For example, we perceive yellow when the receptors for red and green are firing.

In 1870, another German physiologist, Ewald Hering, proposed the **opponent-process theory** of color vision: There are three types of color receptors, but they are not sensitive only to red, green, and blue, as Helmholtz had

afterimage
the lingering visual impression made by a stimulus that has been removed

trichromatic theory
the theory that color vision is made possible by three types of cones, some of which respond to red light, some to green, and some to blue

opponent-process theory
the theory that color vision is made possible by three types of cones, some of which respond to red or green light, some to blue or yellow, and some to the intensity of light

Sensation and Perception   65

trichromat
a person with normal color vision

monochromat
a person who is sensitive to black and white only and hence color-blind

dichromat
a person who is sensitive to black–white and either red–green or blue–yellow and hence is partially color-blind

claimed. Hering suggested instead that afterimages (such as that of the American flag shown in Figure 3.6) are made possible by three types of color receptors: red–green, blue–yellow, and a type that perceives differences in brightness. According to Hering, a red–green cone cannot transmit messages for red and green at the same time. Therefore, staring at the green, black, and yellow flag for 30 seconds will disturb the balance of neural activity. The afterimage of red, white, and blue would represent the eye's attempt to reestablish a balance.

Research suggests that each theory of color vision is partially correct. For example, research shows that some cones are sensitive to blue, some to green, and some to red (Pang et al., 2010). However, cones appear to be connected by bipolar and ganglion neurons such that the messages produced by the cones are transmitted to the brain in an opponent-process fashion (Yin et al., 2009).

A neural rebound effect apparently helps explain the occurrence of afterimages. That is, a green-sensitive ganglion that had been excited by green light for half a minute or so might switch briefly to inhibitory activity when the light is shut off. The effect would be to perceive red even though no red light is present (Hornstein et al., 2004).

3-2e COLOR BLINDNESS

If you can discriminate among the colors of the visible spectrum, you have normal color vision and are labeled a **trichromat**. This means that you are sensitive to red–green, blue–yellow, and light–dark. People who are totally color-blind, called **monochromats**, are sensitive only to lightness and darkness. Total color blindness is rare. Fully color-blind individuals see the world as trichromats would in a black-and-white movie.

Partial color blindness is a sex-linked trait that affects mostly males. Partially color-blind people are called **dichromats**. They can discriminate only between two colors—red and green or blue and yellow—and the colors that are derived from mixing these colors (Loop et al., 2003). Figure 3.7 shows the types of tests that are used to diagnose color blindness.

A dichromat might put on one red sock and one green sock, but would not mix red and blue socks. Monochromats might put on socks of any color. They would not notice a difference as long as the socks' colors did not differ in intensity—that is, brightness.

FIGURE 3.7 | Plates from a Test for Color Blindness

Can you see the numbers in these plates from a test for color blindness? A person with red–green color blindness would not be able to see the 6, and a person with blue–yellow color blindness would probably not discern the 12. (Caution: These reproductions cannot be used for actual testing of color blindness.)

© Cengage Learning 2012

FIGURE 3.8 | Closure

Meaningless splotches of ink, or a horse and rider? This figure illustrates the Gestalt principle of closure.

© Cengage Learning 2012

3-3 Visual Perception

What do you see in Figure 3.8—meaningless splotches of ink or a rider on horseback? If you perceive a horse and rider, it is not just because of the visual sensations provided by the drawing. Each of the blobs is meaningless in and of itself, and the pattern is vague. Despite the lack of clarity, however, you may still perceive a horse and rider.

Visual perception is the process by which we organize or make sense of the sensory impressions caused by the light that strikes our eyes. Visual perception involves our knowledge, expectations, and motivations. Whereas sensation may be thought of as a mechanical process (e.g., light stimulating the rods and cones of our retina), perception is an active process through which we interpret the world around us.

You organize bits of visual information into meaningful wholes by means of your general knowledge and your desire to fit incoming bits and pieces of information into familiar patterns. In the case of the horse and rider, your integration of disconnected pieces of information into a meaningful whole also reflects the principle of **closure**—that is, the tendency to perceive a complete or whole figure even when there are gaps in the sensory input.

3-3a PERCEPTUAL ORGANIZATION

Early in the 20th century, Gestalt psychologists noted certain consistencies in the way we integrate bits and pieces of sensory stimulation into meaningful wholes. They attempted to identify the rules that govern these processes. As a group, these rules are referred to as the laws of **perceptual organization**.

Figure–Ground Perception

If you look out your window, you may see people, buildings, cars, and streets, or perhaps grass, trees, birds, and clouds. These objects tend to be perceived as figures against backgrounds. For instance, individual cars seen against the background of the street are easier to pick out than cars piled on top of one another in a junkyard.

When figure–ground relationships are *ambiguous*, or capable of being interpreted in various ways, our perceptions tend to be unstable and shift back and forth (Bull et al., 2003).

Figure 3.9 shows a Rubin vase, one of psychologists' favorite illustrations of figure–ground relationships. The figure–ground relationship in part A of the figure is ambiguous. There are no cues that suggest which area must be the figure. For this reason, our perception may shift from seeing the vase to seeing two profiles. There

FIGURE 3.9 | The Rubin Vase

A. B. C.

© Cengage Learning 2012

proximity
nearness; the perceptual tendency to group together objects that are near one another

similarity
the perceptual tendency to group together objects that are similar in appearance

continuity
the tendency to perceive a series of points or lines as having unity

common fate
the tendency to perceive elements that move together as belonging together

top-down processing
the use of contextual information or knowledge of a pattern in order to organize parts of the pattern

bottom-up processing
the organization of the parts of a pattern to recognize, or form an image of, the pattern they compose

is no such problem in part B. Because it seems that a blue vase has been brought forward against a colored ground, we are more likely to perceive the vase than the profiles. In part C, we are more likely to perceive the profiles than the vase, because the profiles are complete and the vase is broken against the background. Of course, if we wish to, we can still perceive the vase in part C, because experience has shown us where it is.

Other Gestalt Rules for Organization

Gestalt psychologists have noted that our perceptions are also guided by rules or laws of *proximity*, *similarity*, *continuity*, and *common fate*.

Let's try a mini-experiment. Without reading further, describe part A of Figure 3.10. Did you say it consists of six lines or of three groups of two parallel lines? If you said three sets of lines, you were influenced by the **proximity**, or nearness, of some of the lines. There is no other reason for perceiving them in pairs or subgroups: All lines are parallel and equal in length.

Now describe part B of Figure 3.10. Did you perceive the figure as a six-by-six grid, or as three columns of X's and three columns of O's? According to the law of **similarity**, we perceive similar objects as belonging together. For this reason, you may have been more likely

to describe part B in terms of columns than in terms of rows or a grid.

What of part C? Is it a circle with two lines stemming from it, or is it a (broken) line that goes through a circle? If you saw it as a single (broken) line, you were probably organizing your perceptions according to the rule of **continuity**. That is, we perceive a series of points or a broken line as having unity.

According to the law of **common fate**, elements seen moving together are perceived as belonging together. A group of people running in the same direction appears unified in purpose. Part D of Figure 3.10 provides another example of the law of closure. The arcs tend to be perceived as a circle (or a circle with gaps) rather than as just a series of arcs.

Top-Down Versus Bottom-Up Processing

Imagine that you are trying to put together a thousand-piece jigsaw puzzle. Now imagine that you are trying to accomplish it after someone has walked off with the box showing the picture formed by the completed puzzle.

If you use the picture on the box, you're engaging in **top-down processing**—using the completed image to search for the proper pieces. Similarly, we may form more lasting relationships when we search with an idea of the qualities we will find compatible in another person. Or we may make better investments when we have a retirement financial goal and date in mind. With **bottom-up processing**, we begin with bits and pieces of information and try to assemble them in a pattern—in jigsaw puzzles and, perhaps, by being thrown into a social or vocational situation. In bottom-up processing, we do not have a clear idea of where we are going, and perhaps we try to make the best of things.

FIGURE 3.10 | Some Gestalt Laws of Perceptual Organization

These drawings illustrate the Gestalt laws of proximity, similarity, continuity, and closure.

A. Proximity

B. Similarity

C. Continuity

D. Closure

© Cengage Learning 2012

In a motion picture, viewing a series of stationary images at the rate of about 16 to 22 frames per second provides an illusion of movement termed stroboscopic motion. The actual movement that is occurring is the rapid switching of stationary images.

3-3b PERCEPTION OF MOTION

Imagine yourself on a train that has begun to pull out of the station while the train on the next track stays still. If your own train does not lurch as it accelerates, it might seem that the other train is moving. Or you might not be sure whether your train is moving forward or the other train is moving back.

The visual perception of movement is based on change of position relative to other objects. To early scientists, whose only tool for visual observation was the naked eye, it seemed logical that the sun circled the earth. You have to be able to imagine the movement of the earth around the sun as seen from a theoretical point in outer space; you cannot observe it directly.

How, then, can you be certain which train is moving? One way is to look for objects that you know are still, such as platform columns, houses, signs, or trees. If your position does not change in relation to them, your train is not moving. You might also try to sense the motion of the train in your body. You probably know from experience how to do these things quite well.

We have been considering the perception of real movement. Psychologists have also studied several types of apparent movement, or **illusions** of movement. One of these illusions is stroboscopic motion.

Stroboscopic Motion

So-called motion pictures do not really consist of images that move. Rather, the audience is shown 16 to 22 pictures, or *frames*, per second. Each frame differs slightly from the preceding one. Showing the frames in rapid succession provides the illusion of movement. This illusion of motion is termed **stroboscopic motion**.

At the rate of at least 16 frames per second, the "motion" in a film seems smooth and natural. With fewer than 16 or so frames per second, the movement looks jumpy and unnatural. That is why slow motion is usu-

ally achieved by filming 100 or more frames per second. When they are played back at about 22 frames per second, the movement seems slowed down, but still smooth and natural.

3-3c DEPTH PERCEPTION

Monocular and *binocular cues* help us perceive the depth of objects—that is, their distance from us.

Monocular Cues

Artists use **monocular cues** called pictorial cues to create an illusion of depth. These cues can be perceived by one eye (*mono* means "one"). They include perspective, relative size, clearness, overlapping, shadows, and texture gradient, and they cause some objects to seem more distant than others even though they are all drawn or painted on a flat surface.

Distant objects stimulate smaller areas on the retina than nearby ones, even though they may be the same size. The distances between far-off objects also appear to be smaller than equivalent distances between nearby objects. For this reason, the phenomenon known as **perspective** occurs. That is, we tend to perceive parallel lines as coming closer together, or converging, as they recede from us. As we will see when we discuss *size constancy*, however, experience teaches us that distant objects that look small are larger when they are close. In this way, their relative size also becomes a cue to their distance.

Artists normally use *relative size*—the fact that distant objects look smaller than nearby objects of the same size—to suggest depth in their works.

The *clearness* of an object suggests its distance. Experience teaches us that we sense more details of nearby objects. For this reason, artists can suggest that objects are closer to the viewer by depicting them in greater detail.

illusions
sensations that give rise to misperceptions

stroboscopic motion
a visual illusion in which the perception of motion is generated by a series of stationary images that are presented in rapid succession

monocular cues
stimuli suggestive of depth that can be perceived with only one eye

perspective
a monocular cue for depth based on the convergence (coming together) of parallel lines as they recede into the distance

texture gradient

a monocular cue for depth based on the perception that closer objects appear to have rougher (more detailed) surfaces

motion parallax

a monocular cue for depth based on the perception that nearby objects appear to move more rapidly in relation to our own motion

binocular cues

stimuli suggestive of depth that involve simultaneous perception by both eyes

retinal disparity

a binocular cue for depth based on the difference in the image cast by an object on the retinas of the eyes as the object moves closer or farther away

We also learn that nearby objects can block our view of more distant objects. *Overlapping* is the placing of one object in front of another. Experience teaches us that partly covered objects are farther away than the objects that obscure them (see Figure 3.11).

Additional information about depth is provided by *shadowing* and is based on the fact that opaque objects block light and produce shadows. Shadows and highlights give us information about an object's three-dimensional shape and its relationship to the source of light. For example, in the right part of Figure 3.11, the left circle is perceived as a two-dimensional circle, but the right circle tends to be perceived as a three-dimensional sphere because of the highlight on its surface and the shadow underneath. In the "sphere," the highlighted central area is perceived as closest to us, with the surface receding to the edges.

Another monocular cue is **texture gradient**. (A gradient is a progressive change.) Closer objects are perceived as having rougher textures.

Motion cues are another kind of monocular cue. If you have ever driven in the country, you have probably noticed that distant objects such as mountains and stars appear to move along with you. Objects at an in-termediate distance seem to be stationary, but nearby objects such as roadside markers, rocks, and trees seem to go by quite rapidly. The tendency of objects to seem to move backward or forward as a function of their distance is known as **motion parallax**. We learn to perceive objects that appear to move with us as being at greater distances.

We noted that nearby objects cause the lens of the eye to accommodate or bend more in order to bring them into focus. The sensations of tension in the eye muscles also provide a monocular cue to depth, especially when we are within about four feet of the objects.

Binocular Cues

Binocular cues, or cues that involve both eyes, also help us perceive depth. Two binocular cues are *retinal disparity* and *convergence*.

Try an experiment. Hold your right index finger at arm's length. Now hold your left index finger about a foot closer, but in a direct line. If you keep your eyes relaxed as you do so, you will see first one finger and then the other. An image of each finger will be projected onto the retina of each eye, and each image will be slightly different because the finger will be seen from different angles. The difference between the projected images is referred to as **retinal disparity** and serves as a binocular cue for depth perception. Note that in the case of the closer finger, the "two fingers" appear to be farther apart. Closer objects have greater retinal disparity.

If we try to maintain a single image of the closer finger, our eyes must turn inward, or converge on it, mak-

---

FIGURE 3.11 | **Overlapping and Shadowing as Cues for Depth**

Overlapping as a Cue for Depth

The four circles are all the same size. Which circles seem closer? The complete circles or the circles with chunks bitten out of them?

Shadowing as a Cue for Depth

Shadowing makes the circle on the right look three-dimensional.

Although this woman's hand looks as though it is larger than her head, we recognize that this is an illusion created by the fact that her hand is closer to us than her head.

© Enamul Hoque/Getty Images

convergence
a binocular cue for depth based on the inward movement of the eyes as they attempt to focus on an object that is drawing nearer

size constancy
the tendency to perceive an object as being the same size even as the size of its retinal image changes according to the object's distance

color constancy
the tendency to perceive an object as being the same color even though lighting conditions change its appearance

brightness constancy
the tendency to perceive an object as being just as bright even though lighting conditions change its intensity

ing us cross-eyed. **Convergence** causes feelings of tension in the eye muscles and provides another binocular cue for depth. (After convergence occurs, try looking at the finger first with one eye closed, then the other. You will readily see how different the images are in each eye.) The binocular cues of retinal disparity and convergence are strongest when objects are close.

3-3d PERCEPTUAL CONSTANCIES

Think how confusing it would be if you believed that a door was a trapezoid and not a rectangle because it is ajar. Fortunately, perceptual constancies enable us to recognize objects even when their apparent shape or size differs.

Size Constancy

There are a number of perceptual constancies, including that of **size constancy**. The image of a dog seen from 20 feet away occupies about the same amount of space on your retina as an inch-long insect crawling on your hand. Yet you do not perceive the dog to be as small as the insect. Through your visual experiences you have acquired size constancy—that is, the tendency to *perceive* an object as the same size even though the size of its image on your retina varies as a function of its distance. Experience teaches us about perspective—that the same object seen at a distance appears to be smaller than when it is nearby.

Color Constancy

Color constancy is the tendency to perceive objects as retaining their color even though lighting conditions may alter their appearance. Your bright- yellow car may edge toward gray as the hours wend their way through

twilight. But when you finally locate the car in the parking lot, you may still think of it as yellow. You expect to find a yellow car and still judge it to be "more yellow" than the (twilight-faded) red and green cars on either side of it.

Brightness Constancy

Brightness constancy is similar to color constancy. Consider Figure 3.12. The orange squares within the blue squares are equally bright, yet the one within the dark-blue square is perceived as brighter. Why? Again, consider the role of experience. If it were nighttime, we would expect orange to fade to gray. The fact that the orange within the dark square stimulates the eye with equal intensity suggests that it must be much brighter than the orange within the lighter square.

FIGURE 3.12 | Brightness Constancy

The orange squares within the blue squares are the same hue, yet the orange within the dark blue square is perceived as brighter. Why?

© Cengage Learning 2012

Shape Constancy

Shape constancy is the tendency to perceive objects as maintaining their shape, even if we look at them from different angles so that the shape of their image on the retina changes dramatically. You perceive the top of a coffee cup or a glass to be a circle even though it is a circle only when seen from above. When seen from an angle, it is an ellipse. When the cup or glass is seen on edge, its retinal image is the same as that of a straight line. So why do you still describe the rim of the cup or glass as a circle? Perhaps for two reasons: First, experience has taught you that the cup will look circular when seen from above. Second, you may have labeled the cup as circular or round.

Let's return to the door that "changes shape" when it is ajar. The door is a rectangle only when viewed straight on. When we move to the side or open it, the left or right edge comes closer and appears to be larger, changing the retinal image to a trapezoid. Yet we continue to think of doors as rectangles. In the photo on the previous page, we see a woman with a very large hand, but because of experience, we recognize that the hand only appears to be out of proportion to the rest of her because it is pushed toward us.

3-3e VISUAL ILLUSIONS

The principles of perceptual organization make it possible for our eyes to "play tricks" on us. That is, the perceptual constancies trick the eye through *visual illusions*.

The *Hering–Helmholtz* and *Müller–Lyer illusions* (see Figure 3.13) are named after the people who devised them. In the Hering–Helmholtz illusion (part A), the horizontal lines are straight and parallel. However, the radiating lines cause them to appear to be bent outward near the center. The two lines in the Müller–Lyer illusion (part B) are the same length, but the line on the right, with its reversed arrowheads, looks longer.

Let's try to explain these illusions. Because of our experience and lifelong use of perceptual cues, we tend to perceive the Hering–Helmholtz drawing as three-dimensional. Because of our tendency to perceive bits of sensory information as figures against grounds, we perceive the blue area in the center as a circle in front of a series of radiating lines, all of which lie in front of a blue ground. Next, because of our experience with perspective, we perceive the radiating lines as parallel. We perceive the two horizontal lines as intersecting the "receding" lines, and we know that they would have to appear bent out at the center if they were to be equidistant at all points from the center of the circle.

Experience probably compels us to perceive the vertical lines in the Müller–Lyer illusion as the corners of a building (see Figure 3.13, part B). We interpret the length of the lines based on our experience with corners of buildings.

3-4 Hearing

Consider the advertising slogan for the classic science fiction film *Alien*: "In space, no one can hear you scream." It's true. Space is an almost perfect vacuum. Hearing requires a medium through which sound can travel, such as air or water.

FIGURE 3.13 | The Hering–Helmholtz and Müller–Lyer Illusions

In the Hering–Helmholtz illusion, are the horizontal lines straight or curved? In the Müller–Lyer illusion, are the vertical lines equal in length?

A. The Hering–Helmholtz Illusion

B. The Müller–Lyer Illusion

© Cengage Learning 2012

FIGURE 3.14 | Sound Waves of Various Frequencies and Amplitudes

Which sounds have the highest pitch? Which are loudest?

Low frequency

Higher frequency

Low amplitude

Higher amplitude

© Cengage Learning 2012

The pitch of women's voices is usually higher than that of men's voices because women's vocal cords are usually shorter and therefore vibrate at a greater frequency. Also, the strings of a violin are shorter than those of a viola or double bass. Pitch detectors in the brain allow us to tell differences in pitch.

The loudness of a sound roughly corresponds to the height, or amplitude, of sound waves. Figure 3.14 shows records of sound waves that vary in frequency and amplitude. Frequency and amplitude are independent. That is, both high- and low-pitched sounds can be either high or low in loudness. The loudness of a sound is expressed in **decibels (dB)**. Zero dB is equivalent to the threshold of hearing—the lowest sound that the typical person can hear. How loud is that? It's about as

"The empty vessel makes the greatest sound."

—WILLIAM SHAKESPEARE

Sound, or *auditory stimulation*, is the vibration of molecules in a medium such as air or water. Sound travels through the medium like waves, or like ripples in a pond when you toss in a pebble. The molecules of the medium are alternately compressed and expanded like the movements of an accordion. If you were listening under water, you would also hear the splash because of changes in the pressure of the water. In either case, the changes in pressure are vibrations that approach your ears in waves. These vibrations—sound waves—can also be created by a ringing bell, your vocal cords, guitar strings, or the slam of a book thrown down on a desk. A single cycle of compression and expansion is one wave of sound. Sound waves can occur many times in one second. The human ear is sensitive to sound waves with frequencies of from 20 to 20,000 cycles per second.

3-4a PITCH AND LOUDNESS

Pitch and loudness are two psychological dimensions of sound. The pitch of a sound is determined by its frequency, or the number of cycles per second as expressed in the unit **hertz (Hz)**. One cycle per second is 1 Hz. The greater the number of cycles per second (Hz), the higher the pitch of the sound.

✳ iPods on Campus: The Sounds of Oblivion?

The majority of university students own iPods, and most others have another personal listening device (Danhauer, 2009). Because these devices can produce outputs at 130 dB and higher, listeners may be at risk for hearing loss. To combat hearing loss, Fligor and Cox (2004) recommend the "60–60 rule"—that people should listen at no more than 60% of full volume for no more than 60 minutes per day. There are other dangers, such as "iPod oblivion," in which listeners pay less attention to their environments when they are listening. Two pedestrian deaths in New York within four months were attributed to iPod oblivion (Kuntzman, 2007).

Jeffrey Danhauer (2009) surveyed students drawn from universities across the United States and found that their reasons for using iPods included listening to music (95%), avoiding bothering other people with their music (77%), relaxing (75%), fighting boredom (74%), isolating themselves from the people around them (55%), and helping them concentrate on things such as schoolwork (46%).

© Tetra Images/Corbis

cochlea

the inner ear; the bony tube that contains the basilar membrane and the organ of Corti

basilar membrane

a membrane that lies coiled within the cochlea

organ of Corti

the receptor for hearing that lies on the basilar membrane in the cochlea

auditory nerve

the axon bundle that transmits neural impulses from the organ of Corti to the brain

loud as the ticking of a watch 20 feet away in a very quiet room.

The decibel equivalents of familiar sounds are shown in Figure 3.15. Twenty-five dB is equivalent in loudness to a whisper at five feet. Thirty dB is roughly the limit of loudness at which your librarian would like to keep your college library. You may suffer hearing damage if you are exposed to sounds of 85 to 90 dB for long periods.

FIGURE 3.15 | Decibel Ratings of Familiar Sounds

Zero dB is the threshold of hearing. You may suffer hearing loss if you incur prolonged exposure to sounds of 85 to 90 dB.

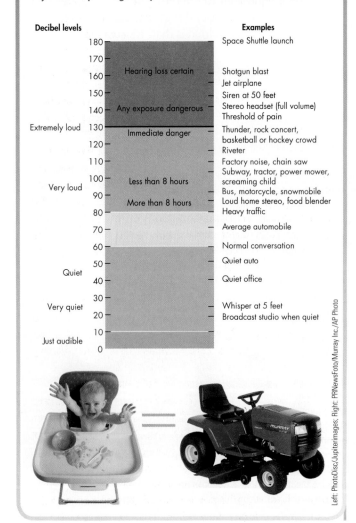

Decibel levels

		Examples
180		Space Shuttle launch
170		
160	Hearing loss certain	Shotgun blast
150		Jet airplane
		Siren at 50 feet
140	Any exposure dangerous	Stereo headset (full volume)
		Threshold of pain
Extremely loud 130	Immediate danger	Thunder, rock concert, basketball or hockey crowd
120		Riveter
110		Factory noise, chain saw
		Subway, tractor, power mower, screaming child
Very loud 100	Less than 8 hours	
90	More than 8 hours	Bus, motorcycle, snowmobile
80		Loud home stereo, food blender
		Heavy traffic
70		Average automobile
60		Normal conversation
Quiet 50		Quiet auto
40		Quiet office
Very quiet 30		
20		Whisper at 5 feet
10		Broadcast studio when quiet
Just audible 0		

Left: PhotoDisc/Jupiterimages; Right: PRNewsFoto/Murray Inc./AP Photo

3-4b THE EAR

The ear is shaped and structured to capture sound waves, vibrate in sympathy with them, and transmit them to the brain. In this way, you not only hear something, you can also figure out what it is. The ear has three parts: the outer ear, the middle ear, and the inner ear (see Figure 3.16).

The outer ear is shaped to funnel sound waves to the *eardrum*, a thin membrane that vibrates in response to sound waves, and thereby transmits them to the middle and inner ears. The middle ear contains the eardrum and three small bones, which also transmit sound by vibrating. These bones were given their Latin names (*malleus*, *incus*, and *stapes* [pronounced STAYpeas], which translate as "hammer," "anvil," and "stirrup") because of their shapes. The middle ear functions as an amplifier, increasing the pressure of the air entering the ear.

The stirrup is attached to another vibrating membrane, the *oval window*. The oval window works in conjunction with the round window, which balances the pressure in the inner ear (see Figure 3.16). The round window pushes outward when the oval window pushes in, and is pulled inward when the oval window vibrates outward.

The oval window transmits vibrations into the inner ear, the bony tube called the **cochlea** (from the Greek word for "snail"). The cochlea, which is shaped like a snail shell, contains two longitudinal membranes that divide it into three fluid-filled chambers. One of the membranes that lies coiled within the cochlea is called the **basilar membrane**. Vibrations in the fluids within the chambers of the inner ear press against the basilar membrane.

The **organ of Corti**, sometimes referred to as the "command post" of hearing, is attached to the basilar membrane. Some 16,000 receptor cells—called *hair cells* because they project like hair from the organ of Corti—are found in each ear. Hair cells "dance" in response to the vibrations of the basilar membrane (Hwang et al., 2010). Their movements generate neural impulses, which are transmitted to the brain via the **auditory nerve**. Auditory input is then projected onto the hearing areas of the temporal lobes of the cerebral cortex.

3-4c LOCATING SOUNDS

There is a resemblance between balancing a set of stereo speakers and locating sounds. A sound that is louder in the right ear is perceived as coming from the right. A sound coming from the right also reaches the right ear first. Both loudness and the sequence in which the sounds reach the ears provide directional cues.

FIGURE 3.16 | The Human Ear

Organ of Corti

Section through cochlea

Basilar membrane

Tectorial membrane

Hair cells

Hammer (malleus)

Anvil (incus)

Stirrup (stapes)

Semicircular canals

Auditory nerve

Oval window

Cochlea

Auditory nerve

Round window

Eardrum

Middle ear

Outer ear (auditory canal)

Eustachian tube

© Cengage Learning 2012

But it may not be easy to locate a sound coming from in front or in back of you or above. Such sounds are equally distant from each ear and equally loud. So what do we do? Simple—we turn our head slightly to determine in which ear the sound increases. If you turn your head to the right and the loudness increases in your left ear, the sound is likely coming from in front.

3-4d PERCEPTION OF LOUDNESS AND PITCH

Sounds are heard because they cause vibration in parts of the ear and information about these vibrations is transmitted to the brain. The loudness and pitch of sounds appear to be related to the number of receptor neurons on the organ of Corti that fire and how often they fire. Psychologists generally agree that sounds are perceived as louder when more of these sensory neurons fire.

As discussed earlier, it takes two processes to explain perception of color: *trichromatic theory* and *opponent-process theory*. For pitch perception—that is, percep-

tion of sound waves that vary in frequency from 20 to 20,000 cycles per second—it takes three processes: *place theory, frequency theory,* and the *volley principle.*

Hermann von Helmholtz helped develop the place theory of pitch discrimination as well as the trichromatic theory of color vision. **Place theory** holds that the pitch of a sound is sensed according to the place along the basilar membrane that vibrates in response to it. In research that led to the award of a Nobel Prize, Georg von Békésy (1957) found that receptors at different sites along the membrane fire in response to tones of differing frequencies. Receptor neurons appear to be lined up along the basilar membrane like piano keys. The higher the pitch of a sound, the closer the responsive neurons lie to the oval window (Erixon et al., 2009). However, place theory appears to apply only to pitches that are at least 4,000 Hz. But what about lower pitches? That's where frequency theory comes in.

Frequency theory notes that for us to perceive lower pitches, we need to match the frequency of the sound waves with our neural impulses. That is, in response to low pitches—say 20 to 1,000 cycles per second—hair cells on the basilar membrane fire at the same frequencies as the sound waves. However, neurons cannot fire more that 1,000 times per second. Therefore, frequency theory best explains perception of pitches between 20 and 1,000 cycles per second. In actuality, frequency the-

flavor
a complex quality of food and other substances that is based on their odor, texture, and temperature as well their taste

olfactory nerve
the nerve that transmits information concerning odors from olfactory receptors to the brain

taste cells
receptor cells that are sensitive to taste

taste buds
the sensory organs for taste; they contain taste cells and are located mostly on the tongue

ory appears to account only for pitch perception between 20 and a few hundred cycles per second.

The *volley principle* accounts for pitch discrimination between a few hundred and 4,000 cycles per second (Ebeling, 2008; Machery & Carlyon, 2010). In response to sound waves of these frequencies, groups of neurons take turns firing in the way that one row of soldiers used to fire rifles while another row knelt to reload. Alternating firing—that is, volleying—appears to transmit sensory information about pitches in the intermediate range.

3-4e DEAFNESS

More than 1 in 10 Americans have a hearing impairment, and 1 in 100 cannot hear at all (Erixon et al., 2009). Two major types of deafness are *conductive deafness* and *sensorineural deafness*. *Conductive deafness* stems from damage to the structures of the middle ear—either to the eardrum or to the bones that conduct (and amplify) sound waves from the outer ear to the inner ear (Daud et al., 2010; Erixon et al., 2009). This is the hearing impairment often found among older people. Hearing aids amplify sound and often help people with conductive deafness.

Sensorineural deafness usually stems from damage to the structures of the inner ear, most often the loss of hair cells. Sensorineural deafness can also stem from damage to the auditory nerve, caused by such factors as disease or exposure to very loud sounds. In sensorineural deafness, people tend to be more sensitive to some pitches than others. In so-called Hunter's notch, the loss is limited to the frequencies of the sound waves generated by a gun firing. Prolonged exposure to 85 dB can cause hearing loss. People who attend rock concerts, where sounds may reach 140 dB, risk damaging their ears, as do workers who run pneumatic drills or drive noisy vehicles. The ringing sensation that often follows exposure to loud sounds probably means that hair cells in the inner ear have been damaged.

Cochlear implants, or "artificial ears," contain microphones that sense sounds and electronic equipment that transmits sounds past damaged hair cells to stimulate the auditory nerve. Such implants have helped many people with sensorineural deafness (Tait et al., 2010). However, they cannot assume the functions of damaged auditory nerves.

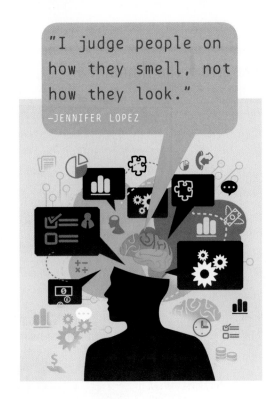

"I judge people on how they smell, not how they look."
—JENNIFER LOPEZ

(3-5) The Chemical Senses: Smell and Taste

Smell and taste are the chemical senses. In vision and hearing, physical energy strikes our sensory receptors. In smell and taste, we sample molecules of substances.

3-5a SMELL

Smell has an important role in human behavior. It contributes to the **flavor** of foods, for example. If you did not have a sense of smell, an onion and an apple might taste the same to you. People's sense of smell may be deficient when compared with that of a dog, but we can detect the odor of 1 one-millionth of a milligram of vanilla in a liter of air.

The sense of smell detects odors. An odor is a sample of molecules of a substance in the air. Odors trigger firing of receptor neurons in the *olfactory membrane* high in each nostril. Receptor neurons can detect even a few molecules of the substance in gaseous form. The receptor neurons transmit information about odors to the brain via the **olfactory nerve**.

3-5b TASTE

As in the case of smell, the sense of taste samples molecules of a substance. Taste is sensed through **taste cells**—receptor neurons located on **taste buds**. You have about

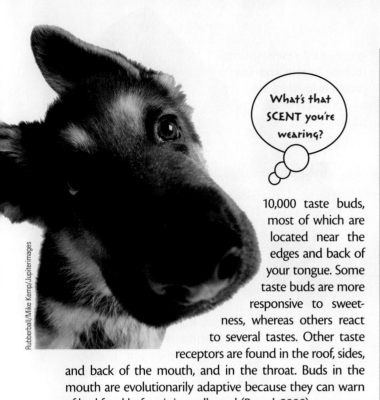

What's that SCENT you're wearing?

10,000 taste buds, most of which are located near the edges and back of your tongue. Some taste buds are more responsive to sweetness, whereas others react to several tastes. Other taste receptors are found in the roof, sides, and back of the mouth, and in the throat. Buds in the mouth are evolutionarily adaptive because they can warn of bad food before it is swallowed (Brand, 2000).

Researchers generally agree on at least four primary taste qualities: sweet, sour, salty, and bitter. Many argue that more basic tastes exist, including *umami*, which is pronounced *ooh-mommy* in Japanese and means "meaty" or "savory" (Rolls, 2009; Yamamoto et al., 2009). Regardless of the number of basic tastes, the flavor of a food is more complex than taste alone. *Flavor* depends on odor, texture, and temperature as well as on taste. Apples and onions are similar in taste, but their flavors differ greatly.

Just as some people see better than others, some people taste better than others—but their superiority may be limited to one or more basic tastes. Those of us with low sensitivity for sweetness may require twice the sugar to sweeten our food as those who are more sensitive. Those of us who claim to enjoy bitter foods may actually be taste-blind to them. Sensitivities to various tastes

Apples and onions are similar in taste, but their flavors differ greatly.

have a genetic component (Bartoshuk, 2000; Snyder & Bartoshuk, 2009).

3-6 The Skin Senses

The skin senses include touch, pressure, warmth, cold, and pain. We have distinct sensory receptors for pressure, temperature, and pain, but some nerve endings may receive more than one type of sensory input. Let's focus on touch, pressure, temperature, and pain.

3-6a TOUCH AND PRESSURE

Sensory receptors embedded in the skin fire when the surface of the skin is touched. There may be several kinds of receptors for touch, some that respond to constant pressure, some that respond to intermittent pressure, as in tapping the skin. *Active touching* means continuously moving your hand along the surface of an object so that you continue to receive sensory input from the object. If you are trying to "get the feel of" a fabric or the texture of a friend's hair, you must move your hand over it. Otherwise, the sensations quickly fade. If you pass your hand over the fabric or hair and then hold it still, the sensations of touching will fade. Active touching receives information concerning pressure, temperature, texture, and feedback from the muscles involved in movements of our hands.

Different parts of the body are more sensitive to touch and pressure than others. The parts of the body that "cover" more than their fair share of somatosensory cortex are most sensitive to touch. These parts include the hands, face, and some other regions of the body. Our fingertips, lips, noses, and cheeks are more sensitive than our shoulders, thighs, and calves. Why the difference in sensitivity? First, nerve endings are more densely packed in the fingertips and face than in other locations. Second, more sensory cortex is devoted to the perception of sensations in the fingertips and face (see Figure 2.11 on page 41).

3-6b TEMPERATURE

The receptors for temperature are neurons located just beneath the skin. When skin temperature increases, the receptors for warmth fire. Decreases in skin temperature cause receptors for cold to fire.

Sensations of temperature are relative. When we are at normal body temperature, we might perceive another person's skin as warm. When we are feverish, though, the other person's skin might seem cool. We also adapt to differences in temperature. When we enter a swimming pool, the water may seem cold because it is below body temperature. Yet after a few moments an 80°F pool may seem quite warm. In fact, we may chide a newcomer for not diving right in.

3-6c PAIN

For most people, pain is a frequent visitor. Headaches, backaches, toothaches—these are only a few of the types of pain that most of us encounter from time to time. According to a national Gallup survey of more than 2,000 adults (Arthritis Foundation, 2000), 89% experience pain at least once a month. More than half (55%) of people aged 65 and above say they experience pain daily. People aged 65 and above are most likely to attribute pain to getting older (88%) and to assume they can do nothing about disabilities such as arthritis. By contrast, people aged 18 to 34 are more likely to attribute pain to tension or stress (73%), overwork (64%), or their lifestyle (51%). When we assume that there is nothing we can do about pain, we are less likely to try. Yet 43% of Americans say that pain curtails their activities, and 50% say that pain puts them in a bad mood.

Pain results when neurons called *nociceptors* in the skin are stimulated. Evolutionary psychologists would point out that pain is adaptive, if unpleasant, because it motivates us to do something about it. For some of us, however, chronic pain—pain that lasts once injuries or illnesses have cleared—saps our vitality and interferes with the pleasures of everyday life (Fenton, 2010; Gatchel & Kishino, 2010).

We can sense pain throughout most of the body, but pain is usually sharpest where nerve endings are densely packed, as in the fingers and face. Pain can also be felt deep within the body, as in the cases of abdominal pain and back pain. Even though headaches may seem to originate deep inside the head, there are no nerve endings for pain in the brain.

Pain usually originates at the point of contact, as when you bang a knee. But it reverberates throughout the nervous system. The pain message to the brain is facilitated by the release of chemicals such as prostaglandins, bradykinin, and P (yes, P stands for "pain"). *Prostaglandins* facilitate transmission of the pain message to the brain and heighten circulation to the injured area, causing the redness and swelling that we call inflammation. Inflammation attracts infection-fighting blood cells to the injury to protect it against invading germs. Pain-relieving drugs such as aspirin and ibuprofen help by inhibiting production of prostaglandins.

The pain message is relayed from the spinal cord to the thalamus and then projected to the cerebral cortex, making us aware of the location and intensity of the damage. Ronald Melzack speaks of a "neuromatrix" that includes these chemical reactions but involves other aspects of our physiology and psychology in our reaction to pain (Gatchel et al., 2012). For example, visual and other sensory inputs tell us what is happening and affect our interpretation of the situation. Our emotional response affects the degree of pain, and so do the ways in which we respond to stress. If, for instance, the pain derives from an object we fear, perhaps a knife or a needle, we may experience more pain. If we perceive that there is nothing we can do to change the situation, perception of pain may increase. If we have self-confidence and a history of successful response to stress, perception of pain may diminish.

Phantom Limb Pain

One of the more intriguing topics in the study of pain is phantom limb pain. About two out of three combat veterans with amputated limbs report feeling pain in such missing, or "phantom," limbs (Nampiaparampil, 2008). Although the pain occurs in the absence of the limb, it is real enough. The pain sometimes involves activation of nerves in the stump of the missing limb, but local anesthesia does not always eliminate the pain.

TRUTH?
FICTION?

MANY PEOPLE DO FEEL AS THOUGH THEY EXPERIENCE PAIN IN LIMBS THAT HAVE BEEN AMPUTATED (SO-CALLED *PHANTOM LIMB PAIN*). HOWEVER, THE LIMBS ARE GONE, SO THAT PAIN CANNOT ACTUALLY BE "IN" THE LIMB.

Researchers have found that many people who experience phantom limb pain have also undergone reorganization of the motor and somatosensory cortex that is consistent with the pain (Melzack & Katz, 2006).

Gate Theory

Simple remedies like rubbing a banged knee frequently help relieve pain. Why? According to the *gate theory* of pain originated by Ronald Melzack and Patrick Wall, the nervous system can process only a limited amount of stimulation at a time. Rubbing the knee transmits sensations to the brain that "compete" for the attention of neurons. Many nerves are thus prevented from transmitting pain messages to the brain. It is like shutting down a "gate" in the spinal cord, or like a switchboard being flooded with calls.

Acupuncture

Thousands of years ago, the Chinese began mapping the body to learn where pins might be placed to deaden pain. This practice is termed acupuncture. Traditional acupuncturists believe that the practice balances the body's flow of energy, but research has shown that it stimulates nerves that reach the hypothalamus and may also cause the release of endorphins and cortisol (Spelts & Gaynor, 2010). Endorphins are neurotransmitters that are similar in effect to the narcotic morphine. Cortisol is a stress hormone.

(3-7) Kinesthesis and the Vestibular Sense

Try an experiment. Close your eyes and then touch your nose with your finger. If you weren't right on target, I'm sure you came close. But how? You didn't see your hand moving, and you didn't hear your arm swishing through the air. Humans and many other animals have senses that alert them to their movements and body position without relying on vision, including *kinesthesis* and the *vestibular sense*.

3-7a KINESTHESIS

Kinesthesis is the sense that informs you about the position and motion of parts of the body. The term is derived from the ancient Greek words for "motion"

(kinesis) and "perception" (aisthesis). In kinesthesis, sensory information is fed back to the brain from sensory organs in the joints, tendons, and muscles. You were able to bring your finger to your nose easily by employing your kinesthetic sense. When you make a muscle in your arm, the sensations of tightness and hardness are also provided by kinesthesis.

Imagine going for a walk without kinesthesis. You would have to watch the forward motion of each leg to be certain you had raised it high enough to clear the curb. And if you had tried the brief nose-to-finger experiment without the kinesthetic sense, you would have had no sensory feedback until you felt the pressure of your finger against your nose (or cheek, or eye, or forehead), and you probably would have missed dozens of times.

3-7b THE VESTIBULAR SENSE

It is your **vestibular sense** that provides your brain with information as to whether or not you are physically upright. Sensory organs located in the semicircular canals and elsewhere in the ears monitor your body's motion and position in relation to gravity. They tell you whether you are falling and provide cues to whether your body is changing speed, such as when you are in an accelerating airplane or automobile.

(3-8) ESP: Is There Perception Without Sensation?

Imagine the wealth you could amass if you had *precognition*, that is, if you were able to perceive future events in advance. Perhaps you would check the next week's stock market reports and know what to buy or sell. Or you could bet with confidence on who would win the next Super Bowl or World Series. Or think of the power you would have if you were capable of *psychokinesis*, that is, mentally manipulating or moving objects. Precognition and psychokinesis are two concepts associated with extrasensory perception (ESP). Two other theoretical forms of ESP are *telepathy*, or direct trans-

kinesthesis
the sense that informs us about the positions and motion of parts of our bodies

vestibular sense
the sense of equilibrium that informs us about our bodies' positions relative to gravity

© Photolink/Getty Images

extrasensory perception (ESP)
perception of objects or events through means other than the recognized sensory organs

mission of thoughts or ideas from one person to another, and *clairvoyance*, or the perception of objects that do not stimulate the known sensory organs. An example of clairvoyance is "seeing" what card will be dealt next, even though it is still in the deck and unseen even by the dealer.

ESP—also referred to as *parapsychological* or *psi phenomena*—refers to the perception of objects or events through means other than the known sensory organs. *Parapsychological (psi)* means standing alongside psychology, not being a part of psychology. Psychological communication occurs verbally or by means of body language. *Psi communication* refers to the transfer of information through an irregular or unusual process—not through the usual senses.

Many psychologists do not believe ESP is an appropriate area for scientific inquiry. Psychologist Ray Hyman (2011) argues that "It's craziness, pure craziness." Scientists study natural events, but ESP smacks of the supernatural, even the occult. Extrasensory perception also has the flavor of a nightclub act in which a blindfolded "clairvoyant" calls out the contents of an audience member's pocketbook. Other psychologists, however, believe that there is nothing wrong with investigating ESP. The issue for them is not whether ESP is sensationalistic but whether its existence can be demonstrated in the laboratory.

Perhaps the best known of the ESP researchers was Joseph Banks Rhine, who studied ESP for several decades beginning in the late 1920s (Viulli, 2008). In a typical experiment in clairvoyance, Rhine would use a pack of 25 Zener cards, which contained five sets of simple symbols. Pigeons' pecking randomly to indicate which one was about to be turned up would be "correct" 20% of the time. Rhine found that some people guessed correctly significantly more often than the 20% chance rate. He concluded that these individuals might have some degree of ESP.

A more current method for studying *telepathy* (direct communication between minds) is the *ganzfeld procedure* (Howard et al., 2009). In this method, one person acts as a "sender" and the other as a "receiver." The sender views randomly selected visual stimuli such as photographs or videotapes, while the receiver, who is in another room and whose eyes are covered and ears are blocked, tries to mentally tune in to the sender. After a session, the receiver is shown four visual stimuli and asked to select the one transmitted by the sender. A person guessing which stimulus was "trans-

FICTION THERE IS NO ADEQUATE SCIENTIFIC EVIDENCE THAT PEOPLE CAN READ OTHER PEOPLE'S MINDS.

mitted" would be correct 25% of the time (1 time in 4) by chance alone. An analysis of 28 experiments using the ganzfeld procedure, however, found that receivers correctly identified the visual stimulus 38% of the time (Honorton, 1985), a percentage unlikely to be due to chance.

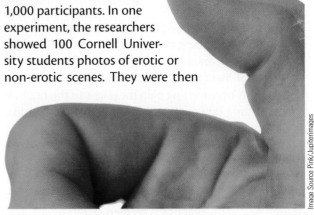

Image Source Pink/Jupiterimages

An article by Daryl Bem (2011) reported the results of several experiments with more than 1,000 participants. In one experiment, the researchers showed 100 Cornell University students photos of erotic or non-erotic scenes. They were then shown the photos again, in random order, but asked to predict whether the next photo would have erotic or non-erotic content. Since half were erotic and half were not, a chance result would be 50–50. Participants correctly predicted the erotic photos 53.1% of the time, whereas their hit rate on predicting non-erotic photos was just 50–50, a chance result. The chances that the 53.1% success rate was due to chance alone were less than 1 in 20. However, no single individual was correct every time.

Overall, there are many reasons for skepticism of ESP. First is the *file-drawer problem* (Howard et al., 2009). Buyers of supermarket magazines tend to forget "psychics'" predictions when they fail to come true (that is, they have "filed" them away). Similarly, ESP researchers are less likely to report research results that show failure. Therefore, we would expect unusual findings (for example, a subject with a high success rate at psi-communication tasks over a period of several days) to appear in the research literature. In other words, if you flip a coin indefinitely, eventually you will flip 10 heads in a row. The odds against it are high, but if you report only your success and not the weeks of failure, you appear to have unique coin-flipping ability.

Then, too, people who appear to have demonstrated ESP with one researcher have failed to do so with another researcher or have refused to participate in other studies (Howard et al., 2009). Moreover, in all of these studies, *not one person has emerged who can reliably show ESP from one occasion to another and from one researcher to another.* In sum, most psychologists do not grant ESP research much credibility. They prefer to study perception that involves sensation. After all, what is life without sensation?

By the Numbers

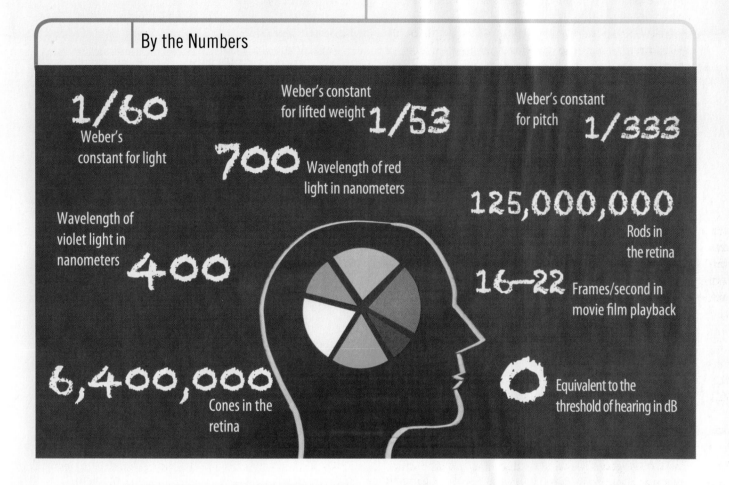

1/60 Weber's constant for light

1/53 Weber's constant for lifted weight

1/333 Weber's constant for pitch

700 Wavelength of red light in nanometers

400 Wavelength of violet light in nanometers

125,000,000 Rods in the retina

16–22 Frames/second in movie film playback

6,400,000 Cones in the retina

0 Equivalent to the threshold of hearing in dB

STUDY TOOLS ▶ 3

Ready to study? In the book, you can:

❍ Review what you've read with Fill-Ins and Multiple Choice quizzes (below).

❍ Rip out Chapter Review card (in the back).

Or you can go online to CourseMate at www.cengagebrain.com for these resources:

❍ Complete Practices Quizzes to prepare for tests.

❍ Review Key Terms Flash Cards (online or print).

❍ Play games to master concepts.

FILL-INS

Answers can be found in the back of the book, starting on page 368.

1. _____ is the organization of sensations into an inner representation of the world; it reflects learning and expectations as well as sensations.

2. The _____ threshold for a stimulus, such as light, is the lowest intensity at which it can be detected.

3. The retina is made up of photoreceptors called _____ and _____.

4. The axons of ganglion cells make up the _____ nerve, which conducts visual information to the brain.

5. We perceive movement by sensing motion across the _____ of the eye and change of position in relation to other objects.

6. Odors are detected by the _____ membrane in each nostril.

7. The receptor neurons for taste are called _____ cells, which are located in taste buds on the tongue.

8. Kinesthesis is the sensing of bodily _____ and movement.

9. The vestibular sense is housed mainly in the _____ canals of the ears.

10. One reason for skepticism about ESP is the _____-_____ problem; that is, researchers are less likely to report research results that show failure.

82   Sensation and Perception

1. _____ is to mechanical stimulation as perception is to mental representation.
   a. Adaptation   c. Sensation
   b. Organization   d. Cognition

2. Which of the following accommodates to an image by changing thickness and focusing light onto the retina?
   a. Sclera   c. Iris
   b. Lens   d. Cornea

3. Which of the following colors is longest in wavelength?
   a. Red   c. Violet
   b. Yellow   d. Green

4. The Gestalt rule describing the perceptual tendency to see objects that are near each other as belonging to a set is termed _____; while the tendency to see like objects as belonging together is termed _____.
   a. proximity; continuity
   b. closure; constancy
   c. continuity; similarity
   d. proximity; similarity

5. The normal human ear can hear sounds varying in frequency from _____ to _____ cycles per second (Hz).
   a. 2 to 2,000
   b. 20 to 2,000
   c. 20 to 20,000
   d. 200 to 20,000

6. Which of the following is *not* involved in explaining the perception of pitch?
   a. Place theory
   b. The volley principle
   c. Opponent-process theory
   d. Frequency theory

7. The following are considered to be basic tastes, with the exception of
   a. savory.
   b. sweet.
   c. sour.
   d. salty.

8. Because one odor can mask another, people use _____.
   a. air fresheners   c. incense burners
   b. perfumes   d. all of the above

9. The sensory receptors for kinesthesis are located in the
   a. tendons, muscles, and joints.
   b. semicircular canals.
   c. bony frame of the body.
   d. skin and hair.

10. Most psychologists do not believe in extrasensory perception because
    a. scientists have not defined what is meant by extrasensory perception.
    b. there is no evidence to support the existence of extrasensory perception.
    c. extrasensory perception would give those who have it unfair advantages.
    d. it is a sensationalistic concept.

Colin Anderson/Jupiter Images

LEARNING OUTCOMES

4-1 Define consciousness

4-2 Explain the nature of sleep and various sleep disorders

4-3 Explain the natures and uses of hypnosis, meditation, and biofeedback in altering consciousness

4-4 Define substance abuse and dependence, identify categories of psychoactive drugs, and explain their allures and dangers

 STUDY TOOLS ▶

After you read the chapter, go to the Study Tools at the end of the chapter, page 107.

CHAPTER 4

Consciousness

When you talk to yourself, who talks, and who listens?

This is the type of question posed by philosophers and scientists who study consciousness. Although it might seem that psychologists, who study the brain and mental processes, are best equipped to look into consciousness, they banished this topic from their field for many years. In 1904, for example, William James wrote an article with the intriguing title "Does Consciousness Exist?" James did not think consciousness was a proper area of study for psychologists because scientific methods could not directly observe or measure another person's consciousness.

John Watson, the "father of modern behaviorism," agreed. Watson insisted that only observable, measurable behavior is the province of psychology: "The time seems to have come when psychology must discard all references to consciousness" (1913, p. 163). When Watson became the president of the American Psychological Association in 1914, his view was further cemented in the minds of many psychologists.

But the past few decades have seen a cognitive revolution, and thousands of psychologists now believe we cannot capture the richness of human experience without referring to consciousness (Sternberg, 2009). We are flooded with studies of consciousness by psychologists, biologists, neuroscientists, physicists, even computer scientists. Yet we still cannot directly observe the consciousness of another person, and so we rely on self-reports of consciousness as we observe events such as neural activity in the brain.

4-1   What Is Consciousness?

Mental concepts such as consciousness acquire scientific status by being tied to observable behavior whenever possible. The concept of consciousness has various meanings, and psychologists use it in many ways.

When you talk to yourself, who talks, and who listens?

TRUTH OR FICTION

WHAT DO YOU THINK? FOLKLORE, COMMON SENSE, OR NONSENSE? CIRCLE THE T FOR "TRUTH" OR THE F FOR "FICTION," AND CHECK THE ACCURACY OF YOUR ANSWERS AS YOU READ THROUGH THE CHAPTER.

T	F	WE ACT OUT OUR FORBIDDEN FANTASIES IN OUR DREAMS.
T	F	INSOMNIA CAN BE CAUSED BY TRYING TOO HARD TO FALL ASLEEP.
T	F	IT IS DANGEROUS TO AWAKEN A SLEEPWALKER.
T	F	YOU CAN BE HYPNOTIZED AGAINST YOUR WILL.
T	F	YOU CAN TEACH A RAT TO RAISE OR LOWER ITS HEART RATE.
T	F	HEROIN WAS ONCE USED AS A CURE FOR ADDICTION TO MORPHINE.
T	F	MANY HEALTH PROFESSIONALS CALM DOWN HYPERACTIVE CHILDREN BY GIVING THEM A STIMULANT.
T	F	COCA-COLA ONCE "ADDED LIFE" TO ITS SIGNATURE DRINK THROUGH THE USE OF A POWERFUL—BUT NOW ILLEGAL—STIMULANT.
T	F	THE NUMBER OF PEOPLE WHO DIE FROM SMOKING-RELATED CAUSES IS GREATER THAN THE NUMBER LOST TO MOTOR-VEHICLE ACCIDENTS, ABUSE OF ALCOHOL AND ALL OTHER DRUGS, SUICIDE, HOMICIDE, AND AIDS *COMBINED*.

4-1a CONSCIOUSNESS AS AWARENESS

One meaning of **consciousness** is *sensory awareness* of the environment. The sense of vision enables us to see, or be *conscious* of, the sun gleaming on the snow. The sense of hearing allows us to hear, or be conscious of, a concert. Yet sometimes we are not aware of sensory stimulation. We may be unaware, or unconscious, of sensory stimulation when we do not pay attention to it. The world is abuzz with signals, yet you are conscious of or focusing on only the words on this page (I hope).

Therefore, another aspect of consciousness is **selective attention**. Selective attention means focusing one's consciousness on a particular stimulus. Selective attention is a key to self-control. To keep your car on the road, you must pay more attention to driving conditions than to your hunger pangs or a cellphone call.

Adaptation to our environment involves learning which stimuli must be attended to and which can be safely ignored. Selective attention makes our senses keener (Kerlin et al., 2010; McLachlan & Wilson, 2010). This is why we can pick out the speech of a single per-

son across a room at a cocktail party, a phenomenon aptly termed the *cocktail party effect*. Selective attention also plays a role in the advertisements and marketing ploys we notice.

How do advertisers of running shoes, automobiles, or beer use these facts to get "into" our consciousness and, they hope, our pocketbooks? Think of some TV commercials that captured your attention. What kinds of stimuli made them front and center in your awareness?

Yet another meaning of consciousness is that of **direct inner awareness**. Close your eyes and imagine spilling a can of bright-red paint across a black tabletop. Watch it spread across the black, shiny surface and then spill onto the floor. Although this image may be vivid, you did not "see" it literally. Neither your eyes nor any other sensory organs were involved. You were conscious of the image through direct inner awareness.

We are conscious of—or have direct inner awareness of—our own thoughts, images, emotions, and memories. However, we may not be able to measure direct inner awareness scientifically. Nevertheless, many psychologists would argue that if you have it, you know it. Self-awareness is connected with the firing of billions of neurons hundreds of times per second. Even so, we detect psychological processes but not neural events (Roth, 2000).

4-1b CONSCIOUS, PRECONSCIOUS, UNCONSCIOUS, AND NONCONSCIOUS

Sigmund Freud, the founder of psychoanalysis, differentiated between thoughts and feelings of which we are conscious and those that are preconscious and unconscious.

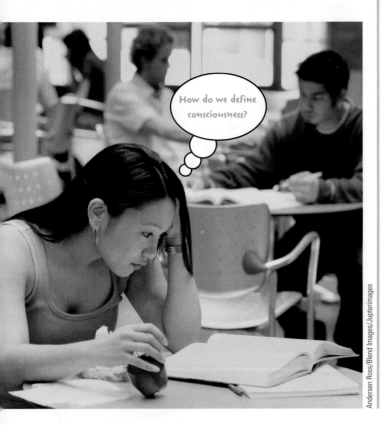

How do we define consciousness?

Andersen Ross/Blend Images/Jupterimages

> "Consciousness comes in many flavors. Anyone who has taught an introductory psychology class, or attended one at eight o'clock Friday morning, has seen them all. There may be a couple of party-hearty frat boys in the back row, dozing after a long night spent celebrating the upcoming weekend. These two are not conscious. Up a couple of rows is the scammer checking out [someone] across the aisle and wondering if he can get a date. He is conscious, but not of you; nor are the three girls down the way who are passing notes to each other and suppressing their merriment. Another student has a tape recorder going and is finishing up a paper for another class, and he will be conscious of you later. The front-row kids are sippin' their coffee, taking notes furiously and occasionally nodding in agreement; at least they are conscious of you."
>
> —MICHAEL S. GAZZANIGA, 2008, P. 277.

Preconscious material is not currently in awareness but is readily available. For example, if you answer the following questions, you will summon up "preconscious" information: What did you eat for breakfast? What is your phone number? You can make these preconscious bits of information conscious by directing your attention to them.

According to Freud, still other mental events are **unconscious**, or unavailable to awareness under most circumstances. Freud believed that some painful memories and sexual and aggressive impulses are unacceptable to us, so we *automatically* (unconsciously) eject them from awareness. That is, we *repress* them. **Repression** of these memories and impulses allows us to avoid feelings of anxiety, guilt, or shame.

Related, non-Freudian concepts include *suppression* and *nonconscious*. When people choose to stop thinking about unacceptable ideas or distractions, they are using **suppression**. When we consciously eject unwanted mental events from awareness, we are using suppression. We may, for example, suppress thoughts of an upcoming party when we need to study for a test. We may also try to suppress thoughts of the test while we are at the party!

Some bodily processes, such as the firing of neurons, are **nonconscious**. They cannot be experienced through sensory awareness or direct inner awareness. Growing hair and carrying oxygen in the blood are nonconscious. We can see that our hair has grown, but we have no sense receptors that provide sensations of growing. We feel the need to breathe but do not experience the exchange of carbon dioxide and oxygen.

4-1c CONSCIOUSNESS AS PERSONAL UNITY

As we develop, we differentiate ourselves from that which is not us. We develop a sense of being persons, individuals. There is a totality to our impressions, thoughts, and feelings that makes up our consciousness—our continuing sense of self in the world. That self forms intentions and guides behavior. In this usage of the word, consciousness *is* self.

4-1d CONSCIOUSNESS AS THE WAKING STATE

The word *conscious* also refers to the waking state as opposed, for example, to sleep. From this perspective, sleep, meditation, the hypnotic "trance," and the distorted perceptions that can accompany use of consciousness-altering drugs are considered *altered states of consciousness*.

The remainder of the chapter explores various altered states of consciousness, including sleep and dreams; hypnosis, meditation, and biofeedback; and, finally, the effects of psychoactive drugs.

preconscious in psychodynamic theory, descriptive of material that is not in awareness but can be brought into awareness by focusing one's attention

unconscious in psychodynamic theory, descriptive of ideas and feelings that are not available to awareness; also: without consciousness

repression in psychodynamic theory, the automatic (unconscious) ejection of anxiety-evoking ideas, impulses, or images from awareness

suppression the deliberate, or conscious, placing of certain ideas, impulses, or images out of awareness

nonconscious descriptive of bodily processes, such as growing hair, of which we cannot become conscious; we may "recognize" that our hair is growing, but we cannot directly experience the biological process

One of the meanings of consciousness is the continuing sense of self in the world.

circadian rhythm
a cycle that is connected with the twenty-four-hour period of the earth's rotation

4-2 Sleep and Dreams

Sleep is a fascinating topic. After all, we spend about one-third of our adult lives asleep. Sleep experts recommend that adults get eight hours of sleep a night, but according to the National Sleep Foundation (2009), adults in the United States typically get about 6.8 hours of sleep. About one-third get six hours or less of sleep a night during the workweek. One-third admit that lack of sleep impairs their ability to function during the day, and nearly one in five admits to falling asleep at the wheel.

Yes, we spend one-third of our lives in sleep—or would if we could. As you can see in Figure 4.1, some animals get much more sleep than we do, and some obtain much less. Why? It might have something to do with evolutionary forces. Animals that are most at risk of being hunted by predators tend to sleep less—an adaptive response to the realities of life and death.

FIGURE 4.1 | Sleep Times for Mammals

Different mammals require different amounts of sleep. Reasons remain uncertain, but evolution apparently plays a role: Animals more prone to being attacked by predators sleep less.

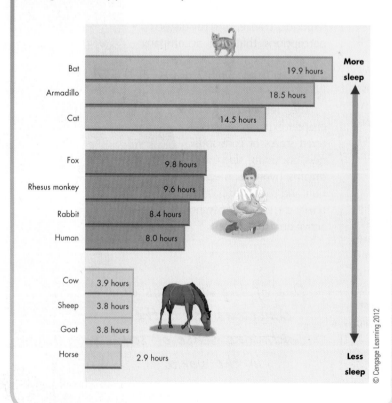

Bat	19.9 hours
Armadillo	18.5 hours
Cat	14.5 hours
Fox	9.8 hours
Rhesus monkey	9.6 hours
Rabbit	8.4 hours
Human	8.0 hours
Cow	3.9 hours
Sheep	3.8 hours
Goat	3.8 hours
Horse	2.9 hours

More sleep → Less sleep

© Cengage Learning 2012

4-2a BIOLOGICAL AND CIRCADIAN RHYTHMS

We and other animals are subject to rhythms, and they are related to the rotation and revolutions of the planet. Many birds (and people who can afford it!) migrate south in the fall and north in the spring. A number of animals hibernate for the winter and emerge when buds are once again about to blossom.

Alternating periods of wakefulness and sleep reflect an internally generated *circadian rhythm*. A **circadian rhythm** is a cycle that is connected with the 24-hour period of the earth's rotation. A cycle of wakefulness and sleep is normally 24 hours long. When people are removed from cues that signal day or night, however, a cycle tends to become extended to about 25 hours, and people sleep nearly 10 of them (National Sleep Foundation, 2009). Why? We do not know. And during a night of sleep, we typically undergo a series of 90-minute cycles in which we run through the stages of sleep. In the morning, the shining sun adjusts the timing of the circadian clock by activating proteins in the retinas of the eyes. The proteins then signal tiny structures in the hypothalamus called the *suprachiasmatic nucleus (SCN)*. In turn, the SCN stimulates the pineal gland to decrease its output of the hormone melatonin, which promotes sleep.

Some of us, known as "morning people," function best in the morning; others function best in the afternoon. Some of us are "night owls," who are at our best when most neighbors are sound asleep.

Why do we sleep? Why do we dream? Let's explore the nature of sleep, dreams, and sleep disorders.

4-2b THE STAGES OF SLEEP

When we sleep, we slip from consciousness to unconsciousness. When we are conscious, our brains emit waves characterized by certain *frequencies* (numbers of waves per second) and *amplitudes* (heights—an index of strength). Brain waves are rough indicators of the activity of large numbers of neurons. The strength, or energy, of brain waves is expressed in volts (an electrical unit). When we sleep, our brain waves differ from those emitted when we are conscious. The electroencephalograph (EEG; see Figure 2.7 on page 37) has enabled researchers to measure brain waves. Figure 4.2 shows EEG patterns that reflect the frequency and strength of brain waves during the waking state, when we are relaxed, and when we are in the various stages of sleep. Brain waves, like other waves, are cyclical. The printouts in Figure 4.2 show what happens during a period of 15 seconds or so.

High-frequency brain waves are associated with wakefulness. When we move deeper into sleep, their frequency decreases and their amplitude (strength) increases. When we close our eyes and begin to relax before going to sleep, our brains emit **alpha waves**—low-amplitude brain waves of about 8 to 13 cycles per second.

Figure 4.2 shows five stages of sleep. The first four sleep stages are considered **nonrapid eye movement (NREM) sleep**. These contrast with the fifth stage, **rapid eye movement (REM) sleep**, so called because our eyes dart back and forth beneath our eyelids.

As we enter stage 1 sleep, our brain waves slow down from the alpha rhythm and enter a pattern of **theta waves**. Theta waves, with a frequency of about 6 to 8 cycles per second, are accompanied by slow, rolling eye movements. The transition from alpha waves to theta waves may be accompanied by a *hypnagogic state* dur-

ing which we may experience brief but vivid dreamlike images. Stage 1 sleep is the lightest stage of sleep. If we are awakened from stage 1 sleep, we may feel we were not sleeping at all.

After 30 to 40 minutes of stage 1 sleep, we undergo a steep descent into stages 2, 3, and 4 (see Figure 4.3). During stage 2, brain waves are medium in amplitude with a frequency of about 4 to 7 cycles per second, but these are punctuated by *sleep spindles*, brief bursts of brain activity that have a frequency of 12 to 16 cycles per second.

During deep sleep stages 3 and 4, our brains produce slower **delta waves**, which reach relatively great amplitude. During stage 3, the delta waves have a frequency of 1 to 3 cycles per second. Stage 4 is the deepest stage of sleep, from which it is the most difficult to be awakened. During

alpha waves
rapid low-amplitude brain waves that have been linked to feelings of relaxation

nonrapid eye movement (NREM) sleep
the first four stages of sleep

rapid eye movement (REM) sleep
a stage of sleep characterized by rapid eye movements, which have been linked to dreaming

theta waves
slow brain waves produced during the hypnagogic state

delta waves
strong, slow brain waves usually emitted during stage 4 sleep

---

FIGURE 4.2 | The Stages of Sleep

This figure illustrates typical EEG patterns for the stages of sleep. During REM sleep, EEG patterns resemble those of the waking state. For this reason, REM sleep is often termed *paradoxical sleep*. As sleep progresses from stage 1 to stage 4, brain waves become slower, and their amplitude increases. Dreams, including normal nightmares, are most vivid during REM sleep. More disturbing sleep terrors tend to occur during deep stage 4 sleep.

Awake — beta waves
(low amplitude, high frequency)

Awake

Drowsy — alpha waves
(higher amplitude, slower frequency)

Stage 1 sleep — theta waves
(low frequency, low amplitude)

Sleep spindle   K complex

Stage 2 sleep — sleep spindles
and the K complex

**NREM
Sleep**

Stage 3 sleep — beginning of
delta waves (low frequency,
high amplitude)

Stage 4 sleep — delta waves
continue to increase
in amplitude

REM Sleep
Occurs when we re-enter
Stage 1, about ninety minutes
after falling asleep (frequently
called *paradoxical sleep*)

REM sleep — brain-wave
patterns are very similar
to those of initial
NREM stage 1

© Cengage Learning 2012

FIGURE 4.3 | Sleep Cycles

This figure illustrates the alternation of REM and non-REM sleep for the typical sleeper. There are about five periods of REM sleep during an 8-hour night. Sleep is deeper earlier in the night, and REM sleep tends to become prolonged toward morning.

| Sleep stage | A | 1 | 2 | 3 | 4 | 3 | 2 | REM | 1 | 2 | 3 | 4 | 3 | 2 | 3 | 2 | REM | 1 |

11 PM   12 AM   1 AM   2 AM

stage 4 sleep, the delta waves slow to about 0.5 to 2 cycles per second, and their amplitude is greatest.

After perhaps half an hour of deep stage 4 sleep, we begin a relatively rapid journey back upward through the stages until we enter REM sleep (see Figure 4.3). During REM sleep, we produce relatively rapid, low-amplitude brain waves that resemble those of light stage 1 sleep. REM sleep is also called *paradoxical sleep* because the EEG patterns observed suggest a level of arousal similar to that of the waking state (see Figure 4.2). However, it is difficult to awaken a person during REM sleep. When people are awakened during REM sleep, as is the practice in sleep research, about 80% of the time they report that they have been dreaming. (People report dreaming only about 20% of the time when awakened during NREM sleep.)

Each night we tend to undergo five cycles through the stages of sleep (see Figure 4.3). Five cycles include five periods of REM sleep. Our first journey through stage 4 sleep is usually the longest. Sleep tends to become lighter as the night wears on; periods of REM sleep lengthen and we may not enter the deepest stages of sleep. Toward morning our last period of REM sleep may last about half an hour.

4-2c THE FUNCTIONS OF SLEEP

Researchers do not have all the answers as to why we sleep, but sleep seems to serve several purposes: It rejuvenates the body, helps us recover from stress, helps us consolidate learning, and may promote development of infants' brains.

Consider the hypothesis that sleep helps rejuvenate a tired body. Most of us have had the experience of going without sleep for a night and feeling "wrecked" or "out of it" the following day. Perhaps the next evening we went to bed early to "catch up on our sleep." What happens to you if you do not sleep for one night? For several nights? Compare people who are highly sleep-deprived with people who have been drinking heavily. Sleepless people's abilities to concentrate and perform may be seriously impaired, but they may not recognize their limitations.

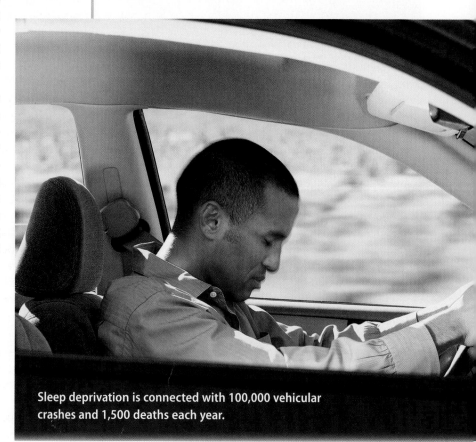

Sleep deprivation is connected with 100,000 vehicular crashes and 1,500 deaths each year.

3 AM			4 AM			5 AM			6 AM			7 AM
2	3	2	REM	1	2	3 2 A 1		REM	A 1 A	2		REM

© Cengage Learning 2012

Many students can pull "all-nighters" in which they cram for a test through the night and perform reasonably well the following day. But they begin to show deficits in psychological functions such as attention, learning, and memory, especially if they go sleepless for more than one night (Dubiela et al., 2010; Ward et al., 2009). Sleep deprivation also makes for dangerous driving (M. L. Jackson, 2009). It is estimated to be connected with 100,000 vehicular crashes and 1,500 deaths each year (S. Clark, 2009). To combat sleep deprivation during the week, many people sleep late or nap on their days off (National Sleep Foundation, 2009).

Why Do You Need the Amount of Sleep You Need?

The amount of sleep we need seems to be in part genetically determined (Cirelli, 2009). People also need more sleep when they are under stress, such as a change of job or an episode of depression (Mayers et al., 2009; Rosekind et al., 2010). In fact, sleep seems to help us recover from stress.

Newborn babies may sleep 16 hours a day, and teenagers may sleep 12 hours or more. It is widely believed that older people need less sleep than younger adults do, but sleep in older people is often interrupted by physical discomfort or the need to go to the bathroom. To make up for sleep lost at night, older people may "nod off " during the day.

Sleep, Learning, and Memory

REM sleep and deep sleep are both connected with the consolidation of learning and memory (Dubiela et al., 2010; Ward et al., 2009). In fact, fetuses have periods of waking and sleeping, and REM sleep may foster the development of the brain before birth (Fifer & Moon, 2003; Uhlhaas et al., 2010). In some studies, animals or people have been deprived of REM sleep. Under deprivation of REM sleep, animals and people learn more slowly and

forget what they have learned more quickly. REM-sleep-deprived people and animals tend to show *REM rebound*, meaning that they spend more time in REM sleep during subsequent sleep periods. They "catch up."

4-2d DREAMS

Like memories and fantasies, dreams are imagery in the absence of external stimulation and can seem real. In college, I often had "anxiety dreams" the night before a test. I would dream that I had taken the test and it was all over. (Imagine my disappointment when I awakened and realized the test still lay before me!)

Dreams are most likely to be vivid during REM sleep, whereas images are vaguer and more fleeting during NREM sleep. If you sleep for eight hours and undergo five sleep cycles, you may have five dreams. Dreams may compress time the way a movie does, by skipping hours or days to a future time, but the actual action tends to take place in "real time." Fifteen minutes of events fills about 15 minutes of dreaming. Furthermore, your dream theater is quite flexible. You can dream in black and white or in full color.

Some dreams are nightmares. One common nightmare is that you are falling. Another is that you are trying to run away from a threat but cannot gain your footing or coordinate your legs. Nightmares, like most pleasant dreams, are products of REM sleep.

There are many theories about why we dream what we dream. Some are psychological, and others are more biologically oriented.

Dreams as "the Residue of the Day"

You may recall dreams involving fantastic adventures, but most dreams involve memories of the activities and problems of the day (Morewedge & Norton, 2009). If we are preoccupied with illness or death, sexual or aggressive urges, or moral dilemmas, we are likely to dream about them. The characters in our dreams are more likely to be friends and neighbors than spies, monsters, and princes—subjects that have been referred to, poetically, as "the residue of the day."

Traumatic events, however, can spawn nightmares, as reported in the aftermath of the terrorist attacks on the World Trade Center and Pentagon in 2001 (Roberts et al., 2009; Singareddy & Balon, 2002). People who have frequent nightmares are more likely than others to also suffer from anxiety, depression, and other psychological problems (Roberts et al., 2009).

Dreams as the Expression of Unconscious Desires

In the Disney film *Cinderella*, a song lyric goes, "A dream is a wish your heart makes." Freud theorized that dreams reflect unconscious wishes and urges. He argued that dreams express impulses we would censor during the

FICTION THERE IS NO EVIDENCE THAT WE ACT OUT FORBIDDEN FANTASIES IN OUR DREAMS.

day, although researchers find no evidence for this assertion. Moreover, he said that the content of dreams is symbolic of unconscious fantasized objects such as the genitals. In his method of psychoanalysis, Freud would interpret his clients' dreams.

The Activation–Synthesis Model of Dreams

There are also biological views of the "meanings" of dreams. According to the **activation–synthesis model**, acetylcholine (a neurotransmitter) and the pons (see Figure 2.11 on page 41) stimulate responses that lead to dreaming (Hobson, 2003, 2009; Stuart & Conduit, 2009). One is *activation* of the reticular formation, which arouses us, but not to waking. During the waking state, firing of these cells is linked to movement, particularly the movements in walking, running, and other physical acts. But during REM sleep, neurotransmitters tend to inhibit activity so we usually do not thrash about as we dream (Stuart & Conduit, 2009). In this way, we save ourselves—and our bed partners—some wear and tear.

Most dreams involve memories of the day gone by—or, poetically, "the residue of the day."

Blend Images/Jupiterimages

But the eye muscles are stimulated and show the REM activity associated with dreaming. The reticular formation also stimulates parts of the cortex involved in memory. The cortex then *synthesizes*, or puts together, these sources of stimulation to yield the stuff of dreams. Yet research with the PET scan shows that the frontal lobes of the brain, which seem to be where we make sense of experience, are relatively inactive during sleep (Wade, 1998). Dreams are therefore more likely to be emotionally gripping than coherent in plot.

Because recent events are most likely to be reverberating in our brains, we are most likely to dream about them. With the brain cut off from the world outside, learning experiences and memories are replayed and consolidated during sleep (Siegel, 2009). It's useful to get a night of sleep between studying and test-taking, if you can.

4-2e SLEEP DISORDERS

Although nightmares are unpleasant, they do not qualify as sleep disorders. The term *sleep disorder* is reserved for other problems that can seriously interfere with our functioning. Some sleep disorders, like insomnia, are all too familiar, experienced by at least half of American adults. Others, like apnea (pauses in breathing) affect fewer than 10% of us (National Sleep Foundation, 2009). In this section we discuss insomnia and less common sleep disorders: narcolepsy, apnea, sleep terrors, bed-wetting, and sleepwalking.

Insomnia

According to the National Sleep Foundation (2009), more than half of American adults and about two-thirds of older adults are affected by insomnia in any given year. Trying to get to sleep can compound sleep problems by creating autonomic activity and muscle tension. You cannot force or will yourself to go to sleep. You can only set the stage for sleep by relaxing when you are tired.

Narcolepsy

A person with **narcolepsy** falls asleep suddenly. Narcolepsy afflicts as many as 100,000 people in the United States and seems to run in families. The "sleep attack" may last 15 minutes or so, after which the person feels refreshed. Nevertheless, sleep attacks are dangerous and upsetting. They can occur while driving or working with sharp tools. They may be accompanied by the collapse of muscle groups or the entire body—a condition called *sleep paralysis*. In sleep paralysis, the person cannot move during the transition from consciousness to sleep, and hallucinations (as of a person or object sitting on the chest) occur.

Narcolepsy is thought to be a disorder of REM-sleep functioning. Stimulants and antidepressant drugs have helped many people with the problem (Mamelak, 2009).

Sleep Apnea

Sleep apnea is a dangerous sleep disorder in which the air passages are obstructed. People with apnea stop breathing periodically, up to several hundred times per night. Obstruction may cause the sleeper to sit up and gasp for air before falling back asleep. People with sleep apnea are stimulated nearly, but not quite, to waking by the buildup of carbon dioxide. Sleep apnea is associated with obesity and chronic snoring. It can lead to high blood pressure, heart attacks, and strokes (Sekizuka et al., 2010).

Causes of sleep apnea include anatomical deformities that clog the air passageways, such as a thick palate, and problems in the breathing centers in the brain. Sleep apnea is treated by such measures as weight loss, surgery, and continuous positive airway pressure (CPAP), which is supplied by a mask that provides air pressure that keeps the airway open during sleep.

Deep-Sleep Disorders: Sleep Terrors, Bed-Wetting, and Sleepwalking

Sleep terrors, bed-wetting, and sleepwalking all occur during deep (stage 3 or 4) sleep. They are more common among children and may reflect immaturity of the nervous system (Kotagal, 2009; Nir & Tononi, 2010). **Sleep terrors** are similar to, but more severe than, nightmares, which occur during REM sleep. Sleep terrors usually occur during the first two sleep cycles of the night, whereas nightmares are more likely to occur toward morning. Experiencing a surge in the heart and respiration rates,

narcolepsy
a "sleep attack" in which a person falls asleep suddenly and irresistibly

sleep apnea
temporary absence or cessation of breathing while sleeping

sleep terrors
frightening dreamlike experiences that occur during the deepest stage of NREM sleep; nightmares, in contrast, occur during REM sleep

"**Fatigue** is the best pillow."
—BENJAMIN FRANKLIN

hypnosis
an altered state of consciousness in which people are highly suggestible and behave as though they are in a trance

the person may suddenly sit up, talk incoherently, and thrash about. He or she is never fully awake, returns to sleep, and may recall a vague image as of someone pressing on his or her chest. (Memories of nightmares tend to be more detailed.) Sleep terrors are often decreased by a minor tranquilizer at bedtime, which reduces the amount of time spent in stage 4 sleep.

Bed-wetting probably reflects immaturity of the nervous system. In most cases, it resolves itself before adolescence, often by age eight. Methods that condition children to awaken when they are about to urinate have been helpful (E. C. Jackson, 2009). The drug imipramine often helps. Sometimes all that is needed is reassurance that no one is to blame for bed-wetting and that most children outgrow it.

Perhaps half of children talk in their sleep now and then. Adults occasionally do so, too. Surveys suggest that some 7% to 15% of children walk in their sleep—a behavior pattern that is technically termed *somnambulism* (Cotton & Richdale, 2010; Li et al., 2009). Only 2% of a random sample of nearly 5,000 people aged 15 to 100 did so (Ohayon et al., 1999). Sleepwalkers may roam about nightly while their parents fret about possible accidents. Sleepwalkers typically do not remember their excursions, although they may respond to questions while they are up and about. Mild tranquilizers and maturity typically put an end to it.

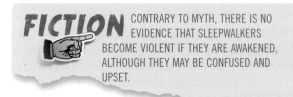

FICTION CONTRARY TO MYTH, THERE IS NO EVIDENCE THAT SLEEPWALKERS BECOME VIOLENT IF THEY ARE AWAKENED, ALTHOUGH THEY MAY BE CONFUSED AND UPSET.

4-3 Altering Consciousness Through Hypnosis, Meditation, and Biofeedback

Perhaps you have watched a fellow student try to place a friend in a "trance" after reading a book on hypnosis. Or perhaps you have seen an audience member hypnotized in a nightclub act. If so, chances are the person acted as if he or she had returned to childhood, imagined that a snake was about to have a nip, or lay rigid

between two chairs for a while. In this section we deal with three altered states of consciousness: hypnosis, meditation, and biofeedback. Each of these is an *altered state of consciousness* because they involve focusing on stimuli that are not common parts of our daily lives.

4-3a HYPNOSIS

Of these altered states, the one we hear of most is hypnosis. The word **hypnosis** is derived from the Greek word for *sleep*. It is an altered state of consciousness in which people are suggestible and behave as though they are in a trance. Modern hypnosis evolves from the ideas of Franz Mesmer in the 18th century. Mesmer asserted that everything in the universe was connected by forms of magnetism—which actually may not be far off the mark. However, he also claimed that people, too, could be drawn to one another by "animal magnetism." Not so. Mesmer used bizarre props to bring people under his "spell" and managed a respectable cure rate for minor ailments. Scientists now attribute his successes to the placebo effect, not animal magnetism.

Today, hypnotism is more than a nightclub act. It is also used as an anesthetic in dentistry, childbirth, and medical procedures (Vanhaudenhuyse et al., 2009). Some psychologists use hypnosis to help clients reduce anxiety, overcome fears, or lessen the perception of chronic pain (Dufresne et al., 2009). A study with 241 surgery patients shows how hypnosis can help people deal with pain and anxiety. The patients underwent procedures that used only local anesthetics (Lang et al., 2000). They could use as much pain medication as they wished. Patients who were hypnotized needed less additional pain medication and experienced less anxiety as measured by blood pressure and heart rate. The hypnotized patients focused on pleasant imagery rather than the surgery.

© Imagestopshop/Alamy

Hypnosis as an aid in relaxation training also helps people cope with stress and enhance the functioning of their immune systems (Jensen et al., 2009; Kiecolt-Glaser et al., 2001). Research also shows that hypnosis can be a useful supplement to other forms of therapy, especially in helping people control their weight and stop smoking (Tønnesen, 2009). Some police departments even use hypnosis to prompt the memories of witnesses.

The state of consciousness called the *hypnotic trance* has traditionally been induced by asking people to narrow their attention to a small light, a spot on the wall, an object held by the hypnotist, or the hypnotist's voice. The hypnotist usually suggests that the person's limbs are becoming warm, heavy, and relaxed. People may also be told that they are becoming sleepy or falling asleep. But hypnosis is *not* sleep, as shown by differences between EEG recordings for the hypnotic trance and the stages of sleep. (Subjects understand that the word *sleep* suggests a hypnotic trance.) Researchers are also studying changes in the brain that result from hypnosis. For example, Rainville and his colleagues (2002) used PET scans on people being hypnotized and found that mental absorption and mental relaxation are associated with changes in blood flow in the cerebral cortex (absorption) and parts of the brain involved in arousal and attention (relaxation).

People who are easily hypnotized are said to have *hypnotic suggestibility*. Part of "suggestibility" is knowledge of what is expected during the "trance state." Generally speaking, suggestible people are prone to fantasy and want to cooperate with the hypnotist (Dienes et al., 2009). As a result, they pay close attention to the instructions.

Explaining Hypnosis

Hypnotism is no longer explained in terms of animal magnetism, but others have offered explanations. According to Freud, hypnotized adults permit themselves to return to childish modes of responding that emphasize fantasy and impulse rather than fact and logic. Modern views of hypnosis are quite different.

Theodore Sarbin offers a **role theory** view of hypnosis (Lynn et al., 2008; Sarbin & Coe, 1972). He points out that the changes in behavior attributed to the hypnotic trance can be successfully imitated when people are instructed to behave *as though* they were hypnotized. For example, people can lie rigid between two chairs whether they are hypnotized or not. Also, people cannot be hypnotized unless they are familiar with the hypnotic "role"—the behavior that constitutes the trance. Sarbin is not saying that subjects *fake* the hypnotic role. Instead, Sarbin is suggesting that people *allow* themselves to enact this role under the hypnotist's directions.

The **response set theory** of hypnosis is related to role theory. It suggests that expectations play a role in the production of experiences suggested by the hypnotist (Lynn et al., 2008). A positive response to each suggestion of the hypnotist sets the stage—creates a *response set*—in which the subject is more likely to follow further suggestions.

Role theory and response set theory appear to be supported by research evidence that "suggestible" people want to be hypnotized, are good role players, have vivid imaginations, and know what is expected of them (Cavallaro et al., 2010; Lynn et al., 2008). By making suggestions that the subject follows, the hypnotist gets his or her "foot in the door," increasing the likelihood that the subject will follow additional suggestions. The fact that the behaviors shown by hypnotized people can be mimicked by people who know what is expected of them means that we need not resort to the concept of the "hypnotic trance"—an unusual and mystifying altered state of awareness—to explain hypnotic events.

Let's now consider two other altered states of consciousness that involve different ways of focusing our attention: meditation and biofeedback.

4-3b MEDITATION

The dictionary defines *meditation* as the act or process of thinking. But the concept usually suggests thinking deeply about the universe or about one's place in the world, often within a spiritual context. As the term is commonly used by psychologists, however, meditation refers to various ways of focusing one's consciousness to alter one's relationship to the world. In this use, ironically, *meditation* can also refer to a process by which people seem to suspend thinking and allow the world to fade away.

The kinds of meditation that psychologists and other kinds of helping professionals speak of are not the first definition you find in the dictionary. Rather, they tend to refer to rituals, exercises, even passive observation—activities that alter the normal relationship between the person and the environment. They are methods of suspending problem solving, planning, worries, and awareness of the events of the day. These methods alter consciousness—the normal focus of

FICTION DESPITE THE EXISTENCE OF HYPNOTIC SUGGESTIBILITY, IT IS EXTREMELY UNLIKELY THAT SOMEONE COULD BE HYPNOTIZED AGAINST HIS OR HER WILL (BARBER, 2000).

role theory
a theory that explains hypnotic events in terms of the person's ability to act *as though* he or she were hypnotized

response set theory
the view that response expectancies play a key role in the production of the experiences suggested by the hypnotist

attention—and help people cope with stress by inducing feelings of relaxation.

One common form of meditation, **transcendental meditation (TM)**, was brought to the United States by the Maharishi Mahesh Yogi in 1959. People practice TM by concentrating on *mantras*—words or sounds that are claimed to help the person achieve an altered state of consciousness. TM has some goals that cannot be assessed scientifically, such as expanding consciousness to encompass spiritual experiences, but there are also measurable goals, such as reducing anxiety and lowering blood pressure. For example, Herbert Benson (1975) found that TM lowered heart and respiration rates and produced what he labeled a *relaxation response* (A. Taylor et al., 2010). The blood pressure of people with hypertension—a risk factor in cardiovascular disease—decreased. Meditators produced more frequent alpha waves—brain waves associated with feelings of relaxation. Meditation has also been shown to increase nighttime concentrations of the hormone melatonin, which helps people get to sleep (Rubia, 2009). Research in brain imaging has shown that meditation activates neural structures involved in attention and control of the autonomic nervous system as well, helping produce feelings of relaxation (Rubia, 2009).

Psychologist Jon Kabat-Zinn, founder of the Stress Reduction Clinic at the University of Massachusetts Medical Center, has promoted the use of **mindfulness meditation (MM)** in cognitive and behavior therapy. MM, as opposed to TM, makes no pretense of achieving spiritual goals. Instead, MM provides clients with mantra-like techniques they can use to focus on the

present moment rather than ruminate about problems (Heidenreich & Michalak, 2003; Salmon et al., 2004). MM holds promise for helping clients cope with problems such as depression as well as reducing stress (Ramel et al., 2004).

4-3c BIOFEEDBACK

Psychologist Neal E. Miller (1909–2002) trained laboratory rats to increase or decrease their heart rates. How? His procedure was simple but ingenious. As discovered by James Olds and Peter Milner (1954), there is a "pleasure center" in the rat's hypothalamus. A small burst of electricity in this center is strongly reinforcing: Rats learn to do what they can, such as pressing a lever, to obtain this "reward."

Neal Miller (1969) implanted electrodes in the rats' pleasure centers. Some rats were then given a burst of electricity whenever their heart rates happened to increase. Other rats received the burst when their heart rates decreased. After a 90-minute training session, the rats learned to alter their heart rates by as much as 20% in the direction for which they had been rewarded.

Miller's research was an example of **biofeedback training (BFT)**. Biofeedback is a system that provides, or "feeds back," information about a bodily function. Miller used electrical stimulation of the brain to feed back information to rats when they had engaged in a targeted bodily response—in this case, raised or lowered their heart rates.

Similarly, people have learned to change some bodily functions voluntarily, including heart rate, that were once considered beyond conscious control. However, electrodes are not implanted in people's brains. Rather, people hear a "blip" or receive some other signal that informs them the targeted response is being displayed.

BFT is used in many ways, including helping people combat stress, tension, and anxiety. For example, people can learn to emit alpha waves through EEG feedback and feel more relaxed. The psychologist asks the person to "make the blip go faster." A blip may blink faster whenever alpha waves are being emitted. An **electromyograph (EMG)** monitors muscle tension. The EMG can be used to help people become more aware of muscle tension in the forehead, fingers, and else-

Biofeedback is a system that provides, or "feeds back," information about a bodily function to an organism. Through biofeedback training, people have learned to gain voluntary control over a number of functions that are normally automatic, such as heart rate and blood pressure.

where and to learn to lower tension (Pluess et al., 2009). Through the use of other instruments, people have learned to lower their heart rates, blood pressure, and sweating (Greenhalgh et al., 2010). Biofeedback is widely used by sports psychologists to teach athletes how to relax muscle groups that are unessential to the task at hand so that the athletes can control anxiety and tension.

4-4 Altering Consciousness Through Drugs

The world is a supermarket of **psychoactive substances**, or drugs. The United States is flooded with drugs that distort perceptions and change mood—drugs that take you up, let you down, and move you across town. Some of these drugs are legal, others illegal. Some are used recreationally, others medically. Some are safe if used correctly and dangerous if they are not. Some people use drugs because their friends do or because their parents tell them not to. Some are seeking pleasure; others are seeking inner truth or escape.

Young people often become involved with drugs that impair their ability to learn at school and are con-

nected with reckless behavior (Pani et al., 2010). Alcohol is the most popular drug on high school and college campuses (Johnston et al., 2009). More than one in six people of college age smokes marijuana (Johnston et al., 2010). Many Americans take **depressants** to get to sleep at night and **stimulants** to get going in the morning. Cocaine was once a toy of the well-to-do, but price breaks have brought it into the lockers of high school students.

4-4a SUBSTANCE ABUSE AND DEPENDENCE

Where does drug use end and abuse begin? The American Psychiatric Association (2000) defines **substance abuse** as repeated use of a substance despite the fact that it is causing or compounding social, occupational, psychological, or physical problems.* If you are missing school or work because you are drunk or "sleeping it off," you are abusing alcohol. The amount you drink is not as crucial as the fact that your pattern of use disrupts your life. Binge drinking, for example, is abusive because it has been associated with health problems such as heart failure and interpersonal problems such as rape (McCauley et al., 2010; Zagrosek et al., 2010).

Substance dependence is more severe than substance abuse and has behavioral and biological aspects (American Psychiatric Association, 2000).* Behaviorally, dependence is characterized by loss of control over one's use of the substance. Dependent people may organize their lives around getting and using a substance. Biological or physiological dependence is typified by tolerance, withdrawal symptoms, or both. **Tolerance** is the body's habituation to a substance so that, with regular usage, higher doses are needed to achieve similar effects. There is also an **abstinence syndrome**—that is, a characteristic

IT IS TRUE THAT, THROUGH BIOFEEDBACK TRAINING, YOU CAN TEACH A RAT TO RAISE OR LOWER ITS HEART RATE.

---

*The DSM content has been adapted for the particular audience and is intended for educational purposes only.

psychoactive substances
drugs that have psychological effects such as stimulation or distortion of perceptions

depressant
a drug that lowers the rate of activity of the nervous system

stimulant
a drug that increases activity of the nervous system

substance abuse
persistent use of a substance even though it is causing or compounding problems in meeting the demands of life

substance dependence
loss of control over use of a substance; biologically speaking, dependence is typified by tolerance, withdrawal symptoms, or both

tolerance
habituation to a drug, with the result that increasingly higher doses of the drug are needed to achieve similar effects

abstinence syndrome
a characteristic cluster of withdrawal symptoms that results from sudden decrease in an addictive drug's level of usage

group of withdrawal symptoms—when the level of usage of a substance suddenly drops off. Withdrawal symptoms for alcohol include anxiety, tremors, restlessness, rapid pulse, and high blood pressure.

When doing without a drug, people who are *psychologically* dependent show signs of anxiety such as shakiness, rapid pulse, and sweating that may be similar to withdrawal symptoms. Because of these signs, they may believe that they are physiologically dependent on—or addicted to—a drug when they are psychologically dependent. But symptoms of abstinence from some drugs are unmistakably physiological. One is *delirium tremens* ("the DTs"), experienced by some chronic alcoholics when they suddenly lower their intake of alcohol. People with DTs have heavy sweating, restlessness, disorientation, and frightening hallucinations—often of crawling animals.

Causal Factors in Substance Abuse and Dependence

Substance abuse and dependence usually begin with experimental use in adolescence (Marlatt, 2010; Schulte et al., 2009). People experiment with drugs for various reasons, including curiosity, conformity to peer pressure, parental use, rebelliousness, escape from boredom or pressure, and excitement or pleasure (T. T. Clark, 2010; Lindgren et al., 2010; Yang et al., 2009).

Social–cognitive theorists suggest that people often try alcohol and tranquilizers such as Valium (the

generic name is diazepam) on the basis of a recommendation or observation of others. Use of a substance may be reinforced by peers or by the drug's positive effects on mood and its reduction of anxiety, fear, and stress (Griffin et al., 2004). Many people use drugs as self-medication for anxiety, depression, even low self-esteem. Parents who use drugs may increase their children's knowledge of drugs. They also, in effect, show their children when to use them—for example, by drinking alcohol to cope with tension or to lessen the anxiety associated with meeting people at parties and other get-togethers (Power et al., 2005).

People may have a genetic predisposition toward physiological dependence on various substances, including alcohol, opioids, cocaine, and nicotine (Agrawal et al., 2010; Dick et al., 2009; Farrer et al., 2009; Kuo et al., 2010). For example, the biological children of alcoholics who are reared by adoptive parents seem more likely to develop alcohol-related problems than the natural children of the adoptive parents. An inherited tendency toward alcoholism may involve greater sensitivity to alcohol (that is, greater enjoyment of it) and greater tolerance of it (Radcliffe et al., 2009). College students with alcoholic parents exhibit better muscular control and visual–motor coordination when they drink than do college students whose parents are not alcoholics. They also feel less intoxicated when they drink (Pihl et al., 1990).

Now that we have learned about substance abuse and dependence, let's consider different kinds of psychoactive drugs. Some are depressants, others stimulants, and still others hallucinogens.

> "The chains of habit are too weak to be felt until they are too strong to be broken."
>
> —SAMUEL JOHNSON

The amount you drink is not as crucial as the fact that your pattern of use disrupts your life.

4-4b DEPRESSANTS

Depressant drugs generally act by slowing the activity of the central nervous system. There are also effects specific to each depressant drug. In this section, we consider the effects of alcohol, opiates, and barbiturates.

Alcohol

No drug has meant so much to so many as alcohol. Alcohol is our dinnertime relaxant, our bedtime sedative, our cocktail-party social facilitator. We use alcohol to celebrate holy days, applaud our accomplishments, and express joyous wishes. The young assert their maturity with alcohol. Alcohol is used at least occasionally by the majority of high school and college students (Johnston et al., 2010). Alcohol even kills germs on surface wounds.

People use alcohol like a Swiss Army knife. It does it all. It is the all-purpose medicine you can buy without prescription. It is the relief from anxiety, depression, or loneliness that you can swallow in public without criticism or stigma. A man who takes a Valium tablet may look weak. A man who downs a bottle of beer may be perceived as "macho."

But the army knife also has a sharp blade. No drug has been so abused as alcohol. Ten million to 20 million Americans are alcoholics. In contrast, 750,000 to 1 million use heroin regularly, and about 800,000 use cocaine regularly (Johnston et al., 2010). Excessive drinking has been linked to lower productivity, loss of employment, and downward movement in social status. Yet, half of all Americans use alcohol regularly.

What about alcohol on campus? About four college students die *each day* from alcohol-related causes (Hingson et al., 2002). *Binge drinking*—defined as having five or more drinks in a row for a male, or four or more for a female—is connected with aggressive behavior, poor grades, sexual promiscuity, and accidents (McCauley et al., 2010; Randolph et al.,

About four college students die *each day* from alcohol-related causes.

2009; Swartout & White, 2010). Nevertheless, nearly half of college men and three in ten college women binge at least twice a month (Johnston et al., 2010). The media pay more attention to deaths due to heroin and cocaine overdoses, but more college students die each year from causes related to drinking, including accidents and overdoses (Hingson et al., 2002; Hustad et al., 2010).

The effects of alcohol vary with the dose and duration of use. Low doses may be stimulating because alcohol dilates blood vessels, which ferry sugar through the body. Higher doses have a sedative effect, which is why alcohol is classified as a depressant. Alcohol relaxes people and deadens minor aches and pains. Alcohol impairs cognitive functioning, slurs the speech, and impairs coordination.

Alcohol lowers inhibitions. Drinkers may do things they would not do if they were sober, such as having unprotected sex (Collins et al., 2010; S. B. Johnson et al., 2010; Lam et al., 2009). When drunk, people may be less able to foresee the consequences of their behavior. They may also be less likely to summon up their moral beliefs. Then, too, alcohol induces feelings of elation and euphoria that may wash away doubts. Alcohol is also associated with a liberated social role in our culture. Drinkers may place the blame on alcohol ("It's the alcohol, not me"), even though they choose to drink.

Men are more likely than women to become alcoholics. Why? A cultural explanation is that tighter social constraints are usually placed on women. A biological explanation is that alcohol hits women harder, discouraging them from overindulging. If you have the impression that alcohol "goes to women's heads" more quickly than to men's, you are probably right. Women seem more affected by alcohol because they have less of an enzyme—*aldehyde dehydrogenase*—that metabolizes alcohol in the stomach than men do (M. A. Miller et al., 2009; Oertelt-Prigione & Regitz-Zagrosek, 2009). Thus, alcohol reaches women's bloodstream and brain relatively intact.

Levels of aldehyde dehydrogenase are also associated with levels of drinking in some ethnic groups. Asians and Asian Americans, who have lower levels of aldehyde dehydrogenase than Europeans do, are more likely than Europeans and European Americans to show a "flushing response" to alcohol, as evidenced by redness of the face, rapid heart rate, dizziness, and headaches (Kawano, 2010). Such sensitivity to alcohol may inhibit immoderate drinking among Asian Americans as well as women in general.

Regardless of how or why one starts drinking, regular drinking can lead to physiological dependence. People are then motivated to drink to avoid withdrawal symp-

toms. Still, even when alcoholics have "dried out"—withdrawn from alcohol—many return to drinking. Perhaps they still want to use alcohol as a way of coping with stress or as an excuse for failure.

Opiates

Opiates are a group of **narcotics** derived from the opium poppy, from which they obtain their name. The ancient Sumerians gave the opium poppy its name: It means "plant of joy." **Opioids** are similar in chemical

✳ Do You Have a Problem with Alcohol?

How can you tell whether you have a drinking problem? Answering the following four questions can help you figure it out (National Institute on Alcohol Abuse and Alcoholism, 2005):

Yes No Have you ever felt you should cut down on your drinking?

Yes No Have people annoyed you by criticizing your drinking?

Yes No Have you ever felt bad or guilty about your drinking?

Yes No Have you ever had a drink first thing in the morning (as an "eye opener") to steady your nerves or get rid of a hangover?

Just one "yes" answer suggests a possible alcohol problem. Two or more "yes" answers make it highly likely that a problem exists. In either case, it is advisable to discuss your answers with your doctor or another health-care provider.

WOMEN AND ALCOHOL

Women have less of an enzyme—aldehyde dehydrogenase—that metabolizes alcohol in the stomach than men do. Therefore, alcohol "goes to their heads" more quickly. Asians also have less of the enzyme than Europeans do, placing them at increased risk of a "flushing response" when they drink.

structure but made in a laboratory. Opiates include morphine, heroin, codeine, Demerol, and similar drugs. The major medical application of opiates is relief from pain.

Heroin can provide a strong euphoric "rush." Users claim that it is so pleasurable it can eradicate thoughts of food or sex. High doses can cause drowsiness and stupor, alter time perception, and impair judgment. With regular use of opiates, the brain stops producing neurotransmitters that are chemically similar to opiates—the pain-relieving endorphins.

As a result, people can become physiologically dependent on opiates, such that going without them can be agonizing. Withdrawal syndromes may begin with flulike symptoms and progress through tremors, cramps, chills alternating with sweating, rapid pulse, high blood pressure, insomnia, vomiting, and diarrhea. This information seems to have gotten through to high school students; most disapprove of using heroin (Johnston et al., 2010).

Heroin was once used as a cure for addiction to morphine. Now we have methadone, a synthetic opioid that is used to treat physiological dependence on heroin. Methadone is slower acting than heroin and does not provide the thrilling rush, but it does prevent withdrawal symptoms.

TRUTH IT IS TRUE THAT, SOON AFTER ITS DISCOVERY, HEROIN WAS HAILED AS A CURE FOR ADDICTION TO MORPHINE. IT WAS NOT YET REALIZED HOW ADDICTIVE HEROIN WAS.

Barbiturates

Barbiturates like Nembutal and Seconal are depressants with several medical uses, including relief from anxiety, tension, and pain, and treatment of epilepsy, high blood pressure, and insomnia. With regular use, barbiturates lead rapidly to physiological and psychological dependence. Physicians therefore provide them with caution.

Barbiturates are popular as street drugs because they are relaxing and produce mild euphoria. High doses result in drowsiness, motor impairment, slurred speech, irritability, and poor judgment. A highly physiologically dependent person who is withdrawn abruptly from barbiturates may experience convulsions and die. Because of additive effects, it is dangerous to mix alcohol and other depressants.

4-4c STIMULANTS

Stimulants increase the activity of the nervous system. Some of their effects can be positive. For example, amphetamines stimulate cognitive

TRUTH IT IS TRUE THAT SIMULANTS ARE OFTEN PRESCRIBED TO CALM HYPERACTIVE CHILDREN.

activity and apparently help people control impulses (Wilner et al., 2009). Some stimulants are appealing as street drugs because they contribute to feelings of euphoria and self-confidence. But they also have their risks. In this section, we discuss amphetamines, cocaine, and nicotine.

Amphetamines and Related Stimulants

Amphetamines are a group of stimulants that were first used by soldiers during World War II to help them stay alert at night. Truck drivers have also used them to drive through the night. Students sometimes use amphetamines for all-night cram sessions, whereas dieters sometimes use them because they reduce hunger.

Amphetamines are often abused for the euphoric rush high doses can produce. Some people swallow amphetamines in pill form or inject liquid Methedrine, the strongest form, into their veins. As a result, they may stay awake and high for days on end. But such highs must end. People who have been on prolonged highs sometimes "crash," or fall into a deep sleep or depression. Some commit suicide when crashing.

On the other hand, physicians frequently prescribe stimulants in an effort to help hyperactive children control their behavior. Stimulants such as Ritalin and Adderall are widely used to treat attention-deficit/hyperactivity disorder (ADHD) in children. They have been shown to increase the attention span, decrease aggressive and disruptive behavior, and lead to academic gains (May & Kratochvil, 2010; Wanchoo et al., 2010). Why should these stimulants calm children? Hyperactivity may be connected with immaturity of the cerebral cortex, and these drugs may stimulate the cortex to exercise control over more primitive parts of the brain. On the other hand, these stimulants place children—and adults who may continue to use them—at increased risk for sleep disorders and loss of appetite (Meijer et al., 2009).

Tolerance for amphetamines develops quickly, and users can become dependent on them, especially when they use them to medicate themselves for depression. Whether these stimulants cause physical addiction has been a subject of controversy. It is widely accepted, however, that high doses can cause restlessness, insomnia, loss of appetite,

barbiturate
an addictive depressant used to relieve anxiety or induce sleep

amphetamines
stimulants derived from *a*lpha-*m*ethyl-*b*eta-*ph*enyl-*eth*yl*amine*, a colorless liquid consisting of carbon, hydrogen, and nitrogen

hallucinations, paranoid delusions (e.g., false ideas that others are eavesdropping or intend them harm), and irritability.

Cocaine

Cocaine is derived from coca leaves—the plant from which the soft drink took its name. Do you recall commercials claiming that "Coke adds life"? Given its caffeine and sugar content, "Coke"—Coca-Cola, that is—should provide quite a lift. It is true that Coca-Cola once "added life" through the use of cocaine—legal then but illegal today. But Coca-Cola hasn't been "the real thing" since 1906, when the company stopped using cocaine in its formula.

Cocaine is a stimulant that produces euphoria, reduces hunger, deadens pain, and boosts self-confidence. As shown in Figure 4.4, cocaine apparently works by binding to sites on sending neurons that normally reuptake molecules of the neurotransmitters norepineph-

"I CAN RESIST EVERYTHING EXCEPT TEMPTATION."
–OSCAR WILDE (LADY WINDERMERE'S FAN)

rine, dopamine, and serotonin. As a result, molecules of these transmitters remain longer in the synaptic cleft, enhancing their mood-altering effects and producing a "rush." But when cocaine levels drop, lower absorption of neurotransmitters by receiving neurons causes the user's mood to "crash."

Cocaine may be brewed from coca leaves as a "tea," snorted in powder form, or injected in liquid form. Repeated snorting constricts blood vessels in the nose, drying the skin and sometimes exposing cartilage and perforating the nasal septum. These problems require

TRUTH IT IS TRUE THAT COCA-COLA ONCE NUMBERED COCAINE AMONG ITS INGREDIENTS, BUT IT WAS NOT ILLEGAL AT THE TIME. NOR WERE PEOPLE YET AWARE OF COCAINE'S HAZARDS.

FIGURE 4.4 | How Cocaine Produces Euphoria and Why People "Crash"

A. In the normal functioning of the nervous system, neurotransmitters are released into the synaptic cleft by vesicles in terminal buttons of sending neurons. Many are taken up by receptor sites in receiving neurons. **B.** In the process called reuptake, sending neurons typically reabsorb excess molecules of neurotransmitters. **C.** Molecules of cocaine bind to the sites on sending neurons that normally reuptake molecules of neurotransmitters. As a result, molecules of norepinephrine, dopamine, and serotonin remain longer in the synaptic cleft, increasing their typical mood-altering effects and providing a euphoric "rush." When the person stops using cocaine, the lessened absorption of neurotransmitters by receiving neurons causes his or her mood to "crash."

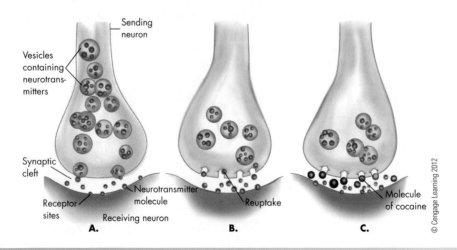

cosmetic surgery. The potent cocaine derivatives known as "crack" and "bazooka" are inexpensive because they are unrefined.

Physical dangers include sudden rises in blood pressure, which constricts the coronary arteries and decreases the oxygen supply to the heart, and quickens the heart rate, events that can lead to respiratory and cardiovascular collapse, as in the sudden deaths of some young athletes (Lange & Hillis, 2010). Overdoses can cause restlessness and insomnia, tremors, headaches, nausea, convulsions, hallucinations, and delusions. Use of crack has been connected with strokes. Only about 4% of adolescents aged 15 to 19 use cocaine regularly, and most believe that it is harmful (Johnston et al., 2010). Cocaine causes physiological as well as psychological dependence.

Cocaine—also called *snow* and *coke*—has been used as a local anesthetic since the early 1800s. In 1884 cocaine came to the attention of Sigmund Freud, who used it to fight his own depression and published an article about it: "Song of Praise." Freud's early ardor was tempered when he learned that cocaine is habit-forming and can cause hallucinations and delusions.

Nicotine

Nicotine is the stimulant in tobacco smoke. Nicotine stimulates discharge of the hormone adrenaline and the release of neurotransmitters, including dopamine, acetylcholine, GABA, and endorphins (Haustein & Groneberg, 2009). Adrenaline creates a burst of autonomic activity that accelerates the heart rate and pours sugar into the blood. Acetylcholine is vital in memory formation, and nicotine appears to enhance memory and attention; improve performance on simple, repetitive tasks; and enhance the mood (Froeliger et al., 2009; Greenwood et al., 2009). Although it is a stimulant, because of GABA and endorphins, nicotine has a relaxing effect (A. Cohen et al., 2009). It depresses the appetite and raises the metabolic rate. Thus, some people smoke cigarettes to control their weight.

Nicotine may be as addictive as heroin or cocaine (Franklin et al., 2009). It is the agent that creates physiological dependence on tobacco products (Small et al., 2010). Symptoms of withdrawal include nervousness, drowsiness, loss of energy, headaches, irregular bowel movements, lightheadedness, insomnia,

The perils of cigarette smoking are widely known today. One surgeon general declared that cigarette smoking is the chief preventable cause of death in the United States. The number of Americans who die from smoking are comparable to the number of lives that would be lost if two jumbo jets crashed *every day*. If flying were that unsafe, would the government ground all flights? Would the public continue to make airline reservations?

hydrocarbons
chemical compounds consisting of hydrogen and carbon

secondhand smoke
smoke from the tobacco products and exhalations of other people; also referred to as *passive smoking*

hallucinogenic
a substance that causes hallucinations

marijuana
the dried vegetable matter of the *Cannabis sativa* plant

 TRUTH SMOKING-RELATED DEATHS ARE IN FACT HIGHER THAN THE NUMBER OF PEOPLE WHO DIE FROM MOTOR VEHICLE ACCIDENTS, ALCOHOL AND DRUG ABUSE, SUICIDE, HOMICIDE, AND AIDS COMBINED.

dizziness, cramps, palpitations, tremors, and sweating.

It's no secret. Cigarette packs sold in the United States carry messages like "Warning: The Surgeon General Has Determined That Cigarette Smoking Is Dangerous to Your Health." Cigarette advertising has been banned on radio and television. Nearly 400,000 Americans die from smoking-related illnesses each year (American Lung Association, 2010). This number is greater than the equivalent of two jumbo jets colliding in midair each day with all passengers lost.

The carbon monoxide in cigarette smoke impairs the blood's ability to carry oxygen, causing shortness of breath. The **hydrocarbons** ("tars") in cigarette and cigar smoke lead to lung cancer (American Lung Association, 2010). Cigarette smoking also stiffens arteries (Campbell et al., 2010) and is linked to death from heart disease, chronic lung and respiratory diseases, and other health problems. Women who smoke show reduced bone density, increasing the risk of fracture of the hip and

"As an example to others, and not that I care for moderation myself, it has always been my rule never to smoke when asleep, and never to refrain from smoking when awake."
—MARK TWAIN

back (American Lung Association, 2010). Pregnant women who smoke have a higher risk of miscarriage, preterm births, stillborn babies, and children with learning problems (American Lung Association, 2010).

Secondhand smoke—smoke inhaled from other people's tobacco products—is also connected with respiratory illnesses, asthma, and other health problems. Prolonged exposure to secondhand smoke (also referred to as *passive smoking*) during childhood is a risk factor for lung cancer (American Cancer Society, 2010). Because of the effects of second-hand smoke, smoking has been banished from many airplanes, restaurants, and other public spaces.

The incidence of smoking is connected with gender and level of education (see Table 4.1). Better-educated people are less likely to smoke and more likely to quit if they do smoke.

4-4d HALLUCINOGENICS

Hallucinogenics are so named because they produce hallucinations—that is, sensations and perceptions in the absence of external stimulation. Hallucinogenics may also have additional effects such as relaxation, euphoria, or, in some cases, panic. In this section, we discuss marijuana, LSD, and other hallucinogenics.

Marijuana

Marijuana is a substance that is produced from the *Cannabis sativa* plant, which grows wild in many parts of the world. Marijuana helps some people relax and can elevate their mood. It also sometimes produces mild hallucinations, which is why we discuss it as a hallucinogen. The major psychedelic substance in marijuana is delta-9-tetrahydrocannabinol, or THC. THC is found in the branches and leaves of the plant, but it is highly concentrated in the resin. *Hashish*, or "hash," is derived from the resin and is more potent than marijuana.

Some users report that marijuana helps them socialize. Moderate to strong intoxication is linked to reports of sharpened perceptions, increases in self-insight, creative thinking, and empathy for others. Time seems to slow. A song might seem to last an hour rather than minutes. There is increased awareness of bodily sensations such as heartbeat. Marijuana users also report that strong intoxication heightens sexual sensations. Visual hallucinations may occur, and strong intoxication may cause disorientation. If the smoker's mood is euphoric, disorientation may be interpreted as "harmony" with the universe, but some users find disorientation threatening and fear they will not regain their identity (Bonn-Miller et al., 2007).

Marijuana carries a number of health risks. For example, it impairs the perceptual–motor coordination used in driving and operating machines. It impairs short-term memory and slows learning (Egerton et al., 2006). Strong intoxication can cause nausea and vomiting. Regular users may experience tolerance and withdrawal symptoms (Budney et al., 2007). Brain imaging studies suggest that males who begin using marijuana in adolescence may have smaller brains and less gray matter than other males (Ashtari et al., 2009). Both males and females who started marijuana use early may be generally smaller in height and weight than other people. These differences may reflect the effect of marijuana on pituitary and sex hormones.

LSD and Other Hallucinogenics

LSD is the abbreviation for lysergic acid diethylamide, a synthetic hallucinogen. Users of "acid" claim that it "expands consciousness" and opens up new worlds to them. Sometimes people say they have achieved great insights while using LSD, but when it wears off they cannot apply or recall them. LSD produces vivid, colorful hallucinations.

Some LSD users have **flashbacks**—distorted perceptions or hallucinations that mimic the LSD "trip" but occur days, weeks, or longer after usage. The experiencing of flashbacks is more technically termed *hallucinogen persisting perception disorder* (HPPD) by the American Psychiatric Association (2000).* The psychological explanation of "flashbacks" is that people who would use LSD regularly are also more likely to allow flights of fancy. Yet research with 38 people with HPPD suggests that following extensive use of LSD, the brain may fail to inhibit certain internal sources of visionlike experiences, especially when the eyes are closed (Catts & Catts, 2009).

Other hallucinogens include **mescaline** (derived from the peyote cactus) and **phencyclidine (PCP)**. PCP was developed as an anesthetic and an animal tranquilizer. It goes by the street names "angel dust," "ozone," "wack," and "rocket fuel." The street terms "killer joints" and "crystal super grass" refer to PCP combined with marijuana.

Regular use of hallucinogens may lead to tolerance and psychological dependence, but hallucinogens are not known to create physiological dependence. High doses may impair coordination, cloud judgment, change the mood, and cause frightening hallucinations and paranoid delusions. Table 4.2 summarizes the effects of various psychoactive drugs.

LSD
lysergic acid diethylamide; a hallucinogen

flashbacks
distorted perceptions or hallucinations that occur days or weeks after LSD usage but mimic the LSD experience

mescaline
a hallucinogen derived from the mescal (peyote) cactus

phencyclidine (PCP)
another hallucinogen whose name is an acronym for its chemical structure

---

*The DSM content has been adapted for the particular audience and is intended for educational purposes only.

TABLE 4.1
Snapshot, U.S.A.: Gender, Level of Education, and Smoking

FACTOR	GROUP	PERCENT WHO SMOKE
Gender	Women	18.3
	Men	23.1
Level of education	Fewer than 12 years	27.5
	College graduate and above	10.6

Data based on reports of persons aged 18 and above.

Source: Dube, S. R., Asman, K., Malarcher, A., & Carabollo, R. (2009). Cigarette smoking among adults and trends in smoking cessation—United States. *Morbidity and Mortality Weekly Report, 58*(44), 1227–1232.

TABLE 4.2 | Psychoactive Drugs and Their Effects

DRUG	TYPE	HOW TAKEN	DESIRED EFFECTS	TOLERANCE	ABSTINENCE SYNDROME	SIDE EFFECTS
Alcohol	Depressant	By mouth	Relaxation, euphoria, lowered inhibitions	Yes	Yes	Impaired coordination, poor judgment, hangover
Opiates	Depressants	Injected, smoked, by mouth	Relaxation, euphoria, relief from anxiety and pain	Yes	Yes	Impaired coordination and mental functioning, drowsiness, lethargy
Barbiturates	Depressant	By mouth, injected	Relaxation, sleep, euphoria, lowered inhibitions	Yes	Yes	Impaired coordination and mental functioning, drowsiness, lethargy
Amphetamines	Stimulants	By mouth, injected	Alertness, euphoria	Yes	?	Restlessness, loss of appetite, psychotic symptoms
Cocaine	Stimulant	By mouth, snorted, injected	Euphoria, self-confidence	Yes	Yes	Restlessness, loss of appetite, convulsions, strokes, psychotic symptoms
Nicotine	Stimulant	By tobacco (smoked, chewed, or sniffed)	Relaxation, stimulation, weight control	Yes	Yes	Cancer, heart disease, lung and respiratory diseases
Marijuana	Hallucinogenic	Smoked, by mouth	Relaxation, perceptual distortions, enhancement of experience	?	?	Impaired coordination and learning, respiratory problems, panic
LSD, Mescaline, PCP	Hallucinogenic	By mouth	Perceptual distortions, vivid hallucinations	Yes	No	Impaired coordination, psychotic symptoms, panic

© Paul Taylor/Corbis

Veer/Kristopher Grunert/Getty Images

© Alloy Photography/Veer

© David Young-Wolff/PhotoEdit Inc.

© Corbis Photography/Veer

© Fancy Photography/Veer

STUDY TOOLS ▶ 4

Ready to study? In the book, you can:

- ● Review what you've read with Fill-Ins and Multiple Choice quizzes (below).
- ● Rip out Chapter Review card (in the back).

Or you can go online to CourseMate at www.cengagebrain.com for these resources:

- ● Complete Practices Quizzes to prepare for tests.
- ● Review Key Terms Flash Cards (online or print).
- ● Play games to master concepts.

FILL-INS

Answers can be found in the back of the book, starting on page 368.

1. *Consciousness* has several meanings, including sensory awareness, the selective aspect of attention, direct inner _____, personal unity, and the waking state.

2. Because EEG patterns during REM sleep resemble those of the waking state, REM sleep is also called _____ sleep.

3. During a typical 8-hour night, we undergo (how many?) _____ trips through the different stages of sleep.

4. According to the _____–synthesis model, dreams reflect neural activity.

5. Hypnosis is an altered state of consciousness in which people are suggestible and behave as though they are in a _____.

6. In meditation, one focuses on a _____ to alter the normal person–environment relationship.

7. Substance _____ is characterized by repeated use of a substance although it is impairing functioning.

8. Physiological dependence is evidenced by tolerance or by an _____ syndrome when one discontinues use of the substance.

9. _____ is a stimulant that boosts self-confidence but also triggers rises in blood pressure and constricts the coronary arteries.

10. _____ substances distort perceptions.

1. When we say that we are "conscious of" seeing something or hearing a sound, we are referring to consciousness as

   a. a stream.
   b. a behavioral concept.
   c. the sense of personal unity.
   d. sensory awareness.

2. The notion that animals that are most at risk from predators sleep less is taken from which of the following perspectives?

   a. Behaviorist   c. Evolutionary
   b. Environmental   d. Developmental

3. Which of the following statements is correct concerning brain waves and the sleep cycle?

   a. Low-frequency brains waves are associated with being awake.
   b. High-frequency brains waves are associated with being awake.
   c. There are no recordable brain waves when we sleep.
   d. It is difficult to tell the difference between "sleep" brain waves and "awake" brain waves.

4. Allegra is said to have hypnotic suggestibility. She is likely to

   a. be prone to fantasy.
   b. have no idea as to what is expected in the trance state.
   c. attend to her own internal feelings rather than the instructions of the hypnotist.
   d. all of the above

5. In his classic study of transcendental meditation, Benson found that meditation leads to

   a. spiritual awakening.
   b. expanded consciousness.
   c. a relaxation response.
   d. more intense hypnagogic states.

6. Which of the following are children most likely to "outgrow"?

   a. Insomnia
   b. Bed-wetting
   c. Sleep apnea
   d. Narcolepsy

7. When Clay joined AA in order to stop drinking, he received a pamphlet that described the symptoms of alcohol withdrawal. These included

   a. high blood pressure and rapid pulse.
   b. restlessness and tremors.
   c. anxiety and weakness.
   d. all of the above

8. The most popular drug on college campuses is

   a. alcohol.
   b. marijuana.
   c. cocaine.
   d. LSD.

9. Elyse is a college student who has developed a tolerance to heroin and experiences withdrawal symptoms whenever she doesn't have a "fix" at least every eight hours. She feels that she has lost control and has to organize her life around her habit. She would be classified as having

   a. substance abuse.
   b. substance dependence.
   c. substance use.
   d. an anxiety disorder.

10. Which of the following is most likely to be prescribed for use with hyperactive children?

   a. Ritalin
   b. Morphine
   c. Dopamine
   d. Tranquilizers

LEARNING OUTCOMES

5-1 Define learning

5-2 Describe principles and methods of classical conditioning

5-3 Describe principles and methods of operant conditioning

5-4 Discuss cognitive factors in learning

STUDY TOOLS ▶ After you read the chapter, go to the Study Tools at the end of the chapter, page 132.

CHAPTER 5

Learning

Now, I'm going to teach a psychologist how to fetch a ball.

Masterfile (Royalty-Free Div.)

I was showing my daughter Allyn how to teach our new dog, Phoebe, to fetch. I bought a soft yellow ball for the dog that squeaked when she bit into it. She enjoyed playing with it, and I assumed she would want to run after it. (Wrong!) I waved it under her nose. She sniffed at it, barked, and wagged her tail excitedly.

As my daughter watched, I tossed the ball about 20 feet away. "Fetch!" I said to Phoebe as the ball bounced invitingly in the grass.

Phoebe just stared.

My daughter scoffed. I ran after the ball, picked it up, and waved it under Phoebe's nose again. She barked and wagged her tail rapidly like a reed in a brisk wind.

"Fetch!" I said and tossed the ball again.

Again Phoebe refused to run. She barked and snapped at my legs again. "This is ridiculous," I muttered, and I went to get the ball. As I brought it back to Phoebe, Allyn said, "Don't you see what's happening?"

"What?"

"Phoebe's teaching you to fetch."

5-1 Learning, Experience, and Change

One could say that Phoebe was teaching me what to do by showing excitement when I did the "right" thing—that is, fetch the ball. She was teaching, and I was learning. Learning is a key area in psychology.

Learning is defined in psychology as more than listening to teachers, honing skateboard jumps, or mastering the use of an iPad. From the strict behaviorist perspective, **learning** is a relatively permanent change in behavior that arises from practice or experience. The behaviorist perspective plays down the roles of cognition and choice. It suggests that psychologists learn to run after balls because they have been rewarded or reinforced for doing so.

Cognitive psychologists define learning as the process by which organisms make relatively permanent changes in the way they represent the environment because of

WHAT DO YOU THINK? FOLKLORE, COMMON SENSE, OR NONSENSE? CIRCLE THE T FOR "TRUTH" OR THE F FOR "FICTION," AND CHECK THE ACCURACY OF YOUR ANSWERS AS YOU READ THROUGH THE CHAPTER.

T	F	A SINGLE NAUSEATING MEAL CAN GIVE RISE TO A TASTE AVERSION THAT LASTS FOR YEARS.
T	F	PSYCHOLOGISTS HELPED A YOUNG BOY OVERCOME HIS FEAR OF RABBITS BY HAVING HIM EAT COOKIES WHILE A RABBIT WAS BROUGHT CLOSER AND CLOSER.
T	F	DURING WORLD WAR II, A PSYCHOLOGIST CREATED A MISSILE THAT WOULD USE PIGEONS TO GUIDE THE MISSILE TO ITS TARGET.
T	F	SLOT-MACHINE PLAYERS POP COINS INTO THE MACHINES MOST RAPIDLY WHEN THEY HAVE NO IDEA WHEN THEY MIGHT WIN.
T	F	YOU CAN TRAIN A RAT TO CLIMB A RAMP, CROSS A BRIDGE, CLIMB A LADDER, PEDAL A TOY CAR, AND DO SEVERAL OTHER TASKS—ALL IN PROPER SEQUENCE.
T	F	YOU HAVE TO MAKE MISTAKES TO LEARN.
T	F	DESPITE ALL THE MEDIA HOOPLA, NO SCIENTIFIC CONNECTION HAS BEEN ESTABLISHED BETWEEN VIOLENCE IN THE MEDIA AND REAL-LIFE AGGRESSION.

learning (1) according to behaviorists, a relatively permanent change in behavior that results from experience; (2) according to cognitive theorists, the process by which organisms make relatively permanent changes in the way they represent the environment because of experience

classical conditioning a simple form of learning in which a neutral stimulus comes to evoke the response usually evoked by another stimulus by being paired repeatedly with the other stimulus

reflex a simple unlearned response to a stimulus

stimulus an environmental condition that elicits a response

experience. These changes influence the organism's behavior but do not fully determine it. From this perspective, I knew that I would earn Phoebe's attention by running after the ball, but I could have chosen not to do it. Learning, for cognitive psychologists, may be *shown* by changes in behavior, but learning itself is a mental process. Cognitive psychologists suggest that people choose whether or not to imitate the aggressive and other behaviors they observe, and that people are most likely to imitate behaviors that are consistent with their values.

Sometimes learning experiences are direct, as when we are praised for doing something properly. But we can also learn from the experiences of others—by watching their behavior and hearing their life stories. We learn, too, from books and audiovisual media. In this chapter, we consider various kinds of learning, including conditioning and learning in which cognition plays a more central role.

5-2 Classical Conditioning: Learning What Is Linked to What

Classical conditioning involves ways in which we learn to associate events with other events. It is involuntary, automatic learning. For example, we generally prefer grades of A to grades of F and are more likely to stop for red lights than green lights. Why? We are not born with instinctive attitudes toward letter grades or stoplights. Rather, we learn the meanings of these symbols because they have been associated with other events. A's are associated with the approval of our teachers and caregivers. Because of experience in crossing streets or riding in cars, we associate green lights with the word "go" and red lights with "stop."

Ivan Pavlov and His Associates— Including a "Professional Furry Salivator" (the Dog).

Classical conditioning is a simple form of associative learning in which organisms come to anticipate or associate events with one another. If the name Ivan Pavlov rings a bell with us, it is most likely because of his research in learning with dogs. Ivan Pavlov (1927) made his great contribution to the psychology of learning by accident. Pavlov was actually attempting to identify neural receptors in the mouth that triggered a response from the salivary glands. But his efforts were hampered by the dogs' annoying tendency to salivate at undesired times, such as when a laboratory assistant was clumsy and banged the metal food trays.

Just as you salivate after you've taken a bite of cake, a dog salivates if meat powder is placed on its tongue. Pavlov was dosing his dogs with meat powder for his research because he knew that salivation in response to meat powder is a **reflex**. Reflexes are unlearned and evoked by certain **stimuli**. Pavlov discovered that reflexes can also be learned, or *conditioned*, by association. His dogs began salivating in response to clanging food trays because clanging, in the past, had been repeatedly paired with arrival of food. The dogs would also salivate when an assistant entered the laboratory. Why? In the past, the assistant had brought food.

Pavlov at first viewed the extra salivation of his dogs as a hindrance to his research. But then it dawned on him that this "problem" might be worth looking into. He found out that he could train, or condition, his dogs to salivate in response to any stimulus.

In his initial experiments, Pavlov trained dogs to salivate when he sounded a tone or a bell. Pavlov termed these trained salivary responses *conditional reflexes*. The reflexes were *conditional* on the repeated pairing of a previously neutral stimulus (such as the clanging of a food tray) and a stimulus (in this case, food) that evoked the target response (in this case, salivation). Today, conditional reflexes are generally referred to as *conditioned responses*.

Pavlov demonstrated conditioned responses by showing that when meat powder was placed on a dog's tongue, the dog salivated. Pavlov repeated the process several times, with one difference. He preceded the meat powder by half a second or so with the sounding

© Bettman/Corbis

of a tone on each occasion. After several pairings of the meat powder and the tone, Pavlov sounded the tone but did *not* follow it with the meat powder. Still the dog salivated. It had learned to salivate in response to the tone.

5-2a EXPLAINING CLASSICAL CONDITIONING

Behaviorists explain the outcome of *classical conditioning* in terms of the publicly observable conditions of learning. For them, classical conditioning is a simple form of learning in which one stimulus comes to evoke the response usually evoked by another stimulus. Why? Because the stimuli are paired repeatedly. In Pavlov's demonstration, the dog learned to salivate in response to the tone *because* the tone had been paired with meat powder. Behaviorists do *not* say that the dog "knew" food was on the way. How can we guess what a dog "knows"? We can only outline the conditions under which targeted behaviors occur.

Cognitive psychologists view classical conditioning as the learning of relationships among events. The relationships allow organisms to mentally represent their environments and make predictions (Pickens & Holland, 2004). In Pavlov's demonstration, the dog salivated in response to the tone *because* the tone became mentally connected with the meat. The cognitive focus is on *the information learned by the organism*. Organisms are seen as seekers of information that generate and test rules about relationships among events.

5-2b STIMULI AND RESPONSES IN CLASSICAL CONDITIONING

In Pavlov's experiment, the meat powder is an **unconditioned stimulus (UCS)**. Salivation in response to the meat powder is an unlearned, or **unconditioned, response (UCR)**. The tone was at first a meaningless or neutral stimulus. It might have caused the dog to look in the direction of the sound—an **orienting reflex**. But the tone was not yet associated with food. Then, through repeated association with the meat powder, the tone became a learned, or **conditioned, stimulus (CS)** for the salivation response. Salivation in response to the tone (or conditioned stimulus) is a learned, or **conditioned, response (CR)**. Therefore, salivation can be either a conditioned response or an unconditioned response, depending on the method used to evoke the response (see Figure 5.1).

Here is a mini-experiment that many adults have tried. They smile at infants, say something like "kitchie-coo" (don't ask me why), and then tickle the infant's foot. Perhaps the infant laughs and perhaps curls or retracts the foot. After a few repetitions—which psychologists call "trials"—the adult's simply saying "kitchie-coo" is likely to be enough to cause the infant to laugh and retract its foot.

unconditioned stimulus (UCS) a stimulus that elicits a response from an organism prior to conditioning

unconditioned response (UCR) an unlearned response to an unconditioned stimulus

orienting reflex an unlearned response in which an organism attends to a stimulus

conditioned stimulus (CS) a previously neutral stimulus that elicits a conditioned response because it has been paired repeatedly with a stimulus that already elicited that response

conditioned response (CR) a learned response to a conditioned stimulus

FIGURE 5.1 | A Schematic Representation of Classical Conditioning

Prior to conditioning, food elicits salivation. The tone, a neutral stimulus, elicits either no response or an orienting response. During conditioning, the tone is rung just before meat powder is placed on the dog's tongue. After several repetitions, the tone, now a CS, elicits salivation, the CR.

5-2c TASTE AVERSION

When I was a child in the Bronx, my friends and I would go to the movies on Saturday mornings. One day my friends dared me to eat two huge containers of buttered popcorn by myself. I had no problem with the first enormous basket of buttered popcorn. More slowly—much more slowly—I forced down the second basket. I felt bloated and nauseated. The taste of the butter, corn, and salt lingered in my mouth and nose, and my head spun. It was obvious to me that no one could talk me into even another handful of popcorn that day. But I was surprised that I couldn't face buttered popcorn again for a year.

Years later I learned that psychologists refer to my response to buttered popcorn as a *taste aversion*. Many decades have now passed, and the distinctive odor of buttered popcorn still turns my stomach. A single nauseating meal can give rise to a taste aversion that lasts for years.

Taste aversions are intriguing examples of classical conditioning. They are adaptive because they motivate organisms to avoid harmful foods. Taste aversions differ from other kinds of classical conditioning in a couple of ways. First, only one association may be required. A single overdose of popcorn left me with a lifetime aversion. Second, whereas most kinds of classical conditioning require that the unconditioned stimulus and conditioned stimulus be close together in time, in taste aversion the unconditioned stimulus (in this case, nausea) can occur hours after the conditioned stimulus (in this case, the flavor of food).

The Evolution of Taste Aversion

Research on taste aversion also challenges the view that organisms learn to associate any stimuli that are linked in time. In reality, not all stimuli are created equal. The evolutionary perspective suggests that animals (and humans) would be *biologically prepared* to develop aversions that

TRUTH IT IS TRUE THAT A SINGLE NAUSEATING MEAL CAN GIVE RISE TO A TASTE AVERSION THAT LASTS FOR YEARS.

are adaptive in their environments (Bouton, 2010; Öhman & Mineka, 2001). Those of us who acquire taste aversions quickly are less likely to eat poisonous food, more likely to survive, and more likely to contribute our genes to future generations.

In a classic study, Garcia and Koelling (1966) conditioned two groups of rats. Each group was exposed to the same three-part conditioned stimulus: a taste of sweetened water, a light, and a clicker. Afterward, one group of rats was induced to experience nausea by radiation or poison, and the other group received electric shock.

After conditioning, the rats that had been nauseated showed an aversion for sweetened water but not to the light or clicker. Although all three stimuli had been presented at the same time, *the rats had acquired only the taste aversion*. After conditioning, the rats that had been shocked avoided both the light and the clicker, *but they did not show a taste aversion to the sweetened water*. For each group of rats, the conditioning that took place was adaptive. In the natural scheme of things, nausea is more likely to stem from poisoned food than from lights or sounds. So, for nauseated rats, acquiring the taste aversion was appropriate. Sharp pain, in contrast, is more likely to stem from natural events involving lights (e.g., fire, lightning) and sharp sounds (e.g., twigs snapping, things falling). Therefore, it was more appropriate for the shocked animals to develop an aversion to the light and the clicker than the sweetened water.

In classical conditioning, organisms learn to connect stimuli, such as the sound of a tone with food. Now let's consider various factors in classical conditioning, beginning with what happens when the connection between stimuli is broken.

Formation of a Taste Aversion? Taste aversions can be acquired by means of a single pairing of the US and the CS. Evolutionary psychologists point out that the rapid acquisition of a taste aversion makes it more likely that a human or an animal will survive and reproduce.

5-2d EXTINCTION AND SPONTANEOUS RECOVERY

Extinction and *spontaneous recovery* are aspects of conditioning that help us adapt by updating our expectations or revising our thinking about (representations of) the changing environment. For example, a child may learn to connect hearing a car pull into the driveway (a conditioned stimulus) with the arrival of his or her parents (an unconditioned stimulus). Thus, the child may squeal with delight (squealing is a conditioned response) when he or she hears the car.

Extinction enters the picture when times—and the relationships between events—change. After moving to a new house, the child's parents may commute by public transportation. The sound of a car in a nearby driveway may signal a neighbor's, not a parent's, homecoming. When a conditioned stimulus (such as the sound of a car) is no longer followed by an unconditioned stimulus (a parent's homecoming), the conditioned stimulus loses its ability to elicit a conditioned response. In this way, the organism adapts to a changing environment.

In classical conditioning, **extinction is the process by which conditioned stimuli lose the ability to elicit conditioned responses because the conditioned stimuli are no longer associated with unconditioned stimuli.** That is, the toddler is no longer gleeful at the sounds of the car in the driveway. From the cognitive perspective, extinction changes the child's mental representation of its environment because the conditioned stimulus no longer allows the child to make the same prediction.

In experiments on the extinction of conditioned responses, Pavlov found that repeated presentations of the conditioned stimulus (in this case, the tone) without the unconditioned stimulus (in this case, meat powder) led to extinction of the conditioned response (salivation in response to the tone). Basically, the dog stopped salivating at the sound of the tone. Interestingly, Figure 5.2 shows that after the initial conditioning, a dog's responsive salivation increased for a while and then leveled off. The dog was conditioned to begin to salivate in response to a tone after two or three pairings of the tone with meat powder. Continued pairings of the stimuli led to increased salivation (measured in number of drops of saliva). After seven or eight trials, salivation leveled off at 11 to 12 drops.

In the next series of experiments, salivation in response to the tone was extinguished through several trials in which the tone was presented without the meat powder. After about 10 extinction trials, the animal no longer salivated. That is, it no longer showed the conditioned response when the tone was sounded.

What would happen if we were to allow a day or two to pass after we had extinguished salivation in Pavlov's dog and then again sounded the tone? Where would you place your bet? Would the dog salivate or not?

If you bet that the dog would again show the conditioned response (in this case, salivation in response to the tone), you were correct. Organisms tend to show **spontaneous recovery** of extinguished conditioned responses as a function of the passage of time. For this reason, the term *extinction* may be a bit misleading. When a species of animal becomes extinct, all members of that species capable of reproducing have died. The species vanishes. But the experimental extinction of conditioned responses does not lead to their permanent eradication. Rather, extinction merely *inhibits* the response. The response remains available for the future under the "right" conditions.

> **extinction**
> the process by which stimuli lose their ability to evoke learned responses because the events that had followed the stimuli no longer occur (The learned responses are said to be *extinguished*.)
>
> **spontaneous recovery**
> the recurrence of an extinguished response as a function of the passage of time

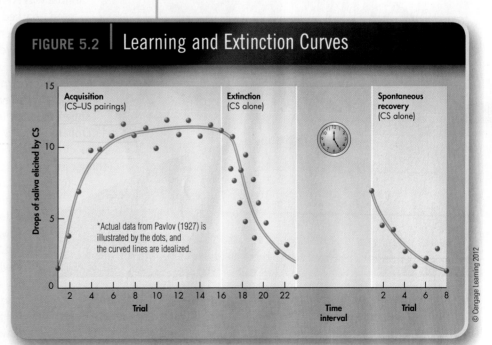

FIGURE 5.2 | Learning and Extinction Curves

Acquisition (CS–US pairings) Extinction (CS alone) Spontaneous recovery (CS alone)

Drops of saliva elicited by CS

*Actual data from Pavlov (1927) is illustrated by the dots, and the curved lines are idealized.

Trial Time interval Trial

© Cengage Learning 2012

Evolutionary psychologists note that spontaneous recovery, like extinction, is adaptive. In the wild, a water hole may contain water for only a couple of months during the year. But evolution would favor the survival of animals that associate the water hole with the thirst drive from time to time so that they return to it when it again holds water. As time passes and the seasons change, things sometimes follow circular paths and arrive where they were before. Spontaneous recovery helps organisms adapt to situations that recur from time to time.

5-2e GENERALIZATION AND DISCRIMINATION

No two things are exactly alike. Traffic lights are hung at slightly different heights, and shades of red and green differ a little. The barking of two dogs differs, and the sound of the same animal differs slightly from one bark to the next. Rustling sounds in the undergrowth differ, but evolution would favor the survival of rabbits and deer that flee when they perceive any one of many possible rustling sounds. Adaptation requires us to respond similarly (or *generalize*) to stimuli that are equivalent in function and to respond differently to (or *discriminate* between) stimuli that are not.

Pavlov noted that responding to different stimuli as though they were functionally equivalent—*generalizing*—is adaptive for animals. **Generalization** is the tendency for a conditioned response to be evoked by stimuli that are similar to the stimulus to which the response was conditioned. For example, Pavlov demonstrated generalization by getting his dog to salivate when it was shown a circle. Then later the dog salivated in response to being shown closed geometric figures—even squares. The more closely the figure resembled a circle, however, the greater the *strength* of the response (as measured by drops of saliva).

But what happens if food follows the presentation of a circle but not a square? Organisms must also learn that (1) many stimuli perceived as being similar are functionally different, and (2) they must respond adaptively to each. During the first couple of months of life, for example, babies can discriminate their mother's voice from those of other women. They often stop crying when they hear their mother but not when they hear a stranger.

Pavlov showed that a dog conditioned to salivate in response to circles could be trained *not* to salivate in response to ellipses. After a while, the dog no longer salivated in response to the ellipses. Instead, it showed **discrimination**: It salivated only in response to circles. Pavlov found that increasing the difficulty of the discrimination task apparently tormented the dog. After the dog was trained to salivate in response to circles but not ellipses, Pavlov showed it a series of progressively rounder ellipses. Eventually the dog could no longer distinguish the ellipses from circles. The animal was so stressed that it urinated, defecated, barked profusely, and snapped at laboratory personnel.

How do we explain the dog's belligerent behavior? In *Frustration and Aggression*, a classic work written more than 70 years ago, a group of behaviorally oriented psychologists suggested that frustration induces aggression (Dollard et al., 1939). Why is failure to discriminate circles from ellipses frustrating? For one thing, in such experiments, rewards—such as food—are usually contingent on correct discrimination. That is, if the dog errs, it doesn't eat. Cognitive theorists, however, disagree (Rescorla, 1988). They would say that in Pavlov's experiment, the dog lost its ability to adjust its mental map of the environment as the ellipses grew more circular. Thus, it was frustrated.

Evolution would favor the survival of animals that associate a water hole with the thirst drive from time to time so that they return to it when it once more holds water.

Jeremy Woodhouse/Getty Images

Daily life requires generalization and discrimination. No two hotels are alike, but when we travel from one city to another, it is adaptive to expect to stay in a hotel. It is encouraging that a green light in Washington has the same meaning as a green light in Paris. But returning home in the evening requires the ability to discriminate between our home and those of others. Imagine the confusion that would occur if we could not discriminate among our friends, mates, or coworkers from other people.

5-2f HIGHER-ORDER CONDITIONING

Consider a child who is burned by touching a hot stove. After this experience, the sight of the stove may evoke fear. And because hearing the word *stove* may evoke a mental image of the stove, just hearing the word may evoke fear.

Recall the mini-experiment in which an adult smiles, says "kitchie-coo," and then tickles an infant's foot. After a few repetitions, just smiling at the infant may cause the infant to retract its foot. In fact, just walking into the room may have the same effect! The experiences with touching the hot stove and tickling the infant's foot are examples of *higher-order conditioning*.

In **higher-order conditioning**, a previously neutral stimulus (for example, hearing the word *stove* or seeing the adult who had done the tickling enter the room) comes to serve as a learned, or conditioned, stimulus after being paired repeatedly with a stimulus that has already become a learned, or conditioned, stimulus (for example, seeing the stove or hearing the phrase "kitchie-coo"). Pavlov demonstrated higher-order conditioning by first conditioning a dog to salivate in response to a tone. He then repeatedly paired the shining of a light with the sounding of the tone. After several pairings, shining the light (the higher-order conditioned stimulus) came to evoke the response (salivation) that had been elicited by the tone (the first-order conditioned stimulus).

5-2g APPLICATIONS OF CLASSICAL CONDITIONING

Some of the most important applications of classical conditioning involve the conditioning of fear and the counter-conditioning, or extinction, of fear. The fear-reduction

methods we discuss are part of behavior therapy and are elaborated on in Chapter 13.

"Little Albert": Classical Conditioning of Emotional Responses

In 1920, John B. Watson and his future wife, Rosalie Rayner, published an article describing their demonstration that emotional reactions such as fears can be acquired through principles of classical conditioning. The subject of their demonstration was a lad known in psychological literature by the name of Little Albert. Albert was a phlegmatic fellow at the age of 11 months, not given to ready displays of emotion. But prior to the study, the infant did enjoy playing with a laboratory rat.

Using a method that some psychologists have criticized as unethical, Watson startled Little Albert by clanging steel bars behind his head when he played with the rat. After seven pairings, Albert showed fear of the rat even though clanging was suspended. Albert's fear was also generalized to objects similar in appearance to the rat, such as a rabbit and the fur collar on his mother's coat. Albert's conditioned fear of rats may never have become extinguished because extinction would have required perceiving rats (the conditioned stimuli) without painful consequences (in the absence of the unconditioned stimuli). But Albert's mother removed him from the laboratory before Watson and Rayner could attempt to countercondition the boy's acquired fear. And once outside the laboratory, fear might have prevented Albert from facing furry animals.

higher-order conditioning

a classical conditioning procedure in which a previously neutral stimulus comes to elicit the response brought forth by a *conditioned* stimulus by being paired repeatedly with that conditioned stimulus

Watson and Rayner conditioned "Little Albert" to fear a rat by clanging steel bars behind his head when he played with the rat.

And as we shall see in the section on operant conditioning, avoiding furry animals might have been *reinforced* by reduction of fear.

Preparedness and the Conditioning of Fear

Little Albert developed his fear of rats easily enough, but would Watson and Rayner have been able to condition him to fear flowers or potted plants? Perhaps not. As suggested by Arne Öhman and Susan Mineka (2003), humans (and other primates) may be **biologically prepared** by evolutionary forces to rapidly develop fears of certain animals, including snakes, that could do them harm. People also seem to be prepared to fear thunder, threatening faces, sharp objects, darkness, and heights—all of which would have been sources of danger to our ancestors and which, to some degree, may still threaten us (Gerdes et al., 2009; Mineka & Oehlberg, 2008; Starratt & Shackelford, 2010).

Counterconditioning

In **counterconditioning**, an organism learns to respond to a stimulus in a way that is incompatible with a response that was conditioned earlier. For example, relaxation is incompatible with a fear response. The reasoning behind counterconditioning is this: If fears, as Watson had shown, could be conditioned by painful experiences like a clanging noise, perhaps fears could be counterconditioned by substituting pleasant experiences. In 1924, Watson's protégé Mary Cover Jones attempted to countercondition fear in a two-year-old boy named Peter.

Peter had an intense fear of rabbits.

© Michael Newman/Photo Edit

Jones had a rabbit gradually brought closer to Peter while he munched candy and cookies. Jones first placed the rabbit in a far corner of the room while Peter munched and crunched. Peter cast a wary eye, but he continued to consume the treats. Over a couple of months, the animal was brought closer until Peter simultaneously ate and touched the rabbit. Jones theorized that the joy of eating was incompatible with fear and thus counterconditioned it.

TRUTH IT IS TRUE THAT PSYCHOLOGISTS HELPED A YOUNG BOY OVERCOME HIS FEAR OF RABBITS BY HAVING HIM EAT COOKIES WHILE A RABBIT WAS BROUGHT CLOSER AND CLOSER.

Flooding and Systematic Desensitization

If Mary Cover Jones had simply plopped the rabbit on Peter's lap rather than bring it gradually closer, she would have been using the method of **flooding**. Flooding, like counterconditioning, is a behavior therapy method for reducing fears. It is based on the classical conditioning principle of extinction (Mystkowski & Mineka, 2007). In flooding, the client is exposed to the fear-evoking stimulus until fear is extinguished. Little Albert, for example, might have been placed in close contact with a rat until his fear had become extinguished. In extinction, the conditioned stimulus (in this case, the rat) is presented repeatedly in the absence of the unconditioned stimulus (the clanging of the steel bars) until the conditioned response (fear) is no longer evoked.

Although flooding is usually effective, it is unpleasant. (When you are fearful of rats, being placed in a room with one is no picnic.) For this reason, behavior therapists frequently prefer to use **systematic desensitization**, in which the client is gradually exposed to fear-evoking stimuli under circumstances in which he or she remains relaxed. For example, while feeling relaxed, Little Albert might have been given an opportunity to look at photos of rats or to see rats from a distance before they were brought closer. Systematic desensitization takes longer than flooding but is not as unpleasant.

In any event, people can learn by means of simple association. In terms of the evolutionary perspective, organisms that can learn by several routes—including conditioning and conscious reflection—would stand a greater chance of survival than organisms whose learning is limited to conditioning.

5-3 Operant Conditioning: Learning What Does What to What

Through classical conditioning, we learn to associate stimuli. As a result, a simple, usually passive response made to one stimulus is then made in response to the other. In the case of Little Albert, clanging noises were associated with a rat. As a result, the rat came to elicit the fear caused by the clanging. However, classical conditioning is only one kind of learning that occurs in these situations. After Little Albert acquired his fear of the rat, his voluntary behavior changed: He tried to avoid the rat as a way of reducing his fear. Thus, Little Albert engaged in another kind of learning— *operant conditioning.*

In operant conditioning, organisms learn to do things—or *not* to do things—because of the consequences of their behavior. For example, I avoided buttered popcorn to prevent nausea. But we also seek fluids when we are thirsty, sex when we are aroused, and an ambient temperature of 68° to 70°F when we feel too hot or too cold. *Classical conditioning focuses on how organisms form anticipations about their environments. Operant conditioning focuses on what they do about them.* Let's look at the contributions of Edward L. Thorndike and B. F. Skinner to operant conditioning.

5-3a EDWARD L. THORNDIKE AND THE LAW OF EFFECT

In the 1890s, stray cats were mysteriously disappearing from the alleyways of Harlem. Some of them, it turned out, were being brought to the quarters of Columbia University doctoral student Edward

Thorndike. Thorndike was using them as subjects in experiments on the effects of rewards and punishments on learning.

Thorndike placed a cat in a "puzzle box." If it pulled a dangling string, a latch would be released, allowing it to jump out and reach a bowl of food. When first placed in a puzzle box, a cat would claw and bite at the bars and wire. Through such random behavior, it might take 3 to 4 minutes for the cat to chance upon the response of pulling the string. When placed back in the cage, it might again take several minutes for the cat to pull the string. But with repetition, it took less time, and after seven or eight tries, the cat might pull the string immediately.

Thorndike explained the cat's learning to pull the string in terms of his **law of effect**: A response (such as string pulling) would be—to use Thorndike's term— "stamped in" (that is, strengthened) in a particular situation (such as being inside a puzzle box) by a reward (escaping from the box and eating). But punishments— using Thorndike's terminology once again—"stamp out" response. That is, organisms would learn not to behave in ways that bring on punishment. Later, we shall see that the effects of punishment on learning are not so certain.

5-3b B. F. SKINNER AND REINFORCEMENT

When it comes to unusual war stories, few will top that of B. F. Skinner. One of Skinner's wartime efforts was "Project Pigeon." During World War II, Skinner proposed that pigeons be trained to guide missiles to their targets. In their training, the pigeons would be **reinforced** with food pellets for pecking at targets projected onto a screen (see Figure 5.3). Once trained, the pigeons would be placed in missiles. Their pecking

FIGURE 5.3
Project Pigeon

© Cengage Learning 2012

TRUTH IT WAS B. F. SKINNER WHO CREATED A MISSILE THAT COULD USE PIGEONS TO GUIDE THE MISSILE TO ITS TARGET DURING WORLD WAR II.

at similar targets displayed on a screen would correct the missile's flight path, resulting in a "hit" and a sacrificed pigeon. However, plans for building the necessary missile—for some reason called the *Pelican* and not the *Pigeon*—were scrapped. The pigeon equipment was too bulky, and Skinner's suggestion was not taken seriously.

Project Pigeon may have been scrapped, but the principles of learning Skinner applied to the project have found wide application. Skinner taught pigeons and other animals to engage in **operant behavior**, behavior that operates on, or manipulates, the environment. In classical conditioning, involuntary responses such as salivation or eyeblinks are often conditioned. In operant conditioning, *voluntary* responses such as pecking at a target, pressing a lever, or skills required for playing tennis are acquired, or conditioned.

Operant conditioning is therefore defined as a simple form of learning in which an organism learns to engage in certain behavior because of the effects of that behavior. In operant conditioning, we learn to engage in operant behaviors, also known simply as **operants**, that result in presumably desirable outcomes such as food, a hug, an A on a test, attention, or social approval. For example, some children learn to conform to social rules to earn the attention and approval of their parents and teachers. Ironically, other children may learn to "misbehave" because misbehavior also gets attention. In particular, children may learn to be "bad" when their "good" behavior is routinely ignored. Some children who do not do well in school seek the approval of deviant peers (Patterson et al., 2000).

5-3c METHODS OF OPERANT CONDITIONING

Skinner (1938) made many theoretical and technological innovations. Among them was his focus on discrete behaviors, such as lever pressing, as the *unit*, or type, of behavior to be studied. Other psychologists might focus on how organisms think or "feel." Skinner focused on measurable things they *do*. Many psychologists have found these kinds of behavior inconsequential, especially when it comes to explaining and predicting human behavior. But Skinner's supporters point out that focusing on discrete behavior creates the potential for helpful changes. For example, in helping people combat depression, one psychologist might focus on their "feelings." A Skinnerian would focus on cataloging (and

FIGURE 5.4 | A Rat in a "Skinner Box"

Water Light Screen

Food pellet dispenser

Food tray Lever

© Cengage Learning 2012

modifying) the types of things that "depressed people" *do*. Directly modifying depressive behavior might also brighten clients' self-reports about their "feelings of depression."

To study operant behavior, Skinner devised an animal cage (or "operant chamber") that has been dubbed the *Skinner box*. (Skinner himself repeatedly requested that his operant chamber *not* be called a Skinner box, but history has thus far failed to honor his wishes.) Such a box is shown in Figure 5.4. The cage is ideal for laboratory experimentation because experimental conditions can be carefully introduced and removed, and their effects on laboratory animals can be observed.

The rat in Figure 5.4 was deprived of food and placed in a Skinner box with a lever at one end. At first it sniffed its way around the cage and engaged in random behavior. The rat's first pressing of the lever was accidental. However, because of this action, a food pellet dropped into the cage. The arrival of the food pellet increased the probability that the rat would press the lever again. The pellet is thus said to have *reinforced* lever pressing.

In operant conditioning, it matters little why or how the first "correct" response is made. The animal can happen on it by chance or be physically guided to make the response. You may command your dog to "Sit!" and then press its backside down until it is sitting. Finally, you reinforce sitting with food or a pat on the head and a kind word. Animal trainers use physical guiding or coaxing to bring about the first "correct" response. Can you imagine how long it would take to train your dog if you waited for it to sit or roll over and then seized the opportunity to command it to sit or roll over?

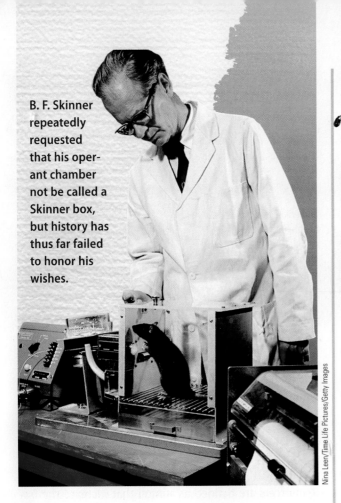

B. F. Skinner repeatedly requested that his operant chamber not be called a Skinner box, but history has thus far failed to honor his wishes.

People, of course, can be verbally guided into desired responses when they are learning tasks such as spelling, adding numbers, or operating a machine. But they need to be informed when they have made the correct response. Knowledge of results often is all the reinforcement people need to learn new skills.

5-3d TYPES OF REINFORCERS

Any stimulus that increases the probability that responses preceding it—whether pecking a button in a Skinner box or studying for a quiz—will be repeated serves as a reinforcer. Reinforcers include food pellets when an animal has been deprived of food, water when it has been deprived of liquid, the opportunity to mate, and the sound of a tone that has previously been associated with eating. Skinner distinguished between *positive* and *negative* reinforcers and *primary* and *secondary* reinforcers.

Positive and Negative Reinforcers

Positive reinforcers increase the probability that a behavior will occur when they are applied. Food and approval usually serve as positive reinforcers. Negative reinforcers increase the probability that a behavior will occur when the reinforcers are *removed* (see Figure 5.5). People often learn to plan ahead so that they need not fear that things will go wrong. In such cases, fear acts as a negative reinforcer because *removal* of fear increases the probability that the behaviors preceding it (such as planning ahead) will be repeated.

Immediate Versus Delayed Reinforcers

Immediate reinforcers are more effective than delayed reinforcers. Therefore, the short-term consequences of behavior often provide more of an incentive than the long-term consequences.

For example, some students socialize when they should be studying because the pleasure of socializing is immediate. Studying may not pay off until the final exam or graduation. (This is why younger students do better with frequent tests.) It is difficult to quit smoking cigarettes because the reinforcement of nicotine is immediate and the health hazards of smoking are more distant. Focusing on short-term reinforcement is also connected with risky sex, such as engaging in sexual activity with a stranger or failing to prevent pregnancy (Castor et al., 2010; Shuper et al., 2010). One of the aspects of being human is the ability to foresee the long-range consequences of one's behavior and to make choices. But

positive reinforcer a reinforcer that when *presented* increases the frequency of an operant

negative reinforcer a reinforcer that when *removed* increases the frequency of an operant

FIGURE 5.5 | Positive Versus Negative Reinforcers

Procedure	Behavior	Consequence	Change in behavior
Use of positive reinforcement	Behavior (Studying)	Positive reinforcer (Teacher approval) is *presented* when student studies	Frequency of behavior *increases* (Student studies more)
Use of negative reinforcement	Behavior (Studying)	Negative reinforcer (Teacher disapproval) is *removed* when student studies	Frequency of behavior *increases* (Student studies more)

© Cengage Learning 2012

Nina Leen/Time Life Pictures/Getty Images

primary reinforcer an unlearned reinforcer whose effectiveness is based on the biological makeup of the organism and not on learning

secondary reinforcer a stimulus that gains reinforcement value through association with established reinforcers

conditioned reinforcer another term for a secondary reinforcer

immediate reinforcers—such as those cookies staring in the face of the would-be dieter—can be powerful temptations indeed.

Primary and Secondary Reinforcers

We can also distinguish between primary and secondary, or conditioned, reinforcers. **Primary reinforcers** are effective because of the organism's biological makeup. For example, food, water, warmth (positive reinforcers), and pain (a negative reinforcer) all serve as primary reinforcers. **Secondary reinforcers** acquire their value through being associated with established reinforcers. For this reason they are also termed **conditioned reinforcers**. We may seek money because we have learned that it may be exchanged for primary reinforcers.

5-3e EXTINCTION AND SPONTANEOUS RECOVERY IN OPERANT CONDITIONING

Keisha's teacher writes "Good" on all of her homework assignments before returning them. One day, her teacher no longer writes anything on the assignments—the reinforcement ends. Reinforcers are used to strengthen responses. What happens when reinforcement stops?

In Pavlov's experiment, the meat powder was the event that followed and confirmed the appropriateness of salivation. In operant conditioning, the ensuing events are reinforcers. The extinction of learned responses results from the repeated performance of operant behavior without reinforcement. Keisha might stop doing her homework if she is not reinforced for completing it. In other words, reinforcers maintain operant behavior or strengthen habitual behavior in operant conditioning. With humans, fortunately, people can reinforce themselves for desired behavior by telling themselves they did a good job—or in Keisha's case, she may tell herself that she is doing the right thing regardless of whether her teacher recognizes it.

Spontaneous recovery of learned responses occurs in operant conditioning as well as in classical conditioning. Spontaneous recovery is adaptive in

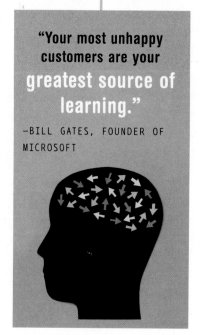

"Your most unhappy customers are your **greatest source of learning.**"

—BILL GATES, FOUNDER OF MICROSOFT

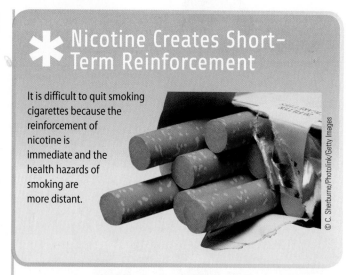

✳ Nicotine Creates Short-Term Reinforcement

It is difficult to quit smoking cigarettes because the reinforcement of nicotine is immediate and the health hazards of smoking are more distant.

© C. Sherburne/Photolink/Getty Images

operant conditioning as well as in classical conditioning. Reinforcers may once again become available after time elapses, just as there are new tender sprouts on twigs when the spring arrives.

5-3f REINFORCERS VERSUS REWARDS AND PUNISHMENTS

Reinforcers are defined as stimuli that increase the frequency of behavior. Skinner distinguished between reinforcers, on the one hand, and rewards and punishments, on the other. *Reinforcers* are known by their effects, whereas *rewards* and *punishments* are more known by how they feel. It may be that most reinforcers—food, hugs, having the other person admit to starting the argument, and so on—feel good, or are pleasant events. Yet things that we might assume would feel bad, such as a slap on the hand, disapproval from a teacher, even suspensions and detention may be positively reinforcing to some people—perhaps because such experiences confirm negative feelings toward teachers or one's belonging within a deviant subculture (Atkins et al., 2002).

Skinner preferred the concept of reinforcement to that of reward because reinforcement does not suggest trying to "get inside the head" of an organism (whether a human or lower animal) to guess what it would find pleasant or unpleasant. A list of reinforcers is arrived at scientifically and *empirically*—that is, by observing what sorts of stimuli increase the frequency of the behavior.

Whereas *reinforcers*—even negative reinforcers—increase the frequency of the behavior they follow, *punishments* decrease it (see Figure 5.6). Punishment can rapidly suppress undesirable behavior (Gershoff, 2002) and may be warranted in "emergencies," such as when a child tries to run into the street.

Psychologists distinguish between *positive punishments* and *negative punishments*. Both kinds of punishments are aversive events, and both decrease the frequency of the behavior they follow (see Figure 5.8). *Positive punishment* is the application of an aversive stimulus to decrease unwanted behavior, such as spanking, scolding, or a parking ticket. *Negative punishment* is the removal of a pleasant stimulus, such as removing a student's opportunity to talk with friends in class by seating them apart, or removing a student's opportunity to mentally escape from class by taking his or her iPhone or iPad. "Time out" is a form of negative punishment because it places a misbehaving child in an environment in which she or he cannot experience rewards.

5-3g DISCRIMINATIVE STIMULI

Skinner might not have succeeded in getting his pigeons into the drivers' seats of missiles, but he had no problem training them to respond to traffic lights. Imagine yourself trying the following experiment: Place a pigeon in a Skinner box with a button on the wall. Deprive it of food for a while. Drop a food pellet into the cage whenever it pecks the button. Soon it will learn to peck the button. Now you place a small green light in the cage and turn it on and off intermittently throughout the day. Reinforce button pecking with food whenever the green light is on, but not when the light is off. It will not take long for the pigeon to learn that it will gain as much by grooming itself or cooing and flapping around as it will by pecking the button when the light is off.

"Education is what survives when what has been learned has been forgotten."
—B. F. SKINNER

The green light has become a discriminative stimulus. **Discriminative stimuli**, such as green or red lights, indicate whether behavior (in the case of the pigeon, pecking a button) will be reinforced (by a food pellet being dropped into the cage). Behaviors (or operants) that are not reinforced tend to be extinguished. For the pigeon in our experiment, the behavior of pecking the button *when the light is off* is extinguished.

A moment's reflection will suggest many ways in which discriminative stimuli influence our behavior. Isn't it more efficient to answer the telephone when it is ringing? Do you think it is wise to ask someone for a favor when she or he is displaying anger and disapproval toward you?

We noted that a pigeon learns to peck a button if food drops into its cage when it does so. What if you want the pigeon to continue to peck the button, but you're running out of food? Do not despair. As we see in the following section, you can keep that bird pecking away indefinitely, even as you hold up on most of the food.

5-3h SCHEDULES OF REINFORCEMENT

In operant conditioning, some responses are maintained by means of **continuous reinforcement**. You probably become warmer every time you put on heavy clothing. You probably become less thirsty every time you drink water. Yet if you have ever watched people toss their money down the maws of slot machines, you know that behavior can also be maintained by means of **partial reinforcement**.

discriminative stimulus in operant conditioning, a stimulus that indicates that reinforcement is available

continuous reinforcement a schedule of reinforcement in which every correct response is reinforced

partial reinforcement one of several reinforcement schedules in which not every correct response is reinforced

FIGURE 5.6 | Negative Reinforcers Versus Punishments

Procedure	Behavior	Consequence	Change in behavior
Use of negative reinforcement	Behavior (Studying)	Negative reinforcer (Teacher disapproval) is *removed* when student studies	Frequency of behavior *increases* (Student studies more)
Use of punishment	Behavior (Talking in class)	Punishment (Detention) is *presented* when student talks in class	Frequency of behavior *decreases* (Student talks less in class)

© Cengage Learning 2012

Folklore about gambling is based on solid learning theory. You can get a person "hooked" on gambling by fixing the game to allow heavy winnings at first. Then you gradually space out the winnings (reinforcements) until gambling is maintained by infrequent winning—or even no winning at all. Partial reinforcement schedules can maintain gambling, like other behavior, for a great deal of time, even though it goes unreinforced (Pulley, 1998).

Responses that have been maintained by partial reinforcement are more resistant to extinction than responses that have been maintained by continuous reinforcement (Rescorla, 1999). From the cognitive perspective, we could suggest that organisms that have experienced partial reinforcement do not expect reinforcement every time they engage in a response. Therefore, they are more likely to persist in the absence of reinforcement.

There are four basic reinforcement schedules: *fixed-interval*, *variable-interval*, *fixed-ratio*, and *variable-ratio*.

Interval Schedules

In a **fixed-interval schedule**, a fixed amount of time—say, a minute—must elapse before the correct response will result in a reinforcer. With a fixed-interval schedule, an organism's response rate falls off after each reinforcement and then picks up again as the time when reinforcement will occur approaches. For example, in a one-minute fixed-interval schedule, a rat is reinforced with, say, a food pellet for the first operant—for example, the first pressing of a lever—that occurs after one minute has elapsed. After each reinforcement, the rat's rate of lever pressing slows down, but as the end of the one-minute interval draws near, lever pressing increases in frequency, as suggested in Figure 5.7. It is as if the rat has learned that it must wait awhile before it is reinforced. The resultant record on the *cumulative recorder* shows a typical series of upward waves, or scallops, which are called *fixed-interval scallops*.

Car dealers use fixed-interval reinforcement schedules when they offer in-

centives for buying up the remainder of the year's line in summer and fall. In a sense, they are suppressing buying at other times, except for consumers whose current cars are in their death throes or those with little self-control. Similarly, you learn to check your e-mail only at a certain time of day if your correspondent writes at that time each day.

Reinforcement is more unpredictable in a **variable-interval schedule**. Therefore, the response rate is lower, but it is also steadier. If the boss calls us in for a weekly report, we probably work hard to pull things together just before the report is to be given, just as we might cram the night before a weekly quiz. But if we know that the boss might call us in for a report on the progress of a certain project at any time (variable-interval schedule), we are likely to keep things in a state of reasonable readiness at all times. However, our efforts are unlikely to have the intensity they would in a fixed-interval schedule (for example, a weekly report). Similarly, we are less likely to cram for unpredictable pop quizzes than to study for regularly scheduled quizzes. But we are likely to do at least some studying on a regular basis in preparation for pop quizzes. Likewise, if you receive e-mail from your correspondent irregularly, you are likely to check your e-mail regularly for his or her communication, but with less eagerness.

Ratio Schedules

In a **fixed-ratio schedule**, reinforcement is provided after a *fixed* number of correct responses have been made. In a **variable-ratio schedule**, reinforcement is

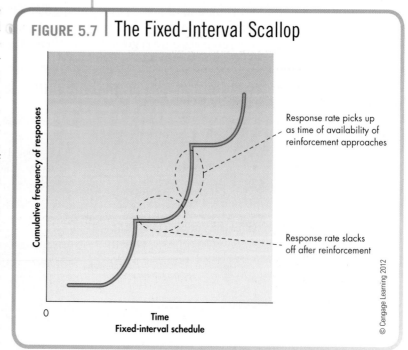

FIGURE 5.7 | The Fixed-Interval Scallop

Cumulative frequency of responses

Time
Fixed-interval schedule

Response rate picks up as time of availability of reinforcement approaches

Response rate slacks off after reinforcement

© Cengage Learning 2012

shaping
a procedure for teaching complex behaviors that at first reinforces approximations of the target behavior

successive approximations
behaviors that are progressively closer to a target behavior

TRUTH SLOT-MACHINE PLAYERS POP COINS INTO THE MACHINES MOST RAPIDLY WHEN THEY HAVE NO IDEA WHEN THEY MIGHT WIN.

provided after a *variable* number of correct responses have been made. In a 10:1 ratio schedule, the mean number of correct responses that would have to be made before a subsequent correct response would be reinforced is 10, but the ratio of correct responses to reinforcements might be allowed to vary from, say, 1:1 to 20:1 on a random basis.

Fixed- and variable-ratio schedules both maintain a high response rate. With a fixed-ratio schedule, it is as if the organism learns that it must make several responses before being reinforced. It then "gets them out of the way" as rapidly as possible. Consider the example of piecework. If a worker must sew five shirts to receive $10, he or she is on a fixed-ratio (5:1) schedule and is likely to sew at a uniformly high rate, although there might be a brief pause after each reinforcement. With a variable-ratio schedule, reinforcement can come at any time. This unpredictability also maintains a high response rate. Slot machines tend to pay off on variable-ratio schedules, and players can be seen popping coins into them and yanking their "arms" with barely a pause. For gamblers, the unpredictability of winning maintains a high response rate. I have seen players who do not even stop to pick up their winnings. Instead, they continue to pop in the coins, either from their original stack or from the winnings tray.

5-3i SHAPING

If you are teaching hip-hop dancing to people who have never danced, do not wait until they have performed it precisely before telling them they're on the right track. The foxtrot will be back in style before they have learned a thing.

We can teach complex behaviors by **shaping**. Shaping reinforces progressive steps toward the behavioral goal. At first, for example, it may be wise to smile and say, "Good," when a reluctant newcomer gathers the courage to get out on the dance floor, even if your feet are flattened by his initial clumsiness. If you are teaching someone to drive a car with a standard shift, at first generously reinforce the learner simply for shifting gears without stalling.

But as training proceeds, we come to expect more before we are willing to provide reinforcement. We reinforce **successive approximations** of the goal. If you want to train a rat to climb a ladder, first reinforce it with a food pellet when it turns toward the ladder. Then wait until it approaches the ladder before giving it a pellet. Then do not drop a pellet into the cage until the rat touches the ladder. In this way, the rat will reach the top of the ladder more quickly than if you had waited for the target behavior to occur at random.

Have you ever driven home and suddenly realized that you couldn't recall exactly how you got there? Your entire trip may seem "lost." Were you in great danger? How could you al-low such a thing to happen? Actually, your driving and your responses to the demands of the route may have become so habitual that you did not have to focus on them. As you drove,

TRUTH IT IS TRUE THAT YOU CAN TRAIN A RAT TO DO SEVERAL THINGS IN SEQUENCE—SUCH AS CROSSING A BRIDGE, CLIMBING A RAMP, AND SO ON—BY USING SHAPING.

you were able to think about dinner, work, or the weekend. But if something unusual had occurred on the way, such as an engine problem or a rainstorm, you would have devoted as much attention to your driving as was needed to arrive home. Your trip was probably quite safe after all.

5-3j APPLICATIONS OF OPERANT CONDITIONING

Operant conditioning, like classical conditioning, is not just an exotic laboratory procedure. We use it every day in our efforts to influence other people. Parents and peers induce children to acquire so-called gender-appropriate behavior patterns through rewards and punishments. Peers influence peers by playing with those who are generous and nonaggressive and by avoiding those who are not (Warman & Cohen, 2000).

Operant conditioning also plays a role in attitude formation. Adults often reward children for expressing attitudes that coincide with their own and punish or ignore them for expressing contradictory attitudes. Let's now consider some specific applications of operant conditioning.

TRUTH IN THE METHOD OF PROGRAMMED LEARNING, THE LEARNER CAN IDEALLY LEARN WITHOUT MAKING ANY MISTAKES AT ALL.

Biofeedback Training

Biofeedback training (BFT) is based on operant conditioning. It has enabled people and lower animals to learn to control autonomic responses to attain reinforcement (N. E. Miller, 1969; Vernon et al., 2003). In BFT, people receive reinforcement in the form of *information*. For example, we can learn to emit alpha waves—the kind of brain wave associated with relaxation—through feedback from an electroencephalograph, which measures brain waves. People use other instruments to learn to lower muscle tension, heart rates, and blood pressure.

Behavior Modification

Remember that *reinforcers* are not *defined* as pleasant events but rather as stimuli that increase the frequency of behavior. Ironically, adults frequently reinforce undesirable behavior in children by paying attention to them, or punishing them, when they misbehave but ignoring them when they behave in desirable ways. Similarly, teachers who raise their voices when children misbehave may be unintentionally conferring hero status on those pupils in the eyes of their peers. To the teacher's surprise, some children may then go out of their way to earn disapproval. But teachers can learn to use *behavior modification* to reinforce children when they are behaving appropriately and, when possible, to extinguish misbehavior by ignoring it.

Teachers also frequently use time out from positive reinforcement to discourage misbehavior. In this method, children are placed in a drab, restrictive environment for a specified period, usually about 10 minutes, when they behave disruptively. While isolated, they cannot earn the attention of peers or teachers, and no reinforcers are present.

Programmed Learning

B. F. Skinner developed an educational method called *programmed learning* that is based on operant conditioning. This method assumes that any complex task can be broken down into a number of small steps. These steps can be shaped individually and then combined in sequence to form the correct behavioral chain.

Programmed learning does not punish errors. Instead, correct responses are reinforced, usually with immediate feedback. Every child earns a 100, but at her or his own pace. Programmed learning also assumes it is the task of the teacher (or program) to structure the learning experience in such a way that errors will not be made. In programmed learning, one can learn without making mistakes.

This woman is using biofeedback training to relax muscles in her forehead, which, in turn, will reduce anxiety.

WILL & DENI MCINTYRE/Photo Researchers/Getty Images

5-4 Cognitive Factors in Learning

Classical and operant conditioning were originally conceived of as relatively simple forms of learning. Much of conditioning's appeal is that it can be said to meet the behaviorist objective of explaining behavior in terms of observable events—in this case, laboratory conditions. Building on this theoretical base, some psychologists have suggested that the most complex human behavior involves the summation of a series of instances of conditioning. Many psychologists believe, however, that conditioning is too mechanical a process to explain all instances of learned behavior, even in laboratory rats (Weiner, 2006). They turn to cognitive factors to describe and explain additional findings in the psychology of learning.

In addition to concepts such as *association* and *reinforcement*, cognitive psychologists use concepts such as *mental structures*, *schemas*, *templates*, and *information processing*. Cognitive psychologists see people as searching for information, weighing evidence, and making decisions. Let's consider some classic research that points to cognitive factors in learning, as opposed to mechanical associations. These cognitive factors are not limited to humans—although, of course, humans are the only species that can talk about them.

5-4a LATENT LEARNING: FORMING COGNITIVE MAPS

Many behaviorists argue that organisms acquire only responses, or operants, for which they are reinforced. E. C. Tolman, however, showed that rats also learn about their environment in the absence of reinforcement. In doing so, he showed that rats must form **cognitive maps** of their surroundings.

Tolman trained some rats to run through mazes for standard food goals. Other rats were allowed to explore the same mazes for several days without food goals or other rewards. After the unrewarded rats had been allowed to explore the mazes for 10 days, food rewards were placed in a box at the far end of the maze. The previously unrewarded rats reached the food box as quickly as the rewarded rats after only one or two trials (Tolman & Honzik, 1930).

Tolman concluded that the rats had learned about the mazes by exploring them even when they were unrewarded for doing so. He distinguished between *learning* and *performance*. Rats apparently created a cognitive map of a maze. Even though they were not externally motivated to follow a rapid route through the maze, they would learn fast routes just by exploring it. Yet this learning might remain hidden, or be considered **latent learning**, until food motivated them to take the rapid routes.

5-4b CONTINGENCY THEORY

Behaviorists and cognitive psychologists interpret classical conditioning in different ways. Behaviorists explain it in terms of the pairing of stimuli. Cognitive psychologists explain classical conditioning in terms of the ways in which stimuli provide information that allows organisms to form or revise mental representations of their environment. Robert Rescorla conducted research in an effort to demonstrate which view is more accurate. His viewpoint, **contingency theory,** suggests that learning occurs only when the conditioned stimulus (CS) provides *information* about the unconditioned stimulus (US).

In classical conditioning of dogs, Rescorla (1967) obtained some results that are difficult to explain without reference to cognitive concepts. Each phase of his work paired a tone (a CS) with an electric shock (a US), but in different ways. With one group of animals, the shock was consistently presented after the tone. That is, the unconditioned stimulus followed on the heels of the conditioned stimulus, as in Pavlov's studies. The dogs in this group learned to show a fear response when the tone was presented.

A second group of dogs heard an equal number of tones and received an equal number of electric shocks, but the shock never immediately followed the tone. In other words, the tone and the shock were not paired. Now, from the behaviorist perspective, the dogs should not have learned to associate the tone and the shock because one did not predict the other. Actually, the dogs learned quite a lot: They learned that they had nothing to fear when the tone was sounded! They showed vigilance and fear when the laboratory was quiet—for the shock might come at any time—but they were calm in the presence of the tone.

The third group of dogs also received equal numbers of tones and shocks, but the stimuli were presented at random intervals. Occasionally, they were paired, but most often, they were not. According to Rescorla, behaviorists might argue that intermittent pairing of the tones and shocks should have brought about some

cognitive map
a mental representation of the layout of one's environment

latent learning
learning that is hidden or concealed

contingency theory
the view that learning occurs when stimuli provide information about the likelihood of the occurrence of other stimuli

observational learning
the acquisition of knowledge and skills through the observation of others (who are called *models*) rather than by means of direct experience

model
an organism that engages in a response that is then imitated by another organism

learning. Yet it did not. The animals showed no fear in response to the tone. Rescorla suggests that the animals in this group learned nothing because the tones did not allow them to make predictions about electric shock. Rescorla concluded that learning occurs only when the CS (in this case, the tone) provides information about the US (in this case, the shock).

5-4c OBSERVATIONAL LEARNING

How many things have you learned from watching other people in real life, in films, and on television? From films and television, you may have gathered vague ideas about how to skydive, ride a surfboard, and dust for fingerprints, even if you have never tried them yourself. How do people learn by observing others?

In experiments on **observational learning**, Albert Bandura and his colleagues conducted experiments (e.g., Bandura et al., 1963) that show that we can acquire skills by observing the behavior of others. In the terminology of observational learning, a person who engages in a response that is imitated is a **model**. When we see modeled behavior being reinforced, we are said to be *vicariously* reinforced. Engaging in the behavior thus becomes more likely for us as well as for the model. Observational learning occurs when, as children, we watch our parents cook or clean. Observational learning takes place when we watch teachers solve problems on the blackboard or hear them speak in a foreign language. Observational learning is not acquired through

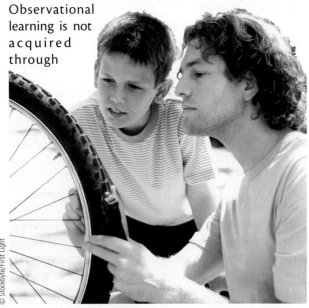
© Stockbyte/First Light

To what degree are gender roles learned by observation?

reinforcement. We can learn through observation without engaging in overt responses at all. It appears sufficient to pay attention to the behavior. We may need some practice to refine the skills we acquire. We may also allow these skills to lie dormant or latent. For example, we may not imitate aggressive behavior unless we are provoked and believe that we are more likely to be rewarded than punished for it.

But is there something in us (and monkeys and apes) that leads us to *automatically* imitate the behavior of others? The answer is apparently yes. We are referring to *mirror neurons*—neurons that fire when an animal observes the behavior of another and that tend to stimulate imitative behavior (Gallese et al., 1996). Mirror neurons are apparently involved when newborn babies return the favor if their caregivers stick out their tongues at them, but as babies develop, this automatic imitation tends to drop out (Meltzoff & Prinz, 2002). Nevertheless, mirror neurons also allow us to anticipate other people's intentions when they reach for things. Mirror neurons may also be a reason that we tend to yawn when people around us yawn, or why laughter is sometimes "contagious."

5-4d VIOLENCE IN THE MEDIA AND AGGRESSION

The debate as to whether violence in media such as films, television, and video games fuels violence in the real world has been going on for more than 50 years. However, research strongly suggests that media violence is a risk factor for increasing emotional arousal, aggressive behavior, and violent thoughts (Anderson et al., 2008; Dubow et al., 2010; Fanti et al., 2009).

We should be particularly concerned about violent video games such as Grand Theft Auto because they require audience participation (Anderson et al., 2008). Players don't just watch; they participate. Some games reward players for killing police, prostitutes, or bystanders. Virtual weapons include guns, knives, flamethrowers, swords, clubs, cars, hands, and feet. Sometimes, the player assumes the role of a hero, but it is also common for the player to assume the role of a criminal.

Television is one of our major sources of informal observational learning. Children are routinely exposed to murders, beatings, and sexual assaults—just by turning on the TV set (Huesmann et al., 2003; Potter, 2008). If children watch two to four hours of TV a day, they will have seen 8,000 murders and another 100,000 acts of violence by the time they have finished elementary school (Eron, 1993). Are kids less likely to be exposed to violence by going to the movies? No. One study found that virtually all G-rated animated films have scenes of

What do we *learn* from violence in video games and other media? The research suggests that we learn a great deal—not only aggressive skills, but also the idea that violence is the normal state of affairs.

violence (Yokota & Thompson, 2000). Other media that contain violence include movies, music, music videos, advertising, video games, the Internet, and comic books.

Why all this violence? Simple: Violence sells. But does violence do more than sell? That is, does media violence cause real violence? If so, what can parents and educators do to prevent the fictional from spilling over into the real world?

Bandura: Research on the Effects of Violence in the Media

A classic experiment by Bandura, Ross, and Ross (1963) suggests the powerful influence of televised models. One group of preschool children observed a film of an adult model hitting and kicking an inflated Bobo doll, while a control group saw an aggression-free film. The experimental and control children were then left alone in a room with the same doll as hidden observers recorded their behavior. The children who had observed the aggressive model showed significantly more aggressive behavior toward the doll themselves (see Figure 5.8). Many children imitated bizarre attack behaviors devised for the model in this experiment—behaviors that they would not have thought up themselves.

The children exposed to the aggressive model also showed aggressive behavior patterns that had not been modeled. Observing the model, therefore, not only led

FIGURE 5.8 | Classic Research on the Imitation of Aggressive Models

Albert Bandura and his colleagues showed that children frequently imitate the aggressive behavior that they observe. In the top row, an adult model strikes a clown doll. The lower rows show a boy and a girl imitating the aggressive behavior.

to imitation of modeled behavior patterns but also apparently disinhibited previously learned aggressive responses. The results were similar whether children observed human or cartoon models on film.

Consensus on the Effects of Violence in the Media?

In any event, most organizations of health professionals agree that media violence does contribute to aggression (Bushman & Anderson, 2007). This relationship has been found for girls and boys of different ages, social classes, ethnic groups, and cultures (Huesmann et al., 2003). Consider a number of ways that depictions of violence make such a contribution (Anderson et al., 2010; Bushman & Anderson, 2007):

- *Observational learning*: Children learn from observation. Television violence supplies models of aggressive "skills," which children may acquire. In fact, children are more likely to imitate what others do than to heed what they say.

- *Disinhibition*: Punishment inhibits behavior. Conversely, media violence may disinhibit aggressive behavior, especially when media characters "get away" with violence or are rewarded for it.

- *Increased emotional arousal*: Media violence and aggressive video games increase viewers' level of emotional arousal. It "works them up." We are more likely to be aggressive when we are highly aroused.

- *Priming of aggressive thoughts and memories*: Media violence triggers aggressive ideas and memories.

- *Habituation*: We become used to repeated stimuli. Repeated exposure to media violence may decrease viewers' sensitivity to real violence. If children perceive violence as the norm, they may be more tolerant of it and place less value on restraining aggressive urges.

Violent video games are also connected with aggressive behavior, including juvenile delinquency (Dubow et al., 2010). Playing violent video games increases aggressive thoughts and behavior in the laboratory

(Anderson et al., 2010). However, males are relatively more likely than females to act aggressively after playing violent video games and are more likely to see the world as a hostile place. Students who obtain higher grades are also less likely to behave aggressively following exposure to violent video games. Thus, cultural stereotyping of males and females, possible biological sex differences, and moderating variables like academic achievement also figure into the effects of media violence.

There seems to be a circular relationship between exposure to media violence and aggressive behavior (Anderson et al., 2010). Yes, TV violence and violent video games contribute to aggressive behavior, but aggressive youngsters are also more likely to seek it out. Figure 5.9 explores the possible connections between TV violence and aggressive behavior.

The family also affects the likelihood that children will imitate media violence. Studies find that parental substance abuse, paternal physical punishments, and single parenting contribute to the likelihood of aggression in early childhood (Brook et al., 2001; Gupta et al.,

FIGURE 5.9 | What Are the Connections Between Media Violence and Aggressive Behavior?

Does media violence cause aggressive behavior? Do aggressive children prefer to tune in to violent shows? Or do other factors, such as personality traits that create a disposition toward aggression, contribute both to aggressive behavior and the interest in media violence?

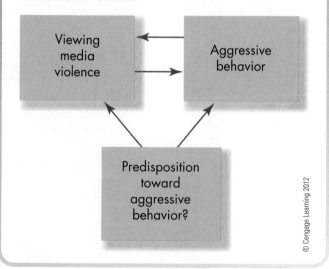

2001). Parental rejection and use of physical punishment further increase the likelihood of aggression in children (Eron, 1982). These family factors suggest that the parents of aggressive children may be absent or unlikely to help young children understand that the kinds of socially inappropriate behaviors they see in the media are not for them. A harsh home life may also confirm the TV viewer's or game player's vision of the world as a violent place.

If children believe violence to be inappropriate for them, they will be less likely to act aggressively, even if they have acquired aggressive skills from exposure to the media or other sources. It would be of little use to talk about learning if we couldn't remember what we learn from second to second or from day to day. In the next chapter, we turn our attention to memory. In Chapter 8, we see how learning is intertwined with thinking, language, and intelligence.

Teaching Children Not to Imitate Media Violence

Children are going to be exposed to media violence—if not in Saturday-morning cartoon shows, then in evening dramas and in the news. Or they'll hear about violence from friends or watch other children get into fights. If all those sources of violence were somehow hidden from view, they would learn about violence in *Hamlet*, *Macbeth*, and the Bible. The notion of preventing children from being exposed to violent models may be impractical.

What, then, should be done? Parents and educators can do many things to tone down the impact of media violence. Children who watch violent shows may act less aggressively when they are informed that:

- The violent behavior they observe in the media does not represent the behavior of most people.
- The apparently aggressive behaviors they watch are not real. They reflect camera tricks, special effects, and stunts.
- Most people resolve conflicts by nonviolent means.
- The real-life consequences of violence are harmful to the victim and often to the aggressor.

Despite our history of evolutionary forces, and despite the fact that in most species, successful aggression usually wins individuals the right to transmit their genes to future generations, humans are thinking beings. If children consider violence to be inappropriate for them, they will be less likely to act aggressively, even when they have acquired aggressive skills from exposure to the media or other sources.

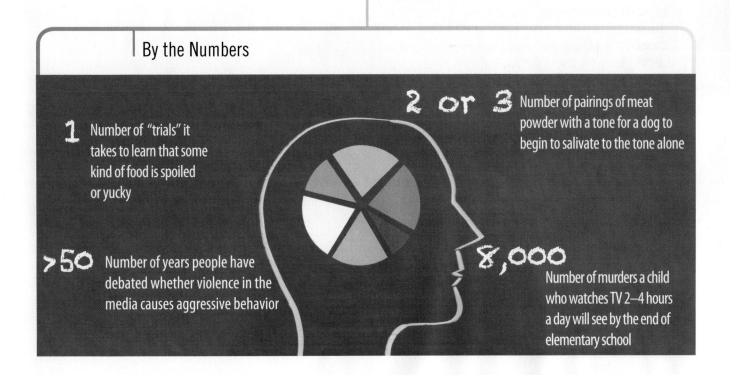

By the Numbers

1 Number of "trials" it takes to learn that some kind of food is spoiled or yucky

2 or 3 Number of pairings of meat powder with a tone for a dog to begin to salivate to the tone alone

>50 Number of years people have debated whether violence in the media causes aggressive behavior

8,000 Number of murders a child who watches TV 2–4 hours a day will see by the end of elementary school

STUDY TOOLS ▶ 5

Ready to study? In the book, you can:
- ❍ Review what you've read with Fill-Ins and Multiple Choice quizzes (below).
- ❍ Rip out Chapter Review card (in the back).

Or you can go online to CourseMate at www.cengagebrain.com for these resources:
- ❍ Complete Practices Quizzes to prepare for tests.
- ❍ Review Key Terms Flash Cards (online or print).
- ❍ Play games to master concepts.

FILL-INS

Answers can be found in the back of the book, starting on page 368.

1. A response to an unconditioned stimulus is called a(n) _____ response.

2. A response to a conditioned stimulus is termed a(n) _____ response.

3. Repeated presentation of a CS (such as a tone) without the UCS (such as meat) will_____ the CR (salivation).

4. Extinguished responses often show _____ recovery as a function of the passage of time.

5. John B. Watson and Rosalie Rayner used conditioning to teach a boy who is known as "Little _____" to fear rats.

6. In the behavior-therapy method of _____, a client is continuously exposed to a fear-evoking stimulus until the fear response is extinguished.

7. _____ reinforcers increase the probability that operants will occur when they are removed.

8. In a _____-_____ schedule, a specific amount of time must elapse since a previous correct response before reinforcement again becomes available.

9. _____ learning breaks down learning tasks into small steps and reinforces correct performance of each step.

10. According to _____ theory, learning occurs because a CS indicates that the UCS is likely to follow.

1. According to behaviorists, _____ is a relatively permanent change in an organism's behavior that occurs because of experience.

   a. extinction
   b. learning
   c. acquisition
   d. higher-order conditioning

2. While attempting to identify neural receptors that trigger salivary glands, Ivan Pavlov inadvertently found that responses can be learned through

   a. operant conditioning.
   b. observation.
   c. instinct.
   d. association.

3. Roberto kept seeing signs on the highway advertising Pizza Hut. He started to salivate at the possibility of having a pizza. The signs were

   a. unconditioned stimuli.
   b. unconditioned responses.
   c. conditioned stimuli.
   d. conditioned responses.

4. Johnny was tormented in the schoolyard every day by a bully with bright red frizzy hair. One day, Johnny's father brought his boss, Mr. Dale, home. The boss had bright red frizzy hair, and Johnny ran to his room, crying. Mr. Dale's hair functioned as a _____, and Johnny's fear was a _____.

   a. US; CR
   c. CS; CR
   b. US; UR
   d. CR; CS

5. Spotted Zebras learn to stop going to a particular water hole after approaching it several times and finding that it is dry. However, after a month or two passes, they may return to the water hole. Learning to stop going to the water hole because it is dry, but then returning to it after time passes, is an example of _____ followed by _____.

   a. extinction, spontaneous recovery
   b. shaping, successive approximations
   c. discrimination training, generalization
   d. contingency theory, latent learning

6. Which of the following best illustrates operant conditioning according to Skinner?

   a. A dog salivates at the sound of a dinner bell.
   b. A cat comes running when it hears the sound of the can opener.
   c. A dolphin is given a fish every time it jumps through a hoop.
   d. The mating behavior of salmon.

7. When a behavior is followed by negative reinforcement, the behavior is likely to

   a. be extinguished.
   c. decrease.
   b. be suppressed.
   d. increase.

8. Slot machines tend to keep gamblers playing by using a _____ schedule of reinforcement.

   a. fixed-interval
   b. variable-interval
   c. fixed-ratio
   d. variable-ratio

9. Professor Fournier gives a quiz every Monday. His students would then tend to _____ because they are on a _____ schedule of reinforcement.

   a. start studying immediately after the quiz; fixed-ratio
   b. study regularly through the week; fixed-interval
   c. study on Sunday nights; fixed-interval
   d. pay attention in class; variable-interval

10. Johnny watches TV violence for an hour or two a day, but he is not violent outside the home. Then one day Billy attacks him on the way home from school, and Johnny imitates the behavior he saw on TV to fight Billy off and teach Billy never to attack him again. Although Johnny had not shown violent behavior until he was attacked, we can assume that when watching TV, he was engaging in

    a. latent learning.
    b. shaping.
    c. discrimination training.
    d. operant conditioning.

gabczi/Shutterstock.com

LEARNING OUTCOMES

6-1 Define memory and differentiate between types of memories

6-2 Explain the processes of memory

6-3 Explain the stages of memory

6-4 Identify contributors to forgetting

6-5 Describe the biological aspects of memory

 STUDY TOOLS ▶ After you read the chapter, go to the Study Tools at the end of the chapter, page 158.

CHAPTER 6

MEMORY:
Remembrance of Things Past—and Future

Jeff would never forget his sudden loss of memory. He watched in horror as his cell phone slipped from his pocket and fell to the floor of the Blockbuster store in Boston. Before he could grab it, it shattered into pieces. A New York college student, Jeff experienced the trauma of phone loss on his winter break.

Why was the loss traumatic? Why was it a memory problem? Simple: There was no way for Jeff to retrieve his phone book. "I was at the store and it was snowing out and I suddenly realized that I had no way of getting in touch with anyone," he explains (Metz, 2005). Jeff now copies every cell-phone entry in a little black book—made of paper. Other people back up their phone books—and their pictures and downloads—on servers provided by cellular telephone operating companies or cellphone manufacturers. iPhones have backups available. Verizon's method is called Backup Assistant. Most people transfer their memories from their old cellphone to the new one when they make a change.

What's the problem with remembering all those phone numbers? The answer lies partly in their length. Psychologist George Miller (1956) researched the amount of information people can keep in mind at once, and he found that the average person is comfortable with digesting about seven digits at a time. Most people have little trouble recalling five pieces of information, as in a ZIP code. Some can remember nine, which is, for most, an upper limit. So seven pieces of information, plus or minus one or two, is the "magic" number.

This chapter is all about the "backup assistant" in your brain—your memory. Without memory, there is no past. Without memory, experience is trivial and learning is lost. Let's see what psychologists have learned about the ways in which we remember things—other than keying them into a cellphone's memory chip.

> *Without memory, there is no past.*

TRUTH OR *FICTION*

WHAT DO YOU THINK? FOLKLORE, COMMON SENSE, OR NONSENSE? CIRCLE THE T FOR "TRUTH" OR THE F FOR "FICTION," AND CHECK THE ACCURACY OF YOUR ANSWERS AS YOU READ THROUGH THE CHAPTER.

T	F	A WOMAN WHO COULD NOT REMEMBER WHO SHE WAS AUTOMATICALLY DIALED HER MOTHER'S NUMBER WHEN THE POLICE GAVE HER A TELEPHONE.
T	F	LEARNING MUST BE MEANINGFUL IF WE ARE TO REMEMBER IT.
T	F	IF YOU CAN SEE, YOU HAVE A PHOTOGRAPHIC MEMORY.
T	F	ALL OF OUR EXPERIENCES ARE PERMANENTLY IMPRINTED ON THE BRAIN, SO THE PROPER STIMULUS CAN CAUSE US TO REMEMBER THEM EXACTLY.
T	F	IT MAY BE EASIER FOR YOU TO RECALL THE NAME OF YOUR FIRST-GRADE TEACHER THAN THE NAME OF SOMEONE YOU JUST MET AT A PARTY.
T	F	YOU MAY ALWAYS RECALL WHERE YOU WERE AND WHAT YOU WERE DOING ON THE MORNING OF SEPTEMBER 11, 2001.
T	F	IF YOU STUDY WITH THE STEREO ON, YOU WOULD PROBABLY DO BETTER TO TAKE THE TEST WITH THE STEREO ON.
T	F	LEARNING SPANISH CAN MAKE IT HARDER TO REMEMBER FRENCH—AND VICE VERSA.

explicit memory
memory that clearly and distinctly expresses (explicates) specific information

episodic memory
memories of events that happen to a person or that take place in the person's presence

semantic memory
general knowledge, as opposed to episodic memory

6-1 Kinds of Memory

Jeff remembered a thing he had personally done, like drop his cellphone in Boston on a blustery day in January. Remembering dropping one's cellphone is an *episodic memory*—a memory of an event in one's life. According to psychologists who have extensively researched memory, episodic memory is one kind of memory system (Carver & Cluver, 2009; Dickerson & Eichenbaum, 2009). And when I learned of Jeff's experience, I tried to remind myself repeatedly not to forget to jot down notes about it and write it up as soon as I could. (I was trying to jog my *prospective memory*—remembering to do something in the future.) Let's consider several memory systems.

6-1a EXPLICIT MEMORY

Explicit memory—also referred to as *declarative memory*—is memory for specific information. Things that are *explicit* are clear, or clearly stated or explained. The use of the term *declarative* indicates that these memories state or reveal (that is, *declare*) specific information. The information may be autobiographical or refer to general knowledge.

Psychologist Endel Tulving (1985) describes two kinds of explicit memories: episodic and semantic. They are identified according to the type of information they hold.

Episodic Memory (I remember . . .)

Episodic memories are types of explicit memories. They are memories of the things that happen to us or take place in our presence (Dickerson & Eichenbaum, 2009; Grillon et al., 2010). Episodic memory is also referred to as *autobiographical memory*. Your memories of what you ate for breakfast and of what your professor said in class today are episodic memories. We tend to use the phrase "I remember …" when we are referring to episodic memories, as in "I remember the blizzard of 2004."

Semantic Memory (I know . . .)

General knowledge is referred to as **semantic memory**—another kind of explicit memory. *Semantics* concerns meanings. You can "know" that the United States has 50 states without visiting them and personally adding them up. You "know" who authored *Hamlet*, although you were not looking over Shakespeare's shoulder as he did so. These are examples of semantic memory.

Five Memory Challenges

Let's challenge your memory. This is not an actual memory test of the sort used by psychologists to determine whether people's memory functioning is within normal limits. Instead, it will provide you with some insight into how your memory works and may also be fun.

Directions: Find four sheets of blank paper and number them 1 through 4. Also use a watch with a second hand. Then follow these instructions:

1. Following are 10 letters. Look at them for 15 seconds. Later in the chapter I will ask you if you can write them on sheet number 1. (No cheating! Don't do it now.)

THUNSTOFAM

2. Look at these nine figures for 30 seconds. Then try to draw them in the proper sequence on sheet number 2, right after you have finished looking at them. (We'll talk about your drawings later.)

3. Look at the following list of 17 letters for 60 seconds and then see whether you can reproduce it on sheet number 3.

GMC-BSI-BMA-TTC-IAF-BI

4. Which of these pennies is an accurate reproduction of the Lincoln penny you see every day? This time there's nothing to draw on another sheet; just circle or put a checkmark by the penny that you think resembles the ones you throw in the back of the drawer.

A   B   C   D   E   F

5. Examine the following drawings for 1 minute. Then copy the *names* of the figures on sheet number 4. When you're finished, just keep reading. Soon I'll be asking you to draw those figures.

eyeglasses   hourglass   seven   gun

That's it. You'll find out about the results of these memory challenges as you read through the chapter.

Your future recollection that there are several memory systems is more likely to be semantic than episodic. That is, you are more likely to "know" that there are several types of memory than to recall where you were and how you were sitting. We are more likely to say "I know …" in reference to semantic memories, as in "I *know* about—" (or "I heard about—") "—the blizzard of 1898." Put another way, you may *remember* that you wrote to your mother, but you *know* that Shakespeare wrote *Hamlet*.

6-1b IMPLICIT MEMORY

Implicit memory—also referred to as *nondeclarative memory*—is memory of how to perform a task. It is the act itself, doing something, like riding a bike, accessing your cellphone contacts list, and texting a message (Schacter et al., 1993). Implicit memories are suggested (or implied) but not plainly stated or verbally expressed. Implicit memories are illustrated by the things that people *do* but not by the things they state clearly. Implicit memories involve procedures and skills, cognitive and physical, and are also referred to as *procedural* or *skill memories.*

Implicit memories can endure even when we have not used them for years. Getting to class "by habit"—without paying attention to landmarks or directions—is another instance of implicit memory. If someone asked you what 2 times 2 is, the number 4 would probably "pop" into mind without conscious calculation. After going over the alphabet or multiplication tables hundreds of times, our memory of them becomes automatic or implicit. We need not focus on them to use them.

Your memory of the alphabet or the multiplication tables is the result of a great deal of repetition that makes associations automatic, a phenomenon that psychologists refer to as **priming**. Studies involving brain imaging reveal that priming makes it possible for people to carry out mental tasks with less neural activity (Koenig et al., 2008; Spencer et al., 2009). Years of priming help people make complete words out of the following word fragments (Friedrich et al., 2009; Schacter et al., 2007). Even though the cues in the following fragments are limited, you might make them into words:

PYGY TXT BUFL

Sample answers are "pygmy," "text," and "buffalo." Can you think of others?

Daniel Schacter (1992) illustrates implicit memory with the story of a woman with amnesia who was wandering the streets. The police picked her up and found that she could not remember who she was and that she had no identification. After fruitless interviewing, the police hit on the idea of asking her to dial phone numbers—just any number at all. When asked for the phone numbers of people she knew, she

had no answer. She could not *declare* her mother's phone number. She could not make the number *explicit*. She could not even remember her mother's name, or whether she had a mother. But dialing her mother's phone number was a habit, and she did it "on automatic pilot." We can assume that she had been *primed* for this task by dialing the number hundreds of times. Implicit memory reveals the effects of experience when we are not specifically trying to recall information.

6-1b RETROSPECTIVE MEMORY VERSUS PROSPECTIVE MEMORY

Retrospective memory is the recalling of information that has been previously learned. *Episodic, semantic,* and *implicit memories* involve remembering things that were learned. **Prospective memory** refers to remembering to do things in the future, such as remembering to pay your bills or to withdraw some cash.

Most of us have had failures of prospective memory in which we felt we were supposed to do something but couldn't remember what. Prospective memory may fail when we are preoccupied, distracted, or "stressed out" about time (Knight & Titov, 2009).

There are various kinds of prospective memory tasks. For example, *habitual tasks* such as getting to class on time are easier to remember than occasional tasks such as meeting someone for coffee at an arbitrary time (Henry et al., 2004). But motivation also plays a role. You are more likely to remember the coffee date if the person you are meeting excites you. Psychologists also

implicit memory
memory that is suggested (implied) but not plainly expressed, as illustrated in the things that people *do* but do not state clearly

priming
the activation of specific associations in memory, often as a result of repetition and without making a conscious effort to access the memory

retrospective memory
memory for past events, activities, and learning experiences, as shown by explicit (episodic and semantic) and implicit memories

prospective memory
memory to perform an act in the future, as at a certain time or when a certain event occurs

© Ocean/Corbis

encoding
modifying information so that it can be placed in memory; the first stage of information processing

storage
the maintenance of information over time; the second stage of information processing

distinguish between event-based and time-based prospective memory tasks (Fortin et al., 2002). *Event-based tasks* are triggered by events, such as remembering to take one's medicine at breakfast or to brush one's teeth after eating. *Time-based tasks* are to be performed at a certain time or after a certain amount of time has elapsed between occurrences, such as tuning in to a favorite news program at 7:30 p.m. or taking a pill every four hours (Marsh et al., 2005).

An age-related decline takes place in retrospective and prospective memories (Old & Naveh-Benjamin, 2008). Generally speaking, the decline in older adults may be related to their speed of cognitive processing rather than the "loss" of information per se. In the case of prospective memory, older adults appear about equally aware of specific cues or reminders as young adults; however, it takes them longer to respond to the cues or reminders (Old & Naveh-Benjamin, 2008). That is, if they meet with a friend, they are likely to remember that they were supposed to ask something, but it may take longer for them to remember the particular question.

Moods and attitudes affect prospective memory (Villa & Abeles, 2000). For example, depressed people are less likely to push to remind themselves to do what they intend to do (Rude et al., 1999).

Before moving to the next section, why don't you turn to the piece of paper on which you wrote the names of the four figures—that is, sheet 4—and draw them from memory as exactly as you can. Hold on to the drawings. We'll talk about them soon.

(6-2) Processes of Memory

Both psychologists and computer scientists speak of processing information. Think of using a computer to write a term paper. Once the system is up and operating, you begin to enter information. You can enter information into the computer's memory by, for example, typing alphanumeric characters on a keyboard or—in the case of voice recognition technology—speaking. But if you were to do some major surgery on your computer and open up its memory, you wouldn't find these

characters or sounds inside it. This is because the computer is programmed to change the characters or sounds—the information you have entered—into a form that can be placed in its electronic memory. Similarly, when we perceive information, we must change it into a form that can be remembered if we are to place it in our memory.

6-2a ENCODING

Information about the outside world reaches our senses in the form of physical and chemical stimuli. The first stage of information processing is changing information so that we can place it in memory: **encoding**. When we encode information, we transform it into psychological formats that can be represented mentally. To do so, we commonly use visual, acoustic, and semantic codes.

Let's illustrate the uses of coding by referring to the list of letters you first saw in the section on challenges to memory. Try to write the letters on sheet number 1. Go on, take a minute, and then come back.

If you had used a *visual code* to try to remember the list, you would have mentally represented it as a picture. That is, you would have maintained—or attempted to maintain—a mental image of the letters.

You may also have decided to read the list of letters to yourself—that is, to silently say them in sequence: "t," "h," "u," and so on. By so doing, you would have been using an *acoustic code*, or representing the stimuli as a sequence of sounds. You may also have read the list as a three-syllable word, "thun-sto-fam." This is an acoustic code, but it also involves the "meaning" of the letters, in the sense that you are interpreting the list as a word. This approach has elements of a semantic code.

Semantic codes represent stimuli in terms of their meaning. Our 10 letters were meaningless in and of themselves. However, they can also serve as an acronym—a term made up of the first letters of a phrase that is pronounced as a word—for the familiar phrase "THe UNited STates OF AMerica." This observation lends them meaning.

6-2b STORAGE

The second memory process is *storage*. **Storage** means maintaining information over time. If you were given the task of storing the list of letters—that is, told

> **FICTION** 👉 LEARNING NEED NOT ALWAYS BE MEANINGFUL IF WE ARE TO REMEMBER IT. MAINTENANCE REHEARSAL OFTEN WORKS AS WELL.

to remember it—how would you attempt to place it in storage? One way would be by **maintenance rehearsal**—by mentally repeating the list, or saying it to yourself.

You could also encode the list of letters by relating it to something that you already know. This coding is called **elaborative rehearsal**. You are "elaborating" or extending the semantic meaning of the letters you are trying to remember. For example, as mentioned above, the list of 10 letters is an acronym for "The United States of America." That is, you take the first two letters of each of the words in the phrase and string them together to make up the 10 letters of THUNSTOFAM. If you had recognized this, storage of the list of letters might have been almost instantaneous, and it would probably have been permanent. But enough maintenance rehearsal can do the job.

6-2c RETRIEVAL

The third memory process is *retrieval*. **Retrieval** of stored information means locating it and returning it to consciousness. With well-known information such as our names and occupations, retrieval is effortless and rapid. But when we are trying to remember large amounts of information, or information that is not perfectly understood, retrieval can be difficult or fail. It is easiest to retrieve information stored in a computer by using the name of the file. Similarly, retrieval of information from our memories requires knowledge of the proper *retrieval cues*.

If you had encoded THUNSTOFAM as a three-syllable word, your retrieval strategy would involve recollection of the word and rules for decoding. In other words, you would say the "word" *thun-sto-fam* and then decode it by spelling it out. You might err in that "thun" sounds like "thumb" and "sto" could also be spelled "stow." However, using the semantic code, or recognition of the acronym for "The United States of America," could lead to flawless recollection.

I predicted that you would immediately and permanently store the list if you recognized it as an acronym. Here, too, there would be recollection (of the name of a nation) and rules for decoding. That is, to "remember" the 10 letters, you would have to envision the phrase ("The United States of America") and read off the first two letters of each word. In this case, you are actually reconstructing the list of 10 letters.

But what if you were not able to remember the list of 10 letters? What would have gone wrong? In terms of the three processes of memory, it could be that you had (a) not encoded the list in a useful way, (b) not entered the encoded information into storage, or (c) stored the information but forgotten the cues for remembering it—such as the phrase "The United States of America" or the rule for decoding the phrase.

You may have noticed that we have come a long way into this chapter, but I have not yet *defined* memory. No apologies—we weren't ready. Now that we have explored some basic concepts, let's give it a try: **Memory** is the processes by which information is encoded, stored, and retrieved.

6-3 Stages of Memory

William James (1890) was intrigued by the fact that some memories are unreliable. They would "go in one ear and out the other," while other memories stuck for a lifetime. The world is a dazzling array of sights and

"THE STREAM OF THOUGHT FLOWS ON, BUT MOST OF ITS ELEMENTS FALL INTO THE BOTTOMLESS PIT OF OBLIVION. OF SOME, NO ELEMENT SURVIVES THE INSTANT OF THEIR PASSAGE. OF OTHERS, IT IS CONFINED TO A FEW MOMENTS, HOURS, OR DAYS. OTHERS, AGAIN, LEAVE VESTIGES WHICH ARE INDESTRUCTIBLE, AND BY MEANS OF WHICH THEY MAY BE RECALLED AS LONG AS LIFE ENDURES."

—WILLIAM JAMES

maintenance rehearsal
mental repetition of information to keep it in memory

elaborative rehearsal
the kind of coding in which new information is related to information that is already known

retrieval
the location of stored information and its return to consciousness; the third stage of information processing

memory
the processes by which information is encoded, stored, and retrieved

sensory memory
the type or stage of memory first encountered by a stimulus; sensory memory holds impressions briefly, but long enough so that series of perceptions are psychologically continuous

sounds and other sources of sensory information, but only some of it is remembered. Psychologists Richard Atkinson and Richard Shiffrin (1968) suggested a model for how some information is lost immediately, other information is held briefly, and still other information is held for a lifetime. As shown in Figure 6.1, they proposed three stages of memory that determine whether (and how long) information is retained: *sensory memory*, *short-term memory* (STM), and *long-term memory* (LTM).

6-3a SENSORY MEMORY

When we look at a visual stimulus, our impressions may seem fluid enough. Actually, however, they consist of a series of eye fixations referred to as *saccadic eye movements*. These movements jump from one point to another about four times each second. Yet the visual sensations seem continuous, or streamlike, because of **sensory memory**. Sensory memory is the type or stage of memory that is first encountered by a stimulus. Although sensory memory holds impressions briefly, it is long enough so that a series of perceptions seem to be connected.

FIGURE 6.1 | Three Stages of Memory: The Atkinson–Shiffrin Model

The Atkinson–Shiffrin model proposes that there are three stages of memory: (a) sensory memory, (b) short-term memory, and (c) long-term memory. Part A shows that sensory information impacts on the registers of the sensory memory. Memory traces are held briefly in sensory memory before decaying. If we attend to the information, much of it can be transferred to short-term memory (STM). Part B: Information may be maintained in STM through maintenance rehearsal or elaborative rehearsal. Otherwise, it may decay or be displaced. Part C: Once information is transferred to long-term memory (LTM), it may be filed away indefinitely. However, if the information in LTM is organized poorly, or if we cannot find cues to retrieve it, it can be lost.

© Cengage Learning 2012

To understand the functioning of sensory memory, let's return to our list of letters: THUNSTOFAM. If the list were flashed on a screen for a fraction of a second, the visual impression, or **memory trace**, of the stimulus would also last for only a fraction of a second afterward. Psychologists speak of the memory trace of the list as being held in a visual *sensory register*.

If the letters had been flashed on a screen for, say, 1/10th of a second, your ability to remember them on the basis of sensory memory alone would be limited. Your memory would be based on a single eye fixation, and the trace of the image would vanish before a single second had passed. A century ago, psychologist William McDougall (1904) engaged in research in which he showed people one to 12 letters arranged in rows—just long enough to allow a single eye fixation. Under these conditions, people could typically remember only four or five letters. Thus, recollection of THUNSTOFAM, a list of 10 letters arranged in a single row, would probably depend on whether one had encoded it so that it could be processed further.

George Sperling (1960) modified McDougall's experimental method and showed that there is a difference between what people can see and what they can report. McDougall had used a *whole-report procedure,* in which people were asked to report every letter they saw in the array. Sperling used a modified *partial-report procedure,* in which people were asked to report the contents of one of three rows of letters. In a typical procedure, Sperling flashed three rows of letters like the following on a screen for 50 milliseconds (1/20th of a second):

A G R E

V L S B

N K B T

Using the whole-report procedure, people could report an average of four letters from the entire display (one out of three). But if immediately after presenting the display Sperling pointed an arrow at a row he wanted viewers to report, they usually reported most of the letters in the row successfully.

"The true art of memory is the art of attention."

—DR. SAMUEL JOHNSON

If Sperling presented six letters arrayed in two rows, people could usually report either row without error. If people were flashed three rows of four letters each—a total of 12—they reported correctly an average of three of four letters in the designated row, suggesting that about nine of the 12 letters had been perceived.

Sperling found that the amount of time that elapsed before he pointed to the row to be reported affected people's memory. If he delayed pointing for a few fractions of a second after showing the letters, people were less successful in reporting the letters in the row. If he allowed a full second to elapse, the arrow did not help people remember at all. Sperling concluded that the memory trace of visual stimuli *decays* within a second (see Figure 6.1). With a single eye fixation, people can *see* most of a display of 12 letters clearly, as shown by their ability to immediately read off most of the letters in a designated row. Yet as fractions of a second are elapsing, the memory trace of the letters is fading. By the time a full second elapses, the trace is gone.

Iconic Memory

Psychologists believe we possess a sensory register for each sense. The mental representations of visual stimuli are referred to as **icons**. The sensory register that holds icons is labeled **iconic memory**. Iconic memories are accurate, photographic memories. If you can see and are not neurologically impaired, you have a "photographic memory." But such memories are brief. What most of us usually think of as a photographic memory—the ability to retain exact mental representations of visual stimuli over long periods—is technically termed **eidetic imagery**. Only a few people are capable of eidetic imagery.

memory trace
an assumed change in the nervous system that reflects the impression made by a stimulus

icon
a mental representation of a visual stimulus that is held briefly in sensory memory

iconic memory
the sensory register that briefly holds mental representations of visual stimuli

eidetic imagery
the maintenance of detailed visual memories over several minutes

Iconic Memory and Saccadic Eye Movements

As mentioned previously, saccadic eye movements occur about four times a second. But iconic memory holds icons for up to a second. For this reason, the flow of visual information seems smooth and continuous. Your impression that the words you are reading flow across the page, rather than jumping across in spurts, is a product of your iconic memory. Similarly, motion pictures present 16 to 22 separate frames, or still images, each second, but iconic memory allows you to perceive the imagery in the film as being seamless (Demeyer et al., 2009).

Echoic Memory

Mental representations of sounds, or auditory stimuli, are called **echoes**. **Echoic memory** is the sensory register that holds echoes.

The memory traces of auditory stimuli—echoes—can last for several seconds, many times longer than the traces of visual stimuli (icons). This difference is one of the reasons that acoustic codes aid in the retention of information that has been presented visually—or why saying the letters or syllables of THUNSTOFAM makes the list easier to remember.

❿ 6-3b SHORT-TERM MEMORY

Imagine you are completing a writing assignment, and you key or speak words and phrases into your word-processing program. They appear on your monitor as a sign that your computer has them in *memory*. Your word-processing program allows you to add words, delete words, check whether they are spelled correctly, add images, and move paragraphs from place to place. Although you can manipulate the information in your computer's memory, it isn't saved. It hasn't been entered into storage. If the program or the computer crashes, the information is gone. The computer's memory is a short-term affair. To maintain a long-term connection with the information, you have to save it. Saving it means giving it a name—hopefully, a name that you will remember so that you can later find and retrieve the information—and instructing your computer to save it (keep it in storage until told otherwise).

If you focus on a stimulus in the sensory register, you will tend to retain it in your own **short-term memory**—also referred to as **working memory**—for a minute or so after the trace of the stimulus decays. As one researcher describes it, "Working memory is the mental glue that links a thought through time from its beginning to its end" (Goldman-Rakic, 1995). When you are given a new phone number and write it down or immediately dial the number, you are retaining the number in your short-term memory. When you are told the name of someone at a party and then use that name immediately in addressing that person, you are retaining the name in short-term memory. In short-term memory, the image tends to fade significantly after 10 to 12 seconds if it is not repeated or rehearsed. It is possible to focus on maintaining a visual image in the short-term memory, but it is more common to encode visual stimuli as sounds, or auditory stimuli. Then the sounds can be rehearsed, or repeated.

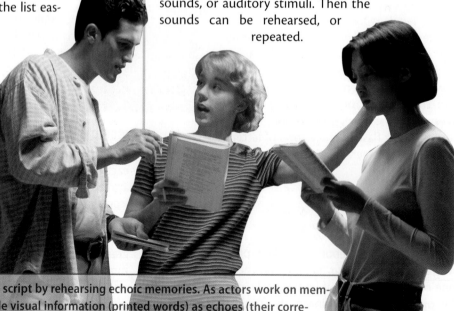

These actors are memorizing a script by rehearsing echoic memories. As actors work on memorizing scripts, they first encode visual information (printed words) as echoes (their corresponding sounds within the brain). Then they commit the echoes to memory by rehearsing (repeating) them, referring back to the visual information as necessary. Eventually, the lines of other actors become cues that trigger memory of an actor's own lines.

Comstock/Jupiterimages

Once information is in our short-term memories, we can work on it. Like the information in the word-processing program, we can manipulate it. But it isn't necessarily saved. If we don't do something to save—such as write down a new telephone number or key it into your cellphone's contact list—it can be gone forever. You need to rehearse new information to "save" it, but you may need only the proper cue to retrieve information from long-term memory.

Let's now return to the task of remembering the first list of letters in the challenges to memory at the beginning of the chapter. If you had encoded the letters as the three-syllable "word" THUN-STO-FAM, you would probably have recalled them by mentally rehearsing (saying to yourself) the three-syllable "word" and then spelling it out from the sounds. A few minutes later, if someone asked whether the letters had been uppercase (THUNSTOFAM) or lowercase (thunstofam), you might not have been able to answer with confidence. You used an acoustic code to help recall the list, and uppercase and lowercase letters sound alike.

Because it can be pronounced, THUNSTOFAM is not too difficult to retain in short-term memory. But what if the list of letters had been TBXLFNTSDK? This list of letters cannot be pronounced as it is. You would have to find a complex acronym to code these letters, and do so within a fraction of a second—most likely an impossible task. To aid recall, you would probably choose to try to repeat the letters rapidly—to read each one as many times as possible before the memory trace fades. You might visualize each letter as you say it and try to get back to it (that is, to run through the entire list) before it decays.

Let's assume that you encoded the letters as sounds and then rehearsed the sounds. When asked to report the list, you might mistakenly say T-V-X-L-F-N-T-S-T-K. This would be an understandable error because the incorrect *V* and *T* sounds are similar, respectively, to the correct *B* and *D* sounds.

The Serial-Position Effect

If asked to recall the list of letters TBXLFNTSDK, you would be likely to recall the first and last letters in the series, *T* and *K*, more accurately than the others. The tendency to recall the first and last items in a series is known as the **serial-position effect**. This effect may occur because we pay more attention to the first and last stimuli in a series. They serve as the visual or auditory boundaries for the other stimuli. In addition, the first items are likely to be rehearsed more frequently (repeated more times) than other items. The last items are likely to have been rehearsed most recently and hence are most likely to be retained in short-term memory.

Chunking

Rapidly rehearsing 10 meaningless letters is not an easy task. With TBXLFNTSDK there are 10 discrete elements, or **chunks**, of information that must be kept in short-term memory. When we encode THUNSTOFAM as three syllables, there are only three chunks to memorize at once—a memory task that is much easier on the digestion.

As noted earlier, psychologist George Miller (1956) found that the average person is comfortable with remembering about seven integers at a time, the number of integers in a telephone number. Businesses pay the phone company hefty premiums so that they can attain numbers with two or three zeroes or repeated digits—for example, 592-2000 or 272-3333. These numbers include fewer chunks of information and so are easier to remember. Customer recollection of business phone numbers increases sales. A financial services company might use the toll-free number CALL-IRA, which reduces the task to two chunks of information that also happen to be meaningfully related (semantically coded) to the nature of the business.

Return to the third challenge to memory presented earlier. Were you able to remember the six groups of letters (GMC-BSI-BMA-TTC-IAF-BI)? Would your task have been simpler if you had grouped them differently? How about moving the dashes forward by a letter, so that they read GM-CBS-IBM-ATT-CIA-FBI? If we do this, we have the same list of letters, but we also have six chunks of information that can be coded semantically (according to what they mean). You may have also been able to generate the list by remembering a rule, such as "big corporations and government agencies."

Reconsider the second challenge to memory presented earlier. You were asked to remember nine chunks of visual information. Perhaps you could have used the acoustic codes "L" and "Square" for chunks three and five, but no obvious codes are available for the seven other chunks. Now look at Figure 6.2. If you had recognized that the elements in the challenge could be arranged as the familiar tic-tac-toe grid, remembering the nine elements might have required two chunks of information. The first would have been the mental image of the grid, and the second would have been the rule for decoding: Each element corresponds to the shape of a section of the grid if read like words on a page (from upper left to lower right). The number sequence 1 through 9 would not in itself present a problem, because you learned this series by rote many years ago and have rehearsed it in countless calculations since then.

displace
in memory theory, to cause information to be lost from short-term memory by adding new information

long-term memory
the type or stage of memory capable of relatively permanent storage

repression
in Freud's psychodynamic theory, the ejection of anxiety-evoking ideas from conscious awareness

---

FIGURE 6.2 | A Familiar Grid

The nine drawings in the second challenge to memory form this familiar tic-tac-toe grid when the numbers are placed inside them and they are arranged in order. This method for recalling the shapes collapses nine chunks of information into two. One is the tic-tac-toe grid. The second is the rule for decoding the drawings from the grid.

© Cengage Learning 2012

Interference in Short-Term Memory

In a classic experiment with college students, Lloyd and Margaret Peterson (1959) demonstrated how prevention of rehearsal can wreak havoc with short-term memory. They asked students to remember three-letter combinations such as HGB—normally, three easy chunks of information. They then had the students count backward from an arbitrary number, such as 181, by threes (that is, 181, 178, 175, 172, and so on). The students were told to stop counting and to report the letter sequence after the intervals of time shown in Figure 6.3. The percentage of correctly recalled letter combinations fell dramatically within seconds. Counting backward for 18 seconds had dislodged the letter sequences in almost all of these bright students' memories.

Psychologists say that the appearance of new information in short-term memory **displaces** the old infor-

mation. Remember: Only a few bits of information can be retained in short-term memory at the same time.

6-3c LONG-TERM MEMORY

Long-term memory is the third stage of information processing (refer back to Figure 6.1). Think of your long-term memory as a vast storehouse of information containing names, dates, places, what Johnny did to you in second grade, and what Susan said about you when you were 12.

Some psychologists (Freud was one) believed that nearly all of our perceptions and ideas are stored permanently. We might not be able to retrieve all of them, however. Some memories might be "lost" because of lack of proper cues. Still others might be kept unconscious by the forces of **repression**. Adherents to this view often pointed to the work of neurosurgeon Wilder Penfield (1969). When parts of their brains were electrically stimulated, many of Penfield's patients reported the appearance of images that had something of the feel of memories.

Today, most psychologists view this notion as exaggerated. Memory researcher Elizabeth Loftus, for example, notes that the "memories" stimulated by Penfield's probes lacked detail and were sometimes incorrect (e.g., Bernstein & Loftus, 2009). Therefore, it has *not* been

---

FIGURE 6.3 | The Effect of Interference on Short-Term Memory

182,179,176, 173,170,167...

H, G, B

In this experiment, college students were asked to remember a series of three letters while they counted backward by threes. After just three seconds, retention was cut by half. Ability to recall the words was almost completely lost by 15 seconds.

© Muhamed Gaff/Corbis

Graph: Percent recalled (y-axis, 0 to 100) vs. Elapsed time (seconds) (x-axis, 0 to 18), showing a declining curve.

© Cengage Learning 2012

shown that all of our experiences are permanently imprinted on the brain. Now let's consider some other questions about long-term memory.

How Accurate Are Long-Term Memories?

Psychologist Elizabeth Loftus notes that memories are distorted by our biases and needs—by the ways in which we conceptualize our worlds. We represent much of our world in the form of **schemas**. A *schema* is a way of mentally representing the world, such as a belief or expectation, that can influence our perception of persons, objects, and situations.

FICTION NOT ALL EXPERIENCES ARE PERMANENTLY IMPRINTED ON THE BRAIN.

Now, retrieve sheet number 4. You drew the figures "from memory" according to instructions on page 136. Now look at Figure 6.4. Are your drawings closer in form to those in group 1 or to those in group 2? I wouldn't be surprised if they were more like those in group 1—if, for example, your first drawing looked more like eyeglasses than a dumbbell. After all, they were labeled like the drawings in group 1. The labels serve as *schemas* for the drawings—ways of organizing your knowledge of them—and these schemas may have influenced your recollections. By the way, take out a penny and look at it. Did you pick the correct penny when you answered the challenges to memory?

How Much Information Can Be Stored in Long-Term Memory?

How many terabytes of storage are there in your most personal computer—your brain? Unlike a computer, the human ability to store information is, for all practical purposes, unlimited (Voss, 2009; Y. Wang et al., 2009). Even the largest hard drives fill up when we save Web pages, pictures, or videos. Yet how many "movies" of the past have you saved in your own long-term memory? How many thousands of scenes and stories can you rerun at will? And, assuming that you have an intact sensory system, the movies in your personal storage bins not only have color and sound but also aromas, tactile sensations, and more. *Your long-term memory is a biochemical "hard drive" with no known limits on the amount of information it can store.*

New information may replace older information in short-term memory, but there is no evidence that long-term memories—those in "storage"—are lost by displacement. Long-term memories may endure a lifetime. Now and then, it may seem that we have forgotten, or "lost," a long-term memory such as the names of elementary-school classmates, yet it may be that we

schema
a way of mentally representing the world, such as a belief or an expectation, that can influence perception of persons, objects, and situations

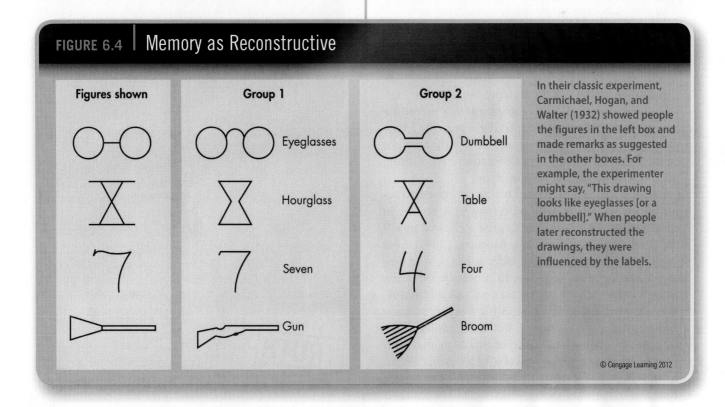

FIGURE 6.4 | Memory as Reconstructive

Figures shown	Group 1	Group 2
	Eyeglasses	Dumbbell
	Hourglass	Table
	Seven	Four
	Gun	Broom

In their classic experiment, Carmichael, Hogan, and Walter (1932) showed people the figures in the left box and made remarks as suggested in the other boxes. For example, the experimenter might say, "This drawing looks like eyeglasses [or a dumbbell]." When people later reconstructed the drawings, they were influenced by the labels.

© Cengage Learning 2012

cannot find the proper cues to retrieve them. However, if you drive by your elementary school (a cue) you might suddenly recall the long-lost names of schoolteachers.

Levels of Processing Information

People who use elaborative rehearsal (the kind of coding in which new information is related to information that is already known) to remember things are *processing information at a deeper level* than people who use maintenance rehearsal (mental repetition of information to keep it in memory). Fergus Craik and Robert Lockhart (2008) pioneered the *levels-of-processing model of memory*, which holds that memories tend to endure when information is processed *deeply*—attended to, encoded carefully, pondered, and related to things we already know. Remembering relies on how carefully they attend to information and how *deeply* they process it, not on whether memories are transferred from one *stage* of memory to another. If you are bombarded by one name after another at a cocktail party, it may be easier for you to recall the name of your first-grade teacher—someone with whom you had countless interactions—than the name of someone you just met.

> **TRUTH** IT IS TRUE THAT IT MAY BE EASIER TO RECALL THE NAME OF YOUR FIRST GRADE TEACHER THAN THOSE OF PEOPLE YOU HAVE JUST MET. YOU LEARNED THEIR NAMES MORE RECENTLY, BUT YOU HAD COUNTLESS MEANINGFUL INTERACTIONS WITH YOUR FIRST GRADE TEACHER.

Think of all the math problems we solved in high school. Each problem is an application of a procedure and, perhaps, of certain formulas. By repeatedly applying the procedures and formulas in slightly different contexts, we rehearse them elaboratively. As a result, we are more likely to remember them.

There is also a good deal of biologically oriented research that connects deep processing with activity in certain parts of the brain, notably the prefrontal area of the cerebral cortex (Barbey & Barsalou, 2009; Luo & Craik, 2009). One reason that older adults show memory loss is that they tend not to process information quite as deeply as younger people do (Craik & Bialystok, 2006; Schneider-Garces et al., 2010). Deep processing requires sustained attention, and older adults, along with people who have suffered brain injuries and strokes, are apparently not capable of focusing their attention as well as they had previously (Willmott et al., 2009).

Flashbulb Memories

Why are some events, like the attack of September 11, 2001, etched in memory for a lifetime? It appears that we tend to remember events that are surprising, important, and emotionally stirring more clearly. Such events can create *flashbulb memories*, which preserve experiences in detail (Hirst et al., 2009) even if those details are sometimes reconstructed, as is the case with other memories (Kvavilashvili et al., 2009). Why is the memory etched when the "flashbulb" goes off? One factor is the distinctness of the memory. It is easier to discriminate stimuli that stand out. Such events are striking in themselves. The feelings caused by them are also special. It is thus relatively easy to pick them out from the storehouse of memories. Major events such as the assassination of a president or the loss of a close relative also tend to have important effects on our lives. We are likely to dwell on them and form networks of associations. That is, we are likely to rehearse them elaboratively. Our rehearsal may include great expectations, or deep fears, for the future. Therefore, you may always recall where you were and what you were doing on the morning of September 11, 2001, when terrorists attacked the World Trade Center and the Pentagon.

Why is it that some events, such as the terrorist attack of September 11, 2001, can be etched in memory for a lifetime?

AP Photo/Carmen Taylor

> **TRUTH** IT IS TRUE THAT THE "FLASHBULB" IN YOUR MEMORY PROBABLY WENT OFF ON SEPTEMBER 11, 2001, EVEN THOUGH YOU WERE QUITE A BIT YOUNGER THAN YOU ARE NOW AND THAT EVENT OCCURRED MORE THAN 10 YEARS AGO. YOU MAY RECALL WHERE YOU WERE AND WHAT YOU WERE DOING AT THE TIME FOR DECADES TO COME.

Biology is intimately connected with psychology. Strong feelings are connected with the secretion of stress hormones, and stress hormones help carve events into memory—"as almost to leave a scar upon the cerebral tissues," as noted by William James.

Organization in Long-Term Memory

The storehouse of long-term memory is usually well organized. Items are not just piled on the floor or thrown into closets. We tend to gather information about rats and cats into a certain section of the storehouse, perhaps the animal or mammal section. We put information about oaks, maples, and eucalyptus into the tree section. Such categorization of stimuli is a basic cognitive function. It allows us to make predictions about specific instances and to store information efficiently.

We tend to organize information according to a *hierarchical structure*, as shown in Figure 6.5. A *hierarchy* is an arrangement of items (or chunks of information) into groups or classes according to common or distinct features. As we work our way up the hierarchy shown in the figure, we find more encompassing, or *superordinate*, classes to which the items below them belong. For example, all mammals are animals, but there are many types of animals other than mammals.

When items are correctly organized in long-term memory, you are more likely to recall—or know—accurate information about them. For example, do you "remember" whether whales breathe underwater? If you did not know that whales are mammals (or in Figure 6.5, *subordinate* to mammals), or if you knew nothing about mammals, a correct answer might depend on some remote instance of rote learning. That is, you might be depending on chancy episodic memory rather than on reliable semantic memory. For example, you might recall some details from a TV documentary on whales. If you *did* know that whales are mammals, however, you would also know—or remember—that whales do not breathe underwater. How? You would reconstruct information about whales from knowledge about mammals, the group to which whales are subordinate. Similarly, you would know, or remember, that because they are mammals, whales are warm-blooded, nurse their young, and are a good deal more intelligent than, say, tunas and sharks, which are fish. Had you incorrectly classified whales as fish, you might have searched your memory and constructed the incorrect answer that they do breathe underwater.

Your memory is thus organized according to a remarkably complex filing system that has a certain inter-

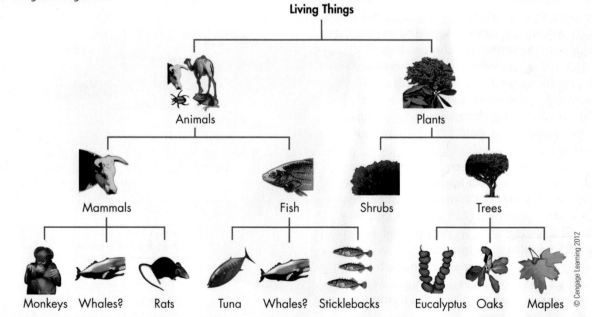

FIGURE 6.5 | The Hierarchical Structure of Long-Term Memory

Where are whales filed in the hierarchical cabinets of your memory? Your classification of whales may influence your answers to these questions: Do whales breathe underwater? Are they warm-blooded? Do they nurse their young? A note to biological purists: This figure is not intended to represent phyla, classes, orders, and so on accurately. Rather, it shows how an individual's classification scheme might be organized.

Living Things

Animals — Plants

Mammals — Fish — Shrubs — Trees

Monkeys — Whales? — Rats — Tuna — Whales? — Sticklebacks — Eucalyptus — Oaks — Maples

© Cengage Learning 2012

tip-of-the-tongue (TOT) phenomenon
the feeling that information is stored in memory although it cannot be readily retrieved; also called the *feeling-of-knowing experience*

context-dependent memory
information that is better retrieved in the context in which it was encoded and stored, or learned

nal logic. If you place a piece of information into the wrong file, it is probably not the fault of the filing system itself. Nevertheless, you may "lose" the information in the sense of not being able to find the best cues to retrieve it.

"It's **déjà vu** all over again."

—YOGI BERRA

The Tip-of-the-Tongue Phenomenon

Having something on the tip of your tongue can be a frustrating experience. Psychologists term this experience the **tip-of-the-tongue (TOT) phenomenon**, or the *feeling-of-knowing experience*.

Research provides insight into the TOT phenomenon (Brown & McNeill, 1966; Galdo-Alvarez et al., 2009; Schwartz, 2008). In classic research, Brown and McNeill (1966) defined some rather unusual words for students, such as *sampan*, a small riverboat used in China and Japan. The students were then asked to recall the words they had learned. Some of the students often had the right word "on the tip of their tongue" but reported words with similar meanings such as *junk, barge,* or *houseboat*. Still other students reported words that sounded similar, such as *Saipan, Siam, sarong,* and *sanching*. Why?

To begin with, the words were unfamiliar, so elaborative rehearsal did not take place. The students did not have an opportunity to relate the words to other things they knew. Brown and McNeill also suggested that our storage systems are indexed according to cues that include both the sounds and the meanings of words—that is, according to both acoustic and semantic codes. By scanning words similar in sound and meaning to the word on the tip of the tongue, we sometimes find a useful cue and retrieve the word for which we are searching.

Sometimes an answer seems to be on the tip of our tongue because our learning of the topic is incomplete. We may not know the exact answer, but we know something. (As a matter of fact, if we have good writing skills, we may present our incomplete knowledge so forcefully that we earn a good grade on an essay question on the topic!) At such times, the problem lies not in retrieval but in the original processes of learning and memory—that is, encoding and storage.

Context-Dependent Memory

The context in which we acquire information can also play a role in retrieval. I remember walking down the halls of the apartment building where I had lived as a child. Cooking odors triggered a sudden assault of images of playing under the staircase, of falling against a radiator, of the shrill voice of a former neighbor calling for her child at dinnertime. Odors, it turns out, are particularly likely to trigger related memories (Lee et al., 2009).

My experience was an example of a **context-dependent memory**. My memories were particularly clear in the context in which they were formed. It could also be helpful, if possible, to study in the same room in which a test will be given. Being in the proper context—for example, studying in the exam room or under the same conditions—can dramatically enhance recall (Isarida & Isarida, 2006).

According to a study with 20 bilingual Cornell students, the "context" for memory extends to language (Marian & Neisser, 2000). The students emigrated from Russia at an average age of 14 and were an average of about 22 years old at the time of the experiment. They were asked to recall the details of experiences in Russia and the United States. When they were interviewed in Russian, they were better able to retrieve experiences from their lives in Russia. Similarly, when they were interviewed in English, they were better able to recall events that happened in the United States.

Datacraft Co Ltd/imagenavi/Jupiterimages

TRUTH IF YOU STUDY WITH THE STEREO ON, YOU MIGHT WELL DO BETTER TAKING THE TEST WITH MUSIC ON—AS WITH EARBUDS. (OF COURSE, YOUR PROFESSOR MIGHT OBJECT TO YOUR USING AN MP3 PLAYER DURING AN EXAM.)

State-Dependent Memory

State-dependent memory is an extension of context-dependent memory. We sometimes retrieve information better when we are in a biological or emotional state similar to the one in which we encoded and stored the information. Feeling the rush of love may trigger other images of falling in love. The grip of anger may prompt memories of incidents of frustration. The research in this area extends to states in which we are sober or inebriated.

6-4 Forgetting

What do DAL, RIK, BOF, and ZEX have in common? They are all **nonsense syllables**. Nonsense syllables are meaningless sets of two consonants with a vowel sandwiched in between. They were first used by Hermann Ebbinghaus (1885/1913) to study memory and forgetting. Because nonsense syllables are intended to be meaningless, remembering them should depend on simple acoustic coding and maintenance rehearsal rather than on elaborative rehearsal, semantic coding, or other ways of making learning meaningful. They are thus well suited for use in the measurement of forgetting.

6-4a MEMORY TASKS USED IN MEASURING FORGETTING

Three basic memory tasks have been used by psychologists to measure forgetting: recognition, recall, and relearning. Nonsense syllables have been used in studying each of them. The study of these memory tasks has led to several conclusions about the nature of forgetting.

Recognition

One aspect of forgetting is failure to recognize something we have experienced. There are many ways of measuring *recognition*. In many studies, psychologists ask subjects to read a list of nonsense syllables. The subjects then read a second list of nonsense syllables and indicate whether they recognize any of the syllables as having appeared on the first list. Forgetting is defined as failure to recognize a syllable that has been read before.

In another kind of recognition study, Harry Bahrick and his colleagues (1975) studied high-school graduates who had been out of school for various lengths of time. They interspersed photos of the graduates' classmates with four times as many photos of strangers. Recent graduates correctly recognized former classmates 90% of the time. Those who had been out of school for 40 years recognized former classmates 75% of the time. A chance level of recognition would have been only 20% (one photo in five was of an actual classmate). Thus, even older people showed rather solid long-term recognition ability.

Recognition is the easiest type of memory task. This is why multiple-choice tests are easier than fill-in-the-blank or essay tests. We can recognize correct answers more easily than we can recall them unaided.

Recall

In his own studies of *recall*, another memory task, Ebbinghaus (1885/1913) would read lists of nonsense syllables aloud to the beat of a metronome and then see how many he could produce from memory. After reading through a list once, he usually would be able to recall seven syllables—the typical limit for short-term memory.

Psychologists also often use lists of pairs of nonsense syllables, called **paired associates**, to measure recall. A list of paired associates is shown in Figure 6.6. Subjects read through the lists pair by pair. Later they are shown the first member of each pair and are asked to recall the second. Recall is more difficult than recognition. In a recognition task, one simply indicates whether an item has been seen before or which of a number of items is

state-dependent memory information that is better retrieved in the physiological or emotional state in which it was encoded and stored, or learned

nonsense syllables meaningless sets of two consonants, with a vowel sandwiched in between, that are used to study memory

paired associates nonsense syllables presented in pairs in experiments that measure recall

FIGURE 6.6 | Paired Associates

WOM	CEG
GOR	NIF
XAR	MUP
JEK	BAC
HOK	MIB

© Cengage Learning 2012

paired with a stimulus (as in a multiple-choice test). In a recall task, the person must retrieve a syllable, with another syllable serving as a cue.

Retrieval is made easier if the two syllables can be meaningfully linked—that is, encoded semantically—even if the "meaning" is stretched. Consider the first pair of nonsense syllables in Figure 6.6. The image of a WOMan smoking a CEG-arette may make CEG easier to retrieve when the person is presented with the cue WOM.

Harry Bahrick (Bahrick et al., 2008) conducted a study to see whether people could recall college grades from 1 to 50 years earlier. The researchers recruited 276 alumni of Ohio Wesleyan University who had graduated 1 to 50 years earlier. Participants were asked to recall their college grades, and their recollections were checked against their actual grades. The alumni accurately recalled 3,025 of 3,967 college grades. As you can see in Figure 6.7, the number of correct recollections fell off with the age of the respondent, generally due to errors of omission. But graduates who were out of school more than 40 years made no more errors of commission—that is, entered no more wrong grades—than those who were out of school about eight years. Students who received better grades made fewer errors. Eighty-one percent of wrong entries inflated the grade. The researchers suggest that we bring in relevant generic memories to fill in gaps ("I was sort of a good student; I got a B+.") after our actual episodic memory fails and that most of us distort our memories in a more emotionally gratifying fashion.

FIGURE 6.7 | Memory for College Grades, Half a Century Later

© Cengage Learning 2014

FIGURE 6.8 | Ebbinghaus's Classic Curve of Forgetting

Recollection of lists of words drops precipitously during the first hour after learning. Losses of learning then become more gradual. Retention drops by half within the first hour. It takes a month (31 days), however, for retention to be cut in half again.

© Cengage Learning 2012

Relearning

Relearning is a third method of measuring retention. Do you remember having to learn all of the state capitals in grade school? What were the capitals of Wyoming and Delaware? Even when we cannot recall or recognize material that had once been learned, such as Cheyenne for Wyoming and Dover for Delaware, we can relearn it more rapidly the second time.

To study the efficiency of relearning, Ebbinghaus (1885/1913) devised the **method of savings**. First he recorded the number of repetitions required to learn a list of nonsense syllables or words. Then he recorded the number of repetitions required to relearn the list after a certain amount of time had elapsed. Next he computed the difference in the number of repetitions to determine the **savings**. If a list had to be repeated 20 times before it was learned, and 20 times again after a year had passed, there were no savings. Relearning, that is, was as tedious as the initial learning. If the list could be learned with only 10 repetitions after a year had elapsed, however, half the number of repetitions required for learning had been saved.

Figure 6.8 shows Ebbinghaus's classic curve of forgetting. As you can see, there was no loss of memory as measured by savings immediately after a list had been learned. However, recollection dropped quite a bit, by half, during the first hour after learning a list. Losses of learning then became more gradual. It took a month (31 days) for retention to be cut in half again. That is, forgetting occurred most rapidly right after material was learned. We continue to forget material as time elapses but at a slower pace.

6-4b INTERFERENCE THEORY

When we do not attend to, encode, and rehearse sensory input, we may forget it through decay of the trace of the image. Material in short-term memory, like material in sensory memory, can be lost through decay. It can also be lost through displacement, as may happen when we try to remember several new names at a party.

Why can learning Spanish make it harder to remember French? The answer may be found in **interference theory**. According to this view, we also forget material in short-term and long-term memory because newly learned material interferes with it. The two basic types of interference are retroactive interference (also called *retroactive inhibition*) and proactive interference (also called *proactive inhibition*).

Retroactive Interference

In **retroactive interference**, new learning interferes with the retrieval of old learning. For example, a medical student may memorize the names of the bones in the leg through rote repetition. Later he or she may find that learning the names of the bones in the arm makes it more difficult to retrieve the names of the leg bones, especially if the names are similar in sound or in relative location on each limb.

Proactive Interference

In **proactive interference**, older learning interferes with the capacity to retrieve more recently learned material. High-school Spanish may pop in when you are trying to retrieve college French or Italian words. All three are Romance languages, with similar roots and spellings. Previously learned Japanese words probably would not interfere with your ability to retrieve more recently learned French or Italian, because the roots and sounds of Japanese differ considerably from those of the Romance languages.

6-4c REPRESSION

According to Freud, we are motivated to forget painful memories and unacceptable ideas because they produce anxiety, guilt, and shame. Repression, according to Freud, is the automatic ejection of painful memories and unacceptable urges from conscious awareness. It is motivated by the desire to avoid facing painful memories and emotions. Psychoanalysts believe that repression is at the heart of disorders such as **dissociative amnesia**, which is discussed in Chapter 12. There is a current controversy in psychology about whether repression (motivated forgetting) exists and, if it does, how it works.

TRUTH IT IS TRUE THAT LEARNING A ROMANCE LANGUAGE SUCH AS SPANISH OR ITALIAN COULD INTERFERE WITH YOUR LEARNING FRENCH LATER ON, AND VICE VERSA.

There is much research on repression, often in the form of case studies that are found in psychoanalytic journals (e.g., Eagle, 2000). Much has been made of case studies in which veterans have supposedly forgotten traumatic battlefield experiences, developed post-traumatic stress disorder (once called "battlefield neurosis"), and then "felt better" once they recalled and discussed the traumatic events. Critics argue that the evidence for such repression and recovery of memories is weak and that this kind of "memory" can be implanted by the suggestions of interviewers (Loftus & Davis, 2006; A. K. Thomas & Loftus, 2002; van de Wetering et al., 2002). The issue remains controversial, as we see next.

Do People Really Recover Repressed Memories of Childhood?

Despite shaky scientific support, there are cases of so-called recovered memories, especially memories of childhood sexual abuse by a relative, teacher, or friend. The question is whether these memories are induced by therapists who foster beliefs that become so deeply ingrained they seem like authentic memories. "We don't know what percent of these recovered memories are real and what percent are pseudomemories," notes psychiatrist Harold Lief (cited in Brody, 2000), one of the first to challenge such memories.

Psychologist Elizabeth Loftus (Loftus & Davis, 2006) cited numerous studies that demonstrated how easy it was to implant a false memory. In one study, researchers were able to readily convince half the subjects that they had been lost in a mall or hospitalized with severe pain as children.

6-4d INFANTILE AMNESIA

When he interviewed people about their early experiences, Freud discovered that they could not recall episodes that had happened prior to the age of three or so and that recall was cloudy through the age of five. This phenomenon is referred to as **infantile amnesia**.

Infantile amnesia has little to do with the fact that the episodes occurred in the distant

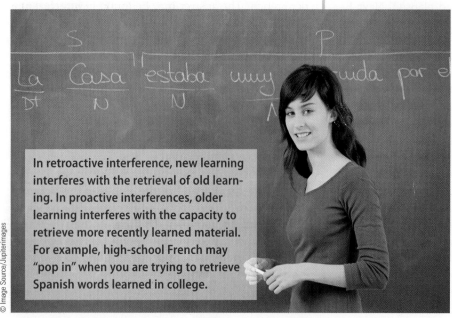

In retroactive interference, new learning interferes with the retrieval of old learning. In proactive interferences, older learning interferes with the capacity to retrieve more recently learned material. For example, high-school French may "pop in" when you are trying to retrieve Spanish words learned in college.

© Image Source/Jupiterimages

past. Middle-aged and older people have vivid memories from the ages of 6 through 10, yet the events happened many decades ago. But 18-year-olds show steep declines in memory when they try to recall episodes that occurred earlier than the age of 6, even though they happened less than 18 years earlier (Wetzler & Sweeney, 1986).

Freud believed that young children have aggressive impulses and perverse lusts toward their parents. He attributed infantile amnesia to repression of these impulses. The episodes lost to infantile amnesia, however, are not weighted in the direction of such "primitive" impulses. In fact, infantile amnesia probably reflects the interaction of physiological and cognitive factors. For example, a structure of the limbic system (the **hippocampus**) that is involved in the storage of memories does not become mature until we are about two years old (Shrager et al., 2008; Wais et al., 2006). In addition, myelination of brain pathways is incomplete for the first few years, contributing to the inefficiency of information processing and memory formation.

There are also cognitive explanations for infantile amnesia (Piolino et al., 2009; Q. Wang, 2008):

- Infants are not particularly interested in remembering the past.
- Infants, in contrast to older children, tend not to weave episodes together into meaningful stories of their own lives. Information about specific episodes thus tends to be lost. Research shows that when parents reminisce about the past with children, the children's memories of being infants are strengthened.
- Infants do not make reliable use of language to symbolize or classify events. Their ability to *encode* sensory input—that is, to apply the auditory and semantic codes that facilitate memory formation—is therefore limited. Yet research shows that young infants can recall events throughout the period when infantile amnesia is presumed to occur if they are now and then exposed to objects they played with or photos of events.

In any event, we are unlikely to remember episodes from the first two years of life unless we are reminded of them from time to time as we develop. Many early childhood memories that seem so clear today might be reconstructed and hold many inaccuracies. They might also be memories of events that occurred later than the period to which we attribute them. Yet there is no evidence that such early memories are systematically repressed.

6-4e ANTEROGRADE AND RETROGRADE AMNESIA

Adults also experience amnesia, although usually for biological reasons, as in the cases of anterograde and retrograde amnesia (Kikuchi et al., 2010). In so-called **anterograde amnesia**, there are memory lapses for the period following a trauma such as a blow to the head, an electric shock, or an operation. In some cases the trauma seems to interfere with all the processes of memory. The ability to pay attention, the encoding of sensory input, and rehearsal are all impaired. A number of investigators have linked certain kinds of brain damage—such as damage to the hippocampus—to amnesia (Epp et al., 2008; Travis et al., 2010).

In **retrograde amnesia**, the source of trauma prevents people from remembering events that took place before the accident (Wheeler & McMillan, 2001). In one well-known case of retrograde amnesia, a man received a head injury in a motorcycle accident (Baddeley, 1982). When he regained consciousness, he had lost memory for all events that had occurred after the age of 11. In fact, he appeared to believe that he was still 11 years old. During the next few months he gradually recovered more knowledge of his past. He moved toward the present year by year, up until the critical motorcycle ride.

But he never did recover the events just prior to the accident. The accident had apparently prevented the information that was rapidly unfolding before him from being transferred to long-term memory. In terms of stages of memory, it may be that our perceptions and ideas need to consolidate, or rest undisturbed for a while, if they are to be transferred to long-term memory (Nader et al., 2000).

6-5 The Biology of Memory

Psychologists know that mental processes such as the encoding, storage, and retrieval of information—that is, memory—are accompanied by changes in the brain (Kandel, 2006). Early in the 20th century, many psychologists used the concept of the **engram** in their study of memory. Engrams were viewed as electrical circuits in the brain that corresponded to memory traces—neurological processes that paralleled experi-

hippocampus
a structure in the limbic system that plays an important role in the formation of new memories

anterograde amnesia
failure to remember events that occurred after physical trauma because of the effects of the trauma

retrograde amnesia
failure to remember events that occurred prior to physical trauma because of the effects of the trauma

engram
an assumed electrical circuit in the brain that corresponds to a memory trace

**long-term
potentiation (LTP)**
enhanced efficiency in synaptic transmission that follows brief, rapid stimulation

ences. Yet biological psychologists such as Karl Lashley (1950)
spent many fruitless years searching for such circuits or for the
structures of the brain in which they might be housed.
Much research on the biology of memory focuses today
on the roles of stimulants, neurons, neurotransmitters,
hormones, and structures in the brain.

6-5a NEURAL ACTIVITY AND MEMORY

Rats that are reared in stimulating environments provide some insight into the neural events that are involved in memory. The animals develop more dendrites
and synapses in the cerebral cortex than rats reared in
impoverished environments (Kolb et al., 2009). Moreover, visually stimulating rats increases the number of
synapses in their visual cortex (Inaba et al., 2009). Therefore, the storage of experience does involve avenues of
communication among brain cells.

Information received through other senses is just as
likely to lead to corresponding changes in the cortical
regions that represent them. For example, sounds may

Courtesy of Diana Copeland

Forever 27

Thalamus

Hippocampus

The hippocampus is essential to the formation of new memories. Consider
the classic case of a man called "H. M." Parts of the brain are sometimes
lesioned to help people with epilepsy. In H.M.'s case, a section of the
hippocampus was removed (Milner, 1966). Right after the operation,
H. M.'s mental functioning appeared normal. As time went on, however,
it became clear that he had problems processing new information. For
example, two years after the operation, H. M. believed he was 27—his age
at the time of the operation. When his family moved to a new address,
H. M. could not find his new home or remember the new address. He
responded with appropriate grief to the death of his uncle, yet he then
began to ask about his uncle and why he did not visit. Each time he was
reminded of his uncle's passing, he grieved as if he were hearing it for
the first time. H. M.'s operation apparently prevented him from
transferring information from short-term to long-term memory.

**FIGURE 6.9 | One Avenue to Long-Term
Potentiation (LTP)**

LTP can occur via the action of neurotransmitters such as
serotonin and glutamate at synapses. Structurally, LTP
can also occur as shown in Parts A and B, when dendrites
sprout new branches that connect with transmitting
axons, increasing the amount of stimulation they receive.

© Cengage Learning 2012

Part A   Part B

similarly cause changes in the auditory cortex. Experiences perceived by several senses are apparently stored
in numerous parts of the cortex. The recall of sensory
experiences apparently involves neural activity in related regions of the brain.

Research with sea snails such as *Aplysia* and *Hermis-
senda* offers more insight into the biology of memory.
Aplysia has only some 20,000 neurons compared with
humans' *billions*. As a result, researchers have been able
to study how experience is reflected at the synapses of
specific neurons. The sea snail will reflexively withdraw
its gills when it receives electric shock, in the way a
person will reflexively withdraw a hand from a hot
stove or a thorn. In one kind of experiment, researchers
precede the shock with a squirt of water. After a few
repetitions, the sea snail becomes conditioned to withdraw its gills when squirted with the water. When sea
snails are conditioned, they release more serotonin at
certain synapses. As a consequence, transmission at
these synapses becomes more efficient as trials (learning) progress (Mechner, 2009; Squire & Kandel, 2008).
This greater efficiency is termed **long-term potentiation (LTP)**. As shown in Figure 6.9, dendrites can also
participate in LTP by sprouting new branches that attach to the transmitting axon. Rats that are given substances that enhance LTP learn mazes with fewer errors;
that is, they are less likely to turn down the wrong alley
(Adams et al., 2009; Uzakov et al., 2005).

Serotonin and many other naturally occurring chemical substances, including adrenaline, noradrenaline,
acetylcholine, glutamate, antidiuretic hormone, even
the sex hormones estrogen and testosterone have also
been shown to play roles in memory.

6-5b BRAIN STRUCTURES AND MEMORY

Memory does not reside in a single structure of the brain. Memory relies on complex neural networks that draw on various parts of the brain (Nyberg et al., 2000). However, some parts of the brain play more specific roles in memory. The hippocampus is vital in storing new information even if we can retrieve old information without it (Squire, 2009). But the hippocampus is not a storage bin. Rather, it is involved in relaying sensory information to parts of the cortex.

Where are the storage bins? The brain stores parts of memories in the appropriate areas of the sensory cortex. Sights are stored in the visual cortex, sounds in the auditory cortex, and so on. The limbic system is largely responsible for integrating these pieces of information when we recall an event. However, the frontal lobes apparently store information about where and when events occur (Chafee & Goldman-Rakic, 2000; C. R. E. Wilson et al., 2008).

But what of the decision to try to recall something? What of the spark of consciousness that drives us to move backward in time or to strive to remember to do something in the future? The prefrontal cortex (see

misinformation effect the shaping of bogus or slanted memories by providing inaccurate information as, for example, in the form of "leading questions"

✳ Can We Trust Eyewitness Testimony?

Jean Piaget, the investigator of children's cognitive development, distinctly remembered an attempt to kidnap him from his baby carriage as he was being wheeled along the Champs Élysées. He recalled the excited throng, the abrasions on the face of the nurse who rescued him, the police officer's white baton, and the flight of the assailant. Although they were graphic, Piaget's memories were false. Years later, the nurse admitted that she had made up the tale. Piaget had fallen victim to an example of what psychologists term the **misinformation effect**. The false information provided by his nurse became implanted in his own memory.

Can eyewitness testimony be trusted? Is there reason to believe that the statements of eyewitnesses are any more factual than Piaget's?

One problem with eyewitness testimony is that the words chosen by an experimenter—and those chosen by a lawyer interrogating a witness—have been shown to influence the reconstruction of memories (Cutler & Kovera, 2010). For example, as in the experiment described earlier, an attorney for the plaintiff might ask the witness, "How fast was the defendant's car going when it *smashed into* the plaintiff's car?" In such a case, the car might be reported as going faster than if the question had been: "How fast was the defendant's car going when the accident occurred?" (Loftus & Palmer, 1974). Could the attorney for the defendant claim that the use of the word *smashed* biased the witness? What about jurors who heard the word *smashed*? Would they be biased toward assuming that the driver had been reckless?

Children tend to be more suggestible witnesses than adults, and preschoolers are more suggestible than older children (Ceci et al., 2007;

How trustworthy is eyewitness testimony? Memories are reconstructive rather than photographic. The wording of questions also influences the content of the memory. Attorneys therefore are sometimes instructed not to phrase questions in such a way that they "lead" the witness.

© Rubberball/Corbis

Cutler & Kovera, 2010; Krähenbühl et al., 2009). But when questioned properly, even young children may provide accurate and useful testimony (Ceci et al., 2007; Krähenbühl et al., 2009).

There are also problems in the identification of criminals by eyewitnesses. For one thing, witnesses may pay more attention to the suspect's clothing than to more meaningful characteristics such as facial features, height, and weight. In one experiment, viewers of a videotaped crime incorrectly identified a man as the criminal because he wore the eyeglasses and T-shirt that had been worn by the perpetrator on the tape. The man who had actually committed the crime was identified less often (Sanders, 1984).

Other problems with eyewitness testimony include the following (Cutler & Kovera, 2010):

• Identification is less accurate when suspects belong to ethnic or racial groups that differ from that of the witness.

• Identification of suspects is compromised when interrogators make misleading suggestions.

• Witnesses are seen as more credible when they claim to be certain in their testimony, but there is little evidence that claims of certainty are accurate.

Thus, there are many problems with eyewitness testimony. Yet even Elizabeth Loftus (e.g., Wright & Loftus, 2008), who has extensively studied the accuracy of eyewitness testimony, agrees that it is a valuable tool in the courtroom. After all, identifications made by eyewitnesses are frequently correct, and what, Loftus asks, would be the alternative to the use of eyewitnesses? If we were to prevent eyewitnesses from testifying, how many criminals would go free?

✳ The Relationships Among the Various Kinds of Memories

Memories can address past events (*retrospective memories*) or future events (*prospective memories*). Memories of the past can be *explicit* (declarative) or *implicit* (nondeclarative). Explicit memories include memories of personal episodes (which are called *episodic or autobiographical memories*) or of general information (*semantic memories*).

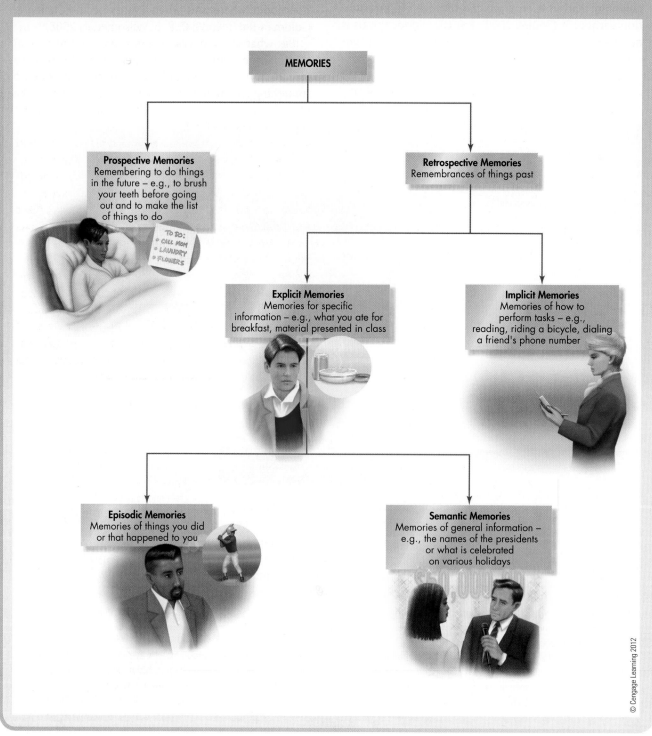

MEMORIES

Prospective Memories
Remembering to do things in the future – e.g., to brush your teeth before going out and to make the list of things to do

TO DO:
° CALL MOM
° LAUNDRY
° FLOWERS

Retrospective Memories
Remembrances of things past

Explicit Memories
Memories for specific information – e.g., what you ate for breakfast, material presented in class

Implicit Memories
Memories of how to perform tasks – e.g., reading, riding a bicycle, dialing a friend's phone number

Episodic Memories
Memories of things you did or that happened to you

Semantic Memories
Memories of general information – e.g., the names of the presidents or what is celebrated on various holidays

© Cengage Learning 2012

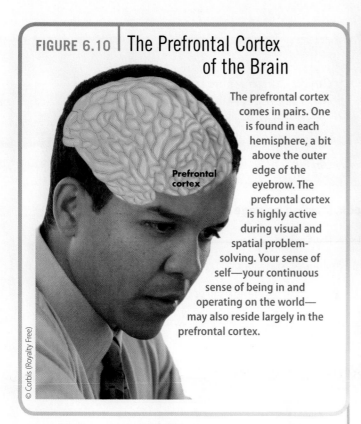

FIGURE 6.10 | The Prefrontal Cortex of the Brain

The prefrontal cortex comes in pairs. One is found in each hemisphere, a bit above the outer edge of the eyebrow. The prefrontal cortex is highly active during visual and spatial problem-solving. Your sense of self—your continuous sense of being in and operating on the world—may also reside largely in the prefrontal cortex.

Prefrontal cortex

© Corbis (Royalty Free)

Figure 6.10) is the executive center in memory (Christ et al., 2009; Wheeler & Treisman, 2002). It appears to empower people with consciousness—the ability to mentally represent and become aware of experiences that occur in the past, present, and future. It enables people to mentally travel back in time to reexperience the personal, autobiographical past. It enables people to focus on the things they intend to do in the future, such as mail a letter on the way to class or brush their teeth before going to bed.

The hippocampus is also involved in the where and when of things (Eichenbaum & Fortin, 2003). The hippocampus does not become mature until we are about two years old. Immaturity may be connected with infantile amnesia. Adults with hippocampal damage may be able to form new procedural memories, even though they cannot form new episodic ("where and when") memories (Fields, 2005). They can develop new skills even though they cannot recall the practice sessions (Squire & Kandel, 2008).

The thalamus is involved in the formation of verbal memories. Part of the thalamus of an Air Force cadet known as N. A. was damaged in a fencing accident. Afterward, N. A. could no longer form verbal memories, but he could form visual memories (Squire, 2004). (One might measure visual memory by showing people pictures, allowing time to pass, and then asking them to point out those they have been shown.)

The encoding, storage, and retrieval of information thus involve biological activity. As we learn, new synapses are developed, and changes occur at existing synapses. Parts of the brain are also involved in the formation of memories. In the next chapter, we see how people manipulate information they have stored to adapt to the environment or create new environments.

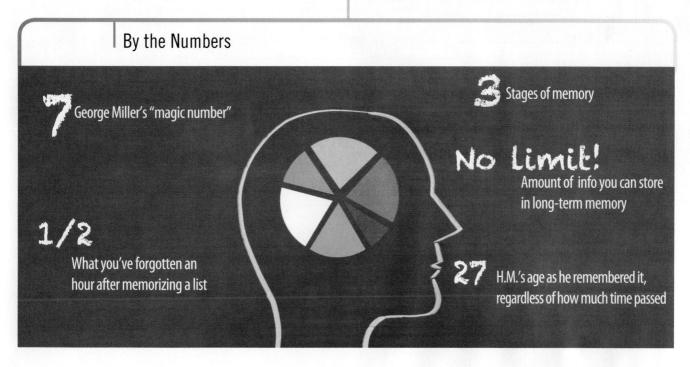

By the Numbers

7 George Miller's "magic number"

3 Stages of memory

No Limit! Amount of info you can store in long-term memory

1/2 What you've forgotten an hour after memorizing a list

27 H.M.'s age as he remembered it, regardless of how much time passed

STUDY TOOLS ▶ 6

Ready to study? In the book, you can:
- ➋ Review what you've read with Fill-Ins and Multiple Choice quizzes (below).
- ➋ Rip out Chapter Review card (in the back).

Or you can go online to CourseMate at www.cengagebrain.com for these resources:
- ➋ Complete Practices Quizzes to prepare for tests.
- ➋ Review Key Terms Flash Cards (online or print).
- ➋ Play games to master concepts.

Answers can be found in the back of the book, starting on page 368.

FILL-INS

1. Memories of the events that happen to a person are _____ memories.

2. _____ memories concern generalized knowledge.

3. One way of storing information is by _____ rehearsal, or by mentally repeating it.

4. Another way of storing information is by _____ rehearsal, when we relate new information to things we already know.

5. The Atkinson–Shiffrin model hypothesizes three stages of memory: _____, _____-_____, and _____-_____.

6. _____ imagery is the ability to retain exact mental representations of visual stimuli over long periods of time.

7. Detailed memories of surprising, important, and emotional events are termed _____ memories.

8. In _____ interference, new learning interferes with the retrieval of old learning.

9. In _____ interference, older learning interferes with the capacity to retrieve more recently learned material.

10. Experience enhances the avenues of communication among brain cells by development of dendrites and _____.

1. Remembering what you had for dinner is an example of _____. memory.

   a. implicit   c. dependent
   b. episodic   d. semantic

2. Hamilton told himself to remember to get three things at the corner deli. On the way to the store, he ran into Jason and chatted for a few minutes. Afterward, he could only remember two of the items. Chatting with Jason had apparently interfered with Hamilton's

   a. episodic memory.
   b. semantic memory.
   c. prospective memory.
   d. implicit memory.

3. You recall what you ate for breakfast this morning, but you know who wrote Hamlet. Your knowledge that Shakespeare wrote Hamlet is an example of

   a. episodic memory.
   b. prospective memory.
   c. implicit memory.
   d. semantic memory.

4. Breaking THUNSTOFAM into three syllables THUN-STO-FAM and then repeating them many times in an effort to remember the ten letters is an example of using the techniques of

   a. chunking and maintenance rehearsal.
   b. encoding and elaborative rehearsal.
   c. sensory memory and short-term memory.
   d. working memory and semantic memory.

5. Tracy took tennis lessons when she was very young but had not played tennis for years when she decided to enroll in a tennis class at college. A moment after she picked up her racket, she realized with surprise that she had shifted it to the correct forehand grip without even thinking. Tracy's _____. memory made this possible.

   a. implicit   c. psychomotor
   b. episodic   d. semantic

6. If you learn how to do something once, and then forget it, what is most likely to happen if you attempt to relearn it?

   a. **Anxiety will interfere with your ability to relearn it.**
   b. **The original learning will be on the tip of your tongue.**
   c. **Your hippocampus will be flooded with dopamine.**
   d. **You will relearn it more quickly than you originally learned it.**

7. The process of modifying information so that we can place it in memory is called

   a. **storing.**
   b. **memorizing.**
   c. **encoding.**
   d. **programming.**

8. Mentally repeating a list or saying it to yourself refers to

   a. **metamemory.**
   b. **elaborative rehearsal.**
   c. **retrospective memory.**
   d. **maintenance rehearsal.**

9. Evan met Lesley at a party three weeks ago. He bumps into her on the way to class. He feels as though he knows her name but he just can't retrieve the information. This experience is referred to as

   a. **mnemonic failure.**
   b. **tip-of-the-tongue phenomenon.**
   c. **consolidation.**
   d. **déjà vu.**

10. From the clinical evidence on brain injury, it appears that storage bins for long-term memories are located in

    a. **the hippocampus.**
    b. **one specific brain area.**
    c. **different brain areas.**
    d. **the frontal lobe and thalamus.**

© Science Faction/SuperStock

LEARNING OUTCOMES

7-1 Define thinking and the various concepts involved in thinking

7-2 Describe how language develops

7-3 Identify the concept of intelligence and the techniques used to measure intelligence

7-4 Describe the controversy surrounding intelligence testing

 STUDY TOOLS ▶ After you read the chapter, go to the Study Tools at the end of the chapter, page 187.

CHAPTER 7

Thinking, Language, and Intelligence

What form of life is so adaptive that it can survive in desert temperatures of 120°F or Arctic climes of −40°F? What form of life can run, walk, climb, swim, live underwater for months on end, and fly to the moon and back? I won't keep you in suspense any longer. We are that form of life. Yet our unclad bodies do not allow us to adapt to these extremes of temperature. Brute strength does not allow us to live underwater or travel to the moon. Rather, it is our cognitive processes of thinking, language, and intelligence that permit us to adapt to these conditions and surpass our physical limitations.

Our cognitive processes are the key assets that have enabled humans to survive and prosper. Other species may be stronger, run faster, smell more keenly, even live longer, but only humans have produced literature, music, mathematics, and science. Our cognitive processes have made these achievements possible. In this chapter, we look at these three related areas of **cognition**: thinking, language, and intelligence.

7-1 Thinking

The Greek philosopher Aristotle pointed out that people differ from lower organisms in their capacity for rational thinking. *What is thinking?* **Thinking** means paying attention to information, representing it mentally, reasoning about it, and making judgments and decisions about it. Thinking refers to conscious, *planned* attempts to make sense of and change the world. By contrast, mental processes such as dreaming and daydreaming do not represent thinking; they may be unplanned and proceed more or less on their own.

We begin with concepts, which provide many of the building blocks for thinking.

7-1a CONCEPTS

Concepts are mental categories used to group together objects, relations, events, abstractions, or qualities that have common properties. Concepts are crucial to cog-

> *Intelligence may be the most controversial topic in psychology.*

TRUTH OR *FICTION*

WHAT DO YOU THINK? FOLKLORE, COMMON SENSE, OR NONSENSE? CIRCLE THE T FOR "TRUTH" OR THE F FOR "FICTION," AND CHECK THE ACCURACY OF YOUR ANSWERS AS YOU READ THROUGH THE CHAPTER.

T	F	ONLY HUMANS CAN USE INSIGHT TO SOLVE PROBLEMS.
T	F	CRYING IS A CHILD'S FIRST USE OF LANGUAGE.
T	F	YOUNG CHILDREN SAY THINGS LIKE "DADDY GOED AWAY" AND "MOMMY SITTED DOWN" BECAUSE THEY *DO* UNDERSTAND RULES OF GRAMMAR.
T	F	"STREET SMARTS" ARE A SIGN OF INTELLIGENCE.
T	F	CREATIVE PEOPLE ARE HIGHLY INTELLIGENT.
T	F	HIGHLY INTELLIGENT PEOPLE ARE CREATIVE.
T	F	TWO CHILDREN CAN ANSWER EXACTLY THE SAME ITEMS ON AN INTELLIGENCE TEST CORRECTLY, YET ONE CHILD CAN OBTAIN AN ABOVE AVERAGE IN IQ, AND THE OTHER CAN OBTAIN A BELOW AVERAGE IQ.
T	F	INTELLIGENCE TESTS MEASURE MANY THINGS OTHER THAN INTELLIGENCE.

nition. They can represent objects, events, and activities—and visions of things that never were or cannot be measured, such as Middle Earth in *The Lord of the Rings* or the land of Oz in *The Wizard of Oz*.

Labels for objects depend on experience with them and on one's cultural setting (Sloman et al., 2002). Concepts such as *square*, *circle*, and *triangle* are not all that common in nature, and some peoples who do not construct houses with these shapes, such as the Himba of northern Namibia, have no words for them (Davidoff et al., 2008; Roberson et al., 2002). But these shapes are concepts that are basic to geometry. Much thinking has to do with categorizing new concepts and manipulating relationships among concepts, as in problems in geometry.

We tend to organize concepts in *hierarchies* (see Figure 7.1). For example, the newspaper category includes objects such as your school paper and the *Los Angeles Times*. Newspapers, college textbooks, and catalogs can be combined into higher-order categories such as *printed matter* or *printed devices that store information*. If you add iPods, hard drives, and DVDs, you can create a still higher category—*objects that store information*. Now consider a question that requires categorical thinking: How are a newspaper and a DVD alike? Answers to such questions entail supplying the category that includes both objects. In this case, we can say that both objects store information. Their functions are alike, even if their technology differs.

Prototypes are good examples. They best match the key features of categories (Machery, 2009). Which animal seems more birdlike to you: a robin or an ostrich? Why? Which better fits the prototype of a fish: a sea horse or a tuna? Why?

Many simple prototypes, such as *dog* and *red*, are taught by means of examples, or **exemplars**. Research suggests that it is more efficient for most of us to learn what *fruits* and *vegetables* are from experience with

FIGURE 7.1 | Organization of Concepts into Hierarchies

People may have a concept, "objects that store information." This concept may include concepts such as iPod, DVD, and printed matter. Within the concept of printed matter, people may include newspapers, college textbooks (certainly the most important object that stores information!), novels, and catalogs. The concept of newspaper may include one's school newspaper and various commercial newspapers.

OBJECTS THAT STORE INFORMATION

Printed matter — iPod — DVDs

Newspapers — College textbooks — Novels — Catalogs

© Cengage Learning 2014

exemplars of each, rather than by working from definitions of them (Freund, 2009; Voorspoels et al., 2008). We point to a dog and tell a child "dog" or "This is a dog." Dogs are *positive instances* of the dog concept. *Negative instances*—things that are *not* dogs—are then shown to the child while we say, "This is *not* a dog." Negative instances of one concept may be positive instances of another. So, in teaching a child, we may be more likely to say, "This is not a dog—it's a cat" than simply, "This is not a dog."

Children may at first include horses and other four-legged animals within the dog concept until the differences between dogs and horses are pointed out. In language development, such overinclusion of instances in a category (reference to horses as dogs) is labeled *overextension*. Children's prototypes become refined after they are shown positive and negative instances and given explanations. Abstract concepts such as *bachelor* or *square root* tend to be formed through explanations that involve more basic concepts.

7-1b PROBLEM SOLVING

Problem solving is an important aspect of thinking. Here's a problem for you to solve. What are the next two letters in this series?

O T T F F S S E _ _ ?

How did you try to find the answer? Did you search your personal memory banks and ask yourself what O can stand for, then T, and so on? Did you try to think of some phrase the letters might represent? Perhaps the first letters of the stars in a constellation? [If you don't resort to a search engine answer and do not arrive at the answer on your own, I'll be discussing it within a few pages.]

7-1c UNDERSTANDING THE PROBLEM

Successful understanding of a problem generally requires three features:

- *The parts or elements of our mental representation of the problem relate to one another in a meaningful way.* If we are trying to solve a problem in geometry, our mental triangles, like actual triangles, should have angles that total 180 degrees.

How Do You Go about Understanding a Problem? This student is apparently seeking to boost her storehouse of background knowledge. Will doing so help her focus on the answer efficiently?

- *The elements of our mental representation of the problem correspond to the elements of the problem in the outer world.* If we are assessing a patient in the emergency room of a hospital, we want to arrive at a diagnosis of what might be wrong before we make a treatment plan. To do so, we take the patient's vital signs, including heart rate, temperature, and blood pressure, so that our mental picture of the patient conforms to what is going on in his or her body.

- *We have a storehouse of background knowledge that we can apply to the problem.* We have the necessary experience or course work to solve the problem.

The Use of Algorithms

An **algorithm** is a specific procedure for solving a type of problem. An algorithm invariably leads to the solution—if it is used properly, that is. Mathematical formulas like the Pythagorean theorem are examples of algorithms. They yield correct answers to problems *as long as the right formula is used*. Finding the right formula to solve a problem may require scanning one's memory for all formulas that contain variables that represent one or more of the elements in the problem. The Pythagorean theorem concerns right triangles. Therefore, it is appropriate to consider using this formula for problems concerning right triangles, but not others.

If you are going to be meeting someone for the first time and want to make a good impression, you consider the nature of the encounter (for example, a job interview or a blind date) and then consider how to dress and behave for the encounter. If it's a job interview, the algorithm may be to dress neatly, to be well groomed, and not to wear too much cologne or perfume. If it's a date, you may ditch the suit but hike up the cologne or perfume a notch. In either case, smile and make eye contact—it's all part of the formula.

Anagrams are scrambled words. *Korc* is an anagram for *rock* or *cork*. The task in anagram problems is to try to reorganize jumbles or groups of letters into words. Some anagram problems require us to use every letter from the pool of letters; others allow us to use only some of the letters. How many words can you make from the pool of letters *DWARG*? If you were to use the

Johner Photography/Veer

systematic random search
an algorithm for solving problems in which each possible solution is tested according to a particular set of rules

heuristics
rules of thumb that help us simplify and solve problems

means–end analysis
a heuristic device in which we try to solve a problem by evaluating the difference between the current situation and the goal

systematic random search algorithm, you would list every possible letter combination, using from one to all five letters. You could use a dictionary or a spell-checking program to see whether each result is, in fact, a word. The method might take awhile, but it would work.

The Use of Heuristic Devices

Sometimes people use shortcuts to "jump to conclusions"—and these are often correct conclusions. The shortcuts are called **heuristics**, or heuristic devices—rules of thumb that help us simplify and solve problems. Heuristics are often based on strategies that worked in the past (Mair et al., 2009).

In contrast to algorithms, heuristics do not guarantee a correct solution. But when they work, they permit more rapid solutions. A heuristic device for solving the anagram problem would be to look for familiar letter combinations and then check the remaining letters for words that include these combinations. In *DWARG*, for example, we find some familiar combinations: *dr* and *gr*. We may then quickly find *draw*, *drag*, and *grad*. The drawback to this method is that we might miss some words.

One type of heuristic device is the **means–end analysis**. In using this heuristic device, we assess the difference between our current situation and our goals and do what we can to reduce this difference. Let's say that you are out in your car and have gotten lost. One heuristic device based on analysis of what you need to do to get to where you want to go might be to ask for directions. This approach requires no "sense of direction." An algorithm might be more complicated and require some scientific knowledge. For example, if you know your destination is west of your current location you might try driving toward the setting sun.

The Use of Analogies

An *analogy* is a partial similarity among things that are different in other ways. The analogy heuristic applies the solution of an earlier problem to the solution of a new one. We use the analogy heuristic whenever we try to solve a new problem by referring to a previous problem (Mair et al., 2009; Wang & Chiew, 2010).

Let's see whether you can use the analogy heuristic to your advantage in the following number-series problem. Look at the following series of numbers and find the rule that governs their order:

8, 5, 4, 9, 1, 7, 6, 3, 2, 0

This is rather abstract and mathematical. Actually, you use the analogy heuristic regularly. For example, when you begin a new term with a new instructor, you probably consider who the instructor reminds you of. Then, perhaps, you recall the things that helped you get along with the analogous instructor and try them on the new one. We tend to look for things—analogies—that have helped us in similar situations. When we considered OTTFFSSENT, we used the first letters of the numbers one through ten. When we consider the first 10 digits in the following order—8, 5, 4, 9, 1, 7, 6, 3, 2, and 0—we can again think of their first letters when they are spelled out. It happens that they are in alphabetical order (*eight*, *five*, *four*, and so on).

Factors That Affect Problem Solving

The way you approach a problem is central to how effective you are at solving it. Other factors also influence your effectiveness. Three factors that can make it easier or harder to solve problems reside within you: your level of expertise, whether you fall prey to a mental set, and whether you develop insight into the problem.

Expertise To appreciate the role of expertise in problem solving, unscramble the following anagrams, taken from Novick and Coté (1992). In each case use all of the letters to form an actual English word:

DNSUO

RCWDO

IASYD

How long did it take you to unscramble each anagram ("sound," "crowd," and "daisy")? Would a person whose native language is English—that is, an "expert"—unscramble each anagram more efficiently than a bilingual person who spoke another language in the home? Why or why not?

Experts solve problems more efficiently and rapidly than novices do. Generally speaking, people who are experts at solving a certain kind of problem share the following characteristics (Bassok & Novick, 2012; Mair et al., 2009; Nokes & VanLehn, 2008):

- They know the particular area well.
- They have a good memory for the elements in the problems.
- They form *mental images* or representations that facilitate problem solving.
- They relate the problem to similar problems.
- They are more goal-directed and have efficient methods for problem solving.

These factors are interrelated. Art historians, for example, acquire a database that permits them to understand the intricacies of paintings. As a result, their memory for details of paintings mushrooms.

Novick and Coté (1992) found that the solutions to the anagram problems seemed to "pop out" in under two seconds among experts. The experts apparently used more efficient methods than the novices. Experts seemed to use *parallel processing*. That is, they dealt simultaneously with two or more elements of the problems. In the case of DNSUO, for example, they may have played with the order of the vowels (*UO* or *OU*) at the same time that they tested which consonant (D, N, or S) was likely to precede them, arriving quickly at *sou* and *sound*. Novices were more likely to engage in *serial processing*—that is, to handle one element of the problem at a time.

Mental Sets   The tendency to respond to a new problem with the same approach that helped solve similar problems is termed a **mental set**. Mental sets usually make our work easier, but they can mislead us when the similarity between problems is illusory.

Insight   To gain insight into the role of **insight** in problem solving, consider the following problem, posed by Metcalfe (1986):

> *A stranger approached a museum curator and offered him an ancient bronze coin. The coin had an authentic appearance and was marked with the date 544 BCE. The curator had happily made acquisitions from suspicious sources before, but this time he promptly called the police and had the stranger arrested. Why?*

I'm not going to give you the answer to this problem. But I'll make a guarantee. When you arrive at the solution, it will hit you all at once. You'll think "Of course!" It will seem as though the pieces of information in the problem have suddenly been reorganized so that the solution leaps out—in a flash.

Bismarck, one of psychologist N. R. F. Maier's rats, appeared to suddenly reorganize the pieces of information in a problem with which he was presented, showing evidence of insight in his species (Maier & Schneirla, 1935). Bismarck had been trained to climb a ladder to a tabletop where food was placed. On one occasion, Maier used a mesh barrier to prevent the rat from reaching his goal. But, as shown in Figure 7.2, a second ladder was provided and was visible to the animal. At first Bismarck sniffed and scratched and tried to find a path through the mesh. Then he spent some time washing his face, an activity that may signal frustration in rats. Suddenly he jumped into the air, turned, ran down the familiar ladder and around to the new ladder, ran up the new ladder, and claimed his just desserts. Did Bismarck suddenly perceive the relationships between the elements of the problem so that the solution occurred by insight? He seems to have had what Gestalt psychologists have termed an "Aha! experience."

mental set
the tendency to respond to a new problem with an approach that was successfully used with similar problems

insight
in Gestalt psychology, a sudden perception of relationships among elements of the mentally represented elements of a problem that permits its solution

FICTION   IT APPEARS THAT HUMANS ARE NOT THE ONLY SPECIES WHO USE INSIGHT TO SOLVE PROBLEMS, AS SHOWN IN MAIER'S RESEARCH WITH "BISMARCK."

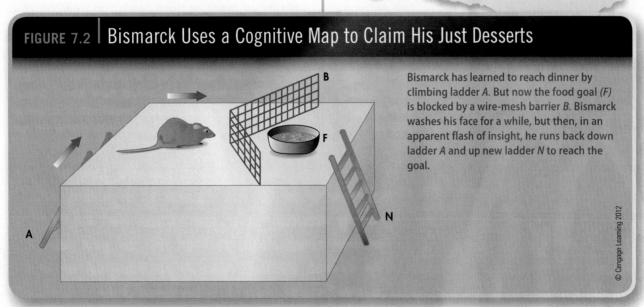

FIGURE 7.2 | Bismarck Uses a Cognitive Map to Claim His Just Desserts

Bismarck has learned to reach dinner by climbing ladder *A*. But now the food goal (*F*) is blocked by a wire-mesh barrier *B*. Bismarck washes his face for a while, but then, in an apparent flash of insight, he runs back down ladder *A* and up new ladder *N* to reach the goal.

© Cengage Learning 2012

Incubation An incubator warms chicken eggs so that they will hatch. **Incubation** in problem solving refers to standing back from the problem for a while as some process within may continue to work on it. Later, the answer may come to us in a flash of insight. Standing back from the problem may help by distancing us from unprofitable but persistent mental sets (Kohn & Smith, 2009; Sio & Ormerod, 2009).

Functional Fixedness **Functional fixedness** may hinder problem solving. For example, first ask yourself what a pair of pliers is. Is it a tool for grasping, a paperweight, or a weapon?

A pair of pliers could function as any of these, but your tendency to think of it as a grasping tool is fostered by your experience with it. You have probably used pliers only for grasping things. Functional fixedness is the tendency to think of an object in terms of its name or its familiar function. It can be similar to a mental set in that it makes it difficult to use familiar objects to solve problems in novel ways.

7-1d JUDGMENT AND DECISION MAKING

You might like to think that people are so rational that they carefully weigh the pros and cons when they make judgments or decisions. Or you might think that they insist on finding and examining all the relevant information. Actually, people make most of their decisions on the basis of limited information. They take shortcuts. They use heuristic devices— rules of thumb—in judgments and decision making just as they do in problem solving (Gigerenzer et al.,

2008). For example, they may let a financial advisor select stocks for them rather than research the companies themselves. Or they may see a doctor recommended by a friend rather than look at the doctor's credentials. In this section we consider various factors in judgment and decision making.

Heuristics in Decision Making

Imagine that you flip a coin six times. In the following three possible outcomes, H stands for heads and T for tails. Circle the most likely sequence:

H H H H H H

H H H T T T

T H H T H T

Did you select T H H T H T as the most likely sequence of events? Most people do. Why? There are two reasons. First, people recognize that the sequence of six heads in a row is unlikely. (The probability of achieving it is $1/2 \times 1/2 \times 1/2 \times 1/2 \times 1/2 \times 1/2$, or 1/64th.) Three heads and three tails are more likely than six heads (or six tails). Second, people recognize that the sequence of heads and tails ought to appear random. T H H T H T has a random look to it, whereas H H H T T T does not.

People tend to select T H H T H T because of the **representativeness heuristic**. According to this decision-making heuristic, people make judgments about events (samples) according to the populations of events that they appear to represent (Nilsson et al., 2008). In this case, the sample of events is six coin tosses. The "population" is an infinite number of random coin tosses. But guess what? *Each* sequence is equally likely (or unlikely). If the question had been whether six heads or three heads and three tails had been more likely, the correct answer would have been three and three.

If the question had been whether heads and tails would be more likely to be consecutive or in random order, the correct answer would have been random order. But each of the three sequences is a *specific* sequence. What is the probability of attaining the *spe-*

How Do You Choose a Doctor? Do you go by reputation or the advice of a friend or family member? Do you check out his or her credentials online? Or do you have no choice because you're on campus or in a particular health insurance plan?

cific sequence T H H T H T? The probability that the first coin toss will result in a tail is 1/2. The probability that the second will result in a head is 1/2, and so on. Thus, the probability of attaining the exact sequence T H H T H T is identical to that of achieving any other specific sequence: $1/2 \times 1/2 \times 1/2 \times 1/2 \times 1/2 \times 1/2 = 1/64$th. (Try this out on a friend.)

Another heuristic device used in decision making is the **availability heuristic**. According to this heuristic, our estimates of frequency or probability are based on how easy it is to find examples of relevant events. Let me ask you whether there are more art majors or sociology majors at your college. Unless you are familiar with the enrollment statistics, you will probably answer on the basis of the numbers of art majors and sociology majors that you know.

The **anchoring and adjustment heuristic** suggests that there can be a good deal of inertia in our judgments. In forming opinions or making estimates, we have an initial view, or presumption. This is the anchor. As we receive additional information, we make adjustments, sometimes grudgingly. That is, if you grow up believing that one religion or one political party is the "right" one, that belief serves as a cognitive anchor. When inconsistencies show up in your religion or political party, you may adjust your views of them, but perhaps not very willingly.

Let's illustrate further by means of a math problem. Write each of the following multiplication problems on a separate piece of paper:

A. $8 \times 7 \times 6 \times 5 \times 4 \times 3 \times 2 \times 1$

B. $1 \times 2 \times 3 \times 4 \times 5 \times 6 \times 7 \times 8$

Show problem A to a few friends. Give them each 5 seconds to estimate the answer. Show problem B to some other friends and give them 5 seconds to estimate the answer.

The answers to the multiplication problems are the same because the order of quantities being multiplied does not change the outcome. However, when Amos Tversky and Daniel Kahneman (1982, 2003) showed these problems to high-school students, the average estimate given by students who were shown version A was significantly higher than that given by students who were shown version B. Students who saw 8 in the first position offered an average estimate of 2,250. Students who saw 1 in the first position gave an average estimate of 512. That is, the estimate was larger when 8 served as the anchor. By the way, what is the correct answer to the multiplication problems? Can you use the anchoring and adjustment heuristic to explain why both groups were so far off?

The Framing Effect

The **framing effect** refers to the way in which wording, or the context in which information is presented, affects decision making (Li & Chapman, 2009; Tetlock & McGraw, 2005). Political groups, like advertisers, are aware of the framing effect and choose their words accordingly. For example, proponents of legalized abortion refer to themselves as "pro-choice" and opponents refer to themselves as "pro-life." Each group frames itself in a positive way ("pro" something) and refers to a popular value (freedom or life).

Overconfidence

Whether our decisions are correct or incorrect, most of us tend to be overconfident about them. We also tend to view our situations with 20-20 hindsight. When we are proven wrong, we frequently find a way to show that we "knew it all along." We also become overconfident that we would have known the actual outcome if we had had access to the information that became available after the event. For example, if we had known that a key player would pull a hamstring muscle, we would have predicted a different outcome for the football game. If we had known that it would be blustery on Election Day, we would have predicted a smaller voter turnout and a different outcome. There are several reasons for overconfidence, even when our judgments are wrong:

- We tend to be unaware of how flimsy our assumptions may be.

- We tend to focus on examples that confirm our judgments and ignore those that do not.

- Because our working memories have limited space, we tend to forget information that runs counter to our judgments.

- We work to bring about the events we believe in, so they sometimes become self-fulfilling prophecies.

7-2 Language

Oscar Wilde, the Irish playwright, wrote "It is only by language that we rise above [the lower animals]—by language, which is the parent, not the child, of thought."

availability heuristic
a decision-making heuristic in which our estimates of frequency or probability of events are based on how easy it is to find examples

anchoring and adjustment heuristic
a decision-making heuristic in which a presumption or first estimate serves as a cognitive anchor; as we receive additional information, we make adjustments but tend to remain in the proximity of the anchor

framing effect
the influence of wording, or the context in which information is presented, on decision making

He gave us quite a bit to think about. Are humans the only species to use language? We'll grapple with that question in a moment. And then, which comes first: language or thinking? Can you think without using language? (Give it a try.) We'll come back to that question later too. For the moment, let's consider whether apes can use language, and also whether language is for the birds—more specifically, the African Grey parrot.

7-2a COMMUNICATION BY NONHUMANS

In recent years, the exclusive human claim to language has been brought into question by studies of communication with various animal species. The African Grey parrot, like many other parrots, can mimic human speech, but it is also suspected of being intelligent enough to understand some of the words it imitates. It has long been suspected that spontaneous language development occurs among many species of dolphins and whales, but we lack solid scientific evidence. Monkeys signal the peril of nearby predators with characteristic hoots. But none of these sounds contains *symbols*.

A language is a system of symbols along with rules that are used to manipulate the symbols. Symbols such as words stand for or represent other objects, events, or ideas. Because chimpanzees and gorillas have been taught to communicate by making signs with their hands, the question as to whether or not they are actually using language in the way that humans do is much more complex.

Chimpanzees are our closest genetic relatives, sharing an estimated 98.42% of their genetic code with humans (Zimmer, 2002–2003). Magnetic resonance imaging (MRI) studies with chimpanzees and gorillas show that most of them, like humans, show enlargement in the left hemisphere of the cerebral cortex, in part of Broca's area (Cantalupo & Hopkins, 2001; Keller et al., 2009). The differences that remain between humans and chimps are at least in part associated with capabilities such as fine control of the mouth and larynx that are not found in apes (Sherwood et al., 2008). The genetic differences between chimps and humans probably explain why chimps cannot articulate speech but also apparently give chimps and other apes some meaningful ability to use language (Sherwood et al., 2008).

"MAN INVENTED LANGUAGE TO SATISFY HIS DEEP NEED TO COMPLAIN."

–LILY TOMLIN

Do Apes Really Use Language?

Although apes do not speak, they have been taught to use American Sign Language and other symbol systems. For example, a chimpanzee named Washoe, who was a pioneer in the effort to teach apes to use language, was using 181 signs by the age of 32 (King, 2008). Loulis, a baby chimp adopted by Washoe, gained the ability to use signs just by observing Washoe and some other chimps that had been trained in sign language. Other chimps have used plastic symbols or pressed keys on a computer keyboard to communicate.

Sue Savage-Rumbaugh and her colleagues (Segerdahl et al., 2006; Washburn et al., 2007) believe that pygmy chimpanzees can understand some of the *semantic* subtleties of language. She claims that one chimp, Kanzi, picked up language from observing another chimp being trained and has the grammatical abilities of a 2½-year-old child. Kanzi also understands several words spoken by humans. Kanzi held a toy snake to a toy dog's mouth when asked to make the dog bite the snake.

Critics of the view that apes can learn to produce language, such as Herbert Terrace (Terrace & Metcalfe, 2005) and Steven Pinker (1994a, 2011), note that:

- Apes can string together signs in a given sequence to earn rewards, but animals lower on the evolutionary ladder, such as pigeons, can also peck buttons in a certain sequence to obtain a reward.
- It takes apes longer to learn new signs than it takes children to learn new words.
- Apes are unreliable in their sequencing of signs, suggesting that by and large they do not comprehend rules of grammar.
- People observing apes signing may be subject to *observer bias*—that is, they may be seeing what they want to see.

Scientists will continue to debate how well chimpanzees and gorillas understand and produce language, but there is little doubt that they have learned to use symbols to communicate (Segerdahl et al., 2006).

7-2b WHAT IS LANGUAGE?

As you can see from the discussion of apes and language, the way in which one defines language is no small matter. If we define language simply as a system of communication, many animals have language, including the birds and the bees. Through particular chirps and shrieks, birds may communicate that they have taken possession of a tree or bush. The waggle dances of bees inform other bees of the location of a food source or a predator. All of these are instinctive communication patterns but not what we mean by language.

With language, sounds or signs are symbols for objects and actions. Apes have been taught to use symbols to communicate, but is such usage an adequate definition of language? Many language experts require one more piece. They define **language** as the communication of thoughts and feelings by means of symbols *that are arranged according to rules of grammar*. Instinctive waggle dances and shrieks have no symbols and no grammar. By these rigorous rules, only humans use language. Whether apes can handle rules of grammar is under debate.

Language makes it possible for one person to communicate knowledge to another and for one generation to communicate to another. It creates a vehicle for recording experiences. It allows us to put ourselves in the shoes of other people, to learn more than we could learn from direct experience. Language also provides many units of thinking.

True language is distinguished from the communication systems of lower animals by properties such as semanticity, infinite creativity, and displacement (Hoff, 2005):

- **Semanticity**: The sounds (or signs) of a language have meaning. Words serve as symbols for actions, objects, relational concepts (*over, in, more,* and so on), and other ideas. The communication systems of the birds and the bees do not use words and symbols. Therefore, they lack semanticity.

- **Infinite creativity**: The capacity to create rather than imitate sentences.

- **Displacement**: The capacity to communicate information about events and objects in another time or place. Language makes it possible to transmit knowledge from one person to another and from one generation to another, furthering human adaptation.

7-2c LANGUAGE AND COGNITION

The relationships between language and thinking are complex and not always obvious. For example, can you think *without* using language? Would you be able to solve problems without using words or sentences?

Jean Piaget (Inhelder & Piaget, 1958) believed that language reflects knowledge of the world but that much knowledge can be acquired without language. For example, it is possible to understand the concepts of roundness or redness even when we do not know or use the words *round* or *red*.

language
the communication of information by means of symbols arranged according to rules of grammar

semanticity
meaning; the quality of language in which words are used as symbols for objects, events, or ideas

infinite creativity
the capacity to combine words into original sentences

displacement
the quality of language that permits one to communicate information about objects and events in another time and place

Joyce Butler of Columbia University shows chimpanzee "Nim Chimpsky"— named humorously after linguist Noam Chomsky— the sign for "drink," and Nim imitates her.

7-2d LANGUAGE AND CULTURE

Different languages have different words for the same concepts, and concepts do not necessarily overlap. As noted earlier, concepts expressed in our own language (such as *square* and *triangle*) may not exist in the language of another culture—and vice versa. Is it possible for English speakers to share the thoughts experienced by people who speak other languages? The answer is probably yes in many or most cases, but in some cases, no. In any event, the question brings us to the linguistic-relativity hypothesis.

The Linguistic-Relativity Hypothesis

The **linguistic-relativity hypothesis** was proposed by Benjamin Whorf (1956). Whorf believed that language structures the way we perceive the world. That is, the categories and relationships we use to understand the world are derived from our language. Therefore, speakers of various languages conceptualize the world in different ways.

Thus, most English speakers' ability to think about snow may be limited compared with that of the Inuit (Eskimos). We have only a few words for snow, whereas the Inuit have many. The Inuit's words differ according to whether the snow is hard packed, falling, melting, covered by ice, and so on. When we think about snow, we have fewer words to choose from and have to search for descrip-

How many words do you know for snow?

tive adjectives. The Inuit, however, can readily find a single word that describes a complex weather condition. Is it therefore easier for them to think about this variety of snow? Similarly, the Hanunoo people of the Philippines use 92 words for rice depending on whether the rice is husked or unhusked and on how it is prepared. And whereas we have one word for camel, Arabs have more than 250.

In English, we have hundreds of words to describe colors. There is about a 95% overlap in perception and labeling of colors among English speakers and Chinese people (Moore et al., 2002). It has been pointed out, however, that Shona-speaking people use only three words for colors, and Bassa speakers use only two corresponding to light and dark. Nevertheless, studies of languages spoken in nonindustrialized societies find overlaps for white, black, red, green, yellow, and blue (Regier, 2005; Tohidian, 2009). Moreover, people who use only a few words to distinguish among colors seem to perceive the same color variations as people with more words. For example, the Dani of New Guinea have just two words for colors: one that refers to yellows and reds and one that refers to greens and blues. Yet performance on matching and memory tasks shows that the Dani can discriminate the many colors of the spectrum.

Most cognitive scientists no longer accept the linguistic-relativity hypothesis (Pinker, 2007, 2011). For one thing, adults use images and abstract logical propositions, as well as words, as units of thought. Infants, moreover, display considerable intelligence before they have learned to speak. Another criticism is that a language's vocabulary suggests the range of concepts that the speakers of the language have traditionally found important, not their cognitive limits. For example, people who were magically lifted from the 19th century and placed inside an airplane probably would not think they were flying inside a bird or a large insect, even if their language lacked a word for airplane.

7-2e LANGUAGE DEVELOPMENT: THE TWO-YEAR EXPLOSION

Languages around the world develop in a specific sequence of steps, beginning with the *prelinguistic* vocalizations of crying, cooing, and babbling. These sounds are not symbols. That is, they do not represent objects or events. Therefore, they are *prelinguistic*, not linguistic.

Prelinguistic Vocalizations

As parents are well aware, newborn children have one inborn, highly effective form of verbal expression: crying—and more crying. But crying does not represent language; it is a prelinguistic event. During the second month, babies begin *cooing*, another form of prelinguistic expression that appears to be linked to feelings of pleasure. By the fifth or sixth month, children begin to *babble*. Children babble sounds that occur in many languages, including the throaty German *ch*, the clicks of certain African languages, and rolling *r*'s. Babies' babbling frequently combines consonants and vowels, as in "ba," "ga," and, sometimes, the much-valued "dada" (McCardle et al., 2009). "Dada" at first is purely coincidental (sorry, dads), despite the family's delight over its appearance.

Babbling, like crying and cooing, is inborn and prelinguistic. Deaf children babble, and children from cultures whose languages sound very different all seem to babble the same sounds (Hoff, 2005). But children single out the sounds used in the home within a few months. By the age of 9 or 10 months, they are repeating the sounds regularly, and foreign sounds are dropping out. In fact, early experience in acquiring the phonemes (that is, meaningful units of sound) native to one's own language can make it difficult to pronounce and even discriminate the phonemes used in other languages later in life (Iverson et al., 2003).

Children tend to utter their first word at 11 to 13 months, but a range of 8 to 18 months is normal (McCardle et al., 2009; Tamis-LeMonda et al., 2006). Parents often miss the first word because it is not pronounced clearly. The growth of vocabulary is slow at first. It may take children 3 to 4 months to achieve a 10-word vocabulary after they have spoken their first word. By about 18 months, children are producing a couple of dozen words.

FICTION CRYING DOES *NOT* REPRESENT LANGUAGE; IT IS A PRELINGUISTIC EVENT.

Although crying can effectively communicate discomfort and the desire to have a caregiver present—now—cries do not possess symbols and are thus not an example of true language.

holophrase a single word used to express complex meanings

Development of Grammar

The first linguistic utterances of children around the globe are single words that can express complex meanings. These initial utterances of children are called **holophrases**. For example, *mama* may be used by the child to signify meanings as varied as "There goes Mama," "Come here, Mama," and "You are my Mama." Similarly, *cat* can signify "There is a cat," "That stuffed animal looks just like my cat," or "I want you to give me my cat right now!" Most children show their parents what they intend by augmenting their holophrases with gestures and intonations. That is, they act delighted when parents do as requested and howl when they do not.

Toward the end of the second year, children begin to speak two-word sentences. These sentences are termed *telegraphic speech* because they resemble telegrams. Telegrams cut out the "unnecessary" words. "Home Tuesday" might stand for "I expect to be home on Tuesday." Two-word utterances seem to appear at about the same time in the development of all languages (Saffran, 2009; Slobin, 1983). Two-word utterances are brief but grammatically correct. The child says, "Sit chair" to tell a parent to sit in a chair, not "Chair sit." The child says, "My shoe," not "Shoe my," to show possession. "Mommy go" means Mommy is leaving. "Go Mommy" expresses the wish for Mommy to go away.

There are different kinds of two-word utterances. Some, for example, contain nouns or pronouns and verbs ("Daddy sit"). Others contain verbs and objects ("Hit ball"). The sequence of emergence of the various kinds of two-word utterances is also apparently the same in all languages—languages as diverse as English, Luo (an African tongue), German, Russian, and Turkish (Slobin, 1983). The invariance of this sequence has implications for theories of language development, as we will see.

overregularization
the application of regular grammatical rules for forming inflections (e.g., past tense and plurals) to irregular verbs and nouns

Overregularization

Overregularization is an important development for understanding the roles of nature and nurture in language development (E. V. Clark & Nikitina, 2009). In English, we add *d* or *ed* to make the past tense of regular verbs and *s* or *z* sounds to make regular nouns plural. Thus, *walk* becomes *walked*, and *look* becomes *looked*. *Cat* becomes *cats*, and *doggy* becomes *doggies*. There are also irregular verbs and nouns. For example, *see* becomes *saw*, *sit* becomes *sat*, and *go* becomes *went*. *Sheep* remains *sheep* (plural) and *child* becomes *children*.

At first children learn irregular verbs and nouns by imitating older people. Two-year-olds tend to form them correctly—at first! Then they become aware of the grammatical rules for forming the past tense and plurals. As a result, they tend to make charming errors (Pinker, 2011). A three- to five-year-old, for example, may be more likely to say "I seed it" than "I saw it," and more likely to say "Mommy sitted down" than "Mommy sat down." They are likely to talk about the "gooses" and "sheeps" they "seed" on the farm and about all the "childs" they ran into at the playground. This tendency to regularize the irregular is what is meant by overregularization.

Should parents be concerned about overregularization? Not at all. Overregularization reflects knowledge of grammar, not faulty language development. In another year or two, *mouses* will be boringly transformed into *mice*, and Mommy will no longer have *sitted* down. Parents might as well enjoy overregularization while they can.

Other Developments

By the age of six, children's vocabularies have expanded to 10,000 words, give or take a few thousand. By seven to nine, most children realize that words can have more than one meaning, and they are entertained by riddles and jokes that require some sophistication with language.

TRUTH YOUNG CHILDREN SAY THINGS LIKE "DADDY GOED AWAY" AND "MOMMY SITTED DOWN" BECAUSE THEY *DO* UNDERSTAND RULES OF GRAMMAR.

"Since all normal humans talk but no house pets or house plants do, no matter how pampered, heredity must be involved in language. But since a child growing up in Japan speaks Japanese whereas the same child brought up in California would speak English, the environment is also crucial."

—STEVEN PINKER,
THE LANGUAGE INSTINCT

Between the elementary school and high school years, language grows more complex, and children rapidly add to their vocabularies. Vocabulary, in fact, can grow for a lifetime, especially in one's fields of specialization and interest.

7-2f NATURE AND NURTURE IN LANGUAGE DEVELOPMENT

Billions of children have acquired the languages spoken by their parents and passed them down, with minor changes, from generation to generation. Language development, like many other areas of development, apparently reflects the interactions between nature and nurture.

Learning Theory and Language Development

Learning theorists see language as developing according to laws of learning (Hoff, 2005). They usually refer to the concepts of imitation and reinforcement. From a social-cognitive perspective, parents serve as *models*. Children learn language, at least in part, through observation and imitation. Many words, especially nouns and verbs (including irregular verbs), are apparently learned by imitation.

Children initially repeat the irregular verb forms they have heard accurately, apparently as a result of modeling. Modeling, however, does not explain all of the events in language learning. As noted previously, children later overregularize irregular verb forms because they have developed an understanding of grammar. Nor can learning by imitation explain how children come to utter phrases and sentences they have *not* observed. Parents, for example, are unlikely to model utterances such as "Bye-bye sock" and "All gone Daddy," but children say them.

Learning theory cannot account for the unchanging sequence of language development and the spurts in children's language acquisition. Even the types of two-word utterances emerge in a consistent pattern in diverse cultures. Although timing differs from one child to another, the types of questions used, passive versus active sentences, and so on, all emerge in the same order.

The Nativist Approach to Language Development

The nativist theory of language development holds that the innate factors—which make up children's *nature*—cause children to attend to and acquire language in certain ways. From this perspective, children bring neurological "prewiring" to language learning (A. Clark & Misyak, 2009; Pinker, 2011).

According to **psycholinguistic theory**, language acquisition involves the interaction of environmental influences—such as exposure to parental speech and reinforcement—and the inborn tendency to acquire language. Noam Chomsky (see Cherniak, 2009) refers to the inborn tendency as a **language acquisition device (LAD)**. Evidence for an LAD is found in the universality of human language abilities and in the specific sequence of language development (Cherniak, 2009; A. Clark & Misyak, 2009).

The LAD prepares the nervous system to learn grammar. On the surface, languages differ a great deal. However, the LAD serves children all over the world because languages share what Chomsky refers to as a "universal grammar"—an underlying set of rules for turning ideas into sentences (Pinker, 2011).

psycholinguistic theory
the view that language learning involves an interaction between environmental factors and an inborn tendency to acquire language

language acquisition device (LAD)
in psycholinguistic theory, neural "prewiring" that facilitates the child's learning of grammar

"Motherese"—Of "Yummy Yummy" and "Kitty Cats"

One way that adults attempt to prompt the language development of children is by using baby talk, or "motherese," referred to more technically as *infant-directed speech (IDS)* (Meltzoff & Brooks, 2009; Singh et al., 2009). Motherese is a limiting term because grandparents, fathers, siblings, and unrelated people have also been observed using IDS (Braarud & Stormark, 2008). Moreover, women (but usually not men) often talk to their pets as if they were infants (Prato-Previde et al., 2006). Infant-directed speech is used in languages as diverse as Arabic, English, Comanche, Italian, French, German, Xhosa (an African tongue), Japanese, Mandarin Chinese, and even a Thai sign language (Lee et al., 2010; Nonaka, 2004).

IDS has the following characteristics (Matsuda et al., 2011; Meltzoff & Brooks, 2009):

- It is spoken more slowly, at a higher pitch, and includes pauses between ideas.

- Sentences are brief, and the focus is on nouns, verbs, and just a few modifiers.

- Key words are placed at the ends of sentences and spoken in a higher, louder voice.

- The diminutive *y* is frequently added to nouns. *Dad* becomes *Daddy*; *horse* becomes *horsey*.

- Adults repeat sentences, sometimes using minor variations, as in "Show me your nose." "Where is your nose?"

- It includes duplication. *Yummy* becomes *yummy-yummy*. *Daddy* may alternate with *Da-da*.

- Much IDS focuses on naming objects (Meltzoff & Brooks, 2009). Vocabulary is concrete and refers to the child's environment. For example, stuffed lions may be called "kitties."

- Objects may be overdescribed with compound labels. Rabbits may become "bunny rabbits," and cats may become "kitty cats." Users of IDS try to ensure they are using at least one label the child will recognize.

- Parents speak for the children, as in "Is baby tired?" "Oh, we're so tired." Parents seem to be helping children express themselves by offering them models of sentences they can use.

Does IDS encourage communication and foster language development? Research supports its use. Infants as young as two days old prefer IDS to adult talk (N. A. Smith & Trainor, 2008). The short, simple sentences and high pitch are more likely to produce a response from the child and enhance vocabulary development than complex sentences and those spoken in a lower pitch (Matsuda et al., 2011). Repetition of children's vocalizations appears to encourage vocalizing.

intelligence

a general mental capability that involves the ability to reason, plan, solve problems, think abstractly, comprehend complex ideas, learn quickly, and learn from experience

g

Spearman's symbol for general intelligence, which he believed underlay more specific abilities

s

Spearman's symbol for *specific* factors, or *s factors,* which he believed accounted for individual abilities

primary mental abilities

according to Thurstone, the basic abilities that make up intelligence examples include word fluency and numerical ability

In the following section, we see that some aspects of language development—particularly vocabulary development—are strongly related to intelligence. Numerous researchers suggest that language learning occurs during one or more *sensitive periods,* which begin at about 18 to 24 months and last until puberty (Bates, 2001). During these sensitive periods, neural development (as in the differentiating of brain structures) provides plasticity that facilitates language learning.

7-3 Intelligence

The concept of intelligence is closely related to thinking. Whereas thinking involves the understanding and manipulating of information, **intelligence** is the underlying ability to understand the world and cope with its challenges (Cornoldi, 2006; Sternberg et al., 2005). That is, intelligence is seen as making thinking possible. Although these concepts overlap, psychologists tend to be concerned with *how* we think, but laypeople and psychologists are often concerned with *how much* intelligence we have. Although intelligence, like thinking, cannot be directly seen or touched, psychologists tie the concept to achievements such as school performance and occupational status (Nisbett, 2009).

7-3a THEORIES OF INTELLIGENCE

Although psychologists have engaged in thousands of studies on intelligence, they do not quite agree on what intelligence is. Psychologists have therefore developed theories to help them understand and define intelligence.

Factor Theories

Many investigators have viewed intelligence as consisting of one or more *factors.* Factor theories argue that intelligence is made up of a number of mental abilities, ranging from one kind of ability to hundreds.

In 1904, British psychologist Charles Spearman suggested that the behaviors we consider intelligent have a common underlying factor that he labeled ***g,*** for "general intelligence" or broad reasoning and problem-solving abilities. Spearman supported his view by noting that people who excel in one area (such as vocabulary) are also likely to excel in others (such as math). But he also noted that even the most capable people are relatively superior in some areas—such as music or business or poetry. For this reason, he suggested that specific, or ***s,*** factors account for specific abilities.

Contemporary psychologists continue to use the term *g* in research, speaking, for example, of the extent to which they believe a particular kind of test, such as the SATs, measure *g* (Lubinski & Benbow, 2006).

American psychologist Louis Thurstone (1938) analyzed tests of specific abilities and concluded that Spearman had oversimplified intelligence. Thurstone's data suggested the presence of eight specific factors, which he labeled **primary mental abilities** (see Table 7.1). Thurstone's primary mental abilities contain the types of items measured on the most widely used intelligence tests today. The question remains as to whether his primary mental abilities are distinct or whether they are different ways of assessing *g*.

The Theory of Multiple Intelligences

Thurstone wrote about various factors or components of intelligence. Howard Gardner's (1983/1993, 2009) *theory of multiple intelligences* proposes, instead, that there are a number of *intelligences,* not just one. Gardner

TABLE 7.1

Primary Mental Abilities, According to Thurstone

ABILITY	DEFINITION
Visual and spatial abilities	Visualizing forms and spatial relationships
Perceptual speed	Grasping perceptual details rapidly, perceiving similarities and differences between stimuli
Numerical ability	Computing numbers
Verbal meaning	Knowing the meanings of words
Memory	Recalling information (e.g., words and sentences)
Word fluency	Thinking of words quickly (e.g., rhyming and doing crossword puzzles)
Deductive reasoning	Deriving examples from general rules
Inductive reasoning	Inferring general rules from examples

© Cengage Learning 2012

refers to each kind of intelligence in his theory as "an intelligence" because they can differ so much. Two of these "intelligences" are familiar ones: language ability and logical–mathematical ability. Gardner also refers, however, to bodily–kinesthetic talents (of the sort shown by dancers and athletes), musical talent, spatial–relations skills, and two kinds of personal intelligence: awareness of one's own inner feelings and sensitivity to other people's feelings. Gardner (2001) more recently added "naturalist intelligence" and "existential intelligence." Naturalist intelligence refers to the ability to look at natural events, such as kinds of animals and plants, or the stars above, and to develop insights into their nature and the laws that govern their behavior. Existential intelligence means dealing with the larger philosophical issues of life. According to Gardner, one can compose symphonies or advance mathematical theory yet be average in, say, language and personal skills.

Critics of Gardner's view agree that people function more intelligently in some aspects of life than in others. They also agree that many people have special talents, such as bodily–kinesthetic talents, even if their overall intelligence is average. But these critics question whether such talents are best thought of as "intelligences" or special talents (Neisser et al., 1996). Language skills, reasoning ability, and ability to solve math problems seem to be more closely related than musical or gymnastic talent to what most people mean by intelligence.

The Triarchic Theory of Intelligence

Psychologist Robert Sternberg (2000; 2006) has constructed a three-pronged or *triarchic theory of intelligence* that resembles a view proposed by the Greek philosopher Aristotle (Tigner & Tigner, 2000). The three prongs include *analytical, creative*, and *practical intelligence* (see Figure 7.3).

Analytical intelligence is similar to Aristotle's "theoretical intelligence" and can be defined as academic ability. It enables us to solve problems and acquire new knowledge. It is the type of intelligence measured by standard intelligence tests. Problem-solving skills include encoding information, combining and comparing bits of information, and generating a solution. Consider Sternberg's analogy problem:

Washington is to *1* as *Lincoln* is to
(a) 5, (b) 10, (c) 15, (d) 50?

To solve the analogy, we must first correctly *encode* the elements—*Washington, 1,* and *Lincoln*—by identifying them and comparing them to other information. We can first encode *Washington* and *Lincoln* as the names of presidents and then try to combine *Washington* and *1* in a meaningful manner. (There are other possibilities: Both are also the names of memorials and cities, for example.) If we do encode the names as presidents, two possibilities quickly come to mind. Washington was the first president, and his picture is on the $1 bill. We can then generate two possible solutions and try them out. First, was Lincoln the 5th, 10th, 15th, or 50th president? Second, on what bill is Lincoln's picture found? (Do you need to consult a history book or peek into your wallet at this point?) The answer is (a) 5, because Lincoln's likeness is found on the $5 bill. (He was the nation's 16th president, not 15th president.)

Creative intelligence is similar to Aristotle's "productive intelligence" and is defined by the ability to cope with novel situations and generate many possible solutions to problems. It is creative to quickly relate novel situations to familiar situations (that is, to perceive similarities and differences). Psychologists who consider creativity to be separate from analytical intelligence or academic ability note that there is only a moderate relationship between academic ability and creativity (Simonton, 2009). To Sternberg, however, creativity *is* a form of intelligence.

Aristotle and Sternberg both speak of practical intelligence ("street smarts"). Practical intelligence enables people to deal with other people, including difficult people, and to meet the demands of their environment. For example, keeping a job by adapting one's behavior to the employer's requirements is adaptive. But if the employer is making unreasonable demands, finding a more suitable job is also adaptive. Street smarts appear to help people get by in the real world, especially with other people, but are not particularly predictive of academic success (Heng, 2000).

Emotional Intelligence

Psychologists Peter Salovey and John Mayer developed the theory of emotional intelligence, which was popularized by psychologist Daniel Goleman (1995). The theory holds that social and emotional skills, like academic skills, are a form of intelligence (Mayer et al., 2008; Salovey et al., 2008). Emotional intelligence resembles two of Gardner's "intelligences"—intrapersonal

FIGURE 7.3 | Sternberg's Theory of Intelligence

According to Robert Sternberg, there are three types of intelligence: analytical (academic ability), creative, and practical ("street smarts"). Psychologists discuss the relationships between intelligence and creativity, but within Sternberg's model, creativity is a *type* of intellectual functioning.

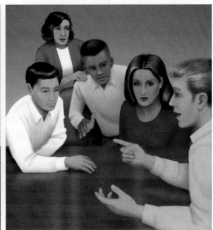

Analytical intelligence
(Academic ability)
Abilities to solve problems, compare and contrast, judge, evaluate, and criticize

Creative intelligence
(Creativity and insight)
Abilities to invent, discover, suppose, or theorize

Practical intelligence
("Street smarts")
Abilities to adapt to the demands of one's environment and apply knowledge in practical situations

© Cengage Learning 2012

skills and interpersonal skills (including insight into the feelings of other people). It also involves self-insight and self-control—the abilities to recognize and regulate one's moods (Salovey et al., 2008). Failure to develop emotional intelligence is connected with poor ability to cope with stress, depression, and aggressive behavior (Brackett et al., 2011).

But *is* emotional intelligence a form of intelligence? Psychologist Ulric Neisser (1997b) says that "the skills that Goleman describes … are certainly important for determining life outcomes, but nothing is to be gained by calling them forms of intelligence."

There are thus many views of intelligence—what intelligence is and how many kinds of intelligence there may be. We do not yet have the final word on the nature of intelligence, but I would like to share psychologist Linda Gottfredson's definition: Intelligence is "a very general mental capability that, among other things, involves the ability to reason, plan, solve problems, think abstractly, comprehend complex ideas, learn quickly and learn from experience. It is not merely book learning, a narrow academic skill, or test-taking smarts. Rather it reflects a broader and deeper capability for comprehending our surroundings—'catching on,' 'making sense,' of things, or 'figuring out what to do'" (in Nisbett, 2009, p. 4).

7-3b CREATIVITY AND INTELLIGENCE

Think of artists, musicians, poets, scientists who innovate research methods, and other creative individuals. Like the concept of intelligence, the concept of creativity has been difficult to define. One issue is whether creativity is distinct from intelligence, or is, as Sternberg suggests, a type of intelligence. For example, we would not ask the question, "Do creative people tend to be intelligent?" unless we saw creativity as distinct from intelligence. If you consider creativity to be an aspect of intelligence, then the two concepts—intelligence and creativity—overlap. But if you think of intelligence as more closely related to academic ability, it is not always true that a highly intelligent person is creative or that a creative person is highly intelligent. Research findings suggest that the relationship between intelligence test

TRUTH ~~**FICTION**~~

(DEPENDS)

THE ANSWER TO WHETHER AN INTELLIGENT PERSON IS CREATIVE OR A CREATIVE PERSON IS INTELLIGENT PARTLY DEPENDS ON DEFINITIONS OF THE TERMS. WHICH PSYCHOLOGIST CONSIDERS CREATIVITY TO BE A KIND OF INTELLIGENCE?

scores and standard measures of creativity is only moderate (Simonton, 2009).

Within his triarchic theory, Sternberg defines **creativity** as the ability to do things that are novel and useful (Sternberg et al., 2012). Creative people can solve problems to which there are no preexisting solutions and no proven formulas. Creative people share a number of qualities (Sternberg et al., 2012): They take chances. They refuse to accept limitations. They appreciate art and music. They use common materials to make unique things. They challenge social norms and take unpopular stands. They challenge ideas that other people accept at face value.

Creative problem solving demands divergent rather than convergent thinking. In **convergent thinking**, thought is limited to present facts; the problem-solver narrows his or her thinking to find the best solution. (You use convergent thinking to arrive at the right answer to a multiple-choice question.) In **divergent thinking**, the problem-solver associates freely to the elements of the problem, allowing "leads" to run a nearly limitless course. (You may use divergent thinking when you are trying to generate ideas to answer an essay question on a test.) Problem solving can involve both kinds of thinking. At first, divergent thinking helps generate many possible solutions. Convergent thinking is then used to select likely solutions and reject others.

Intelligence test questions usually require analytical, convergent thinking to focus in on the one right answer. Tests of creativity determine how flexible a person's thinking is (Simonton, 2009). Here is an item from a test used by Getzels and Jackson (1962) to measure associative ability, a factor in creativity: "Write as many meanings as you can for each of the following words: (a) duck; (b) sack; (c) pitch; (d) fair." Those who write several meanings for each word, rather than only one, are rated as potentially more creative.

Now that we have begun speaking of scores on intelligence tests, let's see how psychologists go about measuring intelligence. We will also see how psychologists attempt to *validate* their measures of intelligence—that is, how they try to demonstrate that they are in fact measuring intelligence.

7-3c THE MEASUREMENT OF INTELLIGENCE

Although psychologists disagree about the nature of intelligence, laypeople and educators are concerned with "how much" intelligence people have, because the issue affects educational and occupational choices. In this section we consider two of the most widely used intelligence tests.

The Stanford–Binet Intelligence Scale

Many of the concepts of psychology have their origins in common sense. The commonsense notion that academic achievement depends on children's intelligence led Alfred Binet and Theodore Simon to invent measures of intelligence.

Early in the 20th century, the French public school system was looking for a test that could identify children who were unlikely to benefit from regular classroom instruction. If these children were identified, they could be given special attention. The first version of that test, the Binet–Simon scale, came into use in 1905. Since that time it has undergone extensive revision and refinement. The current version is the Stanford–Binet Intelligence Scale (SBIS).

Binet assumed that intelligence increases with age, so older children should get more items right than younger children. Binet therefore included a series of age-graded questions, as in Table 7.2, arranged in order of difficulty.

The Binet–Simon scale yielded a score called a **mental age (MA)**. The MA shows the intellectual level at which a child is functioning. For example, a child with an MA of six is functioning intellectually like the average six-year-old. In taking the test, children earned "months" of credit for each correct answer. Their MA was determined by adding up the years and months of credit they attained.

Louis Terman adapted the Binet–Simon scale for use with American children at Stanford University. The first version of the resultant Stanford–Binet Intelligence Scale was published in 1916. The SBIS included more items than the original test and was used with children aged 2 to 16. The SBIS also yielded an **intelligence quotient (IQ)** rather than an MA. As a result, American educators developed interest in learning the IQs of their pupils. The SBIS is used today with children from the age of two upward and with adults.

The IQ reflects the relationship between a child's mental age and his or her actual or chronological age (CA). Use of this ratio reflects the fact that the same MA score has different implications for children of dif-

creativity
the ability to generate novel and useful solutions to problems

convergent thinking
a thought process that narrows in on the single best solution to a problem

divergent thinking
a thought process that attempts to generate multiple solutions to problems

mental age (MA)
the accumulated months of credit that a person earns on the Stanford–Binet Intelligence Scale

intelligence quotient (IQ)
(a) originally, a ratio obtained by dividing a child's score (or mental age) on an intelligence test by chronological age. (b) generally, a score on an intelligence test

TABLE 7.2

Items Similar to Those on the Stanford–Binet Intelligence Scale

LEVEL (YEARS)	ITEM
2	1. Children show knowledge of basic vocabulary words by identifying parts of a doll, such as the mouth, ears, and hair.
	2. Children show counting and spatial skills along with visual–motor coordination by building a tower of four blocks to match a model.
4	1. Children show word fluency and categorical thinking by filling in the missing words when they are asked questions such as: "Father is a man; mother is a _____?" "Hamburgers are hot; ice cream is_____?"
	2. Children show comprehension by answering correctly when they are asked questions such as: "Why do people have automobiles?" "Why do people have medicine?"
9	1. Children can point out verbal absurdities, as in this question: "In an old cemetery, scientists unearthed a skull which they think was that of George Washington when he was only five years of age. What is silly about that?"
	2. Children display fluency with words, as shown by answering these questions: "Can you tell me a number that rhymes with snore?" "Can you tell me a color that rhymes with glue?"
Adult	1. Adults show knowledge of the meanings of words and conceptual thinking by correctly explaining the differences between word pairs like "sickness and misery," "house and home," and "integrity and prestige."
	2. Adults show spatial skills by correctly answering questions like: "If a car turned to the right to head north, in what direction was it heading before it turned?"

Rubberball/Mike Kemp/Jupiterimages

ferent ages. That is, an MA of 8 is an above-average score for a 6-year-old but below average for a 10-year-old. In 1912, German psychologist Wilhelm Stern suggested the IQ as a way to deal with this problem. Stern computed IQ using the formula

$$IQ = \frac{\text{Mental age (MA)}}{\text{Chronological age (CA)}} \times 100.$$

According to this formula, a child with an MA of 6 and a CA of 6 would have an IQ of 100. Children who can handle intellectual problems as well as older children do have IQs above 100. For example, an 8-year-old who does as well on the SBIS as the average 10-year-old would attain an IQ of 125. Children who do not answer as many items correctly as other children of the same age attain MAs lower than their CAs. Thus, their IQ scores are below 100.

IQ scores on the SBIS today are derived by comparing their results to those of other people of the same age. People who answer more items correctly than the average for people of the same age attain IQ scores above 100. People who answer fewer

items correctly than the average for their age attain scores below 100. Therefore, two children can answer exactly the same items on an intelligence test correctly, yet one can be above average in IQ. This is because the ages of the children may differ. The more intelligent child would be the younger of the two.

The Wechsler Scales

In contrast to the SBIS, David Wechsler developed a series of scales for use with children and adults. The Wechsler scales group test questions into a number of separate subtests (see Figure 7.4). Each subtest measures a different intellectual task. For this reason, the test shows how well a person does on one type of task (such as defining words) as compared with another (such as using blocks to construct geometric designs). In this way, the Wechsler scales highlight children's relative strengths and weaknesses, as well as measure overall intellectual functioning.

Wechsler described some of his scales as measuring *verbal* tasks and others as assessing *performance* tasks. In general, verbal subtests re-

TRUTH TWO CHILDREN CAN ANSWER EXACTLY THE SAME ITEMS ON AN INTELLIGENCE TEST CORRECTLY, YET ONE CAN BE ABOVE AVERAGE AND THE OTHER BELOW AVERAGE IN IQ.

quire knowledge of verbal concepts, whereas performance subtests require familiarity with spatial–relations concepts. Wechsler's scales permit the computation of verbal and performance IQs. Nontechnically oriented college students often attain higher verbal than performance IQs. Less-well-educated people often obtain higher performance than verbal IQs.

Wechsler also introduced the concept of the *deviation IQ*. Instead of dividing mental age by chronological age to compute an IQ, he based IQ scores on how a person's answers compared with those attained by people in the same age group. The average test result at any age level is defined as an IQ score of 100. Wechsler distributed IQ scores so that the middle 50% were defined as the "broad average range" of 90 to 110. As you can see in Figure 7.5, IQ scores cluster around the average. Only 4% of the population have IQ scores of above 130 or below 70.

FIGURE 7.4 | Items Similar to Those on the Wechsler Adult Intelligence Scale

Picture arrangement

These pictures tell a story, but they are in the wrong order. Put them in the right order so that they tell a story.

Picture completion

What part is missing from this picture?

Block design

Put the blocks together to make this picture.

Object assembly

Put the pieces together as quickly as you can.

© Cengage Learning 2012

Group Tests

The SBIS and Wechsler scales are administered to one person at a time. This one-to-one ratio is optimal because it allows the examiner to observe the test taker closely. Examiners are alerted to factors that impair performance, such as language difficulties, illness, or a noisy or poorly lit room. But large institutions with few trained examiners, such as the public schools and armed forces, require tests that can be administered simultaneously to large groups.

Group tests for children were first developed during World War I. At first these tests were hailed as remarkable instruments because they helped school administrators place children. As the years passed, however, group tests came under attack because many administrators relied on them exclusively and did not seek other sources of information about children's abilities.

At their best, intelligence tests provide only one source of information about individual children. Numbers alone, and especially IQ scores, cannot adequately define children's special abilities and talents.

The Reliability and Validity of Intelligence Tests

Over the years, the SBIS and the Wechsler scales have been shown to be reliable and valid. In terms of *reliability*, the scores are rather consistent from testing to testing. This kind of reliability is called *test–retest reliability*. The tests also show *validity* in that the scores correlate moderately to highly with the variables they are supposed to predict, such as school performance, even though motivation and adjustment to the school setting are also involved (Kaplan & Saccuzzo, 2008; Roid & Tippin, 2009).

FIGURE 7.5 | Approximate Distribution of IQ Scores

Approximate percentage of population

25
16
7
2

Low average   High average

Dull normal

Borderline

Intellectually deficient

This bell-shaped curve is also referred to as a normal curve.

Above average

Superior

Very superior

Below 70 70–79 80–89 90–99 100–109 110–119 120–129 130 and above

Range of IQ scores

© Cengage Learning 2012

7-3d DIFFERENCES IN INTELLECTUAL FUNCTIONING

The average IQ score in the United States is very close to 100. Yet for some socioeconomic and ethnic groups in the United States, the average is higher, and for others, it is lower. Questions have also been raised about whether males or females are more intelligent overall, and whether there are gender differences in the kinds of intellectual or cognitive skills valued in society. Tests of intellectual functioning have thus been seen as divisive and as maintaining a class system or social order that is based on prejudices and "tradition" as much as on science. In this section we discuss (a) socioeconomic and ethnic differences and (b) gender differences in cognitive skills.

Socioeconomic and Ethnic Differences

There is a body of research suggestive of differences in intelligence—or, more precisely, intelligence test scores—between socioeconomic and ethnic groups. Lower-class U.S. children obtain IQ scores some 10 to 15 points lower than those obtained by middle- and upper-class children. African American children tend to obtain IQ scores some 15 points lower than those obtained by their European American age-mates (Helms, 2006; Neisser et al., 1996). Latin American and Native American children also tend to score below the norms for European Americans (Neisser et al., 1996; Sternberg, 2007).

Many studies of IQ confuse the factors of social class and ethnicity because disproportionate numbers of African Americans, Latin Americans, and Native Americans are found among the lower socioeconomic classes (Helms, 2006; Nisbett, 2009). When we limit our observations to particular ethnic groups, we still find an effect for social class. That is, middle-class European Americans outscore poorer European Americans. Middle-class African Americans, Latin Americans, and Native Americans outscore poorer members of their own ethnic groups. *Washington Post* columnist Eugene Robinson (2011) notes that "a gap has opened up between an educated middle-class Black America and a poor, undereducated Black America." In other words, it would be a mistake to lump all African Americans together.

There may also be intellectual differences between Asians and Caucasians. Asian Americans, for example, frequently outscore European Americans on the math portion of the Scholastic Aptitude Test. Students in China (Taiwan) and Japan also outscore European Americans on achievement tests in math and science (Nisbett, 2009). In the United States, moreover, people of Asian Indian, Korean, Japanese, Filipino, and Chinese descent are more likely than European Americans, African Americans, and Latin Americans to graduate from high school and complete college (Sternberg, 2007; Xie & Goyette, 2003; Yeh & Chang, 2004). They are also overrepresented in competitive colleges and universities (Knapp et al., 2011; Liu, 2009). For example, Asian Americans make up 12% of the population of California, but they comprise 41% of the student population of the state's highest-ranked public university: the University of California at Berkeley.

Most psychologists believe that such ethnic differences reflect cultural attitudes toward education rather than inborn racial differences (Nisbett, 2009). That is, the Asian children may be more motivated to work in school. Research shows that Chinese and Japanese students and their mothers tend to attribute academic successes to hard work (Bae et al., 2008). European Americans are more likely to attribute their children's academic successes to "natural" ability (Bae et al., 2008).

Intelligence tests may be said to have a *cultural bias* because children reared in African American or Latin American neighborhoods are at a cultural disadvantage in intelligence testing (Dotson et al., 2009). Many psychologists, including Raymond B. Cattell (1949) and Florence Goodenough (1926; now revised as the Goodenough–Harris Drawing Test), have tried to construct culture-free intelligence tests. Cattell's Culture-Fair Intelligence Test evaluates reasoning through the child's ability to understand and use the rules that govern a progression of geometric designs (see Figure 7.6). Goodenough's Draw-A-Person test is based on the premise that children from all cultural backgrounds have had the opportunity to observe people and note the relationships between the parts and the whole. Her instructions simply require children to draw a picture of a man or woman.

Ironically, European American children outperform African American children on "culture-free" tests (Rushton et al., 2003), perhaps because they are more likely than disadvantaged children to have played with blocks (practice relevant to the Cattell test) and to have sketched animals, people, and things (practice relevant to the Goodenough test). Nor do culture-free tests predict academic success as well as other intelligence tests.

Gender Differences

It was once widely believed that males were more intelligent than females because of their greater knowledge of world affairs and their skills in science and industry. But these differences did not reflect differences in cognitive ability. Rather, they reflected exclusion of females from world affairs, science, and industry. Moreover, intelligence tests do not show overall gender differences in cognitive abilities (Halpern & LaMay, 2000).

Reviews of the research suggest that girls are somewhat superior to boys in verbal abilities, such as vocabulary, ability to generate sentences and words that are similar in meaning to other words, spelling, knowledge of foreign languages, and pronunciation (Andreano & Cahill, 2009; Lohman & Lakin, 2009). Girls seem to acquire language somewhat faster than boys do. Also, in the United States, more boys than girls have reading problems, ranging from reading below grade level to severe disabilities (Brun et al., 2009).

Males seem to do somewhat better at manipulating visual images in working memory. Males as a group excel in visual–spatial abilities of the sort used in math, science, and map-reading (Andreano & Cahill, 2009; Yazzie, 2010).

For half a century or more, it has been believed that male adolescents generally outperform females in mathematics, and research has tended to support that belief (Collaer & Hill, 2006; Halpern et al., 2007). But a study by Janet Hyde and her colleagues (2008) of some 7 million children in second through eleventh grade found no gender differences for performance in mathematics on standardized tests. Although there are no overall gender differences in average scores on math tests in the United States, males are apparently more likely than females to perform at the extremes, as in the percentage of individuals who obtain scores under 300 or over 700 on the quantitative scale of the SAT (Else-Quest et al., 2010). Nevertheless, most Americans have different expectations for boys and girls, and these expectations may still dissuade some math-proficient

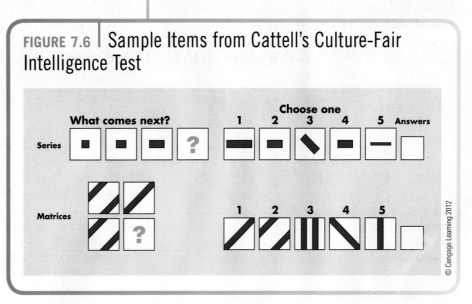

FIGURE 7.6 Sample Items from Cattell's Culture-Fair Intelligence Test

© Cengage Learning 2012

girls from entering so-called STEM (science, technology, engineering, and mathematics) fields (Hyde & Mertz, 2009).

But note that the reported gender differences are *group* differences. There is greater variation in these skills between individuals *within* the groups than between males and females (Halpern, 2003). That is, there may be a greater difference in, say, verbal skills between two women than between the typical woman and the typical man. Millions of females outdistance the "average" male in math and spatial abilities. Men have produced their verbally adept Shakespeares. Moreover, in most cases, gender differences in cognitive skills are small (Else-Quest & Grabe, 2012). Differences in verbal, math, and visual–spatial abilities also appear to be narrowing as more females pursue course work in fields that had been typically populated by males.

While scholars sit around and debate gender differences in intellectual functioning, women are voting on the issue by flooding fields once populated almost exclusively by men (Cox & Alm, 2005). Figure 7.7 shows that women are tossing these stereotypes out the window by entering the sciences and professional fields ranging from business to law to medicine in increasing numbers.

7-4 Nature and Nurture in Intelligence

If different ethnic groups tend to score differently on intelligence tests, psychologists—like educators and other people involved in public life—want to know why. We will see that this is one debate that can make use of key empirical findings. Psychologists can point with pride to a rich mine of research on the roles of nature (genetic influences) and nurture (environmental influences) in the development of intelligence.

7-4a GENETIC INFLUENCES ON INTELLIGENCE

Research on genetic influences has employed kinship studies, twin studies, and adoptee studies. Let's consider each of these to see whether heredity affects intellectual functioning.

We can examine the IQ scores of closely and distantly related people who have been reared together or apart. If heredity is involved in human intelligence, closely related people ought to have more similar IQs than distantly related or unrelated people, even when they are reared separately (Petrill et al., 2010).

Figure 7.8 is a composite of the results of more than a hundred studies of IQ and heredity in human beings (McGue et al., 1993; Plomin & Spinath, 2004; Plomin et al., 2008). The IQ scores of identical (monozygotic, or MZ) twins are more alike than scores for any other pairs, even when the twins have been reared apart. There are moderate correlations between the IQ scores of fraternal (dizygotic, or DZ) twins, between those of siblings, and between those of parents and their children. Correlations between the scores of children and their foster parents and between those of cousins are weak.

The results of large-scale twin studies are consistent with the data in Figure 7.8 (e.g., Haworth et al., 2009). A classic

FIGURE 7.7 | Women Flood Professions Once Populated Almost Exclusively by Men

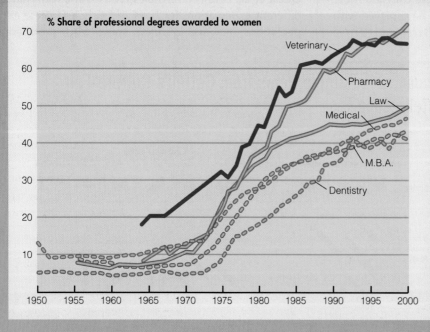

% Share of professional degrees awarded to women

© Cengage Learning 2012

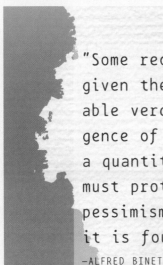

"Some recent philosophers seem to have given their moral approval to these deplorable verdicts that affirm that the intelligence of an individual is a fixed quantity, a quantity that cannot be augmented. We must protest and react against this brutal pessimism; we will try to demonstrate that it is founded on nothing."

—ALFRED BINET

study of 500 pairs of MZ and DZ twins in Louisville, Kentucky (Wilson, 1983), found that the correlations in intelligence for MZ twins were higher than those for DZ twins. The correlations in intelligence between DZ twin pairs were the same as those between other siblings. The MacArthur Longitudinal Twin Study examined the intellectual abilities of 200 fourteen-month-old pairs of twins (Oliver & Plomin, 2007). The study found that MZ twins were more similar than DZ twins in spatial memory, ability to categorize things, and word comprehension.

In sum, studies generally suggest that the **heritability** of intelligence is between 40% and 60% (Haworth et al., 2009; Neisser et al., 1996). In other words, about half of the difference between your IQ score and the IQ scores of other people can be explained by heredity.

Note, too, that genetic pairs (such as MZ twins) who were reared together show higher correlations in their IQ scores than similar genetic pairs (such as other MZ twins) who were reared apart. This finding holds for DZ twins, siblings, parents and their children, and unrelated people. Being reared together is, therefore, related with similarities in IQ. *For this reason, the same group of studies used to demonstrate a role for the heritability of IQ scores also suggests that the environment plays a role in determining IQ scores.*

Another strategy for exploring genetic influences on intelligence is to compare the correlations between the IQ scores of adopted children and those of their biological and adoptive parents. When children are separated from their biological parents at an early age, one can argue that strong relationships between their IQs and those of their natural parents reflect genetic influences. Strong relationships between the children's IQs and those of their adoptive parents might reflect environmental influences.

Several studies with one- and two-year-old children in Colorado (Baker et al., 1983), Texas (Horn, 1983), and Minnesota (Scarr & Weinberg, 1983) have found a stronger relationship between the IQ scores of adopted children and those of their biological parents than between the children's scores and those of their adoptive parents.

7-4b ENVIRONMENTAL INFLUENCES ON INTELLIGENCE

Let's now look at studies of environmental influences on intelligence, which also employ a variety of research strategies. These include observation of the role of the home environment and evaluation of the effects of educational programs.

The Home Environment

The home environment and styles of parenting also affect IQ scores (Bradley, 2006). Children of parents who are emotionally and verbally responsive, furnish appropriate play materials, are involved with their children, encourage independence, and provide varied daily experiences obtain higher IQ scores later on (Bradley, 2006). Organization and safety in the home have also been linked to higher IQs and achievement test scores (Bradley et al., 1989; Petrill et al., 2010).

Other studies support the view that children's early environment is linked to IQ scores and academic achievement. For example, Victoria Molfese and her colleagues (1997) found that the home environment was the single most important predictor of scores on IQ tests among children aged three to eight.

FIGURE 7.8 | Findings of Studies of the Relationship Between IQ Scores and Heredity

The data represent a composite of several studies. By and large, correlations are higher between people who are more closely related, yet people who are reared together have more similar IQ scores than people who are reared apart. Such findings suggest that both genetic and environmental factors contribute to IQ scores.

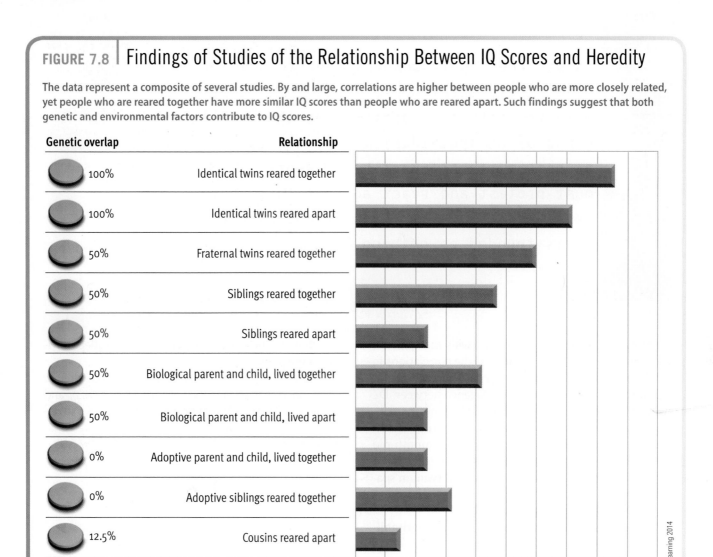

Education

Although intelligence is viewed as permitting people to profit from education, education also apparently contributes to intelligence. Government-funded efforts to provide preschoolers with enriched early environments have led to intellectual gains. Head Start programs, for example, enhance the IQ scores, achievement test scores, and academic skills of disadvantaged children (Bierman et al., 2008) by exposing them to materials and activities that middle-class children take for granted. These include letters and words, numbers, books, exercises in drawing, pegs and pegboards, puzzles, toy animals, and dolls. On the other hand, many children's IQ scores and achievements tend to decrease again in the years following the Head Start experience if they return to the less intellectually stimulating environment that preceded Head Start (Nisbett, 2009).

Later schooling also contributes to IQ. When children of about the same age start school a year apart because of admissions standards related to their date of birth, children who have been in school longer obtain higher IQ scores (Neisser et al., 1996). Moreover, test scores tend to decrease during the summer vacation (Neisser et al., 1996).

The findings on intelligence, the home environment, and educational experiences show that much indeed can be done to enhance intellectual functioning in children.

The Flynn Effect

Philosopher and researcher John Flynn (2003) found that IQ scores in the Western world increased substantially between 1947 and 2002, some 18 points in the United States. Psychologist Richard Nisbett (2009) argues that our genetic codes could not possibly have changed enough in half a century to account for this enormous difference and concludes that social and cultural factors such as the effects of improved educational systems and the penetration of the mass media must be among the reasons for the change.

If such environmental factors are capable of producing changes of this magnitude over time for the entire American population, they can also produce significant differences between subpopulations, such as between

Theories of Intelligence Summary Chart

Theory	Basic Information	Comments
General versus specific factors (proponent: Charles Spearman) © Archives of the History of American Psychology—The University of Akron	▪ Spearman created factor analysis to study intelligence. ▪ There is strong evidence for the general factor (g) in intelligence. ▪ s factors are specific abilities, skills, and talents	▪ Concept of g remains in use today—a century later.
Primary mental abilities (proponent: Louis Thurstone) George Skadding/Time Life Pictures/Getty Images	▪ Thurstone used factor analysis. ▪ There are many "primary" abilities. ▪ All abilities and factors are academically oriented.	▪ Other researchers (e.g., Guilford) claim to have found hundreds of factors. ▪ The more factors that are claimed, the more they overlap.
Triarchic theory (proponent: Robert Sternberg) Courtesy of Tufts University	▪ Intelligence is three-pronged—with analytical, creative, and practical components. ▪ Analytical intelligence is analogous to academic ability.	▪ The theory coincides with the views of Aristotle. ▪ Critics do not view creativity as a component of intelligence.
Multiple intelligences (proponent: Howard Gardner) ©2003 Jay Gardner	▪ Gardner theorized distinct "intelligences." ▪ Intelligences include academic intelligences, personal and social intelligences, talents, and philosophical intelligences. ▪ The theory posits different bases in the brain for different intelligences	▪ Proponents continue to expand the number of "intelligences." ▪ Critics see little value in theorizing "intelligences" rather than aspects of intelligence. ▪ Most critics consider musical and bodily skills to be special talents, not "intelligences"

FIGURE 7.9 | The Complex Web of Factors That Affect Intellectual Functioning

Intellectual functioning appears to be influenced by the interaction of genetic factors, health, personality, and sociocultural factors.

Genetic factors

A stimulating environment in the home and in the schools

Health
Socioeconomic status
Flexibility
Achievement motivation
Academic/educational adjustment
Belief that education and achievement are keys to self-development and fulfillment

© Cengage Learning 2012

African Americans and European Americans. For example, the difference in IQ scores between the two racial groups has decreased from 15 points to 9.5 points over the past 30 years (Nisbett, 2007), which is again too large a difference to reflect genetic factors. Instead, it would suggest that the educational gap between the races may be narrowing.

All in all, intellectual functioning appears to reflect the interaction of a complex web of genetic, physical, personal, and sociocultural factors, as suggested in Figure 7.9.

Perhaps we need not be so concerned with whether we can sort out exactly how much of a person's intelligence is due to heredity and how much is due to environmental influences. Psychology has traditionally supported the dignity of the individual. It might be more appropriate for us to try to identify children of all ethnic groups who are at risk of failure and to do what we can to enrich their environments.

By the Numbers

$1/2 \times 1/2 \times 1/2 \times 1/2 \times 1/2 \times 1/2$ Probability of flipping six heads in a row

$8 \times 7 \times 6 \times 5 \times 4 \times 3 \times 2 \times 1 = 1 \times 2 \times 3 \times 4 \times 5 \times 6 \times 7 \times 8$

98.42% Human overlap in genes with chimpanzees

8 Number of primary mental abilities, according to Thurstone

10,000 Approximate number of words understood by a 6-year-old

100 Mean IQ score

50 Percentage of people obtaining IQ scores between 90 and 110

STUDY TOOLS ▸ 7

Ready to study? In the book, you can:

- Review what you've read with Fill-Ins and Multiple Choice quizzes (below).
- Rip out Chapter Review card (in the back).

Or you can go online to CourseMate at www.cengagebrain.com for these resources:

- Complete Practices Quizzes to prepare for tests.
- Review Key Terms Flash Cards (online or print).
- Play games to master concepts.

FILL-INS

Answers can be found in the back of the book, starting on page 368.

1. _____ are mental categories used to class objects, relations, or events with common properties.

2. A(n) _____ is a specific procedure for solving a type of problem.

3. _____ devices are rules of thumb that serve as shortcuts to rapid solutions.

4. A _____ set is the tendency to respond to a new problem with the same approach that helped solve similar problems.

5. According to the _____-relativity hypothesis, language structures the way we perceive the world.

6. Children's use of sentences such as "I standed up" and "Mommy sitted down" are examples of _____.

7. Spearman suggested that intelligent behaviors have a common underlying factor, which he labeled _____, and specific factors that account for specific abilities.

8. Gardner proposes the existence of _____ intelligences, each of which is based in a different area of the brain.

9. Sternberg constructed a "triarchic" model of intelligence, including analytical, creative, and _____ intelligence.

10. The Stanford–Binet Intelligence Scale yields a score called a(n) _____ _____ (IQ).

1. Eight-year-old Stephanie understands that her dog Boodles is a dog and that all dogs are animals. Stephanie's concept of animal is best characterized as

   a. intuitive.
   b. ideational.
   c. overextended.
   d. hierarchical.

2. Algorithms are usually time consuming, whereas _____ provide a more rapid solution when they work.

   a. anagrams
   b. formulas
   c. systematic random searches
   d. heuristics

3. What conclusion may be drawn about problem solving from Maier's studies with Bismarck?

   a. Only humans can solve problems by means of insight.
   b. A rat has demonstrated insight under laboratory conditions.
   c. A rat has demonstrated trial-and-error learning under laboratory conditions.
   d. Rats are capable of insight under a variety of conditions.

4. One plausible explanation of the incubation effect is

   a. the tendency to allow the unconscious to free up insights.
   b. distancing problem solvers from persistent but unproductive mental sets.
   c. conscious searching for heuristic devices.
   d. spontaneous means-end analysis.

5. True language is distinguished from the communications systems of lower animals by all of the following except

   a. infinite creativity.
   b. displacement.
   c. making sounds.
   d. semanticity.

6. When reading the sentences, "The chicken is ready for dinner," and "The lion is ready for dinner," if you understand which is ready to eat and which is ready to be eaten, you are using the phrase "is ready to eat" with different _____ in each case.

   a. morphemes
   b. phonemes
   c. factors
   d. semanticity

7. Jamie's mother was concerned that her 4-year-old daughter overregularized plurals and tenses. She took Jamie to Dr. Acton, a noted learning theorist, who advised her to

   a. wait for Jamie's speech to correct itself.
   b. take her to a speech therapist.
   c. correct her grammar through imitation and repetition.
   d. begin instruction in another language.

8. According to Robert Sternberg, the three types of intelligence are

   a. logical, musical, emotional.
   b. experimental, logical, verbal.
   c. verbal, performance, problem solving.
   d. analytical, creative, practical.

9. The ability to do things that are unique and beneficial and to generate novel combinations out of existing elements describes

   a. insight.
   b. creativity.
   c. intelligence.
   d. expertise.

10. According to the text, Janet Hyde and her colleagues studied the performance of some 7 million children in second through eleventh grades in mathematics and found that

    a. boys obtained higher scores than girls.
    b. girls obtained higher scores than boys.
    c. there were no overall gender differences in scores.
    d. European Americans obtained higher scores than any other racial or ethnic group.

THE IN-CROWD

Share your 4LTR Press story on Facebook at
www.facebook.com/4ltrpress for a chance to win.

To learn more about the
In-Crowd opportunity 'like'
us on Facebook.

© age fotostock / SuperStock

LEARNING OUTCOMES

8-1 Define motivation including needs, drives, and incentives

8-2 Identify the theories of motivation

8-3 Describe the biological and psychological contributions to hunger

8-4 Explain the role of sex hormones and the sexual response cycle in human sexuality

8-5 Describe achievement motivation

8-6 Identify the theoretical explanations of emotions

After you read the chapter, go to the Study Tools at the end of the chapter, page 214.

CHAPTER 8

Motivation and EMOTION

The Seekers had received word that the world was coming to an end on December 21st. A great flood would engulf their city and the rest of the Earth. Now they were gathered around their leader, Marian Keech, in her home, as she recorded messages that she said were sent to her by the Guardians from outer space. The messages were received through "automatic writing"; that is, the Guardians communicated through Ms. Keech, who wrote down their words without awareness. Another message brought good news, however. Because of their faith, the Seekers would be saved by flying saucers at the stroke of midnight on the 21st.

In their classic observational study, Leon Festinger and his colleagues (1956) described how they managed to be present in Ms. Keech's household at the fateful hour by pretending to belong to the group. Their purpose was to observe the behavior of the Seekers during and following the prophecy's failure. The cognitive theory of motivation that the researchers were working on—*cognitive-dissonance theory*—suggested that there would be a discrepancy or conflict between two key cognitions: (1) Ms. Keech is a prophet, and (2) Ms. Keech is wrong.

How might the conflict be resolved? One way would be for the Seekers to lose faith in Ms. Keech. But the researchers expected that according to their theory, the Seekers could also be motivated to resolve the conflict by going out to spread the word and find additional converts. Otherwise, the group would be painfully embarrassed.

Let's return to the momentous night. Many members of the group had quit their jobs and gone on spending sprees before the anticipated end. Now, as midnight approached, they fidgeted, awaiting the flying saucers. Midnight came, but there were no saucers. Anxious glances were exchanged. There was silence, and then some coughs. Minutes passed, torturously slowly. Watches were checked, more glances exchanged.

At 4:00 a.m., a bitter and frantic Ms. Keech complained that she sensed that members of the group were doubting her. At 4:45 a.m., however, she seemed suddenly relieved. Another message was arriving, and Ms. Keech was spelling it out through automatic writ-

> *When a prophecy fails, how do its believers respond? Why?*

WHAT DO YOU THINK? FOLKLORE, COMMON SENSE, OR NONSENSE? CIRCLE THE T FOR "TRUTH" OR THE F FOR "FICTION," AND CHECK THE ACCURACY OF YOUR ANSWERS AS YOU READ THROUGH THE CHAPTER.

T	F	GETTING AWAY FROM IT ALL BY GOING ON A VACATION FROM ALL SENSORY INPUT FOR A FEW HOURS IS RELAXING.
T	F	PEOPLE FEEL HUNGER DUE TO CONTRACTIONS ("PANGS") IN THE STOMACH.
T	F	FASHION MAGAZINES CAN CONTRIBUTE TO EATING DISORDERS AMONG WOMEN.
T	F	MONEY CAN'T BUY YOU HAPPINESS.
T	F	YOU MAY BE ABLE TO FOOL A LIE DETECTOR BY BITING YOUR TONGUE OR SQUIGGLING YOUR TOES.

ing! The Seekers, it turned out, had managed to save the world through their faith. The universal powers had decided to let the world travel on along its sinful way for a while longer. Why? Because of the faith of the Seekers, there was hope!

With their faith restored, the followers called wire services and newspapers to spread the word. The three psychologists from the University of Minnesota went home, weary but enlightened. They wrote a book enti-

Glossary

motivation
the state in which an organism experiences an inducement or incentive to do something

motive
a hypothetical state within an organism that propels the organism toward a goal

need
a state of deprivation

drive
a condition of arousal in an organism that is associated with a need

incentive
an object, person, or situation perceived as capable of satisfying a need or as desirable for its own sake

instinct
an inherited disposition to activate specific behavior patterns that are designed to reach certain goals

tled *When Prophecy Fails*, which serves as one of the key documents of their theory.

8-1 The Psychology of Motivation

The psychology of **motivation** is concerned with the *why* of behavior. Why do we eat? Why do some of us strive to get ahead? Why do some of us ride motorcycles at breakneck speeds? Why are some people aggressive? Why were the Seekers in a state of discomfort when the prophecy failed?

To answer these questions, psychologists use concepts such as *motives, needs, drives,* and *incentives.* **Motives** are hypothetical states that activate behavior, propelling us toward goals. We call them "hypothetical states" because motives are not seen and measured directly. They are inferred from behavior. Motives may take the form of *needs, drives,* and *incentives,* which are also inferred from behavior.

Psychologists speak of physiological and psychological **needs**. We must meet physiological needs to survive. Examples include the needs for oxygen, food, drink, pain avoidance, proper temperature, and elimination of waste products. Some physiological needs, such as hunger and thirst, are states of physical deprivation. When we have not eaten or drunk for a while, we develop needs for food and water. The body also needs oxygen, vitamins, and so on.

Psychological needs include needs for achievement, power, self-esteem, social approval, and belonging. Psychological needs are not necessarily based on states of deprivation. A person with a need for achievement may already have a history of successful achievements. Because people's biological makeups are similar, we share similar physiological needs. But because we are influenced by our cultural settings, our needs may be expressed in different ways. We all need food, but some prefer a vegetarian diet whereas others prefer meat. Because learning enters into psychological needs, they can differ markedly from one person to another.

Needs give rise to **drives**. Depletion of food gives rise to the hunger drive, and depletion of liquids gives rise to the thirst drive. *Physiological drives* are the counterparts of physiological needs. When we have gone without food and water, our body may *need* these substances. However, our *experience* of the drives of hunger and thirst is psychological. Drives arouse us to action and tend to be stronger when we have been deprived longer. We are hungrier when we haven't eaten for 10 hours than 1 hour.

Psychological needs for approval, achievement, and belonging also give rise to drives. We can have a drive to get ahead in the business world just as we have a drive to eat. Psychologists are working to learn more about the origins of these drives. We do know that we can also be driven to obtain *incentives*. An **incentive** is an object, a person, or a situation that can satisfy a need or is desirable for its own sake. Money, food, a sexually attractive person, social approval, and attention can all act as incentives.

8-2 Theories of Motivation

Although psychologists agree that it is important to understand why humans and lower animals do things, they do not agree about the precise nature of motivation. Let's consider various theoretical perspectives on motivation.

8-2a THE EVOLUTIONARY PERSPECTIVE

The evolutionary perspective notes that many animals are neurally "prewired"—that is, born with preprogrammed tendencies—to respond to certain situations in certain ways (Burghardt, 2009; Confer et al., 2010). Spiders spin webs instinctively. Bees "dance" instinctively to communicate the location of food to other bees.

These instinctive behaviors are found in particular species. They are *species-specific*. Species-specific behaviors are also called **instincts** and are inborn. They are genetically transmitted from generation to generation.

Psychologists have asked whether humans have instincts, and if so, how many. More than a

In the presence of another male, Siamese fighting fish *(Betta splendens)* assume stereotypical threatening postures in which they extend their fins and gills and circle one another. If neither male retreats, there will be conflict.

© George Diebold/Photodisc/Getty Images

century ago, psychologists William James (1890) and William McDougall (1908) argued that humans have instincts that foster survival and social behavior. James numbered love, sympathy, and modesty as social instincts. McDougall compiled 12 "basic" instincts, including hunger, sex, and self-assertion. Other psychologists have made longer lists, and still others deny that people have instincts. The question of whether people have instincts—and what they might be—remains unresolved.

8-2b DRIVE-REDUCTIONISM AND HOMEOSTASIS

Sigmund Freud believed that tension motivates us to behave in ways that restore us to a resting state. His views are similar to those of the **drive-reduction theory** of learning, as set forth by psychologist Clark Hull in the 1930s.

According to Hull, *primary drives* such as hunger, thirst, and pain trigger arousal (tension) and activate behavior. We learn to engage in behaviors that reduce the tension. We also acquire drives—called *acquired drives*—through experience. We may acquire a drive for money because money enables us to obtain food, drink, and homes, which protect us from crime and extremes of temperature. We might acquire drives for social approval and affiliation because other people, and their goodwill, help us reduce primary drives, especially when we are infants. In all cases, reduction of tension is the goal. Yet some people appear to acquire what could be considered excessive drives for money or affiliation. They gather money long after their material needs have been met, and some people find it difficult to be alone, even briefly.

Primary drives like hunger are triggered when we are in a state of deprivation. Sensations of hunger motivate us to act in ways that will restore the bodily balance. This tendency to maintain a steady state is called **homeostasis** Homeostasis works like a thermostat. When the temperature in a room drops below the *set point*, the heating system turns on. The heat stays on until the set point is reached. Similarly, most animals eat until they are no longer hungry. But many people eat "recreationally"—as when they see an appealing dessert—suggesting there is more to eating than drive reduction.

8-2c THE SEARCH FOR STIMULATION

Physical needs give rise to drives like hunger and thirst. In such cases, we are motivated to *reduce* the tension or stimulation that impinges on us. However, in the case of *stimulus motives*, organisms seek to *increase* stimulation.

A classic study conducted at McGill University in Montreal during the 1950s suggests the importance

"Such is the state of life, that none are happy but by the anticipation of change: the change itself is nothing; when we have made it, the next wish is to change again."

—DR. SAMUEL JOHNSON

of sensory stimulation and activity. Some "lucky" students were paid $20 a day (which, with inflation, would now be more like $200) for doing nothing—literally. Would you like to "work" by doing nothing for $200 a day? Don't answer too quickly. According to the results of this study you might not like it at all.

In this experiment, student volunteers were placed in quiet cubicles and blindfolded (Bexton et al., 1954). Their arms were bandaged so that they felt little if anything with their hands. They could hear nothing but the dull, continuous hum of air conditioning. Many slept for a while, but after a few hours of sensory-deprived wakefulness, most felt bored and irritable. As time went on, many grew more uncomfortable. Many students quit the experiment during the first day despite the financial incentive. Many of those who remained for a

Dr. Neal Miller/Yale University

Do organisms have innate drives to obtain sensory stimulation, manipulate objects (like these young rhesus monkeys), and explore the environment?

self-actualization
according to Maslow and other humanistic psychologists, self-initiated striving to become what one is capable of being

FICTION GENERALLY, IT IS NOT TRUE THAT GETTING AWAY FROM IT ALL BY GOING ON A VACATION FROM ALL SENSORY INPUT FOR A FEW HOURS IS RELAXING.

few days found it hard to concentrate on simple problems for days afterward. For many, the experiment did not provide a relaxing vacation. Instead, it produced boredom, discomfort, and disorientation.

Humans and other animals appear motivated to seek novel stimulation. Even when they have been deprived of food, rats may explore unfamiliar arms of mazes rather than head straight for the food source. Animals that have just copulated and thereby reduced their primary sex drives often show renewed interest in sex when presented with a novel sex partner. People (and nonhumans) take in more calories at buffets and smorgasbords than when fewer kinds of food are available (Szentirmai et al., 2010). Children spend hour after hour playing video games for the pleasure of zapping virtual people or monsters.

Stimulus motives provide an evolutionary advantage. Animals that are active and motivated to explore and manipulate their environment are more likely to survive. If you know where the nearest tall tree is, you're more likely to escape a leopard and transmit your genes to future generations.

But note that survival is more or less a question of defending oneself or one's group against dangers of one kind or another. In the following section, we see that many psychologists believe people are also motivated to develop their unique potentials, even in the absence of any external threat.

8-2d HUMANISTIC THEORY

Humanistic psychologists such as Abraham Maslow (1908–1970) suggest that human behavior is not just mechanical and aimed toward survival and the reduction of tension. Maslow believed that people are also motivated by a conscious desire for personal growth. Humanists note that people tolerate pain, hunger, and many other kinds of tension to obtain personal fulfillment.

Maslow believed that we are separated from other animals by our capacity for **self-actualization**, or self-initiated striving to become what we believe we are capable of being. Maslow considered self-actualization to be as important a need in humans as hunger. The need for self-actualization pushes people to strive to

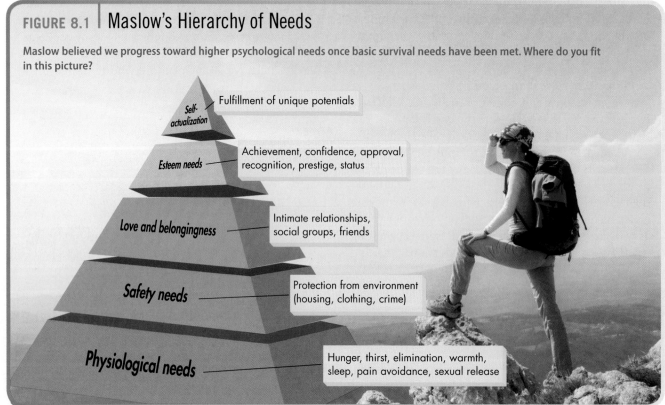

FIGURE 8.1 | Maslow's Hierarchy of Needs

Maslow believed we progress toward higher psychological needs once basic survival needs have been met. Where do you fit in this picture?

Self-actualization — Fulfillment of unique potentials

Esteem needs — Achievement, confidence, approval, recognition, prestige, status

Love and belongingness — Intimate relationships, social groups, friends

Safety needs — Protection from environment (housing, clothing, crime)

Physiological needs — Hunger, thirst, elimination, warmth, sleep, pain avoidance, sexual release

iStockphoto.com/gaspr13

become concert pianists, chief executive officers, or best-selling authors—even when they have plenty of money to live on.

Maslow (1970) organized human needs into a hierarchy. Maslow's **hierarchy of needs** ranges from physiological needs such as hunger and thirst, through self-actualization (see Figure 8.1). He believed that we naturally strive to climb this hierarchy.

Critics of Maslow's theory argue that there is too much individual variation for the hierarchy of motives to apply to everyone (Cooke, 2008). Some people whose physiological, safety, and love needs are met show little interest in achievement and recognition. And some artists devote themselves fully to their craft, even if they have to pass up the comforts of a warm home or alienate their families.

8-2e COGNITIVE PERSPECTIVES ON MOTIVATION

Cognitive theorists note that people represent their worlds mentally. As in Piaget's cognitive developmental theory, they see people as natural scientists who strive to understand the world so that they can predict and control events. Therefore, people try to eliminate inconsistencies—or, as we saw in the case of the Seekers at the beginning of the chapter—discrepancies in information so that their ability to make sense of the world remains whole.

Children also attempt to create consistency between their own gender and what experience teaches them that boys and girls are expected to do in their cultural settings. As soon as they come to understand whether they are male or female, they begin to imitate the behavior of older people of the same gender (Ruble et al., 2006). According to *cognitive-dissonance theory*, people are generally motivated to hold consistent beliefs and to justify their behavior. That is why we are generally more likely to appreciate what we must work to obtain.

Each theory of motivation may have something to offer. Drive-reduction theory may explain why we drink when thirsty, but stimulus motives might explain why we go clubbing and drink alcohol. Each theory might apply to certain aspects of behavior. As the chapter progresses, we will describe research that lends support to each theory.

"IN GENERAL MY CHILDREN REFUSE TO EAT ANYTHING THAT HASN'T DANCED ON TELEVISION."

—ERMA BOMBECK

8-3 Hunger

We need food to survive, but for many of us, food means more than survival. Food is a symbol of family togetherness and caring. We associate food with the nurturance of the parent–child relationship and with visits home on holidays. Friends and relatives offer us food when we enter their homes, and saying no may be viewed as a personal rejection. Bacon and eggs, coffee with cream and sugar, meat and mashed potatoes—all seem to be part of sharing American values and abundance.

8-3a BIOLOGICAL INFLUENCES ON HUNGER

In considering the bodily mechanisms that regulate hunger, let's begin with the mouth, where we get signals of **satiety** that regulate our eating. We also get signals of satiety from the digestive tract, although it takes longer for these signals to reach the brain. Therefore, if we did not receive signals of satiety from chewing and swallowing, we might eat for a long time after we had taken in enough food.

hierarchy of needs
Maslow's ordering of needs from most basic (physiological needs such as hunger and thirst) to most elaborate and sophisticated (self-actualization)

satiety
the state of being satisfied; fullness

What triggers your hunger drive? Are you only interested in eating when your blood sugar level falls, or do the sights and aromas of foods stimulate you to eat?

© Alloy Photography/Veer

ventromedial nucleus (VMN)
a central area on the underside of the hypothalamus that appears to function as a stop-eating center

hyperphagic
characterized by excessive eating

lateral hypothalamus
an area at the side of the hypothalamus that appears to function as a start-eating center

To demonstrate that chewing and swallowing provide feelings of satiety, researchers conducted classic "sham feeding" experiments with dogs. They implanted a tube in the animals' throats so that any food swallowed fell out of the body. Even though no food reached the stomach, the animals stopped feeding after a while (Janowitz & Grossman, 1949). Thus, sensations of chewing and swallowing must provide some feelings of satiety. However, the dogs in the study resumed feeding sooner than animals whose food did reach the stomach. Let's proceed to the stomach, too, as we seek further regulatory factors in hunger.

An empty stomach leads to stomach contractions, which we call *hunger pangs*. Classic research suggested that stomach contractions are crucial to hunger. A man (A. L. Washburn) swallowed a balloon that was inflated in his stomach. His stomach contractions squeezed the balloon, so the contractions could be recorded by observers. Washburn also pressed a key when he felt hungry, and the researchers found a correspondence between his stomach contractions and his feelings of hunger (Cannon & Washburn, 1912).

Medical observations and classic research find that humans and nonhumans whose stomachs have been removed still regulate food intake so as to maintain a normal weight (Tsang, 1938). (Food is absorbed through their intestines.) This finding led to the discovery of other mechanisms that regulate hunger, including the hypothalamus, blood sugar level, and receptors in the liver. When we are deprived of food, the level of sugar in the blood drops. The drop in blood sugar is communicated to the hypothalamus, which stokes the hunger drive.

The hypothalamus is a pea-sized structure in the brain that's involved in many aspects of motivation, including sex, aggression, and hunger. Two parts of it that involve the hunger drive are of particular interest. When a researcher destroys the **ventromedial nucleus (VMN)** of a rat's hypothalamus during surgery, the rat will grope toward food as soon as its eyes open (Fetissov & Meguid, 2010). Then it eats vast quantities of Purina Rat Chow or whatever is available. Investigators have concluded that the VMN functions like a "stop-eating center" in the rat's brain. If the VMN is electri-

"There is no sincerer love than the love of food."
—GEORGE BERNARD SHAW

cally stimulated—that is, "switched on"—the rat stops eating until the current is turned off. When the VMN is destroyed, the rat becomes **hyperphagic** (see Figure 8.2). That is, it continues to eat until it has about doubled its normal weight. Then it will level off its eating rate and maintain the higher weight. It is as if the set point of the stop-eating center has been raised to a higher level, like turning up the thermostat in a house from 65°F to 70°F. Some people develop tumors near the base of the brain that damage the VMN and apparently cause them to overeat and grow obese (Chance et al., 2007).

By contrast, the **lateral hypothalamus** may function like a "start-eating center." If you electrically stimulate the lateral hypothalamus, the rat starts to eat (N. E. Miller, 1995). If you destroy the lateral hypothala-

FIGURE 8.2 | A Hyperphagic Rat

This rodent winner of the basketball look-alike contest went on a binge after it received a lesion in the ventromedial nucleus (VMN) of the hypothalamus. It is as if the lesion pushed the "set point" for the body weight up several notches; the rat's weight is now about five times normal. But now it eats only enough to maintain its pleasantly plump figure, so you need not be concerned that it will eventually burst. If the lesion had been made in the lateral hypothalamus, the animal might have become the Calista Flockhart of the rat world.

Dr. Neal Miller/Yale University

mus, the rat may stop eating altogether—that is, become **aphagic**. If you force-feed an aphagic rat for a while, however, it begins to eat on its own and levels off at a relatively low body weight. It is as if you have lowered the rat's set point. It is like turning down the thermostat from, say, 70°F to 40°F.

8-3b PSYCHOLOGICAL INFLUENCES ON HUNGER

Although many areas of the body work in concert to regulate the hunger drive, this is only part of the story. In human beings, the hunger drive is more complex. Psychological as well as physiological factors play an important role. How many times have you been made hungry by the sight or aroma of food? How many times have you eaten not because you were hungry but because you were at a relative's home or hanging around a cafeteria or coffee shop? Or because you felt anxious or depressed? Or simply because you were bored?

TRUTH IT IS TRUE THAT PANGS IN THE STOMACH ARE CONNECTED WITH FEELINGS OF HUNGER, *BUT* STOMACH CONTRACTIONS ARE NOT AS INFLUENTIAL AS FORMERLY THOUGHT.

One study confirmed what most of us already assumed—that watching television increases the amount of food we eat (Higgs & Woodward, 2009). One reason is that watching television can distract us from bodily changes that signal fullness and from cognitive awareness of how much we have already eaten. The same reason seems to hold true for gorging on popcorn, candy, and soft drinks at the movies. Watching television also interferes with memory formation of how much we have eaten, making us vulnerable to overeating at subsequent meals.

8-3c BEING OVERWEIGHT: A SERIOUS AND PERVASIVE PROBLEM

Consider some facts about being overweight (Flegal et al., 2010):

- More than two out of three adult Americans are overweight, according to the national *body mass index (BMI)* guidelines, and one in three are obese.

- Problems with unhealthy weight gain have been on the upswing in the United States; for example, 68% of Americans were overweight in 2008 as compared with 60% in 1988–1994.

- More than 78% of African American women and 81% of Latina Americans, age 40 and older, are overweight, and about half are obese.

- Obesity is a risk in various chronic medical conditions including type 2 diabetes, hypertension (high blood pressure), high cholesterol levels, stroke, heart disease, some cancers, and arthritis.

- Weight control is elusive for most people, who regain most of the weight they have lost, even when they have dieted "successfully" (Apovian, 2010; Heber, 2010).

aphagic characterized by undereating

Studies using data obtained by the federal government find that extremely obese people, whose BMIs are greater than or equal to 40, live shorter lives than people who are normal in weight (Finkelstein et al., 2010; see Table 8.1). With all the health problems connected to obesity, why are so many people obese?

Factors in Becoming Overweight

Many biological and psychological factors are involved in obesity. Being overweight runs in families. A study of Scandinavian adoptees by Albert Stunkard and his colleagues (1990) found that children bear a closer resemblance in weight to their biological parents than to their adoptive parents. Today, it is widely accepted that heredity plays a role in obesity in humans (Bouchard, 2010) and other animals, including monkeys and rats (Felsted et al., 2010).

The efforts of overweight people to maintain a slender profile may be sabotaged by an adaptive mechanism that would help preserve life in times of famine—*adaptive thermogenesis*. This mechanism causes the body to produce less energy (burn fewer calories) when someone goes on a diet (Apovian, 2010; Heber, 2010). This does not mean that overweight people will not lose weight by dieting; it means that it will take longer than expected.

TABLE 8.1

Years of Life Lost by an Extremely Obese, Non-smoking 40-Year-Old, Compared with a Normal-Weight Person of the Same Age

	EUROPEAN AMERICAN	AFRICAN AMERICAN
Male	9	8
Female	7	5

Source of data: Finkelstein, E. A., Brown, D. S., Wrage, L. A., Allaire, B. T., & Hoerger, T. J. (2010). Individual and Aggregate Years-of-life-lost Associated with Overweight and Obesity. *Obesity*, *18*(2), 333–339.

anorexia nervosa
a life-threatening eating
disorder characterized by
dramatic weight loss and a
distorted body image

Fatty tissue in the body also metabolizes (burns) food more slowly than muscle does. For this reason, a person with a high fat-to-muscle ratio metabolizes food more slowly than a person of the same weight with more muscle (Apovian, 2010; Heber, 2010). That is, two people of the same weight may metabolize food at different rates, depending on their distribution of muscle and fat. Meanwhile, the normal distribution of fat cells is different for men and women. The average man is 40% muscle and 15% fat. The average woman is 23% muscle and 25% fat. If a man and a woman with typical distributions of muscle and fat are of equal weight, therefore, the woman—who has more fat cells—must eat less to maintain that weight.

We also live in an "obesogenic environment" (Apovian, 2010; Heber, 2010). Foods high in sugar and fat are everywhere. Children in the United States are exposed to an average of 10,000 food commercials a year. More than nine of ten of these commercials are for fast foods, sugared cereals, candy, and soft drinks (Harris et al., 2009; Sixsmith & Furnham, 2010). Psychological factors, such as observational learning, stress, and emotional

© Mike Kemp/Rubberball/Getty Images

states, also "bombard" us and play a role in obesity (Apovian, 2010). Situations contribute as well. Family celebrations, watching television, arguments, and tension at work can all lead to overeating or going off a diet. Efforts to diet may also be impeded by negative emotions such as depression and anxiety, which can lead to binge eating (Ricca et al., 2009).

8-3d EATING DISORDERS

Consider some facts about eating and eating disorders in the United States, as reported by the National Eating Disorders Association (2010):

- More than half of teenage girls and nearly one third of teenage boys use unhealthful methods to try to control their weight, including fasting, skipping meals, smoking cigarettes, vomiting, and using laxatives.

- About two out of five first- through third-grade girls would like to be thinner.

- More than four out of five 10-year-old girls report fear of being fat.

- Nearly half of 9- to 11-year old girls are "sometimes" or "very often" dieting.

- More than 90% of college women have dieted at some time.

Eating disorders are characterized by persistent, gross disturbances in eating patterns. In this section, we focus on an eating disorder in which individuals are too thin, *anorexia nervosa*, and one in which the person may be normal in weight, but certainly not in the methods used to maintain that weight—*bulimia nervosa*.

Anorexia Nervosa

Anorexia nervosa is a life-threatening eating disorder characterized by extreme fear of being too heavy, dramatic weight loss, a distorted body image, and resistance to eating enough to reach or maintain a healthful weight. Anorexia nervosa mostly afflicts women during adolescence and young adulthood (Ackard et al., 2007). The typical person with anorexia is a young European American female of higher socio-economic status. Affluent females have greater access to fitness centers and health clubs and are more likely to subscribe to the magazines that idealize slender bodies and shop in the boutiques that cater to svelte women. They are regularly confronted with unrealistic standards of slimness that make them dissatisfied with their own figures (Ackard et al., 2007).

Females with anorexia nervosa can drop 25% or more of their weight within a year. Severe weight loss can prevent ovulation and cause respiratory and cardiovascular problems (Andersen & Ryan, 2009; Gardini et al., 2009; Papadopoulos et al., 2009). Females with anorexia are also at risk for premature development of osteoporosis, a condition characterized by loss of bone density that usually afflicts people in late adulthood (Andersen & Ryan, 2009). Given these problems, the mortality rate for females with anorexia nervosa is approximately 5%.

In one common pattern, the girl sees that she has gained some weight after reaching puberty, and she resolves that she must lose it. But even after the weight is gone, she maintains her pattern of dieting and, in many cases, exercises at a fever pitch. This pattern continues as she plunges below her "desirable" weight. Girls with the disorder are in denial about health problems; some point to feverish exercise routines as evidence of strength. Distortion of the body image—seeing oneself as heavier than one is—is a major feature of the disorder (Hrabosky et al., 2009; Miyake et al., 2010).

Bulimia Nervosa

Bulimia nervosa entails repeated cycles of binge eating and purging. Like anorexia, it tends to afflict women during adolescence and young adulthood (Bravender et al., 2010). Binge eating often follows on the heels of food restriction—as in dieting (Cifani et al., 2009; White et al., 2009). There are various methods of purging. Some people vomit. Other avenues include strict dieting or fasting, the use of laxatives, and engaging in demanding, prolonged exercise regimens. Individuals with eating disorders tend to be perfectionists about their bodies. They will not settle for less than their idealized body shape and weight (Franco et al., 2009; Watson et al., 2011). Bulimia, like anorexia, triggers hormonal imbalances: Many women with bulimia nervosa have irregular menstrual cycles (Mendelsohn, & Warren, 2010). Eating disorders are upsetting and dangerous in themselves, of course, but they are also often connected with deep depression (Wilson et al., 2010).

Origins of the Eating Disorders

Health professionals have done a great deal of research into the origins of eating disorders, but they admit that many questions about them remain unanswered.

Many parents are obsessed with getting their children—especially their infants—to eat. Thus, some psychologists suggest that children now and then refuse to eat as a way of engaging in warfare with their parents. ("You have to eat something!" "I'm not hungry!") It often seems that warfare does occur in the families of adolescents with eating disorders. Parents in such families are often unhappy with the family's functioning. They frequently have issues with eating and

> **TRUTH**
>
> IT IS TRUE THAT FASHION MAGAZINES CAN CONTRIBUTE TO EATING DISORDERS AMONG WOMEN.

dieting themselves. They also "act out" against their daughters—letting them know that they consider them unattractive and, prior to the development of the eating disorder, letting them know that they think they should lose weight (Cooper et al., 2001; Crittenden & Dallos, 2009).

A particularly disturbing risk factor for eating disorders in adolescent females is a history of child abuse, particularly sexual abuse (Leung et al., 2010; Maniglio, 2009). One study found a history of childhood sexual abuse in about half of women with bulimia nervosa, as opposed to a rate of about 7% among women without the disorder (Deep et al., 1999).

The sociocultural climate also affects eating behavior. Slimness is idealized in the United States. When you check out current fashion magazines and catalogs, you are looking at models who, on average, are 9% taller and 16% thinner than the typical female—and who still manage to have ample bust lines. Miss America, the annually renewed American role model, has also been slenderizing across the years. Over the past 80 years, the winner has added only 2% in height but has lost 12 pounds in weight. In the 1920s, Miss America's weight relative to her height yielded a body mass index (BMI) of 20 to 25, which is considered normal by the World Health Organization (WHO). The WHO labels people as malnourished when their BMIs are lower than 18.5. Recent Miss Americas, however, come in at a BMI near 17 (Ludescher et al., 2009). As the cultural ideal slenderizes, women with average body weights according to the health charts feel overweight, and more-than-average women feel gargantuan.

Kristian Dowling/Getty Images

The Model Figure for the 2010s? The great majority of women who compare themselves to the idealized embodiment of the tall, slender model are likely to be disappointed. The models' body mass index (BMI) is about 17, and nearly two of three American women have a BMI in excess of 25.

> **bulimia nervosa**
> an eating disorder characterized by repeated cycles of binge eating and purging

Glossary

activating effect
the arousal-producing effects of sex hormones that increase the likelihood of sexual behavior

estrus
the periodic sexual excitement of many female mammals as governed by levels of sex hormones

sexual response cycle
Masters and Johnson's model of sexual response, which consists of four stages or phases: excitement, plateau, orgasm, and resolution

vasocongestion
engorgement of blood vessels with blood, which swells the genitals and breasts during sexual arousal

myotonia
muscle tension

excitement phase
the first phase of the sexual response cycle, which is characterized by muscle tension, increases in the heart rate, and erection in the male and vaginal lubrication in the female

8-4 Sexual Motivation and Sexual Orientation

In a TV comedy, a mother referred to her teenage son as "a hormone with feet." She recognized that her son had become obsessed with sex, which is normal enough for adolescents in our culture. It is also now widely understood that the adolescent preoccupation with sex is strongly related to the surge in sex hormones that occurs at puberty. The phrase "a hormone with feet" implies movement as well as motivation, and movement means direction. We will see that sex hormones tend to propel us in certain directions as well as provide the driving force.

8-4a HORMONES AND SEXUAL MOTIVATION

Sex hormones can be said to fuel the sex drive. Research with men who produce little testosterone—due to age or health problems—shows that their sex drive increases when they receive testosterone replacement therapy (Muraleedharan & Jones, 2010). The most common sexual problem among women is lack of sexual desire or interest, and the sex drive in women is also connected to testosterone levels (Downey, 2009). Although men produce 7 to 10 times the testosterone produced by women, women produce androgens ("male" sex hormones) in the adrenal glands and the ovaries. Testosterone injections, patches, or pills can heighten the sex drive in women who do not produce enough of the hormone (Brand & van der Schouw, 2010).

Sex hormones promote the development of male and female sex organs and regulate the menstrual cycle. They also have *activating* and *organizing* effects on sexual behavior. They affect the sex drive and promote sexual response; these are **activating effects**. Female mice, rats, cats, and dogs are receptive to males only during **estrus**, when female sex hormones are plentiful.

During estrus, female rats respond to males by hopping, wiggling their ears, and arching their backs with their tails to one side, thus enabling males to penetrate them.

8-4b SEXUAL RESPONSE AND SEXUAL BEHAVIOR

Men show more interest in sex than women do (Fisher et al., 2012; Schmitt et al., 2012). A survey of more than 1,000 undergraduates found that men reported being more interested than women in casual sex and multiple sex partners (Schmitt et al., 2012). Women are more likely to want to combine sex with a romantic relationship (Fisher et al., 2012).

Although we may be more culturally attuned to focus on sex differences rather than similarities, William Masters and Virginia Johnson (1966) found that the biological responses of males and females to sexual stimulation are quite similar. Masters and Johnson use the term **sexual response cycle** to describe the changes that occur in the body as men and women become sexually aroused. They divide the sexual response cycle into four phases: *excitement*, *plateau*, *orgasm*, and *resolution*.

The sexual response cycle is characterized by *vasocongestion* and *myotonia*. **Vasocongestion** is the swelling of the genital tissues with blood, causing erection of the penis and swelling of the area surrounding the vaginal opening. The testes and the nipples swell as blood vessels dilate in these areas. **Myotonia** is muscle tension, which causes grimaces, spasms in the hands and feet, and the spasms of orgasm.

Erection, vaginal lubrication, and orgasm are all reflexes. That is, they occur automatically in response to adequate sexual stimulation.

Excitement Phase

Vasocongestion during the **excitement phase** cause erection in men. The scrotal skin thickens, becoming less baggy. The testes increase in size and become elevated.

In the female, excitement is characterized by vaginal lubrication, which may start 10 to 30 seconds after sexual stimulation begins. Vasocongestion swells the clitoris, flattens and spreads the vaginal lips, and expands the inner part of the vagina. The breasts enlarge, and blood vessels near the surface become more prominent. The nipples may erect in both men and women. Heart rate and blood pressure increase.

Plateau Phase

The level of sexual arousal remains somewhat stable during the **plateau phase** of the cycle. Because of vasocongestion, the circumference of the head of the penis increases somewhat. The testes are elevated into position for **ejaculation** and may reach one-and-a-half times their unaroused size.

In women, vasocongestion swells the outer part of the vagina and the inner vagina expands further. The clitoris withdraws beneath the clitoral hood and shortens. Breathing becomes rapid, like panting. Heart rate may increase to 100 to 160 beats per minute. Blood pressure continues to rise.

Orgasmic Phase

During **orgasm** in the male, muscle contractions propel semen from the body. Sensations of pleasure tend to be related to the strength of the contractions and the amount of seminal fluid. The first three to four contractions are generally most intense and occur at 0.8-second intervals (five contractions every four seconds). Additional contractions occur more slowly.

Orgasm in the female is manifested by three to fifteen contractions of the pelvic muscles that surround the vaginal barrel. As with males, the contractions first occur at 0.8-second intervals. Weaker and slower contractions follow.

Blood pressure and heart rate reach a peak, with the heart beating up to 180 times per minute. Respiration may increase to 40 breaths per minute.

Resolution Phase

In the **resolution phase**, after orgasm, the body returns to its unaroused state. Men enter a **refractory period** during which they cannot experience another orgasm or ejaculate. Women do not undergo a refractory period and therefore can become quickly rearoused to the point of repeated (multiple) orgasm if they desire and receive continued sexual stimulation.

The sexual response cycle describes what happens when females and males are exposed to sexual stimulation. But what kinds of sexual experiences do people seek? How many sex partners do they have? Who are their partners? What do we know about the sex lives of people in the United States?

8-4c SURVEYS OF SEXUAL BEHAVIOR

The well-known Kinsey reports (Kinsey et al., 1948, 1953) interviewed 5,300 males and 5,940 females in the United States between 1938 and 1949. Interviewers asked about sexual experiences including masturbation, oral sex, and premarital sex. The nation was astounded to learn that most males masturbated and had had sexual intercourse prior to marriage. Moreover, significant minorities of females reported these behaviors. But Kinsey had not obtained a random sample of the population. His samples underrepresented people of color, people in rural areas, older people, poor people, Catholics, and Jews. There is thus no way of knowing whether or not Kinsey's results accurately mirrored general American sexual behavior at the time. But the *relationships* Kinsey uncovered, such as the positive link between level of education and premarital sex, may be accurate enough.

If you're trying to report accurately on sex in the United States, you have to give everyone in the country an equal chance of participating. That never happens perfectly. What if you want to interview college students and use listed phone numbers to reach them? In doing so, you've just left out all students who use cellphones only. The researchers who published the recent National Survey of Sexual Health and Behavior (NSSHB) took measures to prevent that type of thing from happening (Reece et al., 2010). All in all, they surveyed 5,865 adolescents and adults, aged 14 to 94, and derived what most researchers believe is a reasonably accurate snapshot of

plateau phase the second phase of the sexual response cycle, which is characterized by increases in vasocongestion, muscle tension, heart rate, and blood pressure in preparation for orgasm

ejaculation the process of propelling seminal fluid (semen) from the penis

orgasm the height or climax of sexual excitement, involving involuntary muscle contractions, release of sexual tensions, and usually, subjective feelings of pleasure

resolution phase the fourth phase of the sexual response cycle, during which the body gradually returns to its prearoused state

refractory period in the sexual response cycle, a period of time following orgasm during which an individual is not responsive to sexual stimulation

Walter Lockwood Photography/Getty Images

FIGURE 8.3 | Percentage of Americans Performing Certain Sexual Behaviors in the Past Year (N=5865)

Sexual Behaviors	Age Groups																			
	14-15		16-17		18-19		20-24		25-29		30-39		40-49		50-59		60-69		70+	
	Men	Women	Men	Women	Men	Women	Men	Women	Men	Women	Men	Women	Men	Women	Men	Women	Men	Women	Men	Women
Masturbated Alone	62%	40%	75%	45%	81%	60%	83%	64%	84%	72%	80%	63%	76%	65%	72%	54%	61%	47%	46%	33%
Masturbated with Partner	5%	8%	16%	19%	42%	36%	44%	36%	49%	48%	45%	43%	38%	35%	28%	18%	17%	13%	13%	5%
Received Oral from Women	12%	1%	31%	5%	54%	4%	63%	9%	77%	3%	78%	5%	62%	2%	49%	1%	38%	1%	19%	2%
Received Oral from Men	1%	10%	3%	24%	6%	58%	6%	70%	5%	72%	6%	59%	6%	52%	8%	34%	3%	25%	2%	8%
Gave Oral to Women	8%	2%	18%	7%	51%	2%	55%	9%	74%	3%	69%	4%	57%	3%	44%	1%	34%	1%	24%	2%
Gave Oral to Men	1%	12%	2%	22%	4%	59%	7%	74%	5%	76%	5%	59%	7%	53%	8%	36%	3%	23%	3%	7%
Vaginal Intercourse	9%	11%	30%	30%	53%	62%	63%	80%	86%	87%	85%	74%	74%	70%	58%	51%	54%	42%	43%	22%
Received Penis in Anus	1%	4%	1%	5%	4%	18%	5%	23%	4%	21%	3%	22%	4%	12%	5%	6%	1%	4%	2%	1%
Inserted Penis into Anus	3%		6%		6%		11%		27%		24%		21%		11%		6%		2%	

Source: Center for Sexual Health Promotion. (2011). *National Survey of Sexual Health and Behavior (NSSHB)*. Indiana University, Bloomington: School of Health, Physical Education, and Recreation. http://www.nationalsexstudy.indiana.edu/graph.html (Accessed February 22, 2012)

the American population—or at least a reasonably accurate picture of what people are willing to report.

You'll find a quick overview of some of the researchers' results in Figure 8.3. The kinds of sexual behaviors they surveyed are listed in the first column. The ages of the respondents are indicted in the row at the top. Respondents are broken down by sex (men and women) as well as by age. Let's take a look at the first sexual behavior in the list, masturbation, and see what we find.

For every age group, men are more likely to report masturbating alone in the past year than women are. Why do you think that is so? Also, the incidence of masturbation alone generally rises through the late twenties and then begins to decline. How would you explain that?

Despite the availability of methods of contraception and disease prevention, and despite the widespread portrayal of casual sex in the media, a survey by the Centers for Disease Control and Prevention (Martinez et al., 2011) finds that fewer teenagers are having unmarried sex now than they did in the 1980s through the early 2000s (see Figure 8.4). According to the survey, 43% of unmarried female teens and 42% of unmarried male teens have had sex at least one time in the years 2006–2010, whereas the percentages were 52% for girls and 60% for boys as recently as 2002. Teenage pregnancy has also been undergoing a steady decline as unmarried teens have also become more likely to use condoms.

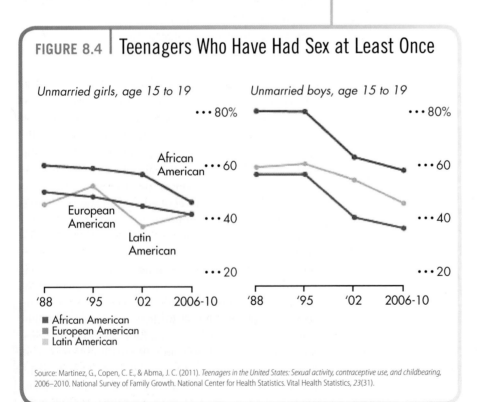

FIGURE 8.4 | Teenagers Who Have Had Sex at Least Once

Unmarried girls, age 15 to 19

Unmarried boys, age 15 to 19

African American
European American
Latin American

African American
European American
Latin American

Source: Martinez, G., Copen, C. E., & Abma, J. C. (2011). *Teenagers in the United States: Sexual activity, contraceptive use, and childbearing, 2006–2010*. National Survey of Family Growth. National Center for Health Statistics. Vital Health Statistics, *23*(31).

8-4d SEXUAL ORIENTATION

Earlier we discussed that sex hormones have *activating* effects. However, they also have

> "Bisexuality immediately doubles your chances for a date on Saturday night."
>
> —WOODY ALLEN

directional or **organizing effects**. That is, they predispose lower animals toward stereotypical masculine or feminine mating patterns. Sex hormones are thus likely candidates for influencing the development of sexual orientation (De Rooij et al., 2009).

One's **sexual orientation** refers to the direction of his or her sexual and romantic interests—toward people of the other sex or toward people of the same sex. The great majority of people have a **heterosexual** orientation; they are sexually attracted to and interested in forming romantic relationships with people of the other sex. Some people, however, have a **homosexual** orientation; they are attracted to and interested in forming romantic relationships with people of their own sex. Males with a homosexual orientation are referred to as *gay males*. Homosexual females are referred to as *lesbians*. *Bisexual* people are attracted to both females and males.

About 7% of American men and women define themselves as being "other than heterosexual," but as noted earlier, the behavior of the other 93% doesn't exactly match up with the way people label themselves. For example, nearly twice as many people—about 14%—say they have had oral sex with a person of the same gender (Herbenick et al., 2010a, 2010b, 2010c; Reece et al., 2010). Estimates of the prevalence of various sexual orientations in our culture remain somewhat speculative.

Theories of the Origins of Sexual Orientation

Theories of the origins of sexual orientation look both at nature and nurture—the biological makeup of the individual and environmental influences. Several theories bridge the two.

Social-cognitive theorists look for the roles of factors such as reinforcement and observational learning. From this perspective, reinforcement of sexual behavior with members of one's own gender—as in reaching orgasm with them when members of the other gender are unavailable—might affect one's sexual orientation. Similarly, childhood sexual abuse by someone of the same gender could lead to fantasies about sex with people of one's own gender and affect sexual orientation. Observation of others en-

organizing effect
the directional effect of sex hormones—for example, along typical male or female patterns of mating

sexual orientation
the directionality of one's sexual and romantic interests; that is, whether one is sexually attracted to, and desires to form a romantic relationship with, members of the other gender or of one's own gender

heterosexual
referring to people who are sexually aroused by, and interested in forming romantic relationships with, people of the other gender

homosexual
referring to people who are sexually aroused by, and interested in forming romantic relationships with, people of the same gender

Ryan Pierse/Getty Images

gaged in enjoyable male–male or female–female sexual encounters could also affect the development of sexual orientation. But critics point out that most individuals become aware of their sexual orientation before they have sexual contacts with other people of either gender (Savin-Williams & Cohen, 2007). Moreover, in a society that generally condemns homosexuality, young people are unlikely to believe that male–male or female–female contacts will have positive effects for them.

There is evidence for genetic factors in sexual orientation (Dawood et al., 2009; Ramagopalan et al., 2010). About 52% of identical (MZ) twin pairs, whose genetic codes are completely the same, share a gay male sexual orientation as compared with 22% of fraternal (DZ) twins, whose genetic codes overlap only 50%, and 11% for adoptive brothers (Dawood et al., 2009).

In many families of animals, such as rodents, there is little room for thinking about sex and deciding whether an individual will pursue sexual relationships with males or females. Sexual motivation comes under the governance of sex hormones (Henley et al., 2010; Piffer et al., 2009). Furthermore, much sexual motivation is determined by whether the brains and sex organs of fetuses are bathed in large doses of testosterone in the uterus. In male fetuses, testosterone is normally produced by the developing testes. Yet female fetuses are exposed to testosterone when they share the uterus with many male siblings. Researchers have also injected male sex hormones into the uteruses of rodents. When they do, the sex organs of females become masculinized in appearance, and they show a tendency toward masculine-type behavior patterns at maturity, including mating with other females (Phoenix, 2009).

It has been shown, then, that sex hormones predispose nonhumans to stereotypical masculine or feminine mating patterns. Do sex hormones influence the developing human embryo and fetus as they affect rodents (Garcia-Falgueras & Swaab, 2010)? The evidence is somewhat mixed, and this possibility continues to receive intensive study (Dawood et al., 2009). And if prenatal hormones affect the sexual orientation of the fetus, what causes the fluctuation in hormone levels? Hormone levels in utero can be influenced by genetic factors, maternal stress, drinking alcohol, and other factors. We must confess that much about the development of sexual orientation remains speculative.

8-5 Achievement Motivation

Many students persist in studying despite being surrounded by distractions. Many people strive relentlessly to get ahead, to "make it," to earn large sums of money,

to invent, to accomplish the impossible. Psychological research has pointed to these people having something called *achievement motivation*.

Psychologist David McClelland (1958) helped pioneer the assessment of achievement motivation through evaluation of fantasies. One method involves the Thematic Apperception Test (TAT), developed by Henry Murray. The test contains cards with pictures and drawings that are subject to various interpretations. Individuals are shown one or more test cards and asked to construct stories about the pictured theme: to indicate what led up to it, what the characters are thinking and feeling, and what is likely to happen.

One test card is similar to that in Figure 8.5. The meaning of the card is ambiguous—unclear. Is the girl sleeping, thinking about the book, wishing she were out with friends?

Consider two stories that could be told about this card:

- *Story 1:* "She's upset that she's got to read the book because she's behind in her assignments and doesn't particularly like to work. She'd much rather be out with her friends, and she may very well sneak out to do just that."

- *Story 2:* "She's thinking, 'Someday I'll be a great scholar. I'll write books like this, and everybody will be proud of me.' She reads all the time."

The second story suggests more achievement motivation than the first. Classic studies find that people

FIGURE 8.5 | A Drawing Similar to Those on TAT Cards

© Cengage Learning 2012

with high achievement motivation earn higher grades than people with comparable learning ability but lower achievement motivation. They are more likely to earn high salaries and be promoted than less motivated people with similar opportunities (Story et al., 2009; E. A. Turner et al., 2009).

McClelland (1965) used the Thematic Apperception Test to sort college students into groups—students with high achievement motivation and students with low achievement motivation. He found that 83% of college graduates with high achievement motivation found jobs in occupations characterized by risk, decision-making, and the chance for great success, such as business management, sales, or self-employment. Most (70%) of the graduates who chose nonentrepreneurial positions showed low achievement motivation. People with high achievement motivation seem to prefer challenges and are willing to take moderate risks to achieve their goals.

8-5a EXTRINSIC VERSUS INTRINSIC MOTIVES

Do you want to do well in this course? If you do, why? Carol Dweck (2009; Dweck & Master, 2008) finds that achievement motivation can be driven by performance or learning goals, or both. For example, are you motivated mainly by performance goals, such as your grade in the course? If so, it may be in part because your motives concern tangible rewards such as getting into graduate school, landing a good job, reaping approval from your parents or your instructor, or avoiding criticism. Performance goals are usually met through *extrinsic rewards* such as praise and income. Parents of children who develop performance goals are likely to respond to good grades with rewards such as toys or money and to respond to poor grades with anger and removal of privileges.

Or is it learning goals that mainly motivate you to do well? That is, is your central motive the enhancing of your knowledge and skills—your ability to understand and master the subject matter? Learning goals usually lead to *intrinsic rewards*, such as self-satisfaction. Students who develop learning goals often have parents with strong achievement motivation who encourage their children to think and act independently. Parents and teachers help children develop learning goals by showing warmth and praising them for their efforts to learn, exposing them to novel and stimulating experiences, and encouraging persistence (Dweck, 2006, 2009). Children who are stimulated in this way tend to set high standards for themselves, associate their achievements with self-worth, and attribute their achievements to their own efforts rather than to chance or to the intervention of others.

Many of us strive to meet both performance and learning goals in our courses as well as in other areas of life. Grades are important because they are connected with tangible benefits, but learning for its own sake is also of value and can provide great pleasure.

"When I was young I thought that **money was the most important** thing in life; now that I am old I know that it is."

—OSCAR WILDE

8-6 Emotion

Emotions color our lives. We are green with envy, red with anger, blue with sorrow. Positive emotions such as love and desire can fill our days with pleasure. Negative emotions such as fear, depression, and anger can fill us with dread and make each day a chore. Sometimes our emotions "lurk in the background." Sometimes they seize control of the day. And *emotion* can be hard to define (Solomon, 2008).

An emotion can be a response to a situation, in the way that fear is a response to a threat. An emotion can motivate behavior, as anger can motivate aggression. An emotion can also be a goal in itself. We may behave in ways that will lead us to experience happiness or love. Emotions are thus intertwined with motivation. We are driven by emotions, and meeting—or failing to meet—our needs can have powerful emotional results.

Emotions are defined as feeling states with physiological, cognitive, and behavioral components (Solomon, 2008). Strong emotions are associated with arousal of the **autonomic nervous system (ANS)** (LeDoux & Phelps, 2008). The greater the arousal, the more intense the emotion. It also appears that the type of arousal affects the emotion being experienced. Although the word *emotion* might seem to be about feeling and not about thinking, cognitions—particularly interpretations of the meanings of events—are impor-

emotion
a state of feeling that has cognitive, physiological, and behavioral components

autonomic nervous system (ANS)
the division of the peripheral nervous system that regulates glands and activities such as heartbeat, respiration, digestion, and dilation of the pupils

TABLE 8.2 | Components of Emotions

EMOTION	PHYSIOLOGICAL	COGNITIVE	BEHAVIORAL
Fear	Sympathetic arousal	Belief that one is in danger	Avoidance tendencies
Anger	Sympathetic and para-sympathetic arousal	Frustration or belief that one is being mistreated	Attack tendencies
Depression	Parasympathetic arousal	Thoughts of helplessness, hopelessness, worthlessness	Inactivity, possible self-destructive tendencies

© Cengage Learning 2012

tant aspects of emotions. *Fear*, which usually occurs in response to a threat, involves cognitions that one is in danger as well as arousal of the **sympathetic nervous system** (e.g., rapid heartbeat and breathing, sweating, muscle tension).

Emotions also involve behavioral tendencies. Fear is connected with behavioral tendencies to avoid or escape a situation (see Table 8.2). As a response to a social provocation, *anger* involves cognitions that the provocateur should be paid back, arousal of both the sympathetic and **parasympathetic nervous systems**, and tendencies to attack (Carver & Harmon-Jones, 2009). *Depression* usually involves cognitions of helplessness and hopelessness, parasympathetic arousal, and tendencies toward inactivity—or sometimes self-destruction. *Happiness, grief, jealousy, disgust, embarrassment, liking*—all have cognitive, physiological, and behavioral components.

8-6a THE EXPRESSION OF EMOTIONS

Happiness and sadness are found in all cultures, but do people around the world express emotions in the same way? It turns out that the expression of many emotions may be universal (Ekman, 2003). Smiling is apparently a universal sign of friendliness and approval. Baring the teeth, as noted by Charles Darwin (1872) in the 19th century, may be a universal sign of anger. As the originator of the theory of evolution, Darwin believed that the universal recognition of facial expressions would have survival value. For example, in the absence of language, facial expressions could signal the approach of enemies (or friends).

Most investigators agree that certain facial expressions suggest the same emotions in people who are reared in diverse cultures (Matsumoto et al., 2008; Sebe et al., 2007). Moreover, people in diverse cultures recognize the emotions indicated by certain facial expressions. Paul Ekman (1980) took photographs of people exhibiting anger, disgust, fear, happiness, sadness, and surprise

FIGURE 8.6 | Photographs Used in Research by Paul Ekman

Ekman's research suggests that the facial expressions connected with several important emotions such as happiness, anger, surprise, and fear are universally recognized.

©1976 Paul Ekman/Human Interaction Laboratory

(see Figure 8.6). He then asked people around the world to say what emotions were being depicted. Those queried ranged from European college students to members of the Fore, a tribe that dwells in the New Guinea highlands.

All groups, including the Fore, who had almost no contact with Western culture, agreed on the emotions. The Fore also displayed familiar facial expressions when asked how they would respond if they were the characters in stories that called for basic emotional responses. Ekman and his colleagues (1987) obtained similar results in a study of 10 cultures.

On the other hand, there is no perfect one-to-one relationship between facial expressions and emotions (Matsumoto et al., 2008). Facial expressions sometimes occur in the absence of the emotion they are thought to accompany (Porter & ten Brinke, 2008). The voice, posture, and gestures also provide clues to what people are feeling and are about to do (Campos, 2000).

Happy people
• believe in their ability to effect change
• are open to new experience
• are willing to risk developing new relationships

8-6b POSITIVE PSYCHOLOGY

Ted Lewis, the Great Depression–era bandleader, used to begin his act by asking, "Is evvvvrybody happy?" Well, everybody is not happy, but surveys do suggest that most people in developed nations are reasonably satisfied with their lives (Cummins & Nistico, 2002). Many people might think that psychologists are interested only in negative emotions such as anxiety, depression, and anger. Not at all. An area of psychology called **positive psychology** deals with positive emotions such as happiness and love, optimism and hope, and joy and sensual pleasures.

Are some people just "born happy," or do life experiences determine happiness? What factors interfere with happiness? Some psychologists, such as David Lykken (Lykken & Csikszentmihalyi, 2001), believe that genetic factors play a powerful role in happiness. They note that happiness tends to run in families and that we tend to have a more or less stable level of happiness throughout much of our lives (W. Johnson & Krueger, 2006). Positive events such as learning that the person we love also loves us or receiving recognition for our work can certainly raise our level of happiness at the moment (Feeney, 2004). Similarly, negative life events, such as the loss of a loved one, financial reverses, or injuries can depress us—and un-

derstandably so. Yet we may tend to bounce back to a more or less characteristic level of happiness, as did the actor Christopher Reeve following the accident—being thrown from a horse—that paralyzed him.

Which life experiences contribute to happiness? Despite the saying "Money can't buy you happiness," people tend to be happier when they live in affluent societies and earn decent incomes (W. Johnson & Krueger, 2006). Perhaps money doesn't make people happy in itself, but people who have it at least do not have to worry about money. Money aside, Chinese students tend to think of happiness in terms of feelings of contentment, inner harmony, personal achievement, physical wellness, spiritual enhancement, hopefulness about the future, generosity, and self-development (Lu, 2001). People who are married or in enduring relationships tend to be happier than loners (Waite et al., 2009; Wienke & Hill, 2009). Happy people are also more open to new experiences and new relationships (Demir & Weitekamp, 2007).

Then there are the attitudinal aspects of happiness. People at any income level can make themselves miserable when they compare themselves to people with more (Cheung & Leung, 2008). Happiness also tends to be accompanied by optimism—a cognitive bias toward assuming that things will work out (Ho et al., 2010; Wilhelm et al., 2010). But the "bias" is not groundless, because happy people often believe in their ability to effect change and then try harder. They are also willing to pat themselves on the back for their successes and are not quick to blame themselves when things go wrong—attitudes that contribute to self-esteem, another factor in happiness.

FICTION DESPITE THE SAYING THAT "MONEY CAN'T BUY YOU HAPPINESS," SURVEYS IN THE UNITED STATES, RUSSIA, CHINA, AND LATIN AMERICA SUGGEST THAT PEOPLE TEND TO BE HAPPIER WHEN THEY LIVE IN AFFLUENT SOCIETIES OR EARN DECENT INCOMES.

8-6c THE FACIAL-FEEDBACK HYPOTHESIS

The face has a special place among visual stimuli. Social animals like humans need to be able to differentiate and recognize members of their group, and in people, the face is the most distinctive key to identity (Parr et al., 2000). Faces are also a key to social communication. Facial expressions reflect emotional states, and our ability to "read" these expressions enables us to interact appropriately with other people.

It is known that various emotional states give rise to certain patterns of electrical activity in the facial muscles and in the brain (Davis et al., 2009; Porter & ten Brinke, 2008). But can it work the other way around? The **facial-feedback hypothesis** argues that facial expressions can also affect our emotional state; that is, the causal relationship between emotions and facial expressions can also work in the opposite direction.

Psychological research has yielded some interesting findings concerning the facial-feedback hypothesis. Inducing people to smile, for example, leads them to report more positive feelings and to rate cartoons as more humorous (Soussignan, 2002). When induced to frown, they rate cartoons as more aggressive. When people exhibit pain through facial expressions, they rate electric shocks as more painful.

What are the possible links between facial feedback and emotion? One is arousal. Intense contraction of facial muscles such as those used in signifying fear heightens arousal, which, in turn, boosts emotional response. Feedback from the contraction of facial muscles may also induce emotions. Engaging in the "Duchenne smile," characterized by "crow's feet wrinkles around the eyes and a subtle drop in the eye cover fold so that the skin above the eye moves down slightly toward the eyeball" can induce pleasant feelings (Ekman, 2003; Soussignan, 2002; see Figure 8.7).

You may have heard the British expression "Keep a stiff upper lip" as a recommendation for handling stress. It might be that a "stiff" lip suppresses emotional response—as long as the lip is relaxed rather than quivering with fear or tension. But when the lip is stiffened through strong muscle tension, facial feedback may heighten emotional response.

8-6d THEORIES OF EMOTION

David, 32, is not sleeping well. He wakes before dawn and cannot get back to sleep. His appetite is off, his energy level is low, and he has started smoking again. He has a couple of drinks at lunch and muses that it's lucky that any more alcohol makes him sick to his stomach—otherwise, he'd probably be drinking too much, too. Then he thinks, "So what difference would it make?" Sometimes he is sexually frustrated; at other times he wonders whether he has any sex drive left. Although he's awake, each day it's getting harder to drag himself out of bed in the morning. This week he missed one day of work and was late twice. His supervisor has suggested in a nonthreatening way that he "do something about it." David knows that her next warning will not be nonthreatening. It's been going downhill since Sue walked out. Suicide has even crossed David's mind. He wonders if he's going crazy.

David is experiencing the emotion of depression, and seriously so. Depression is to be expected following a loss, such as the end of a relationship, but David's feelings have lingered. His friends tell him that he should get out and do things, but David is so down that he

Smiling is usually a response to feeling good within, but experimental research into the facial-feedback hypothesis suggests that the act of smiling can also enhance our moods.

FIGURE 8.7 | We May Smile When We Are Pleased, but Can Smiling Make Us Feel Good about Things?

According to the facial-feedback hypothesis, smiling just might have that effect. When people are compelled to smile because they are holding a pen between their teeth, they are more likely to rate comic strips as funny (see part A). Holding the pen between their lips forces a frown, and the rating of the cartoons plummets (part B).

A.

B.

© Kathleen Olson/Kofoto

hasn't the motivation to do much at all. After much prompting by family and friends, David consults a psychologist who ironically also pushes him to get out and do things—the things he used to enjoy. The psychologist also shows David that part of his problem is that he sees himself as a failure who cannot make meaningful changes.

The "commonsense theory" of emotions is that something happens (a situation) that is cognitively appraised (interpreted) by the person, and the feeling state (a combination of arousal and thoughts) follows. For example, you meet someone new, you appraise that person as delightful, and feelings of attraction follow. Or, as in the case of David, a social relationship comes to an end, you recognize your loss, feel powerless to change it, and feel down in the dumps.

However, both historic and contemporary theories of how the components of emotions interact are at variance with this commonsense view. Let's consider a number of theories and see whether we can arrive at some useful conclusions.

The James–Lange Theory

A century ago, William James suggested that our emotions follow, rather than cause, our behavioral responses to events. At about the same time this view was also proposed by the Danish physiologist Karl G. Lange. It is therefore termed the *James–Lange theory of emotion*.

According to James and Lange, certain external stimuli instinctively trigger specific patterns of arousal and action, such as fighting or fleeing (see Figure 8.8, part A). We then become angry *because* we are acting aggressively or become afraid *because* we are running away. Emotions are simply the cognitive representations (or by-products) of automatic physiological and behavioral responses.

The James–Lange theory is consistent with the facial-feedback hypothesis. That is, smiling apparently can induce pleasant feelings, even if the effect may not be strong enough to overcome deep feelings of sadness. The theory also suggests that we may be able to change our feelings by changing our behavior. Changing one's behavior to change one's feelings is one aspect of behavior therapy. When David's psychologist urges him to get out and do things, she is assuming that by changing his behavior, David can have a positive effect on the way he feels.

Walter Cannon (1927) criticized the James–Lange assertion that each emotion has distinct physiological correlates. He argued that the physiological arousal associated with emotion A is not as distinct from the arousal associated with emotion B as the theory asserts. Note that the James–Lange view downplays the importance of human cognition; it denies the roles of cognitive appraisal, personal values, and personal choice in our behavioral and emotional responses to events.

FIGURE 8.8 | Theories of Emotion

A. **James–Lange**	B. **Cannon–Bard**	C. **Cognitive appraisal**
Events trigger specific arousal patterns and actions. Emotions result from our appraisal of our body responses.	Events are first processed by the brain. Body patterns of arousal, action, and our emotional responses are then triggered simultaneously.	Events and arousal are appraised by the individual. The emotional response stems from the person's appraisal of the situation and his or her level of arousal.

© Cengage Learning 2012

The Cannon–Bard Theory

Walter Cannon (1927) and Philip Bard (1934) suggested that an event might *simultaneously* trigger bodily responses (arousal and action) and the experience of an emotion. As shown in Figure 8.8 (part B), when an event is perceived (processed by the brain), the brain stimulates autonomic and muscular activity (arousal and action) *and* cognitive activity (experience of the emotion). Thus, according to the *Cannon–Bard theory of emotion*, emotions *accompany* bodily responses. They are not *produced by* bodily changes, as in the James–Lange theory.

The central criticism of the Cannon–Bard theory focuses on whether bodily responses (arousal and action) and emotions are in fact stimulated simultaneously. For example, pain or the perception of danger may trigger arousal before we begin to feel distress or fear. Also, many of us have had the experience of having a "narrow escape" and becoming aroused and shaky afterward, when we have had time to consider the damage that might have occurred. What is needed is a theory that allows for an ongoing interaction of external events, physiological changes (such as autonomic arousal and muscular activity), and cognitive activities.

The Theory of Cognitive Appraisal

More recent theoretical approaches to emotion stress cognitive factors. For example, Stanley Schachter asserts that many emotions have similar patterns of bodily arousal but that the labels we give them depend largely on our cognitive appraisal of our situations. Cognitive appraisal is based on many factors, including our perception of events and the ways other people respond to those events (see Figure 8.8, part C). When other people are present, we engage in social comparison to arrive at a response.

In a classic experiment, Schachter and Singer (1962) showed that arousal can be labeled quite differently, depending on the situation. The investigators told participants they wanted to determine the effects of a vitamin on vision. Half the participants received an injection of adrenaline, a hormone that stimulates the sympathetic branch of the autonomic nervous system. A control group received an injection of a placebo. Those who had been given adrenaline received one of three "cognitive manipulations." Group 1 was told nothing about possible emotional effects of the "vitamin." Group 2 was deliberately misinformed; members of this group were led to expect itching, numbness, or other irrelevant symptoms. Group 3 was informed accurately about the increased arousal they would experience. Group 4 was a control group injected with a placebo and given no information about its effects.

After receiving injections and cognitive manipulations, the participants were asked to wait in pairs while the experimental apparatus was being set up. The participants did not know that the person with whom they were waiting was a confederate of the experimenter. The confederate's purpose was to respond in a way that the participant would believe was caused by the injection.

Some participants waited with a confederate who acted happy-go-lucky. He flew paper airplanes about the room and tossed paper balls into a wastebasket. Other participants waited with a confederate who acted angry. He complained about the experiment, tore up a questionnaire, and stormed out of the room. As the confederates worked for their Oscar awards, the real participants were observed through a one-way mirror.

The people in groups 1 and 2 were likely to imitate the behavior of the confederate. Those who were exposed to the happy-go-lucky confederate acted jovial and content. Those who were exposed to the angry confederate imitated that person's complaining, aggressive behavior. But those in groups 3 and 4 were less influenced by the confederate's behavior.

Schachter and Singer concluded that participants in groups 1 and 2 were in an ambiguous situation. Members of these groups felt arousal from the adrenaline injection but couldn't label it as a specific emotion. Social comparison with a confederate led them to attribute their arousal either to happiness or to anger. Members of group 3 expected arousal from the injection, but no particular emotional consequences. These participants did not imitate the confederate's display of happiness or anger because they were not in an ambiguous situation; they knew their arousal was caused by adrenaline. Members of group 4 had no arousal for which they needed an

attribution, except perhaps for some arousal induced by observing the confederate. Nor did they imitate the behavior of the confederate.

Now, happiness and anger are very different emotions. Yet Schachter and Singer suggest that the bodily differences between these two emotions are slight enough that different views of the situation can lead one person to label arousal as happiness and another person to label it as anger. The Schachter–Singer view could not be further removed from the James–Lange theory, which holds that each emotion is associated with specific and readily recognized body sensations. The truth, it happens, may lie somewhere in between.

In science, it must be possible to replicate experiments and attain identical or similar results; otherwise, a theory cannot be considered valid. The Schachter and Singer study has been replicated, but with *different* results (Ekman, 1993). For example, some studies found that participants were less likely to imitate the behavior of the confederate and were likely to perceive unexplained arousal negatively, attributing it to nervousness or anger (Zimbardo et al., 1993).

The connections between arousal and emotions have led to the development of many kinds of lie detection, as we see in the following section.

The Polygraph: Just What Do Lie Detectors Detect?

Lying, for better or worse, is a part of life. People admit to lying in 14% of their emails, 27% of their face-to-face interactions, and 37% of their phone calls (Hancock, 2007). Political leaders lie to get elected. When people communicate with online "matches," men are most likely to lie about their personal assets and their goals for a relationship (Hall et al., 2010). Women are most likely to lie about their weight (Hall et al., 2010). Most people lie to their lovers, usually about other relationships (Toma et al., 2008). People also lie about their qualifications to get jobs, and of course, some people lie about whether or not they have committed a crime.

Facial expressions often offer clues to deceit, but some people can lie with a straight face—or a smile. As Shakespeare pointed out in Hamlet, "One may smile, and smile, and be a

© Blend Images / SuperStock

One way to fool a lie detector test is to bite your tongue—less obviously than this, perhaps.

villain." The use of devices to detect lies has a long if not laudable history:

> *The Bedouins of Arabia ... until quite recently required conflicting witnesses to lick a hot iron; the one whose tongue was burned was thought to be lying. The Chinese, it is said, had a similar method for detecting lying: Suspects were forced to chew rice powder and spit it out; if the powder was dry, the suspect was guilty (Kleinmuntz & Szucko, 1984, pp. 766–767).*

These methods may sound primitive, even bizarre, but they are broadly consistent with modern psychological knowledge. Anxiety about being caught in a lie is linked to arousal of the sympathetic division of the autonomic nervous system. One sign of sympathetic arousal is lack of saliva, or dryness in the mouth. The emotions of fear and guilt are also linked to sympathetic arousal and hence to dryness in the mouth.

Polygraphs, or lie detectors, monitor indicators of sympathetic arousal during an interrogation: heart rate, blood pressure, respiration rate, and electrodermal response (sweating). But questions have been raised about the validity of assessing truth or fiction by means of polygraphs (Iacono, 2008).

The American Polygraph Association claims that use of the polygraph is 85% to 95% accurate. Critics find polygraph testing to be less accurate and claim that it is sensitive to more than lies (Iacono, 2008). Factors such as tense muscles, drugs, and previous experience with polygraph tests can significantly reduce their accuracy rate. In one experiment, people were able to reduce the accuracy of polygraph-based judgments to about 50% by biting their tongues (to produce pain) or pressing their toes against the floor (to tense muscles) while being interrogated (Honts & Handler, 2011). You might thus give the examiner the impression that you are lying even when you are telling the truth, throwing off the test's results.

It appears that no specific pattern of bodily responses pinpoints lying (Honts & Handler, 2011). Because of validity problems, results of polygraph examinations are no longer admitted as evidence in many courts.

Evaluation

What can we make of all this? Research suggests that the patterns of arousal connected with various emotions are more specific than suggested by Schachter and Singer—although less so than suggested by James and Lange (Larsen et al., 2008). Research with brain imaging suggests that different emotions, such as happiness and sadness, involve different structures in the brain (Lane et al., 2009; Pollatos et al., 2007; Suslow et al., 2010). Even so, researchers have not found brain cells that respond to but a single emotion. The emotion of disgust apparently has the most specific location, the primary taste cortex. It makes sense that an emotion related to "distasteful" experiences would be centered here.

Regarding the Schachter and Singer study, Zimbardo and his colleagues (1993) note that lack of control over our feelings and lack of understanding what is going on are disturbing experiences. Thus, our cognitive appraisal of situations does affect our emotional responses, but perhaps not as Schachter and Singer believed.

In sum, various components of an experience—cognitive, physiological, and behavioral—contribute to our emotional responses. Our bodies may become aroused in a given situation, but people also appraise those situations; arousal in itself does not appear to directly cause one emotion or another. The fact that none of the theories of emotion we have discussed applies to all people in all situations is comforting. Apparently our emotions are not quite as easily understood, manipulated, or—as in the case of the polygraph—even detected, as some theorists have suggested.

TRUTH IT IS TRUE THAT YOU MIGHT BE ABLE TO FOOL A LIE DETECTOR BY BITING YOUR TONGUE OR WIGGLING YOUR TOES.

By the Numbers

3/10 Fraction that represents the number of obese American adults

Total number of additional calories Americans consume than needed to maintain their weights—every day
200 billion

Total number of daily calories needed to feed a nation of 80 million people
200 billion

23 Percentage of body weight made of muscle in the average woman

6:1 Ratio of women to men who have an eating disorder

Percentage of body weight made of muscle in the average man
40

60 Percent of Americans who believe it is sometimes necessary to lie

7 Percentage of Americans who define themselves as being "other than heterosexual"

Percent of APA respondents who believe that polygraph should not be admitted as evidence in courts of law
74

STUDY TOOLS ▶ 8

Ready to study? In the book, you can:

❍ Review what you've read with Fill-Ins and Multiple Choice quizzes (below).

❍ Rip out Chapter Review card (in the back).

Or you can go online to CourseMate at www.cengagebrain.com for these resources:

❍ Complete Practices Quizzes to prepare for tests.

❍ Review Key Terms Flash Cards (online or print).

❍ Play games to master concepts.

FILL-INS

Answers can be found in the back of the book, starting on page 368.

1. _____ are hypothetical states that activate behavior and direct organisms toward goals.

2. A(n) _____ is an object, person, or situation that is perceived as capable of satisfying a need.

3. Drives help the body maintain a steady state, a tendency that is called _____.

4. Maslow argued that people have a hierarchy of needs, the highest of which is the need for _____.

5. _____ nervosa is a life-threatening eating disorder characterized by dramatic weight loss and a distorted body image.

6. Masters and Johnson divide the sexual response cycle into four phases: the _____, plateau, orgasm, and resolution phases.

7. Sex hormones have activating and _____ effects on sexual behavior.

8. McClelland used the Thematic _____ Test to measure achievement motivation.

9. Students with _____ goals are mainly motivated by factors such as good grades, rewards from parents, and the prospect of landing a good job.

10. According to the James–Lange theory, emotions have specific patterns of arousal and _____.

1. Money, food, and a sexually attractive person can all be viewed as
   a. drives.
   b. physiological.
   c. incentives.
   d. psychological.

2. Drive-reduction theory defines hunger, pain, and thirst as
   a. primary drives.
   b. instincts.
   c. secondary drives.
   d. acquired motives.

3. The _____ is signaled when there is a drop in blood sugar due to food deprivation.
   a. hypothalamus
   b. basilar membrane
   c. corpus callosum
   d. medulla

4. Whenever Farah eats, she immediately excuses herself and goes to the rest room and vomits. Farah is most likely to be diagnosed with
   a. anorexia nervosa.
   b. bulimia nervosa.
   c. aphagia.
   d. a disorder in the thyroid gland.

5. Performance goals are to _____ rewards as learning goals are to _____ rewards.
   a. intrinsic; extrinsic
   b. satisfaction with self; prestige
   c. extrinsic; intrinsic
   d. none of these

6. According to the text, which of the following hormones is most strongly connected with the sex drive in women?
   a. Estrogen   c. Oxytocin
   b. Prolactin   d. Testosterone

7. Identical (MZ) twins have the same sexual orientation about _____ percent of the time.
   a. 12   c. 52
   b. 32   d. 72

8. Fear involves activation of the _____ nervous system, but depression involves activation of the _____ nervous system.
   a. peripheral; somatic
   b. somatic; peripheral
   c. parasympathetic; sympathetic
   d. sympathetic; parasympathetic

9. Which of the following quotes supports the research regarding socioeconomic factors and happiness?
   a. "Money can't buy you love."
   b. "Good nature is worth more than money."
   c. "Happiness is a warm puppy."
   d. "Having money is better than poverty if for only financial reasons."

10. Which of the following is correct concerning relationships and happiness?
    a. People who are married or in enduring relationships report the highest level of happiness.
    b. People who are divorced or separated are happiest.
    c. People who are single are happiest.
    d. People who have a series of casual sexual relationships are happiest.

LEARNING OUTCOMES

9-1 Explain prenatal development and the role that sex hormones play

9-2 Explain the physical, cognitive, moral, social, and emotional development of children

9-3 Explain the physical, cognitive, moral, social, and emotional development of adolescents

9-4 Explain the features of emerging adulthood

9-5 Explain the physical, cognitive, moral, social, and emotional development of adults

STUDY TOOLS ▶ After you read the chapter, go to the Study Tools at the end of the chapter, page 240.

CHAPTER 9

The Voyage Through the LIFE SPAN

We have a story to tell. An important story. A fascinating story about the remarkable voyage you have already taken through childhood and adolescence. It is about the unfolding of your adult life. Billions have made this voyage before. Yet you are unique, and things will happen to you that have never happened before.

Developmental psychologists are interested in studying our voyage through the life span for several reasons. The discovery of early influences and developmental sequences helps psychologists understand adults. Psychologists are also interested in the effects of genetic factors, early interactions with parents and siblings, and the school and community on traits such as aggressiveness and intelligence.

Developmental psychologists also seek to learn the causes of developmental abnormalities. For example, should pregnant women abstain from smoking and drinking? (Yes.) What factors contribute to child abuse? Other developmental psychologists focus on adult development. For example, what can we expect as we voyage through our 30s, 40s, 50s, and beyond? The information developmental psychologists acquire can help us make decisions about how we rear our children and lead our own lives.

Let's now turn to prenatal developments—the changes that occur between conception and birth. They are spectacular, but they occur "out of sight."

> *"There is no cure for life or death save to enjoy the interval."*
> —GEORGE SANTAYANA

> *Billions make the voyage, yet each is unique.*

TRUTH OR **FICTION**

WHAT DO YOU THINK? FOLKLORE, COMMON SENSE, OR NONSENSE? CIRCLE THE T FOR "TRUTH" OR THE F FOR "FICTION," AND CHECK THE ACCURACY OF YOUR ANSWERS AS YOU READ THROUGH THE CHAPTER.

T	F	YOUR HEART STARTED BEATING WHEN YOU WERE ONLY ONE-FIFTH OF AN INCH LONG AND WEIGHED A FRACTION OF AN OUNCE.
T	F	PRIOR TO SIX MONTHS OR SO OF AGE, "OUT OF SIGHT" IS LITERALLY "OUT OF MIND."
T	F	THE ARCHITECT FRANK LLOYD WRIGHT DESIGNED NEW YORK'S INNOVATIVE SPIRAL-SHAPED GUGGENHEIM MUSEUM WHEN HE WAS 65 YEARS OLD.
T	F	ALZHEIMER'S DISEASE IS A NORMAL PART OF AGING.
T	F	MOST PARENTS SUFFER FROM THE "EMPTY-NEST SYNDROME" WHEN THEIR YOUNGEST CHILD LEAVES HOME.

9-1 Prenatal Development

The most dramatic gains in height and weight occur during prenatal development. Within nine months, the newly conceived organism develops from a nearly microscopic cell to a *neonate* (newborn) about 20 inches long. Its weight increases a billionfold!

During the months following conception, the single cell formed by the union of sperm and egg—the **zygote**—multiplies, becoming two cells, then four, then eight, and so on. Following conception (which takes place in the fallopian tube), the zygote divides repeatedly as it proceeds on its 3- to 4-day voyage to

zygote
a fertilized ovum (egg cell)

germinal stage
the first stage of prenatal development, during which the dividing mass of cells has not become implanted in the uterine wall

amniotic sac
a sac within the uterus that contains the embryo or fetus

placenta
a membrane that permits the exchange of nutrients and waste products between the mother and her developing child but does not allow the maternal and fetal bloodstreams to mix

umbilical cord
a tube between the mother and her developing child through which nutrients and waste products are conducted

the uterus. The ball-like mass of multiplying cells wanders about the uterus for another three to four days before beginning to implant in the uterine wall. Implantation takes another week or so. The period from conception to implantation is called the **germinal stage**.

The *embryonic stage* lasts from implantation until about the eighth week of development. During this stage, the major body organ systems take form. As you can see from Figure 9.1, the growth of the head precedes that of other parts of the body. The growth of the organs—heart, lungs, and so on—also precedes the growth of the extremities. The relatively early *maturation* of the brain and the organ systems allows them to participate in the nourishment and further development of the embryo. The heart will continue to beat without rest every minute of every day for most of a century, perhaps longer.

During the second month, the nervous system begins to transmit messages. By five to six weeks, the embryo is only a quarter-inch to a half-inch long, yet nondescript sex organs have formed. By about the sev-

enth week, the genetic code (XY or XX) begins to assert itself, causing the sex organs to differentiate. If a Y sex chromosome is present, testes form and begin to produce *androgens* (male sex hormones), which further masculinize the sex organs. In the absence of these hormones, the embryo develops sex organs typical of the female, regardless of its genetic code. By the end of the second month, the head has become rounded and the facial features distinct—all in an embryo that is about one inch long and weighs 1/30th of an ounce.

As it develops, the embryo is suspended within a protective **amniotic sac** in the mother's uterus. The sac is surrounded by a clear membrane and contains amniotic fluid. The fluid is a sort of natural air bag, allowing the child to move or even jerk around without injury. It also helps maintain an even temperature.

From now until birth, the embryo exchanges nutrients and wastes with the mother through the **placenta**. The embryo is connected to the placenta by the **umbilical cord**. The placenta is connected to the mother by blood vessels in the uterine wall.

The *fetal stage* lasts from the beginning of the third month until birth. By the end of the third month, the major organ systems and the fingers and toes have formed. In the middle of the fourth month, the mother usually detects the first fetal movements. By the end of the sixth month, the fetus moves its limbs so vigorously that mothers often feel that they are being kicked. The fetus opens and shuts its eyes, sucks its thumb, and alternates between periods of wakefulness and sleep.

FIGURE 9.1

A Human Fetus at Twelve Weeks

By the end of the first trimester, formation of all the major organ systems is complete. Fingers and toes are fully formed, and the sex of the fetus can be determined visually.

Claude Edelmann/Photo Researchers, Inc.

A Human Fetus at Four Months

At this midway point between conception and birth, the fetus is covered with fine, downy hair, called *lanugo*.

Petit Format/Photo Researchers, Inc.

During the three months prior to birth, the organ systems of the fetus continue to mature. The heart and lungs become increasingly capable of sustaining independent life. The fetus gains about 5½ pounds and doubles in length. Newborn boys average about 7½ pounds and newborn girls about 7 pounds.

TRUTH DURING THE FOURTH WEEK, A PRIMITIVE HEART BEGINS TO BEAT AND PUMP BLOOD—IN AN ORGANISM THAT IS ONE-FIFTH OF AN INCH LONG.

9-2 Childhood

Childhood begins with birth. When my children are enjoying themselves, I kid them and say, "Stop having fun. You're a child, and childhood is the worst time of life." I get a laugh because they know that childhood is supposed to be the best time of life—a time for play and learning and endless possibilities. In this section we see that childhood is an exciting time of physical, cognitive, and social and emotional developments.

9-2a PHYSICAL DEVELOPMENT

During infancy—the first two years of childhood—dramatic gains in height and weight continue. Babies usually double their birth weight in about five months and triple it by their first birthday (Kuczmarski et al., 2000). Their height increases by about 10 inches in the first year. Children grow another four to six inches during the second year and gain some four to seven pounds. After that, they gain about two to three inches a year until they reach the adolescent growth spurt. Weight gains also remain fairly even at about four to six pounds per year until the spurt. Other aspects of physical development in childhood include reflexes and perceptual development.

Reflexes

Soon after you were born, a doctor or nurse probably pressed her fingers against the palms of your hands. Most likely you grasped the fingers firmly—so firmly that you could have been lifted from your cradle! Grasping at birth is inborn, an example of the importance of nature in human development. Grasping is one of the baby's reflexes. **Reflexes** are simple, inborn responses elicited by specific stimuli. Reflexes are essential to survival and occur automatically—that is, without thinking about them.

Newborn children do not know that it is necessary to eat to survive. Fortunately, rooting and sucking reflexes cause them to eat. They turn their head toward stimuli that prod or stroke the cheek, chin, or corner of the mouth. This

is termed **rooting**. They also automatically suck objects that touch their lips.

Newborns use the *withdrawal reflex* to avoid painful stimuli. In the *startle*, or *Moro*, *reflex*, they draw up their legs and arch their backs in response to sudden noises, bumps, or loss of support while being held. They grasp objects that press against the palms of their hands (the *grasp*, or *palmar*, *reflex*). They fan their toes when the soles of their feet are stimulated (the *Babinski reflex*). Pediatricians test these reflexes to assess babies' neural functioning. Babies also breathe, sneeze, cough, yawn, blink, defecate, and urinate reflexively.

Motor Development

The motor development of the child refers to the progression from simple acts like lifting the head to running around. Maturation and experience both play key roles in motor development (Brown et al., 2009; Spittle et al., 2009). Maturation of the brain is a key to motor development. Motor development provides some of the most fascinating changes in infants, in part because so much seems to happen so quickly—and so much of it during the first year. Children go through a sequence that includes rolling over, sitting up, crawling, creeping, walking, and running. The ages at which infants first engage in these activities vary, but the sequence generally remains the same (see Figure 9.2). Invariant sequences suggest an unfolding of the genetic code (maturation).

The role of maturation in areas such as physical development (for example, gains in height and weight and the effects of puberty), language development, and motor development is clear. But environmental factors are also involved. Children may have certain genetic potentials for body size and growth rates, but they do not reach them unless environmental factors such as nutrition, relatively clean air, and so on are available. Children do not understand or produce language until their genetic codes spark the development of certain structures and processes in the brain. But the environment is also involved. Children learn the languages used in their homes and communities. They do not speak foreign tongues without being exposed to them.

Perceptual Development

Newborn children spend about 16 hours a day sleeping and do not have much opportunity to learn about the world. Yet they perceive the world reasonably well soon after birth. Within a couple of days, infants can follow, or

reflex
a simple inborn response to a stimulus

rooting
the turning of an infant's head toward a touch, such as by the mother's nipple

fixation time
the amount of time spent
looking at a visual stimulus

"track," a moving light with their eyes. By three months, they can discriminate most colors. Newborns are nearsighted (that is, they focus better on nearby than distant objects), but by about four months, infants focus on distant objects about as well as adults do.

The visual preferences of infants are measured by the amount of time, termed **fixation time**, they spend looking at one stimulus instead of another. In classic research by Robert Fantz (1961), two-month-old infants preferred visual stimuli that resembled the human face to newsprint, a bull's-eye, and featureless red, white, and yellow disks (see Figure 9.3).

Classic research has shown that infants tend to respond to cues for depth by the time they are able to crawl (at about six to eight months). Most also have the good sense to avoid crawling off ledges and tabletops into open space (Campos et al., 1978).

Normal newborns hear well. Most newborns reflexively turn their heads toward unusual sounds. This finding, along with findings about visual tracking, suggests that infants are preprogrammed to survey their environments. Speaking or singing softly in a low-pitched tone soothes infants. This is why lullabies help infants fall asleep.

Research indicates that neonates prefer their mother's voice to those of other women, but they do not show a preference for their father's voice (DeCasper & Prescott, 1984; Freeman et al., 1993). Babies, of course, have had months of "experience" in the uterus. For at least two or three months before birth, they have been able to hear. Because they are predominantly exposed to sounds produced by their mother, learning may contribute to newborn preferences. Neonates can also discriminate distinct odors, and their preferences are quite similar to those of older children and adults (Werner & Bernstein, 2001).

9-2b COGNITIVE DEVELOPMENT

This section explores the ways in which children mentally represent and think about the world—that is, their *cognitive development*. Because cognitive functioning develops over many years, young children have ideas about the

FIGURE 9.2 | Motor Development

Age (weeks)

- Turns from stomach to side
- Turns from stomach to back
- Turns from back to stomach
- Crawls
- Creeps
- Sits up
- Kneels up
- Stands up
- Starts walking
- Full walking

© Cengage Learning 2012

FIGURE 9.3 | Two-Month-Olds' Preferences for Visual Stimuli

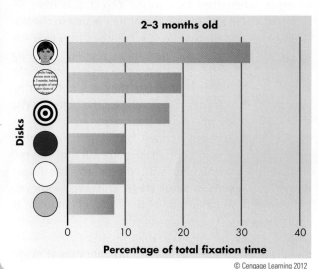

© Cengage Learning 2012

world that differ considerably from those of adults. Many of these ideas are charming but illogical—at least to adults. Let's consider three views of cognitive development. We begin with Jean Piaget's stage theory of cognitive development. Next we turn to the views of the Russian psychologist Lev Semenovich Vygotsky. Then we focus on Lawrence Kohlberg's theory of moral development.

Jean Piaget's Cognitive–Developmental Theory

Jean Piaget (1896–1980) earned his Ph.D. in biology. In 1920 he obtained a job at the Binet Institute in Paris, where work on intelligence tests was being conducted. His first task was to adapt English verbal reasoning items for use with French children. To do so, he had to try out the items on children in various age groups and see whether they could arrive at correct answers. The task was boring until Piaget became intrigued by the children's *wrong* answers. Another investigator might have shrugged them off, but Piaget perceived patterns in the children's "mistakes." The wrong answers reflected consistent, if illogical, cognitive processes. Piaget's observations led to his theory of cognitive development.

Assimilation Piaget described human thought, or intelligence, in terms of the concepts of assimilation and accommodation. **Assimilation** means responding to a new stimulus through existing cognitive structures.

Infants, for example, usually try to place new objects in their mouth to suck, feel, or explore. Piaget would say that the child is assimilating a new toy to the sucking schema. A **schema** is a pattern of action or a "mental structure" involved in acquiring or organizing knowledge.

Accommodation **Accommodation** is the creation of new ways of responding to objects or looking at the world. With accommodation, children transform existing schemas to incorporate new events. For example, children who study biology learn that whales cannot be assimilated into the "fish" schema. They accommodate by constructing new schemas, such as "mammals without legs that live in the sea." The ability to accommodate to novel stimuli advances as a result of maturation and experience. Let's apply these concepts to the stages of cognitive development.

Piaget's Stages of Cognitive Development

Piaget hypothesized that children's cognitive processes develop in an orderly sequence. Some children may be more advanced than others, but the sequence remains the same. Piaget (1963) identified four major stages of cognitive development: *sensorimotor*, *preoperational*, *concrete operational*, and *formal operational*.

The Sensorimotor Stage The newborn infant is capable of assimilating novel stimuli only to existing reflexes (or ready-made schemas) such as the rooting and sucking reflexes. But by the time an infant reaches the age of one month, he or she already shows purposeful behavior by repeating behavior patterns that are pleasurable, such as sucking his or her hand. During the first month or so, an infant apparently does not connect stimuli

JEAN PIAGET

assimilation
according to Piaget, the inclusion of a new event into an existing schema

schema
according to Piaget, a hypothetical mental structure that permits the classification and organization of new information

accommodation
according to Piaget, the modification of schemas so that information inconsistent with existing schemas can be integrated or understood

object permanence
recognition that objects removed from sight still exist, as demonstrated in young children by continued pursuit

sensorimotor stage
the first of Piaget's stages of cognitive development, characterized by coordination of sensory information and motor activity, early exploration of the environment, and lack of language

preoperational stage
the second of Piaget's stages, characterized by illogical use of words and symbols, spotty logic, and egocentrism

egocentrism
according to Piaget, the assumption that others view the world as one does oneself

perceived through different senses. Reflexive turning toward sources of auditory and olfactory stimulation cannot be considered purposeful searching. But within the first few months, the infant begins to coordinate vision with grasping to look at the object being held or touched.

TRUTH IT IS TRUE THAT "OUT OF SIGHT" IS TRULY "OUT OF MIND" PRIOR TO THE AGE OF 6 MONTHS OR SO.

A three- or four-month-old infant may be fascinated by her own hands and legs. The infant may become absorbed in watching herself open and close her fists. The infant becomes increasingly interested in acting on the environment to make interesting results (such as the sound of a rattle) last longer or occur again. Behavior becomes increasingly intentional and purposeful. Between four and eight months of age, the infant explores cause-and-effect relationships such as the thump made by tossing an object or the swinging that results from kicking a hanging toy.

For most infants younger than six months, objects are not yet represented mentally. For this reason, as you can see in Figure 9.4, a child makes no effort to search for an object that has been removed or placed behind a screen. By the age of 8 to 12 months, however, infants realize that objects removed from sight still exist and attempt to find them. In this way, they show what is known as **object permanence**, thereby making it possible to play peekaboo.

Between one and two years of age, children begin to show interest in how things are constructed. It may be for this reason that they persistently touch and finger

their parents' faces and their own. Toward the end of the second year, children begin to engage in mental trial and error before they try out overt behaviors. For example, when they look for an object you have removed, they will no longer begin their search in the last place they saw it. Rather, they may follow you, assuming you are carrying the object even though it is not visible. It is as though they are anticipating failure in searching for the object in the place where they last saw it.

Because the first stage of development is dominated by learning to coordinate perception of the self and of the environment with motor activity, Piaget termed it the **sensorimotor stage**. This stage comes to a close with the acquisition of the basics of language at about age two.

The Preoperational Stage The **preoperational stage** is characterized by the use of words and symbols to represent objects and relationships among them. But be warned—any resemblance between the logic of children between the ages of two and seven and your own logic may be coincidental. Children may use the same words as adults, but this does not mean their views of the world are the same. Preoperational children tend to think one-dimensionally—to focus on one aspect of a problem or situation at a time.

One consequence of one-dimensional thinking is **egocentrism**. Preoperational children cannot understand that other people do not see things the same way they do. When my daughter Allyn was 2½, I asked her to tell me about a trip to the store with her mother. "You tell me," she replied. It seemed she did not understand that I could not see the world through her eyes.

To egocentric preoperational children, all the world's a stage that has been erected to meet their needs and amuse them. When asked, "What are television sets

---

FIGURE 9.4 | Object Permanence

To this infant, who is in the early part of the sensorimotor stage, out of sight is truly out of mind. Once a sheet of paper is placed between the infant and the toy animal, the infant loses all interest in it. The toy is apparently not yet mentally represented.

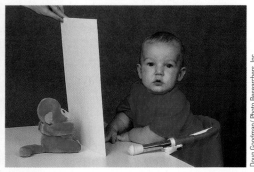

Doug Goodman/ Photo Researchers, Inc.

TABLE 9.1

Examples of Preoperational Thought

TYPE OF THOUGHT	SAMPLE QUESTIONS	TYPICAL ANSWERS
EGOCENTRISM	Why does it get dark out?	So I can go to sleep.
	Why does the sun shine?	To keep me warm.
	Why is there snow?	For me to play in.
ANIMISM	Why do trees have leaves?	To keep them warm.
	Why do stars twinkle?	Because they're happy and cheerful.
ARTIFICIALISM	What makes it rain?	Someone emptying a watering can.
	Why is the sky blue?	Somebody painted it.
	What is the wind?	A man blowing.

© Cengage Learning 2012

conservation
according to Piaget, recognition that basic properties of substances such as weight and mass remain the same when superficial features change

objective responsibility
according to Piaget, the assignment of blame according to the amount of damage done rather than the motives of the actor

for?", they may answer, "To watch my favorite shows and cartoons." Preoperational children also show *animism*. They attribute life and consciousness to physical objects like the sun and the moon. In addition, they also show *artificialism*. They believe that environmental events like rain and thunder are human inventions. Asked what causes thunder, a four-year-old may reply "A man grumbling." Examples of egocentrism, animism, and artificialism are shown in Table 9.1.

To gain further insight into preoperational thinking, find a three- or four-year-old and try these miniexperiments:

- Pour water from a tall, thin glass into a low, wide glass. Now, ask the child whether the low, wide glass contains more, less, or the same amount of water that was in the tall, thin glass. If the child says that they hold the same amount of water, the child is correct. But if the child errs, why do you think this is so?

- Now flatten a ball of clay into a pancake, and ask the child whether you wind up with more, less, or the same amount of clay. If the child errs again, why do you think this is so?

To arrive at the correct answers to these questions, children must understand the law of **conservation**. This law holds that basic properties of substances such as mass, weight, and volume remain the same—that is, are *conserved*—when one changes superficial properties such as their shape or arrangement.

Conservation requires the ability to think about, or *center* on, two aspects of a situation at once, such as height and width. Conserving the mass, weight, or volume of a substance requires the recognition that a change in one dimension can compensate for a change in another. But the preoperational boy in Figure 9.5 focuses on only one dimension at a time. First he is shown two short, squat glasses of water and agrees that they contain the same amount of water. Then, while he watches, water is poured from a squat glass into a tall, thin glass.

Now he is asked which glass contains more water. After mulling over the problem, he points to the tall glass. Why? Because when he looks at the glasses he is "overwhelmed" by the fact that the thinner glass is taller. The preoperational child focuses on the most apparent dimension of the situation—in this case, the greater height of the thinner glass. He does not realize that the increased width of the squat glass compensates for the decreased height.

Piaget (1997) found that the moral judgment of preoperational children is also one-dimensional. Five-year-olds tend to be slaves to rules and authority. When you ask them why something should be done in a certain way, they may insist, "Because that's the way to do it!" or "Because Mommy says so!" Right is right and wrong is wrong. Why? "Because!"—that's why.

According to most older children and adults, an act is a crime only when there is criminal intent. Accidents may be hurtful, but the perpetrators are usually seen as blameless. But in the court of the one-dimensional, preoperational

To a preoperational child, right is right and wrong is wrong. Why? "Because!"—that's why.

child, there is **objective responsibility**. People are sentenced (and harshly!) on the basis of the amount of damage they have done, not their motives or intentions. To demonstrate objective responsibility, Piaget would tell children stories and ask them which character was naughtier and why. John, for example, accidentally breaks 15 cups when he opens a door. Henry breaks one

Comstock/Jupiterimages

concrete operational stage
Piaget's third stage, characterized by logical thought concerning tangible objects, conservation, and subjective morality

decentration
simultaneous focusing on more than one dimension of a problem, so that flexible, reversible thought becomes possible

subjective moral judgment
according to Piaget, moral judgment that is based on the motives of the perpetrator

cup when he sneaks into a kitchen cabinet to find forbidden jam. The preoperational child usually judges John to be naughtier. Why? Because he broke more cups.

The Concrete Operational Stage
By about age seven, the typical child is entering the stage of **concrete operations**. In this stage, which lasts until about age 12, children show the beginnings of the capacity for adult logic. However, their logical thoughts, or *operations*, generally involve tangible objects rather than abstract ideas.

Concrete operational children are capable of **decentration**; they can center on two dimensions of a problem at once. This attainment has implications for moral judgments, conservation, and other intellectual undertakings.

Children now become **subjective** in their moral judgments. When assigning guilt, they center on the motives of wrongdoers as well as on the amount of damage done. Concrete operational children judge Henry more harshly than John because John's misdeed was an accident.

Concrete operational children understand the laws of conservation. The boy in Figure 9.5, now a few years older, would say that the squat glass still contains the same amount of juice. If asked why, he might reply, "Because you can pour it back into the other one." Such an answer

also suggests awareness of the concept of *reversibility*—the recognition that many processes can be reversed or undone so that things are restored to their previous condition. Centering simultaneously on the height and the width of the glasses, the boy recognizes that the loss in height compensates for the gain in width.

Children in this stage are less egocentric. They are able to take on the roles of others and to view the world, and themselves, from other people's perspectives. They recognize that people see things in different ways because of different situations and sets of values.

During the concrete operational stage, children's own sets of values begin to emerge and acquire stability. Children come to understand that feelings of love between them and their parents can endure even when someone is temporarily angry or disappointed. We continue our discussion of Piaget's theory—his stage of *formal operations*—later in the chapter in the section on adolescence.

Evaluation of Piaget's Theory A number of questions have been raised concerning the accuracy of Piaget's views. Among them are these:

- *Was Piaget's timing accurate?* Some critics argue that Piaget's methods led him to underestimate children's abilities (Bjorklund, 2000; Meltzoff & Gopnik, 1997). Other researchers using different methods have found, for example, that preschoolers are less egocentric and that children are capable of conservation at earlier ages than Piaget thought.

FIGURE 9.5 | Conservation

A.   B.   C.

© Cengage Learning 2012

(a) The boy in this illustration agreed that the amount of water in two identical containers is equal. (b) He then watched as water from one container was poured into a tall, thin container. (c) When asked whether the amounts of water in the two containers are now the same, he says no.

- *Does cognitive development occur in stages?* Cognitive events such as egocentrism and conservation appear to develop more continuously than Piaget thought—that is, they may not occur in stages (Bjorklund, 2000; Flavell, 2000). Although cognitive developments appear to build on previous cognitive developments, the process may be more gradual than stagelike.

- *Are developmental sequences always the same?* Here, Piaget's views have fared better. It seems there is no variation in the sequence in which cognitive developments occur.

In sum, Piaget's theoretical edifice has been rocked, but it has not been reduced to rubble. Now let's consider the views of Lev Vygotsky (1896–1934), a Russian psychologist whose work was banned in communist Russia. Unlike Piaget, Vygotsky was not a stage theorist. Instead, he saw the transmission of knowledge from generation to generation as cumulative, and focused on the ways in which children's interactions with their elders enhance their cognitive development.

Lev Vygotsky's Sociocultural Theory

The term *sociocultural theory* has different meanings. For example, the term can refer to the roles of factors such as ethnicity and gender in behavior and mental processes. But Vygotsky's sociocultural theory focuses instead on the ways in which children's cognitive development is influenced by the cultures in which they are reared and the people who teach them.

Vygotsky's theory (1978) focuses on the transmission of information and cognitive skills from generation to generation. The transmission of skills involves teaching and learning, but Vygotsky did not view learning as a mechanical process that can be described in terms of conditioning. Rather, he focused more generally on how the child's social interaction with adults, largely in the home, organized a child's learning experiences in such a way that the child can obtain cognitive skills—such as computation or reading skills—and use them to acquire information. Like Piaget, Vygotsky saw the child's functioning as adaptive (Piaget & Smith, 2000), and the child adapts to his or her social and cultural interactions.

Key concepts in Vygotsky's theory include the *zone of proximal development* and *scaffolding*. The word *proximal* means "nearby" or "close," as in the words *approximate* and *proximity*. The **zone of proximal development (ZPD)** refers to a range of tasks that a child can carry out with the help of someone who is more skilled (Haenen, 2001). The "zone" refers to the relationship between the child's abilities and what she or he can do with help from others. Adults or older children best guide the child through this zone by gearing their assistance to the child's capabilities (Flavell et al., 2002).

Within the zone, the child works with and learns from others (Meijer & Elshout, 2001). When learning with others, the child tends to internalize—or bring inward—the conversations and explanations that help him or her gain skills (Murata & Fuson, 2006; Umek et al., 2005). Children not only learn the meanings of words from teachers but also learn ways of talking to themselves about solving problems within a cultural context. Outer speech becomes inner speech. What was the teacher's becomes the child's. What was a social and cultural context becomes embedded within the child; thus we have the term, *sociocultural theory*.

A *scaffold* is a temporary skeletal structure that enables workers to fabricate a building, bridge, or other, more permanent, structure. Cognitive **scaffolding** refers to the temporary support provided by a parent or teacher to a child who is learning to perform a task. The amount of guidance decreases as the child becomes more skilled and self-sufficient. In Vygotsky's theory, teachers and parents provide children with problem-solving methods that serve as cognitive scaffolding while the child gains the ability to function independently.

Piaget's focus was largely maturational. It was assumed that maturation of the brain allowed the child to experience new levels of insights and suddenly develop new kinds of problem solving. Vygotsky focused on the processes in the teacher–learner relationship. To Vygotsky,

Brand X Pictures/Jupiterimages

According to Vygotsky's theory, teachers and parents provide children with problem-solving methods that serve as cognitive scaffolding.

zone of proximal development (ZPD) Vygotsky's term for the situation in which a child carries out tasks with the help of someone who is more skilled, frequently an adult who represents the culture in which the child develops

scaffolding Vygotsky's term for temporary cognitive structures or methods of solving problems that help the child as he or she learns to function independently

preconventional level
according to Kohlberg, a period during which moral
judgments are based largely
on expectation of rewards or
punishments

conventional level
according to Kohlberg, a period during which moral
judgments largely reflect social conventions; a "law and
order" approach to morality

cognitive development was about culture and social interaction (Montero & De Dios, 2006; Norton & D'Ambrosio, 2008). Let's now turn to another aspect of cognitive development—the ways in which children (and adults) arrive at judgments about what is right and what is wrong.

Lawrence Kohlberg's Theory of Moral Development

Cognitive–developmental theorist Lawrence Kohlberg (1981) used the following tale in his research into children's moral reasoning:

> In Europe a woman was near death from a special kind of cancer. There was one drug that the doctors thought might save her. It was a form of radium that a druggist in the same town had recently discovered. The drug was expensive to make, but the druggist was charging 10 times what the drug cost him to make. He paid $200 for the radium and charged $2,000 for a small dose of the drug. The sick woman's husband, Heinz, went to everyone he knew to borrow the money, but he could only get together about $1,000, which was half of what it cost. He told the druggist that his wife was dying and asked him to sell it cheaper or let him pay later. But the druggist said: "No, I discovered the drug, and I'm going to make money from it." So Heinz got desperate and broke into the man's store to steal the drug for his wife (Kohlberg, 1969).

Heinz is caught in a moral dilemma. A legal or social rule (in this case, the law forbidding stealing) is pitted against a strong human need (his desire to save his wife). Children and adults arrive at yes or no answers for different reasons. According to Kohlberg, the reasons can be classified according to their level of moral development.

As a stage theorist, Kohlberg argues that the stages of moral reasoning follow a specific sequence. Children progress at different rates, and not all children (or adults) reach the highest stage. But the sequence is always the same: Children must go through stage 1 before they enter stage 2, and so on. According to Kohlberg, there are three levels of moral development and two stages within each level.

When it comes to the dilemma of Heinz, Kohlberg believed that people could justify Heinz's theft of the drug or his decision not to steal it by the reasoning of any level or stage of moral development. In other words, Kohlberg was not as interested in the eventual "yes" or "no" as he was in *how a person reasoned* to arrive at yes or no.

"We find delight in the beauty and happiness of children that makes the heart too big for the body."

—RALPH WALDO EMERSON

The Preconventional Level   The **preconventional level** applies to most children through about the age of nine. Children at this level base their moral judgments on the consequences of behavior. For example, stage 1 is oriented toward obedience and punishment. Good behavior is obedient and allows one to avoid punishment. However, a child in stage 1 can decide that Heinz should or should not steal the drug.

In stage 2, good behavior allows people to satisfy their needs and those of others. (Heinz's wife needs the drug; therefore, stealing it—the only way of obtaining it—is not wrong.)

The Conventional Level   In the **conventional level** of moral reasoning, right and wrong are judged by conformity to conventional (familial, religious, societal) standards of right and wrong. According to the stage 3 "good-boy orientation," moral behavior is that which meets the needs and expectations of others. Moral behavior is what is "normal"—what the majority does. (Heinz should steal the drug because that is what a "good husband" would do. It is "natural" or "normal" to try to help one's wife. *Or* Heinz should *not* steal the drug because "good people do not steal.")

In stage 4, moral judgments are based on rules that maintain the social order. Showing respect for authority and doing one's duty are valued highly. (Heinz *must* steal the drug; it would be his fault if he let his wife die. He would pay the druggist later, when he had the money.) Many people do not mature beyond the conventional level.

The Postconventional Level Postconventional moral reasoning is more complex and focuses on dilemmas in which individual needs are pitted against the need to maintain the social order and on personal conscience. We discuss the postconventional level later in the chapter in the section on adolescence.

Evaluation of Kohlberg's Theory As Kohlberg's theory predicts, evidence supports the view that the moral judgments of children develop in an upward sequence (Boom et al., 2007). Postconventional thought, if found at all, first occurs in adolescence. Formal-operational thinking is apparently a prerequisite, and education is likely to play a role (Boom et al., 2007). Postconventional reasoning involves understanding of abstract moral principles and empathy with the views and feelings of others.

Kohlberg believed that the stages of moral development were universal, but he may have underestimated the influence of social, cultural, and educational institutions (Dawson, 2002). Parents are also important. Using reason in discipline and discussing the feelings of others advance moral reasoning (Dawson, 2002).

9-2c SOCIAL AND EMOTIONAL DEVELOPMENT

Social relationships are crucial to us as children. When we are infants, our very survival depends on them. Later in life, they contribute to our feelings of happiness and satisfaction. In this section, we discuss social development in childhood.

Erik Erikson's Stages of Psychosocial Development

According to Erik Erikson, we undergo several stages of psychosocial development. During Erikson's first stage, *trust versus mistrust*, we depend on our primary caregivers (usually our parents) and come to expect that our environments will—or will not—meet our needs. Toddlers through about the age of three are said to be in the stage of *autonomy versus shame and doubt*. During this period, their relationships with parents and friends can encourage the development of self-direction and initiative, or feelings of shame and guilt. Children in this stage need to develop feelings of self-control over physical functions—such as toileting—and a sense of independence. One of the ways that many children demonstrate their growing autonomy, much to the dismay of their parents, is by refusing to comply with parental requests or commands.

Erikson believed that children are in the stage of *initiative versus guilt* through about the age of five, in which they begin to assert control over the environment and strive to master adult skills. Erikson labeled the years of about 6 to 12 the stage of *industry versus inferiority*, during which children meet academic and social challenges in school. A positive outcome contributes to a sense of industry, whereas setbacks can lead to feelings of inferiority. Later we will see that Erikson's theory includes four more stages and straddles the life span.

Attachment

Psychologist Mary D. Salter Ainsworth (1913–1999) defined **attachment** as an emotional tie that is formed between one animal or person and another specific individual. Attachment keeps organisms together—it is vital to the survival of the infant—and it tends to endure. The behaviors that define attachment include (1) attempts to maintain contact or nearness, and (2) shows of anxiety when separated. Babies and children try to maintain contact with caregivers to whom they are attached. They engage in eye contact, pull and tug at them, ask to be picked up, and may even jump in front of them in such a way that they will be "run over" if they are not picked up.

The Strange Situation and Patterns of Attachment

The ways in which infants behave in strange situations are connected with their bonds of attachment with their caregivers. Given this fact, Ainsworth and her colleagues (1978) innovated the *strange situation method* to learn how infants respond to separations and reunions with a caregiver (usually the mother) and a stranger. Using this method, Ainsworth and her colleagues identified three

attachment
the enduring affectional tie that binds one person to another

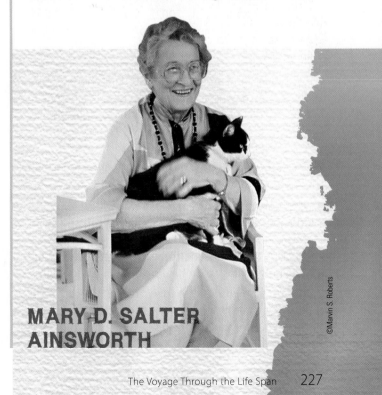

MARY D. SALTER AINSWORTH

©Marvin S. Roberts

major types of attachment, including secure attachment and two types of insecure attachment:

1. *Secure attachment.* Securely attached infants mildly protest their mother's departure, seek interaction upon reunion, and are readily comforted by her.

2. *Avoidant attachment.* Infants who show avoidant attachment are least distressed by their mother's departure. They play by themselves without fuss and ignore their mothers when they return.

3. *Ambivalent/resistant attachment.* Infants with ambivalent/resistant attachment are the most emotional. They show severe signs of distress when their mother leaves and show ambivalence upon reunion by alternately clinging to and pushing their mother away when she returns.

Attachment is connected with the quality of care that infants receive. The parents of securely attached children are more likely to be affectionate and reliable caregivers (Posada et al., 2002). A wealth of research literature speaks of the benefits of secure attachment. For example, secure children are happier, more sociable, and more cooperative with parents; they get along better with peers and are better adjusted in school (Belsky, 2006; McCartney et al., 2004). Insecure attachment in infancy predicts psychological disorders during adolescence (Lee & Hankin, 2009; Sroufe, 1998; Steele, 2005).

Phases of Attachment   Ainsworth also identified three *phases* of attachment:

1. *The initial-preattachment phase,* which lasts from birth to about three months and is characterized by indiscriminate attachment. That is, they prefer being held or being with someone to being alone, but they are generally willing to be held by unfamiliar people.

2. *The attachment-in-the-making phase,* which occurs at about three or four months and is characterized by preference for familiar figures.

FIGURE 9.6 | Attachment in Infant Monkeys

Nina Leen/Time Life Pictures/Getty Images

Although this rhesus monkey infant is fed by the wire "mother," it spends most of its time clinging to the soft, cuddly, terry cloth "mother." It knows where to get a meal, but contact comfort is apparently more important than food in the development of attachment in infant monkeys (and infant humans).

3. *The clear-cut-attachment phase,* which occurs at about six or seven months and is characterized by intensified dependence on the primary caregiver.

John Bowlby (1988), a colleague of Ainsworth, believed that attachment is also characterized by fear of strangers ("stranger anxiety"). That is, at about 8 to 10 months of age, children may cry and cling to their parents when strangers try to befriend them. But not all children develop fear of strangers. It therefore does not seem necessary to include fear of strangers as an essential part of the process of attachment.

Theoretical Views of Attachment   Early in the 20th century, behaviorists argued that attachment behaviors are learned through experience. Caregivers feed their infants and tend to their other physiological needs. Thus, infants associate their caregivers with gratification of needs and learn to approach them to meet their needs. The feelings of gratification associated with the meeting of basic needs generalize into feelings of security when the caregiver is present.

Classic research by psychologist Harry F. Harlow suggests that skin contact may be more important than learning experiences. Harlow noted that infant rhesus monkeys reared without mothers or companions became attached to pieces of cloth in their cages. They maintained contact with them and showed distress when separated from them. Harlow conducted a series of experiments to find out why (Harlow, 1959).

In one study, Harlow placed infant rhesus monkeys in cages with two surrogate mothers, as shown in Figure 9.6. One "mother" was made of wire mesh from which a baby bottle was extended. The other surrogate mother was made of soft, cuddly terry cloth. The infant monkeys spent most of their time clinging to the cloth mother, even though "she" did not gratify their need for food. Harlow concluded that monkeys—and perhaps humans—have an inborn need for **contact comfort** that is as basic as the need for food. Gratification of the need for contact comfort, rather than food, might be why infant monkeys (and humans) cling to their mothers.

Other researchers, such as **ethologist** Konrad Lorenz, argue that for many animals, attachment is an instinct—inborn. (Ethologists study the behavioral characteristics of various species of animals.) Attachment, like other instincts, is theorized to occur in the presence of a specific stimulus and during a **critical period** of life—that is, a period during which the animal is sensitive to the stimulus.

Some animals become attached to the first moving object they encounter. The formation of an attachment in this manner is therefore called **imprinting**. Lorenz (1981) became well known when pictures of his "family" of goslings were made public. How did Lorenz acquire his following? He was present when the goslings hatched and during their critical period, and he allowed them to follow him. The critical period for geese and some other animals is bounded, at the younger end, by the age at which they first walk and, at the older end, by the age at which they develop fear of strangers. The goslings followed Lorenz persistently, ran to him when frightened, honked with distress at his departure, and tried to overcome barriers between them. If you substitute crying for honking, it all sounds rather human.

Ainsworth and Bowlby (1991) consider attachment to be instinctive in humans. However, among humans attachment is less related to issues such as locomotion and fear of strangers (which is not universal). Moreover, the critical period with humans is quite extended.

Parenting Styles

Many psychologists have been concerned about the relationships between parenting styles and the personality development of the child. Diana Baumrind (1989; 2005) has been particularly interested in the connections between parental behavior and the development of children's *instrumental competence*—the ability to manipulate the environment to achieve one's goals. Baumrind has focused largely on four aspects of parental behavior: (1) restrictiveness; (2) demands for the child to achieve intellectual, emotional, and social maturity; (3) communication ability; and (4) warmth and involvement. She labeled the three parenting styles the *authoritative*, *authoritarian*, and *permissive* styles. Other researchers also speak of the *uninvolved* style. These four styles are defined in the following ways:

1. *Authoritative parents.* The parents of the most competent children rate high in all four areas of behavior. Such **authoritative parents** are strict (restrictive) and demand mature behavior. However, they temper their strictness with a desire to reason with their children and with love and support. They expect much, but they explain why and offer help.

2. *Authoritarian parents.* **Authoritarian parents** have strict guidelines about what is right and wrong, and they demand that their children follow those guidelines. Both authoritative and authoritarian parents adhere to strict standards of conduct, but authoritative parents explain their demands and are supportive, whereas authoritarian parents rely on force and

contact comfort
a hypothesized primary drive to seek physical comfort through contact with another

ethologist
a scientist who studies the characteristic behavior patterns of species of animals

critical period
a period of time when an instinctive response can be elicited by a particular stimulus

imprinting
a process occurring during a critical period in the development of an organism, in which that organism responds to a stimulus in a manner that will afterward be difficult to modify

authoritative parents
parents who are strict and warm; authoritative parents demand mature behavior but use reason rather than force in discipline

authoritarian parents
parents who are rigid in their rules and who demand obedience for the sake of obedience

Konrad Lorenz and His Family of Goslings

permissive parents
parents who impose few, if any, rules and who do not supervise their children closely

uninvolved parents
parents who generally leave their children to themselves

adolescence
the period of life bounded by puberty and the assumption of adult responsibilities

puberty
the period of physical development during which sexual reproduction first becomes possible

secondary sex characteristics
characteristics that distinguish females from males, such as distribution of body hair and depth of voice, but that are not directly involved in reproduction

communicate poorly with their children. Authoritarian parents do not respect their children's points of view, and they may be cold and rejecting.

3. *Permissive parents.* **Permissive parents** are generally easygoing with their children. As a result, the children do pretty much what the children want. Permissive parents are warm and supportive, but poor at communicating.

4. *Uninvolved parents.* **Uninvolved parents** tend to leave their children on their own. They make few demands and show little warmth or encouragement.

Research shows that the children of warm parents are more likely to be socially and emotionally well adjusted (Lau et al., 2006; Murray et al., 2009). They are also more likely to internalize moral standards—that is, to develop a conscience (Bender et al., 2007; Lau et al., 2006).

"CHILDREN BEGIN BY LOVING THEIR PARENTS; AS THEY GROW OLDER THEY JUDGE THEM; SOMETIMES THEY FORGIVE THEM."
—OSCAR WILDE

Strictness seems to pay off, provided it is tempered with reason and warmth. Children of authorit*ative* parents have greater self-reliance, self-esteem, social competence, and achievement motivation than other children (Grusec, 2006). Children of authorit*arian* parents are often withdrawn or aggressive and usually do not do as well in school as children of authoritative parents (Paulussen-Hoogeboom et al., 2007; Rudy & Grusec, 2006). Children of permissive parents seem to be less mature. They are often impulsive, moody, and aggressive. In adolescence, lack of parental monitoring

is often linked to delinquency and poor academic performance. Children of uninvolved parents tend to obtain poorer grades than children whose parents make demands on them. The children of uninvolved parents also tend to be more likely to hang out with crowds who "party" a good deal and use drugs. The message? Children profit when parents make reasonable demands, show warmth and encouragement, and spend time with them.

RubberBall Photography/Veer

9-3 Adolescence

Perhaps no other period of life is as exciting—and as bewildering—as adolescence. **Adolescence** is bounded by puberty and the assumption of adult responsibilities. Except for infancy, more changes occur during adolescence than during any other time. Like childhood, adolescence entails physical, cognitive, social, and emotional changes.

9-3a PHYSICAL DEVELOPMENT

One of the most noticeable physical developments of adolescence is a growth spurt that lasts two to three years and ends the gradual changes in height and weight that characterize most of childhood. Within this short span of years, adolescents grow some 8 to 12 inches. Most boys wind up taller and heavier than most girls.

Puberty: More Than "Just a Phase"?

Puberty is the period during which the body becomes sexually mature. It heralds the onset of adolescence. Puberty begins with the appearance of **secondary sex characteristics** such as body hair, deepening of the voice in males, and rounding of the breasts and hips in females. In boys, pituitary hormones stimulate the testes to increase the output of testosterone, which in turn causes enlargement of the penis and testes and the appearance of body hair. By the early teens, erections become common, and boys may ejaculate. Ejaculatory ability usually precedes the presence of mature sperm by at least a year. Ejaculation thus is not evidence of reproductive capacity.

In girls, a critical body weight in the neighborhood of 100 pounds is thought to trigger a cascade of hormonal secretions in the brain that cause the ovaries to secrete higher levels of the female sex hormone, estrogen (Frisch, 1997). Estrogen stimulates the growth of breast tissue and tissue in the hips and buttocks. The pelvis widens, rounding the hips. Small amounts of androgens produced by the adrenal glands, along with estrogen, spur the growth of pubic and underarm hair. Estrogen and androgens also stoke the development of female sex organs. Estrogen production becomes cyclical during puberty and regulates the menstrual cycle. The beginning of menstruation, or **menarche**, usually occurs between 11 and 14. Girls cannot become pregnant until they ovulate, however, and ovulation may begin two years after menarche.

Brain Development

What happens to the brains of adolescents who spend hours a day practicing the piano or the violin? Their learning translates physically into increases in the thickness of the parts of the cerebral cortex that are being used (Bermudez et al., 2009; Johnson et al., 2008). The gains in thickness of the cerebral cortex represent increases in gray matter, which consists of associative neurons that transmit messages back and forth in the brain when we are engaged in thought and sensorimotor activities.

Many adolescents show poor judgment, at least from time to time, and take risks that most adults would avoid, such as excessive drinking, reckless driving, violence, disordered eating behavior, and unprotected sexual activity (Berten & Rossem, 2009). Brain immaturity may play a role. Deborah Yurgelun-Todd and her colleagues (Sava & Yurgelun-Todd, 2008) showed pictures of people with fearful expressions to adolescents ranging in age from 11 to 17 while the adolescents' brains were scanned by functional magnetic resonance imaging (fMRI). Compared to adults, the adolescents' frontal lobes (the seat of executive functioning) were less active, and their amygdalas (a part of the limbic system involved in discriminating emotions, including fear) were more active. The adolescents often misread the facial expressions, with those younger than 14 more often inferring sadness, anger, or confusion rather than fear. The researchers suggest that one reason many adolescents fail to show the judgment, insight, and reasoning ability of adults is immaturity of the frontal lobes (Yurgelun-Todd, 2007).

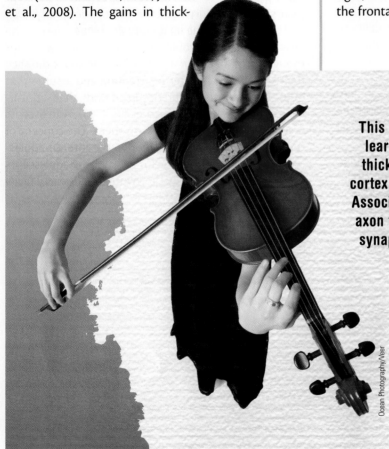

Ocean Photography/Veer

This adolescent musician is not only learning to play the violin but also thickening the parts of her cerebral cortex that are being used in the effort. Associative neurons are sprouting new axon tips and dendrites, creating new synapses, and enhancing the flow of information.

formal operational stage

Piaget's fourth stage, characterized by abstract logical thought and deduction from principles

imaginary audience

an aspect of adolescent egocentrism; the belief that other people are as concerned with our thoughts and behaviors as we are

9-3b COGNITIVE DEVELOPMENT

The adolescent thinker approaches problems differently from the elementary school child. A younger child sticks to the facts, to concrete reality. Speculating about abstract possibilities and what might be is very difficult. The adolescent, on the other hand, is able to deal with the abstract and the hypothetical. In this section, we explore some of the cognitive developments of adolescence by referring to the views of Piaget and Kohlberg.

The Stage of Formal Operations

According to Piaget, children undergo three stages of cognitive development prior to adolescence: sensorimotor, preoperational, and concrete operational. The stage of **formal operations** is the final stage in Piaget's theory, and it represents cognitive maturity. For many children in Western societies, formal operational thought begins at about the beginning of adolescence—the age of 11 or 12. Some people enter this stage later, however, and some never do.

The major achievements of the stage of formal operations involve classification, logical thought, and the ability to hypothesize. Central features are the ability to think about ideas as well as objects and to group and classify ideas—symbols, statements, entire theories. Adolescents can generally follow arguments from premises to conclusions and back again. They can generally appreciate both the outer environment and the world of the imagination: they engage in hypothetical thinking and deductive reasoning.

Formal operational adolescents (and adults) think abstractly. They solve geometric problems about circles and squares without reference to what the circles and squares may represent in the real world. Adolescents in this stage derive rules for behavior from general principles and can focus, or center, on multiple aspects of a situation at once to solve problems.

During the stage of formal operations, adolescents become capable of dealing with hypothetical situations. They realize that situations can have different outcomes, and they think ahead, imagining those outcomes. Adolescents also conduct social "experiments" to test their hypotheses. They may try out various tones of voice and ways of treating others to see what works best for them.

Adolescent Egocentrism

Adolescents in the formal operational stage can reason deductively. They classify objects or people and then draw conclusions about them. Adolescents can be proud of their new logical abilities, leading to a new sort of egocentrism: They demand acceptance of their logic without recognizing the exceptions or practical problems that may be considered by adults. Consider this example: "It is wrong to hurt people. Company A hurts people (perhaps through pollution). Therefore, Company A must be severely punished or shut down." This thinking is logical. But by impatiently demanding major changes or severe penalties, one may not fully consider various practical problems such as the thousands of workers who might be laid off if the company were shut down. Adults have often had life experiences that encourage them to see shades of gray rather than black and white.

The thought of preschoolers is characterized by egocentrism in which they cannot take another's point of view. Adolescent thought is marked by an egocentrism in which they can understand the thoughts of others but still have trouble separating things that are of concern to others and those that are of concern only to themselves (Elkind, 1967, 1985). Adolescent egocentrism gives rise to two interesting cognitive developments: the *imaginary audience* and the *personal fable*.

The concept of the **imaginary audience** refers to the belief that other people are as concerned with our thoughts and behavior as we are. Adolescents thus see themselves as the center of attention and assume that other people are also preoccupied with their appearance and behavior (Milstead et al., 1993). Adolescents may feel onstage with all eyes on them. The concept of the imaginary audience may drive the intense adolescent desire for privacy. It helps explain why adolescents are so self-conscious, why they worry about every facial

Clarissa Leahy/Stone/Getty Images

blemish and spend hours grooming. Self-consciousness seems to peak at about 13 and then decline. Girls tend to be more self-conscious than boys (Elkind & Bowen, 1979).

The **personal fable** is the belief that our feelings and ideas are special, even unique, and that we are invulnerable. The personal fable seems to underlie adolescent showing off and risk taking (Alberts et al., 2007).

The Postconventional Level of Moral Reasoning

Kohlberg's theory of moral reasoning involves three levels: preconventional, conventional, and postconventional. Individuals can arrive at the same decision as to whether Heinz should save his wife by taking the drug without paying for it for different reasons. Deciding not to steal the drug for fear of punishment is less cognitively complex than deciding not to because of the belief that doing could have negative consequences for the social order.

None of Kohlberg's levels is tied to a person's age. Although postconventional reasoning is the highest level, most adolescents and adults never reach it. But if postconventional reasoning emerges, it usually does so in adolescence. Kohlberg's (1969) research found postconventional moral judgments were absent among 7- to 10-year-olds. But by age 16, stage 5 reasoning is shown by about 20% of adolescents, and stage 6 reasoning by about 5%.

At the **postconventional level**, moral reasoning is based on the person's own moral standards. Moral judgments are derived from personal values, not from conventional standards or authority figures. In the contractual, legalistic orientation characteristic of stage 5, it is recognized that laws stem from agreed-upon procedures and that the rule of law is in general good for society; therefore, laws should not be violated except under pressing circumstances. (Although it is illegal for Heinz to steal the drug, in this case it is the right thing to do.)

Stage 6 moral reasoning demands adherence to supposedly universal ethical principles such as the sanctity of human life, individual dignity, justice, and the Golden Rule ("Do unto others as you would have them do unto you"). If a law is unjust or contradicts the rights of the individual, it is wrong to obey it.

People at the postconventional level see their conscience as the highest moral authority. This point has created confusion. To some it suggests that it is right to

break the law when it is convenient, but this interpretation is wrong. Kohlberg means that people at this level feel they must do what they think is right even if they break the law or must sacrifice themselves.

"The best way to keep children home is to make the home atmosphere pleasant—and let the air out of the tires."

—DOROTHY PARKER

9-3c SOCIAL AND EMOTIONAL DEVELOPMENT

In terms of social and emotional development, adolescence has been associated with turbulence. In the 19th century, psychologist G. Stanley Hall described adolescence as a time of *Sturm und Drang*—storm and stress. Current views challenge the assumption that "storm and stress" is the norm (Griffin, 2001). Many adolescents experience a rather calm and joyous period of development. We need to consider individual differences and cultural variations (Arnett, 1999).

Certainly, many American teenagers abuse drugs, get pregnant, contract sexually transmitted infections, get involved in violence, fail in school, even attempt suicide (Miniño, 2010). The U.S. Centers for Disease Control and Prevention (Miniño, 2010) reported that 73% of all deaths among people aged 12 to 19 years result from three causes: motor vehicle and other accidents (48%), homicide (13%), and suicide (12%). Nevertheless, the majority of Americans make it through adolescence quite well.

Relationships with Parents and Peers

Adolescents spend much less time with their parents than they did as children (Halpern, 2005; Staff et al., 2004). Adolescents interact more with their mothers than their fathers and thus have more conflict with their mothers. But they also view their mothers as more supportive and more likely to accept their opinions (Costigan et al., 2007; Sheeber et al., 2007).

The decrease in time spent with family may reflect a striving for independence, yet most adolescents maintain love, loyalty, and respect for their parents (Collins & Laursen, 2006). And adolescents who feel close to their parents are more likely to show greater independence, higher self-esteem, better school performance, and fewer psychological problems (Costigan et al., 2007; Flouri & Buchanan, 2003).

ego identity
Erikson's term for a firm sense of who one is and what one stands for

role diffusion
Erikson's term for lack of clarity in one's life roles (due to failure to develop ego identity)

emerging adulthood
period of development, roughly spanning the ages of 18 to 25, during which time many young people in affluent nations attend college and graduate school, sort out identity issues, and create life plans

Parent–adolescent conflict is greatest during puberty and declines in later adolescence (Smetana et al., 2003, 2006). Conflicts typically center on the everyday details of family life, such as chores, homework, curfews, personal appearance, finances, and dating, but parents and adolescents are usually similar in their beliefs regarding social, political, religious, and economic issues (Collins & Laursen, 2006).

Although relationships with parents generally remain positive, the role of peers as a source of activities, influence, and support increases during the teen years (Kirke, 2009). Adolescents stress the importance of acceptance, self-disclosure, mutual understanding, and loyalty in their friendships (Gonzalez et al., 2004). Adolescents and their friends are typically the same age and the same race (Castelli et al., 2009). Friends are also often alike in their school attitudes, educational aspirations, school achievement, and attitudes about drinking, drug use, and sexual activity (Snijders et al., 2007).

Parents often worry that their teenagers will fall in with the wrong crowd and engage in behavior that is self-destructive or goes against parental wishes. But research shows that most adolescents' friends are not bad influences (Allen & Antonishak, 2008; Reis & Youniss, 2004). Many peers reinforce positive behaviors, such as academic achievement (Allen & Antonishak, 2008).

Ego Identity Versus Role Diffusion

According to Erik Erikson (1963), we undergo eight stages of psychosocial development, each of which is characterized by a certain "crisis." Four of them, beginning with trust versus mistrust, occur in childhood. The fifth, that of *ego identity versus role diffusion*, occurs in adolescence. **Ego identity** is a firm sense of who one is and what one stands for. It can carry one through difficult times and lend meaning to achievements. Adolescents who do not develop ego identity may experience **role diffusion**. They spread themselves too thin, running down one blind alley after another and placing themselves at the mercy of leaders who promise to give them the sense of identity they cannot find for themselves.

In Western society, in which adolescents generally have a good deal of choice in determining what they will become, the creation of an adult identity is a key challenge. Much of this challenge involves learning about one's interests and abilities and connecting them

with an occupation or a role in life. But identity also involves sexual, political, and religious beliefs and commitments. Will the individual be monogamous or sexually active with several people? Will he or she lean left or right along the political spectrum? What role will be played by religion?

9-4 Emerging Adulthood

In earlier days, adolescents made a transition directly into adulthood. Now many of them in affluent nations spend time in what some theorists consider a new period of development, roughly spanning the ages of 18 to 25: **emerging adulthood**. During this time, many young people attend college and graduate school, sort out identity issues, and create meaningful life plans. But even in the United States, of course, many people cannot afford the luxury of sojourning in emerging adulthood.

Jeffrey Arnett (2012; Tanner & Arnett, 2011) hypothesizes that five features distinguish the stage of emerging adulthood that is sandwiched between the stages of adolescence, which precedes it, and young adulthood, which follows it:

- *The age of identity exploration.* Many people of the ages from 18 or 20 to about 25 or 30 are on the path to making vital choices in terms of their love lives and their career lives. They are experimenting with romantic partners and career possibilities.

- *The age of instability.* Americans today average about seven different jobs between 20 and 29. They frequently change romantic partners—sometimes by choice, sometimes because the partner decides to move on. They may move from place to place with little if any furniture. And they frequently change educational directions, finding what they like, finding what they can do, finding what is available.

- *The age of self-focus.* People are exceptionally self-focused during emerging adulthood (Arnett, 2012; Tanner & Arnett, 2011). They are freer to make decisions than they are as children or adolescents; they are more mature, more independent from parental influences, and usually have more resources.

- *The age of feeling in-between.* Emerging adults are similar to adolescents in one way: Whereas adolescents may feel that they exist somewhere between childhood and adulthood, emerging adults are likely to think that they are swimming between adolescence and "real" adulthood. They are likely to be out of school—that is, high school or undergraduate college—but obtaining further training or educa-

Oliver Rossi/Photographer's Choice RF/Getty Images

Emerging adults tend to be self-focused. They recognize that they are freer to make decisions than they were as children and adolescents.

tion. They are beyond the sometimes silly flirtations of adolescence but not yet in long-term, or at least permanent, relationships. They may not be completely dependent on caregivers, but they are just as unlikely to be self-supporting. They may be between roommates or apartments. When they are asked whether they think they have become adults, Arnett (2000) found the most common answer of 18- to 25-year-olds to be something like "In some respects yes and in other respects no." Many think that they have developed beyond the conflicts and exploratory voyages of adolescence, but they may not yet have the ability—or desire—to assume the financial and interpersonal responsibilities they associate with adulthood.

- *The age of possibilities.* Emerging adults typically feel that the world lies open before them. Like the majority of adults, they have an optimistic bias (Arnett, 2012). They believe that things will work out. Yet some of them have a "revolving door" existence: they leave home and then return, according to the ebb and flow of financial and emotional resources.

9-5 Adulthood

Development continues throughout the life span. Many theorists believe that adult concerns and involvements follow observable patterns, so that we can speak of "stages" of adult development. Others argue that there may no longer be a standard life cycle with predictable stages or phases. Age now has an "elastic quality"—

being 50, 60, 70, 80, or even 90 no longer necessarily means loss of cognitive or physical ability, or even wrinkling. People are living longer than ever before and are freer than ever to choose their own destiny.

9-5a PHYSICAL DEVELOPMENT

The most obvious aspects of development during adulthood are physical. Let's consider the physical developments that take place in early adulthood, which spans the ages of 20 to 40; middle adulthood, which spans the ages of 40 to 65; and late adulthood, which begins at 65.

Early Adulthood

Physical development peaks in early adulthood. Most people are at their height of sensory sharpness, strength, reaction time, and cardiovascular fitness. Young adults are at their tallest, and height remains stable through middle adulthood, declining somewhat in late adulthood. Physical strength in both men and women peaks in the 20s and early 30s and then slowly declines (Markham, 2006). Most athletes experience a decline in their 30s, and most athletes retire by age 40. Sexually speaking, most people in early adulthood become readily aroused. They tend to attain and maintain erections as desired and to lubricate readily.

Middle Adulthood

In our middle years, we are unlikely to possess the strength, coordination, and stamina that we had during our 20s and 30s. Still, the years between 40 and 60 are reasonably stable. There is gradual physical decline, but it is minor and likely to be of concern only if a person competes with young adults—or with idealized memories of oneself. Because the physical decline in middle adulthood is gradual, people who begin to eat more nutritious diets and to exercise may find themselves looking and feeling better than they did in early adulthood.

For women, **menopause** is usually considered to be the single most important change of life that occurs during middle adulthood. Menopause usually occurs during the late 40s or early 50s. Menopause is the final phase of the *climacteric*, which is caused by a decline in secretion of female sex hormones. Ovulation comes to an end, and there is some loss of breast tissue and skin elasticity. Loss of bone density can lead to osteoporosis (brittle bones). During the climacteric, many women experience hot flashes, loss of sleep, and some anxiety and depression. Women's experiences during and following the climacteric reflect the intensity of their physical symptoms—which vary considerably—and the extent to which their self-concept was wrapped up with their reproductive capacity (Rathus et al., 2011).

Late Adulthood

An agequake is coming. People age 65 and older are the most rapidly growing segment of the U.S. population (National Center for Health Statistics, 2010). In 1900, only one person in twenty-five was over the age of 65. Today, that figure has more than tripled to one in eight. By midcentury, more than one in five Americans will be 65 years of age or older (National Center for Health Statistics, 2010).

Various changes—some of them troublesome—do occur during the later years (see Figure 9.7). Changes in calcium metabolism increase the brittleness of the bones and heighten the risk of breaks due to falls. The skin becomes less elastic and subject to wrinkles and folds. Older people see and hear less acutely. Because of a decline in the sense of smell, they may use more spice to flavor their food. Older people need more time to respond to stimuli. Older drivers, for example, need more time to respond to changing road conditions. As we grow older, our immune system functions less effectively, leaving us more vulnerable to disease. Age-related changes impact sexual functioning, yet most people can enjoy sex for a lifetime if they remain generally healthy and adjust their expectations.

9-5b COGNITIVE DEVELOPMENT

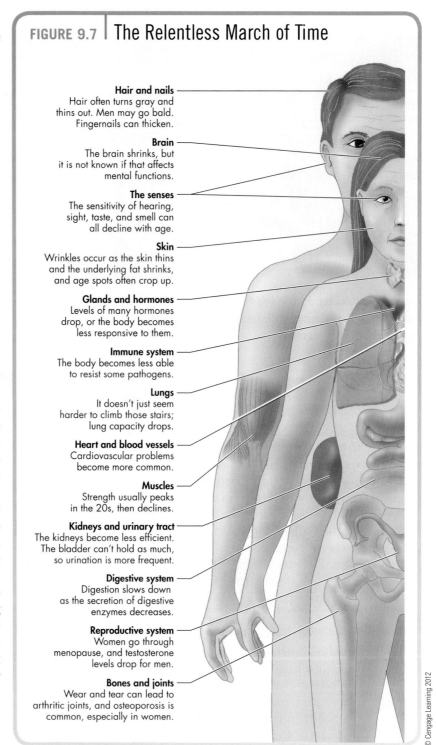

FIGURE 9.7 | The Relentless March of Time

Hair and nails
Hair often turns gray and thins out. Men may go bald. Fingernails can thicken.

Brain
The brain shrinks, but it is not known if that affects mental functions.

The senses
The sensitivity of hearing, sight, taste, and smell can all decline with age.

Skin
Wrinkles occur as the skin thins and the underlying fat shrinks, and age spots often crop up.

Glands and hormones
Levels of many hormones drop, or the body becomes less responsive to them.

Immune system
The body becomes less able to resist some pathogens.

Lungs
It doesn't just seem harder to climb those stairs; lung capacity drops.

Heart and blood vessels
Cardiovascular problems become more common.

Muscles
Strength usually peaks in the 20s, then declines.

Kidneys and urinary tract
The kidneys become less efficient. The bladder can't hold as much, so urination is more frequent.

Digestive system
Digestion slows down as the secretion of digestive enzymes decreases.

Reproductive system
Women go through menopause, and testosterone levels drop for men.

Bones and joints
Wear and tear can lead to arthritic joints, and osteoporosis is common, especially in women.

© Cengage Learning 2012

As in the case of physical development, people are also at the height of their cognitive powers during early adulthood. Cognitive development in adulthood has many aspects—creativity, memory functioning, and intelligence.

People can be creative for a lifetime. At the age of 80, Merce Cunningham choreographed a dance that made use of computer- generated digital images (Teachout, 2000). Hans Hofmann created some of his most vibrant

paintings at 85, and Pablo Picasso was painting in his 90s. Grandma Moses did not even begin painting until she was 78 years old. Giuseppe Verdi wrote his joyous opera *Falstaff* at the age of 79.

Memory functioning does decline with age. But declines in memory are not usually as large as people assume and are often reversible (Villa & Abeles, 2000). Memory tests usually measure ability to recall meaningless information. Older people show better mem-

Architect Frank Lloyd Wright with a model of his Guggenheim Museum.

Ben Schnall/Time & Life Pictures/Getty Images

ory functioning in areas in which they can apply their experience, especially their specialties, to new challenges. For example, who would do a better job of learning and remembering how to solve problems in chemistry—a college history major or a retired professor of chemistry? You might choose the chemistry professor because of his or her *crystallized intelligence*, not his or her *fluid intelligence*.

Crystallized intelligence is defined as a cluster of knowledge and skills that depend on accumulated information and experience, awareness of social conventions, and the capacity to make good decisions. We are using the example of knowledge of chemistry, but crystallized intelligence is shown more generally by vocabulary and accumulated facts about world affairs. Therefore, crystallized intelligence can increase over the decades. **Fluid intelligence** is defined as mental flexibility, demonstrated by the ability to process information rapidly, as in learning and solving problems in new areas. It is the sort of intellectual functioning that is typically measured on intelligence tests, especially with problems that have time limits.

In the absence of senile dementias, crystallized intelligence com-monly increases throughout the life span, along with scores on verbal subtests of standardized intelligence tests. The same studies that indicate that crystallized intelligence tends to increase throughout adulthood tend to show a decline for fluid intelligence (Escorial et al., 2003; Salthouse, 2001).

One of the most severe assaults on intellectual functioning, especially among older people, is **Alzheimer's disease**, a progressive and irreversible brain disease affecting 4–5 million Americans. About one in ten Americans between the ages of 65 and 74 is diagnosed with AD, jumping to more than one in two among those in the 75- to 84-year-old category (Henderson, 2009). Although Alzheimer's is connected with aging, it is a disease rather than a normal progression.

crystallized intelligence one's lifetime of intellectual achievement, as shown largely through vocabulary and knowledge of world affairs

fluid intelligence mental flexibility as shown in learning rapidly to solve new kinds of problems

Alzheimer's disease a progressive form of mental deterioration characterized by loss of memory, language, problem solving, and other cognitive functions

9-5c SOCIAL AND EMOTIONAL DEVELOPMENT

Changes in social and emotional development during adulthood are probably the most "elastic" or fluid. These changes are affected by cultural expectations and individual behavior patterns. As a result, there is much variety. Let's look at some changes that take place at different stages of adulthood.

Early Adulthood

Many theorists suggest that early adulthood is the period of life during which people tend to establish themselves as independent members of society. At some point during their 20s, many people become fueled by ambition. Many strive to advance in their careers. Those who seek professional careers may spend much of their 20s acquiring the skills that will enable them to succeed (Levinson et al., 1978; Levinson, 1996). It is largely during the 20s that people become generally responsible for

"I've yet to be on a campus where most women weren't worrying about some aspect of combining marriage, children, and a career. I've yet to find one where many men were worrying about the same thing."
—GLORIA STEINEM

empty-nest syndrome
a sense of depression and loss of purpose felt by some parents when the youngest child leaves home

sandwich generation
people in middle adulthood who are responsible for meeting the needs of their children yet also responsible for aging parents

 IT IS NOT TRUE THAT MOST PARENTS EXPERIENCE AN EMPTY-NEST SYNDROME WHEN THE YOUNGEST CHILD LEAVES HOME.

their own support, make their own choices, and are freed from parental influences. Many young adults adopt what theorist Daniel Levinson and his colleagues (1978) call *the Dream*—the drive to "become" someone, to leave their mark on history—which serves as a tentative blueprint for life.

During young adulthood, people tend to leave their families of origin and create families of their own. Erik Erikson (1963) characterized young adulthood as the stage of *intimacy versus isolation*. Erikson saw the establishment of intimate relationships as central to young adulthood. Young adults who have evolved a firm sense of identity during adolescence are ready to "fuse" their identities with those of other people through marriage and abiding friendships. People who do not reach out to develop intimate relationships risk retreating into isolation and loneliness.

At age 30 or so, many people reassess their lives, asking themselves, "Where is my life going?" "Why am I doing this?" (Levinson et al., 1978). It is not uncommon for them to switch careers or form new intimate relationships. The later 30s are often characterized by settling down—planting roots. They become focused on career advancement, children, and long-term mortgages.

Middle Adulthood

Erikson (1963) labeled the life crisis of the middle years *generativity versus stagnation*. *Generativity* involves doing things that we believe are worthwhile, such as rearing children or producing on the job. He theorized that generativity enhances and maintains self-esteem. Generativity also involves making the world a better place through joining church or civic groups. *Stagnation* means treading water, as in keeping the same job at the same pay for 30 years or neglecting to rear one's children. Stagnation damages self-esteem.

According to Levinson and colleagues (1978), whose research involved case studies of 40 men, there is a *midlife transition* at about 40 to 45 characterized by a shift in psychological perspective from how many years one has lived to how many years one has left. Research suggests that women may undergo a midlife transition earlier than men do (Zucker et al., 2002). Why? Much of it is related to the winding down of the "biological clock"—their ability to bear children. Yet many women today are having children in their 40s and, now and then, beyond.

In both women and men, according to Levinson, the midlife transition may trigger a *midlife crisis*. The middle-level, middle-aged businessperson looking ahead to another 10 to 20 years of grinding out accounts in a cubbyhole may encounter depression. The homemaker with two teenagers and an empty house from 8 a.m. to 4 p.m. may feel that she or he is coming apart at the seams. Both feel a sense of entrapment and loss of purpose.

Yet many Americans find that these years present opportunities for new direction and fulfillment. Many people are at the height of their productive powers during this period. Many, perhaps most, of today's robust middle-aged adults can look forward to another 30 to 40 healthy years.

The Empty-Nest Syndrome? In earlier decades, psychologists placed emphasis on the so-called **empty-nest syndrome**. This concept was applied most often to women. It was assumed that women experience a sense of loss when their youngest child goes off to college, gets married, or moves out of the home (Stewart & Ostrove, 1998). However, research does not find that parents suffer from an empty-nest syndrome when the youngest child leaves home. Both parents can feel some sense of loss, but once their children become adults, most American parents are content to "launch" their children to live on their own. In fact, many mothers report increased marital satisfaction and personal changes such as greater mellowness, self-confidence, and stability once the children have left home (Etaugh & Bridges, 2006).

Middle-Aged Children and Aging Parents: The "Sandwich Generation" Because of increasing life expectancy, more than half of the middle-aged people in developed nations have at least one living parent, and they frequently go on to late adulthood together (Callahan, 2007; U.S. Bureau of the Census, 2008). Two-thirds of aging American parents have a residence near a child (U.S. Bureau of the Census, 2008), and there are frequent visits and phone calls. The relationships between middle-aged and older parents can grow quite close, especially as tensions and expectations from earlier years tend to slip into history. If the aging parents require assistance, the task usually falls to a middle-aged daughter, who then becomes what has been dubbed part of the **sandwich generation**. She is sandwiched between caring for or contributing to the support of her children or grandchildren at the same time she is caring for her parents (Grundy & Henretta, 2006). Given that she is also likely to be in the workforce, her role overload is multiplied (Gans & Silverstein, 2006).

Eric Lowenbach/Flickr/Getty Images

The woman pushing this wheelchair may be thought of as being in the "sandwich generation." She is "sandwiched" between the needs of her adolescent children and those of her aging parents.

Late Adulthood

Generativity does not end with middle age. Research suggests that many individuals in late adulthood continue to be creative and also to maintain a firm sense of who they are and what they stand for (Webster, 2003). The Greek philosopher Plato was so optimistic about late adulthood that he argued that one could achieve great plea- sure in one's later years, engage in meaningful public service, and also achieve wisdom.

According to psychologist Erik Erikson, late adulthood is the stage of *ego integrity versus despair*. The basic challenge is to maintain the belief that life is meaningful and worthwhile as one ages and faces the inevitability of death. Erikson, like Plato, spoke of the importance of wisdom. He believed that ego integrity derives from wisdom, which can be defined as expert knowledge about the meaning of life, balancing one's own needs and those of others, and pushing toward excellence in one's behavior and achievements (Baltes & Staudinger, 2000; Sternberg, 2000). Erikson also believed that wisdom enables people to accept their life

span as occurring at a certain point in the sweep of history and as being limited. We spend most of our lives accumulating objects and relationships, and Erikson argues that adjustment in the later years requires the ability to let go of them. Other views of late adulthood stress the importance of creating new challenges; however, biological and social realities may require older people to become more selective in their pursuits.

The American poet William Cullen Bryant is best known for his poem "Thanatopsis," which he composed at the age of 18. "Thanatopsis" expresses Erik Erikson's goal of ego integrity—optimism that we can maintain a sense of trust through life. By meeting squarely the challenges of our adult lives, perhaps we can take our leave with dignity. And when our time comes to "join the innumerable caravan"—the billions who have died before us—perhaps we can depart life with integrity as well.

"Live," wrote the poet, so that
. . . *when thy summons comes to join*

The innumerable caravan that moves
To that mysterious realm, where each shall take

His chamber in the silent halls of death,
Thou go not, like the quarry-slave at night,

Scourged to his dungeon, but, sustained and soothed
By an unfaltering trust, approach thy grave

Like one that wraps the drapery of his couch
About him, and lies down to pleasant dreams.

Bryant, of course, wrote "Thanatopsis" at age 18, not at 85, the age at which he died. At that advanced age, his feelings—and his verse—might have differed. But literature and poetry, unlike science, need not perfectly mirror reality. They can serve to inspire and warm us.

Ready to study? In the book, you can:

❍ Review what you've read with Fill-Ins and Multiple Choice quizzes (below).

❍ Rip out Chapter Review card (in the back).

Or you can go online to CourseMate at www.cengagebrain.com for these resources:

❍ Complete Practices Quizzes to prepare for tests.

❍ Review Key Terms Flash Cards (online or print).

❍ Play games to master concepts.

FILL-INS

Answers can be found in the back of the book, starting on page 368.

1. Neonates show _____, which are simple, unlearned, stereotypical responses elicited by specific stimuli.

2. Piaget's _____-operational period is characterized by conservation and reversibility.

3. Vygotsky used the concepts of scaffolding and the _____ of proximal development to explain cognitive development.

4. Ainsworth identified three stages of attachment: The _____ phase, the attachment-in-the-making phase, and the clear-cut-attachment phase.

5. Puberty begins with the appearance of _____ sex characteristics, such as the deepening of the voice in males and rounding of the breasts and hips in females.

6. _____-operational thought is characterized by hypothetical thinking and deductive logic.

7. Adolescent egocentrism gives rise to the _____ audience and the personal fable.

8. Erik Erikson considers the life crisis of adolescence to be ego identity versus role _____.

9. _____ intelligence is mental flexibility as shown by the ability to solve new kinds of problems.

10. Research shows that most parents (do or do not?) suffer from the empty-nest syndrome.

1. A newborn shows a preference for his/her mother's voice rather than the father's voice. This is most likely the result of

   a. an inability to hear until after birth.
   b. learning to recognize the mother's voice because of more exposure to these sounds before birth.
   c. an inability to hear lower pitched tones as in a male's voice.
   d. liking mom more than they like dad.

2. Piaget's stages of cognitive development are, in order of increasing age,

   a. sensorimotor, preoperational, concrete operational, formal operational.
   b. sensorimotor, concrete operational, formal operational, preoperational.
   c. preoperational, operational, postoperational, formal operational.
   d. assimilation, adaptation, accommodation.

3. An adult who chooses not to park in a handicap space because they want to avoid a ticket and fine, is operating at the _____ level of Kohlberg's theory.

   a. nonconventional   c. preconventional
   b. postconvention   d. conventional

4. According to Ainsworth, babies who demonstrate proximity to their mother and separation anxiety when apart are showing indications of

   a. socialization.   c. association.
   b. neuroticism.   d. attachment.

5. Harry Harlow (1959) demonstrated that attachment in rhesus monkeys was related to

   a. feeding only.   c. learning experiences.
   b. contact comfort.   d. insecurity.

6. Menarche is the term used to describe

   a. adolescence.
   b. the beginning of adolescent growth spurts.
   c. the first menstruation.
   d. the onset of male secondary sex characteristics.

7. Formal operations allow adolescents to think

   a. symbolically.
   b. in terms of cause and effect.
   c. concretely.
   d. hypothetically.

8. An adolescent's belief that other people are as concerned with their thoughts and behavior as they are is called the

   a. personal fable.
   b. imaginary audience.
   c. pretend view.
   d. personal fantasy.

9. Intelligence associated with the intellectual attainments of a lifetime or acquired knowledge is called

   a. fluid intelligence.
   b. creative intelligence.
   c. crystallized intelligence.
   d. flexible intelligence.

10. Erikson labeled the life crisis of the middle years as

    a. trust versus mistrust.
    b. generativity versus stagnation.
    c. identity versus stagnation.
    d. midlife transition versus despair.

LEARNING OUTCOMES

10-1 Describe the psychoanalytical perspective and how it contributed to the study of personality

10-2 Explain the trait perspective and the "Big Five" trait model

10-3 Identify the contributions of learning theory to understanding personality

10-4 Describe the humanistic-existential perspective on personality

10-5 Describe the sociocultural perspective on personality

10-6 Describe the different kinds of tests psychologists use to measure personality

STUDY TOOLS ▶ After you read the chapter, go to the Study Tools at the end of the chapter, page 264.

CHAPTER 10

PERSONALITY:
Theory and Measurement

Nearly 1,000 years ago, an Islamic poet, Rumi, wrote of the fable of *The Blind Men and the Elephant*:

Once upon a time, a group of blind men heard that an unusual animal called an elephant had come to their country. Since they had no idea what an elephant looked like and had never even heard its name, they resolved that they would obtain a "picture" of sorts, and the knowledge they sought, by feeling the animal. After all, that was the only possibility available to them. They sought out the elephant, and its handler kindly permitted them to touch the beast. One blind man stroked its leg, the other a tusk, the third an ear, and believing that they now had knowledge of the elephant, they returned home satisfied. But when they were questioned by others, they provided very different descriptions. The one who had felt the leg said that the elephant was firm, strong, and upright, like a pillar. The one who had felt the tusk disagreed. He described the elephant as hard and smooth, clearly not as stout as a pillar, and sharp at the end. Now spoke the third blind man, who had held the ear of the elephant. "By my faith," he asserted, "the elephant is soft and rough." It was neither pillar-like nor hard and smooth. It was broad, thick, and leathery. And so the three argued about the true nature of the beast. Each was right in part, but none grasped the real nature of the elephant. Yet each was fervent in his belief that he knew the animal.

Each of the blind men had come to know the elephant from a different angle. Each was bound by his first experience and blind to the beliefs of his fellows and to the real nature of the beast—not just because of his physical limitations, but also because his initial encounter led him to think of the elephant in a certain way.

> Can there ever be one true portrait of human personality?

WHAT DO YOU THINK? FOLKLORE, COMMON SENSE, OR NONSENSE? CIRCLE THE T FOR "TRUTH" OR THE F FOR "FICTION," AND CHECK THE ACCURACY OF YOUR ANSWERS AS YOU READ THROUGH THE CHAPTER.

T	F	BITING ONE'S FINGERNAILS OR SMOKING CIGARETTES IS A SIGN OF CONFLICT EXPERIENCED DURING EARLY CHILDHOOD.
T	F	BLOODLETTING AND VOMITING WERE ONCE RECOMMENDED AS WAYS OF COPING WITH DEPRESSION.
T	F	TWENTY-FIVE HUNDRED YEARS AGO, A GREEK PHYSICIAN DEVISED A WAY OF LOOKING AT PERSONALITY THAT—WITH A LITTLE "TWEAKING"—REMAINS IN USE TODAY.
T	F	ACTUALLY, THERE ARE NO BASIC PERSONALITY TRAITS. WE ARE ALL CONDITIONED BY SOCIETY TO BEHAVE IN CERTAIN WAYS.
T	F	THE MOST WELL-ADJUSTED IMMIGRANTS ARE THOSE WHO ABANDON THE LANGUAGE AND CUSTOMS OF THEIR COUNTRY OF ORIGIN AND BECOME LIKE MEMBERS OF THE DOMINANT CULTURE IN THEIR NEW HOST COUNTRY.
T	F	PSYCHOLOGISTS CAN DETERMINE WHETHER A PERSON HAS TOLD THE TRUTH ON A PERSONALITY TEST.
T	F	THERE IS A PSYCHOLOGICAL TEST MADE UP OF INKBLOTS, AND TEST-TAKERS ARE ASKED TO SAY WHAT THE BLOTS LOOK LIKE TO THEM.

personality
the reasonably stable patterns of emotions, motives, and behavior that distinguish one person from another

psychodynamic theory
Sigmund Freud's perspective, which emphasizes the importance of unconscious motives and conflicts as forces that determine behavior

Our own conceptions about people, and about ourselves, may be similarly bound up with our own perspectives and initial beliefs. Some think of personality as consisting of the person's most striking traits, as in "This person has an outgoing personality" or "That person has an agreeable personality." But many psychological theorists look deeper.

Those schooled in the Freudian tradition look at personality as consisting of underlying mental structures that jockey for supremacy outside the range of our ordinary awareness. Other theorists focus on how personality is shaped by learning. And to the humanistic theorists, personality is not something people *have* but rather something they *create* to give meaning and direction to their lives. Then, too, sociocultural theorists remind us that we must always consider the influences of culture, race, and ethnicity on personality.

Sometimes even psychologists prefer the first theory of personality they learn about. The Islamic theologian taught his pupils the legend of the blind men and the elephant to illustrate that no person can have a complete view of religious truths; we must therefore remain flexible in our thinking and open to new ideas. It may also be that none of the views of personality presented in this chapter will offer the one true portrait of human personality, but each may have something to contribute to our understanding. So let's approach our study with an open mind, because years from now psychologists may well be teaching new ideas about personality.

While the blind men could touch the elephant, researchers cannot touch a personality; therefore, personality is even harder to describe and understand. Before we discuss psychologists' various approaches to personality, let's define our subject matter: psychologists define **personality** as the reasonably stable patterns of emotions, motives, and behavior that distinguish one person from another.

10-1 The Psychodynamic Perspective

There are several **psychodynamic theories** of personality, each of which owes its origin to Sigmund Freud. Each teaches that personality is characterized by con-

flict. At first the conflict is external: Drives like sex, aggression, and the need for superiority come into conflict with laws, social rules, and moral codes. But at some point laws and social rules are brought inward—that is, *internalized*. The conflict is then between opposing *inner* forces. At any given moment our behavior, our thoughts, and our emotions represent the outcome of these inner contests.

10-1a SIGMUND FREUD'S THEORY OF PSYCHOSEXUAL DEVELOPMENT

Sigmund Freud (1856–1939) was a mass of contradictions. Some have lauded him as one of the greatest thinkers of the 20th century. Others have criticized him as overrated. He preached liberal views on sexuality but was himself a model of sexual restraint. He invented a popular form of psychotherapy but experienced lifelong psychologically related problems such as migraine headaches, fainting under stress, and hatred of the telephone. He smoked 20 cigars a day and could not break the habit even after he developed cancer of the jaw.

SIGMUND FREUD

Imagno/Getty Images

Tim Flach/Stone+/Getty Images

Freud was trained as a physician. Early in his practice, he was surprised to find that some people apparently experienced loss of feeling in a hand or paralysis of the legs even though they had no medical disorder. These odd symptoms often disappeared once the person recalled and discussed stressful events and feelings of guilt or anxiety that seemed to be related to the symptoms. Although these events and feelings lay hidden beneath the surface of awareness, they could influence behavior.

From this sort of clinical evidence, Freud concluded that the human mind is like an iceberg. Only the tip of an iceberg rises above the surface of the water; the great mass of it lies hidden in the depths (see Figure 10.1). Freud came to believe that people, similarly, are aware of only a small part of the ideas and impulses that dwell within their minds. He argued that a much greater portion of the mind—one that contained our deepest images, thoughts, fears, and urges—remains beneath the surface of conscious awareness, where little light illumines them.

Freud labeled the region that pokes into the light of awareness the *conscious* part of the mind. He called the regions below the surface the *preconscious* and the *unconscious*. The preconscious mind contains ideas that are out of awareness but can be made conscious by focusing on them. The unconscious mind is shrouded in mystery. It contains primitive instincts such as sex and aggression. Some unconscious urges cannot be experienced consciously because mental images and words cannot portray them in all their color and fury. Other unconscious urges may be kept below the surface by repression because they would create anxiety.

Repression is defined as the automatic ejection of anxiety-evoking ideas from awareness. People forget many ugly experiences, and some research evidence suggests that people *might* repress them (Furnham et al., 2003; Myers & Brewin, 1994). Other investigators allow that forgetting and distortion of memory occurs, but view the concept of repression as nothing but a myth (Kihlstrom, 2002).

In the unconscious mind, primitive drives seek expression, while learned values try to keep them in check. The conflict can arouse emotional outbursts and psychological problems. To explore the unconscious mind, Freud used a form of mental detective work called *psychoanalysis*. For this reason, his theory of personality is also referred to as *psychoanalytic theory*. In psychoanalysis, people are encouraged to talk about anything that pops into their mind while they remain comfortable and relaxed.

The Structure of Personality

Freud spoke of mental or *psychic structures* to describe the clashing forces of personality. Psychic structures cannot be seen or measured directly, but their presence is suggested by behavior, expressed thoughts, and emotions. Freud believed that there are three psychic structures: the *id*, the *ego*, and the *superego*.

The **id** is present at birth. It represents biological drives and is entirely unconscious. Freud described the id as "a chaos, a cauldron of seething excitations" (1927/1964, p. 73). The conscious mind might find it inconsistent to love and hate the same person, but such conflicting emotions can dwell side by side in the id. In the id, one can hate one's mother for failing to gratify immediately all of one's needs while also loving her. The id follows what Freud termed the *pleasure principle*. It demands instant gratification without consideration for law, social custom, or other people.

id
the psychic structure, present at birth, that represents physiological drives and is fully unconscious

---

FIGURE 10.1 | The Human Iceberg According to Freud

According to psychodynamic theory, only the tip of human personality rises above the surface of the mind into conscious awareness. Material in the preconscious can become conscious if we direct our attention to it. Unconscious material tends to remain shrouded in mystery.

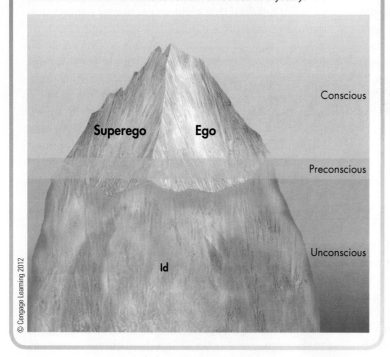

© Cengage Learning 2012

ego
the second psychic structure to develop, characterized by self-awareness, planning, and delay of gratification

superego
the third psychic structure, which functions as a moral guardian and sets forth high standards for behavior

psychosexual development
in psychodynamic theory, the process by which libidinal energy is expressed through different erogenous zones during different stages of development

oral stage
the first stage of psychosexual development, during which gratification is hypothesized to be attained primarily through oral activities

anal stage
the second stage of psychosexual development, when gratification is attained through anal activities

The **ego** begins to develop during the first year of life, largely because a child's demands for gratification cannot all be met immediately. The ego stands for reason and good sense, for rational ways of coping with frustration. The ego is guided by the *reality principle*. It curbs the appetites of the id and seeks ways to find gratification yet avoid social disapproval. The id informs you that you are hungry, but the ego decides to microwave enchiladas. The ego takes into account what is practical along with what is urged by the id. The ego also provides the conscious sense of self.

Although most of the ego is conscious, some of its business is carried out unconsciously. For example, the ego also acts as a censor that screens the impulses of the id. When the ego senses that improper impulses are rising into awareness, it may use psychological defenses to prevent them from surfacing. Repression is one such psychological defense, or *defense mechanism*.

The **superego** develops as the child incorporates the moral standards and values of parents and other members of the community. The child does so through *identification*, by trying to become like these people. The superego functions according to the *moral principle*. It holds up shining models of an ideal self and monitors the intentions of the ego, handing out judgments of right and wrong. It floods the ego with feelings of guilt and shame when the verdict is negative.

Freud believed that a healthy personality has found ways to gratify most of the id's demands without seriously offending the superego. Most of these demands are contained or repressed. If the ego is not a good problem solver, or if the superego is too stern, the ego will have a hard time of it.

Stages of Psychosexual Development

Freud stirred controversy by arguing that sexual impulses are a central factor in personality development, even among children. He believed that sexual feelings are closely linked to children's basic ways of relating to the world, such as nursing and moving their bowels.

Freud believed that a major instinct, *eros*, aims to preserve and perpetuate life. Eros is fueled by psycho-

Freud believed that the first year of life is the oral stage of development. During this time, if it fits, into the mouth it goes.

logical, or psychic, energy, which Freud labeled *libido*. Libidinal energy involves sexual impulses, so Freud considered it to be *psychosexual*. As the child develops, this energy is expressed through sexual feelings in different parts of the body, or *erogenous zones*. To Freud, human development involves the transfer of libidinal energy from one erogenous zone to another. He hypothesized five periods of **psychosexual development**: oral, anal, phallic, latency, and genital.

During the first year of life, a child experiences much of her or his world through the mouth. If it fits, into the mouth it goes. This is the **oral stage**. Freud argued that oral activities such as sucking and biting give the child sexual gratification as well as nourishment.

Freud believed that children encounter conflict during each stage of psychosexual development. During the oral stage, conflict centers on the nature and extent of oral gratification. Early weaning (cessation of breastfeeding) can lead to frustration. Excessive gratification, on the other hand, can lead an infant to expect that it will routinely get anything it wants. Insufficient or excessive gratification in any stage could lead to *fixation* in that stage and to the development of traits that are characteristic of the stage. Oral traits include dependency, gullibility, and excessive optimism or pessimism (depending on the child's experiences with gratification).

Freud theorized that adults with an *oral fixation* could experience exaggerated desires for "oral activities," such as smoking, overeating, alcohol abuse, and nail biting. Like the infant whose survival depends on the mercy of an adult, adults with oral fixations may desire clinging, dependent relationships.

The anal stage begins in the second year. During the **anal stage**, gratification is attained through contraction and relaxation of the muscles that control elimination of waste products. Elimination, which is reflexive during most of the first year, comes under voluntary muscular control, even if such control is not reliable at first. During the anal stage, children learn to delay the gratification that comes from eliminating whenever they feel the urge. The general issue of self-control may bring conflict between parent and child. *Anal fixations* may stem from this conflict and lead to either of two sets of traits in adulthood. *Anal-retentive* traits involve excessive use of self-control: perfectionism, a strong need for order, and exaggerated neatness and cleanliness. *Anal-expulsive* traits, on the other hand, "let it all hang out": they include carelessness, messiness, even sadism.

Children enter the **phallic stage** during the third year. The major erogenous zone is the phallic region (the penis in boys and the clitoris in girls). Parent–child conflict is likely to develop over masturbation, to which parents may respond with threats or punishment. During this stage children may develop strong sexual attachments to the parent of the other gender and begin to view the parent of the same gender as a rival for the other parent's affections.

Children have difficulty dealing with feelings of lust and jealousy. These feelings, therefore, remain unconscious, but their influence is felt through fantasies about marriage with the parent of the other gender and hostility toward the parent of the same gender. In boys, this conflict is labeled the **Oedipus complex**, after the legendary Greek king who unwittingly killed his father and married his mother. Similar feelings in girls give rise to the **Electra complex**. According to Greek legend, Electra was the daughter of the king Agamemnon. She longed for him after his death and sought revenge against his slayers—her mother and her mother's lover.

The Oedipus and Electra complexes are resolved by about the ages of five or six. Children repress their hostilities toward the parent of the same gender and begin to identify with her or him. In psychoanalytic theory, identification is the key to gender-typing: It leads children to play the gender roles of the parent of the same gender and to internalize his or her values. Sexual feelings toward the parent of the other gender are repressed for several years. When the feelings reemerge during adolescence, they are displaced, or transferred, to socially appropriate members of the other gender.

Freud believed that by the age of five or six, children have been in conflict with their parents over sexual feelings for several years. The pressures of the Oedipus and Electra complexes cause them to repress all sexual urges. In so doing, they enter a period of **latency**, during which their sexual feelings remain unconscious, they prefer playmates of their own gender, and they focus on schoolwork.

Freud believed that we enter the final stage of psychosexual development, the **genital stage**, at puberty. Adolescent males again experience sexual urges toward their mother, and adolescent females experience such urges toward their father. However, the *incest taboo* causes them to repress these impulses and displace them onto other adults or adolescents of the other gender. Boys might seek girls "just like the girl that married dear old Dad." Girls might be attracted to boys who resemble their fathers.

People in the genital stage prefer to find sexual gratification through intercourse with a member of the other gender. In Freud's view, oral or anal stimulation, masturbation, and sexual activity with people of the same gender all represent *pregenital* fixations and immature forms of sexual conduct.

10-1b NEO-FREUDIANS

Several personality theorists—*neo-Freudians*—are among Freud's intellectual heirs. Their theories, like his, include conflict and defense mechanisms. In other respects, they differ considerably.

Carl Jung

Carl Jung (1875–1961) was a Swiss psychiatrist who had been a member of Freud's inner circle. He fell into disfavor with Freud when he developed his own psychodynamic theory—**analytical psychology**. In contrast to Freud, Jung downplayed the importance of sex, which he saw as just one of several important instincts.

Jung, like Freud, was intrigued by unconscious processes. He believed that we not only have a *personal* unconscious that contains repressed memories and impulses, but also a **collective unconscious** containing primitive images, or *archetypes*, that reflect the history of our species. Examples of archetypes are the all-powerful God, the young hero, the fertile and nurturing mother, the wise old man, the hostile brother—even fairy godmothers, wicked witches, and themes of rebirth or resurrection. Arche-

phallic stage
the third stage of psychosexual development, characterized by a shift of libido to the phallic region

Oedipus complex
a conflict of the phallic stage in which the boy wishes to possess his mother sexually and perceives his father as a rival in love

Electra complex
a conflict of the phallic stage in which the girl longs for her father and resents her mother

latency
a phase of psychosexual development characterized by repression of sexual impulses

genital stage
the mature stage of psychosexual development, characterized by preferred expression of libido through intercourse with an adult of the other gender

analytical psychology
Jung's psychodynamic theory, which emphasizes the collective unconscious and archetypes

collective unconscious
Jung's hypothesized store of vague memories that represent the history of humankind

inferiority complex
feelings of inferiority hypothesized by Adler to serve as a central motivating force

creative self
according to Adler, the self-aware aspect of personality that strives to achieve its full potential

individual psychology
Adler's psychoanalytic theory, which emphasizes feelings of inferiority and the creative self

types themselves remain unconscious, but Jung believed they affect our thoughts and feelings and cause us to respond to cultural themes in the media.

Alfred Adler

Alfred Adler (1870–1937), another follower of Freud, also felt that Freud had placed too much emphasis on sex. Adler believed that people are basically motivated by an **inferiority complex**. In some people, feelings of inferiority may be based on physical problems and the need to compensate for them. Adler believed, however, that all of us encounter some feelings of inferiority because of our small size as children, and that these feelings give rise to a *drive for superiority*. As a child, Adler was crippled by rickets and suffered from pneumonia, and it may be that his theory developed in part from his own striving to overcome bouts of illness.

Adler believed that self-awareness plays a major role in the formation of personality. He spoke of a **creative self**, a self-aware aspect of personality that strives to overcome obstacles and develop the person's potential. Because each person's potential is unique, Adler's views have been termed **individual psychology**.

Karen Horney

Karen Horney (1885–1952) was criticized by the New York Psychoanalytic Institute because she took issue with the way in which psychoanalytic theory portrayed

Science Source/Photo Researchers

KAREN HORNEY

Horney, like many of Freud's intellectual descendants, took issue with Freud on many issues. For one thing, Horney did not believe that little girls had penis envy or felt inferior to boys in any other way. She also believed that children's social relationships are more important in their development than unconscious sexual and aggressive impulses.

women. Early in the 20th century, psychoanalytic theory taught that a woman's place was in the home. Women who sought to compete with men in the business world were assumed to be suffering from unconscious *penis envy*. Psychoanalytic theory taught that little girls feel inferior to boys when they learn that boys have a penis and

---

✱ Why Do We Need to Have Sports Heroes?

What have psychologists learned about the appeal of celebrities, and especially sports celebrities? Many people form deep and enduring bonds of attachment with athletes and sports teams. Once they identify with a team, their self-esteem rises and falls with the team's wins and losses (Wann et al., 2011a, 2011b). Wins lead to a surge of testosterone in males (Winegard, 2010; Wood & Stanton, 2011), which is connected with aggressiveness and self-confidence. Wins increase the optimism of both males and females.

Psychodynamic theory suggests that children identify with parents and other "big" people in their lives because big people seem to hold the keys to the resources they need for sustenance and stimulation or excitement. Athletes and entertainers—the rich and famous—have their fan clubs, filled with people who tie their own lights to the brilliant suns of their stars.

Teams and sports heroes provide both entertainment and the kind of gutsy competition that evolutionary psychologists believe whispers to us from our genes, pushing us toward aggression and dominance. If we can't do it on our own, we can do it *through* someone else. In some kind of psychological sense, we can *be* someone who is more effective at climbing the heap of humankind into the sun.

Michael Regan/Getty Images

they do not. But Horney argued that little girls do *not* feel inferior to boys and that these views were founded on Western cultural prejudice, not scientific evidence.

Horney agreed with Freud that childhood experiences are important in psychological development. Like other neo-Freudians, however, she asserted that unconscious sexual and aggressive impulses are less important than social relationships. She also believed that genuine and consistent love can alleviate the effects of a traumatic childhood.

Erik Erikson

Like many other modern psychoanalysts, Erik Erikson (1902–1994) believed that Freud had placed undue emphasis on sex. Like Horney, he believed that social relationships (such as that between a parent and child) are more important determinants of personality than sexual urges. Erikson also believed that to a large extent we are the conscious architects of our own personalities.

Erikson, like Freud, is known for devising a comprehensive theory of personality development. But whereas Freud proposed stages of psycho*sexual* development, Erikson proposed stages of psycho*social* development. Rather than label stages for various erogenous zones, Erikson labeled them for the traits that might be developed during the stages. The first stage of **psychosocial development** is labeled the stage of trust versus mistrust because two outcomes are possible: (1) a warm, loving relationship with the mother and others during infancy might lead to a sense of basic trust in people and the world; or (2) a cold, ungratifying relationship with the mother and others might generate a general sense of mistrust. For Erikson, the goal of adolescence is the attainment of **ego identity**, not genital sexuality. The focus is on who we see ourselves as being and what we stand for, not on sexual interests.

Like other modern-day analysts, Erikson believed that Freud had placed too much emphasis on sex and unconscious conflict. Erikson believed that social relationships were the key to healthful development.

Ted Streshinsky/Time Life Pictures/Getty Images

psychosocial development
Erikson's theory of personality and development, which emphasizes social relationships and eight stages of growth

ego identity
a firm sense of who one is and what one stands for

10-1c EVALUATION OF THE PSYCHODYNAMIC PERSPECTIVE

Psychodynamic theories have tremendous appeal. They are rich in concepts and seem to explain many human traits. Today, concepts such as the *id* and *libido* strike many psychologists as unscientific, but Freud was fighting for the idea that human personality and behavior are subject to scientific analysis. He developed his theory at a time when many people viewed psychological problems as signs of possession by the devil or evil spirits. Freud argued that psychological disorders stem from psychological problems—not evil spirits. His views contributed to the development of compassion for people with psychological disorders and to methods of psychotherapy.

"Freud found sex an outcast in the outhouse, and left it in the living room an honored guest."
—W. BERTRAM WOLFE

Psychodynamic theory also focused attention on the far-reaching effects of childhood events and suggested that parents respond to the emotional needs of their children. Freud has helped us recognize that sexual and aggressive urges are common, and that recognizing them is not the same as acting on them. As W. Bertram Wolfe put it, "Freud found sex an outcast in the outhouse, and left it in the living room an honored guest." On the other hand, his views of girls and women have been seen as sexist, as noted by Karen Horney.

Critics note that "psychic structures"—id, ego, and superego—are too vague to measure scientifically (Hergenhahn, 2009). Nor can they be used to predict behavior. Nor have the stages of psychosexual development escaped criticism. Children begin to masturbate as early as the first year, not in the phallic stage. As parents know from discovering their children playing "doctor," the latency stage is not as sexually latent as Freud believed. Much of Freud's thinking about the Oedipus and Electra complexes remains little more than speculation.

The evidence for Erikson's developmental views seems sturdier. For example, people who fail to develop ego identity in adolescence seem to have problems with intimate relationships later on.

Freud's clinical method of gathering evidence is also suspect (Hergenhahn, 2009). Therapists may subtly guide clients into producing memories and feelings they expect to find. Also, most psychodynamic theorists restricted their evidence gathering to case studies with individuals who sought help, particularly people from the middle and upper classes. People who seek therapy differ from the general population.

Psychoanalytic theory focused on reasons that people develop certain traits. We next discuss trait theory, which is not so much concerned with the origins of traits as with their description and categorization.

10-2 The Trait Perspective

The notion of *traits* is familiar enough. If I asked you to describe yourself, you would probably do so in terms of traits such as bright, sophisticated, and witty. (That is you, is it not?) We also describe other people in terms of traits.

Traits are reasonably stable elements of personality that are inferred from behavior. If you describe a friend as "shy," it may be because you have observed anxiety or withdrawal in that person's social encounters. Traits are assumed to account for consistent behavior in different situations. You probably expect your "shy" friend to be retiring in most social confrontations. The concept of traits is also found in other approaches to personality. Freud linked the development of cer-

tain traits to children's experiences in each stage of psychosexual development.

10-2a FROM HIPPOCRATES TO THE PRESENT

The trait perspective dates at least to the Greek physician Hippocrates (ca. 460–377 BCE). Hippocrates believed that traits were embedded in bodily fluids. In his view, a person's personality depends on the balance of four basic fluids, or "humors," in the body. Yellow bile is associated with a choleric (quick-tempered) disposition; blood with a sanguine (warm, cheerful) one; phlegm with a phlegmatic (sluggish, calm, cool) disposition; and black bile with a melancholic (gloomy, pensive) temperament. Disease was believed to reflect an imbalance among

the humors. Depression, for example, represented an excess of black bile. Methods such as bloodletting and vomiting were recommended to restore the balance (Lander & Pritchett, 2009). Although Hippocrates' theory was speculative, the terms *choleric*, *sanguine*, and so on are still used in descriptions of personality.

More contemporary trait theories assume that traits are heritable and are embedded in the nervous system. These theories rely on the mathematical technique of *factor analysis*, developed by Charles Spearman to study intelligence, to determine which traits are basic to others.

Early in the 20th century, Gordon Allport and a colleague (Allport & Oddbert, 1936) catalogued some 18,000 human traits from a search through word lists like dictionaries. Some were physical traits such as *short*, *weak*, and *brunette*. Others were behavioral traits such as *shy* and *emotional*. Still others were moral traits such as *honest*. This exhaustive list has served as the basis for personality research by many other psychologists.

"In most of us by the age of thirty, the character has set like plaster, and will never soften again."
—WILLIAM JAMES

10-2b HANS EYSENCK'S TRAIT THEORY

British psychologist Hans J. Eysenck (1916–1997) focused much of his research on the relationships between two personality traits: **introversion–extraversion** and emotional stability–instability (Eysenck & Eysenck, 1985). (Emotional *in*stability is also called *neuroticism.*) Carl Jung was the first to distinguish between introverts and extraverts. Eysenck added the dimension of emotional stability–instability to introversion–extraversion. He catalogued various personality traits according to where they are situated along these dimensions (see Figure 10.2). For example, an anxious person would be high in both introversion

introversion
a trait characterized by intense imagination and the tendency to inhibit impulses

extraversion
a trait characterized by tendencies to be socially outgoing and to express feelings and impulses freely

and neuroticism—that is, preoccupied with his or her own thoughts and emotionally unstable.

Eysenck acknowledged that his scheme is similar to Hippocrates'. According to Eysenck's dimensions, the choleric type would be extraverted and unstable; the sanguine type, extraverted and stable; the phlegmatic type, introverted and stable; and the melancholic type, introverted and unstable.

FIGURE 10.2 | Eysenck's Personality Dimensions and Hippocrates' Personality Types

Various personality traits shown in the outer ring fall within the two major dimensions of personality suggested by Hans Eysenck, The inner circle shows how Hippocrates' four major personality types—choleric, sanguine, phlegmatic, and melancholic—fit within Eysenck's dimensions.

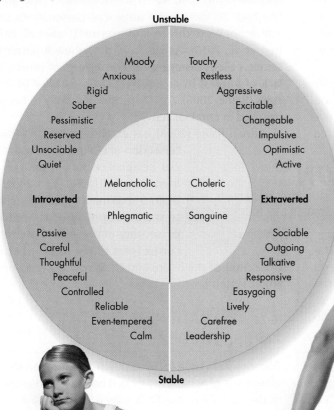

10-2c THE "BIG FIVE": THE FIVE-FACTOR MODEL

More recent research suggests that there may be five basic personality factors, not two. These include the two found by Eysenck—*extraversion* and *neuroticism*—along with *conscientiousness*, *agreeableness*, and *openness to experience* (see Table 10.1).

Many personality theorists, especially Robert McCrae and Paul T. Costa, Jr., played a role in the development of the *five-factor model.* Cross-cultural research has found that these five factors appear to define the personality structure of American, German, Portuguese, Israeli, Chinese, Korean, Japanese, and Philippine people (Katigbak et al., 2002; McCrae & Costa, 1997). A study

TABLE 10.1

The "Big Five": The Five-Factor Model

FACTOR NAME	TRAITS
I. Extraversion	Contrasts talkativeness, assertiveness, and activity with silence, passivity, and reserve
II. Agreeableness	Contrasts kindness, trust, and warmth with hostility, selfishness, and distrust
III. Conscientiousness	Contrasts organization, thoroughness, and reliability with carelessness, negligence, and unreliability
IV. Neuroticism	Contrasts nervousness, moodiness, and sensitivity to negative stimuli with coping ability
V. Openness to experience	Contrasts imagination, curiosity, and creativity with shallowness and lack of perceptiveness

of more than 5,000 German, British, Spanish, Czech, and Turkish people suggests that the factors are related to people's basic temperaments, which are considered to be largely inborn (McCrae et al., 2000). The researchers interpreted the results to suggest that our personalities tend to mature over time rather than be shaped by environmental conditions, although the expression of personality traits is certainly affected by culture.

The five-factor model—also known as the *Big Five model*—is fueling a great deal of research now. Hundreds of studies have correlated scores on the five factors—according to a psychological test constructed by Costa and McCrae (the *NEO Five-Factor Inventory*)—with various behavior patterns, psychological disorders, and kinds of "personalities." Consider driving. Significant negative correlations have been found between the numbers of traffic citations people receive and the accidents they get into, on the one hand, and the factor of agreeableness on the other (Cellar et al., 2000). In other words, it's safer to share the freeway with agreeable people. People who are not judgmental—who will put up with your every whim—tend to score low on conscientiousness (they don't examine you closely) and high on agreeableness (you can be yourself) (Bernardin et al., 2000). Despite the stereotype that older people, especially men, are "crotchety," assessment of 65- to 100-year-olds using the *NEO Five-Factor Inventory* suggests that people, especially men, become more agreeable as they grow older (Weiss et al., 2005). People who are anxious or depressed tend to score higher on the trait of neuroti-

FICTION ACTUALLY, THERE MAY BE SEVERAL BASIC PERSONALITY TRAITS, AS SUGGESTED BY TRAIT THEORY.

cism (Bienvenu et al., 2005). Introverts are more likely than extraverts to fear public gatherings and public speaking (Bienvenu et al., 2005).

10-2d BIOLOGY AND TRAITS

Researchers have also been investigating biological factors that are connected with, and may give rise to, personality traits. For example, researchers estimate that the heritability of the extraverted personality is 40% to 60% (Smillie et al., 2009). Research suggests that brain levels of the neurotransmitter dopamine are involved with extraversion and that levels tend to be higher in extraverts than in introverts (Smillie et al., 2009; Wacker et al., 2009).

Jerome Kagan and other researchers (Dai et al., 2003; Kagan & Saudino, 2001) have also found evidence that genetic factors are part of a child's basic temperament and are involved in shyness and behavioral inhibition. The *antisocial personality*—characterized by frequent conflict with society and lack of feelings of guilt or anxiety—is the other side of the coin when it comes to personality. Whereas shy children readily acquire fears and are highly reactive to stress, children who are on the path to developing antisocial personalities show low responses to threats and stressors (Gao et al., 2010b; Isen et al., 2010). As children, they show a pattern of deceit, callous disregard for the feelings of others, and lack of interest in conforming their behavior to social rules (Raine, 2008). As adults, they are likely to become involved in criminal activity.

Adrian Raine (2008) has extensively studied the intersection of biology and the antisocial personality. In a review of the literature, he found a number of brain impairments that are related to the development of an antisocial personality in the ventral prefrontal cortex (part of the so-called executive center of the brain) and the amygdala (part of the limbic system).

10-2e EVALUATION OF THE TRAIT PERSPECTIVE

Trait theorists have focused much attention on the development of personality tests. They have also given rise to theories about the fit between personality and certain kinds of jobs (Gottfredson, 2009). The qualities that suit a person for various kinds of work can be expressed in terms of abilities, personality traits, and interests.

One limitation of trait theory is that it has tended to be more descriptive than explanatory. It has historically focused on describing traits rather than on tracing their origins or seeking ways to modify maladaptive personality traits and behavior.

10-3 Learning-Theory Perspectives

Trait theory focused on enduring personality characteristics that were generally presumed to be embedded in the nervous system. Learning theorists tend not to theorize in terms of traits. They focus instead on behaviors and presume that those behaviors are largely learned.

That which is learned is also, in principle, capable of being unlearned. As a result, learning theory and personality theory may not be a perfect fit. Nevertheless, learning theorists—both behaviorists and social cognitive theorists—have contributed to the discussion of personality.

10-3a BEHAVIORISM

At Johns Hopkins University in 1924, John B. Watson sounded the battle cry of the behaviorist movement:

Give me a dozen healthy infants, well-formed, and my own specified world to bring them up in, and I'll guarantee to take any one at random and train him to become any type of specialist I might suggest—doctor, lawyer, merchant-chief and, yes, even beggar-man and thief, regardless of his talents, penchants, tendencies, abilities, vocations, and the race of his ancestors. (p. 82)

This proclamation underscores the behaviorist view that personality is plastic—that situational or environmental influences, not internal, individual variables, are the key shapers of personality. In contrast to the psychoanalysts and structuralists of his day, Watson argued that unseen, undetectable mental structures must be rejected in favor of that which can be seen and measured. In the 1930s, Watson's flag was carried onward by B. F. Skinner, who agreed that psychologists should avoid trying to see into the "black box" of the organism and instead emphasize the effects of reinforcements on behavior.

The views of Watson and Skinner largely ignored the notions of personal freedom, choice, and self-direction. Most of us assume that our wants originate within us. Watson and Skinner suggested that environmental influences such as parental approval and social customs shape us into *wanting* certain things and *not wanting* others.

In his novel *Walden Two*, Skinner (1948) described a Utopian society in which people are happy and content because they are allowed to do as they please. From early childhood, however, they have been trained or conditioned to be cooperative. Because of their reinforcement histories, they *want* to behave in decent, kind, and unselfish ways. They see themselves as free because society makes no effort to force them to behave in particular ways. The American poet Robert Frost wrote, "You have freedom when

✳ Virtuous Traits: Positive Psychology and Trait Theory

Trait theory has found applications within positive psychology, an approach that studies character strengths and virtues such as those just listed. Psychologists are also developing psychological methods that help people increase their happiness and life satisfaction (Sheldon, 2009; Shyrack et al., 2010). Psychologists list six major virtues (see the table below) that were found in countries as different as Azerbaijan and Venezuela, along with the United States and other developed nations (Peterson & Seligman, 2004; Snyder et al., 2010).

The *Character Strengths and Virtues: A Handbook and Classification (the CSV)* was partly developed as a counterpoint to the *DSM*, which is the *Diagnostic and Statistical Manual of the Mental Disorders* of the American Psychiatric Association (2000). Whereas the *DSM* is a catalogue of (nearly) everything that can go wrong with people, the *CSV* is a catalogue of things that go right. Fortunately, there are many of them.

VIRTUE	CORRESPONDING CHARACTER STRENGTHS
Wisdom and knowledge	Creativity, curiosity, open-mindedness, love of learning, perspective (ability to provide other people with sound advice)
Courage	Authenticity (speaking one's mind), bravery, persistence, zest
Humanity	Kindness, love, social intelligence
Justice	Fairness, leadership, teamwork
Temperance	Forgiveness, modesty, prudence, self-regulation
Transcendence	Appreciation of beauty and excellence, gratitude (when appropriate), hope, humor, religiosity (having a belief system about the meaning of life)

Source: Peterson & Seligman, 2004.

social cognitive theory

a cognitively oriented learning theory in which observational learning and person variables such as values and expectancies play major roles in individual differences

gender-typing

the process by which males and females come to display behavior patterns consistent with stereotypical masculine and feminine gender roles

gender-schema theory

a cognitive view of gender-typing that proposes that once girls and boys become aware of their anatomic sex, they begin to blend their self-expectations and self-esteem with the ways in which they fit the gender roles prescribed in a given culture

you're easy in your harness." Society in Skinner's *Walden Two* made children "easy" in their "harnesses," but the harnesses were very real.

Some object to behaviorist notions because they play down the importance of consciousness and choice. Others argue that humans are not blindly ruled by reinforcers (that is, rewards and punishments). In some circumstances, people have rebelled against the so-called necessity of survival by choosing pain and hardship over pleasure, or death over life. Many people have sacrificed their own lives to save those of others. The behaviorist "defense" might be that the apparent choice of pain or death is forced on some just as conformity to social custom is forced on others.

10-3b SOCIAL COGNITIVE THEORY

Social cognitive theory was developed by Albert Bandura (1986, 2008) and other psychologists. In contrast to behaviorism, which focuses on observable behavior and the situations in which behavior occurs, social cognitive theory focuses on learning by observation and on the cognitive processes that underlie personal differences. Social cognitive theorists differ from behaviorists in that they see people as influencing their environment just as their environment affects them. Social cognitive theorists agree with behaviorists that discussions of human nature should be tied to observable behavior, but they assert that variables within people—*person variables*—must also be considered if we are to understand people. *Situational variables* include rewards and punishments. Person variables include

FIGURE 10.3 | Person Variables and Situational Variables in Social-Cognitive Theory

According to social-cognitive theory, person variables and situational variables interact to influence behavior.

© Rubberball

"It is **our attitude** at the beginning of a difficult task which, more than anything else, will affect its successful outcome."

—WILLIAM JAMES

knowledge and skills, ways of interpreting experience, expectancies, emotions, and self-regulatory systems and plans (Bandura, 2008; Rodin et al., 2009; Sherman et al., 2009; see Figure 10.3).

We cannot predict behavior from situational variables alone. Whether a person will behave in a certain way also depends on the person's *expectancies* about the outcomes of that behavior and the perceived or *subjective values* of those outcomes. There are various kinds of expectancies. Some are predictions about what will follow what. For example, people might predict other people's behavior on the basis of body language such as "tight lips" or "shifty eyes." *Self-efficacy expectations* are beliefs that we can accomplish certain things, such as doing a backflip into a swimming pool or solving math problems (Bandura & Locke, 2003). People with positive self-efficacy expectations tend to have high self-esteem (Sanna & Meier, 2000) and achievement motivation (Heimpel

Biology, Social Cognition, and Gender-Typing

Gender-typing is the process by which males and females come to develop personality traits and behavior patterns that society considers to be consistent with their gender, male or female—at least most of the time. Researchers who investigate people's perceptions of gender differences in personality traits tend to find groups of "masculine" and "feminine" traits, such as those shown in Table 10.2. According to evolutionary psychologists, gender differences were fashioned by natural selection in response to problems in adaptation that were repeatedly encountered over thousands of generations (Buss, 2009; Schmitt, 2008). Men, who have generally been the hunters, breadwinners, and warriors, are more likely to be seen as *adventurous, aggressive,* and *assertive* (Amanatullah & Morris, 2010; Guzzetti, 2010; Lippa, 2010). Women, who have more often been the homemakers and caretakers, are more likely to be seen as *affectionate, agreeable,* and *emotional.*

Biology and Gender-Typing

Other researchers suggest that the development of gender differences in personality, along with the development of anatomic gender differences, may be related to prenatal levels of sex hormones. Although results of many studies attempting to correlate prenatal sex hormone levels with subsequent gender-typed play have been mixed, a study of 212 pregnant women conducted by Bonnie Auyeung and her colleagues (2009) found that fetal testosterone was related to masculine or feminine-typed play at the age of 8½ years. Other studies show that children display gender-typed preferences—with boys preferring transportation toys and girls preferring dolls—as early as the age of 13 months (Knickmeyer et al., 2005). Another study investigated the gender-typed visual preferences of 30 human infants at the early ages of three to eight months (Alexander et al., 2009). The researchers assessed interest in a toy truck and a doll by using eye-tracking technology to indicate the direction of visual attention. Girls showed a visual preference for the doll over the truck (that is, they made a greater number of visual fixations on the doll), and boys showed a visual preference for the truck.

Social Cognition and Gender-Typing

Social cognitive theorists find roles for learning in gender-typing, and they suggest that children learn what is considered masculine or feminine in their societies by means of observational learning and socialization (Golombok et al., 2008; Zosuls et al., 2009). Children observe the behavior of adult role models and may come to assume that their behavior should conform to that of adults of the same gender. In social-cognitive theory, rewards and punishments influence children to imitate adult models of the same gender. The child not only imitates

What do this mother's female and male twins have to look forward to in terms of gender-role stereotypes?

the behavior of the model but also tries to become broadly like the model—that is, she or he *identifies* with the model.

Almost from the moment a baby comes into the world, she or he is treated in ways that are consistent with gender stereotypes. Parents tend to talk more to baby girls, and fathers especially engage in more roughhousing with boys. When children are old enough to speak, caregivers and even other children begin to tell them how they are expected to behave. Parents may reward children for behavior they consider gender appropriate and punish (or fail to reinforce) them for behavior they consider inappropriate. Girls are encouraged to practice caregiving, which is intended to prepare them for traditional feminine adult roles. Boys are handed LEGOS® or doctor sets to help prepare them for traditional masculine adult roles.

The Gender-Schema Theory of Gender-Typing

Gender-schema theory emphasizes the role of cognition in gender-typing (Martin et al., 2002; Martin & Ruble, 2004). Gender-schema theory proposes that children develop a **gender schema** as a means of organizing their perceptions of the world. A gender schema is a cluster of ideas about masculine and feminine physical traits. Gender becomes important because of society's emphasis on it. According to gender-schema theory, once children come to see themselves as female or male, they begin to seek information concerning gender-typed traits and try to live up to them (Grace et al., 2008; Most et al., 2007; Tenenbaum et al., 2010). Jack will retaliate when provoked because boys are expected to do so. Jill will be "sugary and sweet" if such is expected of little girls.

Today, most scholars would agree that both biology and social cognition interact to affect most areas of behavior and mental processes—including the complex processes involved in gender-typing.

TABLE 10.2	Stereotypical Masculine and Feminine Traits		
MASCULINE		**FEMININE**	
Adventurous	Determined	Affectionate	Fickle
Aggressive	Hardheaded	Agreeable	Gentle
Assertive	Independent	Cautious	Kind
Capable	Intelligent	Dependent	Patient
Confident	Pleasure-seeking	Emotional	Sensitive
Courageous	Rational	Fearful	Talkative

Sources: Amanatullah & Morris, 2010; Guzzetti, 2010; Lippa, 2010; Schmitt et al., 2008.

humanism
the view that people are capable of free choice, self-fulfillment, and ethical behavior

existentialism
the view that people are completely free and responsible for their own behavior

self-actualization
in humanistic theory, the innate tendency to strive to realize one's potential

et al., 2002). Psychotherapy often motivates people to try new things by changing their self-efficacy expectations from "I can't" to "Perhaps I can" (Bandura, 1999).

Observational Learning

Observational learning (also termed *modeling* or *cognitive learning*) is one of the foundations of social cognitive theory. It refers to acquiring knowledge by observing others. For operant conditioning to occur, an organism must first engage in a response, and that response must be reinforced. However, observational learning occurs even when the learner does not perform the observed behavior. Direct reinforcement is not required either. Observing others extends to reading about them or seeing what they do and what happens to them in books, TV, film, and the Internet.

10-3c EVALUATION OF THE LEARNING PERSPECTIVE

Learning theorists have contributed to the scientific understanding of behavior, but they have left some psychologists dissatisfied. Psychodynamic theorists and trait theorists propose the existence of psychological structures that cannot be seen and measured directly. Learning theorists—particularly behaviorists—have dramatized the importance of referring to publicly observable variables, or behaviors, if psychology is to be accepted as a science.

Similarly, psychodynamic theorists and trait theorists focus on internal variables such as unconscious conflict and traits to explain and predict behavior. Learning theorists emphasize the importance of environmental conditions, or situational variables, as determinants of behavior. They have also elaborated on the conditions that foster learning, including automatic kinds of learning. They have shown that we can learn to do things because of reinforcements and that many behaviors are learned by observing others.

Social cognitive theory does not account for self-awareness, and, like its intellectual forebear, behaviorism, it may not pay enough attention to genetic variation in explaining individual differences in behavior.

"Always remember that you are absolutely unique. Just like everyone else."

—MARGARET MEAD

10-4 The Humanistic-Existential Perspective

Humanists and existentialists dwell on the meaning of life. Self-awareness is the hub of the humanistic–existential search for meaning. The term **humanism** has a long history and many meanings. As a counterpoint (or "third force") to the predominant psychodynamic and behavioral models, it puts self-awareness at the center of consideration and argues that people are capable of free choice, self-fulfillment, and ethical behavior. Humanism also represented a reaction to the "rat race" spawned by industrialization and automation. The humanistic views of Abraham Maslow and Carl Rogers emerged from these concerns.

Existentialism in part reflects the horrors of mass destruction of human life through war and genocide, frequent events in the 20th century. The European existentialist philosophers Jean-Paul Sartre and Martin Heidegger saw human life as trivial in the grand scheme of things. But psychiatrists like Viktor Frankl, Ludwig Binswanger, and Medard Boss argued that seeing human existence as meaningless could give rise to withdrawal and apathy—even suicide. Psychological salvation therefore requires giving personal meaning to things and making personal choices (McDonald, 2008).

10-4a ABRAHAM MASLOW AND THE CHALLENGE OF SELF-ACTUALIZATION

Freud wrote that people are basically motivated to gratify biological drives and that their perceptions are distorted by their psychological needs. The humanistic psychologist Abraham Maslow—whose hierarchy of needs we described in Chapter 8—argued that people also have a conscious need for **self-actualization**, or to become all that they can be. Because people are unique, they must follow unique paths to self-actualization. People are not at the mercy of unconscious, primitive impulses. Rather, the main threat to individual personality development is control by other people. We must each be free to get in touch with and actualize our selves. But self-actualization requires taking risks. Many people are more comfortable with the familiar. But people who adhere to the "tried and true" may find their lives slipping into monotony and mediocrity.

10-4b CARL ROGERS'S SELF THEORY

The humanistic psychologist Carl Rogers (1902–1987) wrote that people shape themselves through free choice and action. Rogers defined the *self* as the center of experience. Your self is your ongoing sense of who and what you are, your sense of how and why you react to the environment and how you choose to act on the environment. Your choices are made on the basis of your values, and your values are also part of your self. Rogers's self theory focuses on the nature of the self and the conditions that allow the self to develop freely. Two of his major concerns are the self-concept and self-esteem.

The Self-Concept and Frames of Reference

Our *self-concepts* consist of our impressions of ourselves and our evaluations of our adequacy. Rogers believed that we all have unique ways of looking at ourselves and the world—that is, unique *frames of reference*. It may be that we each use a different set of dimensions in defining ourselves and that we judge ourselves according to different sets of values. To one person, achievement–failure may be the most important dimension. To another person, the most important dimension may be decency–indecency. A third person may not even think in these terms.

Self-Esteem and Positive Regard

Rogers assumed that we all develop a need for self-regard, or self-esteem. At first, self-esteem reflects the esteem in which others hold us. Parents help children develop self-esteem when they show them **unconditional positive regard**—that is, when they accept them as having intrinsic merit regardless of their behavior at

the moment. Rogers was optimistic about human nature. He believed that people are basically good, and that when they develop in an atmosphere of unconditional positive regard, they will become generous and loving—not selfish. But when parents show children **conditional positive regard**—that is, when they accept them only when they behave in a desired manner—children may develop **conditions of worth**. Therefore, children may come to think that they have merit only if they behave as their parents wish them to behave.

Because each individual has a unique potential, children who develop conditions of worth must be somewhat disappointed in themselves. They cannot fully live up to the wishes of others and be true to themselves. Children in some families learn that it is bad to have ideas of their own, especially about sexual, political, or religious matters. When they perceive their caregivers' disapproval, they may come to see themselves as rebels and label their feelings as selfish, wrong, or evil. If they wish to retain a consistent self-concept and self-esteem, they may have to deny their feelings or disown parts of themselves. In this way, their self-concept becomes distorted. According to Rogers, anxiety often stems from recognition that people have feelings and desires that are inconsistent with their distorted self-concept. Because anxiety is unpleasant, people may deny the existence of their genuine feelings and desires.

Rogers believed that the path to self-actualization requires getting in touch with our genuine feelings, accepting them, and acting on them. This is the goal of Rogers's method of psychotherapy, *client-centered therapy*. Rogers also be-

unconditional positive regard a persistent expression of esteem for the value of a person, but not necessarily an unqualified acceptance of all of the person's behaviors

conditional positive regard judgment of another person's value on the basis of the acceptability of that person's behaviors

conditions of worth standards by which the value of a person is judged

ASP via Getty Images

JUST DOING IT

Many males tie their self-esteem to prowess in athletics. What are the roots of your self-esteem?

lieved that we have mental images of what we are capable of becoming. These are termed *self-ideals*. We are motivated to reduce the difference between our self-concepts and our self-ideals.

"You are unique, and if that is not fulfilled, then something has been lost."
—MARTHA GRAHAM

Gabriela Medina/Blend images/Jupiterimages

10-4c EVALUATION OF THE HUMANISTIC-EXISTENTIAL PERSPECTIVE

Humanistic–existential theories have tremendous appeal for college students because of their focus on the importance of personal experience. We tend to treasure our conscious experiences (our "selves"). For most nonhumans, to live is to move, to process food, to exchange oxygen and carbon dioxide, and to reproduce. But for humans, an essential aspect of life is conscious experience—the sense of oneself as progressing through space and time.

Ironically, the primary strength of the humanistic–existential approaches—their focus on conscious experience—is also their main weakness. Conscious experience is private and subjective. Therefore, the validity of formulating theories in terms of consciousness has been questioned.

Humanistic–existential theories, like learning theories, have little to say about the development of traits and personality types. They assume that we are all unique, but they do not predict the sorts of traits, abilities, and interests we will develop.

10-5 The Sociocultural Perspective

Thirteen-year-old Hannah brought her lunch tray to the table in the cafeteria. Her mother, Julie, eyed with horror the French fries, the plate of mashed potatoes in gravy, the bag of potato chips, and the large paper cup brimming with soda. "You can't eat that!" she said. "It's garbage!"

"Oh come on, Mom! Chill, okay?" Hannah rejoined before taking her tray to sit with some friends rather than with us.

I used to spend Saturdays with my children at the Manhattan School of Music. Not only did they study voice and piano, they—and I—widened our cultural perspective by relating to families and students from all parts of the world.

Julie and Hannah are Korean Americans. Flustered, Julie shook her head and said, "I've now been in the United States longer than I was in Korea, and I still can't get used to the way children act here. When she talks that way, it's embarrassing." I vaguely recall making some unhelpful comments about the ketchup on the French fries having antioxidants and some slightly helpful comments about what is typical of teenagers in the United States. But as I thought about Hannah, I realized that in our multicultural society, personality cannot be understood without reference to the **sociocultural perspective**. Different ethnic groups within the United States have different attitudes, beliefs, norms, self-definitions, and values (Phinney & Baledelomar, 2011; Schwartz et al., 2010).

Hannah was strongly influenced by her peers—she was completely at home with blue jeans and French fries. She was also a daughter in an Asian American immigrant group that views education as the key to success in our culture (Leppel, 2002; Magno, 2010). Belonging to this ethnic group had contributed to her ambition and her hard work in school and on her violin, but had not prevented her from becoming an outspoken American teenager. Behavior that struck me as typical and inoffensive had struck her mother as brazen and inappropriate.

Let's consider how sociocultural factors can affect one's sense of self.

10-5a INDIVIDUALISM VERSUS COLLECTIVISM: WHO AM I (IN THIS CULTURAL SETTING)?

One could say that Julie's complaint was that Hannah saw herself as an individual and an artist to a greater extent than as a family member and a Korean girl. Cross-cultural research reveals that people in the United States and many northern European nations tend to be individualistic. **Individualists** tend to define themselves in terms of their personal identities and to give priority to their personal goals (Brewer & Chen, 2007; Triandis, 2006). When asked to complete the statement "I am . . . ," they are likely to respond in terms of their personality traits ("I am outgoing," "I am artistic") or their occupations ("I am a nurse," "I am a systems analyst") (Triandis & Suh, 2005).

In contrast, many people from cultures in Africa, Asia, and Central and South America tend to be collectivistic (Brewer & Chen, 2007; Triandis, 2006). **Collectivists** tend to define themselves in terms of the groups to which they belong and to give priority to the group's goals (Triandis, 2006). They feel complete in terms of their relationships with others (see Figure 10.4). They are more likely than individualists to conform to group norms and judgments (Brewer & Chen, 2007; Triandis & Suh, 2002). When asked to complete the statement "I am . . . ," collectivists are more likely to respond in terms of their families, gender, or nation ("I am a father," "I am a Buddhist," "I am a Japanese") (Triandis, 2001).

The seeds of individualism and collectivism are found in the culture in which a person grows up. The capitalist system fosters individualism to some degree.

FIGURE 10.4 | The Self in Relation to Others from the Individualist and Collectivist Perspectives

To an individualist, the self is separate from other people (part A). To a collectivist, the self is complete only in terms of relationships to other people (part B). (Based on Markus & Kitayama, 1991).

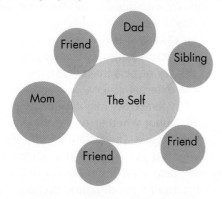

A. Independent view of the self

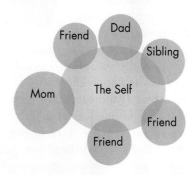

B. Interdependent view of the self

acculturation

the process of adaptation in which immigrants and native groups identify with a new, dominant culture by learning about that culture and making behavioral and attitudinal changes

validity

in psychological testing, the degree to which a test measures what it is supposed to measure

reliability

in psychological testing, the consistency or stability of test scores from one testing to another

The traditional writings of the East have exalted people who resist personal temptations to do their duty and promote the welfare of the group.

Another issue from the sociocultural perspective is *acculturation.* Just how much acculturation is good for you?

10-5b ACCULTURATION, ADJUSTMENT, AND SELF-ESTEEM

Self-esteem is connected with patterns of **acculturation** among immigrants (Phinney & Baledelomar, 2011). Those patterns take various forms. Some immigrants are completely assimilated by the dominant culture. They lose the language and customs of their country of origin and identify with the dominant culture in the new host country. Others maintain almost complete separation. They retain the language and customs of their country of origin and never acclimate to those of the new country. Still others become bicultural. They remain fluent

OSCAR RIVERA/AFP/Getty Images

in the language of their country of origin but also become conversant in the language of their new country. They blend the customs and values of both cultures (Schwartz et al., 2010). They can switch "mental gears"; they apply the values of one culture under some circumstances and apply the values of the other culture under others (Phinney, 2006). Perhaps they relate to other people in one way at work or in school, and in another way at home or in the neighborhood. Research evidence suggests that bicultural people have relatively higher self-esteem than people who completely surrender their traditional backgrounds (David et al., 2009; Schwartz et al., 2010).

FICTION ACTUALLY, RESEARCH EVIDENCE SUGGESTS THAT PEOPLE WHO DO NOT FULLY SURRENDER THEIR TRADITIONAL BACKGROUNDS HAVE HIGHER SELF-ESTEEM THAN THOSE WHO DO.

10-5c EVALUATION OF THE SOCIOCULTURAL PERSPECTIVE

The sociocultural perspective provides valuable insights into the roles of ethnicity, gender, culture, and socioeconomic status in personality formation. It enhances our sensitivity to cultural differences and expectations and allows us to appreciate the richness of human behavior and mental processes.

10-6 Measurement of Personality

Physicians have an easy time of it measuring heart rate and blood pressure. Psychologists, biologists, and neuroscientists find it easier to measure electricity in the brain or substances in the blood than to measure psychological concepts such as intelligence, depression, extraversion, or emotional stability. It may take time, money, and expertise to develop and operate the proper instruments, but once you have them, the measurements tend to be accurate enough.

In Chapter 7 we saw that many critics argue that intelligence tests measure many things other than intelligence, including motivation and familiarity with European American middle-class culture. In Chapter 8 we saw that lie detectors measure four physiological variables and detect much more than lies. The reliability and validity of intelligence tests and lie detectors have been brought into question. So too have the reliability and validity of personality tests.

The **validity** of a test is the extent to which it measures what it is supposed to measure. We usually assess the validity of personality tests by comparing test results to external criteria or standards. For example, a test of hyperactivity might be compared with teachers' reports about whether or not children in their classes are hyperactive. The **reliability** of a test is the stability of one's test results from one testing to another. We usually determine the reliability of tests by comparing testing results on different occasions or at different ages. A reliable IQ test should provide scores during childhood that remain reasonably similar in adolescence and adulthood. Test **standardization** is a process that checks out the scores, validity, and reliability of a test with people of various ages and from various groups. We cannot assess the intellectual functioning of an individual without relating it to other people in the same age group. Such information is made available when tests are professionally developed and scored.

Behavior-rating scales assess behavior in settings such as classrooms or mental hospitals. With behavior-rating scales, trained observers usually check off each occurrence of a specific behavior within a certain time frame—say, 15 minutes. Behavior-rating scales are growing in popularity, especially for use with children (Kamphaus et al., 2000). However, standardized objective and projective tests are used more frequently, and we focus on them in this section.

Measures of personality are used to make important decisions, such as whether a person is suited for a certain type of work, a particular class in school, or a drug to reduce agitation. As part of their admissions process, graduate schools often ask professors to rate prospective students on scales that assess traits such as intelligence, emotional stability, and cooperation. Students may take tests to measure their *aptitudes* and interests to gain insight into whether they are suited for certain occupations. It is assumed that students who share the aptitudes and interests of people who function well in certain positions are also likely to function well in those positions.

Let's consider the two most widely used types of personality tests: objective tests and projective tests.

10-6a OBJECTIVE TESTS

Objective tests present respondents with a standardized group of test items in the form of a questionnaire. Respondents are limited to a specific range of answers. One test might ask respondents to indicate whether items are true or false for them. Another might ask respondents to select the preferred activity from groups of three.

Some tests have a *forced-choice format*, in which respondents are asked to indicate which of two or more statements is more true for them or which of several activities they prefer. The respondents are not usually given the option of answering "none of the above." Forced-choice formats are frequently used in interest inventories, which help predict whether the person would function well in a certain occupation. They are typically the only means of responding to online assessments because the test-taker is usually required to "click" the chosen answer. The following item is similar to those

found in occupational interest inventories:

I would rather
a. be a forest ranger.
b. work in a busy office.
c. play a musical instrument.

The Minnesota Multiphasic Personality Inventory (MMPI)[1] contains hundreds of items presented in a true–false format. The MMPI is designed for use by clinical and counseling psychologists to help diagnose psychological disorders. Accurate measurement of an individual's problems should point to appropriate treatment. The MMPI is the most widely used psychological test in clinical work and is widely used in psychological research.

The MMPI scales were constructed *empirically*—that is, on the basis of actual clinical data rather than psychological theory. A test-item bank of several hundred items was derived from questions that are often asked in clinical interviews. Here are some examples of the kinds of items that were used:

My father was a good man.	T	F
I am very seldom troubled by headaches.	T	F
My hands and feet are usually warm enough.	T	F
I have never done anything dangerous for the thrill of it.	T	F
I work under a great deal of tension.	T	F

The items were administered to people with previously identified symptoms, such as depressive or schizophrenic symptoms. Items that successfully set these people apart were included on scales named for these conditions. Confidence in the MMPI has developed because of its extensive use.

10-6b PROJECTIVE TESTS

Projective tests have no clear specified answers. People are shown ambiguous stimuli such as inkblots or ambiguous drawings and asked to say what they look like or to tell stories about them. Or they are asked to

FICTION IT IS NOT TRUE THAT PSYCHOLOGISTS CAN GUARANTEE THAT THEY CAN DETECT DECEPTION ON A PERSONALITY TEST.

standardization
in psychological testing, the process by which one obtains and organizes test scores from various population groups, so that the results of a person's completing a test can be compared to those of others of his or her gender, in his or her age group, and so on

objective tests
tests whose items must be answered in a specified, limited manner; tests whose items have concrete answers that are considered correct

projective test
a psychological test that presents ambiguous stimuli onto which the test-taker projects his or her own personality in making a response

---

[1]Currently the updated MMPI-2.

complete sentences or to draw pictures of persons. There is no one correct response. It is assumed that people *project* their own personalities into their responses. The meanings they attribute to these stimuli are assumed to reflect their personalities as well as the drawings or blots themselves.

The Rorschach Inkblot Test

There are a number of psychological tests made up of inkblots, and test-takers are asked to say what the blots look like to them. The best known of these is the Rorschach inkblot test, named after its originator, Hermann Rorschach (Archer et al., 2006).

In the Rorschach test, people are given the inkblots, one by one, and are asked what they look like or what they could be. A response that reflects the shape of the blot is considered a sign of adequate *reality testing*. A response that richly integrates several features of the blot is considered a sign of high intellectual functioning. Supporters of the Rorschach believe that it provides insight

into a person's intelligence, interests, cultural background, personality traits, psychological disorders, and many other variables. Critics argue that there is little empirical evidence to support the test's validity (Garb et al., 2005). Even when the Rorschach is being severely challenged as a method of obtaining diagnoses of psychological disorders, researchers continue to claim that it has uses

FIGURE 10.5 | An Inkblot Test

Of all the inkblot tests, the Rorschach is the most widely used projective personality test. What does this inkblot look like to you? What could it be?

Masterfile (Royalty-Free Div.)

in many other areas, including the hiring and selection of personnel in organizations (Del Giudice, 2010), determination of whether individuals are suitable to have child custody (Weiner, 2006), and even in the assessment of children in schools (Hojnoski et al., 2006).

Although there is no single "correct" response to the inkblot shown in Figure 10.5, some responses are not in keeping with the features of the blots and reveal to the examiner that the test-taker is projecting his or her personality onto the test stimuli. The shape of the inkblot in Figure 10.5 might commonly suggest a butterfly or a flower, or many other things. A test-taker who makes unusual or uncommon responses to the features of the blot may be revealing personality problems.

The Thematic Apperception Test

The Thematic Apperception Test (TAT) was developed in the 1930s by Henry Murray and Christiana Morgan. It consists of drawings, like the one shown in Figure 8.5 (see p. 204), that are open to various interpretations. Individuals are given the cards one at a time and asked to make up stories about them.

The TAT is widely used in research on motivation and in clinical practice (Archer et al., 2006; Hojnoski et al., 2006). The assumption is that we are likely to project our own needs into our responses to ambiguous situations, even if we are unaware of them or reluctant to talk about them. The TAT is also widely used to assess attitudes toward other people, especially parents and intimate partners.

By the Numbers

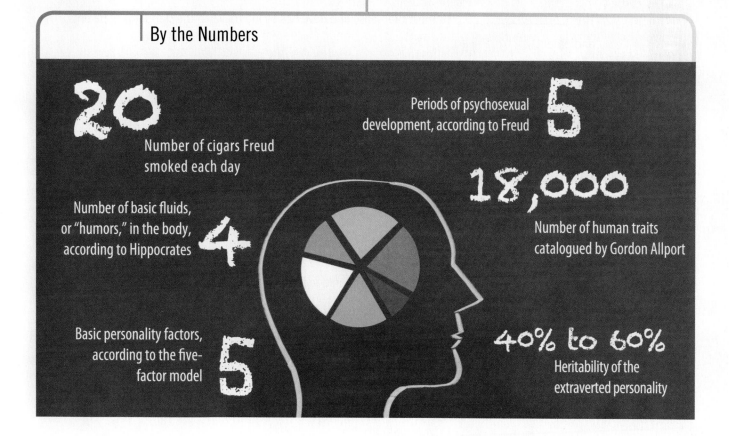

20 Number of cigars Freud smoked each day

4 Number of basic fluids, or "humors," in the body, according to Hippocrates

5 Basic personality factors, according to the five-factor model

5 Periods of psychosexual development, according to Freud

18,000 Number of human traits catalogued by Gordon Allport

40% to 60% Heritability of the extraverted personality

Ready to study? In the book, you can:

- ⊙ Review what you've read with Fill-Ins and Multiple Choice quizzes (below).
- ⊙ Rip out Chapter Review card (in the back).

Or you can go online to CourseMate at www.cengagebrain.com for these resources:

- ⊙ Complete Practices Quizzes to prepare for tests.
- ⊙ Review Key Terms Flash Cards (online or print).
- ⊙ Play games to master concepts.

FILL-INS

Answers can be found in the back of the book, starting on page 368.

1. According to Freud, the unconscious psychic structure called the _____ is present at birth and operates according to the pleasure principle.

2. The _____ is the moral sense and develops by internalizing the standards of parents and others.

3. The stages of psychosexual development include the oral, _____, phallic, latency, and genital stages.

4. Jung believed that in addition to a personal unconscious mind, people also have a(n) _____ unconscious.

5. Adler believed that people are motivated by a(n) _____ complex.

6. Raine found brain impairments that are related to the development of a(n) _____ personality.

7. Maslow argued that people have growth-oriented needs for self-_____.

8. According to Rogers, we see the world through unique frames of _____.

9. According to sociocultural theory, _____ define themselves in terms of the groups to which they belong and give priority to group goals.

10. Projective tests present _____ stimuli and permit the respondent a broad range of answers.

1. Marisa is five months old and always chews her rattle. According to Freud, she is in the _____ stage.

   a. anal
   b. oral
   c. phallic
   d. latency

2. Which best illustrates a child undergoing the Oedipus complex?

   a. Billy acts out to get his mother's attention whenever she is alone with his father.
   b. Kelly seeks out strangers for sexual encounters.
   c. Alan always goes shopping with his father.
   d. Maria has not had conscious sexual desires for the past year.

3. Which of the following is an assumption of most trait theories?

   a. Traits are flexible and change with time.
   b. Traits are generally learned from parents.
   c. Traits are somehow inherited and embedded in the nervous system.
   d. Traits are hard to categorize.

4. The five-factor model includes which five basic personality factors?

   a. depression, obsessiveness, conscientiousness, agreeableness, openness
   b. narcissism, neuroticism, conscientiousness, agreeableness, openness
   c. extraversion, neuroticism, conscientiousness, agreeableness, openness
   d. extraversion, psychosis, conscientiousness, agreeableness, openness

5. The views of Watson and Skinner largely ignore the notion of

   a. environmental variables.
   b. personal freedom.
   c. reinforcement and punishment.
   d. shaping.

6. Social-cognitive theory differs from behaviorism in that social-cognitive theory argues that

   a. rewards shape behaviors.
   b. the ego follows the moral principle.
   c. wants and desires are the result of our environment.
   d. people influence their environments.

7. Lisa is studying musical theater. She is convinced that if she works hard enough, she will one day make it to Broadway. Her sense of conviction is an example of

   a. self-efficacy expectations.
   b. competencies.
   c. modeling.
   d. encoding strategies.

8. Carl Rogers believed that every person has his or her own unique

   a. frame of character.
   b. grey eminence.
   c. frame of reinforcement.
   d. frame of reference.

9. A test in the format of a questionnaire that has specific correct answers is an example of

   a. an acculturated test.
   b. an innate test.
   c. an objective test.
   d. a projective test.

10. The ability to give a response that accurately reflects the shape of the inkblot on the stimulus card is a sign of intact

    a. neuroticism.
    b. reality testing.
    c. acculturation.
    d. collectivism.

LEARNING OUTCOMES

11-1 Define stress and identify various sources of stress

11-2 Identify the psychological moderators of stress

11-3 Describe the impact of stress on the body

11-4 Explain the relationships between psychology and health

After you read the chapter, go to the Study Tools at the end of the chapter, page 282.

Stress, Health, and COPING

The Earth moved. Or, a bit more precisely, in March of 2011, two immense walls of rock that had been pressing against each other for millennia finally budged. As in other places we call "faults," such as California's San Andreas Fault, they had been in combat for millions of years, trying to pass in opposite directions. Nobody saw it happen, because this particular confrontation occurred at the bottom of the ocean, off the northern coast of Japan. But the energy released caused the greatest earthquake experienced in Japan in 140 years, and it drove a wall of water more than 30 feet high—a tsunami—into the coast of Japan.

The earthquake and its aftershocks were felt in To-kyo, 250 miles down the coast. A 26-year-old office worker said, "I thought I was going to die when the earthquake hit. At first the shaking was not so great, but then it grew more violent and we all ducked under our desks. Ceiling tiles rained on us, and machines and reams of paper flew at us from shelves."

That was the least of it. The tsunami hit the shore and swept away boats, houses, cars, trucks, and people, turning villages and small cities into garbage heaps and graveyards. One fishing boat captain, Koji Haga, rode the tsunami inland like a rider clutching to the back of some prehistoric whale, struggling to keep his pitching vessel upright. Somehow he survived, but nearly 20,000 others did not. They were swept out to sea or buried in rubble.

And some were poisoned by radiation. The tsunami also smashed six reactors at a coastal nuclear power plant. Volunteer workers braved exposure to radiation to try to keep overheated, melting fuel rods cooled with water—succeeding here, failing there. They received overdoses of radiation and face radiation poisoning and potential early demise from cancer. Despite the workers' heroism, hundreds of thousands of people had to be evacuated for miles around the plants. Many of them were sudden members of a new group of people in this affluent, well-organized society—the homeless.

Disasters like the tsunami take an emotional as well as a physical toll (Mason et al., 2010; Weems et al., 2010). Studies of communities devastated by earthquakes, oil

> Koji Haga rode the tsunami inland like a rider clutching to the back of some prehistoric whale.

TRUTH OR FICTION

WHAT DO YOU THINK? FOLKLORE, COMMON SENSE, OR NONSENSE? CIRCLE THE T FOR "TRUTH" OR THE F FOR "FICTION," AND CHECK THE ACCURACY OF YOUR ANSWERS AS YOU READ THROUGH THE CHAPTER.

T	F	SOME STRESS IS GOOD FOR US.
T	F	VACATIONS CAN BE STRESSFUL.
T	F	SEARCHING FOR SOCIAL APPROVAL OR PERFECTION IS AN EXCELLENT WAY OF MAKING YOURSELF MISERABLE.
T	F	TYPE A PEOPLE ACHIEVE MORE THAN TYPE B PEOPLE, BUT THEY ARE LESS SATISFIED WITH THEMSELVES.
T	F	HUMOR HELPS US COPE WITH STRESS.
T	F	AT ANY GIVEN MOMENT, COUNTLESS MICROSCOPIC WARRIORS WITHIN OUR BODIES ARE CARRYING OUT SEARCH-AND-DESTROY MISSIONS AGAINST FOREIGN AGENTS.
T	F	IF YOU HAVE A FAMILY HISTORY OF HEART DISEASE OR CANCER, THERE IS LITTLE OR NOTHING YOU CAN DO TO PREVENT DEVELOPING THE ILLNESS YOURSELF.

spills, fires, tsunamis, hurricanes, and other disasters suggest that most survivors eventually adjust to the stress of living with their memories and their grief. But many others have a cluster of symptoms that we call posttraumatic stress disorder: lingering nightmares, flashbacks, de-

stress
the demand that is made on an organism to adapt

eustress (YOU-stress)
stress that is healthful

health psychology
the field of psychology that studies the relationships between psychological factors (e.g., attitudes, beliefs, situational influences, and behavior patterns) and the prevention and treatment of physical illness

pathogen
a microscopic organism (e.g., bacterium or virus) that can cause disease

pression, and irritability that suggest deeper effects of stress.

This chapter is about stress—its origins, its psychological and physical effects, and ways of coping with it.

11-1 Stress: What It Is, Where It Comes From

In physics, stress is defined as a pressure or force exerted on a body. Tons of rock pressing on the earth, one car smashing into another, a rubber band stretching—all are types of physical stress. Psychological forces, or stresses, also press, push, or pull. We may feel "crushed" by the weight of a big decision, "smashed" by adversity, or "stretched" to the point of snapping. In the case of the victims of the earthquake and tsunami in Japan, physical events had psychological and physical consequences. As we will see throughout the chapter, those psychological consequences can also affect our health.

Psychologists define **stress** as the demand made on an organism to adapt, cope, or adjust. Some stress is healthful and necessary to keep us alert and occupied. Stress researcher Hans Selye (1907–1982) referred to such healthful stress as **eustress** (pronounced YOU-stress). We may experience eustress when we begin a sought-after job or are trying to choose the color of an iPad. But intense or prolonged stress, such as that caused by a natural disaster or social or financial problems, can overtax our ability to adjust, affect our moods, impair our ability to experience pleasure, and harm the body (Folkman, 2011; Gotlib & Joormann, 2010).

A study by the UCLA Higher Education Research Institute found that college freshmen are now encountering a record level of stress. Figure 11.1 shows that over the past 25 years, fewer and fewer college freshmen have been reporting that their emotional health is "above average." During the same period, more and more college freshmen have been reporting that they felt overwhelmed during their senior year at high school. Either freshmen are being more

IT IS TRUE THAT SOME STRESS IS HEALTHFUL AND NECESSARY TO KEEP US ALERT AND OCCUPIED.

open about their feelings or we have been living in more and more stressful times—or both.

Stress is one of the key topics in health psychology. **Health psychology** studies the relationships between psychological factors and the prevention and treatment of physical health problems. Health psychologists investigate how:

- psychological factors such as stress, behavior patterns, and attitudes can lead to or aggravate illness;
- people can cope with stress;
- stress and **pathogens** (disease-causing organisms such as bacteria and viruses) interact to influence the immune system;
- people decide whether or not to seek health care; and
- psychological interventions such as health education (for example, concerning nutrition, smoking, and exercise) and behavior modification can contribute to physical health.

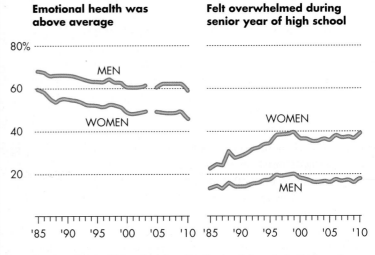

FIGURE 11.1 | College Freshmen's Emotional Health

Freshmen's self-assessment of their emotional health hit a 25-year low in 2010, according to the annual report of the Higher Education Research Institute. A much larger share of students said they had felt frequently overwhelmed with all they had to do as high school seniors. Women were twice as stressed as men.

Source: Tamar Lewin (2011, Jan. 27). Record level of stress found in college freshmen. *The New York Times online.*

11-1a DAILY HASSLES AND LIFE CHANGES

Which straw will break the camel's back? The last straw, according to the saying. Similarly, stresses can pile up until we can no longer cope with them. Some of these stresses are daily hassles (Back et al., 2008; Henderson et al., 2010). *Daily hassles* are regularly occurring conditions and experiences that can threaten or harm our well-being. Lazarus and his colleagues (1985) found that such hassles could be grouped as follows:

- *Household hassles:* preparing meals, shopping, and home maintenance
- *Health hassles:* physical illness, concern about medical treatment, side effects of medication
- *Time-pressure hassles:* having too many things to do and not enough time
- *Inner concern hassles:* being socially isolated, lonely
- *Environmental hassles:* crime, neighborhood deterioration, noise, pollution
- *Financial responsibility hassles:* concern about owing money, such as mortgage payments and loans
- *Work hassles:* job dissatisfaction, not liking one's duties at work, and problems with coworkers
- *Security hassles:* concerns about job security, terrorism, investments, retirement

Life changes differ from daily hassles in two ways:

- Many life changes are positive, whereas all hassles are negative.
- Hassles occur regularly, whereas life changes occur at irregular intervals.

Peggy Blake and her colleagues (1984) constructed a scale of "life-change units" to measure the impact of life changes among college students. Surveys with students revealed that death of a spouse or parent were considered the most stressful life changes (94 and 88 life-change units, respectively). Academic failure (77 units) and

TRUTH IT IS TRUE THAT VACATIONS CAN BE STRESSFUL; THIS IS BECAUSE THEY ARE LIFE CHANGES, AND ANY CHANGE REQUIRES ADJUSTMENT.

graduation from college (68 units) were also considered highly stressful, even though graduation from college is a positive event—considering the alternative. Positive life changes such as an outstanding personal achievement (49 units) and going on vacation (30 units) also made the list.

11-1b HASSLES, LIFE CHANGES, AND HEALTH PROBLEMS

Hassles and life changes—especially negative life changes—can cause us to worry and can affect our moods (McLaughlin et al., 2010; O'Drisscoll & Brough, 2010). Hassles and life changes also predict physical health problems such as heart disease and cancer, and even athletic injuries (Perna et al., 2003; Schneiderman et al., 2005). Holmes and Rahe (1967) found that people who "earned" 300 or more life-change units within a year, according to their scale, were at greater risk for health problems. Eight of ten developed health problems, compared with only one of three people whose totals of life-change units for the year were below 150.

Stress in America: The American Psychological Association Survey

Each year, the American Psychological Association (2012) commissions surveys of stress in America. In 2011, as you can see in Figure 11.2, the respondents

Daily hassles are notable conditions and experiences that are threatening or harmful to a person's well-being. This person is apparently overworked. Perhaps he works so hard because of financial hassles. He probably has time-pressure hassles and health hassles, or given his diet, health hassles may be forthcoming. His work environment also seems to be crashing in on him.

Masterfile (Royalty-Free Div.)

overwhelmingly reported that money and work were their major sources of stress. We will see later that "job strain" is a key contributor to heart disease. When we add in the costs of housing, which are mentioned by nearly half the sample, we find another area in which finances contribute to stress. Health is another major area of concern, mentioned in various ways by more than half of the sample. Intimate relationships are also a source of stress for more than half (59%) of the sample. One might think that intimate relationships would serve as a buffer against external sources of stress for people, *and perhaps they do.* (Life is complex.) However, these relationships can also contribute to stress.

Respondents reported many physical and psychological symptoms of stress. Nearly half (45%) reported that stress made them irritable or angry. Stress made more than two in five (41%) tired, and more than one-third (36%) reported having headaches. More than one in four (26%) had indigestion, and almost one in four (23%) felt tense. About one-third felt depressed (34%) or as though they could cry (30%).

FIGURE 11.2 | Percent of People Who Report the Following as Sources of Stress

Causes of Stress

■2011

Money	75%
Work	70%
The economy	67%
Relationships (e.g., spouse, kids, girl/boy friend)	58%
Family responsibilities	57%
Health problems affecting my family	53%
Personal health concerns	53%
Job stability	49%
Housing costs (e.g., mortgage or rent)	49%
Personal safety	32%

BASE: All respondents 2011 (n=1226)
Q625 Below is a list of things people say cause stress in their lives. For each one, please indicate how significant a source of stress it is in your life.

American Psychological Association (2012). *Stress in America.* Washington, DC: American Psychological Association, p. 17.

The most commonly reported methods of coping with stress were listening to music (49%), exercising or going for walks (48%), spending time with friends or family (46%), and reading (45%). Watching TV or movies was close behind (38%). About one-third reported praying (37%) or napping (34%). One in six (16%) drank, and one in seven (13%) smoked—not a healthful choice.

Not all people report that the same events cause them stress, or course. And, as we see, they respond to stress in many different ways. The stress of an event reflects the meaning of the event to an individual (Buchanan et al., 2010; David et al., 2010). Pregnancy, for example, may seem like a blessing to a well-established couple who has been trying to have a child for many years, but it may seem disastrous to a single teenager without resources. We appraise events, and our responses depend on their perceived danger, our values and goals, our beliefs in our coping ability, and our social situations.

11-1c CONFLICT

Should you eat dessert or try to stick to your diet? Should you live on campus, which is more convenient, or should you rent an apartment, where you may have more independence? Choices like these can place us in conflict. In psychology, **conflict** is the feeling of being pulled in two or more directions by opposing motives. Conflict is stressful. Psychologists often classify conflicts into four types: approach–approach, avoidance–avoidance, approach–avoidance, and multiple approach–avoidance.

Classic experimental research by Neal E. Miller (1944) and others suggests that the *approach–approach conflict* is the least stressful type of conflict. Here, each of two goals is desirable, and both are within reach. You may not be able to decide between pizza or tacos, or a trip to Nassau or Hawaii. I recently had such a conflict in which I was "forced" to choose between triple-chocolate fat-free frozen yogurt and coffee chocolate-chip fat-free frozen yogurt. Such conflicts are usually resolved by making a decision (I took the triple chocolate). Those who experience this type of conflict may vacillate until they make a decision, as shown by people who put off decisions and ruminate about conflicting goals (Emmons & King, 1988).

Avoidance–avoidance conflict is more stressful because you are motivated to avoid each of two negative goals. However, avoiding one requires approaching the other. You may be fearful of visiting the dentist but also afraid that your teeth will decay if you do not make an appointment and go. Each potential outcome in an avoidance–avoidance conflict is undesirable. When an avoidance–avoidance conflict is highly stressful and no resolution is in sight, some people withdraw from the conflict by focusing on other matters or doing nothing.

When the same goal produces both approach and avoidance motives, we have an *approach–avoidance conflict*. People and things have their pluses and minuses, their good points and their bad points. Cheesecake may be delicious, but oh, the calories! Goals that produce mixed motives may seem more attractive from a distance but undesirable from up close (Elliot & Mapes, 2005). Many couples who repeatedly break up and reunite recall each other fondly when apart and swear that they could make the relationship work if they got together again. But after they do spend time together, they again wonder, "How could I ever have believed that this so-and-so would change?"

The most complex form of conflict is the *multiple approach–avoidance conflict*, in which each of several alternative courses of action has pluses and minuses. This sort of conflict might arise on the eve of an examination, when you are faced with the choice of studying or, say, going to a film. Each alternative has both positive and negative aspects: "Studying's a bore, but I won't have to worry about flunking. I'd love to see the movie, but I'd just be worrying about how I'll do tomorrow."

> *"The deepest principle of human nature is the craving to be appreciated."*
> —WILLIAM JAMES

Research has connected internal conflict with various health problems (Freitas et al., 2009). In one study (Emmons & King, 1988), the researchers enlisted 88 college undergraduates and surveyed their personal goals and the degree of conflict experienced between them. They used diaries to assess the students' emotional lives and physical symptoms. Students who reported more conflict and more ambivalence about conflict more often reported feeling anxious and depressed, reported more physical complaints, and made significantly more visits to the college health center over the course of two years.

11-1d IRRATIONAL BELIEFS

Psychologist Albert Ellis (1913–2007) noted that our *beliefs* about events, not just the events themselves, can be stressors (David et al., 2010; Ellis, 2005). Consider a case in which a person is fired from a job and is anxious and depressed about it. It may seem logical that losing the job is responsible for the misery, but Ellis pointed out how the individual's beliefs about the loss compounded his or her misery (Table 11.1).

Consider this situation according to Ellis's A → B → C approach: Losing the job is an *activating event* (A). The

TABLE 11.1 | Irrational Beliefs: Cognitive Doorways to Distress

Irrational Belief 1:	You must have sincere love and approval almost all the time from the people who are important to you.
Irrational Belief 2:	You must prove yourself to be thoroughly competent, adequate, and achieving at something important.
Irrational Belief 3:	Things must go the way you want them to go. Life is awful when you don't get your first choice in everything.
Irrational Belief 4:	Other people must treat everyone fairly and justly. When people act unfairly or unethically, they are rotten.
Irrational Belief 5:	When there is danger or fear in your world, you must be preoccupied with and upset by it.
Irrational Belief 6:	People and things should turn out better than they do. It's awful and horrible when you don't find quick solutions to life's hassles.
Irrational Belief 7:	Your emotional misery stems from external pressures that you have little or no ability to control. Unless these external pressures change, you must remain miserable.
Irrational Belief 8:	It is easier to evade life's responsibilities and problems than to face them and undertake more rewarding forms of self-discipline.
Irrational Belief 9:	Your past influenced you immensely and must therefore continue to determine your feelings and behavior today.
Irrational Belief 10:	You can achieve happiness by inertia and inaction, or by just enjoying yourself from day to day.

catastrophize
to interpret negative events as being disastrous; to "blow out of proportion"

Type A behavior
behavior characterized by a sense of time urgency, competitiveness, and hostility

eventual outcome, or *consequence* (C), is misery. Between the activating event (A) and the consequence (C), however, lie *beliefs* (B), such as these: "This job was the most important thing in my life," "What a no-good failure I am," "My family will starve," "I'll never find a job as good," "There's nothing I can do about it." Such beliefs compound misery, foster helplessness, and divert us from planning and deciding what to do next. The belief that "There's nothing I can do about it" fosters helplessness. The belief that "I am a no-good failure" internalizes the blame and may be an exaggeration. The belief that "My family will starve" may also be an exaggeration. We can diagram the situation like this:

Activating events → Beliefs → Consequences
or A → B → C

Anxieties about the future and depression over a loss are normal and to be expected. The beliefs of the person who lost the job, however, tend to **catastrophize** the extent of the loss and contribute to anxiety and depression—and thus raise the person's blood pressure (David et al., 2010; DiGiuseppe, 2009). By heightening the individual's emotional reaction to the loss and fostering feelings of helplessness, these beliefs also impair coping ability.

Ellis proposed that many of us carry with us the irrational beliefs shown in Table 11.1. They are our personal doorways to distress. In fact, they can give rise to problems in themselves. When problems assault us from other sources, these beliefs can magnify their effect.

Ellis found it understandable that we would want the approval of others but irrational to believe that we cannot survive without it. It would be nice to be competent in everything we do, but it's unreasonable to *expect* it. Sure, it would be nice to be able to serve and volley like a tennis pro, but most of us haven't the time or natural ability to perfect the game. Demanding perfection prevents us from going out on

 TRUTH RESEARCH FINDINGS DO CONFIRM THE CONNECTIONS BETWEEN IRRATIONAL BELIEFS (E.G., EXCESSIVE DEPENDENCE ON SOCIAL APPROVAL AND PERFECTIONISM) AND FEELINGS OF ANXIETY AND DEPRESSION (DAVIES, 2008; DIGIUSEPPE, 2009; WIEBE & MCCABE, 2002).

the court on weekends and batting the ball back and forth just for fun. The belief that one must be preoccupied by threats is a prescription for perpetual emotional upheaval. Believing that we cannot overcome the influences of the past leads to feelings of helplessness and demoralization. Sure, Ellis might say, childhood experiences can explain the origins of irrational beliefs, but it is our own cognitive appraisal—here and now—that causes us to be miserable.

11-1e THE TYPE A BEHAVIOR PATTERN

Some people create stress for themselves through the **Type A behavior** pattern. Type A people are highly driven, competitive, impatient, hostile, and aggressive—so much so that they are prone to getting into auto accidents (Ben-Zur, 2002; Yamada et al., 2008). They feel rushed and pressured and keep one eye glued to the clock. They are not only prompt for appointments but often early. They eat, walk, and talk rapidly. They grow restless when others work slowly. They attempt to dominate group discussions. Type A people find it difficult to surrender control or share power. They are reluctant to delegate authority in the workplace and thus increase their own workloads. They watch their form, perfect their strokes, and strive for continuous self-improvement. They require themselves to achieve in everything they do.

Type B people, in contrast, relax more readily and focus more on the quality of life. They show lower blood pressure than Type A people in response to stressors, which is a key reason that Type A behavior is also referred to as the *coronary-prone behavior pattern* (Glass et al., 2007; Manuck et al., 2007). Type B people are less ambitious and less impatient, and they pace themselves. Type A people earn higher grades and more money than Type B's who are equal in intelligence, but Type A people are more likely to continue to strive for more and more.

TRUTH IT IS TRUE THAT TYPE A PEOPLE ACHIEVE MORE THAN TYPE B PEOPLE BUT ARE LESS SATISFIED WITH THEMSELVES.

11-2 Psychological Moderators of Stress

Psychological factors can influence, or *moderate*, the effects that stressors have on us. In this section, we discuss several psychological moderators of stress: self-efficacy expectations, psychological hardiness, humor, predictability and control, and social support.

11-2a SELF-EFFICACY EXPECTATIONS: "THE LITTLE ENGINE THAT COULD"

Self-efficacy is the ability to make things happen. Our **self-efficacy expectations**—our beliefs that we can bring about desired changes through our own efforts—affect our ability to withstand stress (Luszczynska et al., 2009; Pietrzak et al., 2010).

In a classic experiment, Albert Bandura and his colleagues (1985) assessed participants' self-efficacy, exposed them to fearful stimuli, and then monitored the levels of adrenaline and noradrenaline in their bloodstreams as they did so. Adrenaline and noradrenaline are secreted when we are under stress. They arouse the body in several ways, such as accelerating the heart rate and releasing glucose from the liver. Excessive arousal can distract us from coping with the tasks at hand. Bandura and his colleagues exposed participants to fear-inducing objects and found that high self-efficacy expectations are accompanied by relatively *lower* levels of adrenaline and noradrenaline. People with higher self-efficacy expectations thus have biological as well as psychological reasons for remaining calmer.

People who have higher self-efficacy expectations are less prone to be disturbed by adverse events (Maddi, 2008) and are more likely to lose weight or quit smoking and less likely to relapse afterward (Kalavana et al., 2010; Martinez et al., 2010). They are also better able to function in spite of pain (Howard et al., 2010). A study of Native Americans found that alcohol abuse was correlated with self-efficacy expectations (Walle, 2004). That is, individuals with feelings of powerlessness were more likely to abuse alcohol, perhaps as a way of lessening stress.

Our self-efficacy expectations affect our abilities to withstand stress and make things happen.

11-2b PSYCHOLOGICAL HARDINESS

Psychological hardiness also helps people resist stress (Maddi et al., 2009; Pietrzak et al., 2010). Our understanding of hardiness is derived largely from the pioneering work of Suzanne Kobasa (Maddi, 2008). Kobasa and her colleagues studied business executives who seemed able to resist illness despite stress. In one phase of the research, executives completed a battery of psychological tests, and the researchers found that the psychologically hardy executives had three key characteristics. The characteristics include commitment, challenge, and control (Maddi et al., 2009).

1. *Commitment.* Psychologically hardy executives tended to involve themselves in, rather than feel alienated from, what they were doing or encountering.

2. *Challenge.* Psychologically hardy executives believed that change, rather than stability, is normal in life. They appraised change as an interesting incentive to personal growth, not a threat to security.

3. *Control.* Psychologically hardy executives were high in perceived control over their lives (Pietrzak et al., 2010). Psychologically hardy people tend to have what psychologist Julian B. Rotter (1990) termed an internal **locus of control** (Weiner, 2010).

Psychologically hardy people may be more resistant to stress because they *choose* to face it (Bartone et al., 2008; Maddi et al., 2009). They also interpret stress as making life more interesting. For example, they see a conference with a supervisor as an opportunity to persuade the supervisor rather than as a risk to their position.

11-2c SENSE OF HUMOR

The idea that humor lightens the burdens of life and helps people cope with stress has been with us for millennia. Consider the biblical maxim, "A merry heart doeth good like a medicine" (Proverbs 17: 22). Research suggests that humor can moderate the effects of stress (Marziali et al., 2008). In one classic study, for example, students completed a checklist of negative life events and a measure of mood disturbance (Martin & Lefcourt, 1983). The measure of mood disturbance

self-efficacy expectations
our beliefs that we can bring about desired changes through our own efforts

psychological hardiness
a cluster of traits that buffer stress and are characterized by commitment, challenge, and control

locus of control
the place (locus) to which an individual attributes control over the receiving of reinforcers—either inside or outside the self

TRUTH RESEARCH SUGGESTS THAT HUMOR CAN INDEED MODERATE THE EFFECTS OF STRESS.

yielded a stress score. The students also rated their sense of humor. Students were asked to try to produce humor in an experimental stressful situation, and their ability to do so was rated by the researchers. Students who had a greater sense of humor and were capable of producing humor in the stressful experimental condition were less affected by the stress than other students. Later experimentation found that exposing students to humorous videotapes raised the level of immunoglobin A (a measure of the functioning of the immune system) in their saliva (Lefcourt, 1997; K. L. Smith, 2009).

How does humor help people cope with stress? There are many possibilities. One is that laughter stimulates the output of endorphins, which might enhance the functioning of the immune system. Another is that the benefits of humor may be explained in terms of the positive cognitive shifts they entail and the positive emotions that accompany them.

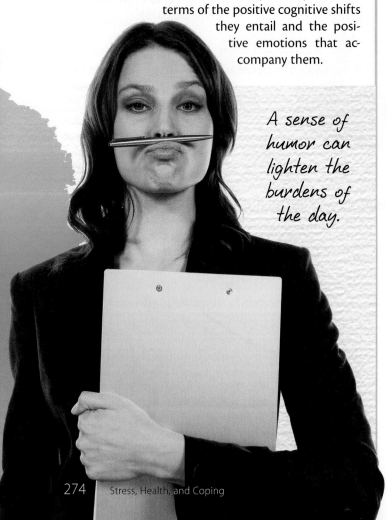

A sense of humor can lighten the burdens of the day.

11-2d PREDICTABILITY AND CONTROL

The ability to predict a stressor apparently moderates its impact. Predictability allows us to brace ourselves for the inevitable and, in many cases, plan ways of coping with it. Control—even the illusion of being in control—allows us to feel that we are not at the mercy of the fates (Folkman & Moskowitz, 2000b; Yartz et al., 2008). There is also a relationship between the desire to assume control over one's situation and the usefulness of information about impending stressors. Predictability is of greater benefit to **internals**—that is, to people who wish to exercise control over their situations—than to **externals**. People who want information about medical procedures and what they will experience cope better with pain when they undergo those procedures (Ludwick-Rosenthal & Neufeld, 1993; Thompson, 2009).

11-2e SOCIAL SUPPORT

People are social beings, and social support also seems to act as a buffer against the effects of stress (Folkman & Moskowitz, 2000a; Pietrzak et al., 2010). The concept of social support has many definitions:

- *Emotional concern:* listening to people's problems and expressing feelings of sympathy, caring, understanding, and reassurance.

- *Instrumental aid:* the material supports and services that facilitate adaptive behavior. For example, after a disaster, relief organizations may provide food, medicines, and temporary living quarters.

- *Information:* guidance and advice that enhance people's ability to cope.

- *Appraisal:* feedback from others about how one is doing. This kind of support involves helping people interpret, or "make sense of," what has happened to them.

- *Socializing:* conversation, recreation, even going shopping with someone. Socializing has beneficial effects, even when it is not oriented toward solving problems.

Research supports the value of social support. Introverts, people who lack social skills, and people who live by themselves seem more prone to developing infectious diseases such as colds under stress (Cohen et al., 2003; Pressman & Cohen, 2005). Social support helps people cope with the stresses of cancer and other health problems (Kahana et al., 2009). Social support helps people cope with the stresses of natural disasters such as hurricanes and earthquakes (Hu et al., 2010; X. Wang et al., 2000). Social support helps women cope with the aftermath of rape (Fisher et al., 2008). Stress is also less likely to lead to high blood pressure or alcohol abuse among people with social support (Dennis et al., 2008; Rodriguez et al., 2008).

How does stress contribute to the development of physical health problems? In the next section, we consider the effects of stress on the body.

11-3 Stress and the Body

Stress is more than a psychological event. It is more than "knowing" it is there; it is more than "feeling" pushed and pulled. Stress also has very definite effects on the body, which, as we will see, can lead to psychological and physical health problems. Stress researcher Hans Selye outlined a number of the bodily effects in his concept of the *general adaptation syndrome* (GAS).

11-3a THE GENERAL ADAPTATION SYNDROME

Selye suggested that under stress, the body is like a clock with an alarm that does not shut off until the clock shakes apart or its energy has been depleted. The body's response to different stressors shows certain similarities whether the stressor is a bacterial invasion, perceived danger, or a major life change (Selye, 1976). For this reason, Selye labeled this response the **general adaptation syndrome (GAS)**. The GAS is a group of bodily changes that occur in three stages: an alarm reaction, a resistance stage, and an exhaustion stage. These changes mobilize the body for action and—like that alarm that goes on ringing—can eventually wear out the body.

The Alarm Reaction

The **alarm reaction** is triggered by perception of a stressor. This reaction mobilizes or arouses the body, biologically speaking. Early in the 20th century, physiologist Walter B. Cannon (1932) argued that this mobilization was the basis for an instinctive **fight-or-flight reaction**. The fight-or-flight response kicks the endocrine, cardiovascular, and musculoskeletal systems into action to enable survival. Short-term stress can enhance the functioning of the immune system as well, thus helping prevent infection from wounds, but chronic or long-term stress can impair the functioning of the immune system (Dhabhar, 2009).

Stress has a domino effect on the endocrine system (Lupien et al., 2009; see Figure 11.3). The hypothalamus secretes corticotrophin-releasing hormone (CRH). CRH causes the pituitary gland to secrete adrenocorticotrophic hormone (ACTH). ACTH then causes the adrenal

general adaptation syndrome (GAS) Selye's term for a hypothesized three-stage response to stress

alarm reaction the first stage of the GAS, which is triggered by the impact of a stressor and characterized by sympathetic activity

fight-or-flight reaction an innate adaptive response to the perception of danger

---

FIGURE 11.3 | Stress and the Endocrine System

Stress has a domino effect on the endocrine system, leading to the release of corticosteroids and a mixture of adrenaline and noradrenaline. Corticosteroids combat allergic reactions (such as difficulty in breathing) and cause inflammation. Adrenaline and noradrenaline arouse the body to cope by accelerating the heart rate and providing energy for the fight-or-flight reaction.

Hypothalamus
Pituitary

The hypothalamus secretes corticotrophin-releasing hormone (CRH)

CRH causes the pituitary gland to secrete adrenocorticotrophic hormone (ACTH)

Stressor

Adrenal glands
Kidneys

ACTH then causes the adrenal cortex to secrete corticosteroids

The adrenal medulla releases a mixture of adrenaline and noradrenaline

resistance stage
the second stage of the GAS, characterized by prolonged sympathetic activity in an effort to restore lost energy and repair damage. Also called the *adaptation stage*

exhaustion stage
the third stage of the GAS, characterized by weakened resistance and possible deterioration

cortex to secrete cortisol and other corticosteroids (steroidal hormones). Corticosteroids help protect the body by combating allergic reactions (such as difficulty in breathing) and producing inflammation. (However, corticosteroids can be harmful to the cardiovascular system, which is one reason that chronic stress can impair one's health and why athletes who use steroids to build muscle mass can experience cardiovascular problems.) Inflammation increases circulation to parts of the body that are injured. It ferries in hordes of white blood cells to fend off invading pathogens.

Two other hormones that play a major role in the alarm reaction are secreted by the adrenal medulla. The sympathetic division of the ANS activates the adrenal medulla, causing it to release a mixture of adrenaline and noradrenaline. This mixture arouses the body by accelerating the heart rate and causing the liver to release glucose (sugar). This provides the energy that fuels the fight-or-flight reaction, which activates the body so that it is prepared to fight or flee from a predator.

The fight-or-flight reaction stems from a period in human prehistory when many stressors were life threatening. It was triggered by the sight of a predator at the edge of a thicket or by a sudden rustling in the undergrowth. Today it may be aroused when you are caught in stop-and-go traffic or learn that your mortgage payments are going to increase. Once the threat is removed, the body returns to a lower state of arousal. Many of the bodily changes that occur in the alarm reaction are outlined in Table 11.2.

The Resistance Stage

According to Selye's theory, if the alarm reaction mobilizes the body and the stressor is not removed, we enter the adaptation or **resistance stage** of the GAS. Levels of endocrine and sympathetic activity are lower than in the alarm reaction but still higher than normal. (It's as if the alarm is still on, but a bit softer.) But make no mistake: The person feels tense, and the body remains under a heavy burden.

The Exhaustion Stage

If the stressor is still not dealt with adequately, we may enter the **exhaustion stage** of the GAS. The muscles become fatigued. The body is depleted of the resources required for combating stress. With exhaustion, the parasympathetic division of the ANS may predominate. As a result, our heartbeat and respiration rate slow down, and many aspects of sympathetic activity are reversed. It might sound as if we would profit from the respite, but remember that we are still under stress—possibly an external threat. Continued stress in the exhaustion stage may lead to what Selye terms "diseases of adaptation." These are connected with constriction of blood vessels and alteration of the heart rhythm and can range from allergies to hives and heart disease—and ultimately, death.

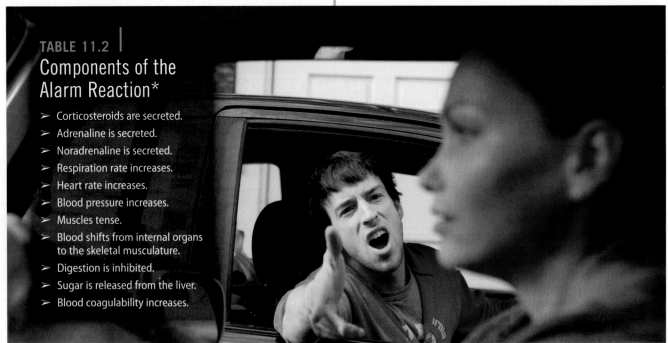

TABLE 11.2
Components of the Alarm Reaction*

➤ Corticosteroids are secreted.
➤ Adrenaline is secreted.
➤ Noradrenaline is secreted.
➤ Respiration rate increases.
➤ Heart rate increases.
➤ Blood pressure increases.
➤ Muscles tense.
➤ Blood shifts from internal organs to the skeletal musculature.
➤ Digestion is inhibited.
➤ Sugar is released from the liver.
➤ Blood coagulability increases.

Cocoon/Photodisc/Jupiter Images

*The alarm reaction is defined by the release of corticosteroids and adrenaline and by activity of the sympathetic branch of the autonomic nervous system.

Discussion of the effects of stress on the immune system paves the way for understanding the links between psychological factors and physical illness.

11-3b EFFECTS OF STRESS ON THE IMMUNE SYSTEM

Psychologists, biologists, and medical researchers have combined their efforts in a field of study called *psychoneuroimmunology* that addresses the relationships among psychological factors, the nervous system, the endocrine system, the immune system, and disease. One of its major concerns is the effect of stress on the immune system (Kemeny, 2009). Research shows that stress suppresses the immune system, as measured by the presence of various substances in the blood that make up the immune system (Calcagni & Elenkov, 2006).

The Immune System

The **immune system** combats disease in several ways (Iwasaki & Medzhitov, 2010). One way is the production of white blood cells, which engulf and kill pathogens such as bacteria, fungi, and viruses, and worn-out and cancerous body cells. The technical term for white blood cells is **leukocytes**. They engage in search-and-destroy missions in which they "recognize" and eradicate foreign agents and unhealthy cells.

Leukocytes recognize foreign substances, or antigens, by their shapes. The body reacts to **antigens** by generating specialized proteins, or **antibodies**. Antibodies attach themselves to the antigens, deactivating them and marking them for destruction. The immune system "remembers" how to battle antigens by maintaining their antibodies in the bloodstream, often for years.[1]

---

[1] A vaccination introduces a weakened form of an antigen (usually a bacteria or a virus) into the body to stimulate the production of antibodies. Antibodies can confer immunity for many years, in some cases for a lifetime.

immune system
the system of the body that recognizes and destroys foreign agents (antigens) that invade the body

leukocytes
white blood cells (derived from the Greek words *leukos*, meaning "white," and *kytos*, literally meaning "a hollow" but used to refer to cells)

antigen
a substance that stimulates the body to mount an immune system response to it (short for *anti*body *gen*erator)

antibodies
substances formed by white blood cells that recognize and destroy antigens

✳ Are There Gender Differences in Response to Stress?

For a century, it has been widely believed that humans are prewired to experience what biologist Walter Cannon labeled a "fight-or-flight" reaction to stress. Cannon believed we are instinctively pumped up to fight like demons or, when advisable, to beat a hasty retreat.

Or are we? According to reviews of the literature by psychologist Shelley E. Taylor and her colleagues (Taylor, 2006; Taylor et al., 2000), women under stress are more likely to care for their children and seek social contact and support from others. The "woman's response" to stress, the "tend-and-befriend" response, involves nurturing and seeking social support rather than fighting or fleeing.

This response may be prewired in female humans and in females of other mammalian species. Evolutionary psychologists might suggest that the tend-and-befriend response may have become sealed in human genes because it promotes the survival of females who are tending their young. Females who choose to fight might die or be separated from their young—no evolutionary brass ring there.

Gender differences in behavior are frequently connected with gender differences in hormones and other biological factors. This one is no different. Taylor (2006) points to the effects of the pituitary hormone oxytocin, which is connected with nurturing behaviors such as cuddling one's young (Taylor, 2006). The literature shows that when oxytocin is released during stress, it tends to have a calming effect on both rats and humans. It makes them less afraid and more social.

But men also release oxytocin when they are under stress. So why the gender difference? The answer may lie in other hormones—estrogen and testosterone. Females have more estrogen than males, and estrogen appears to enhance the effects of oxytocin. Males, on the other hand, have more testosterone than females, and testosterone may mitigate the effects of oxytocin (Taylor, 2006).

It is thus possible that males are more aggressive than females under stress because of the genetic balance of hormones in their bodies. Due to such differences, women tend to outlive men. "Men are more likely than women to respond to stressful experiences by developing certain stress-related disorders, including hypertension, aggressive behavior, or abuse of alcohol or hard drugs," Taylor added in a press release (May 2000).

Torff/plainpicture

inflammation
increased blood flow to an injured area of the body, resulting in redness, warmth, and an increased supply of white blood cells

biopsychosocial
having to do with the interactions of biological, psychological, and sociocultural factors

Inflammation is another function of the immune system. When injury occurs, blood vessels in the area first contract (to stem bleeding) and then dilate. Dilation increases the flow of blood, cells, and natural chemicals to the damaged area, causing the redness, swelling, and warmth that characterize inflammation (Leonard, 2005). The increased blood supply also floods the region with white blood cells to combat invading microscopic lifeforms such as bacteria, which otherwise might use the local damage as a port of entry into the body.

TRUTH LEUKOCYTES CONTINUOUSLY CARRY ON MICROSCOPIC WARFARE, DESTROYING FOREIGN AGENTS (SUCH AS GERMS) AND OTHER HARMFUL FACTORS, SUCH AS CANCEROUS CELLS.

Stress and the Immune System

One of the reasons that stress eventually exhausts us is that it stimulates the production of steroids. Steroids suppress the functioning of the immune system. Suppression has negligible effects when steroids are secreted occasionally. But persistent secretion of steroids decreases inflammation and interferes with the formation of antibodies. As a consequence, we become more vulnerable to infections, including the common cold (Cohen et al., 2012). By weakening the immune system, stress may also be connected with a more rapid progression of HIV infection to AIDS (Cohen et al., 2012).

Studies with college students have shown that the stress of exams depresses the immune system's response to the Epstein-Barr virus, which causes fatigue and other problems (Glaser et al., 1993). Students who were lonely showed greater suppression of the immune system than students who had more social support. The Epstein-Barr virus remains dormant in 90% of people who recover from an episode. Stress elevates blood levels of cortisol and adrenaline (epinephrine) and heightens the probability that the virus will be reactivated (Coskun et al., 2010).

11-4 Psychology and Chronic Health Problems

Why do people become ill? Why do some people develop cancer? Why do others have heart attacks? Why do still others seem to be immune to these illnesses? The **biopsychosocial** approach to health recognizes that there is no single, simple answer to these questions. The likelihood of contracting an illness—be it a case of the flu or cancer—can reflect the interaction of many factors, including biological, psychological, and sociocultural factors (Benke & Fallin, 2010; Schneiderman et al., 2005).

Biological factors such as pathogens, injuries, age, gender, and a family history of disease may strike us as the most obvious causes of illness. Genetics, in particular, tempts some people to assume that there is little they can do about their health. It is true that there are some severe health problems that are unavoidable for people with certain genes. However, in many cases, especially with cardiovascular problems and cancer, genes only create *predispositions* toward the health problem.

Genetic predispositions interact with the environment to express themselves (Benke & Fallin, 2010; Hunter, 2005). For example, genetic factors are involved in breast cancer. However, rates of breast cancer among women who have recently emigrated to the United States from rural Asia are similar to those in their countries of origin and nearly 80% lower than the rates among third-generation Asian American women, whose rates are

Stress Tip Sheet

The American Psychological Association offers tips on how to manage your stress:

- **Identify your sources of stress.** What events or situations trigger stressful feelings? Are they related to your children, family, health, financial decisions, work, relationships, or something else?
- **Learn your own stress signals.** People experience stress in different ways. You may have a hard time concentrating or making decisions, feel angry or irritable, or experience headaches, muscle tension, or a lack of energy. Gauge your stress signals.
- **Recognize how you deal with stress.** Determine whether you are using unhealthy behaviors (such as smoking, drinking alcohol, and over- or under-eating) to cope. Is this a routine behavior, or is it specific to certain events or situations? Do you make unhealthy choices as a result of feeling stressed?
- **Find healthy ways to manage stress.** Consider healthy, stress-reducing activities such as meditation, exercising, or talking things out with friends or family. Keep in mind that unhealthy behaviors develop over time and can be difficult to change. Don't take on too much at once. Focus on changing only one behavior at a time.
- **Take care of yourself.** Eat right, get enough sleep, drink plenty of water, and engage in regular physical activity. Take regular vacations or other breaks from work. No matter how hectic life gets, make time for yourself—even if it's just reading a book or listening to music.
- **Reach out for support.** Accepting help from friends and family can improve your ability to manage stress. If you continue to feel overwhelmed, you may want to talk to a psychologist, who can help you better manage stress and change unhealthy behaviors.

similar to those of European American women (Hoover, 2000; Wu et al., 2009). Thus, factors related to one's lifestyle are also intimately connected with the risk of breast cancer—and most other kinds of cancer.

As shown in Figure 11.4, biological factors (such as genetics and obesity), psychological factors (such as behaviors and personality), sociocultural factors (such as socioeconomic status), environmental factors, and stressors all play roles in health problems such as heart disease and cancer.

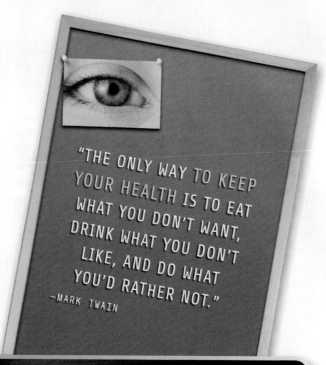

"THE ONLY WAY TO KEEP YOUR HEALTH IS TO EAT WHAT YOU DON'T WANT, DRINK WHAT YOU DON'T LIKE, AND DO WHAT YOU'D RATHER NOT."
—MARK TWAIN

FIGURE 11.4 | Factors in Heart Disease and Cancer

HEART DISEASE

Biological:

Family history

Physiological conditions:
 Obesity
 High serum cholesterol
 Hypertension

Psychological (personality and behavior):

Type A behavior

Hostility and holding in feelings of anger

Job strain

Chronic fatigue, stress, anxiety, depression, and emotional strain

Patterns of consumption:
 Heavy drinking (but a drink a day may be helpful with heart disease)
 Smoking
 Overeating

Sudden stressors

Physical inactivity

Sociocultural:

African Americans are more prone to hypertension and heart disease than European Americans

Access to health care

Timing of diagnosis and treatment

CANCER

Biological:

Family history

Physiological conditions:
 Obesity

Psychological (personality and behavior):

Patterns of consumption:
 Smoking
 Drinking alcohol (especially in women)

Eating animal fats?

Sunbathing (skin cancer)

Prolonged depression

Stress? Especially prolonged stress

Sociocultural:

Socioeconomic status

Access to health care

Timing of diagnosis and treatment

Higher death rates are found in nations with higher rates of fat intake

Goodshoot/Jupiterimages

Many health problems are affected by psychological factors, such as attitudes, emotions, and behavior (Frasure-Smith & Lespérance, 2008; Kiecolt-Glaser et al., 2002b). Nearly one million deaths each year in the United States are preventable (Health, United States, 2002). Stopping smoking, eating right, exercising, and controlling alcohol use would prevent nearly 80% of these. Psychological states such as anxiety and depression can impair the functioning of the immune system, rendering us more vulnerable to physical disorders ranging from viral infections to cancer (Kiecolt-Glaser et al., 2002a; Salovey et al., 2000).

Let's now discuss the chronic health problems of heart disease and cancer. Each involves biological, psychological, and sociocultural factors. Although these are medical problems, we also explore ways in which psychologists have contributed to their prevention and treatment.

11-4a CORONARY HEART DISEASE

Coronary heart disease (CHD) is the leading cause of death in the United States, most often from heart attacks (Arias et al., 2010).

Risk Factors

The risk factors for CHD are as follow (Glynn, 2010):

- *Family history:* People with a family history of CHD are more likely to develop the disease themselves.
- *Physiological conditions:* Obesity, high *serum cholesterol* levels, and *hypertension* (high blood pressure) are risk factors for CHD. About one American in five has hypertension, which can lead to CHD. *Essential hypertension*—that is, hypertension without an identifiable cause—has a genetic component. However, blood pressure is also connected with emotions like depression and anxiety. In addition, it rises when we inhibit the expression of strong feelings or are angry or on guard against threats. When we are under stress, we may believe that we can feel our blood pressure "pounding through the roof," but most people cannot sense hypertension. Therefore, it is important to check blood pressure regularly.
- *Patterns of consumption:* Patterns include heavy drinking, smoking, and overeating. On the other hand, a little alcohol seems to be good for the heart.
- *Type A behavior:* Most studies suggest that there is at least a modest relationship between Type A behavior and CHD. Hostility seems to be the component of the Type A behavior pattern that is most harmful (Chida & Steptoe, 2009). People who are highly prone to anger are about three times as likely

as other people to have heart attacks (J. E. Williams et al., 2000). The stress hormones connected with anger can constrict blood vessels to the heart, leading to a heart attack.

- *Job strain:* Overtime work, assembly line labor, and exposure to conflicting demands can all contribute to CHD. High-strain work, which makes heavy demands on workers but gives them little personal control, puts workers at the highest risk (Aboa-Éboulé et al., 2007; Ferrario et al., 2011).
- *Chronic fatigue, stress, anxiety, depression, and emotional strain.* Depression is connected with irregularities in the heart rate and may make blood platelets "sticky," which may, in turn, cause clots that lead to CHD (Kramer, 2003).
- *A physically inactive lifestyle.*

African Americans are more likely than any other ethnic group in the United States to have heart attacks and to die from them (National Center for Health Statistics, 2010). Figure 11.5 compares the death rates from heart disease of American men and women of various ethnic backgrounds. Asian Americans, Native Americans, and Latin Americans are less likely than European Americans or African Americans to die from heart disease. Early diagnosis and treatment might help decrease the racial gap.

Reducing Risk

Measures such as the following may help reduce the risk of CHD: stopping smoking; eating fewer saturated fats and more fruits, vegetables, and whole grains; reducing hypertension and lowering LDL (harmful) serum cholesterol, through medicine if necessary; modifying Type A behavior; managing feelings of anger; and exercising regularly (get a medical checkup first).

11-4b CANCER

According to the National Vital Statistics Reports, cancer is the second-leading cause of death in the United States (Jemal et al., 2009). Cancer is characterized by the development of abnormal, or mutant, cells that may take root anywhere in the body: in the blood, bones, digestive tract, lungs, and sex organs. If their spread is not controlled early, the cancerous cells may *metastasize*—that is, establish colonies elsewhere in the body. It appears that our bodies develop cancerous cells frequently. However, these are normally destroyed by the immune system. People whose immune system is damaged by physical or psychological factors may be more likely to develop tumors (Antoni & Lutgendorf, 2007; Mantovani & Sica, 2010).

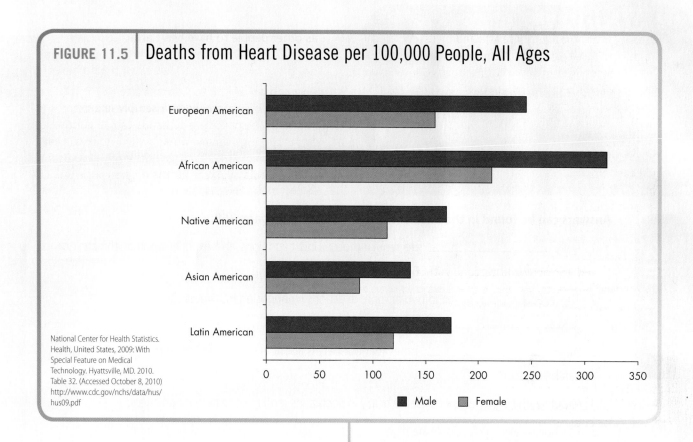

FIGURE 11.5 | Deaths from Heart Disease per 100,000 People, All Ages

National Center for Health Statistics. Health, United States, 2009: With Special Feature on Medical Technology. Hyattsville, MD. 2010. Table 32. (Accessed October 8, 2010) http://www.cdc.gov/nchs/data/hus/hus09.pdf

■ Male ■ Female

Risk Factors

As with many other disorders, people can inherit a disposition toward cancer (Santarius et al., 2010). So-called carcinogenic genes may remove the brakes from cell division, allowing cells to multiply wildly. Or they may allow mutations to accumulate unchecked. Many behavior patterns, however, markedly heighten the risk for cancer. These include smoking, more than a drink or two a day (especially for women), eating animal fats, and sunbathing (which may cause skin cancer due to exposure to ultraviolet light). Prolonged psychological conditions such as depression or stress may heighten the risk of some kinds of cancer by depressing the functioning of the immune system (Antoni & Lutgendorf, 2007; Gross et al., 2010).

African Americans are more likely than European Americans to contract most forms of cancer (National Center for Health Statistics, 2010). Once they contract cancer, African Americans are more likely than European Americans to die from it. The results for African Americans may reflect genetic factors to some degree, but are also connected with their lower socioeconomic status and relative lack of access to health care (Orsi et al., 2010).

Also consider cultural differences in health. Death rates from cancer are higher in such nations as the Netherlands, Denmark, England, Canada, and—yes—the United States, where average rates of daily fat intake are high (Bagchi & Preuss, 2007). Death rates from cancer are lower in such nations as Thailand, the Philippines, and Japan, where fat intake is lower. Thailand, the Philippines, and Japan are Asian nations, but do not assume that the difference is racial! The diets of Japanese Americans are similar in fat content to those of other Americans—and so are their rates of death from cancer.

Researchers have also suggested possible links between stress and cancer (Salovey et al., 2000). For example, Rachel Yehuda (2002) suggests that stress sometimes lowers levels of cortisol and impairs the ability of the immune system to destroy cancer cells. But here, too, the research evidence calls these theoretical links into question.

Reducing Risk

Measures such as the following may help reduce the risk of developing or dying from cancer: getting regular medical checkups to detect cancer early; stopping smoking; eating fewer saturated fats and more fruits, vegetables, and whole grains; and exercising regularly (get a medical checkup first). Cancer is most curable when it is detected early, before it metastasizes.

Ready to study? In the book, you can:

- ● Review what you've read with Fill-Ins and Multiple Choice quizzes (below).
- ● Rip out Chapter Review card (in the back).

Or you can go online to CourseMate at www.cengagebrain.com for these resources:

- ● Complete Practices Quizzes to prepare for tests.
- ● Review Key Terms Flash Cards (online or print).
- ● Play games to master concepts.

FILL-INS

Answers can be found in the back of the book, starting on page 368.

1. Daily _____ are regularly occurring conditions and experiences that threaten or harm our well-being.

2. The feeling of being pulled in two or more directions by opposing motives is called _____.

3. Albert _____ notes that our beliefs about events, as well as the events themselves, can be stressors.

4. People with (higher or lower?) self-efficacy expectations tend to cope better with stress.

5. Psychologically hardy people are high in _____, challenge, and control.

6. The GAS has three stages: _____, resistance, and exhaustion.

7. Cannon dubbed the alarm reaction the _____ or _____ reaction.

8. Women may show a tend-and-_____ response to stress rather than fight-or-flight.

9. Psychological states such as anxiety and depression impair the functioning of the _____ system, rendering us more vulnerable to health problems.

10. Risk factors for coronary heart disease include family history, obesity, hypertension, high levels of serum _____, heavy drinking, smoking, hostility, Type A behavior, and job strain.

1. Life changes that are positive can still be stressful because _____ is required.
   - a. loneliness
   - b. adjustment
   - c. depression
   - d. none of these

2. According to Ellis, a situation like failing a test, which results in stress, is called a(n)
   - a. stimulus event.
   - b. causal event.
   - c. initiating event.
   - d. activation event.

3. Edward's professor told him that his first paper could have been shorter in length. Edward starts sweating and ruminating because he jumps to the conclusion that he does not know how to write papers and will definitely fail this class. This is an example of
   - a. imbibing.
   - b. imbuing.
   - c. catastrophizing.
   - d. impetuous behavior.

4. Which quotation best represents the Type A personality?
   - a. "Do unto others as you would have them do unto you."
   - b. "Winning isn't everything; it's the only thing."
   - c. "Don't worry, be happy."
   - d. "All for one and one for all."

5. Moderators of stress include all of the following except
   - a. pretending that stressors do not exist.
   - b. psychological hardiness.
   - c. sense of humor.
   - d. predictability and control.

6. Psychological hardiness consists of three characteristics. These include
   - a. expectations, humor, and control.
   - b. power, control, and commitment.
   - c. commitment, challenge, and control.
   - d. confidence, competence, and efficacy.

7. Candace has an internal locus of control. This means that she
   - a. can only control her inner emotions.
   - b. can only control her outward appearance.
   - c. feels she is controlled by others.
   - d. feels she can control her own life.

8. The three stages of GAS (in their correct order) are
   - a. alarm, snooze, rest.
   - b. alarm, rest, snooze.
   - c. alarm, resistance, exhaustion.
   - d. resistance, alarm, exhaustion.

9. Boris has been under a great deal of stress. Which of the following is most likely true?
   - a. His immune system is weakened.
   - b. His immune system is strengthened.
   - c. His immune system is unaffected.
   - d. None of the above

10. Clarice wants to assess her risk for coronary heart disease (CHD). Which of the following is a risk factor for CHD?
    - a. low serum cholesterol
    - b. family history
    - c. low blood pressure
    - d. physically active lifestyle

LEARNING OUTCOMES

12-1 Define psychological disorders and describe their prevalence

12-2 Describe the symptoms and possible origins of anxiety disorders

12-3 Describe the symptoms and possible origins of dissociative disorders

12-4 Describe the symptoms and possible origins of somatoform disorders

12-5 Describe the symptoms and possible origins of mood disorders

12-6 Describe the symptoms and possible origins of schizophrenia

12-7 Describe the symptoms and possible origins of personality disorders

 After you read the chapter, go to the Study Tools at the end of the chapter, page 306.

CHAPTER 12

Psychological
DISORDERS

During one long fall semester, the Ohio State campus lived in terror. Four college women were abducted, forced to cash checks or obtain money from automatic teller machines, and then raped. A mysterious phone call led to the arrest of a 23-year-old drifter—let's call him "William"—who had been dismissed from the Navy.

William was not the boy next door.

Psychologists and psychiatrists who interviewed William concluded that 10 personalities—8 male and 2 female—resided within him (Scott, 1994). His personality had been "fractured" by an abusive childhood. His several personalities displayed distinct facial expressions, speech patterns, and memories. They even performed differently on psychological tests.

Arthur, the most rational personality, spoke with a British accent. Danny and Christopher were quiet adolescents. Christine was a 3-year-old girl. Tommy, a 16-year-old, had enlisted in the Navy. Allen was 18 and smoked. Adelena, a 19-year-old lesbian personality, had committed the rapes. Who had made the mysterious phone call? Probably David, 9, an anxious child.

The defense claimed that William's behavior was caused by a psychological disorder termed *dissociative identity disorder* (previously referred to as *multiple personality disorder*). Several distinct identities or personalities dwelled within him. Some of them were aware of the others. Some believed that they were unique. Billy, the core identity, had learned to sleep as a child to avoid his father's abuse. A psychiatrist asserted that Billy had also been "asleep," or in a "psychological coma," during the abductions. Billy should therefore be found not guilty by reason of **insanity**.

William was found not guilty. He was committed to a psychiatric institution and released 6 years later.

In 1982, a man named John Hinckley was also found not guilty of an assassination attempt on President Reagan's life, although the shooting was witnessed on television by millions. Expert witnesses testified that he should be diagnosed with *schizophrenia*. Hinckley, too, was committed to a psychiatric institution. William and

> William was not the boy next door.

TRUTH OR FICTION

WHAT DO YOU THINK? FOLKLORE, COMMON SENSE, OR NONSENSE? CIRCLE THE T FOR "TRUTH" OR THE F FOR "FICTION," AND CHECK THE ACCURACY OF YOUR ANSWERS AS YOU READ THROUGH THE CHAPTER.

T	F	A MAN SHOT THE PRESIDENT OF THE UNITED STATES IN FRONT OF MILLIONS OF TELEVISION WITNESSES AND WAS FOUND NOT GUILTY BY A COURT OF LAW.
T	F	ANXIETY IS ABNORMAL.
T	F	FEELING ELATED IS NOT ALWAYS A GOOD THING.
T	F	PEOPLE WHO THREATEN TO COMMIT SUICIDE ARE JUST SEEKING ATTENTION.
T	F	PEOPLE WITH SCHIZOPHRENIA MAY SEE AND HEAR THINGS THAT ARE NOT REALLY THERE.
T	F	SOME PEOPLE CAN KILL OR MAIM OTHERS WITHOUT ANY FEELINGS OF GUILT.

Hinckley were diagnosed with psychological disorders, which is the topic of this chapter.

12-1 What Are Psychological Disorders?

Psychology is the study of behavior and mental processes. **Psychological disorders** are behaviors or mental processes that are connected with various kinds of

insanity
a legal term descriptive of a person judged to be incapable of recognizing right from wrong or of conforming his or her behavior to the law

psychological disorders
patterns of behavior or mental processes that are connected with emotional distress or significant impairment in functioning

hallucination
a perception in the absence of sensory stimulation that is confused with reality

ideas of persecution
erroneous beliefs that one is being victimized or persecuted

distress or significant impairment in functioning. However, they are not predictable responses to specific events.

Some psychological disorders are characterized by anxiety, but many people are anxious now and then without being considered disordered. For example, it is appropriate to be anxious before a midterm exam. When, then, are feelings like anxiety deemed to be signs of a psychological disorder? For one thing, anxiety may suggest a disorder when it is not appropriate to the situation. For example, there is (usually) no reason to be anxious when looking out a fourth-story window. The magnitude of the problem may also suggest disorder. Some anxiety can be expected before a job interview. However, feeling that your heart is pounding so intensely that it might leap out of your chest—and then avoiding the interview—are not usual.

Behaviors or mental processes are suggestive of psychological disorders when they meet some combination of the following criteria:

1. *They are unusual.* Rarity or statistical deviance may not be sufficient for behavior or mental processes to

FICTION ☞ ANXIETY CAN ACTUALLY BE PERFECTLY NORMAL, AS ON THE EVE OF A BIG TEST OR WHEN ON A FIRST DATE.

be labeled abnormal, but it helps. After all, only a few people obtain a score of 700 or more on the verbal part of the SAT, but that achievement is not considered disordered. Only a few "see things" or "hear things" as Hinckley did, and those behaviors are deemed disordered because of their bizarre quality. We must also consider the situation. Although many of us feel "panicked" when we realize that a term paper is due the next day, most of us do not have panic attacks out of the blue. Unpredictable panic attacks thus are suggestive of psychological disorder.

2. *They suggest faulty perception or interpretation of reality.* Our society considers it normal to be inspired by religious beliefs but abnormal to believe that God is literally speaking to you. "Hearing voices" and "seeing things" are considered **hallucinations**. Similarly, **ideas of persecution**, such as believing that the FBI is "out to get you," are considered signs of disorder. (Unless, of course, they *are* out to get you.) Hinckley testified that he believed he would be impressing a popular young actress, Jodie Foster, by killing the president—an idea that was delusional.

3. *They suggest severe personal distress.* Anxiety, exaggerated fears, and other psychological states cause personal distress, and severe personal distress may be considered abnormal. William and Hinckley

✳ The Insanity Plea

John Hinckley was found not guilty of a 1981 assassination attempt on President Ronald Reagan by reason of insanity. Hinckley was diagnosed with schizophrenia and was committed to a psychiatric institution rather than given a prison term. What does it mean to be "insane"? What is the "insanity plea"?

In pleading insanity, lawyers use the M'Naghten rule, named after Daniel M'Naghten, who tried to assassinate British Prime Minister Robert Peel in 1843. M'Naghten had delusions that Peel was persecuting him, and he killed the minister's secretary in the attempt. The court found M'Naghten not guilty by reason of insanity. That is, the defendant did not understand what he was doing at the time of the act or did not realize it was wrong. The insanity plea is still used in much the same way today (Zapf et al., 2009).

Many people would like to ban the insanity plea because they equate it with people's "getting away with murder." But there may not be all that much cause for concern. The insanity defense is raised in only about 1% of cases (Silver, 1994). Moreover, people found to be not guilty by reason of insanity are institutionalized for indefinite terms—supposedly until they are no longer insane.

AP Photo/Judy Lineberger

While on trial, John Hinckley, Jr., looks on while his father cries and claims responsibility for "John's tragedy" because he prevented his son from coming home when he desperately needed help.

were in distress—although, of course, they victimized other people.

4. *They are self-defeating.* Behavior or mental processes that cause misery rather than happiness and fulfillment may suggest psychological disorder. Those who have depressive disorders suffer a great deal. We might also note that chronic drinking may be deemed abnormal because it threatens one's health and one's social and vocational life.

This medieval woodcut represents the practice of exorcism, in which a demon is expelled from a person who has been "possessed."

5. *They are dangerous.* Behavior or mental processes that are hazardous to the self or others may be considered suggestive of psychological disorders. People who threaten or attempt suicide may be considered abnormal, as may people who threaten or attack others, like William and Hinckley.

6. *The individual's behavior is socially unacceptable.* We must consider the cultural context of a behavior pattern in judging whether it is normal (Lopez & Guarnaccia, 2000). For example, many people in the United States admire women who are self-assertive, yet some Latin American, Asian American, and "traditional" European American groups may see outspoken women as being disrespectful and having personality problems.

12-1a PERSPECTIVES ON PSYCHOLOGICAL DISORDERS

If the standards for defining psychological disorders are complex and influenced by one's culture, so too are the explanations of their origins.

The Demonological Model

If William and John Hinckley had lived in the 17th and 18th centuries, they might have been hanged as witches. At that time, people assumed the behaviors associated with psychological disorders were caused by possession by the Devil. So-called witches were executed for events ranging from a neighbor's infertility to a poor harvest. In fact, throughout all of recorded history, people have attributed unusual behavior and psychological disorders to demons. The ancient Greeks believed that the gods punished humans by causing madness. An exception was the physician Hippocrates, who suggested that psychological disorders are caused by brain abnormalities. The notion that biology could affect thoughts, feelings, and behavior was to lie dormant for about 2,000 years.

The Medical Model

The demonological model led to brutal "treatments"—from drilling holes in the skull to permit evil spirits to escape, as in prehistoric times, to burning at the stake, as practiced during the Middle Ages. During the Age of Reason, many health professionals, such as Philippe Pinel (1745–1826) in France, began to view psychological disorders as diseases of the mind, and they encouraged humane treatment. During the 1800s, it was discovered that the late stages of syphilis can distort the workings of the mind. Since that time, researchers have assumed that other physical abnormalities can have psychological effects. The so-called *medical model* assumes that illnesses have physical or biological causes that can be identified and that people afflicted by them are to be cured through treatment or therapy.

Contemporary Psychological Models

Many contemporary psychologists have joined in the search for biological and physical contributors to psychological disorders. The *diathesis–stress model* assumes that there may be biological differences between individuals—diatheses—that explain why some people develop certain psychological disorders under stress, whereas others do not (Belsky & Pluess, 2009; Eberhart & Hammen, 2010). The *biopsychosocial model* explains psychological disorders in terms of a combination of (a) biological vulnerabilities; (b) psychological factors such as exposure to stress; and (c) sociocultural factors such as family relationships and cultural beliefs (Gilbert,

 ALTHOUGH THEY COMMITTED SERIOUS CRIMES, BOTH WILLIAM AND JOHN HINCKLEY WERE DIAGNOSED WITH SEVERE PSYCHOLOGICAL DISORDERS AND FOUND NOT GUILTY BY A COURT OF LAW.

anxiety disorders
disorders characterized by
excessive worrying, fear of
losing control, nervousness,
and inability to relax

2009; Levine & Schmelkin, 2006). But again, different factors take on different importance among different people. Psychologists today therefore frequently speak of the interaction between the biological *nature* of the individual and his or her life experiences, or *nurture*.

12-1b CLASSIFYING PSYCHOLOGICAL DISORDERS

Classification is at the heart of science. Without classifying psychological disorders, investigators would not be able to communicate, and scientific progress would come to a halt. The most widely used classification scheme for psychological disorders is the *Diagnostic and Statistical Manual (DSM)* of the American Psychiatric Association.

The *DSM* provides information about a person's overall functioning as well as a diagnosis. People may receive diagnoses for clinical syndromes, personality disorders, or both. The *DSM* also includes information about people's medical conditions, psychosocial and environmental problems, and a "global assessment" of functioning. Medical conditions include physical problems that may affect people's response to psychotherapy or drug treatment. Psychosocial and environmental problems include difficulties that may affect the diagnosis, treatment, or outcome of a psychological disorder. The global assessment of functioning allows the clinician to compare the client's current level of functioning with her or his highest previous level to help set treatment goals.

12-1c PREVALENCE OF PSYCHOLOGICAL DISORDERS

At first glance, psychological disorders might seem to affect only a few of us. Relatively few people are admitted to psychiatric hospitals. Most people will never seek the help of a psychologist or psychiatrist. Many of us have "eccentric" relatives or friends, but most of them are not considered "crazy." Nonetheless, psychological disorders affect us all in one way or another.

About half of us will meet the criteria for a *DSM* disorder at some time or another in our lives, with the disorder most often beginning in childhood or adolescence (Kessler et al., 2005a; see Table 12.1). Slightly more than a fourth of us will experience a psychological disorder in any given year (Kessler et al., 2005b; see Table 12.1). But if we include the problems of family members, friends, and coworkers, add in those who foot the bill in health insurance and taxes, and factor in increased product costs due to lost productivity, then perhaps everyone is affected.

Let's now consider the various kinds of psychological disorders.

12-2 Anxiety Disorders

Imagine allowing spiders to crawl over your body or clinging to a beam swinging hundreds of feet above the ground. These are the types of experiences to which many people are exposed on the TV show *Fear Factor*. What makes the show so riveting? Possibly the fact that many of us can't imagine participating in such activities for any amount of money. Discomfort with spiders and extreme heights is common, and sensible. However, there are extreme, irrational fears of objects and situations, such as hypodermic needles and public speaking, that are examples of *phobias*—a type of anxiety disorder.

Anxiety disorders have psychological and physical symptoms. The psychological symptoms include worrying, fear of the worst happening, fear of losing control, nervousness, and inability to relax. The physical symptoms reflect arousal of the sympathetic branch of the autonomic nervous system: trembling, sweat-

TABLE 12.1
Past-Year and Lifetime Prevalences of Psychological Disorders

	ANXIETY DISORDERS	MOOD DISORDERS	BIPOLAR DISORDERS	SUBSTANCE USE DISORDERS	ANY DISORDERS
Prevalence during past year	18.10%	9.50%	2.80%	3.80%	26.20%
Lifetime prevalence	28.80%	20.80%	4.40%	14.60%	46.40%
Median age of onset	11 years	30 years	21 years	20 years	14 years

Sources: Kessler et al., 2005; Merikangas et al., 2007.

Note: The data in this table are based on a nationally representative sample of 9,282 English-speaking U.S. residents aged 18 and above. Respondents could report symptoms of more than one type of disorder. For example, anxiety and mood disorders are often "comorbid"—that is, go together. Anxiety and mood disorders are discussed in this chapter. Substance use disorders include abuse of or dependence on alcohol or other drugs.

> *"I had a great many sex and love cases where people were absolutely devastated when somebody with whom they were compulsively in love didn't love them back. They were killing themselves with anxiety and depression."*
>
> —ALBERT ELLIS

ing, a racing heart, elevated blood pressure (a flushed face), and faintness.

Anxiety is an appropriate response to a real threat, but it can be abnormal when it is excessive, when it comes out of nowhere (that is, when events do not seem to warrant it), and when it prevents us from doing important things such as going for medical exams. The anxiety disorders include *phobic disorders, panic disorder, generalized anxiety, obsessive–compulsive disorder,* and *stress disorders.*

12-2a PHOBIC DISORDERS

There are several types of phobic disorders, including *specific phobias, social phobia,* and *agoraphobia.* Some of them, such as social phobia, can be highly detrimental to one's quality of life (Ohayon & Schatzberg, 2010). **Specific phobias** are excessive, irrational fears of specific objects or situations, such as spiders, snakes, or heights. Consider fear of elevators. Some people will not enter elevators despite the hardships they incur as a result (such as walking up six flights of steps). Yes, the cable *could* break. The ventilation *could* fail. One *could* be stuck in midair waiting for repairs. These problems are uncommon, however, and it does not make sense for most people to walk up and down several flights of stairs to elude them. Similarly, some people with a specific phobia for hypodermic needles will not have injections, even to treat profound illness. Injections can be painful, but most people with a phobia for needles would gladly suffer an even more painful pinch if it would help them fight illness.

Other specific phobias include **claustrophobia** (fear of tight or enclosed places), **acrophobia** (fear of heights), and fear of mice, snakes, and other creepy crawlies. **Social phobias** are persistent fears of scrutiny by others

or of doing something that will be humiliating or embarrassing. Excessive fear of public speaking is a common social phobia.

Agoraphobia may affect 3% to 4% of adults (Kessler et al., 2005). Agoraphobia is derived from the Greek words meaning "fear of the marketplace," or fear of being out in open, busy areas. Some people who receive this diagnosis refuse to venture out of their homes, especially alone. They find it difficult to hold a job or to maintain an ordinary social life.

12-2b PANIC DISORDER

Panic disorder is an abrupt anxiety attack that is apparently unrelated to specific objects or situations. People with panic disorder experience strong cardiac-related sensations: shortness of breath, heavy sweating, tremors, and pounding of the heart (Blechert et al., 2010). Many think they are having a heart attack (Naragon-Gainey, 2010). Levels of cortisol (a stress hormone) in the saliva are elevated during attacks (Bandelow et al., 2000). Many fear suffocation. People with the disorder may also experience choking sensations, nausea, numbness or tingling, flushes or chills, and fear of going crazy or losing control. Panic attacks may last minutes or hours. Afterward, the person usually feels drained.

Many people panic now and then. The diagnosis of panic disorder is reserved for those who undergo multiple attacks or live in fear of attacks. Panic attacks seem to come from nowhere. Thus, some people who have had them stay home for fear of having an attack in public. They are diagnosed as having *panic disorder with agoraphobia* (Schmidt et al., 2010).

specific phobia
persistent fear of a specific object or situation

claustrophobia
fear of tight, small places

acrophobia
fear of high places

social phobia
an irrational, excessive fear of public scrutiny

agoraphobia
fear of open, crowded places

panic disorder
recurrent experiencing of attacks of extreme anxiety in the absence of external stimuli that usually elicit anxiety

© Goodshoot/Jupiterimages

12-2c GENERALIZED ANXIETY DISORDER

generalized anxiety disorder
feelings of dread and foreboding and sympathetic arousal of at least six months' duration

obsessive–compulsive disorder (OCD)
an anxiety disorder defined by recurrent, anxiety-provoking thoughts or images that seem irrational and beyond control (obsessions) and seemingly irresistible urges to engage in thoughts or behaviors that tend to reduce the anxiety (compulsions)

posttraumatic stress disorder (PTSD)
a disorder that follows a distressing event outside the range of normal human experience and that is characterized by features such as intense fear, avoidance

The central symptom of **generalized anxiety disorder** is persistent anxiety. As with panic disorder, the anxiety cannot be attributed to a phobic object, situation, or activity. Rather, it seems to be free floating. The core of the disorder appears to be pervasive worrying about numerous stressors (Behar et al., 2009). Symptoms include motor tension (shakiness, inability to relax, furrowed brow, fidgeting); autonomic overarousal (sweating, dry mouth, racing heart, lightheadedness, frequent urinating, diarrhea); and excessive vigilance, as shown by irritability, insomnia, and a tendency to be easily distracted.

12-2d OBSESSIVE–COMPULSIVE DISORDER

Obsessive–compulsive disorder (OCD) is defined by recurrent, anxiety-provoking thoughts or images that seem irrational and beyond control (*obsessions*) and seemingly irresistible urges to engage in thoughts or behaviors that tend to reduce the anxiety (*compulsions*). Obsessions are so compelling and

Ray Kachatorian/Photodisc/Jupiterimages

A 16-year-old boy with OCD complained that he couldn't get rid of the numbers "in his head."

recurrent that they disrupt daily life. They may include doubts about whether one has locked the doors and shut the windows or images such as one mother's repeated fantasy that her children had been run over on the way home from school. One woman became obsessed with the idea that she had contaminated her hands with Sani-Flush and that the chemicals were spreading to everything she touched. A 16-year-old boy complained that he was distracted by "numbers in my head" when he was about to study or take a test. The more he tried to ignore them, the louder they became.

Compulsions are seemingly irresistible urges to engage in specific acts, often repeatedly, such as elaborate washing after using the bathroom or repeatedly checking that one has locked the door or turned off the gas burners before leaving home. The impulse is recurrent and forceful, interfering with daily life.

Stress Disorders

Sharia dreamed of a man assaulting her in the night at the Superdome in New Orleans, after she had been moved to this "refuge" following Hurricane Katrina in the summer of 2005. Darla, who lives in Oregon, dreamed that she was trapped in a World Trade Center tower when it was hit by an airplane on September 11, 2001. About one in six Iraq or Afghanistan veterans has nightmares and flashbacks to buddies being killed by snipers or explosive devices (Hoge et al., 2004). These all-too-real nightmarish events have caused many bad dreams. Such dreams are part of the experience of posttraumatic stress disorder.

Posttraumatic stress disorder is characterized by a rapid heart rate and feelings of anxiety and helplessness that are caused by a traumatic experience. Such experiences may include a natural or human-made disaster, a threat or assault, or witnessing a death. PTSD may occur months or years after the event. It frequently occurs among firefighters, combat veterans, and people whose homes and communities have been swept away by natural disasters or who have been victims of accidents or interpersonal violence (Chard et al., 2010; McCauley et al., 2010).

The traumatic event is revisited in the form of intrusive memories, recurrent dreams, and flashbacks—the feeling that the event is recurring (McDevitt-Murphy et al., 2010). People with PTSD typically try to avoid thoughts and activities connected to the traumatic event. They may also find it more difficult to enjoy life, and they often have sleep problems, irritable outbursts, difficulty concentrating, extreme vigilance, and an intensified "startle" response. The terrorist attacks of September 11, 2001, took their toll on sleep. According to a poll taken by the National Sleep Foundation (2001) two months after the attacks, nearly

290 Psychological Disorders

FIGURE 12.1 | Sleep Problems Among Americans Before and After September 11, 2001

Insomnia is one of the symptoms of stress disorders. A poll by the National Sleep Foundation found that Americans had a greater frequency of sleep problems after the terrorist attacks of September 11, 2001.

half of Americans had difficulty falling asleep compared with about one-quarter of Americans before the attacks (see Figure 12.1). Women, who are more likely than men to ruminate about stressors (Nolen-Hoeksema et al., 2008), were also more likely than men to report difficulty falling asleep (50% versus 37%).

Acute stress disorder, like PTSD, is characterized by feelings of anxiety and helplessness that are caused by a traumatic event. However, PTSD can occur six months or more after the traumatic event and tends to persist. Acute stress disorder occurs within a month of the event and lasts from two days to four weeks. Women who have been raped, for example, experience acute distress that tends to peak in severity about three weeks after the assault (Bryant, 2006). Yet the same women may go on to experience PTSD (Kilpatrick et al., 2007; Koss et al., 2002).

12-2e ORIGINS OF ANXIETY DISORDERS

What is known about the origins of anxiety disorders?

Psychological Views

Some learning theorists—particularly behaviorists—consider phobias to be conditioned fears that were acquired in early childhood. Avoidance of feared stimuli is reinforced by the reduction of anxiety. Observa-

tional learning may also play a role in the acquisition of fears (Mineka & Oehlberg, 2008). If parents squirm, grimace, and shudder at the sight of mice, blood, or dirt on the kitchen floor, children might assume that these stimuli are awful and imitate their parents' behavior.

Cognitive theorists note that people's appraisals of the magnitude of threats help determine whether they are traumatic and can lead to PTSD (Koster et al., 2009). People with panic attacks tend to misinterpret bodily cues and to view them as threats. Obsessions and compulsions may serve to divert attention from more frightening issues, such as "What am I going to do with my life?" When anxieties are acquired at a young age, we may later interpret them as enduring traits and label ourselves as "someone who fears _____" (you fill it in). We then live up to the labels. We also entertain thoughts that heighten and perpetuate anxiety such as "I've got to get out of here" or "My heart is going to leap out of my chest." Such ideas intensify physical signs of anxiety, disrupt planning, make stimuli seem worse than they really are, motivate avoidance, and decrease self-efficacy expectations. The belief that we will not be able to handle a threat heightens anxiety. The belief that we are in control reduces anxiety (Bandura et al., 1985).

dissociative disorders
disorders in which there are sudden, temporary changes in consciousness or self-identity

dissociative amnesia
a dissociative disorder marked by loss of memory or self-identity; skills and general knowledge are usually retained

dissociative fugue
a dissociative disorder in which one experiences amnesia and then flees to a new location

Evolutionary forces at work? Why do so many people fear spiders?

Biological Views

Genetic factors are implicated in most psychological disorders, including anxiety disorders (Low et al., 2008). Anxiety disorders tend to run in families. Identical (MZ) twins are much more likely to both have the disorder than fraternal (DZ) twins (Kendler et al., 2001). Adoptee studies show that the biological parent places the child at greater risk for anxiety and related traits than does the adoptive parent.

Evolutionary psychologists suggest that anxiety may reflect natural selection. Humans (and nonhuman primates) are genetically predisposed ("biologically prepared") to fear stimuli that may have posed a threat to their ancestors (Gerdes et al., 2009; Mineka & Oehlberg, 2008; Starratt & Shackelford, 2010). Evolutionary forces would have favored the survival of individuals who were predisposed toward acquiring fears of large animals, spiders, snakes, heights, entrapment, sharp objects, and strangers. Thus, people who fearlessly encounter potentially harmful stimuli may be at a disadvantage, evolutionarily speaking, rather than at an advantage.

Perhaps a predisposition toward anxiety—in the form of a highly reactive autonomic nervous system—can be inherited (Beesdo et al., 2010; Binder & Nemeroff, 2009). What might make a nervous system "highly reactive"? The autonomic nervous system may stimulate the production of excessive quantities of adrenaline (epinephrine) and noradrenaline (norepinephrine). These chemicals normally pump up the body in preparation for the fight-or-flight response—both sides of which can make up self-preserving responses to threats. But when their production is so intense that they flood the body, we can feel shaky and drenched with sweat and incapable of doing anything useful.

Biopsychosocial Views

Many cases of anxiety disorders reflect the interaction of biological, psychological, and social factors. Biological imbalances may initially trigger attacks in panic disorder. But subsequent fear of attacks—and of the bodily cues that signal their onset—may heighten discomfort

and give one the idea there is nothing one can do about them (Olatunji & Wolitzky-Taylor, 2009). Feelings of helplessness increase fear. People with panic disorder therefore can be helped by psychological methods that provide ways of reducing physical discomfort—including regular breathing—and show them that there are, after all, things they can do to cope with attacks (Olatunji & Wolitzky-Taylor, 2009).

12-3 Dissociative Disorders

William's disorder, described at the beginning of the chapter, was a dissociative disorder. In the **dissociative disorders**, mental processes such as thoughts, emotions, memory, consciousness, even knowledge of one's own identity—the processes that make a person feel whole—may seem to be split off from one another. The *DSM* lists several dissociative disorders. Among them are dissociative amnesia, dissociative fugue, and dissociative identity disorder (previously termed multiple personality disorder).

12-3a DISSOCIATIVE AMNESIA

A person with **dissociative amnesia** is suddenly unable to recall important personal information (that is, explicit episodic memories). The loss of memory cannot be attributed to organic problems such as a blow to the head or alcoholic intoxication. It is thus a psychological dissociative disorder and not an organic one. In the most common example, the person cannot recall events for a number of hours after a stressful incident, as in warfare or in the case of an uninjured survivor of an accident. In *generalized* dissociative amnesia, people forget their entire lives. Amnesia may last for hours or years.

12-3b DISSOCIATIVE FUGUE

A person with **dissociative fugue** abruptly leaves his or her home or place of work and travels to another place, having lost all memory of his or her past life. While at the new location, the person either does not think about the past or reports a past filled with invented memories. The new personality is often more outgoing and less inhibited than the "real" identity. Following recovery, the events that occurred during the fugue are not recalled.

12-3c DISSOCIATIVE IDENTITY DISORDER

Dissociative identity disorder (DID) (formerly termed **multiple personality disorder**) is the name given to William's disorder. In dissociative identity disorder, two or more identities or personalities, each with distinct traits and memories, "occupy" the same person. Each identity may or may not be aware of the others or of events experienced by the others (Huntjens et al., 2003).

The identities of an individual with dissociative identity disorder might have different eyeglass prescriptions and different allergic responses (Braun, 1988). In one person, an identity named Timmy was not sensitive to orange juice. But when other identities gained control over him and drank orange juice, he would break out with hives. Hives would also erupt if another identity emerged while the juice was being digested. If Timmy reappeared when the allergic reaction was present, the itching of the hives would cease, and the blisters would start to subside. In other cases reported by Braun, different identities within a person might show various responses to the same medicine. Or one identity might exhibit color blindness while others have normal color vision.

12-3d ORIGINS OF DISSOCIATIVE DISORDERS

The dissociative disorders are some of the odder psychological disorders. According to learning theorists and cognitive psychologists, people with dissociative disorders have learned not to think about bad memories or disturbing impulses to avoid feelings of anxiety, guilt, and shame. Both psychodynamic and learning theories suggest that dissociative disorders help people keep disturbing memories or ideas out of mind. Of what could such memories be? Research suggests that many cases involve memories of sexual or physical abuse during childhood, usually by a relative or caregiver (Foote et al., 2006; Ross, 2006; Simeon et al., 2007).

Whereas some disorders—major depressive disorder and schizophrenia among them—are found around the world, most cases of dissociative disorders have been limited to the United States and Canada (Ross, 2006). Perhaps dissociative disorders, especially DID, are culture-bound. It might also be the case, as suggested by skeptics, that many people who claim to have multiple personalities are fabricating it (Kong et al., 2008).

Dissociative identity disorder (DID) (formerly termed **multiple personality disorder**) a disorder in which a person appears to have two or more distinct identities or personalities that may alternately emerge

SHOWTIME/Landov

In the Showtime series *United States of Tara*, Toni Collette plays Tara Gregson, a homemaker with two children and several other personalities. Tara has dissociative identity disorder, and within her "reside" the flirty "T," a suburban housewife plucked from the 1950s, and a beer-guzzling Vietnam veteran named "Buck."

12-4

somatoform disorders
disorders in which people complain of physical (somatic) problems even though no physical abnormality can be found

conversion disorder
a disorder in which anxiety or unconscious conflicts are "converted" into physical symptoms that often have the effect of helping the person cope with anxiety or conflict

la belle indifférence
a French term descriptive of the lack of concern for their (imagined) medical problem sometimes shown by people with conversion disorders

hypochondriasis
a somatoform disorder characterized by persistent belief that one is ill despite lack of medical findings

Somatoform Disorders

People with **somatoform disorders** complain of physical problems such as paralysis, pain, or a persistent belief that they have a serious disease. Yet no evidence of a physical abnormality can be found. In this section, we discuss two somatoform disorders: *conversion disorder* and *hypochondriasis*.

12-4a CONVERSION DISORDER

Conversion disorder is characterized by a major change in, or loss of, physical functioning, although there are no medical findings to explain the loss of functioning. The behaviors are not intentionally produced. That is, the person is not faking. Conversion disorder is so named because it appears to "convert" a source of stress into a physical difficulty.

If you lost the ability to see at night or if your legs became paralyzed, you would understandably show concern. But some people with conversion disorder show indifference to their symptoms, a symptom termed **la belle indifférence**. The lack of concern suggests awareness, on some level, that the physical problems have their benefits.

During World War II, some bomber pilots developed night blindness. They could not carry out their nighttime missions, although no damage to the optic nerves was found. In rare cases, women with large families have been reported to become paralyzed in the legs, again with no medical findings. More recently, a Cambodian woman who had witnessed atrocities became blind as a result.

12-4b HYPOCHONDRIASIS

A more common type of somatoform disorder is **hypochondriasis** (also called *hypochondria*). People with this disorder insist that they are suffering from a serious physical illness, even though no medical evidence of illness can be found. They become preoccupied with minor physical sensations and continue to believe that they are ill despite the reassurance of physicians that they are healthy. They may run from doctor to doctor, seeking the one who will find the causes of the sensations. Fear of illness may disrupt their work or home life.

12-4c ORIGINS OF SOMATOFORM DISORDERS

The somatoform disorders offer a fascinating study in the biopsychosocial perspective. Psychologically speaking, the somatoform disorders have much to do with what one focuses on—actual social and financial problems, for example, or one's body. There is evidence that people with conversion disorder are susceptible to being hypnotized (R. J. Brown et al., 2007), and some investigators consider conversion disorder to be a form of self-hypnosis in which people focus so intently on an imaginary physical problem that they exclude conflicting information (Roelofs et al., 2002). Research evidence suggests that people who develop hypochondriasis are particularly sensitive to bodily sensations and tend to ruminate about them (Marcus et al., 2008).

Biologically speaking, tendencies toward perfectionism and rumination, which are found among many people with somatoform disorders, are thought to be at least partly heritable. Squeamishness about one's body may be too much of a good thing from the evolutionary perspective. That is, concern about bodily harm will presumably encourage one to avoid danger and provide advantages in survival and reproduction. But too much concern may lead to useless preoccupations.

"I DIDN'T KNOW MY MOTHER HAD IT.

I THINK A LOT OF WOMEN DON'T KNOW THEIR MOTHERS HAD IT; THAT'S THE SAD THING ABOUT DEPRESSION. YOU KNOW, YOU DON'T FUNCTION ANYMORE. YOU SHUT DOWN. YOU FEEL LIKE YOU ARE IN A VOID."

—MARIE OSMOND

In 2011, actress Catherine Zeta-Jones revealed that she was seeking treatment for bipolar disorder.

BEN BIRCHALL/PA Photos/Landov

(12-5) Mood Disorders

Mood disorders are characterized by disturbance in expressed emotions. The disruption generally involves sadness or elation. Most instances of sadness are normal, or "run-of-the-mill." If you have failed an important test, if you have lost money in a business venture, or if your closest friend becomes ill, it is understandable and fitting for you to be sad about it. It would be odd, in fact, if you were *not* affected by adversity. In this section, we discuss two mood disorders: *major depressive disorder* and *bipolar disorder*.

12-5a MAJOR DEPRESSIVE DISORDER

People with run-of-the-mill depression may feel sad, blue, or "down in the dumps." They may complain of lack of energy, loss of self-esteem, difficulty concentrating, loss of interest in activities and other people, pessimism, crying, and thoughts of suicide.

These feelings are more intense in people with **major depressive disorder**. According to a nationally representative sample of more than 9,000 adults in the United States, major depressive disorder affects 5% to 7% of us within any given year and one person in six or seven over the course of our lives (Hasin et al., 2005; Kessler et al., 2003). About half of those with major depressive disorder experience severe symptoms such as poor appetite, serious weight loss, and agitation or **psychomotor retardation**. They may be unable to concentrate and make decisions. They may say that they "don't care" anymore and in some cases attempt suicide. A minority may display faulty perception of reality—so-called psychotic behaviors. These include delusions of unworthiness, guilt for imagined wrongdoings, even the notion that one is rotting from disease. There may also be delusions, as of the devil administering deserved punishment, or hallucinations, as of strange bodily sensations.

12-5b BIPOLAR DISORDER

People with **bipolar disorder**, formerly known as *manic–depressive disorder*, have mood swings from ecstatic elation to deep depression. The cycles seem to be unrelated to external events. In the elated, or **manic** phase, the person may show excessive excitement or silliness, carrying jokes too far. The manic person may be argumentative, show poor judgment, destroy property, make huge contributions to charity, or give away expensive possessions. People often find manic individuals abrasive and avoid them. They are often oversexed and too restless to sit still or sleep restfully. They often speak rapidly (showing *pressured speech*) and jump from topic to topic (showing **rapid flight of ideas**). It can be hard to get a word in edgewise.

Depression is the other side of the coin. People with bipolar depression often sleep more than usual and are lethargic. People with major (or unipolar) depression are more likely to have insomnia and agitation. Those with bipolar depression also exhibit social withdrawal and irritability. Some people with bipolar disorder attempt suicide when the mood shifts from the elated phase toward depression (Jamison, 2000). They

mood disorders
a disturbance in expressed emotions, generally involving excessive or inappropriate sadness or elation

major depressive disorder
a serious to severe depressive disorder in which the person may show loss of appetite, psychomotor retardation, and impaired reality testing

psychomotor retardation
slowness in motor activity and (apparently) in thought

bipolar disorder
a disorder in which the mood alternates between two extreme poles (elation and depression); also referred to as *manic depression*

manic
elated, showing excessive excitement

rapid flight of ideas
rapid speech and topic changes, characteristic of manic behavior

learned helplessness
a possible explanation for some depressive behavior, based on findings that organisms in aversive situations learn to show inactivity when their behavior is not reinforced

attributional style
the tendency to attribute one's behavior to internal or external factors, stable or unstable factors, and global or specific factors

neuroticism
a personality trait characterized largely by persistent anxiety

will do almost anything to escape the depths of depression that lie ahead.

12-5c ORIGINS OF MOOD DISORDERS

What is known about the origins of the mood disorders?

Psychological Views

Many learning theorists suggest that depressed people behave as though they cannot obtain reinforcement. For example, they appear to be inactive and apathetic. Many people with depressive disorders have an external locus of control. That is, they do not believe they can control events so as to achieve reinforcements (Tong, 2001; Weinmann et al., 2001).

Research conducted by learning theorists has also found links between depression and **learned helplessness**. In classic research, psychologist Martin Seligman (1975) taught dogs that they were helpless to escape an electric shock. The dogs were prevented from leaving a cage in which they received repeated shocks.

TRUTH IT IS TRUE THAT FEELING "UP" IS NOT ALWAYS A GOOD THING, AS IN THE MANICKY PHASE OF BIPOLAR DISORDER.

Later, a barrier to a safe compartment was removed, offering the animals a way out. When they were shocked again, however, the dogs made no effort to escape. They had apparently learned that they were helpless. Seligman's dogs were also, in a sense, reinforced for doing nothing. That is, the shock *eventually* stopped when the dogs were showing helpless behavior—inactivity and withdrawal. "Reinforcement" might have increased the likelihood of repeating the "successful behavior"—that is, doing nothing—in a similar situation. This helpless behavior resembles that of people who are depressed.

Cognitive factors also contribute to depression. For example, perfectionists set themselves up for depression by making irrational demands on themselves. They are likely to fall short of their (unrealistic) expectations and to feel depressed as a result (Flett et al., 2007).

Still other cognitions involve the ways people explain their failures and shortcomings to themselves. Seligman (1996) suggests that when things go wrong, we may think of the causes of failure as either *internal* or *external*, *stable* or *unstable*, *global* or *specific*. These **attributional styles** can be illustrated using the example of having a date that does not work out. An internal attribution involves self-blame (as in "I really loused it up"). An external attribution places the blame elsewhere (as in "Some couples just don't take to each other," or "She was the wrong sign for me"). A stable attribution ("It's my personality") suggests a problem that cannot be changed. An unstable attribution ("It was because I had a head cold") suggests a temporary condition. A global attribution of failure ("I have no idea what to do when I'm with other people") suggests that the problem is quite large. A specific attribution ("I have problems making small talk at the beginning of a relationship") chops the problem down to a manageable size. How does this connect to depression? Research has shown that people who are depressed are more likely to attribute the causes of their failures to internal, stable, and global factors—factors that they are relatively powerless to change (Safford et al., 2007).

Paul Sutherland/Stone/Getty Images

An internal attribution involves self-blame, as in "I really loused it up." An external attribution places the blame elsewhere.

Biological Views

Researchers are also searching for biological factors in mood disorders. Depression, for example, is often associated with the trait of **neuroticism**, which is heritable (Dunkley et al., 2009). Anxiety is also connected with neuroticism, and mood and anxiety disorders are

The Case of Women and Depression

Women are nearly twice as likely to be diagnosed with depression as men (Keyes & Goodman, 2006; Kramer et al., 2008). This gender difference begins to emerge in adolescence. In any given year, about 12% of women and 7% of men in the United States are diagnosed with depression. It was once assumed that depression was most likely to accompany menopause in women, because women could no longer carry out their "natural" function of childbearing. However, women are more likely to encounter depression during the childbearing years (Deecher et al., 2008; Keyes & Goodman, 2006).

Many people assume that biological sex differences largely explain why women are more likely to become depressed (Deecher et al., 2008). Low levels of estrogen are widely seen as the culprit. Estrogen levels plummet prior to menstruation, and the deficit may trigger psychological changes. How often do we hear degrading remarks such as "It must be that time of the month" when a woman expresses feelings of anger or irritation? Some theorists suggest that women may also have a "cognitive vulnerability" to depression, connected with greater tendencies than men to ruminate about stresses and other negative events (Hughes et al., 2008; Wisco & Nolen-Hoeksema, 2009).

Some of the gender difference may also reflect the greater stresses placed on women, which tend to be maximized when they are working a triple shift—one in the workforce and the others meeting the demands of homemaking, child rearing, and aging parents (Plaisier et al., 2008; Rathus, 2009–2010). Women are more likely to experience physical and sexual abuse, poverty, single parenthood, and sexism. Single mothers, in particular, have lower socioeconomic status than men, and depression and other psychological disorders are more common among poor people (Nicholson et al., 2008). A part of treatment for depressed women, then, is to modify the demands on women. The pain may lie in the individual, but the cause often lies in society.

roman makhmutov/Flickr/Getty Images

frequently found in the same person (Spinhoven et al., 2010). Twin and adoption studies also support a role for genetic factors in bipolar disorder (Willcutt & McQueen, 2010).

Much research into depression focuses on underutilization of the neurotransmitter serotonin in the brain (Artigas, 2008; Leach, 2008). It has been shown, for example, that learned helplessness is connected with lower serotonin levels in rats' brains (Wu et al., 1999). Moreover, people with severe depression often respond to drugs (selective serotonin reuptake inhibitors, or SSRIs) that heighten the action of serotonin (Leonard, 2008).

The Biopsychosocial Perspective

Relationships between mood disorders and biological factors are complex and under intense study. Even if people are biologically predisposed toward depression, self-efficacy expectations and attitudes—particularly attitudes about whether one can change things for the better—may play a role.

Although the mood disorders are connected with processes within the individual, many kinds of situations are also connected with depression. Depression may be a reaction to losses and stress (Cowen, 2002; Mazure et al., 2000). Sources of chronic strain such as marital discord, physical discomfort, and failure or pres-

sure at work all contribute to feelings of depression. We tend to be more depressed by things we bring on ourselves, such as academic and financial problems, unwanted pregnancy, and arguments (Greenberger et al., 2000). However, some people recover from depression less readily than others. People who remain depressed have lower self-esteem (Sherrington et al., 2001), are less likely to be able to solve social problems (Reinecke et al., 2001), and have less social support.

12-5d SUICIDE

Each year about 33,000 people in the United States take their own lives (Centers for Disease Control and Prevention, 2009). Suicide is the third leading cause of death among 15- to 24-year-olds, behind accidents and assaults (Heron & Tejada-Vera, 2009).

We discuss suicide in the section on mood disorders because most suicides are linked to feelings of depression and hopelessness (Dwivedi, 2010; Zaitsoff & Grilo, 2010). Jill Rathus and her colleagues (A. L. Miller et al., 2007) have found that suicidal adolescents experience four kinds of psychological problems: (a) confusion about the self, (b) impulsiveness, (c) emotional instability, and (d) interpersonal problems. Some suicidal teenagers, like suicidal adults, are highly achieving, rigid perfectionists who have set impossibly high expectations for themselves (A. L. Miller et al., 2007). Many people throw themselves into feelings of depression and hopelessness by comparing themselves negatively with others (Barber, 2001).

Contributors to suicidal behavior among adolescents include concerns over sexuality, sexual abuse, grades, problems at home, and substance abuse (Duke et al., 2010; A. L. Miller et al., 2007; Zayas et al., 2010). It is not always a stressful event itself that precipitates suicide but the individual's anxiety or fear of being "found out" about something, such as failing a course or getting arrested. People who consider suicide are apparently less capable of solving problems, especially social problems, than others (A. L. Miller et al., 2007). They are thus less likely to find productive ways of changing the stressful situation. They want a magical solution to problems that require work or else a quick way out (Shneidman, 2001).

There is a tendency for suicide to run in families (Goldston & Compton, 2010). Many suicide attempters have family members with serious psychological problems, and about 25% have family members who have taken their own lives (Sorensen & Rutter, 1991). The

FICTION IT IS NOT TRUE THAT PEOPLE WHO THREATEN SUICIDE ARE ONLY SEEKING ATTENTION.

causal connections are unclear, however. Do people who attempt suicide inherit disorders that can lead to suicide? Does the suicide of a family member give a person the idea of committing suicide or create the impression that he or she is "fated" to commit suicide?

Sociocultural Factors in Suicide

Suicide is connected not only with feelings of depression and stressful events but also with age, educational status, ethnicity, and gender. Suicide is more common among college students than among people of the same age who are not in college. Each year, about 10,000 college students attempt suicide. Although teenage suicides loom large in the media spotlight, older people are more likely to commit suicide (Centers for Disease Control and Prevention, 2009). The suicide rate among older people who are unmarried or divorced is double that of older people who are married.

Rates of suicide and suicide attempts also vary among different ethnic groups and according to gender. For example, about one in every six Native Americans (17%) has attempted suicide—a rate higher than that of other Americans (Centers for Disease Control and Prevention, 2009). About one in eight Latin Americans has attempted suicide and three in ten have considered it. European Americans are next, with 8% attempting and 28% contemplating suicide. African Americans are least likely to attempt suicide (6.5%) or to think about it (20%). The actual suicide rates for African Americans are about two-thirds of those for European Americans, despite the fact that African Americans are more likely to live in poverty and suffer from discrimination (Centers for Disease Control and Prevention, 2009).

About three times as many females as males attempt suicide, but about five times as many males "succeed" (Centers for Disease Control and Prevention, 2009). Males are more likely to shoot or hang themselves; females more often use drugs, such as overdoses of tranquilizers or sleeping pills, or poisons. It takes

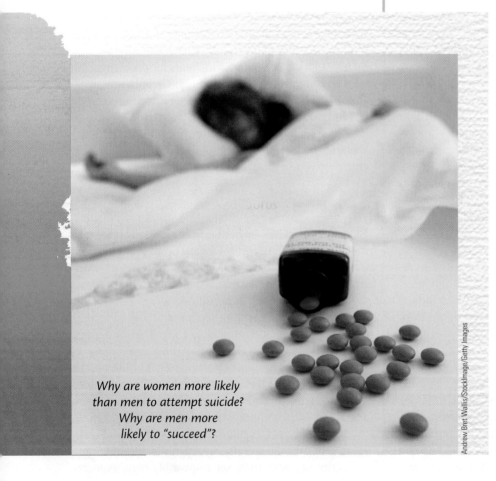

Why are women more likely than men to attempt suicide? Why are men more likely to "succeed"?

Andrew Bret Wallis/StockImage/Getty Images

awhile for drugs to work, giving people the opportunity to find them and intervene.

Myths About Suicide

You may have heard that individuals who threaten suicide are only seeking attention. Those who are serious just do it. Not so. Most people who commit suicide give warnings about their intentions or have made prior attempts (Bakst et al., 2009; Jackson & Nuttall, 2001; Waters, 2000). Contrary to widespread belief, discussing suicide with a person who is depressed does not prompt the person to attempt suicide (National Center for Injury Prevention and Control, 2005). Extracting a promise not to commit suicide before calling or visiting a helping professional seems to prevent some suicides.

Some believe that only "insane" people (meaning people who are out of touch with reality) would take their own lives. However, suicidal thinking is not necessarily a sign of psychosis, neurosis, or personality disorder. Instead, people may consider suicide when they think they have run out of options (Nock & Kazdin, 2002; Townsend et al., 2001).

12-6 Schizophrenia

Schizophrenia is a severe psychological disorder that touches every aspect of a person's life. It is characterized by disturbances in thought and language, perception and attention, motor activity, and mood, as well as withdrawal and absorption in daydreams or fantasy.

Schizophrenia has been referred to as the worst psychological disorder affecting human beings. It afflicts nearly 1% of the population worldwide. Its onset occurs relatively early in life, and its adverse effects tend to endure.

12-6a SYMPTOMS OF SCHIZOPHRENIA

In schizophrenia, whatever can go wrong, psychologically, seems to go wrong. There are disturbances in thinking, language, perception, motor behavior, and social interaction. People with schizophrenia may have *positive symptoms*, *negative symptoms*, or both. **Positive symptoms** are the inappropriate kinds of behavior we find in afflicted people, including, for

"If you talk to God, you are praying. If God talks to you, you have **schizophrenia**."
—THOMAS SZASZ

example, agitated behavior, vivid hallucinations, unshakable delusions, disorganized thinking, and nonsensical speech. **Negative symptoms** are those that reflect the absence of appropriate behavior. We see them in flat, emotionless voices, blank faces, rigid, motionless bodies, and **mutism** (refusal to talk).

Problems in Thinking and Language

Schizophrenia has been called a "thought disorder" because people with schizophrenia have problems in thinking, language, memory, and attention (Cellard et al., 2010). Their thinking and communication ability become unraveled. Their speech may be jumbled. They may combine parts of words into new words or make meaningless rhymes. They may jump from topic to topic, conveying little useful information. They usually do not recognize that their thoughts and behavior are abnormal.

Many people with schizophrenia have unshakeable **delusions** of grandeur, persecution, or reference (Freeman et al., 2010). In the case of *delusions of grandeur*, a person may believe that he is a famous historical figure such as Jesus or a person on a special mission. People with *delusions of persecution* may believe that they are sought by the CIA, FBI, or some other group. Paranoid individuals tend to jump to conclusions that people intend to do them harm based on little evidence (Lincoln et al., 2010). People with *delusions of reference* erroneously believe that other people are talking about them or referring to them. For example, a woman with delusions of reference said that news stories contained coded information about her. Other people with schizophrenia have had delusions that they have committed unpardonable sins, that they were rotting away from disease, or that they or the world did not exist.

Problems in Perception

The perceptual problems of people with schizophrenia often include hallucinations—imagery in the absence of external stimulation that the person cannot

positive symptoms those symptoms of schizophrenia that indicate the presence of inappropriate behavior, such as hallucinations, delusions, agitation, and inappropriate giggling

negative symptoms those symptoms of schizophrenia that reflect the absence of appropriate behavior, such as blank faces, monotonic voices, and motionless bodies

mutism refusal to talk

delusions false, persistent beliefs that are unsubstantiated by sensory or objective evidence

stupor
a condition in which the senses, thought, and movement are dulled

paranoid schizophrenia
a type of schizophrenia characterized primarily by delusions—commonly of persecution—and by vivid hallucinations

disorganized schizophrenia
a type of schizophrenia characterized by disorganized delusions and vivid hallucinations

catatonic schizophrenia
a type of schizophrenia characterized by striking motor impairment

waxy flexibility
a feature of catatonic schizophrenia in which people can be molded into postures that they maintain for quite some time

distinguish from reality. People who experience hallucinations may see colors or even obscene words spelled out in midair. Auditory hallucinations are the most common type.

Problems in Actions, Emotions, and Social Interaction

For individuals with schizophrenia, motor activity may become wild or so slowed that the person is said to be in a **stupor**—that is, a condition in which the senses, thought, and movement are inhibited. There may be strange gestures and facial expressions. The person's emotional responses may be flat or blunted or completely inappropriate—as in giggling upon hearing bad news. People with schizophrenia tend to withdraw from social contacts and become wrapped up in their own thoughts and fantasies (Horan et al., 2010; Mathews & Barch, 2010).

12-6b TYPES OF SCHIZOPHRENIA

All types of schizophrenia involve a thought disorder. However, the three major types of schizophrenia—*paranoid*, *disorganized*, and *catatonic schizophrenia*—have distinct features.

Paranoid Type

People with **paranoid schizophrenia** can have complex delusions and, frequently, related auditory hallucinations. They usually have delusions of grandeur and persecution, but they may also have delusions of jealousy, in which they believe that a spouse or lover has been unfaithful—again, jumping to conclusions with very little evidence (Lincoln et al., 2010). They may show agitation, confusion, and fear and may experience vivid hallucinations that are consistent with their delusions. People with paranoid schizophrenia often construct complex or systematized delusions involving themes of wrongdoing or persecution. John Nash, the character in the true story behind the film *A Beautiful Mind*, believed that the government was recruiting him to decipher coded messages sent by our Cold War enemies.

TRUTH IT IS TRUE THAT PEOPLE WITH SCHIZOPHRENIA MAY SEE AND HEAR THINGS THAT ARE NOT REALLY THERE. THOSE "THINGS" ARE CALLED HALLUCINATIONS.

Disorganized Type

People with **disorganized schizophrenia** show incoherence, disorganized behavior, disorganized delusions, hallucinations, and flat or inappropriate emotional responses. Extreme social impairment is common. People with this type of schizophrenia may also exhibit silliness and giddiness of mood, giggling, and nonsensical speech. They may neglect their appearance and personal hygiene and lose control of their bladder and bowels.

Catatonic Type

Catatonic schizophrenia is one of the most unusual psychological disorders. People with **catatonic schizophrenia** show striking impairment in motor activity. It is characterized by a slowing of activity into a stupor that may suddenly change into an agitated phase. Catatonic individuals may maintain unusual, sometimes difficult postures for hours, even as their limbs grow swollen or stiff. A striking feature of this condition is **waxy flexibility**, in which the person maintains positions into which he or she has been manipulated by others. Catatonic individuals may also show mutism, but afterward, they usually report that they heard what others were saying at the time.

12-6c EXPLAINING SCHIZOPHRENIA

Researchers have investigated various factors that may contribute to schizophrenia, including psychological, sociocultural, and biological factors.

Psychological Views

Most learning theorists have explained schizophrenia in terms of conditioning and observational learning. They have suggested that people engage in schizophrenic behavior when it is more likely to be reinforced than normal behavior. This may occur when a person is reared in a socially unrewarding or punitive situation. Inner fantasies then become more reinforcing than social realities. Patients in a psychiatric hospital may learn what is "expected" by observing others. Hospital staff may reinforce schizophrenic behavior by paying more attention to patients who behave bizarrely. This view is consistent with folklore that the child who disrupts the class attracts more attention from the teacher than the "good" child.

Sociocultural Views

Many investigators have considered whether and how social and cultural factors such as poverty, poor parenting, discrimination, and overcrowding contribute to schizophrenia—especially among people who are genetically vulnerable to the disorder. Although quality of parenting is connected with the development of schizophrenia (Buckley et al., 2000), critics note that many people who are reared in socially punitive settings are apparently immune to the disorder.

Classic research in New Haven, Connecticut, showed that the rate of schizophrenia was twice as high in the lowest socioeconomic class as in the next higher class on the socioeconomic ladder (Hollingshead & Redlich, 1958). It appears that poor-quality housing contributes to psychological disorders (Dunn, 2008). Some sociocultural theorists therefore suggest that treatment of schizophrenia requires alleviation of poverty and other social ills rather than changing people whose behavior is deviant. But critics of this view suggest that low socioeconomic status may be a result, rather than a cause, of schizophrenia. People with schizophrenia may drift downward in social status—winding up in poor neighborhoods—because they lack the social skills and cognitive abilities to function at higher levels.

Although many researchers continue to seek psychological and social risk factors for the development of schizophrenia, research has not discovered any environmental causes that will lead to the development of schizophrenia in people who are unrelated to people with the disorder. Because of this lack of evidence, much focus today is on the biological aspects of schizophrenia—on its nature as a brain disease and on its likely biological origins. Once we have outlined the nature of the biological differences between schizophrenic people and normal people, we will turn to genetic and other biological factors that may produce schizophrenia.

Biological Views

Many studies have shown that the brains of schizophrenic people differ from those of normal people. Studies have focused on the amount of gray matter in the brain (see Figure 12.2), the size of ventricles (hollow spaces), activity levels in the brain, and brain chemistry (for example, neurotransmitters).

Imaging of the brain has shown that people with schizophrenia generally have less gray matter than other people, which suggests deficiencies in attention, working memory, abstract thinking, and language (Takahashi et al., 2009). People with schizophrenia have smaller brains than normal people and, in particular, a smaller prefrontal region of the cortex (Shirayama et al., 2010). PET scans reveal that people with schizophrenia also tend to have a lower level of activity in the prefrontal cortex—the region responsible for planning and decision making (Farzan et al., 2010; Meyer-Lindenberg et al., 2001). Still other research connects the lower activity levels with a loss in synapses (the structures that permit communication between neurons) in the region (Glantz et al., 2010), further decreasing the likelihood that people with schizophrenia will transmit neural messages efficiently.

FIGURE 12.2 | Average Rates of Loss of Gray Matter Among Normal Adolescents and Adolescents Diagnosed with Schizophrenia

High-resolution MRI scans show rates of gray matter loss in normal 13- to 18-year-olds and among adolescents of the same age diagnosed with schizophrenia. Maps of brain changes reveal profound, progressive loss in schizophrenia (right). Loss also occurs in normal adolescents (left), but at a slower rate.

Thompson et al., 2001.

What might account for differences in brain structure and functioning? Schizophrenia, like many other psychological disorders, runs in families (Bolinskey & Gottesman, 2010). People with schizophrenia make up about 1% of the global population, yet children with one schizophrenic parent have about a 6% chance of being diagnosed with it (see Figure 12.3). There is about a 48% agreement rate for the diagnosis among pairs of identical twins, whose genetic codes are the same, compared with a 17% rate among pairs of fraternal twins (Gottesman, 1991). Moreover, adoptee studies find that the biological parent typically places the child at greater risk for schizophrenia than the adoptive parent (Gottesman, 1991). Many studies have been carried out to try to isolate the gene or genes involved in schizophrenia. Some studies find locations for multiple genes on several chromosomes.

In many cases of schizophrenia, a genetic vulnerability may be a necessary factor but insufficient to cause its development. The mothers of many people who develop schizophrenia have undergone complications during pregnancy and birth (Spencer et al., 2008). For example, many mothers had the flu during the 6th or 7th month of pregnancy (Brown & Derkits, 2010; Short et al., 2010). Complications during childbirth, especially prolonged labor, seem to be connected with the larger ventricles—hollow spaces—we find among people with schizophrenia (Spencer et al., 2008). Poor maternal nutrition has been implicated as well (Stein et al., 2009; Susser et al., 2009). People with schizophrenia are also somewhat more likely to have been born during winter than would be predicted by chance; cold weather might heighten the risk of viral and other infections in the mother during late pregnancy and early infancy (Polanczyk et al., 2010).

Numerous chemical substances, including the neurotransmitter dopamine, have been suspected of playing a role in schizophrenia. According to the dopamine theory, people with schizophrenia "over-utilize" dopamine (use more of it than most people do), although they may not produce more of it (Fatemi & Folsom, 2009; Tost et al., 2009). Why? Research suggests that they have increased concentrations of dopamine at the synapses in the brain and

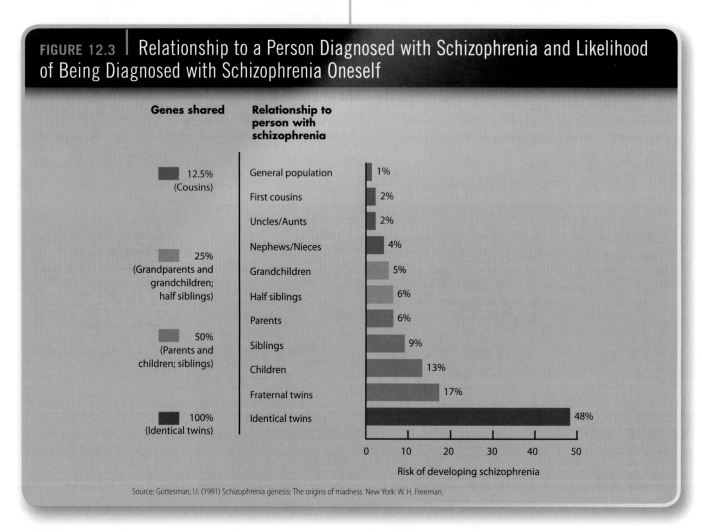

FIGURE 12.3 | Relationship to a Person Diagnosed with Schizophrenia and Likelihood of Being Diagnosed with Schizophrenia Oneself

Source: Gottesman, I.I. (1991) Schizophrenia genesis: The origins of madness. New York: W. H. Freeman.

According to the biopsychosocial model of schizophrenia, people with a genetic vulnerability to the disorder experience increased risk for schizophrenia when they encounter problems such as viral infections, birth complications, stress, and poor parenting. People without the genetic vulnerability would not develop schizophrenia despite such problems.

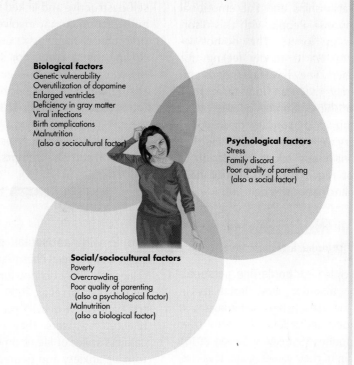

Biological factors
Genetic vulnerability
Overutilization of dopamine
Enlarged ventricles
Deficiency in gray matter
Viral infections
Birth complications
Malnutrition
  (also a sociocultural factor)

Psychological factors
Stress
Family discord
Poor quality of parenting
  (also a social factor)

Social/sociocultural factors
Poverty
Overcrowding
Poor quality of parenting
  (also a psychological factor)
Malnutrition
  (also a biological factor)

personality disorders enduring patterns of maladaptive behavior that are sources of distress to the individual or others

paranoid personality disorder a personality disorder characterized by persistent suspiciousness but not involving the disorganization of paranoid schizophrenia

schizotypal personality disorder a personality disorder characterized by oddities of thought and behavior but not involving bizarre psychotic behaviors

also larger numbers of dopamine receptors (Kegeles et al., 2010). It's a sort of "double hit" of neural transmission that may be connected with the confusion that characterizes schizophrenia.

Biopsychosocial View

Because biological, psychological, and sociocultural factors are implicated in schizophrenia, most investigators today favor the biopsychosocial model. According to this model, genetic factors create a predisposition toward—or vulnerability to—schizophrenia (see Figure 12.4). Genetic vulnerability to the disorder interacts with other factors, such as complications of pregnancy and birth, stress, quality of parenting, and social conditions to give rise to the disorder (Bishop, 2009; Buckley et al., 2000; Sawa & Snyder, 2002).

12-7 Personality Disorders

Personality disorders, like personality traits, are characterized by enduring patterns of behavior. Personality disorders, however, are inflexible and maladaptive. They impair personal or social functioning and are a source of distress to the individual or to other people. There are a number of personality disorders. They include the *paranoid*, *schizotypal*, *schizoid*, *borderline*, *antisocial*, and *avoidant personality disorders*.

12-7a PARANOID PERSONALITY DISORDER

The defining trait of the **paranoid personality disorder** is a tendency to interpret other people's behavior as threatening or demeaning. People with the disorder do not show the grossly disorganized thinking of paranoid schizophrenia. However, they are mistrustful of others, and their relationships suffer for it. They may be suspicious of coworkers and supervisors, but they can generally hold a job.

12-7b SCHIZOTYPAL AND SCHIZOID PERSONALITY DISORDERS

Schizotypal personality disorder is characterized by peculiarities of thought, perception, or behavior, such as excessive fantasy and suspiciousness, feelings of being unreal, or the odd use of words. There are no complex delusions, no hallucinations, and no unusual motor activities, so this disorder is schizo*typal*, not schizophrenic.

© PRNewsFoto/Gentex Corporation

Schizoid personality disorder is characterized by indifference to relationships and flat emotional response. People with this disorder are "loners." They do not develop warm, tender feelings for others. They have few friends and rarely maintain long-term relationships. Some people with schizoid personality disorder do very well on the job provided that continuous social interaction is not required. They do not have hallucinations or delusions.

12-7c BORDERLINE PERSONALITY DISORDER

People with **borderline personality disorder** show instability in their relationships, self-image, and mood and a lack of control over impulses (Stanley & Siever, 2010). They tend to be uncertain of their values, goals, loyalties, careers, choices of friends, and sometimes even their sexual orientations (Roepke et al., 2011). Instability in self-image or identity may leave them with feelings of emptiness and boredom. Many cannot tolerate being alone and make desperate attempts to avoid feelings of abandonment. They may be clinging and demanding in social relationships, but clinging often pushes away the people on whom they depend. They alternate between extremes of adulation in their relationships (when their needs are met) and loathing (when they feel scorned). They tend to view other people as all good or all bad, shifting abruptly from one extreme to the other. As a result, they may flit from partner to partner in brief and stormy relationships. People they had idealized are treated with contempt when they feel the other person has failed them.

Instability of moods is a central characteristic of borderline personality disorder. Moods run the gamut from anger and irritability to depression and anxiety, with each lasting from a few hours to a few days. People with the disorder have difficulty controlling anger and are prone to fights or smashing things. They often act on impulse, like eloping with someone they have just met. This impulsive and unpredictable behavior is often self-destructive and linked to a risk of suicidal attempts and gestures. It may involve spending sprees, gambling, drug abuse, engaging in unsafe sexual activity, reckless driving, binge eating, or shoplifting. People with the disorder may also engage in self-mutilation, such as scratching their wrists or burning their arms with cigarettes (Zanarini et al., 2010). Self-mutilation is sometimes a means of manipulating others, particularly in times of stress. Frequent self-mutilation is also associated with suicide attempts.

12-7d ANTISOCIAL PERSONALITY DISORDER

People with **antisocial personality disorder** often show a superficial charm and are at least average in intelligence. They do not form strong bonds with other people (Kumari et al., 2009; Romero et al., 2001). Though they are often heavily punished by their parents and rejected by peers, they continue in their impulsive, careless styles of life. Women are more likely than men to have anxiety and depressive disorders. However, antisocial personality disorder is more common among men than women (McCormick et al., 2007).

12-7e AVOIDANT PERSONALITY DISORDER

People with **avoidant personality disorder** are generally unwilling to enter a relationship without some assurance of acceptance because they fear rejection and criticism. As a result, they may have few close relationships outside their immediate families. Unlike people with schizoid personality disorder, however, they have some interest in, and feelings of warmth toward, other people.

12-7f ORIGINS OF PERSONALITY DISORDERS

Numerous biological, psychological, and sociocultural factors have been implicated in the personality disorders. Cognitive psychologists find that antisocial adolescents tend to interpret other people's behavior as threatening, even when it is not (Dodge, 2006; Ellis et al., 2009). Aggressive individuals often find it difficult to solve social problems in useful ways (Fontaine et al., 2010).

Biological Factors

Genetic factors are apparently involved in some personality disorders (Jang et al., 2007; Livesley & Jang, 2008). Personality traits are to some degree heritable,

TRUTH IT IS TRUE THAT SOME PEOPLE CAN KILL OR MAIM OTHERS WITH NO FEELINGS OF GUILT AT ALL. WHEN THEY PERSISTENTLY VIOLATE THE RIGHTS OF OTHERS AND ARE IN REPEATED CONFLICT WITH THE LAW, THEY MAY BE DIAGNOSED WITH ANTISOCIAL PERSONALITY DISORDER.

and many personality disorders seem to be extreme variations of normal personality traits. An analysis of 51 twin and adoption studies estimated that genetic factors were the greatest influences on antisocial behavior (Rhee & Waldman, 2002). Referring to the five-factor model of personality, people with schizoid personalities tend to be highly introverted (Widiger & Simonsen, 2005). People with avoidant personalities tend to be both introverted and emotionally unstable (neurotic) (Widiger & Simonsen, 2005).

Perhaps the genetics of antisocial personality involve the prefrontal cortex of the brain, which is connected with emotional responses. There is some evidence that people with antisocial personality, as a group, have less gray matter (associative neurons) in the prefrontal cortex than other people do (Narayan et al., 2007; Raine et al., 2009). Adrian Raine (2008) suggests that specific genes lead to this impairment and also predispose people to antisocial behavior.

Psychological Factors

Learning theorists suggest that childhood experiences can contribute to maladaptive ways of relating to others in adulthood—that is, can lead to personality disorders. Cognitive psychologists find that antisocial adolescents encode social information in ways that bolster their misdeeds. For example, they tend to interpret other people's behavior as threatening, even when it is not (Lochman et al., 2011). Aggressive individuals often find it difficult to solve social problems in useful ways (McMurran et al., 2002). Cognitive therapists have encouraged some antisocial male children and adolescents to view social provocations as problems to be solved rather than as threats to their "manhood," with some favorable initial results (Lochman et al., 2011).

Sociocultural Factors

The label of borderline personality has been applied to people as diverse as Marilyn Monroe and Lawrence of Arabia. Some theorists believe we live in fragmented and alienating times that tend to create problems in forming a stable identity and stable relationships. "Living on the edge," or border, can be seen as a metaphor for an unstable society.

Although the causes of many psychological disorders remain in dispute, various methods of therapy have been devised to deal with them. Those methods are the focus of Chapter 13.

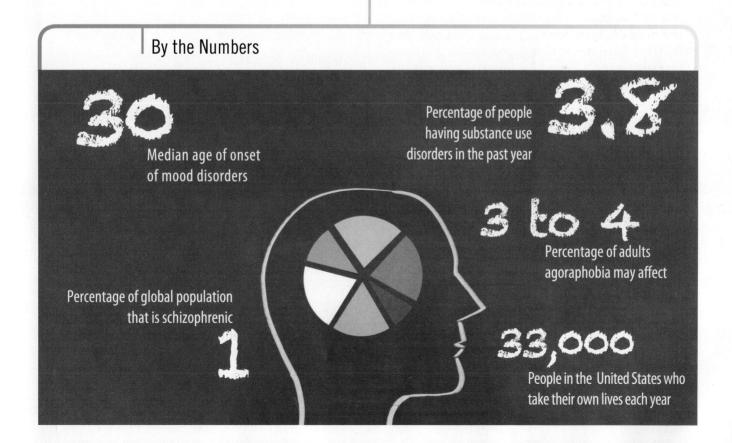

By the Numbers

30
Median age of onset of mood disorders

3.8
Percentage of people having substance use disorders in the past year

3 to 4
Percentage of adults agoraphobia may affect

1
Percentage of global population that is schizophrenic

33,000
People in the United States who take their own lives each year

Ready to study? In the book, you can:

⊙ Review what you've read with Fill-Ins and Multiple Choice quizzes (below).

⊙ Rip out Chapter Review card (in the back).

Or you can go online to CourseMate at www.cengagebrain.com for these resources:

⊙ Complete Practices Quizzes to prepare for tests.

⊙ Review Key Terms Flash Cards (online or print).

⊙ Play games to master concepts.

Answers can be found in the back of the book, starting on page 368.

1. Behavior is labeled abnormal when it is unusual, is socially unacceptable, involves faulty _____ of reality (as with hallucinations), is dangerous, self-defeating, or distressing.

2. A(n) _____ is an irrational, excessive fear.

3. In _____–_____ disorder, people are troubled by intrusive thoughts or impulses to repeat some activity.

4. People with dissociative _____ forget their own identities but retain general knowledge and skills.

5. In dissociative _____ disorder, the person behaves as if distinct personalities occupy the body.

6. In _____ disorders, people complain of physical problems or persist in believing they have a serious disease, even though no medical problem can be found.

7. Manicky people may have grand delusional schemes and show rapid _____ of ideas.

8. Depressed people are more likely than other people to make (internal or external?) attributions for failures.

9. _____ schizophrenia is characterized by impaired motor activity and waxy flexibility.

10. _____ disorders are inflexible, maladaptive behavior patterns that impair personal or social functioning and are a source of distress to the individual or to others.

1. The news just reported that a hurricane is headed toward your home. You feel anxious and can't decide what to do first to prepare. This response is indicative of

    a. **unusual behavior.**   c. **abnormal behavior.**
    b. **normal behavior.**   d. **faulty behavior.**

2. A man cancels an important business trip to the mountains because he cannot control his fear of heights. He goes to a psychologist to discuss the problem. What diagnosis is the psychologist likely to consider?

    a. **agoraphobia**
    b. **acrophobia**
    c. **conversion disorder**
    d. **avoidant personality disorder**

3. A woman has difficulty concentrating on her job at work because of her preoccupation with the possibility that she has left the stove on or the iron plugged in at home. She imagines that her house will catch fire because of her mistake. She confides in her doctor. What diagnosis is the doctor most likely to use to describe her behavior?

    a. **obsessive-compulsive disorder**
    b. **panic disorder**
    c. **specific phobia**
    d. **schizophrenia**

4. Dissociative disorders involve _____ that cannot be attributed to organic problems.

    a. **a loss of memory**
    b. **lack of feelings of guilt and shame**
    c. **hallucinations**
    d. **explosive behavior**

5. For as long as Shelley can remember, grandmother has always been sick. She goes from doctor to doctor even though they keep telling her she is in excellent health. Her grandmother insists the doctors don't know what they are talking about. She is sure she has some terrible disease. Shelley checks her psychology textbook and finds that her grandmother's behavior is closest to fitting the category of

    a. **dissociative amnesia.**
    b. **panic disorder.**
    c. **catatonic schizophrenia.**
    d. **hypochondriasis.**

6. Imagery in the absence of external stimulation is the definition of _____, which are often observed in people with schizophrenia.

    a. **rapid flight of ideas**
    b. **delusions**
    c. **hallucinations**
    d. **stress disorders**

7. The difference between the emotion of sadness and an episode of major depression is that the symptoms of major depression are

    a. **drastically different.**
    b. **more intense.**
    c. **only observed in females.**
    d. **related to stressful situations.**

8. According to the text, which neurotransmitter is associated with depression?

    a. **serotonin**
    b. **dopamine**
    c. **glutamate**
    d. **GABA**

9. Your patient confides that the FBI and the CIA are "out to get me." He has stopped going to work. He keeps his blinds drawn and his doors and windows locked. The truth is that the FBI and CIA are not pursuing him or checking on him at all. Your patient can most likely be diagnosed with

    a. **schizoid personality.**
    b. **dissociative identity disorder.**
    c. **paranoid personality.**
    d. **paranoid schizophrenia.**

10. All of the following are symptoms of borderline personality disorder EXCEPT

    a. **being a loner.**
    b. **unstable moods.**
    c. **fear of abandonment.**
    d. **self mutilation.**

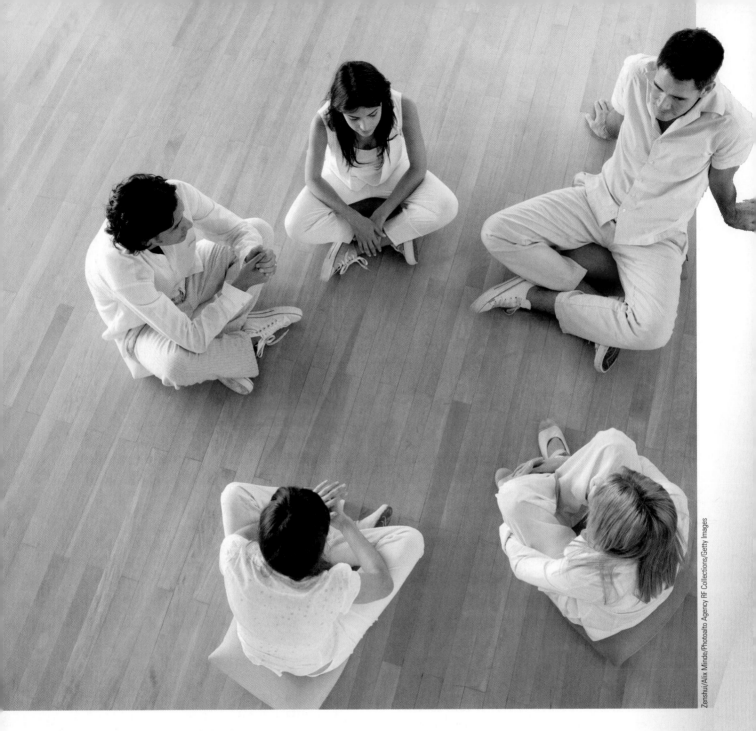

LEARNING OUTCOMES

13-1 Define psychotherapy and describe the history of treatment of psychological disorders

13-2 Describe traditional psychoanalysis and short-term psychodynamic therapies

13-3 Define humanistic therapy and contrast its two main approaches

13-4 Define behavior therapy and identify various behavioral approaches to therapy

13-5 Define cognitive therapy and describe Beck's approach and REBT

13-6 Identify various types of group therapy and discuss their advantages and disadvantages

13-7 Explain whether psychotherapy works and who benefits from it

13-8 Describe methods of biological therapy—their benefits and side effects

STUDY TOOLS ▶
After you read the chapter, go to the Study Tools at the end of the chapter, page 328.

CHAPTER 13

Methods
OF THERAPY

Joanne Cartwright (dubbed "Miss Muffet" by her therapist) had a spider phobia. "I washed my truck every night before I went to work in case there were webs," she said (cited in Robbins, 2000). "I put all my clothes in plastic bags and taped duct tape around my doors so spiders couldn't get in. I thought I was going to have a mental breakdown. I wasn't living." She checked every crack in the sidewalk for spiders—if she could push herself to go outside at all. Finally, her crippling phobia made it all but impossible for her to leave the house. After years of misery, she sought help.

Fortunately for "Miss Muffet," she wound up in the University of Washington's Human Interface Technology Laboratory, where she worked with psychologist Hunter Hoffman. Writing in *Scientific American*, Hoffman (2004) describes an elaborate virtual environment called *SpiderWorld* that helps people with spider phobias overcome their aversion by gradually approaching virtual spiders and reaching out to touch them (see Figure 13.1). A toy spider and a device that tracks the patient's hand movements provide tactile sensations akin to touching a real spider.

Twelve virtual therapy desensitization sessions changed Cartwright's life. "I'm amazed," she notes, "because I am doing all this stuff I could never do," such as camping and hiking.

Joanne Cartwright received virtual therapy to learn to cope with her phobia of spiders. If she had chosen a different kind of therapist, she might have been:

- Lying on a couch, talking about anything that popped into awareness, trying to unearth the possible symbolic meaning of spiders.
- Sitting face to face with a warm, gentle therapist who expressed faith in her ability to cope with her fears.
- Listening to a frank, straightforward therapist assert that she was catastrophizing the awfulness of spiders and compounding her problem by ruminating about it.
- Taking medication.

> *To help people deal with their problems, you must get them exposed to what they fear most.*

TRUTH OR FICTION

WHAT DO YOU THINK? FOLKLORE, COMMON SENSE, OR NONSENSE? CIRCLE THE T FOR "TRUTH" OR THE F FOR "FICTION," AND CHECK THE ACCURACY OF YOUR ANSWERS AS YOU READ THROUGH THE CHAPTER.

T	F	RESIDENTS OF LONDON USED TO VISIT THE LOCAL INSANE ASYLUM FOR A FUN NIGHT OUT ON THE TOWN.
T	F	SOME PSYCHOTHERAPISTS LET THEIR CLIENTS TAKE THE LEAD IN PSYCHOTHERAPY.
T	F	SOME PSYCHOTHERAPISTS TELL THEIR CLIENTS EXACTLY WHAT TO DO.
T	F	LYING IN A RECLINING CHAIR AND FANTASIZING CAN BE AN EFFECTIVE WAY OF CONFRONTING FEARS.
T	F	SMOKING CIGARETTES CAN BE AN EFFECTIVE METHOD FOR HELPING PEOPLE STOP SMOKING CIGARETTES.
T	F	THERE IS NO SCIENTIFIC EVIDENCE THAT PSYCHOTHERAPY HELPS PEOPLE WITH PSYCHOLOGICAL DISORDERS.
T	F	THE ORIGINATOR OF A SURGICAL TECHNIQUE TO REDUCE VIOLENCE LEARNED THAT IT WAS NOT ALWAYS SUCCESSFUL WHEN ONE OF HIS PATIENTS SHOT HIM.

- Participating in some combination of these approaches.

These methods, although different, all represent methods of therapy. In this chapter, we explore methods of psychotherapy and biological therapy.

psychotherapy

a systematic interaction between a therapist and a client that brings psychological
principles to bear on influencing the client's thoughts,
feelings, or behavior to help
the client overcome psychological disorders, adjust to
problems in living, or develop as an individual

asylum

an institution for the care of
the mentally ill

FIGURE 13.1 | Dr. Hunter Hoffman of the University of Washington Uses Virtual Therapy to Treat "Miss Muffet"

"Miss Muffet" is the name playfully given by Hoffman to a woman with a phobia for spiders. She is wearing virtual-reality headgear and sees the scene displayed on the monitor, which shows a large and hairy—but virtual—tarantula.

Mary Levin, UW, with permission from Hunter Hoffman, UW/www.Vrpain.com

(13-1) What Is Psychotherapy?

There are many kinds of psychotherapy, but they have certain common characteristics. **Psychotherapy** is a systematic interaction between a therapist and a client that applies psychological principles to affect the client's thoughts, feelings, or behavior in an effort to help the client overcome psychological disorders, adjust to problems in living, or develop as an individual.

Quite a mouthful? True. But note the essentials:

✔ *Systematic interaction.* Psychotherapy is a systematic interaction between a client and a therapist. The therapist's theoretical point of view interacts with the client's to determine how the therapist and client relate to each other.

✔ *Psychological principles.* Psychotherapy is based on psychological theory and research in areas such as personality, learning, motivation, and emotion.

✔ *Thoughts, feelings, and behavior.* Psychotherapy influences clients' thoughts, feelings, and behavior. It can be aimed at any or all of these aspects of human psychology.

✔ *Psychological disorders, adjustment problems, and personal growth.* Psychotherapy is often used with people who have psychological disorders. Other people seek help in adjusting to problems such as shyness, weight problems, or loss of a life partner. Still other clients want to learn more about themselves and to reach their full potential as individuals, parents, or creative artists.

13-1a THE HISTORY OF THERAPIES

Historically speaking, "treatments" of psychological disorders often reflected the assumption that people who behaved in strange ways were possessed by demons. Because of this belief, treatment tended to involve cruel practices such as exorcism and execution. Some people who could not meet the demands of everyday life were tossed into prisons. Others begged in the streets, stole food, or became prostitutes. A few found their way to monasteries or other retreats that offered a kind word and some support. Generally speaking, they died early.

Asylums

Asylums originated in European monasteries. They were the first institutions meant primarily for people with psychological disorders. But their function was warehousing, not treatment. Their inmate populations mushroomed until the stresses created by noise, overcrowding, and disease aggravated the problems they were meant to ease. Inmates were frequently chained and beaten.

The word *bedlam* derives from St. Mary's of *Bethlehem*, the London asylum that opened its gates in 1547. Here unfortunate people with psychological disorders were chained, whipped, and allowed to lie in their own waste.

Humanitarian reform movements began in the 18th century. In Paris, the physician Philippe Pinel unchained the patients at La Salpêtrière. Rather than run amok, as had been feared, most patients profited from kindness and freedom. Many eventually reentered society. Later movements to reform institutions were led by William Tuke in England and Dorothea Dix in America.

Mental Hospitals

In the United States, mental hospitals gradually replaced asylums. In the mid-1950s more than a million people resided in state, county, Veterans Administration, or private facilities. The mental hospital's function is treatment, not warehousing. Still, because of high patient populations and understaffing, many patients received little attention. Even today, with somewhat improved conditions, one psychiatrist may be responsible for the welfare of several hundred residents on the weekend when other staff are absent.

The Community Mental Health Movement

Since the 1960s, efforts have been made to maintain people with serious psychological disorders in their communities. Community mental health centers attempt to maintain new patients as outpatients and to serve patients who have been released from mental hospitals. Today, most people with chronic psychological disorders live in the community, not in the hospital.

Social critics note that many people who had resided in hospitals for decades were suddenly discharged to "home" communities that seemed foreign and forbidding to them. Many do not receive adequate follow-up care. Many join the ranks of the homeless (Drury, 2003).

psychodynamic therapy
a type of psychotherapy that is based on Freud's thinking and that assumes that psychological problems reflect early childhood experiences and internal conflicts

13-2 Psychodynamic Therapies

Psychodynamic therapies are based on the thinking of Sigmund Freud, the founder of psychodynamic theory. These therapies assume that psychological problems reflect early childhood experiences and internal conflicts. According to Freud, these conflicts involve the shifting of psychic energy among the id, ego, and superego. These shifts of psychic energy determine our behavior. When primitive urges threaten to break through from the id or

The Unchaining of the Patients at La Salpêtrière Philippe Pinel sparked the humanitarian reform movement by unchaining the patients at this asylum in Paris.

Robert-Fleury, Tony (1837-1912) (after)/Bibliotheque des Arts Decoratifs, Paris, France/Archives Charmet/TheBridgeman Art Library

In his consulting room, Freud would sit in a chair by the head of the couch while a client free-associated. The basic rule for free association is that no thought is censored. Freud did not believe that free association was really "free"; he assumed that significant feelings would rise to the surface and demand expression.

© Prisma Bildagentur AG/Alamy

when the superego floods us with excessive guilt, de-fenses are established and distress is created. Freud's therapy method—psychoanalysis—aims to bulwark the ego against the torrents of energy loosed by the id and the superego. With impulses and feelings of guilt and shame placed under greater control, clients are freer to develop adaptive behavior.

13-2a TRADITIONAL PSYCHOANALYSIS

Imagine your therapist asking you to lie on a couch in a slightly darkened room. She or he would sit behind you and encourage you to talk about anything that comes to mind, no matter how trivial, no matter how personal. To avoid interfering with your self-exploration, she or he might say little or nothing for session after session. That would be par for the course. A traditional psychoanalysis can extend for months, even years.

Psychoanalysis is the clinical method devised by Freud. It aims to provide *insight* into the conflicts that are presumed to lie at the roots of a person's problems. Insight means many things, including knowledge of the experiences that lead to conflicts and maladaptive be-havior, recognition of unconscious feelings and con-flicts, and conscious evaluation of one's thoughts, feelings, and behavior.

Psychoanalysis also aims to help the client express feelings and urges that have been repressed. By so doing, Freud believed that the client spilled forth the psychic energy that had been repressed by conflicts and guilt. He called this "spilling forth" **catharsis**. Catharsis would provide relief by alleviating some of the forces assaulting the ego. Freud also sought to replace impulsive and de-fensive behavior with coping behavior. In this way, for example, a man with a phobia for knives might discover

that he had been repressing the urge to harm someone who had taken advantage of him. He might also find ways to confront the person verbally.

Early in his career as a therapist, Freud found that hypnosis allowed his clients to focus on repressed con-flicts and talk about them. He also found, however, that some clients denied the accuracy of this material once they were out of the trance. Others found the memories to be brought out into the open prema-turely and painfully. Freud therefore turned to **free association**, a more gradual method of breaking through the walls of defense that block a client's insight into unconscious processes. In free association, the cli-ent is made comfortable—for example, by lying on a couch—and asked to talk about any topic that comes to mind. No thought is to be censored—that is the basic rule. Psychoanalysts ask their clients to wander "freely" from topic to topic, but they do not believe that the process occurring *within* the client is fully free. Repressed impulses clamor for release.

The ego persists in trying to repress unacceptable impulses and threatening conflicts. As a result, clients might show **resistance** to recalling and discussing threatening ideas. The therapist observes the dynamic struggle between the compulsion to talk about disturb-ing ideas and resistance. Through discreet comments and questions, the analyst hopes to encourage the cli-ent to discuss his or her problems. Talking helps the client gain insight into his or her true wishes and ex-plore ways of fulfilling them.

Transference

Freud believed that clients not only responded to him as an individual but also in ways that reflected their at-titudes and feelings toward other people in their lives.

He labeled this process **transference**. For example, a young woman client might respond to him as a father figure and displace her feelings toward her father onto Freud, perhaps seeking affection and wisdom. Analyzing and working through transference has been considered a key aspect of psychoanalysis.

Dream Analysis

Freud often asked clients to jot down their dreams upon waking so they could discuss them in therapy. Freud considered dreams the "royal road to the unconscious." He believed that the content of dreams is determined by unconscious processes as well as by the events of the day. Unconscious impulses were expressed in dreams as **wish fulfillment**.

13-2b MODERN PSYCHODYNAMIC APPROACHES

Although some psychoanalysts still adhere to Freud's techniques, modern psychodynamic therapy is briefer and less intense and makes treatment available to clients who do not have the time or money for long-term therapy. Some modern psychodynamic therapies continue to focus on revealing unconscious material and breaking through psychological defenses. Nevertheless, they differ from traditional psychoanalysis in that the client and therapist usually sit face to face (i.e., the client does not lie on a couch) (Prochaska & Norcross, 2010). Modern therapists are usually directive as well. They suggest helpful behavior instead of focusing on insight alone. Finally, there is more focus on the ego as the "executive" of personality and less emphasis on the id. For this reason, many modern psychodynamic therapists are called **ego analysts**.

13-3 Humanistic Therapies

Psychoanalytic therapies focus on internal conflicts and unconscious processes. **Humanistic therapies** focus on the quality of the client's subjective, conscious experience. Traditional psychoanalysis focuses on early childhood experiences. Humanistic therapies are more likely to focus on what clients are experiencing here and now.

13-3a CLIENT-CENTERED THERAPY

Carl Rogers (1902–1987) believed that we are free to make choices and control our destinies, despite the burdens of the past. He also believed that we have natural tendencies toward health, growth, and fulfillment. Psychological problems arise from roadblocks placed in the path of self-actualization—that is, what Rogers believed was an inborn tendency to strive to realize one's potential. If, when we are young, other people approve of us only when we are doing what they want us to do, we may learn to disown the parts of ourselves to which they object. We may learn to be seen but not heard—not even by ourselves. As a result, we may experience stress and discomfort and the feeling that we—or the world—are not real.

transference
responding to one person (such as a psychoanalyst) in a way similar to how one responded to another person (such as a parent) in childhood

wish fulfillment
in dreams, the acting out of ideas and impulses that are repressed when one is conscious

ego analyst
a psychodynamically oriented therapist who focuses on the conscious, coping behavior of the ego instead of the hypothesized, unconscious functioning of the id

humanistic therapy
a form of psychotherapy that focuses on the client's subjective, conscious experience in the "here and now"

CARL ROGERS

Rogers believed that our psychological well-being is connected with our freedom to develop our unique frames of reference and potentials. Do you think you can separate your "real self" from your sociocultural experiences and religious training?

client-centered therapy

Carl Rogers's method of psychotherapy, which emphasizes the creation of a warm, therapeutic atmosphere that frees clients to engage in self-exploration and self-expression

By showing the qualities of unconditional positive regard, empathic understanding, and genuineness, client-centered therapists create an atmosphere in which clients can explore their feelings.

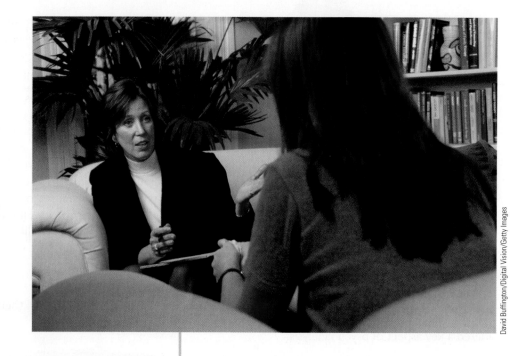

David Buffington/Digital Vision/Getty Images

Client-centered therapy aims to provide insight into the parts of us that we have disowned so that we can feel whole. It creates a warm, therapeutic atmosphere that encourages self-exploration and self-expression. The therapist's acceptance of the client is thought to foster self-acceptance and self-esteem. Self-acceptance frees the client to make choices that develop his or her unique potential.

Client-centered therapy is nondirective. An effective client-centered therapist has several qualities:

TRUTH IT IS TRUE THAT IN CLIENT-CENTERED THERAPY, THE CLIENT TAKES THE LEAD, STATING AND EXPLORING PROBLEMS.

1. *Unconditional positive regard:* respect for clients as human beings with unique values and goals.

2. *Empathy:* recognition of the client's experiences and feelings. Therapists view the world through the client's *frame of reference* by setting aside their own values and listening closely.

3. *Genuineness:* Openness and honesty in responding to the client. Client-centered therapists must be able to tolerate differentness because they believe that every client is different in important ways.

The following excerpt from a therapy session shows how Carl Rogers uses empathetic understanding and paraphrases a client's (Jill's) feelings. His goal is to help her recognize feelings that she has partially disowned:

Jill: *I'm having a lot of problems dealing with my daughter. She's twenty years old; she's in college; I'm having a lot of trouble letting her go.... And I have a lot of guilt feelings about her; I have a real need to hang on to her.*

C. R.: *A need to hang on so you can kind of make up for the things you feel guilty about. Is that part of it?*
Jill: *There's a lot of that.... Also, she's been a real friend to me, and filled my life.... And it's very hard.... a lot of empty places now that she's not with me.*
C. R.: *The old vacuum, sort of, when she's not there.*

Jill: *Yes. Yes. I also would like to be the kind of mother that could be strong and say, you know, "Go and have a good life," and this is really hard for me, to do that.*
C. R.: *It's very hard to give up something that's been so precious in your life, but also something that I guess has caused you pain when you mentioned guilt.*
Jill: *Yeah. And I'm aware that I have some anger toward her that I don't always get what I want. I have needs that are not met. And, uh, I don't feel I have a right to those needs. You know ... she's a daughter; she's not my mother. Though sometimes I feel as if I'd like her to mother me ... it's very difficult for me to ask for that and have a right to it.*
C. R.: *So, it may be unreasonable, but still, when she doesn't meet your needs, it makes you mad.*
Jill: *Yeah, I get very angry, very angry with her.*
C. R.: *(Pauses) You're also feeling a little tension at this point, I guess.*
Jill: *Yeah. Yeah. A lot of conflict.... (C. R.: M-hm.) A lot of pain.*
C. R.: *A lot of pain. Can you say anything more about what that's about? (Farber et al., 1996, pp. 74–75)*

Client-centered therapy is practiced widely in college and university counseling centers, not just to help students experiencing, say, anxieties or depression but also to help them make decisions. Many college students have not yet made career choices, or wonder whether they should become involved with particular people or in sexual activity. Client-centered therapists do not tell clients what to do. Instead, they help clients arrive at their own decisions.

13-3b GESTALT THERAPY

Gestalt therapy was originated by Fritz Perls (1893–1970). Like client-centered therapy, Gestalt therapy assumes that people disown parts of themselves that might meet with social disapproval or rejection. People also don social masks, pretending to be things that they are not. Therapy aims to help individuals integrate conflicting parts of their personality. Perls used the term *Gestalt* to signify his interest in giving the conflicting parts of the personality an integrated form or shape. (The German word *Gestalt* means "unified whole.") Perls adopted the term because he wanted to help clients integrate conflicting parts of their personalities.

TRUTH GESTALT THERAPISTS AND BEHAVIOR THERAPISTS MAY USE SPECIFIC PROCEDURES—TELLING THEIR CLIENTS WHAT TO DO.

"I DO MY THING AND YOU DO YOURS. I AM NOT IN THIS WORLD TO LIVE UP TO YOUR EXPECTATIONS, AND YOU ARE NOT IN THIS WORLD TO MEET UP WITH MINE. YOU ARE YOU AND I AM I, AND IF BY CHANCE WE FIND EACH OTHER, THEN IT IS BEAUTIFUL. IF NOT, IT CAN'T BE HELPED."
—FRITZ PERLS

Although Perls's ideas about conflicting personality elements owe much to psychodynamic theory, his form of therapy, unlike psychoanalysis, focuses on the here and now. Exercises heighten clients' awareness of their current feelings and behavior. Perls also believed, along with Rogers, that people are free to make choices and to direct their personal growth. But the charismatic and forceful Perls was unlike the gentle and accepting Rogers in temperament (Prochaska & Norcross, 2010). Thus, unlike client-centered therapy, Gestalt therapy is directive. The therapist leads the client through planned experiences to heighten their awareness of inner conflict and take responsibility for their behavior.

13-4 Behavior Therapy

Psychodynamic and humanistic forms of therapy tend to focus on what people think and feel. Behavior therapists tend to focus on what people *do*. **Behavior therapy**—also called *behavior modification*—applies principles of learning to directly promote desired behavioral changes. Behavior therapists rely heavily on principles of conditioning and observational learning. They help clients discontinue self-defeating behavior patterns such as overeating, smoking, and phobic avoidance of harmless stimuli. They help clients acquire adaptive behavior patterns such as the social skills required to start social relationships or say no to insistent salespeople.

Behavior therapists may help clients gain "insight" into maladaptive behaviors such as feelings of anxiety by helping the person become aware of the circumstances in which the behaviors occur. They do not help unearth the childhood origins of problems and the symbolic meanings of maladaptive behaviors as psychoanalysts do. Behavior therapists, like other therapists, may also build warm, therapeutic relationships with clients, but they see the effectiveness of behavior therapy as deriving from specific, learning-based procedures (Rachman, 2000). They insist that their methods be established by experimentation and that results be assessed in terms of measurable behavior. In this section we consider some frequently used behavior-therapy techniques.

Gestalt therapy Fritz Perls's form of psychotherapy, which attempts to integrate conflicting parts of the personality through directive methods designed to help clients perceive their whole selves

behavior therapy systematic application of the principles of learning to the direct modification of a client's problem behaviors

systematic desensitization

Wolpe's method for reducing fears by associating a hierarchy of images of fear-evoking stimuli with deep muscle relaxation

modeling

a behavior-therapy technique in which a client observes and imitates a person who approaches and copes with feared objects or situations

13-4a FEAR-REDUCTION METHODS

Many people seek therapy because of fears and phobias that interfere with their functioning. This is one of the areas in which behavior therapy has made great inroads. Behavior-therapy methods for reducing fears include *flooding* (see Chapter 5, page 118), *systematic desensitization*, *virtual therapy*, and *modeling*.

Systematic Desensitization

Adam has a phobia for receiving injections. His behavior therapist treats him as he reclines in a comfortable padded chair. In a state of deep muscle relaxation, Adam observes slides projected on a screen. A slide of a nurse holding a needle has just been shown three times, 30 seconds at a time. Each time Adam has shown no anxiety. So now a slightly more discomforting slide is shown: one of the nurse aiming the needle toward someone's bare arm. After 15 seconds, our armchair adventurer notices twinges of discomfort and raises a finger as a signal (speaking might disturb his relaxation). The projector operator turns off the light, and Adam spends 2 minutes imagining his "safe scene"—lying on a beach beneath the tropical sun. Then the slide is shown again. This time Adam views it for 30 seconds before feeling anxiety.

THE AUTHOR'S FILES

Adam is undergoing **systematic desensitization**, a method for reducing phobic responses originated by

TRUTH USING SYSTEMATIC DESENSITIZATION, A PERSON CAN IN EFFECT CONFRONT HIS OR HER FEAR WHILE LYING IN A RECLINER AND RELAXING.

psychiatrist Joseph Wolpe (1915–1997). Systematic desensitization is a gradual process in which the client learns to handle increasingly disturbing stimuli while anxiety to each one is being counterconditioned. About 10 to 20 stimuli such as slides are arranged in a sequence, or *hierarchy*, according to their capacity to trigger anxiety. In imagination or by being shown photos, the client travels gradually up through this hierarchy, counterconditioning anxiety with relaxation step by step as he or she approaches the target. In Adam's case, the target was the ability to receive an injection without undue anxiety.

Virtual Therapy

Virtual therapy may use more elaborate equipment than slides, but the principle is desensitization. New York Fire Chief Stephen King was in the north tower at the World Trade Center on September 11, 2001, which was hit first by the airplanes. The experience led him to retire from the department, avoid bridges and tunnels, and stay out of Manhattan (King, 2005). "Where I was and what I saw that day—the many people that jumped, the magnitude of it—was just overwhelming."

But virtual therapy has helped King face the past—and his future. Using the technology we find in video games, programs mimic traumatic settings and events—public speaking in an auditorium, flying in an airplane, spiders, or, in King's case, images of the World Trade Center (see Figure 13.2). "The idea behind the treatment," explains Dr. JoAnn Difede (2005), "is to systematically expose the patient to aspects of their experience in a graded fashion so they can confront their fear of the trauma."

Modeling

Modeling relies on observational learning. In this method, clients observe and then imitate people who approach and cope with the objects or situations that the clients fear. Albert Bandura and his colleagues (1969) found that modeling worked as well as systematic desensitization—and more rapidly—in reducing fear of snakes. Clients observed models handling snakes. In the same session, they were able to touch the snakes, pick them up, and let them crawl on their bodies. Modeling also

---

FIGURE 13.2

A Program Containing Images of the World Trade Center Intended to Help People with Posttraumatic Stress Disorder

Virtual therapy clients are exposed to virtual stimuli that represent their source of anxiety and stress to help them gradually confront their fears.

Image and Copyright by Hunter Hoffman, U.W. Virtual World Programmed by Howard Abrams.

increases self-efficacy expectations in coping with feared stimuli.

13-4b AVERSIVE CONDITIONING

Many people also seek behavior therapy because they want to break bad habits, such as smoking, excessive drinking, nail-biting, and the like. One behavior-therapy approach to helping people do so is **aversive conditioning**. Aversive conditioning is a controversial procedure that pairs painful or aversive stimuli with unwanted impulses to make the impulse less appealing. For example, to help people control alcohol intake, tastes of different alcoholic beverages can be paired with drug-induced nausea and vomiting or with electric shock.

 TRUTH IN THE METHOD OF RAPID SMOKING, BEHAVIOR THERAPISTS USE SMOKING AS A WAY OF MAKING CIGARETTE SMOKE UNAPPEALING TO SMOKERS, HELPING THEM TO STOP SMOKING.

Aversive conditioning has been used with problems as diverse as cigarette smoking and sexual abuse. *Rapid smoking* is an aversive conditioning method designed to help smokers quit. In this method, the would-be quitter inhales every six seconds. In another method, the hose of a hair dryer is hooked up to a chamber containing several lit cigarettes. Smoke is blown into the quitter's face as he or she also smokes a cigarette. A third method uses branching pipes so that the smoker draws in smoke from several cigarettes at the same time. In these methods, overexposure makes once-desirable cigarette smoke aversive. The quitter becomes motivated to avoid, rather than seek, cigarettes. Interest in aversive conditioning for quitting smoking has waned, however, because of side effects such as raising blood pressure and the availability of nicotine-replacement techniques.

13-4c OPERANT CONDITIONING PROCEDURES

We tend to repeat behavior that is reinforced. Behavior that is not reinforced tends to become extinguished. Behavior therapists have used these principles of operant conditioning with psychotic patients as well as with clients with milder problems.

The staff at one mental hospital was at a loss about how to encourage withdrawn schizophrenic patients to

eat regularly. Psychologists observed that staff members were making the problem worse by coaxing patients into the dining room and even feeding them. Staff attention apparently reinforced the patients' lack of cooperation. Some rules were changed (Dickerson et al., 2005). Patients who did not arrive at the dining hall within 30 minutes after serving were locked out. Staff could not interact with patients at mealtime. With uncooperative behavior no longer reinforced, patients quickly changed their eating habits. Then patients were required to pay one penny to enter the dining hall. Pennies were earned by interacting with other patients and showing other socially appropriate behaviors. These target behaviors also became more frequent.

Health professionals are concerned about whether people who are, or have been, dependent on alcohol can exercise control over their drinking. One study showed that rewards for remaining abstinent from alcohol can exert a powerful effect (Petry et al., 2000). In the study, one group of alcohol-dependent veterans was given a standard treatment while another group received the treatment *plus* the chance to win prizes for remaining alcohol-free, as measured by a Breathalyzer test. By the end of the eight-week treatment period, 84% of the veterans who could win prizes remained in the program, as compared with 22% of the standard treatment group. The prizes had an average value of $200, far less than what alcohol-related absenteeism from work and other responsibilities can cost.

© Lester Sloan/Woodfin Camp & Associates

In aversive conditioning, unwanted behaviors take on a noxious quality as a result of being repeatedly paired with aversive stimuli. Overexposure is making cigarette smoke aversive to this smoker.

AVERSIVE CONDITIONING

Glossary (margin)

token economy
a controlled environment in which people are reinforced for desired behaviors with tokens (such as poker chips) that may be exchanged for privileges

successive approximations
in operant conditioning, a series of behaviors that gradually become more similar to a target behavior

social skills training
a behavior-therapy method for helping people in their interpersonal relations that uses self-monitoring, behavior rehearsal, and feedback

biofeedback training (BFT)
the systematic feeding back to an organism of information about a bodily function so that the organism can gain control of that function

The Token Economy

Many psychiatric wards and hospitals use **token economies** in which patients need tokens such as poker chips to purchase TV viewing time, extra visits to the canteen, or a private room (Comaty et al., 2001). The tokens are dispensed as reinforcers for productive activities such as making beds, brushing teeth, and socializing. Token economies have not eliminated all symptoms of schizophrenia but have increased patients' activity and cooperation. Tokens have also been used to modify the behavior of children with conduct disorders.

Successive Approximations

The operant conditioning method of **successive approximations** is often used to help clients build good habits. For example: You want to study three hours each evening but can concentrate for only half an hour. Rather than attempting to increase your study time all at once, you could do so gradually by adding, say, five minutes each evening. After every hour or so of studying, you could reinforce yourself with five minutes of people-watching in a busy section of the library.

Social Skills Training

In **social skills training**, behavior therapists decrease social anxiety and build social skills through operant-conditioning procedures that employ *self-monitoring* (keeping a record of one's own behavior to identify problems and record successes), coaching, modeling, role-playing, *behavior rehearsal* (practicing), and *feedback* (receiving information about the effectiveness of behavior). Social skills training has been used to help formerly hospitalized mental patients maintain jobs and apartments in the community. For example, a worker can rehearse politely asking a supervisor for assistance or asking a landlord to fix the plumbing in an apartment. Social skills training is effective in groups. Group members can role-play key people—such as parents, spouses, or potential dates—in the lives of other members.

Biofeedback Training

Through **biofeedback training (BFT)**, therapists help clients become more aware of, and gain control over, various bodily functions. Therapists attach clients to devices that measure bodily functions such as heart rate. "Bleeps" or other electronic signals are used to indicate (and thereby reinforce) changes ("operants") in the desired direction—for example, a slower heart rate. (Knowledge of results is a powerful reinforcer.) One device, the electromyograph (EMG), monitors muscle tension. It has been used to increase control over muscle tension in the forehead and elsewhere, thereby al-

---

✳ Eye-Movement Desensitization and Reprocessing

Helping professionals are often inspired to develop therapy methods based on their personal experiences. As Francine Shapiro (1989) paints it, she had troubling thoughts on her mind when she entered a park. But as her eyes darted about, taking in the scene, she found her troubled thoughts disappearing. Thus, she developed a therapy method called *eye-movement desensitization and reprocessing (EMDR)* to join the arsenal of therapeutic weapons against stress disorders. With this method, the client is asked to imagine a traumatic scene while the therapist moves a finger rapidly back and forth before his or her eyes for about 20–30 seconds. The client follows the finger while keeping the troubling scene in mind. The client tells the therapist what he or she was thinking and how he or she felt during the procedure. The procedure is repeated until the client's anxiety is relieved. Treatment takes about three 90-minute sessions.

Evidence from a number of studies suggests that EMDR helps decrease the anxiety associated with traumatic events (Engelhard et al., 2010; Van der Kolk et al., 2007). One study, for example, compared the effectiveness of EMDR with two alternative treatments: exposure therapy (as in virtual therapy for spider phobia) and relaxation training (Taylor et al., 2003). Another study looked at the effectiveness of EMDR on numerous people following September 11 (Silver et al., 2005). These studies and others suggest that EMDR is effective, but it remains unclear how effective EMDR is and why it works (May, 2005; Schubert & Lee, 2009). Research also challenges the idea that eye movements are necessary (Devilly, 2002; Schubert & Lee, 2009). Perhaps clients receiving EMDR profit from their relationship with the therapist and from expectations of success. Moreover, the client is to some degree exposed to the trauma that haunts him or her under circumstances in which the client believes he or she will be able to manage the trauma.

Conclusion? Exposure helps people cope with trauma. Eye movements may not be needed.

Bananastock/Jupiterimages

---

318   Methods of Therapy

leviating anxiety, stress, and headaches (Nestoriuc et al., 2008).

BFT also helps clients voluntarily regulate functions once thought to be beyond conscious control, such as heart rate and blood pressure. Hypertensive clients use a blood-pressure cuff and electronic signals to gain control over their blood pressure. The electroencephalograph (EEG) monitors brain waves and can be used to teach people how to produce alpha waves, which are associated with relaxation. Some people have overcome insomnia by learning to produce the kinds of brain waves associated with sleep.

13-5 Cognitive Therapies

What thoughts do you have when things go wrong at school or on the job? Do you tell yourself that you're facing a problem that needs a solution? That you've successfully solved problems before and will be able to create a solution this time? Or do you think, "Oh no! This is awful! It's going to get worse, and I'm going to flunk (or get fired)!" If you go the "This is awful" route, you are probably heightening your discomfort and impairing your coping ability. Cognitive therapy focuses directly on your thoughts and encourages ideas that will help you solve problems rather than blow them out of proportion and magnify your discomfort.

"There is nothing either good or bad, but thinking makes it so."
—SHAKESPEARE, HAMLET

Cognitive therapy focuses on changing the beliefs, attitudes, and automatic types of thinking that create and compound people's problems (Butler et al., 2006; David et al., 2010). Cognitive therapists, like psychoanalytic and humanistic therapists, aim to foster self-insight, but they mainly aim to help make people more aware of their *current cognitions*. Cognitive therapists also aim to directly change maladaptive thoughts in an effort to reduce negative feelings and help clients solve problems.

Many behavior therapists incorporate cognitive procedures in their methods. For example, techniques such as systematic desensitization, covert sensitization, and covert reinforcement ask clients to focus on visual imagery. Behavioral methods for treating bulimia nervosa focus on clients' irrational attitudes toward their weight and body shape as well as foster good eating habits. Let's look at the approaches and methods of the cognitive therapists Aaron Beck and Albert Ellis.

13-5a AARON BECK'S COGNITIVE THERAPY

Psychiatrist Aaron Beck began his professional life as a psychoanalyst. He became impatient, however, with analysis's lengthy methods and reluctance to offer specific advice. In his own life he had successfully defeated his fear of blood by assisting in surgical operations and argued himself out of irrational fear of driving through tunnels. Similarly, his methods of cognitive therapy focus on arguing clients out of beliefs that are making them miserable and exposing them to situations they avoid because of irrational fear (Berk et al., 2004; Warman et al., 2005). Beck encourages clients to become their own personal scientists and challenge feelings and beliefs that make no sense.

Beck encourages clients to see the irrationality of their ways of thinking. For example, depressed people tend to minimize their accomplishments and to assume that the worst will happen. Minimizing accomplishments and expecting the worst are (usually) distortions of reality that lead to feelings of depression. Cognitive distortions can be fleeting and automatic, difficult to detect. Beck's methods help clients become aware of such distortions and challenge them.

Beck notes a number of "cognitive errors" that contribute to clients' miseries:

1. Clients may *selectively perceive* the world as a harmful place and ignore evidence to the contrary.

2. Clients may *overgeneralize* on the basis of a few examples. For example, they may perceive themselves as worthless because they were laid off at work or as unattractive because they were refused a date.

3. Clients may *magnify*, or blow out of proportion, the importance of negative events. They may catastrophize failing a test by assuming they will flunk out of college or catastrophize losing a job by believing that they will never find another one and that serious harm will befall their family as a result.

4. Clients may engage in *absolutist thinking*, or looking at the world in black and white rather than in shades of gray. In doing so, a rejection on a date takes on the meaning of a lifetime of loneliness; an uncomfortable illness takes on life-threatening proportions.

cognitive therapy
a form of therapy that focuses on how clients' cognitions (e.g., expectations, attitudes, beliefs) lead to distress and may be modified to relieve distress and promote adaptive behavior

Becoming aware of cognitive errors and modifying catastrophizing thoughts help us cope with stress. Internal, stable, and global attributions of failure lead to depression and feelings of helplessness. Cognitive therapists also alert clients to cognitive errors or irrational thoughts so that the clients can change their attitudes and pave the way for more effective overt behavior.

13-5b ALBERT ELLIS'S RATIONAL EMOTIVE BEHAVIOR THERAPY

In **rational emotive behavior therapy (REBT)**, Albert Ellis (1913–2007) pointed out that our beliefs *about* events, not only the events themselves, shape our responses to them. Moreover, many of us harbor a number of irrational beliefs that can give rise to problems or magnify their impact. Two of the most important ones are the belief that we must have the love and approval of people who are important to us and the belief that we must prove ourselves to be thoroughly competent, adequate, and achieving.

Ellis, like Beck, began his career as a psychoanalyst. And, also like Beck, he became disturbed by the passive role of the analyst and by the slow rate of obtaining results—if they were obtained at all. Ellis's REBT methods are active and directive. He did not sit back like the traditional psychoanalyst and occasionally offer an interpretation. Instead, he urged clients to seek out their irrational beliefs, which can be unconscious, though not as deeply buried as Freud believed. Nevertheless, they can be hard to pinpoint without some di-

Aaron Beck (left) and Albert Ellis (right)

"I get people to truly accept themselves unconditionally, whether or not their therapist or anyone loves them."
—ALBERT ELLIS

rection. Ellis showed clients how those beliefs lead to misery and challenged clients to change them. When Ellis saw clients behaving according to irrational beliefs, he refuted the beliefs by asking "Where is it written that you must …?" or "What evidence do you have that …?" According to Ellis, we need less misery and less blaming in our lives, and more action.

13-5c TOWARD A COGNITIVE-BEHAVIORAL THERAPY

Many theorists consider cognitive therapy to be a collection of techniques that are a part of behavior therapy. Aaron Beck himself appears to be comfortable referring to his approach as *cognitive* in one article and *cognitive-behavioral* in another (Clark & Beck, 2011; Warman & Beck, 2003). We are apparently headed toward an integration of the two approaches that is termed **cognitive-behavioral therapy (CBT)**.

Ellis straddled behavioral and cognitive therapies. He originally dubbed his method of therapy *rational-emotive therapy,* because his focus was on the cognitive—irrational beliefs and how to change them. However,

Group therapy is more economical than individual therapy, group members can practice social skills with one another, and members can learn from the experiences of others.

Manchan/Photographer's Choice RF/Getty Images

Ellis also always promoted behavioral changes to cement cognitive changes. In keeping with his broad philosophy, he recently changed the name of rational-emotive therapy to rational-emotive *behavior* therapy.

13-6 Group Therapies

When a psychotherapist has several clients with similar problems—anxiety, depression, adjustment to divorce, lack of social skills—it often makes sense to treat them in a group rather than in individual sessions. The methods and characteristics of the group reflect the needs of the members and the theoretical orientation of the leader. In group psychoanalysis, clients might interpret one another's dreams. In a client-centered group, they might provide an accepting atmosphere for self-exploration. Members of behavior therapy groups might be jointly desensitized to anxiety-evoking stimuli or might practice social skills together.

Group therapy has the following advantages:

1. It is economical (Prochaska & Norcross, 2010). It allows the therapist to work with several clients at once.

2. Compared with one-to-one therapy, group therapy provides more information and life experience for clients to draw on.

3. Appropriate behavior receives group support. Clients usually appreciate an outpouring of peer approval.

4. When we run into troubles, it is easy to imagine that we are different from other people or inferior to them. Affiliating with people with similar problems is reassuring.

5. Group members who show improvement provide hope for other members.

6. Many individuals seek therapy because of problems in relating to other people. People who seek therapy for other reasons also may be socially inhibited. Members of groups have the opportunity to practice social skills in a relatively nonthreatening atmosphere. In a group consisting of men and women of different ages, group members can role-play one another's employers, employees, spouses, parents, children, and friends. Members can role-play asking one another out on dates, saying no (or yes), and so on.

But group therapy is not for everyone. Some clients fare better with individual treatment. Many prefer not to disclose their problems to a group. They may be overly shy or want individual attention. It is the responsibility of the therapist to insist that group disclosures be kept confidential, to establish a supportive atmosphere, and to ensure that group members obtain the attention they need.

Many types of therapy can be conducted either individually or in groups. Couple therapy and family therapy are conducted only with groups.

13-6a COUPLE THERAPY

Couple therapy helps couples enhance their relationship by improving their communication skills and helping them manage conflict (Prochaska & Norcross, 2010). There are often power imbalances in relationships, and couple therapy helps individuals find "full membership" in the couple. Correcting power imbalances increases happiness and can decrease the incidence of domestic violence. Ironically, in situations of domestic violence, the partner with *less* power in the relationship is usually the violent one. Violence sometimes appears to be a way of compensating for inability to share power in other ways (Rathus & Sanderson, 1999).

Today the main approach to couple therapy is cognitive-behavioral (Rathus & Sanderson, 1999). It teaches couples communications skills (such as how to listen and express feelings), ways of handling feelings like anger, and ways of solving problems.

13-6b FAMILY THERAPY

Family therapy is a form of group therapy in which one or more families constitute the group. Family therapy may be undertaken from various theoretical viewpoints. One is the *systems approach*, in which family interaction is studied and modified to enhance the growth of individual family members and of the family unit as a whole (Prochaska & Norcross, 2010).

Family members with low self-esteem often cannot tolerate different attitudes and behaviors in other family members. Faulty communication within the family also creates problems. In addition, it is not uncommon for the family to present an "identified patient"—that is, the family member who has *the* problem and is *causing* all the trouble. Yet family therapists usually assume that the identified patient is a scapegoat for other problems among family members. It is a sort of myth: Change the "bad apple," or identified patient, and the "barrel," or family, will be functional once more. The family therapist attempts to teach the family to communicate and encourage growth and autonomy in each family member.

> It is a sort of myth: Change the "bad apple," or identified patient, and the "barrel," or family, will be functional once more.

13-6c SELF-HELP AND SUPPORT GROUPS

Millions of people in the United States and elsewhere are involved in self-help and support groups that meet in person, online, or even by telephone. Some self-help and support groups enable people who have been treated for psychological disorders to reach out to others who have had similar experiences (Greidanus & Everall, 2010). These groups tend to be specific, such as groups for parents of children with autistic disorders, intellectual deficiency, or Down syndrome. Members share problems and possible solutions.

The best known of self-help and support groups is Alcoholics Anonymous (AA), whose 12-step program has been used by millions of people in the United States and around the world. Members meet regularly and call other members between meetings when they are tempted to drink. The 12 steps require admitting before the group that one's drinking is out of control, calling upon a higher power for strength, examining injurious behavior, and attempting to make amends.

Does AA work? The organization itself admits that the majority of new recruits drop out within a year. Of greater concern is a meta-analysis that concluded that AA is actually less effective than no treatment at all (Kownacki & Shadish, 1999). But most analyses suggest that AA is as effective as all forms of psychotherapy tested. When treatments, including AA, *are* effective, it seems to be because alcoholics remain in treatment for many years (Moos & Moos, 2006), alleviate feelings of depression (Kelly et al, 2010), and heighten their confidence that they can navigate challenges without drinking (Forcehimes & Tonigan, 2008).

13-7 Does Psychotherapy Work?

In 1952, the British psychologist Hans Eysenck published a review of psychotherapy research—"The Effects of Psychotherapy"—that sent shock waves through the psychotherapy community. On the basis of his review of the research, Eysenck concluded that the rate of improvement among people in psychotherapy was no greater than the rate of "spontaneous remission"—that is, the rate of improvement that would be shown by people with psychological disorders who received no treatment.

Thinkstock Images/Comstock/Jupiterimages

Eysenck was not addressing people with schizophrenia, who typically profit from biological forms of therapy, but he argued that whether or not people with problems such as anxiety and depression received therapy, two of three reported substantial improvement within two years.

That was over half a century ago. Research on the effectiveness of therapy conducted since then has been encouraging (Driessen et al., 2010; Shedler, 2010). In their classic early use of meta-analysis, Mary Lee Smith and Gene Glass (1977) analyzed the results of dozens of studies and concluded that people who obtained psychodynamic therapy showed greater well-being, on average, than 70% to 75% of those who did not obtain treatment. Similarly, nearly 75% of the clients who obtained client-centered therapy were better off than people who did not obtain treatment. Psychodynamic and client-centered therapies appear to be most effective with well-educated, verbal, strongly motivated clients who report problems with anxiety, depression (of light to moderate proportions), and interpersonal relationships. Neither form of therapy appears to be effective with people with psychotic disorders such as major depression, bipolar disorder, and schizophrenia.

FICTION ACTUALLY, THERE IS NOW A GREAT DEAL OF RESEARCH EVIDENCE THAT SHOWS THAT PSYCHOTHERAPY IS EFFECTIVE.

Studies of cognitive therapy have shown that modifying irrational beliefs of the type described by Albert Ellis helps people with problems such as anxiety and depression (David et al., 2010). Modifying self-defeating beliefs of the sort outlined by Aaron Beck also frequently alleviates anxiety and depression (Butler et al., 2006). Cognitive therapy may help people with severe depression, who had been thought responsive only to biological therapies (Hollon & Shelton, 2001; Simons et al., 1995). Cognitive therapy has also helped people with personality disorders (Beck et al., 2001; Trull et al., 2003).

Behavioral and cognitive therapies have provided strategies for treating anxiety disorders, social skills deficits, and problems in self-control (DeRubeis & Crits-Christoph, 1998). These therapies have helped couples and families in distress (Baucom et al., 2002). Moreover, they have modified behaviors related to health problems such as headaches (Verhagen et al., 2009), smoking, chronic pain, and bulimia (Agras et al., 2000; Butler et al., 2006). Cognitive-behavior therapists have innovated treatments for sexual dysfunctions for which there previously were no effective treatments.

13-7a EVIDENCE-BASED PRACTICES

Experimentation is the gold standard for research in psychology, and a number of methods of therapy have been shown to be effective in carefully conducted, random controlled experiments (RCEs)—that is, experiments in which participants are assigned at random to a specific treatment or to a control treatment. The researchers in many of these studies also rely on treatment manuals that concretely outline the treatment methods. Treatment methods that survive these grueling tests are called *evidence-based practices* (Anchin & Pincus, 2010; Bruce & Sanderson, 2004). Table 13.1 shows a number of evidence-based practices and the problems for which they have been found effective. Other treatments may eventually be added as more evidence accumulates.

Many therapists argue that evidence-based practices favor cognitive-behavioral therapies because they are more readily standardized in treatment manuals and can be followed more accurately by practitioners in experiments (Kazdin, 2008; Levy & Ablon, 2009). Alternative treatments, such as psychodynamic therapy, are not so easily standardized or practiced. Therefore, they may not hold up as well in controlled trials. Second, critics assert that most studies supportive of evidence-based practices do not capture the complexity and uniqueness of real clients seen in community settings (Westen et al., 2006). And as we see in the following section on ethnicity and psychotherapy, we must also consider the sociocultural features of clients in determining how to make therapy most effective.

TABLE 13.1

Examples of Evidence-Based Practices

TREATMENT	CONDITION FOR WHICH TREATMENT IS EFFECTIVE
Cognitive therapy	Depression Headache
Behavior therapy or behavior modification	Depression Developmental disabilities Enuresis (bed-wetting)
Cognitive-behavior therapy	Panic disorder with and without agoraphobia Generalized anxiety disorder Bulimia nervosa
Exposure treatment	Agoraphobia and specific phobia
Exposure and response prevention	Obsessive–compulsive disorder
Parent training programs	Children with oppositional behavior

© Cengage Learning 2012

13-7b ETHNICITY AND PSYCHOTHERAPY

Americans from ethnic minority groups are less likely than European Americans to seek therapy (Chen & Rizzo, 2010; Sue et al., 2009). Reasons for their lower participation rate include:

- Lack of awareness that therapy would help
- Lack of information about the availability of professional services or inability to pay for them
- Distrust of professionals, particularly European American professionals and (for women) male professionals
- Language barriers
- Reluctance to open up about personal matters to strangers—especially strangers who are not members of one's own ethnic group
- Cultural inclinations toward other approaches to problem solving, such as religious approaches and psychic healers
- Negative experiences with professionals and authority figures

There are thus many reasons that clinicians need to be sensitive to the cultural heritage, language, and values of their clients. That is, they need to develop multicultural competence (Sue et al., 2009). Let's consider some of the issues involved in conducting psychotherapy with African Americans, Asian Americans, Latin Americans, and Native Americans.

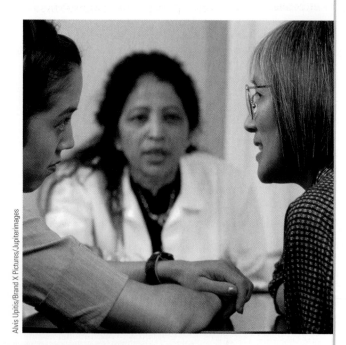

Psychologists need to be sensitive to the cultural heritages, languages, and values of their clients.

African Americans

African Americans often are reluctant to seek psychological help because of cultural assumptions that people should manage their own problems (González et al., 2010; Jackson & Greene, 2000). Many African Americans are also suspicious of their therapists—especially when the therapist is a European American (Mohr et al., 2010). They may withhold personal information because of society's history of racial discrimination (Dana, 2002).

Asian Americans

Asian Americans tend to stigmatize people with psychological disorders. As a result, they may deny problems and refuse to seek help for them (Spencer et al., 2010). Asian Americans, especially recent immigrants, also may not understand or believe in Western approaches to psychotherapy. For example, Western psychotherapy typically encourages people to express their feelings. This mode of behavior may conflict with the Asian tradition of public restraint. Many Asians also experience psychological problems as physical symptoms (Kim & Omizo, 2003; Sue et al., 2009). Rather than thinking of themselves as anxious, they may focus on physical features of anxiety such as a pounding heart and heavy sweating.

Latin Americans

Therapists need to be aware of potential conflicts between the traditional Latin American value of interdependence in the family and the typical European American belief in independence and self-reliance (Garza & Watts, 2010). Measures like the following may help bridge the gaps between psychotherapists and Latin American clients:

- Interacting with clients in the language requested by them or, if this is not possible, referring them to professionals who can do so.
- Using methods that are consistent with the client's values and levels of acculturation, as suggested by fluency in English and level of education.
- Developing therapy methods that incorporate clients' cultural values (Cervantes & Parham, 2005). Malgady and his colleagues (1990), for example, use *cuento therapy* with Puerto Ricans. *Cuento therapy* uses traditional folktales (*cuentos*) with characters who serve as models for adaptive behavior.

Native Americans

Many psychological disorders experienced by Native Americans involve the disruption of their traditional culture caused by European colonization (Olson, 2003; Viets et al., 2009). Loss of cultural identity and social disorganization have set the stage for problems such as alcoholism, substance abuse, and depression. Efforts to prevent psychological disorders do well to focus on strengthening Native American cultural identity, pride, and cohesion.

Psychotherapy is most effective when therapists attend to and respect people's cultural as well as individual differences. Although it is the individual who experiences psychological anguish, the fault can often be traced to cultural issues.

13-8 Biological Therapies

The kinds of therapy we have discussed are psychological in nature—forms of *psycho*therapy. Psychotherapies apply *psychological* principles to treatment, principles based on psychological knowledge of matters such as learning and motivation. However, people with psychological disorders are also often treated with biological therapies. Biological therapies apply what is known of people's *biological* structures and processes to the amelioration of psychological disorders. For example, they may work by altering events in the nervous system, as by changing the action of neurotransmitters. In this section, we discuss three biological, or medical, approaches to treating people with psychological disorders: drug therapy, electroconvulsive therapy, and psychosurgery.

13-8a DRUG THERAPY

In the 1950s, Fats Domino popularized the song "My Blue Heaven." Fats was singing about the sky and happiness. Today, "blue heavens" is one of the street names for the 10-milligram dose of the antianxiety drug Valium. Clinicians prescribe Valium and other drugs for people with various psychological disorders.

rebound anxiety
anxiety that can occur when one discontinues use of a tranquilizer

Antianxiety Drugs

Most antianxiety drugs, such as Valium and Ativan, belong to the chemical class known as *benzodiazepines*. Antianxiety drugs are usually prescribed for outpatients who complain of generalized anxiety or panic attacks, although many people also use them as sleeping pills. Valium and other antianxiety drugs depress the activity of the central nervous system (CNS). The CNS, in turn, decreases sympathetic activity, reducing the heart rate, respiration rate, and feelings of nervousness and tension. Many people come to tolerate antianxiety drugs very quickly. When tolerance occurs, dosages must be increased for the drug to remain effective.

Sedation (feeling of being tired or drowsy) is the most common side effect of antianxiety drugs. Problems associated with withdrawal from these drugs include **rebound anxiety**. That is, some people who have been using these drugs regularly report that their anxiety becomes worse than before once they discontinue them. Antianxiety drugs can induce physical dependence, as evidenced by withdrawal symptoms such as tremors, sweating, insomnia, and rapid heartbeat.

Antipsychotic Drugs

People with schizophrenia are often given antipsychotic drugs (also called *major tranquilizers*). In most cases, these drugs reduce agitation, delusions, and hallucinations. Many antipsychotic drugs, including phenothiazines (e.g., Thorazine) and clozapine (Clozaril) are thought to act by blocking dopamine receptors in the brain (Porsolt

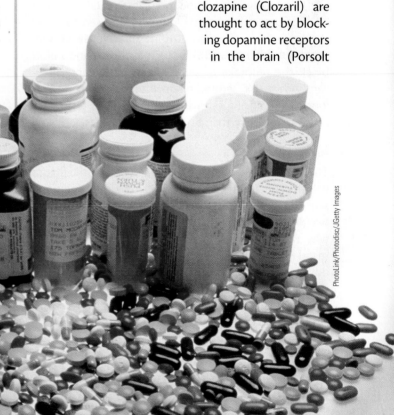

PhotoLink/Photodisc/JGetty Images

antidepressant
acting to relieve depression

selective serotonin-reuptake inhibitors (SSRIs)
antidepressant drugs that work by blocking the reuptake of serotonin by presynaptic neurons, thus increasing the amount of serotonin available to the brain

electroconvulsive therapy (ECT)
treatment of disorders like major depression by passing an electric current (that causes a convulsion) through the head

In electroconvulsive therapy (ECT), electrodes are placed on each side of the patient's head and a current is passed between them, inducing a seizure. ECT is used mainly in cases of major depression when antidepressant drugs and psychotherapy are not sufficient.

WILL MCINTYRE/Photo Researchers/Getty Images

et al., 2010). Research along these lines supports the theory that schizophrenia is connected with overactivity of the neurotransmitter dopamine.

Antidepressants

People with major depression often take so-called **antidepressant** drugs. These drugs are also helpful for some people with eating disorders, panic disorder, obsessive–compulsive disorder (OCD), and social phobia (Zohar & Westenberg, 2007). Problems in the regulation of noradrenaline and serotonin may be involved in eating and panic disorders as well as in depression. Antidepressants are believed to work by increasing levels of these neurotransmitters, which can affect both depression and the appetite (Dagyte et al., 2010).

There are various antidepressants. Each increases the concentration of noradrenaline or serotonin in the brain (Dagyte et al., 2010). **Selective serotonin-reuptake inhibitors (SSRIs)** such as Prozac and Zoloft block the reuptake of serotonin by presynaptic neurons. As a result, serotonin remains in the synaptic cleft longer, influencing receiving neurons. SSRIs appear to be more effective than other antidepressants.

Mood Stabilizers

The ancient Greeks and Romans were among the first to use the metal lithium as a mood stabilizer. They prescribed mineral water—which contains lithium—for people with bipolar disorder. They had no inkling as to why this treatment sometimes helped. A salt of the metal lithium (lithium carbonate), in tablet form, flattens out cycles of manic behavior and depression in most people. It is not known exactly how lithium works, although it affects the functioning of neurotransmitters. Lithium can also be used to strengthen the effects of antidepressant medication (Redrobe & Bourin, 2009).

People with bipolar disorder may have to use lithium indefinitely, as a person with type 1 diabetes must use insulin to control the illness. Many other drugs are also used to help stabilize the moods of patients with bipolar disorder. Among these are divalproex sodium (brand name: Depakote), lamotrigine (Lamictal), carbamazepine (Tegretol), and oxcarbazepine (Trileptal).

13-8b ELECTROCONVULSIVE THERAPY

Electroconvulsive therapy (ECT) is a biological form of therapy for psychological disorders that was introduced by the Italian psychiatrist Ugo Cerletti in 1939. Cerletti had noted that some slaughterhouses used electric shock to render animals unconscious. The shocks also produced convulsions. Along with other European researchers of the period, Cerletti erroneously believed that convulsions were incompatible with schizophrenia and other major psychological disorders.

ECT was originally used for a variety of psychological disorders. Because of the advent of antipsychotic drugs, however, it is now used mainly for people with major depression who do not respond to antidepressants (Piccinni et al., 2009). People typically obtain one ECT treatment three times a week for up to 10 sessions. Electrodes are attached to the temples and an electrical current strong enough to produce a convulsion is induced. The shock causes unconsciousness, so the patient does not recall it. Nevertheless, patients are given a sedative (a drug that relieves nervousness or agitation or puts one to sleep) so that they are asleep during the treatment.

ECT is controversial for many reasons, such as the fact that many professionals are distressed by the thought of passing an electric shock through a patient's head and producing convulsions. There are also side effects, including memory problems. However, research suggests that for most people, cognitive impairment tends to be temporary (Rayner et al., 2009).

13-8c PSYCHOSURGERY

Psychosurgery is more controversial than ECT. The best-known modern technique, **prefrontal lobotomy**, has been used with people with severe disorders. In this method, a picklike instrument severs the nerve pathways that link the prefrontal lobes of the brain to the thalamus. It is intended to sever thought from emotion and enable severely disturbed patients to regain control. The method was pioneered by the Portuguese neurologist Antonio Egas Moniz and was brought to the United States in the 1930s. The theoretical rationale for the operation was vague and misguided, and Moniz's reports of success were exaggerated. Nevertheless, by 1950 prefrontal lobotomies had been performed on thousands of people in an effort to reduce violence and agitation. Anecdotal evidence of the method's unreliable outcomes is found in an ironic footnote to history: one of Dr. Moniz's patients returned to shoot him.

TRUTH ONE OF DR. MONIZ'S "FAILURES" DID INDEED SHOOT HIM, LEAVING A BULLET LODGED IN HIS SPINE AND PARALYZING HIS LEGS.

The prefrontal lobotomy also has side effects, including hyperactivity and distractibility, impaired learning ability, overeating, apathy and withdrawal, epileptic-type seizures, reduced creativity, and, occasionally, death. Because of these side effects, and because of the advent of antipsychotic drugs, the prefrontal lobotomy has been largely discontinued in the United States.

But new methods of psychosurgery are being undertaken with caution and have had mixed success in debilitating cases of OCD and phobias. They are used only when psychotherapy and drug therapy have failed to be of help, and when patients are made fully aware of success rates and potential risks (Carey, 2009). In *gamma knife surgery*, for example, physicians beam streams of radiation deep into the skull, destroying spots of tissue believed to be overactive in severe OCD (Tyagi et al., 2010). Other psychosurgery procedures are also undergoing small-scale trials (Bear et al., 2010). But there are some side effects, and the treatments are not always effective.

13-8d DOES BIOLOGICAL THERAPY WORK?

There are thus a number of biological approaches to treat psychological disorders. But what do we know about the effectiveness of biological therapies?

There is little question that drug therapy has helped many people with psychological disorders. For example,

antipsychotic drugs largely account for the reduced need for the use of restraint and supervision (e.g., padded cells, straitjackets, hospitalization, and so on) with people diagnosed with schizophrenia. Antipsychotic drugs have also enabled many former mental hospital residents to lead largely normal lives in the community, hold jobs, and maintain family lives. Most of the problems related to these drugs concern their side effects.

Comparisons of the effectiveness of psychotherapy and pharmacotherapy (medicine) for depression have yielded mixed results. Cognitive therapy provides coping skills that reduce the risk of recurrence of depression once treatment ends (Hollon & Shelton, 2001). Pim Cuijpers and his colleagues (2009) undertook a meta-analysis of randomly controlled experiments to attempt to answer the question of whether there was a difference in effectiveness of the treatment of depression when an antidepressant drug was added to a psychological treatment. They found that a treatment package that included psychotherapy and pharmacotherapy was more effective than psychological treatment alone, but it was not clear that the antidepressants offered much of an advantage.

In some cases, cognitive-behavior therapy appears to have helped relieve the positive symptoms of schizophrenia (Gregory, 2010; Wykes et al., 2008). Cognitive-behavior therapy is apparently more effective, however, when it is combined with medication in the treatment of schizophrenia (Chadwick & Lowe, 1990).

Many professionals are comfortable with the short-term use of antianxiety drugs in helping clients manage periods of unusual anxiety or tension. However, many people use antianxiety drugs routinely to dull the arousal stemming from anxiety-producing lifestyles or interpersonal problems. Rather than make the often painful decisions required to confront their problems, they take a pill.

Despite the controversies surrounding ECT, it helps many people who do not respond to antidepressant drugs (Piccinni et al., 2009). ECT may be a useful "last resort" when other treatment methods are of no avail.

In sum, drug therapy and perhaps ECT seem to be effective for some disorders that do not respond to psychotherapy alone. Yet common sense and research evidence suggest that psychotherapy is preferable for problems such as anxiety and mild depression. No chemical can show a person how to change an idea or solve an interpersonal problem.

Ready to study? In the book, you can:

- ❍ Review what you've read with Fill-Ins and Multiple Choice quizzes (below).
- ❍ Rip out Chapter Review card (in the back).

Or you can go online to CourseMate at www.cengagebrain.com for these resources:

- ❍ Complete Practices Quizzes to prepare for tests.
- ❍ Review Key Terms Flash Cards (online or print).
- ❍ Play games to master concepts.

FILL-INS

Answers can be found in the back of the book, starting on page 368.

1. Psychotherapy is a systematic interaction between a therapist and a client that applies _____ principles to influence clients' thoughts, feelings, and/or behavior.

2. Freud's method of psychoanalysis attempts to shed light on _____ conflicts that are presumed to lie at the roots of clients' problems.

3. _____-conditioning methods reinforce desired responses and extinguish undesired responses.

4. The chief psychoanalytic method is _____ association.

5. _____ therapies focus on clients' subjective, conscious experience.

6. _____-_____ therapy is a nondirective method that provides clients with an accepting atmosphere that enables them to overcome roadblocks to self-actualization.

7. _____ therapists focus on the beliefs, attitudes, and automatic thoughts that create and compound their clients' problems.

8. Behavior-therapy methods for reducing fears include systematic _____, in which a client is gradually exposed to more fear-arousing stimuli.

9. Albert Ellis's form of therapy confronts clients with the ways in which _____ beliefs contribute to anxiety and depression.

10. (Minor or Major?) tranquilizers are usually prescribed for people who complain of anxiety or tension.

1. Your therapist is accepting and warm. You are encouraged to feel good about yourself and to make choices that develop your potential. Your therapist uses a(n) _____ approach to treatment.

   a. psychoanalytic   c. client-centered
   b. ego analytic   d. behavioral

2. Hannah's therapist believes her anxiety is the result of unconscious impulses breaking through to the conscious level. Her therapist endorses the _____ perspective.

   a. behavioral   c. cognitive
   b. psychodynamic   d. humanistic

3. A client avoids talking about their relationship with their father. The psychoanalyst asks them to talk about this relationship. The client becomes restless and claims, "There is nothing to tell." This is indicative of

   a. transference.   c. catharsis.
   b. resistance.   d. free association.

4. Which of the following examples best represents using operant conditioning to change behavior?

   a. Using electroconvulsive therapy for depression.
   b. Withdrawing attention whenever a child has a temper tantrum.
   c. Fostering insight by using examples.
   d. Giving your sister money to see a therapist.

5. _____ therapists focus on beliefs and attitudes that create and compound their clients' psychological problems.

   a. Cognitive   c. Learning
   b. Psychoanalytic   d. Gestalt

6. Client-centered therapy is to _____ as Gestalt therapy is to _____.

   a. directive; nondirective
   b. nondirective; directive
   c. objective; subjective
   d. present; past

7. Family therapists usually see the "identified patient" as the

   a. cause of the family's problem.
   b. scapegoat for other problems in the family.
   c. key to the family system.
   d. black sheep of the family.

8. Social skills training is facilitated in a group setting because

   a. members of the group can practice the skills with one another.
   b. members can observe and learn from each other.
   c. members can give each other feedback.
   d. all of these

9. Dr. Schwiesow wants to use the best methods when treating her patients with depression. She should search out _____ practices.

   a. evidence-based   c. researched
   b. treatment   d. experimental

10. You have advised a patient to discontinue use of antianxiety drugs. After two weeks, your patient calls to complain that his anxiety symptoms are now worse than before he started to take the drug. You tell the patient that his feelings are a predictable response to discontinuing antianxiety medication. In fact, he is experiencing what is called

    a. addiction.   c. rebound anxiety.
    b. tolerance.   d. relapse.

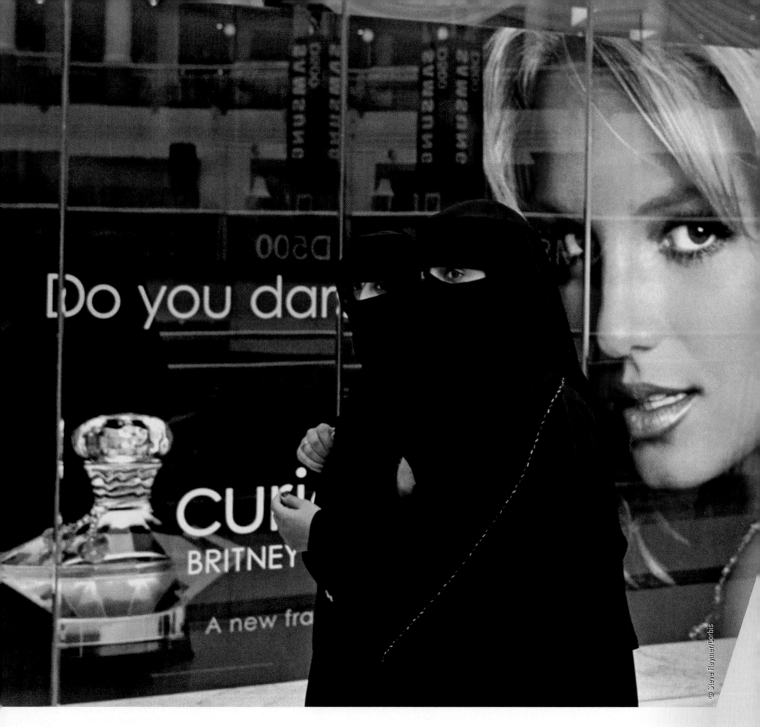

LEARNING OUTCOMES

14-1 Define *attitude* and discuss factors that shape attitudes

14-2 Discuss prejudice and discrimination

14-3 Discuss factors that contribute to interpersonal attraction and love

14-4 Define *social perception* and describe factors that influence it

14-5 Explain why people obey authority figures and conform to social norms

14-6 Discuss factors that contribute to aggression

14-7 Describe differences between the ways in which people behave as individuals and as members of a group

STUDY TOOLS ▶ After you read the chapter, go to the Study Tools at the end of the chapter, page 351.

CHAPTER 14

Social PSYCHOLOGY

Consider some news items from the early years of the 21st century:

- 2011: A suicide bomber drove a car laden with explosives up to a Coptic Christian church in Egypt as worshipers exited a New Year's mass, killing 21 people and wounding at least 80 more.

- 2005: Four suicide bombers blew themselves up aboard three London commuter trains and a bus, killing more than 50 people and wounding 700.

- 2001: And of course, on September 11, 2001, 19 suicide terrorists in the United States used fully fueled airplanes as bombs, flying them into the World Trade Center and the Pentagon, killing nearly 3,000 people.

Although you might think of suicide terrorism as a recent development, it dates back thousands of years (Kazim et al., 2008). The word *suicide* in the phrase "suicide bomber" leads people to turn to psychologists for understanding, with the idea that something must be psychologically wrong with these terrorists. But many social scientists assert that suicide terrorists have no telltale psychological profile (Consortium of Social Science Associations, 2003; Shi & Jia, 2011). Ariel Merari and his colleagues (2010) at the University of Tel Aviv interviewed and tested would-be suicide bombers—people who had been caught in the act and arrested. They found two groups among the would-be suicide terrorists: (1) dependent types with a tendency to follow leaders and public influences, and (2) emotionally unstable and impulsive types. Among both types, some were depressed but would not be diagnosed with major depressive disorder.

Because of the difficulty in identifying suicide terrorists, social psychologist Philip Zimbardo (2004) argues that we must look to the psychology of *social influence* to understand them. As we will see, social psychologist Stanley Milgram (1974), who conducted famous studies on obedience some 50 years ago, concluded, "Often, it is not so much the kind of person a man is, as the kind of situation in which he finds himself that determines how he will act."

> *People can be goaded by social influences into doing things that are not necessarily consistent with their personalities.*

WHAT DO YOU THINK? FOLKLORE, COMMON SENSE, OR NONSENSE? CIRCLE THE T FOR "TRUTH" OR THE F FOR "FICTION," AND CHECK THE ACCURACY OF YOUR ANSWERS AS YOU READ THROUGH THE CHAPTER.

T	F	PEOPLE VOTE THEIR CONSCIENCES.
T	F	WE APPRECIATE THINGS MORE WHEN WE HAVE TO WORK FOR THEM.
T	F	PEOPLE HAVE CONDEMNED BILLIONS OF OTHER PEOPLE WITHOUT EVER MEETING THEM OR LEARNING THEIR NAMES.
T	F	BEAUTY IS IN THE EYE OF THE BEHOLDER.
T	F	OPPOSITES ATTRACT.
T	F	WE TEND TO HOLD OTHERS RESPONSIBLE FOR THEIR MISDEEDS BUT TO SEE OURSELVES AS VICTIMS OF CIRCUMSTANCES WHEN WE MISBEHAVE.
T	F	MOST PEOPLE WILL TORTURE AN INNOCENT PERSON IF THEY ARE ORDERED TO DO SO.
T	F	SEEING IS BELIEVING.
T	F	NEARLY 40 PEOPLE STOOD BY AND DID NOTHING WHILE A WOMAN WAS BEING STABBED TO DEATH.

Social psychology is the field of psychology that studies the nature and causes of behavior and mental processes in social situations. Social psychologists study the ways people can be goaded by social influences into doing things that are not necessarily consistent with their personalities. The social psychological topics we discuss in this chapter include attitudes, social perception, social influence, and group behavior. As we explore each of these, we will ask what they might offer to those of us who have difficulty imagining why people would surrender their own lives to take the lives of others. We begin with attitudes.

"TERRORISM IS ABOUT ONE THING: PSYCHOLOGY. IT IS THE PSYCHOLOGY OF FEAR."

—PHILIP G. ZIMBARDO

14-1 Attitudes

How do you feel about abortion, amnesty for illegal immigrants, and exhibiting the Ten Commandments in public buildings such as courthouses? These are hot-button topics because people have strong attitudes toward them. They each give rise to cognitive evaluations (such as approval or disapproval), feelings (such as liking, disliking, or something stronger), and behavioral tendencies (such as approach or avoidance). Although I asked you how you "feel," attitudes are not just feelings or emotions. Many psychologists view thinking—or judgment—as more basic. Feelings and behavior follow. **Attitudes** are enduring behavioral and cognitive tendencies that are expressed by evaluating particular people, places, or things with favor or disfavor (Bohner & Dickel, 2011).

Attitudes are largely learned. For example, if you learn that an Apple iPad is a wonderful "toy," you may feel the urge to buy one. Attitudes can foster love or hate. They can give rise to helping behavior or to mass destruction. They can lead to social conflict or to the resolution of conflicts. Attitudes can change, but not easily.

14-1a PREDICTING BEHAVIOR FROM ATTITUDES

Our definition of *attitude* implies that our behavior is consistent with our attitudes. But do people really do as they think? When we are free to do as we wish, the answer is often yes. But as indicated by the term **A–B problem**, there are exceptions. In fact, the links between attitudes (A) and behaviors (B) tend to be weak to moderate (Petty et al., 2009a, 2009b). People do not always vote "their consciences." Moreover, research reveals that people who say that drinking alcohol, smoking, and drunken driving are serious threats to their health do not necessarily curb these activities (Kiviniemi & Rothman, 2010).

Several factors affect the likelihood that we can predict behavior from attitudes:

1. *Specificity.* We can better predict specific behavior from specific attitudes than from global attitudes. For example, we can better predict church attendance by knowing people's attitudes toward church attendance than by knowing whether they are Christian.

Do people always vote their "conscience"? This A–B problem refers to the research finding that people do not always act in accord with their attitudes.

Workbook Stock/Jupiterimages/Getty Images

2. *Strength of attitudes.* Strong attitudes are more likely to determine behavior than weak attitudes (DeMarree et al., 2007). A person who believes that the nation's destiny depends on Democrats taking control of Congress is more likely to vote than a person who leans toward that party but does not believe that elections make much difference.

3. *Vested interest.* People are more likely to act on their attitudes when they have a vested interest in the outcome. People are more likely to vote for (or against) unionization of their workplace when they believe that their job security depends on it (Bohner & Dickel, 2011).

4. *Accessibility.* People are more likely to behave in accord with their attitudes when they are accessible—that is, when they are brought to mind (DeMarree et al., 2007). This is why politicians attempt to "get out the vote" by means of media blitzes just prior to an election. Attitudes with a strong emotional impact are more accessible, which is one reason that politicians strive to get their supporters "worked up" over issues.

FICTION ACTUALLY, PEOPLE DO NOT ALWAYS ACT IN ACCORD WITH THEIR CONSCIENCES. THE LINKS BETWEEN ATTITUDES (A) AND BEHAVIORS (B) TEND TO BE WEAK TO MODERATE.

14-1b ATTITUDE FORMATION

You were not born a Republican or a Democrat. You were not born a Christian, Jew, a Muslim, or a Hindu—although your parents may have practiced one of these religions when you came along. Political, religious, and other attitudes are learned or derived from cognitive processes. In this section, we describe some of the processes that result in acquiring attitudes.

Conditioning and Observational Learning

Conditioning may play a role in attitude formation (Walther et al., 2005). Laboratory experiments have shown that attitudes toward national groups can be influenced by associating them with positive words (such as *gift* or *happy*) or negative words (such as *ugly* or *failure*) (De Houwer et al., 2001). Parents often reward children for saying and doing things that agree with their own attitudes. Patriotism is encouraged by showing children approval when they sing the national anthem or wave the flag.

Attitudes formed through direct experience may be stronger and easier to recall, but we also acquire attitudes by observing, listening to, or reading the works of other people. The approval or disapproval of peers leads adolescents to prefer short or long hair, baggy jeans, or preppy sweaters. How do the things you read in newspapers or hear on the radio influence your attitudes?

Cognitive Appraisal

Nevertheless, attitude formation is not fully mechanical. People are also motivated to understand the environment so that they can make predictions and exercise some control over it (Bizer et al., 2004). People also sometimes form or change attitudes on the basis of new information (Petty et al., 2009a, 2009b). For example, we may believe that a car is more reliable than we had thought if a survey by *Consumer Reports* finds that it has an excellent repair record. Even so, initial attitudes act as *cognitive anchors* (Bohner & Dickel, 2011). We often judge new ideas in terms of how much they deviate from our existing attitudes. Accepting larger deviations requires more information processing—that is, more intellectual work (Petty et al., 2009a, 2009b). For this reason, perhaps, great deviations—such as changes from liberal to conservative attitudes, or vice versa—are apt to be resisted.

14-1c CHANGING ATTITUDES THROUGH PERSUASION

Let advertisers spend the same amount of money improving their product that they do on advertising and they wouldn't have to advertise it.

—WILL ROGERS

Will Rogers's comment sounds on the mark, but he was probably wrong. It does little good to have a wonderful product if it remains a secret.

The **elaboration likelihood model** describes the ways in which people respond to persuasive messages (Bohner & Dickel, 2011). Consider two routes to persuading others to change attitudes. The *central route* inspires thoughtful consideration of arguments and evidence. The *peripheral route* associates objects with positive or negative cues. When politicians avow, "This bill is supported by liberals (or conservatives)," they are seeking predictable, knee-jerk reactions rather than careful consideration of a bill's merits. Other cues are rewards (such as a smile or a hug), punishments (such as parental disapproval), and such factors as the trustworthiness and attractiveness of the communicator.

fear appeal
a type of persuasive communication that influences behavior on the basis of arousing fear instead of rational analysis of the issues

selective avoidance
diverting one's attention from information that is inconsistent with one's attitudes

selective exposure
deliberately seeking and attending to information that is consistent with one's attitudes

Advertisements, which are a form of persuasive communication, also rely on central and peripheral routes. Some ads focus on the quality of the product (central route). Others attempt to associate the product with appealing images (peripheral route). For example, ads for Total cereal, which highlight its nutritional benefits, provide information about the quality of the product, but ads that show football players heading for Disney World or choosing a brand of beer offer no information about the product itself.

In this section we look at one central factor in persuasion—the nature of the message—and three peripheral factors: the messenger, the context of the message, and the audience.

The Persuasive Message

How do we respond when TV commercials are repeated until we have memorized the dimples on the actors' faces? Research suggests that familiarity breeds content, not contempt (Bohner & Dickel, 2011; Förster, 2009). It appears that repeated exposure to people and things as diverse as political candidates, photos of college students, and abstract art enhances their appeal (Banaji & Heiphetz, 2008; Reis et al., 2011).

When trying to persuade someone, is it helpful or self-defeating to alert them to the arguments presented by the opposition? In two-sided arguments, the communicator recounts the arguments of the opposition in an effort to refute them. In research concerning a mock trial, college undergraduates were presented with two-sided arguments—those of the prosecution and those of the defendant (McKenzie et al., 2002). When one argument was weak, the college "jurors" expressed more confidence in their decision than when they did not hear the other side at all. Theologians and politicians sometimes forewarn their followers about the arguments of the opposition and then refute each one. Forewarning creates a kind of psychological immunity to them (Eisend, 2007; Taber et al., 2009).

It would be nice to think that people are too sophisticated to be persuaded by emotional factors in attitude formation, but they usually aren't (DeSteno et al., 2004). Consider the **fear appeal**: Women who are warned of the dire risk they run if they fail to be screened for breast cancer are more

"Arguments are to be avoided: they are always vulgar and often convincing."

—OSCAR WILDE

likely to obtain mammograms than women who are informed of the *benefits* of mammography (Ruiter et al., 2001). Interestingly, although sun tanning has been shown to increase the likelihood of skin cancer, warnings against sun tanning were shown to be more effective when students were warned of risks to their *appearance* (e.g., premature aging, wrinkling, and scarring of the skin) than when the warning dealt with the risk to their health. Fear appeals are most effective when the audience believes that the risks are serious—as in causing wrinkles!—and that the audience members can change their behavior to avert the risks—as in preventing cancer or wrinkling (de Hoog et al., 2007; Thompson et al., 2009).

Audiences also tend to believe arguments that appear to run counter to the vested interests of the communicator (Bohner & Dickel, 2011). If the president of Ford or General Motors said that Toyotas and Hondas were superior, you can bet that we would prick up our ears.

The Persuasive Communicator

Would you go to a doctor who admitted that he or she was behind the times? Research shows that persuasive communicators are characterized by expertise, trustworthiness, attractiveness, or similarity to their audiences (Petty et al., 2009a, 2009b). Because of the adoration of their fans, sports superstars such as Peyton Manning are the most valuable endorsers.

People find it painful when they are confronted with information that counters their own views (Garrett, 2009). Therefore, they often show **selective avoidance** and **selective exposure** (Bryant & Davies, 2006). That is, they switch channels when the news coverage runs counter to their own attitudes. They also seek communicators whose outlook coincides with their own. Whom would you prefer to listen to: Rush Limbaugh and Sean Hannity or Chris Matthews and Rachel Maddow?

We often selectively expose ourselves to opinions with which we agree—and vice versa.

Rubberball/Mike Kemp/Jupiterimages

The Context of the Message

You are too shrewd to let someone persuade you by buttering you up, but perhaps someone you know would be influenced by a sip of wine, a bite of cheese, and a sincere compliment. Aspects of the immediate environment, such as music, also increase the likelihood of persuasion. When we are in a good mood, we apparently are less likely to evaluate the situation carefully (Briñol et al., 2007).

It is also counterproductive to call your friends foolish when they differ with you—even though their ideas are bound to be "foolish" if they do not agree with yours. Agreement and praise are more effective ways to encourage others to embrace your views.

The Persuaded Audience

Why can some people say no to salespeople? Why do others enrich the lives of every door-to-door salesperson? It may be that people with high self-esteem and low social anxiety are more likely to resist social pressure (Ellickson et al., 2001).

A classic study by Schwartz and Gottman (1976) describes the cognitive nature of the social anxiety that can make it difficult to refuse requests. They found that people who comply with unreasonable requests are more apt to report thoughts such as:

- "I was worried about what the other person would think of me if I refused."
- "It is better to help others than to be self-centered."
- "The other person might be hurt or insulted if I refused."

People who refuse unreasonable requests reported thoughts like these:

- "It doesn't matter what the other person thinks of me."
- "I am perfectly free to say no."
- "This request is unreasonable."

14-1d CHANGING ATTITUDES AND BEHAVIOR BY MEANS OF COGNITIVE DISSONANCE

According to **cognitive-dissonance theory**, people are thinking creatures who seek consistency in their behaviors and their attitudes—that is, their views of the world. People must apparently mentally represent the world accurately to predict and control events. Consistency in beliefs, attitudes, and behavior helps make the world seem like a predictable place. Therefore, if we find ourselves in the uncomfortable spot

> *"The brain within its groove*
> *Runs evenly and true . . ."*
> —EMILY DICKINSON

where two cherished ideas conflict, we are motivated to reduce the discrepancy.

In the first and still one of the best-known studies on cognitive dissonance, one group of participants received $1 (worth $5 to $10 today) for telling someone else that a boring task was interesting (Festinger & Carlsmith, 1959). Members of a second group received $20 (worth $100 to $200 today) to describe the chore positively. Both groups were paid to engage in **attitude-discrepant behavior**—that is, behavior that ran counter to what they actually thought. After presenting their fake enthusiasm for the boring task, the participants were asked to rate their own liking for it. Ironically, those who were paid *less* rated the task as actually more interesting than their better-paid colleagues reported. Similarly, being compelled by the law to recycle can lead to people's supporting recycling as opposed to throwing out all trash and garbage in a bundle.

Learning theorists might predict that the more we are reinforced for doing something (given more money, for example), the more we should like it (not find the task quite as boring, that is). But that is not what happened here. Cognitive-dissonance theorists rightly predicted that because the ideas (cognitions) of (a) "I was paid very little" and (b) "I told someone that this assignment was interesting" are dissonant, people will tend to engage in **effort justification**. The discomfort of cognitive

cognitive-dissonance theory
the view that we are motivated to make our cognitions or beliefs consistent with each other and with our behavior

attitude-discrepant behavior
behavior inconsistent with an attitude that may have the effect of modifying an attitude

effort justification
in cognitive-dissonance theory, the tendency to seek justification (acceptable reasons) for strenuous efforts

TRUTH WE DO TEND TO APPRECIATE THINGS MORE WHEN WE HAVE TO WORK FOR THEM (STONE & FERNANDEZ, 2008). THIS IS AN EXAMPLE OF EFFORT JUSTIFICATION.

prejudice
an attitude toward a group that leads people to evaluate members of that group negatively

discrimination
hostile behavior that results is directed against groups toward whom one is prejudiced

stereotyping
erroneous assumptions that all members of a group share the same traits or characteristics

dissonance motivates people to explain their behavior to themselves in such a way that unpleas-

ant undertakings seem worth it. Participants who were paid only $1 may have justified their lie by concluding that they may not have been lying in the first place.

14-2 Prejudice and Discrimination

Prejudice is an attitude toward a group that leads people to evaluate members of that group negatively—even though they have never met them. On a cognitive level, prejudice is linked to expectations that members of the target group will behave poorly, say, in the workplace, or engage in criminal behavior or terrorism. On an emotional level, prejudice is associated with negative feelings such as fear, dislike, or hatred. Prejudice is the most troubling kind of attitude.

In behavioral terms, prejudice is connected with avoidance, aggression, and discrimination. **Discrimination** refers to behavior that results from prejudice. Many groups in the United States have

experienced discrimination—women, gays and lesbians, older people, and ethnic groups such as African Americans, Asian Americans, Latin Americans, Irish Americans, Jewish Americans, and Native Americans. Discrimination takes many forms, including denial of access to jobs, the voting booth, and housing.

14-2a STEREOTYPING

Prejudice involves **stereotyping**—that is, erroneous assumptions that all members of a group share the same traits or characteristics. Have people you know characterized African Americans as superstitious and musical? What about gays and lesbians? Are they unfit for military service? Stereotypes may lead people to view members of groups in a biased fashion.

On the other hand, some stereotypes are positive, such as stereotypes about physically attractive people. By and large, we assume that "good things come in pretty packages." Attractive children and adults are judged and treated more positively than their unattractive peers (Langlois et al., 2000). We expect attractive people to be poised, sociable, popular, intelligent, mentally healthy, fulfilled, persuasive, and successful in their jobs and marriages (Principe & Langlois, 2011). Attractive people are also more likely to be judged innocent of crimes in mock jury experiments, and when they are found guilty, they are given less severe sentences (Sporer & Goodman-Delahunty, 2009).

14-2b SOURCES OF PREJUDICE

The sources of prejudice are many and varied:

1. *Dissimilarity.* We are apt to like people who share our attitudes (Cunningham, 2008). People of different religions and races often have different backgrounds, however, giving rise to dissimilar attitudes. Even when people of different races share important values, people may assume that they do not.

2. *Social conflict.* There is often social and economic conflict between people of different races and religions (Reid, 2008).

Here we see convicted murderer Amanda Knox being escorted to a hearing at which her conviction was overturned. Do stereotypes of attractive people lead us to assume that they are less likely to resort to deviant behavior to reach their goals?

OliScarff/Getty Images

3. *Social learning.* Children acquire some attitudes from other people, especially their parents. Children tend to imitate their parents, and parents reinforce their children for doing so (Durlez, 2011). In this way prejudices can be transmitted from generation to generation.

4. *Information processing.* Prejudices act as cognitive filters through which we view the social world. We tend to think of people as "familiar" or "foreign," or "good" or "bad." Our feelings and reactions toward others may be biased by these perceptions (Crisp & Nicel, 2004).

5. *Social categorization.* We also tend to divide our social world into "us" and "them." People usually view those who belong to their own groups—the "in-group"—more favorably than those who do not—the "out-group" (Park & Judd, 2005). Isolation from the out-group makes it easier to maintain our stereotypes.

FICTION ALTHOUGH THERE MAY BE INDIVIDUAL PREFERENCES, IT DOES NOT SEEM THAT STANDARDS FOR BEAUTY ARE SO FLEXIBLE THAT THEY ARE FULLY "IN THE EYE OF THE BEHOLDER."

(14-3) Attraction and Love

Attitudes of liking and loving can lead to important, lasting relationships. They are the flip side of the coin of prejudice—positive attitudes that are associated with interpersonal **attraction** rather than avoidance. Among the factors contributing to attraction are physical appearance, similarity, and reciprocity.

14-3a PHYSICAL APPEARANCE

Physical appearance is a key factor in attraction and in the consideration of romantic partners (Sprecher et al., 2008). What determines physical allure? Are our standards subjective—that is, "in the eye of the beholder"? Or is there general agreement on what is appealing?

Many standards for beauty appear to be cross-cultural (Buss, 2009; Singh & Singh, 2011). For example, a study of people in England and Japan found that both British and Japanese men consider women with large eyes, high cheekbones, and narrow jaws to be most attractive (Perrett et al., 1994). In

his research, Perrett created computer composites of the faces of 60 women and, as shown in part A of Figure 14.1, of the 15 women who were rated the most attractive. He then used computer enhancement to exaggerate the differences between the composite of the 60 and the composite of the 15 most attractive women. He arrived at the image shown in part B of Figure 14.1.

Part B, which shows higher cheekbones and a narrower jaw than Part A, was rated as the most attractive image. Similar results were found for the image of a Japanese woman. Works of art suggest that the ancient Greeks and Egyptians favored similar facial features.

An examination of the Internet dating profiles of 5,810 Yahoo personal ads shows that "thin" is more "in" in the expressed preferences for partners of European Americans and males (Glasser et al., 2009). European American males are more likely than African American

attraction
in social psychology, an attitude of liking or disliking (negative attraction)

FIGURE 14.1

What Features Contribute to Facial Attractiveness?

In both England and Japan, features such as large eyes, high cheekbones, and narrow jaws contribute to perceptions of the attractiveness of women. Part A shows a composite of the faces of 15 women rated as the most attractive of a group of 60. Part B is a composite in which the features of these 15 women are exaggerated—that is, developed further in the direction that separates them from the average of the entire 60.

A.

B.

© Science Photo Library/Photo Researchers, Inc

When It Comes To Sex, Red May Mean "Go"

When you go to buy a box of Valentine's Day candy, what color will the box be? Green? Blue? The answer, of course, is red. What is the most popular color of women's lipstick? Yellow? Brown? Again, the answer is red (Elliot et al., 2007). Red has been the most popular lipstick color since the hot days that saw the construction of the pyramids in ancient Egypt (Elliot & Niesta, 2008). At a traffic light, the color red means stop. But when it comes to sexual attraction, the color red is more likely to mean go.

Why is the color red associated with feelings of attraction? The link between red and physical attraction may be rooted in our biological heritage. Many female primates, including baboons, chimpanzees, gorillas, and rhesus monkeys, show reddened genital regions when they are nearing ovulation—the time of the month when they are fertile (Barelli et al., 2008). Reddening of the skin is caused by elevated estrogen levels, which increase the blood flow under the skin. Male primates are more likely to attempt sexual relations with females who display red (Waitt et al., 2006). Women's estrogen levels are also elevated near ovulation, slightly reddening the skin (Lynn et al., 2007). For men, as with other male primates, the reddening of a woman's skin at the time of ovulation may be a sexual signal.

Experiments find that men rate the same woman as more attractive when her photograph is shown against a red background as opposed to other colors (Elliot & Niesta, 2008). Women also rate photos of men as more attractive when the photos are bordered in red or the men are wearing red clothing (Eliot et al., 2010). The male sex hormone testosterone is involved in oxygenating blood and increasing its flow to the skin—giving off a reddish hue—and to the genitals, leading to sexual excitement. Red coloration can signal good health in men because high blood levels of oxygen are maintained only by organisms in good health (Elliot et al., 2010).

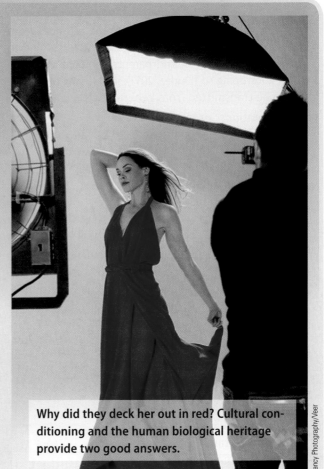

Why did they deck her out in red? Cultural conditioning and the human biological heritage provide two good answers.

Fancy Photography/Veer

and Latinos to want to date slender and buff women. African American and Latino men are significantly more likely to be interested in women with large or thick bodies.

14-3b GENDER DIFFERENCES IN SELECTION OF A ROMANTIC PARTNER

Physical appearance may be a major factor in the selection of a romantic partner, but cross-cultural studies on mate selection find that women tend to place greater emphasis on traits such as professional status, consideration, dependability, kindness, and fondness for children. Men tend to place relatively greater emphasis on physical allure, cooking ability, even thrift (Buss, 2011).

Susan Sprecher and her colleagues (1994) surveyed more than 13,000 Americans, attempting to represent the ethnic diversity we find in the United States. They found that women were more willing than men to marry someone who was not good-looking, but less willing to marry someone who did not hold a steady job.

Why do males tend to place relatively more emphasis than females on physical appearance in mate selection?

Why do females tend to place relatively more emphasis on personal factors such as financial status and reliability? Evolutionary psychologists believe that evolutionary forces favor the survival of women who desire status in their mates and men who emphasize physical allure because these preferences provide reproductive advantages. According to the "parental investment model," a woman's appeal is more strongly connected with her age and health, both of which are markers of reproductive capacity. The value of men as reproducers, however, is more intertwined with factors that contribute to a stable environment for child rearing—such as social standing and reliability (Schmitt, 2003).

14-3c THE ATTRACTION–SIMILARITY HYPOTHESIS

The *attraction–similarity hypothesis* holds that people tend to develop romantic relationships with people who are similar to themselves in physical attractiveness and other traits. Apparently, opposites do *not* attract. Researchers have found that our marital and sex partners tend to be similar to us in race and ethnicity, age, level of education, and religion (Montoya et al., 2008; van Straaten et al., 2009). Note that nearly 95% of marriages and 80% to 90% of cohabiting unions were be-

FICTION ACTUALLY, IT IS NOT TRUE THAT "OPPOSITES ATTRACT." PEOPLE WHO SHARE ATTITUDES ARE MORE LIKELY TO BE ATTRACTED TO ONE ANOTHER.

tween partners
of the same race at the
time of the 2010 U.S. census (U.S. Census Bureau, 2011). Even so, highly educated people are more likely than poorly educated people to marry people of other races (Batson et al., 2006).

Another reason people tend to have partners from the same background is *propinquity*. Marriages are made in the neighborhood and not in heaven (Sprecher & Felmlee, 2008). We tend to live among people who are similar to us in background, and we therefore come into contact with them more often.

Reciprocity is another powerful determinant of attraction (Fehr, 2008). We tend to be more open, warm, and helpful when we are interacting with people who seem to like us (Sprecher et al., 2008).

14-3d LOVE

Love is a strong positive emotion. We had a look at love between children and parents in Chapter 9. Here we will focus on that most dramatic, heated, passionate love we label *romantic love*.

There are a number of theories about romantic love. One theory is Robert Sternberg's (1988) **triangular model of love**, which can be thought of as a love triangle. This love triangle does not refer to two men wooing the same woman. It refers to Sternberg's view that love involves three components: intimacy, passion, and commitment (see Figure 14.2).

Intimacy refers to a couple's closeness, to their mutual concern and sharing of feelings and resources. **Passion** means romance and sexual feelings. **Commitment** means deciding to enhance and maintain the relation-

triangular model of love
Sternberg's view that love involves combinations of three components: intimacy, passion, and commitment

intimacy
close acquaintance and familiarity; a characteristic of a relationship in which partners share their innermost feelings

passion
strong romantic and sexual feelings

commitment
the decision to maintain a relationship

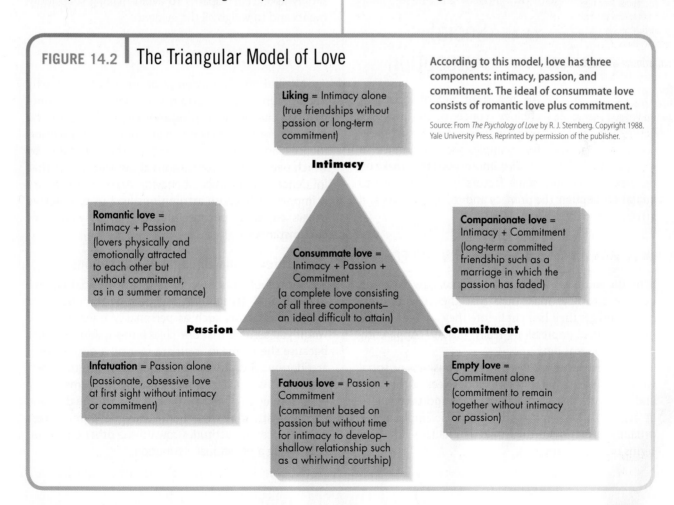

FIGURE 14.2 | **The Triangular Model of Love**

According to this model, love has three components: intimacy, passion, and commitment. The ideal of consummate love consists of romantic love plus commitment.

Source: From *The Psychology of Love* by R. J. Sternberg. Copyright 1988. Yale University Press. Reprinted by permission of the publisher.

Liking = Intimacy alone (true friendships without passion or long-term commitment)

Intimacy

Romantic love =
Intimacy + Passion
(lovers physically and emotionally attracted to each other but without commitment, as in a summer romance)

Consummate love =
Intimacy + Passion + Commitment
(a complete love consisting of all three components—an ideal difficult to attain)

Companionate love =
Intimacy + Commitment
(long-term committed friendship such as a marriage in which the passion has faded)

Passion

Commitment

Infatuation = Passion alone
(passionate, obsessive love at first sight without intimacy or commitment)

Fatuous love = Passion + Commitment
(commitment based on passion but without time for intimacy to develop—shallow relationship such as a whirlwind courtship)

Empty love =
Commitment alone
(commitment to remain together without intimacy or passion)

consummate love
the ideal form of love within Sternberg's model, which combines passion, intimacy, and commitment

romantic love
an intense, positive emotion that involves sexual attraction, feelings of caring, and the belief that one is in love

social perception
a subfield of social psychology that studies the ways in which we form and modify impressions of others

primacy effect
the tendency to evaluate others in terms of first impressions

recency effect
the tendency to evaluate others in terms of the most recent impression

attribution
a belief concerning why people behave in a certain way

dispositional attribution
an assumption that a person's behavior is determined by internal causes such as personal traits

situational attribution
an assumption that a person's behavior is determined by external circumstances such as the social pressure found in a situation

ship. Passion is most crucial in short-term relationships. Intimacy and commitment are more important in enduring relationships. The ideal form of love—**consummate love**—combines all three. Consummate love is made up of romantic love plus commitment.

Romantic love, in Sternberg's scheme, is characterized by passion and intimacy. Passion involves fascination (preoccupation with the loved one), sexual craving, and the desire for exclusiveness (Berscheid, 2009). Intimacy involves closeness and caring—championing the interests of the loved one, even if it entails sacrificing one's own. People are cognitively biased toward evaluating their partners positively (Loving & Agnew, 2001). That is, we idealize those we love.

14-4 Social Perception

An important area of social psychology concerns the ways in which we perceive other people—for example, the importance of the first impressions they make on us. Next we explore some factors that contribute to **social perception**: the primacy and recency effects and attribution theory.

14-4a PRIMACY AND RECENCY EFFECTS

Why do you wear a suit to a job interview? Why do defense attorneys make sure that their clients dress neatly and get their hair cut before they are seen by the jury? Do first impressions really matter? Apparently they do—a great deal.

Whether we are talking about the business or social worlds, or even the relationship between a therapist and a client, first impressions are important (Bidell et al., 2002). First impressions are an example of the **primacy effect**—the tendency to evaluate others in terms of first impressions.

Participants in a classic experiment on the primacy effect read different stories about "Jim" (Luchins, 1957). The stories consisted of one or two paragraphs. The one-paragraph stories portrayed Jim as either friendly or unfriendly. These paragraphs were also used in the two-paragraph stories, but in this case the paragraphs were read in the reverse order. Of those reading only the "friendly" paragraph, 95% rated Jim as friendly. Of those who read just the "unfriendly" paragraph, 3% rated him as friendly. Seventy-eight percent of those who read two-paragraph stories in the "friendly-unfriendly" order labeled Jim as friendly. When participants read the paragraphs in the reverse order, only 18% rated Jim as friendly.

How can we encourage people to pay more attention to impressions occurring after the first encounter? Abraham Luchins accomplished this by allowing time to pass between the presentations of the two paragraphs. In this way, fading memories allowed more recent information to take precedence. The tendency to respond to the most freshly presented piece of information is known as the **recency effect.** Luchins also found a second way to counter first impressions: He simply asked participants to avoid making snap judgments and to weigh all the evidence.

14-4b ATTRIBUTION THEORY

An **attribution** is an assumption or belief about why people behave in a certain way. When you assume that one child is mistreating another child because she is "mean," you are making an attribution. This section focuses on *attribution theory*, or the processes by which people draw conclusions about the factors that influence one another's behavior. Attribution theory is important because attributions lead us to perceive others either as purposeful actors or as victims of circumstances.

Dispositional and Situational Attributions

Social psychologists describe two types of attributions. **Dispositional attributions** ascribe a person's behavior to internal factors such as personality traits and free will. If you assume that one child is mistreating another because she is "mean," you are making a dispositional attribution. **Situational attributions** attribute a person's actions to external factors such as circumstances, social influence, or socialization. If you assume that one child is mistreating the other because her parents have given her certain attitudes toward the other child, you are making a situational attribution.

The Fundamental Attribution Error

In cultures that view the self as independent, such as ours, people tend to make dispositional attributions: they tend to attribute other people's behavior primarily to internal factors such as personality, attitudes, and free will (Chiu & Chao, 2009; Reeder, 2009). This bias in the attribution process is known as the **fundamental attribution error**. For example, if a teenager gets into trouble with the law, individualistic societies are more likely to blame the teenager than the social environment in which the teenager lives.

One reason for the fundamental attribution error is that we tend to infer traits from behavior. But in collectivist cultures that stress interdependence, such as Asian cultures, people are more likely to attribute other people's behavior to that person's social roles and obligations (Basic Behavioral Science Task Force, 1996c). For example, Japanese people might be more likely to attribute a businessperson's extreme competitiveness to the "culture of business" rather than to his or her personality.

The Actor–Observer Effect

We already noted that we are biased toward making dispositional attributions when we are explaining other people's behavior. When we see other people doing things that we do not like, we tend to judge them as willful actors (Baron et al., 2009). But when we find ourselves doing things that we ordinarily disapprove of, we tend to see ourselves as victims of circumstances (Baron et al., 2009). The combination of the tendency to attribute other people's behavior to dispositional factors and our own behavior to situational influences is called the **actor–observer effect**.

Consider an example. Parents and children often argue about the children's choice of friends or dates. When they do, the parents tend to infer traits from behavior and to see the children as stubborn and resistant. The children also infer traits from behavior. Thus, they may see their parents as bossy

and controlling. Parents and children alike attribute the others' behavior to internal causes. That is, both make dispositional attributions about other people's behavior.

How do the parents and teenagers perceive themselves? The parents probably see themselves as being forced into combat by their children's foolishness. If they become insistent, it is in response to the teens' stubbornness. The teenagers probably see themselves as responding to peer pressures. Both parents and children make situational attributions for their own behavior.

The Self-Serving Bias

There is also a **self-serving bias** in the attribution process. We are likely to ascribe our successes to internal, dispositional factors but our failures to external, situational influences (Smith & Weber, 2005). A study with 27 college wrestlers found that they tended to attribute their wins to stable and internal conditions such as their abilities, but their losses to unstable and external conditions such as an error by a referee (De Michele et al., 1998). Sports fans fall into the same trap. They tend to attribute their team's victories to internal conditions and their losses to

TRUTH WE DO TEND TO HOLD OTHERS RESPONSIBLE FOR THEIR MISDEEDS AND TO SEE OURSELVES AS VICTIMS OF CIRCUMSTANCES WHEN WE MISBEHAVE.

fundamental attribution error the assumption that others act predominantly on the basis of their dispositions, even when there is evidence suggesting the importance of their situations

actor–observer effect the tendency to attribute our own behavior to situational factors but to attribute the behavior of others to dispositional factors

self-serving bias the tendency to view one's successes as stemming from internal factors and one's failures as stemming from external factors

Who is at fault here? People tend to make dispositional attributions for other people's behavior, but they tend to see their own behavior as motivated by situational factors. Thus, people are aware of the external forces acting on themselves when they behave, but they tend to attribute other people's behavior to choice and will.

Blend Images Photography/Veer

external conditions (Rees et al., 2005; Wallace & Hinsz, 2009).

Another interesting attribution bias is a gender difference in attributions for friendly behavior. Men are more likely than women to interpret a woman's smile or friendliness toward a man as flirting (Frisby et al., 2010).

14-5 Social Influence

Other people and groups can exert enormous pressure on us to behave according to their norms. **Social influence** is the area of social psychology that studies the ways in which people alter the thoughts, feelings, and behavior of others (Nolan et al., 2008). Let's examine a couple of classic experiments that demonstrate how people influence others to engage in destructive obedience or conform to social norms.

14-5a OBEDIENCE TO AUTHORITY

Throughout history soldiers have followed orders—even when it comes to slaughtering innocent civilians. The Turkish slaughter of Armenians, the Nazi slaughter of Jews, the mutual slaughter of Hutus and Tutsis in Rwanda—these are all examples of the tragedies that can arise from simply following orders. We may say we are horrified by such crimes, and we cannot imagine why people engage in them. But how many of us would refuse to follow orders issued by authority figures?

The Milgram Studies

Yale University psychologist Stanley Milgram also wondered how many people would resist immoral requests made by authority figures. To find out, he undertook a series of classic experiments at the university that have become known as the Milgram studies on obedience.

In an early phase of his work, Milgram (1963) placed ads in local newspapers for people who would be willing to participate in studies on learning and memory. He enlisted 40 people ranging in age from 20 to 50—teachers, engineers, laborers, salespeople, people who had not completed elementary school, and people with graduate degrees.

Let's suppose that you have answered the ad. You show up at the university in exchange for a reasonable fee ($4.50, which in the early 1960s might easily fill your gas tank) and to satisfy your own curiosity. You might be impressed. After all, Yale is a venerable institution that dominates the city. You are no less impressed by the elegant labs, where you meet a distinguished behavioral scientist dressed in a white coat and another person who has responded to the ad. The scientist explains that the purpose of the experiment is to study the *effects of punishment on learning*. The experiment requires a "teacher" and a "learner." By chance, you are appointed the teacher and the other recruit, the learner.

You, the scientist, and the learner enter a laboratory room containing a threatening chair with dangling straps. The scientist straps the learner in. The learner expresses some concern, but this is, after all, for the sake of science. And this is Yale, isn't it? What could happen to a person at Yale?

Suicide Terrorists: Evil? Ordinary? Both?

Why did these men fly into the World Trade Center and the Pentagon? Was it a matter of personality and personal choice? Was it a web of situational factors? Were they evil? Social psychologists who have studied the nature of evil find that many—perhaps most—perpetrators of evil are "ordinary people" (Baumeister, 1996; Berkowitz, 2004). How can this be true? When we seek to "profile" someone, we might be making a fundamental attribution error—that is, we attribute too much of other people's behavior to internal factors such as attitude and choice (Gilovich & Eibach, 2001; Reeder, 2001). Indeed, in 2003, the Consortium of Social Science Associations (COSSA) testified to Congress that they had to conclude there was no clear profile of the suicide terrorist.

The Nineteen Terrorists Who Participated in the Suicide Attacks of September 11, 2001.

FIGURE 14.3 | The Experimental Setup in the Milgram Studies

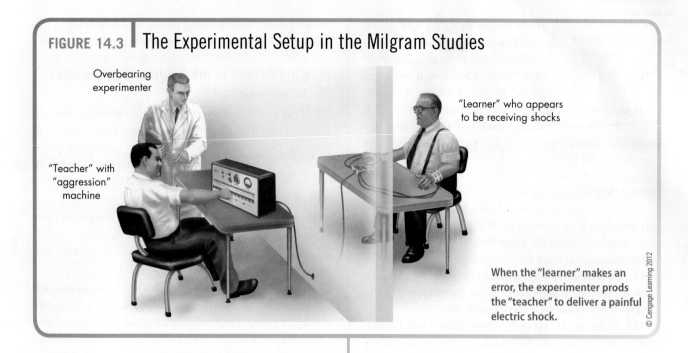

Overbearing experimenter

"Teacher" with "aggression" machine

"Learner" who appears to be receiving shocks

When the "learner" makes an error, the experimenter prods the "teacher" to deliver a painful electric shock.

© Cengage Learning 2012

You follow the scientist to an adjacent room, from which you are to do your "teaching." This teaching promises to have an impact. You are to punish the learner's errors by pressing levers marked from 15 to 450 volts on a fearsome-looking console. Labels describe 28 of the 30 levers as running the gamut from "Slight Shock" to "Danger: Severe Shock." The last two levers are simply labeled "000." Just in case you have no idea what electric shock feels like, the scientist gives you a sample 45-volt shock. It stings. You pity the person who might receive more.

Your learner is expected to learn pairs of words, which are to be read from a list. After hearing the list once, the learner is to produce the word that pairs with the stimulus word from a list of four alternatives. This is done by pressing a switch that lights one of four panels in your room. If it is the correct panel, you proceed to the next stimulus word. If not, you are to deliver an electric shock. With each error, you are to increase the voltage of the shock (see Figure 14.3).

You probably have some misgivings. Electrodes have been strapped to the learner's wrists, and the scientist has applied electrode paste "to avoid blisters and burns." You have also been told that the shocks will cause "no permanent tissue damage," although they might be painful. Still, the learner is going along. And after all, this is Yale.

The learner answers some items correctly and then makes some errors. With mild concern you press the levers up through 45 volts. You've tolerated that much yourself. Then a few more mistakes are made. You press the 60-volt lever, then 75. The learner makes another mistake. You pause and look at the scientist, who is reas-

suring: "Although the shocks may be painful, there is no permanent tissue damage, so please go on." The learner makes more errors, and soon you are up to a shock of 300 volts. But now the learner is pounding on the other side of the wall! Your chest tightens, and you begin to perspire. "Damn science and the $4.50!" you think. You hesitate and the scientist says, "The experiment requires that you continue." After the delivery of the next stimulus word, the learner chooses no answer at all. What are you to do? "Wait for 5 to 10 seconds," the scientist instructs, "and then treat no answer as a wrong answer." But after the next shock the pounding on the wall resumes! Now your heart is racing, and you are convinced you are causing extreme pain and discomfort. Is it possible that no lasting damage is being done? Is the experiment that important, after all? What to do? You hesitate again, and the scientist says, "It is absolutely essential that you continue." His voice is very convincing. "You have no other choice," he says, "you *must* go on." You can barely think straight, and for some unaccountable reason you feel laughter rising in your throat. Your finger shakes above the lever. *What are you to do?*

Milgram had foreseen that some "teachers" in his experiment would hesitate. He had therefore conceived standardized statements that his assistants would use when participants balked—for example: "Although the shocks may be painful, there is no permanent tissue damage, so please go on." "The experiment requires that you continue." "It is absolutely essential that you continue." "You have no other choice: you *must* go on."

To repeat: If you are a teacher in the Milgram study, what do you do? Milgram (1963, 1974) found out what

foot-in-the-door technique

a method for inducing compliance in which a small request is followed by a larger request

most people in his sample would do. The sample was a cross-section of the male population of New Haven. Of the 40 men in this phase of his research, only five refused to go beyond the 300-volt level, the level at which the learner first pounded the wall. Nine other "teachers" defied the scientist within the 300-volt range. But 65% of the participants complied with the scientist throughout the series, believing they were delivering 450-volt, 000-rated shocks.

Were these participants unfeeling? Not at all. Milgram was impressed by their signs of stress. They trembled, they stuttered, they bit their lips. They groaned, they sweated, they dug their fingernails into their flesh. Some had fits of laughter, although laughter was inappropriate. One salesperson's laughter was so convulsive that he could not continue with the experiment.

Milgram's initial research on obedience was limited to a sample of New Haven men. Could he generalize his findings to other men or to women? Would college students, who are considered to be independent thinkers, show more defiance? A replication of Milgram's study with a sample of Yale men yielded similar results. What about women, who are supposedly less aggressive than men? In subsequent research, women, too, administered shocks to the learners. All this took place in a nation that values independence and free will.

On Deception and Truth

I have said that the "teachers" in the Milgram studies *believed* that they were shocking other people when they pressed the levers on the console. They weren't. The only real shock in this experiment was the 45-volt sample given to the teachers. Its purpose was to make the procedure believable.

The learners in the experiment were actually *confederates* of the experimenter. They had not answered the newspaper ads but were in on the truth from the start. The "teachers" were the only real participants. They were led to believe they had been chosen at random for the teacher role, but the choice was rigged so that newspaper recruits would always become teachers.

Milgram debriefed his participants after the experiment was complete. He explained the purpose and methods of his research in detail. He emphasized the fact that they had not actually harmed anyone. But of course the participants did believe that they were hurting other people as the experiment was being carried out. As you can imagine, the ethics of the Milgram studies have been debated by psychologists for de-

TRUTH IT APPEARS TO BE TRUE THAT MOST PEOPLE WILL TORTURE AN INNOCENT PERSON, JUST BECAUSE THEY ARE ORDERED TO DO SO.

cades. College and university review committees might prevent them from being conducted today.

Why Did People in the Milgram Studies Obey the Experimenters?

Many people obey the commands of others even when they are required to perform immoral tasks. But *why?* Why did Germans "just follow orders" during the Holocaust? Why did "teachers" obey the experimenter in Milgram's study? We do not have all the answers, but we can offer a number of hypotheses:

1. *Socialization.* Despite the expressed American ideal of independence, we are socialized from early childhood to obey authority figures such as parents and teachers (Blass, 2009; Twenge, 2009).

2. *Lack of social comparison.* In Milgram's experimental settings, experimenters displayed command of the situation, but "teachers" (participants) did not have the opportunity to compare their ideas and feelings with those of other people in the same situation.

3. *Perception of legitimate authority.* An experimenter at Yale might have appeared to be a highly legitimate authority figure—as might a government official or a high-ranking officer in the military (Blass, 2009). The percentage of individuals who complied with the experimenter's demands dropped from 65% to 48% when Milgram (1974) replicated the study in a dingy storefront in a nearby town. Even in that setting, many people are willing to engage in morally reprehensible acts at the behest of a legitimate-looking authority figure. Hitler and his henchmen were authority figures in Nazi Germany. "Science" and Yale University legitimized the authority of the experimenters in the Milgram studies.

4. *The foot-in-the-door technique.* The **foot-in-the-door technique** might also have contributed to the obedience of the teachers (Burger, 2009). Once they had begun to deliver shocks to learners, they might have found it progressively more difficult to extricate themselves from the situation.

5. *Inaccessibility of values.* People are more likely to act in accordance with their attitudes when their attitudes are readily available, or accessible. Most people believe it is wrong to harm innocent people, but strong emotions impair clear thinking. As the teachers in the Milgram experiments became more emotionally involved, their attitudes might thus have become less "accessible."

6. *Buffers between the perpetrator and the victim.* Several buffers decreased the effect of the learners'

pain on the teachers. For example, the "learners" were in another room. When they were in the same room with the teachers, their compliance rate dropped from 65% to 40%. Moreover, when the teacher held the learner's hand on the shock plate, the compliance rate dropped to 30%.

14-5b CONFORMITY

We are said to *conform* when we change our behavior to adhere to *social norms*. Social norms are widely accepted expectations concerning social behavior. Explicit social norms are often made into rules and laws such as those that require us to whisper in libraries and to slow down when driving past a school. There are also unspoken or implicit social norms, such as those that cause us to face the front in an elevator or to be "fashionably late" for social gatherings. Can you think of some instances in which you have conformed to social pressure?

The tendency to conform to social norms is often good. Many norms have evolved because they promote comfort and survival. Group pressure can also promote maladaptive behavior, as when people engage in risky behavior because "everyone is doing it." Why do so many people tend to follow the crowd? To answer this question, let us look at a classic experiment on conformity conducted by Solomon Asch in the early 1950s.

The Asch Study

Can you believe what you see with your own eyes? Seeing is believing, isn't it? Not if you were a participant in Asch's (1952) study.

Let's say you entered a laboratory room with seven other subjects, supposedly taking part in an experiment on visual discrimination. At the front of the room stood a man holding cards with lines drawn on them.

The eight of you were seated in a series. You were given the seventh seat, a minor fact at the time. The man explained the task. There was a single line on the card on the left. Three lines were drawn on the card at the right (see Figure 14.4). One line on the right card was the same length as the line on the left card. You and the other participants were to call out, one at a time, which of the three lines—1, 2, or 3—was the same length as the one on the card on the left. Simple.

The participants to your right spoke out in order: "3," "3," "3," "3," "3," "3." Now it was your turn. Line 3 was clearly the same length as the line on the first card, so you said "3." The fellow after you then chimed in: "3." That's all there was to it. Then two other cards were set up at the front of the room. This time line 2 was clearly the same length as the line on the first card. The answers were "2," "2," "2," "2," "2," "2." Again it was your turn. You said "2," and perhaps your mind began to wander. Your stomach was gurgling a bit. The fellow after you said "2."

FIGURE 14.4 | Cards Used in the Asch Study on Conformity

Which line on card B (1, 2, or 3) is the same length as the line on card A? Line 2, right? But would you say "2" if you were a member of a group and six people answering ahead of you all said "3"? Are you sure?

A. Standard line

B. Comparison lines

© Cengage Learning 2012

Another pair of cards was held up. Line 3 was clearly the correct answer. The people on your right spoke in turn: "1," "1 … " Wait a second! "… 1," "1." You forgot about dinner and studied the lines briefly. No, line 1 was too short by a good half-inch. But the next two participants said "1" and suddenly it was your turn. Your hands had become sweaty, and there was a lump in your throat. You wanted to say "3," but was it right? There was really no time, and you had already paused noticeably. You said "1," and so did the last fellow.

Now your attention was riveted on the task. Much of the time you agreed with the other judges, but sometimes you did not. And for some reason beyond your understanding, they were in perfect agreement even when they were wrong—assuming you could trust your eyes. The experiment was becoming an uncomfortable experience, and you began to doubt your judgment.

The discomfort in the Asch study was caused by the pressure to conform. Actually, the other seven recruits were confederates of the experimenter. They prearranged a number of incorrect responses. The sole purpose of the study was to see whether you would conform to the erroneous group judgments.

How many people in Asch's study caved in? How many went along with the crowd rather than give what they thought to be the right answer? Seventy-five percent. *Three out of four agreed with the majority's wrong answer at least once.*

14-5c FACTORS THAT INFLUENCE CONFORMITY

Several factors increase the tendency to conform, including belonging to a collectivist rather than an individualistic society (Fukushima et al., 2009), the desire to be liked by other members of the group (but valuing being right over being liked *decreases* the tendency to conform), low self-esteem, social shyness (Wagstaff et al., 2009), and lack of familiarity with the task (Phalet & Schoenpflug, 2001; Wang et al., 2011). Other factors in conformity include group size and social support. The likelihood of conformity, even to incorrect group judgments, increases rapidly as group size grows to five members; it then rises more slowly as the group grows to about eight members. At about that point, the maximum chance of conformity is reached. Yet finding just one other person who supports your minority opinion apparently is enough to encourage you to stick to your guns (Jetten & Hornsey, 2011; Mesoudi, 2009).

FICTION SEEING IS NOT ALWAYS BELIEVING— ESPECIALLY WHEN THE GROUP SEES THINGS DIFFERENTLY.

14-6 Aggression

One could argue that humans are among the most aggressive species on Earth. There are armed conflicts of one kind or another on nearly every continent of the planet. There is murder, and there is battering, often by people's most intimate partners. There is rape. And we praise "controlled" aggression in football and hockey games. Psychologists ask why we are aggressive.

14-6a BIOLOGY, CHEMISTRY, AND AGGRESSION

Evolutionary psychologists believe that "genetic whisperings" influence aggression to some degree (Buss, 2009; Confer et al., 2010). Numerous biological structures and chemicals are involved in aggression. In response to certain stimuli, many nonhumans show instinctive aggres-

sive reactions (Archer, 2009). This behavior is automatic. For example, the male robin responds aggressively to the red breast of another robin. The hypothalamus appears to be involved in this inborn reaction pattern. Electrical stimulation of part of the hypothalamus triggers stereotypical aggressive behaviors in many lower animals, including monkeys. However, in humans, whose brains are more complex, other brain structures apparently moderate possible aggressive instincts.

Chemistry is also involved in aggression, especially in the form of the male sex hormone testosterone. Testosterone appears to affect the tendencies to dominate and control other people. Men have higher testosterone levels than women do and are also (usually) more aggressive than women, especially with male strangers (Crofoot & Wrangham, 2010; Pradhan et al., 2010). Aggressive boys and adolescents are likely to have higher testosterone levels than their less aggressive peers (Popma et al., 2007). James Dabbs and his colleagues (1996) found that members of so-called rambunctious fraternities had higher testosterone levels, on average, than members of more "well-behaved" fraternities. Testosterone levels also vary with the occasion: men's testosterone levels tend to be higher when they are "winning"—whether in athletic competitions such as football or in chess (Carré et al., 2009; Carré & Putnam, 2010).

14-6b PSYCHOLOGICAL ASPECTS OF AGGRESSION

Another reason that males are more likely than females to behave aggressively is that females are more likely to empathize with the victim—to put themselves in the victim's place (Proverbio et al., 2010; Yamasue et al., 2008). Empathy encourages helping behavior, not aggression.

Sigmund Freud, the originator of psychodynamic theory, believed that aggression is a natural and instinctive reaction to the frustrations of daily life. Children (and adults) seek to vent aggressive impulses on other people, including parents, because even the most attentive parents cannot gratify all of their demands immediately. Yet children also fear punishment and loss of love, so they repress most aggressive impulses and store them in the unconscious recesses of the mind.

Cognitive psychologists assert that our behavior is influenced by our values, by how we interpret situations, and by choice. People who believe that aggression is sometimes necessary and justified—as during wartime—are likely to act aggressively. People who believe that a particular war or act of aggression is unjust, or who oppose aggression under all circumstances, are less likely to behave aggressively (Hurka, 2010; Maxwell et al., 2009).

People also decide—sometimes making split-second decisions—whether they will strike out or not on the basis of their interpretation of the other person's motives. But many individuals who act aggressively distort other people's motives. For example, they assume that other people wish them harm when they actually do not (Dodge, 2006; Ellis et al., 2009). We are more likely to respond aggressively to a provocation when we magnify the importance of the "insult" or otherwise stir up feelings of anger (Ellis et al., 2009). How do you respond when someone bumps into you? If you view it as an intentional insult to your honor, you may respond with aggression.

From the behavioral perspective, learning is acquired through reinforcement. Organisms that are reinforced for aggressive behavior are more likely to behave aggressively in situations similar to those in which reinforcement occurs. Strong, agile organisms are likely to be reinforced for aggressive behavior.

Among nonhumans reinforcement is usually physical—for example, food, mating, or escaping a predator. Humans respond to such reinforcements but also to other reinforcers, such as social approval. Children are less likely to act aggressively when teachers and classmates communicate strong disapproval of aggressive behavior (Henry, 2008; Simon et al., 2009). From the social-cognitive perspective, aggressive skills are mainly acquired by observation of other people acting aggressively. However, social-cognitive theorists—like other cognitive theorists—believe that consciousness and choice play key roles in aggressive behavior among humans. Social-cognitive theorists believe that we are not likely to act aggressively unless we believe that aggression is appropriate under the circumstances and likely to be reinforced.

Situational factors also contribute to aggression. The Milgram studies showed us that the majority of "normal" people will act aggressively when they are influenced by other people to do so. In the section on group behavior, we will see that people may also act more aggressively when they are members of a mob.

Do we run faster when we are alone or when we are members of the group?

To be human is to belong to groups. Groups help us satisfy our needs for affection, attention, and belonging. They empower us to do things we could not manage by ourselves. But groups can also pressure us into doing things we might not do if we were acting alone. This section considers ways in which people behave differently as group members than they would as individuals. We begin with social facilitation.

14-7a SOCIAL FACILITATION

When you are given a group assignment, do you work harder or less hard than you would alone? Why? One effect of groups on individual behavior is **social facilitation**, the process by which a person's performance is increased when other members of a group engage in similar behavior. Research suggests that the presence of other people increases our levels of arousal, or motivation (Ito et al., 2011; Thomas et al., 2002). At high levels of arousal, our performance of simple tasks is facilitated. Our performance of complex responses may be impaired, however. For this reason, a well-rehearsed speech may be delivered masterfully before a larger audience, while an impromptu speech may be hampered by a large audience.

Social facilitation may be influenced by **evaluation apprehension** as well as arousal—that is, by concern that they are evaluating us (Rosenberg, 2009; Thomas et al., 2002). When giving a speech, we may "lose our thread" if we are distracted by the audience and focus too much on its apparent reaction. If we believe that we have begun to flounder, evaluation apprehension may skyrocket. As a result, our performance may falter even more.

The presence of others can also impair performance—not when we are acting *before* a group but when we are

social facilitation
the process by which a person's performance is increased when other members of a group engage in similar behavior

evaluation apprehension
concern that others are evaluating our behavior

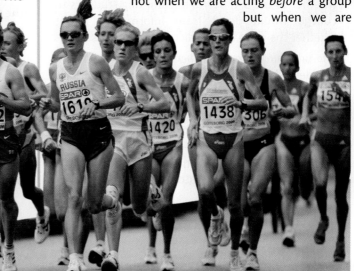

Julian Finney/Getty Images

anonymous members *of* a group (Osborn et al., 2012). Workers, for example, may "goof off" or engage in *social loafing*—that is, failure to make a significant effort because others have made or are making such an effort—when they believe they will not be found out and held accountable. Under these group conditions there is no evaluation apprehension, but rather there may be **diffusion of responsibility** in groups. Each person may feel less obligation to help because others are present, especially if the others are perceived as being capable of doing the job (Abele & Diehl, 2008; Maiden & Perry, 2010). Group members may also reduce their efforts if an apparently capable member makes no contribution but "rides free" on the efforts of others.

14-7b GROUP DECISION MAKING

Organizations use groups such as committees or juries to make decisions in the belief that group decisions are more accurate than individual decisions (Van Swol, 2008). Social psychologists have discovered a number of "rules," or **social decision schemes**, that govern much of group decision making (Stasser, 1999). Here are some examples:

1. *The majority-wins scheme.* In this commonly used scheme, the group arrives at the decision that was initially supported by the majority. This scheme appears to guide decision making most often when there is no single objectively correct decision. An example is a decision about which car models to build when their popularity has not been tested in the court of public opinion.

2. *The truth-wins scheme.* In this scheme, as more information is provided and opinions are discussed, the group comes to recognize that one approach is objectively correct. For example, a group deciding whether to use SAT scores in admitting students to college would profit from information about whether the scores do predict college success.

3. *The two-thirds majority scheme.* Juries tend to convict defendants when two-thirds of the jury initially favors conviction.

4. *The first-shift rule.* In this scheme, the group tends to adopt the decision that reflects the first shift in opinion expressed by any group member. If a jury is deadlocked, the members may eventually follow the lead of the first juror to switch his or her position.

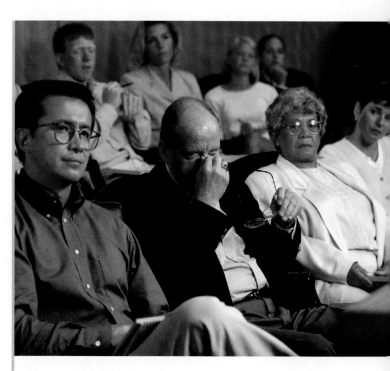

©Guy Call/Corbis

14-7c POLARIZATION AND THE "RISKY SHIFT"

We might assume that a group decision would be more conservative than an individual decision. After all, shouldn't there be an effort to compromise, to "split the difference"? We might also expect that a few mature individuals would be able to balance the opinions of daredevils.

Groups do not always appear to work as we might expect, however. Consider the *polarization* effect. As an individual, you might recommend that your company risk an investment of $500,000 to develop or market a new product. Other company executives, polled individually, might risk similar amounts. If you were gathered together to make a group decision, however, you would probably recommend either an amount well above this figure or nothing at all (Kamalanabhan et al., 2000). This group effect is called *polarization*, or the taking of an extreme position. If you had to gamble on which way the decision would go, however, you would do better to place your money on movement toward the higher sum—that is, to bet on a *risky shift*. Why?

One possibility is that one member of the group may reveal information that the others were not aware of. This information may clearly point in one direction or the other. With doubts removed, the group moves decisively in the appropriate direction. It is also possible that social facilitation occurs in the group setting and that the resulting greater motivation prompts more extreme decisions.

Why, however, do groups tend to take *greater* risks than those their members would take as individuals? One answer is diffusion of responsibility (A. S. Brown, 2007; Kamalanabhan et al., 2000). If the venture flops, the blame will not be placed on you alone.

14-7d GROUPTHINK

Groupthink, a concept originated by Irving Janis (1982), is a problem that may arise in group decision making when group members are swayed more by group cohesiveness and a dynamic leader than by the realities of the situation (Esser & Lindoerfer, 2006; Packer, 2009). Group problem solving may degenerate into groupthink when a group senses an external threat (Underhill, 2008). Groupthink is usually fueled by a dynamic group leader. The threat heightens the cohesiveness of the group and is a source of stress. Under stress, group members tend not to consider all their options carefully and frequently make flawed decisions.

Groupthink has been connected with historic fiascos such as the invasion of Iraq, the botched Bay of Pigs invasion of Cuba, the Watergate scandal in which members of the Nixon administration believed they could cover up a theft, and NASA's decision to launch the *Challenger* space shuttle despite engineers' warnings about the dangers created by unusually cold weather (Brownstein, 2003; Esser & Lindoerfer, 2006).

Janis and other researchers (Brownstein, 2003; Packer, 2009) note characteristics of groupthink that contribute to flawed decisions:

1. *Feelings of invulnerability.* In the Watergate Affair, the decision-making group might have believed that it was beyond the reach of critics or the law because they were powerful people who were close to the President of the United States.

2. *The group's belief in its rightness.* These groups apparently believed in the rightness of what they were doing. In the case of the Iraq invasion, members of the Bush administration believed they had the evidence of weapons of mass destruction (WMDs) that they needed to justify their invasion.

3. *Discrediting information contrary to the group's decision.* Members of the Bush administration discredited reports that raised doubt as to the presence of WMDs.

4. *Pressures on group members to conform.* Striving for unanimity overrides the quest for realism, and authority can trump expertise. After the disastrous invasion of the Bay of Pigs in Cuba, President John F. Kennedy is reported to have said, "How could we have been so stupid?"

5. *Stereotyping members of the out-group.* In the cases of the invasions of the Bay of Pigs and Iraq, proinvasion group members stereotyped members of the out-group as being out of touch with reality.

Groupthink can be averted if group leaders encourage members to remain skeptical about options and to feel free to ask probing questions and disagree with one another.

14-7e MOB BEHAVIOR AND DEINDIVIDUATION

Have you ever done something as a member of a group that you would not have done as an individual? What was it? What motivated you? How do you feel about it? The Frenchman Gustave Le Bon (1895–1960) branded mobs and crowds as irrational, resembling a "beast with many heads." Mob actions such as race riots and lynchings sometimes seem to operate on a

---

✳ Strength in Numbers? Maybe Not

In their classic experiment, Darley and Latané (1968) had male subjects perform meaningless tasks in cubicles. Then, while they were working, they heard a (convincing) recording of a person apparently having an epileptic seizure. When the men thought that four other persons were immediately available, only 31% tried to help the victim. When they thought that no one else was available, however, 85% of them tried to help.

As in other areas of group behavior, it seems that diffusion of responsibility inhibits helping behavior in groups or crowds. When we are in a group, we are often willing to let George (or Georgette) do it. When George isn't around, we are more willing to help others ourselves.

© Digital Vision/PhotoLibrary

deindividuation
the process by which group members may discontinue self-evaluation and adopt group norms and attitudes

altruism
unselfish concern for the welfare of others

bystander effect
the tendency to avoid helping other people in emergencies when other people are also present and apparently capable of helping

psychology of their own. Do mobs "bring out the beast in us"?

When people act as individuals, fear of consequences and self-evaluation tend to prevent them from engaging in antisocial behavior. But in a mob, they may experience **deindividuation**, a state in which they are willing to follow a norm that emerges in a specific situation, even if it means ignoring their own values (Lan & Zuo, 2009; Postmes & Spears, 1998). Many factors lead to deindividuation, including anonymity, diffusion of responsibility, arousal due to noise and crowding, and a focus on emerging group norms rather than on one's own values (S. E. Taylor et al., 2006). Under these circumstances, crowd members behave more aggressively than they would as individuals.

14-7f ALTRUISM AND THE BYSTANDER EFFECT

Altruism—selfless concern for the welfare of others— is connected with some heroic behavior. Humans have sacrificed themselves to ensure the survival of their children or of comrades in battle. So how, one might ask, could the murder of 28-year-old Kitty Genovese have happened? It took place in New York City more than 40 years ago. Murder was not unheard of in the Big Apple, but Kitty had screamed for help as her killer stalked her for more than half an hour and stabbed her in three separate attacks (Manning et al., 2007). Thirty-eight neighbors heard the commotion. Twice, the assault was interrupted by their voices and bedroom lights. Each time the attacker returned. Yet nobody came to the victim's aid. No one even called the police.

Why? Some witnesses said matter-of-factly that they did not want to get involved. One said that he was tired. Still others said, "I don't know." As a nation, are we a callous bunch who would rather watch than help when others are in trouble? Perhaps nobody came to Kitty's aid because of the **bystander effect**; that is, they saw that other people were present or, because the murder took place in crowded New York City, they assumed that other people were also available to help.

TRUTH IT IS TRUE THAT NEARLY 40 PEOPLE STOOD BY AND DID NOTHING WHILE A WOMAN WAS BEING STABBED TO DEATH.

When Do We Help Someone Who Is in Trouble?

Many factors are involved in helping behavior:

1. Observers are more likely to help when they are in a good mood (Schnall et al., 2010). Perhaps good moods impart a sense of personal power—the feeling that we can handle the situation.

2. People who are empathic are more likely to help people in need (Decety & Batson, 2009). Women are more likely than men to be empathic and thus more likely to help people in need (Yamasue et al., 2008).

3. Bystanders may not help unless they believe that an emergency exists (Cocking et al., 2009).

4. Observers must assume the responsibility to act (Piliavin, 2009). A lone person may have been more likely to try to help Kitty Genovese. *Diffusion of responsibility* may inhibit helping behavior in crowds.

5. Observers must know what to do (Baron et al., 2009). Observers who are not sure that they can take charge of the situation may stay on the sidelines for fear of making a social blunder or of getting hurt themselves.

6. Observers are more likely to help people they know (Hopkins & Powers, 2009). Evolutionary psychologists suggest that altruism is selfish from an evolutionary point of view when it helps close relatives or others who are similar to us to survive (Bruene & Ribbert, 2002). It helps us perpetuate a genetic code similar to our own. This view suggests that we are more likely to be altruistic with our relatives rather than strangers, however.

7. Observers are more likely to help people who are similar to themselves. Being able to identify with the person in need promotes helping behavior (Cialdini et al., 1997).

A Note on the Most Prosocial Behavior

Let us not end this chapter and this book on a negative note. Let us think, instead, about the altruism of the firefighters, police officers, and ordinary people who came to the aid of the victims of the suicide terrorism of September 11, 2001. Following the attacks, thousands evacuated lower Manhattan by ferry to New Jersey. Residents of New Jersey drove up and down the streets near the ferry, asking if they could give evacuees rides or help in any other way. And people heading away from the devastation in Manhattan were happy to share their taxicabs, even with strangers. If you know a little about New York City, you know that's rather special—but it's also something done by ordinary people in extraordinary times.

Ready to study? In the book, you can:

❏ Review what you've read with Fill-Ins and Multiple Choice quizzes (below).

❏ Rip out Chapter Review card (in the back).

Or you can go online to CourseMate at www.cengagebrain.com for these resources:

❏ Complete Practices Quizzes to prepare for tests.

❏ Review Key Terms Flash Cards (online or print).

❏ Play games to master concepts.

FILL-INS

Answers can be found in the back of the book, starting on page 368.

1. Attitudes are acquired through conditioning, observational learning, and _____ appraisal.

2. According to cognitive-_____ theory, we are motivated to make our cognitions consistent with one another and with our behavior.

3. One factor in prejudice is social _____, or the tendency to divide the world into us and them.

4. According to the _____-_____ hypothesis, we tend to be attracted to people who are similar to ourselves.

5. According to the triangular model of love, love can include combinations of intimacy, _____, and commitment.

6. The tendency to perceive others in terms of first impressions is an example of the _____ effect.

7. The following factors contribute to obedience: socialization, lack of _____ comparison, perception of experimenters as legitimate authority figures, the foot-in-the-door technique, and inaccessibility of values.

8. Social _____ refers to the enhancement of performance that results from the presence of others.

9. Members of a group may experience _____, which is a state of reduced self-awareness and lowered concern for social evaluation.

10. Kitty Genovese's death has been attributed to the _____ effect.

1. The A–B problem focuses on
   a. activities we do and behaviors we avoid.
   b. attitudes and beliefs.
   c. the relationship between achievement and behavior.
   d. consistency between our attitudes and behavior.

2. Mary prefers living in the country away from the noise and crowds of the city, but her sister Denise prefers the excitement and pace of city life. They differ in _____.
   a. avoidance
   b. attitude
   c. polarization
   d. deindividuation

3. One major reason that groups tend to take greater risks than their members would take as individuals is
   a. diffusion of responsibility.
   b. the reciprocity norm.
   c. group intelligence.
   d. all of these.

4. The _____ route is to facts and research results as the _____ route is to status and prestige.
   a. peripheral; central
   b. central; peripheral
   c. secondary; primary
   d. primary; secondary

5. The "Save the World by Praying" association predicted the world would end on Nov. 1, 1999. When the world did not end on that day their group made a statement that supported the theory of cognitive dissonance. Which of the statements below would fit that description?
   a. "We were wrong, prayer does not help."
   b. "God did not listen to us."
   c. "Our praying must have saved the world."
   d. "We are confused about all this."

6. The first time you met your fiancée you fell down and spilled a glass of wine on her dress. You obviously didn't make a very good first impression. However, it was several months later before you saw her again. Your second meeting went much better and it was almost as if your first encounter never happened. This change in her perception of you is probably due to the
   a. primary effect.
   b. recency effect.
   c. repression.
   d. discrimination.

7. Yevhen is standing in line in school. While he isn't looking, another boy steps on his toe. Yevhen says to himself: "He must have stepped on my toe because it's so crowded in here and somebody else pushed this guy; it was probably an accident." Yevhen is making a _____ attribution.
   a. dispositional
   b. situational
   c. fundamental
   d. motivational

8. If there had been two teachers acting together rather than one in Milgram's experiment, and the teachers could discuss the situation before complying with the demands of the experimenter, this change in procedure would probably have
   a. decreased the level of obedience.
   b. had no affect on obedience.
   c. increased the level of obedience.
   d. none of these

9. The process by which the presence of others improves our performance is known as
   a. reciprocation.
   b. social facilitation.
   c. social lubrication.
   d. reciprocity.

10. The self-serving bias is the tendency to
    a. repeat ourselves when we think we're right.
    b. take care of our own needs first, and worry about others later.
    c. credit our successes to internal, dispositional factors and our failures to situational influences.
    d. describe our successes in greater detail than our failures.

4LTR Press solutions are designed for today's learners through the continuous feedback of students like you. Tell us what you think about PSYCH3 and help us improve the learning experience for future students.

YOUR FEEDBACK MATTERS.

LEARNING OUTCOMES

APP-1 Explain how statistics are used in psychology

APP-2 Calculate values using descriptive statistics

APP-3 Describe and apply the normal curve

APP-4 Calculate values using the correlation coefficient

APP-5 Explain the logic behind inferential statistics

STATISTICS APPENDIX

App-1 Statistics

Imagine that aliens from outer space arrive outside Madison Square Garden in New York City. Their goal this dark winter evening is to learn all they can about planet Earth. They are drawn inside the Garden by lights, shouts, and warmth. The spotlighting inside rivets their attention to a wood-floored arena where the New York Big Apples are hosting the California Quakes in a briskly contested basketball game.

Our visitors use their sophisticated instruments to take measurements of the players. Some statistics are sent back to their home planet: It appears that (1) 100% of Earthlings are male and (2) the height of Earthlings ranges from 6'1" to 7'2".

These measurements are called **statistics**. Statistics is the name given to the science concerned with obtaining and organizing numerical information or measurements. Our visitors have sent home statistics about the gender and size of humans that are at once accurate and misleading. Although they accurately measured the basketball players, their small sample of Earth's population was, shall we say, distorted.

A **population** is a complete group of people, other animals, or measures from which a sample is drawn. For example, all people on Earth could be defined as the population of interest. So could all women, or all women in the United States. A **sample** is a group of measures drawn from a population. Fortunately for us Earthlings, about half of the world's population is female. And the *range* of heights observed by the aliens, of 6'1" to 7'2", is both restricted and too high—much too high. People vary in height by more than 1 foot and 1 inch. And our **average** height is not between 6'1" and 7'2"; rather, it is a number of inches below.

Psychologists, like our imagined visitors, are concerned with measuring human as well as animal characteristics and traits—not just physical characteristics as height, but also psychological traits such as intelligence, aggressiveness, and depression. By observing the *central tendencies* (averages) and variations in measurement

> To what degree do you think the people in your school represent the population of the United States? North America? The world?

TRUTH OR FICTION

WHAT DO YOU THINK? FOLKLORE, COMMON SENSE, OR NONSENSE? CIRCLE THE T FOR "TRUTH" OR THE F FOR "FICTION," AND CHECK THE ACCURACY OF YOUR ANSWERS AS YOU READ THROUGH THE CHAPTER.

T	F	PROFESSIONAL BASKETBALL PLAYERS COULD BE SAID TO BE ABNORMAL.
T	F	BEING A "10" IS NOT ALWAYS A GOOD THING.
T	F	YOU SHOULD NOT ASSUME THAT YOU CAN WALK ACROSS A RIVER WITH AN AVERAGE DEPTH OF 4 FEET.
T	F	ADDING PEOPLE'S INCOMES AND THEN DIVIDING THEM BY THE NUMBER OF PEOPLE CAN BE AN AWFUL WAY OF SHOWING THE AVERAGE INCOME.
T	F	PSYCHOLOGISTS EXPRESS YOUR IQ SCORE IN TERMS OF HOW DEVIANT YOU ARE.
T	F	AN IQ SCORE OF 130 IS MORE IMPRESSIVE THAN AN SAT SCORE OF 500.

statistics
numerical facts assembled in such a manner that they provide useful information about measures or scores (from the Latin *status*, meaning "standing" or "position")

population
a complete group from which a sample is selected

sample
part of a population

average
the central tendency of a group of measures, expressed either as the mean, median, or mode of a distribution

descriptive statistics
the branch of statistics that is concerned with providing descriptive information about a distribution of scores

TRUTH BASKETBALL PLAYERS COULD BE SAID TO BE ABNORMAL IN THE SENSE THAT THEY ARE ARE TALLER, STRONGER, AND MORE AGILE THAN THE REST OF US.

from person to person, psychologists can say that one person is average or above average in intelligence, or that someone else is less anxious than, say, 60% of the population. But psychologists, unlike our aliens, attempt to select a sample that accurately represents the entire population. Professional basketball players do not represent the entire human species.

In this appendix, we survey some statistical methods used by psychologists to draw conclusions about the measurements they take. First we discuss *descriptive statistics* and learn what types of statements we can make about height and other human traits. Then we discuss the *normal curve* and learn why basketball players are abnormal—at least in terms of height. We explain *correlation coefficients* and provide you with some less-than-shocking news: As a group, students who study obtain higher grades than students who do not study. Finally, we have a look at *inferential statistics* and see why basketball players are in fact *statistically significantly* taller than the general population.

Does this basketball player represent all earthlings? In what ways might he do so, and in what ways might he differ?

App-2 Descriptive Statistics

Being told that someone is a "10" may sound great at first. However, it is not very descriptive unless you know something about how the scores on the scale are distributed and how frequently one finds a 10. Fortunately—for 10s, if not for the rest of us—one usually means that the person is a 10 on a scale of from 1 to 10, and that 10 is the highest score. If this is not sufficient, one will also be told that 10s are few and far between—unusual statistical events.

The idea of the scale from 1 to 10 may not be very scientific, but it does suggest something about descriptive statistics. **Descriptive statistics** is the branch of statistics that provides information about distributions of scores. We can use descriptive statistics to clarify our understanding of a distribution of scores such as heights, test grades, IQs, or even increases or decreases in measures of aggressive behavior following the drinking of alcohol. For example, descriptive statistics can help us determine measures of central tendency (averages) and to determine how much fluctuation or variability there is in the scores. Being a 10 loses much of its charm if the average score is an 11. Being a 10 is more remarkable in a distribution whose scores range from 1 to 10 than it is in a distribution whose scores range from 9 to 11.

TRUTH BEING A "10" IS NOT ALWAYS A GOOD THING BECAUSE A SCALE CAN VARY, SAY, FROM 0 TO 100, IN WHICH CASE A SCORE OF 10 WOULD PLACE ONE NEARER TO THE BOTTOM OF THE SCALE, MAKING A SCORE OF 50 THE CENTER POINT OF THE SCALE.

Let's now consider some of the concerns of descriptive statistics: the frequency distribution, measures of central tendency (types of averages), and measures of variability.

Being a 10 may not be such a good thing if the average score is 11.

TABLE A.1 | Roster of Quakes Versus Big Apples at New York

A glance at the rosters for a recent basketball game in which the New York Big Apples "entertained" the California Quakes shows that the heights of the team members, combined, ranged from 6'1" to 7'2". Do the heights of the team members represent those of the general male population? What do you think?

CALIFORNIA QUAKES			NEW YORK BIG APPLES		
2	Callahan	6'7"	3	Roosevelt	6'1"
5	Daly	6'11"	12	Chaffee	6'5"
6	Chico	6'2"	13	Baldwin	6'9"
12	Capistrano	6'3"	25	Delmar	6'6"
21	Brentwood	6'5"	27	Merrick	6'8"
25	Van Nuys	6'3"	28	Hewlett	6'6"
31	Clemente	6'9"	33	Hollis	6'9"
32	Whittier	6'8"	42	Bedford	6'5"
41	Fernando	7'2"	43	Coram	6'2"
43	Watts	6'9"	45	Hampton	6'10"
53	Huntington	6'6"	53	Ardsley	6'10"

© Cengage Learning 2012

TABLE A.2 | Frequency Distribution of Basketball Players (Quakes and Big Apples Combined), with a 1-Inch Class Interval

CLASS INTERVAL	NUMBER OF PLAYERS IN CLASS
6'1"–6'1.9"	1
6'2"–6'2.9"	2
6'3"–6'3.9"	2
6'4"–6'4.9"	0
6'5"–6'5.9"	3
6'6"–6'6.9"	3
6'7"–6'7.9"	1
6'8"–6'8.9"	2
6'9"–6'9.9"	4
6'10"–6'10.9"	2
6'11"–6'11.9"	1
7'0"–7'0.9"	0
7'1"–7'1.9"	0
7'2"–7'2.9"	1

© Cengage Learning 2012

App-2a THE FREQUENCY DISTRIBUTION

A **frequency distribution** takes scores or items of raw data, puts them into order from the lowest to the highest, and indicates how often a score appears. Table A.1 shows the rosters for a recent basketball game between the California Quakes and the New York Big Apples. The players are listed according to the numbers on their uniforms.

It would also be possible to use other class intervals, such as 3 inches, as shown in Table A.3. In determining the size of a class interval, the researcher tries to collapse the data into a small-enough number of classes to ensure that they will be meaningful at a glance. But the researcher also tries to keep a large-enough number of categories (classes) to ensure that important differences are not obscured.

Table A.3 obscures the fact that no players are 6'4" tall. If the researcher believes that this information is important, a class interval of 1 inch may be maintained.

Figure A.1 shows two methods of graphing the information in Table A.3: the **frequency histogram** and the **frequency polygon**. Students sometimes have difficulty interpreting graphs, but the purpose of graphs is to reveal key information about frequency distributions at a glance. Note that in both kinds of graph, the frequency histogram and the frequency polygon, the class intervals are usually drawn along the horizontal line. The horizontal line is also known as the *x*-axis. The numbers of cases (scores, persons, or events) in each class interval are shown along the vertical line, which is also known as the *y*-axis. In the histogram, the number of

frequency distribution
an ordered set of data that indicates the frequency (how often) with which scores appear

frequency histogram
a graphic representation of a frequency distribution that uses rectangular solids (bars) to represent the frequency with which scores appear

frequency polygon
a graphic representation of a frequency distribution that connects the points that show the frequencies with which scores appear, thereby creating a multi-sided geometric figure

TABLE A.3 | Frequency Distribution of Heights of Basketball Players, Using a 3-Inch Class Interval

CLASS INTERVAL	NUMBER OF PLAYERS IN CLASS
6'1"–6'3.9"	5
6'4"–6'6.9"	6
6'7"–6'9.9"	7
6'10"–7'0.9"	3
7'1"–7'3.9"	1

© Cengage Learning 2012

mean
a type of average that is calculated by adding all the scores and then dividing by the number of scores

median
the central score in a frequency distribution; the score beneath which 50% of the cases fall

scores in each class interval is represented by a bar—a rectangular solid—so that the graph looks like a series of steps. In the polygon, the number of scores in each class interval is plotted as a point. The points are connected to form a many-sided geometric figure (polygon). Note that empty class intervals were added at each end of the frequency polygon so that the sides of the figure could be brought down to the *x*-axis to close the geometric figure.

App-2b MEASURES OF CENTRAL TENDENCY

Never try to walk across a river just because it has an average depth of four feet.

—MARTIN FRIEDMAN

Measures of central tendency are "averages" that show the center, or balancing points, of a frequency distribution. There are three commonly used types of measures of central tendency: the *mean*, the *median*, and the *mode*. Each attempts to describe something about the scores in a frequency distribution through the use of a typical or representative number.

A RIVER WITH AN AVERAGE DEPTH OF 4 FEET COULD BE OVER YOUR HEAD IN MANY PLACES; AS SUGGESTED IN THE QUIP BY MARTIN FRIEDMAN, A MEASURE OF CENTRAL TENDENCY CAN SOMETIMES BE MISLEADING.

The **mean** is what most people think of as "the average." We obtain the mean of a distribution by adding up the scores and then dividing the sum by the number of scores. In the case of the basketball players, it would be advisable to first convert the heights into a single unit, such as inches (6'1" becomes 73", and so on). If we add all the heights in inches and then divide by the number of players (22), we obtain a mean height of 78.73". If we convert that number back into units of feet and inches, we obtain 6'6.73".

The **median** is the score of the *middle case* in a distribution. It is the score beneath which 50% of the cases fall. In a distribution with an even number of cases, such as the distribution of the heights of the 22 basketball players as shown in Table A.2, we obtain the median by finding the mean of the two middle cases. When we list the 22 cases in ascending order (moving from lowest to highest), the 11th case is 6'6" and the

FIGURE A.1 | Two Graphical Representations of the Data in Table A.3

The graph on the left is called a frequency histogram, or bar graph. The graph on the right is called a frequency polygon.

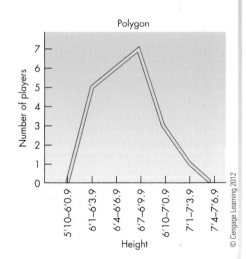

12th case is 6'7". Therefore, the median of the distribution is (6'6" + 6'7") /2, or 6'6.5".

When we analyze the heights of the basketball players, we find that the mean and the median are similar. Either one serves as a useful indicator of the central tendency of the data. But suppose we are trying to find the average savings of 30 families living on a suburban block. Let's assume that 29 of the 30 families have savings between $8,000 and $12,000, adding up to $294,000. But the 30th family has savings of $1,400,000! The mean savings for a family on this block would thus be $56,467. The mean can be greatly distorted by one or two extreme scores. An IQ score of 145 would similarly distort the mean of the IQ scores of a class of 20 students, among whom the other 19 IQ scores ranged from 93 to 112. Then, too, if a few basketball players signed up for one of your classes, the mean of the students' heights would be distorted in an upward direction.

When there are a few extreme scores in a distribution, the median is a better indicator of central tendency. The median savings on our hypothetical block would lie between $8,000 and $12,000. Thus it would be more representative of the central tendency of savings. Studies of the incomes of families in the United States usually report median rather than mean incomes just to avoid the distortion of findings that would occur if the incomes of a handful of billionaires were treated in the same way as more common incomes. On the other hand, one could argue that choosing the median as the average obscures or hides the extreme scores, which are just as "real" as the other scores. Perhaps it is best to use the median and a footnote—a rather big footnote.

TRUTH ADDING PEOPLE'S INCOMES AND THEN DIVIDING THEM BY THE NUMBER OF PEOPLE CAN BE AN AWFUL WAY OF SHOWING THE AVERAGE INCOME. A FEW EXTREMELY HIGH INCOMES, OR IQ SCORES, OR HEIGHTS CAN DISTORT THE AVERAGE OF A GROUP IN AN UPWARD DIRECTION.

The **mode** is simply the most frequently occurring score or measure in a distribution. The mode of the data in Table A.1 is 6'9" because this height occurs most often among the players on the two teams. The median class interval for the data shown in Table A.3 is 6'6.5" to 6'9.5". With this particular distribution, the mode is somewhat higher than the mean or the median.

In some cases the mode is a more appropriate description of the central tendency of a distribution than the mean or the median. Figure A.2 shows a **bimodal** distribution—that is, a distribution with two modes. This is a hypothetical distribution of test scores obtained by a class. The mode at the left indicates the most common class interval (45 to 49) for students who did not study, and the mode to the right shows the most common class interval (65 to 69) for students who did study. (Don't be alarmed. I'm sure that the professor, who is extremely fair, will be delighted to curve the grades so that the interval of 75 to 79 is an A+ and the interval of 65 to 69 is at least a B.) The mean and median test scores would probably lie within the 55 to 59 class interval, yet use of that interval as the measure of central tendency could obscure rather than reveal the important aspects of this distri-

FIGURE A.2 | A Bimodal Distribution

This hypothetical distribution represents students' scores on a test. The mode at the left represents the central tendency of the test scores of students who did not study. The mode at the right represents the mode of the test scores of students who did study.

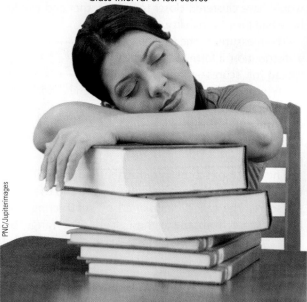

FIGURE A.3 | Hypothetical Distributions of Student Test Scores

Each distribution has the same number of scores, the same mean, even the same range, but the standard deviation (a measure of variability) is greater for the distribution on the left because the scores tend to be farther from the mean.

 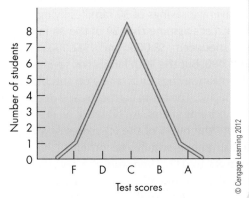

© Cengage Learning 2012

bution of test scores. It might suggest that the test was too hard, not that a number of students chose not to study. Similarly, one of the distribution's modes might be a bit larger than the other, so one could follow the exact rule for finding the mode and report just one of them. But this approach would also hide the meaning of this particular distribution of scores. All in all, it is clearly best to visualize this distribution of scores as bimodal.

App-2c MEASURES OF VARIABILITY

Our hypothetical class obtained test scores ranging from class intervals of 35 to 39 to class intervals of 75 to 79. That is, the scores *varied* from the lower class interval to the higher class interval. Now, if all the students had obtained scores from 55 to 59 or from to 65 to 69, the scores would not have varied as much; that is, they would have clustered closer to one another and would have had lower variability.

The measures of the variability of a distribution inform us about the spread of scores—that is, about the typical distances of scores from the average score. Two commonly used measures of variability are the *range* of scores and the *standard deviation* of scores.

The **range** of scores in a distribution is defined as the difference between the highest score and the lowest score. The range is obtained by subtracting the lowest score from the highest score. The range of

TRUTH PSYCHOLOGISTS MAY EXPRESS YOUR IQ SCORE IN TERMS OF HOW DEVIANT YOU ARE FROM THE AVERAGE OR MEAN SCORE.

heights in Table A.2 is obtained by subtracting 6'1" from 7'2", or 1'1". It is useful to know the range of temperatures when we move to an area with a different climate so that we may anticipate the weather and dress for it appropriately. A teacher must have some understanding of the range of abilities or skills in a class to teach effectively. An understanding of the range of human heights can be used to design doorways, beds, and headroom in automobiles. Even so, the typical doorway is 6'8" high; and, as we saw with the California Quakes and New York Big Apples, some people will have to duck to get through.

The range is an imperfect measure of variability because of the manner in which it is influenced by extreme scores. The range of savings of the 30 families on our suburban block is $1,400,000 minus $8,000, or $1,392,000. This is a large number, and it is certainly true. However, it tells us little about the *typical* variation of savings accounts, which lie within a more restricted range of $8,000 to $12,000.

The **standard deviation** is a statistic that does a better job of showing how the scores in a distribution are distributed (spread) about the mean. It is usually better than the range because it considers every score in the distribution, not just the extreme (highest and lowest) scores. Consider Figure A.3. Each distribution in the figure has the same number of scores, the same mean, and the same range of scores. However, the scores in the distribution on the right side cluster more closely about the mean. Therefore, the standard deviation of the distribution on the right is smaller. That is, the typical score deviates less from the mean score.

The standard deviation is usually abbreviated as S.D. It is calculated by the formula

$$\text{S.D.} = \sqrt{\frac{\text{Sum of } d^2}{N}}$$

where d equals the deviation of each score from the mean of the distribution and N equals the number of scores in the distribution.

Let's find the mean and standard deviation of the IQ scores listed in column 1 of Table A.4. To obtain the mean we add all the scores, attain 1,500, and then divide by the number of scores (15) to obtain a mean of 100. We obtain the deviation score (d) for each IQ score by subtracting the score from 100. The d for an IQ score of 85 equals 100 minus 85, or 15, and so on. Then we

square each d and add the squares. The S.D. equals the square root of the sum of squares (1,426) divided by the number of scores (15), or 9.75.

As an additional exercise, we can show that the S.D. of the test scores on the left (in Figure A.3) is greater than that for the scores on the right. First, we assign the grades a number according to a 4.0 system. Let A = 4, B = 3, C = 2, D = 1, and F = 0. The S.D. for each distribution is computed in Table A.5. The larger S.D. for the distribution on the left indicates that the scores in that distribution are more variable, or tend to be farther from the mean.

TABLE A.4 | Hypothetical Scores Obtained from an IQ Testing

IQ SCORE	d (DEVIATION SCORE)	d^2 (DEVIATION SCORE SQUARED)
85	15	225
87	13	169
89	11	121
90	10	100
93	7	49
97	3	9
97	3	9
100	0	0
101	−1	1
104	−4	16
105	−5	25
110	−10	100
112	−12	144
113	−13	169
117	−17	289

Sum of IQ scores = 1,500   Sum of d^2 scores = 1,426

$$\text{Mean} = \frac{\text{Sum of scores}}{\text{Number of scores}} = \frac{1,500}{15} = 100$$

$$\text{Standard Deviation (S.D.)} = \sqrt{\frac{\text{Sum of } d^2}{N}} = \sqrt{\frac{1,426}{15}} = \sqrt{95.07} = 9.75$$

© Cengage Learning 2012

TABLE A.5 | Computation of Standard Deviations for Test-Score Distributions in Figure A.3

DISTRIBUTION AT LEFT			DISTRIBUTION TO THE RIGHT		
GRADE	d	d^2	GRADE	d	d^2
A (4)	2	4	A (4)	2	4
A (4)	2	4	B (3)	1	1
A (4)	2	4	B (3)	1	1
B (3)	1	1	B (3)	1	1
B (3)	1	1	B (3)	1	1
B (3)	1	1	C (2)	0	0
B (3)	1	1	C (2)	0	0
C (2)	0	0	C (2)	0	0
C (2)	0	0	C (2)	0	0
C (2)	0	0	C (2)	0	0
C (2)	0	0	C (2)	0	0
D (1)	−1	1	C (2)	0	0
D (1)	−1	1	C (2)	0	0
D (1)	−1	1	D (1)	−1	1
D (1)	−1	1	D (1)	−1	1
F (0)	−2	4	D (1)	−1	1
F (0)	−2	4	D (1)	−1	1
F (0)	−2	4	F (0)	−2	4

Sum of grades = 36   Sum of grades = 36
Mean grade = 36/18 = 2   Mean grade = 36/18 = 2
Sum of d^2 = 32   Sum of d^2 = 16
Sum of grades = 36   Sum of grades = 36
Mean grade = 36/18 = 2   Mean grade = 36/18 = 2
Sum of d^2 = 32   Sum of d^2 = 16
S.D. = $\sqrt{32/18}$ = 1.33   S.D. = $\sqrt{16/18}$ = 0.94

© Cengage Learning 2012

normal distribution

a symmetrical distribution that is assumed to reflect chance fluctuations; approximately 68% of cases lie within a standard deviation of the mean

normal curve

graphic presentation of a normal distribution, which shows a characteristic bell shape

App-3 The Normal Curve

Many human traits and characteristics, including height and intelligence, seem to be distributed in a pattern known as a normal distribution. In a **normal distribution**, the mean, the median, and the mode all fall at the same data point or score. Scores cluster most heavily about the mean, fall off rapidly in either direction at first (as shown in Figure A.4), and then taper off more gradually.

The curve in Figure A.4 is bell-shaped. This type of distribution is also called a **normal curve** or bell-shaped curve. This curve is hypothesized as the distribution of variables in which different scores are determined by chance variation. Height is thought to be largely determined by chance combinations of genetic material. A distribution of the heights of a random sample of the population approximates normal distributions for men and women, with the mean of the distribution for men a few inches higher than the mean for women.

Test developers traditionally assumed that intelligence was also randomly or normally distributed among the population. For that reason, they constructed intelligence tests so that scores would be distributed as close to "normal" as possible. In actuality, IQ scores are also influenced by environmental factors and chromosomal abnormalities, so that the resultant curves are not perfectly normal. The means of most IQ tests are defined as scores of 100 points. The Wechsler scales are constructed to have standard deviations of 15 points, as shown in Figure A.4. A standard deviation of 15 points causes 50% of the Wechsler scores to fall between 90 and 110, which is called the "broad average" range. About 68% of scores (two out of three) fall between 85 and 115 (within a standard deviation of the mean), and more than 95% fall between 70 and 130—that is, within two standard deviations of the mean. The more extreme high (and low) IQ scores deviate more from the mean score.

The Scholastic Assessment Tests (SATs) were constructed so that the mean scores would be 500 points and the S.D. would be 100 points. Thus a score of 600 would equal or excel that of some 84% to 85% of the test takers. Because of the complex interaction of variables that determine SAT scores, their distribution is not exactly normal either. Moreover, the actual mean scores and standard deviations tend to vary from year to year, and, in the case of the SAT IIs, from test to test. The normal curve is an idealized curve.

The IQ score of 130 is two standard deviations above the mean and exceeds that of more than 97% of the population. An SAT score of 500 is the mean SAT score and thus equals or excels that of about 50% of the population.

FIGURE A.4 | A Bell-Shaped or Normal Curve

In a normal curve, approximately two out of three cases (68%) lie within a standard deviation (S.D.) from the mean. The mean, median, and mode all lie at the same score. IQ tests and the Scholastic Assessment Tests (SATs) are constructed so that their distributions approximate the normal curve.

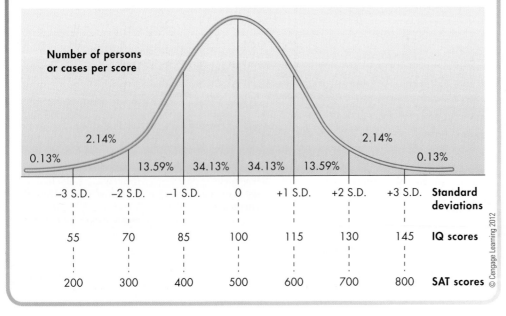

Number of persons or cases per score

0.13%	2.14%	13.59%	34.13% 34.13%	13.59%	2.14%	0.13%

−3 S.D.	−2 S.D.	−1 S.D.	0	+1 S.D.	+2 S.D.	+3 S.D.	**Standard deviations**
55	70	85	100	115	130	145	**IQ scores**
200	300	400	500	600	700	800	**SAT scores**

© Cengage Learning 2012

Mike Dunning/Dorling Kindersley/Getty Images

App-4 The Correlation Coefficient

What is the relationship between intelligence and educational achievement? Between cigarette smoking and lung cancer among humans? Between the personality trait of introversion and numbers of dates among college students? We cannot run experiments to determine whether the relationships between these variables are causal, because we cannot manipulate the independent variable. That is, we cannot assign high or low intelligence at random. Nor can we (ethically) assign some people to smoke cigarettes and others not to smoke. People must be allowed to make their own decisions, so it is possible that the same factors that lead some people to smoke—or to continue to smoke after they have experimented with cigarettes—also lead to lung cancer. (Even if we were to assign a group of people to a nonsmoking condition, could we monitor them continuously to make sure that they weren't sneaking puffs?) Nor can we designate who will be introverted and who will be extraverted. True, we could encourage people to act as if they are introverted or extraverted, but behavior is not the same thing as a personality trait. We cannot run true experiments to answer any of these questions, but the *correlation coefficient* can be used to reveal whether there is a relationship between intelligence and achievement, a relationship between smoking and cancer, or a relationship between personality and dating. Correlational research shows that smoking and cancer are related but does not reveal cause and effect. However, experimental research with animals does strongly suggest that smoking will cause cancer in humans.

AN IQ SCORE OF 130 IS MORE IMPRESSIVE THAN AN SAT SCORE OF 500. THE IQ SCORE IS TWO STANDARD DEVIATIONS ABOVE THE MEAN, AND THE SAT SCORE IS THE MEAN FOR THAT TEST.

The **correlation coefficient** is a statistic that describes the relationship between two variables. A correlation coefficient can vary from +1.00 to −1.00. A correlation coefficient of +1.00 is called a perfect positive correlation, and it describes the relationship between temperatures as measured by the Fahrenheit and Centigrade scales. A correlation coefficient of −1.00 is a perfect negative correlation, and a correlation of 0 (zero) reveals no relationship between variables.

As suggested by Figures A.5 and A.6, most correlation coefficients in psychological research are less than perfect. The left graph in Figure A.5 reveals a positive relationship between time spent studying and grade point averages. Because there is a positive correlation between the variables but the relationship is not perfect, the correlation coefficient will lie between 0.00 and +1.00. Perhaps it is about +0.60 or +0.70. However, we cannot absolutely predict what a person's GPA will be if we know the hours per week that he or she

correlation coefficient a number between −1.00 and +1.00 that indicates the direction (negative or positive) and extent (from none to perfect) of the relationship between two variables

FIGURE A.5 | Positive and Negative Correlations

When there is a positive correlation between variables, as there is between intelligence and achievement, one increases as the other increases. By and large, the more time students spend studying, the better their grades are likely to be, as suggested in the diagram to the left. (Each dot represents the amount of time a student spends studying each week and his or her grade point average.) But there is a negative correlation between grades and juvenile delinquency. As the number of delinquent acts per year increases, one's grade point average tends to decline. Correlational research may suggest but does not demonstrate cause and effect.

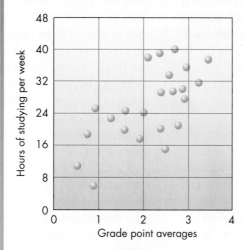

Positive correlation, as found between intelligence and academic achievement

Negative correlation, as found between delinquency and academic achievement

© Cengage Learning 2012

inferential statistics
the branch of statistics that is concerned with the confidence with which conclusions drawn about samples can be extended to the populations from which the samples were drawn

FIGURE A.6 | Correlational Relationships, Cause and Effect

Correlational relationships may suggest but do not demonstrate cause and effect. In part A, there is a correlation between variables X and Y. Does this mean that either variable X causes variable Y or that variable Y causes variable X? Not necessarily. Other factors could affect both variables X and Y. Consider the examples of academic grades (variable X) and time spent studying (variable Y) in part B. There is a positive correlation between the two. Does this mean that studying contributes to good grades? Perhaps. Does it mean that good grades encourage studying? Again, perhaps. But there could also be other variables—such as cultural belief in the value of education, enjoyment of learning, even parental pressure to do well—that contribute both to time spent studying and good grades.

© Cengage Learning 2012

spends studying (nor can we predict exactly how much time the person spends studying on the basis of his or her GPA). Nevertheless, it would seem advisable to place oneself among those who spend a good deal of time studying if one wishes to achieve a good GPA.

The right drawing in Figure A.5 reveals a negative relationship between number of delinquent acts committed per year and GPA. The causal connection is less than perfectly clear. Does delinquency interfere with studying and academic achievement? Does poor achievement weaken a student's commitment to trying to get ahead through work? Do feelings of distance from "the system" contribute both to delinquent behavior and a low GPA? The answers are not to be found in Figure A.5, but the negative correlation between delinquent behavior and GPA does suggest that it is worthwhile to study the issues involved and—for a student—to distance himself or herself from delinquent behavior if he or she wishes to achieve in the academic world.

App-5 Inferential Statistics

Head Start programs have apparently raised children's intellectual functioning, as reflected in their grades and IQ scores. In one such study, children enrolled in a Head Start program obtained a mean IQ score of 99, whereas children similar in background who were not enrolled in Head Start obtained a mean IQ score of 93.

Is this difference of six points in IQ *significant,* or does it represent a chance fluctuation in scores? Inferential statistics help us determine whether we can conclude that the differences between such samples reflect real differences that are found in the populations that they represent.

Descriptive statistics enables us to provide descriptive information about samples of scores. **Inferential statistics** assist us in determining whether we can generalize differences among samples to the populations that they represent.

Figure A.7 shows the distribution of heights of 1,000 men and 1,000 women who were selected at random from the general U.S. population. The mean height for men is greater than the mean height for women. Can we conclude, or *infer,* that this difference in height is not just a chance fluctuation but represents an actual difference between the general populations of men and women? Or must we avoid such an inference and summarize our results by stating only that the mean height of the sample of men in the study was greater than the mean height of the sample of women in the study?

If we could not draw inferences about populations from studies of samples, our research findings would be limited indeed. We could speak only about the specific individuals studied. There would be no point to learning about any study in which you did not participate because it would not apply to you! Fortunately, that is not the case. Inferential statistics permits us to

FIGURE A.7 | Distribution of Heights for Random Samples of Men and Women

Note that the mean height of the men is greater than that of the women. Is the group mean difference in height statistically significant? Researchers use a tool called inferential statistics to determine the answer.

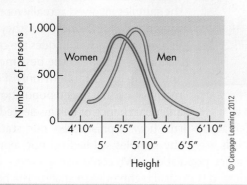

© Cengage Learning 2012

extend findings with samples to the populations from which they were drawn.

App-5a STATISTICALLY SIGNIFICANT DIFFERENCES

We asked whether the differences in height between our samples of men and women were simply a chance fluctuation or whether they represented actual differences between the heights of men and women. Researchers tend not to talk about "real differences" or "actual differences" between groups, however. Instead, they speak of statistically significant differences. Similarly, researchers asked whether differences in IQ scores

between children in Head Start programs and other children from similar backgrounds were chance fluctuations or statistically significant differences.

Statistically significant differences are differences that are unlikely to be due to chance fluctuation. Psychologists usually do not accept a difference as being statistically significant unless the probability (p) that it is due to chance fluctuation is less than 1 in 20 (i.e., $p < .05$). They are more comfortable labeling a difference as statistically significant when the probability (p) that it is due to chance fluctuation is less than 1 in 100 (i.e., $p < .01$).

Psychologists use formulas involving the means (e.g., mean IQ scores of 93 versus 99) and the standard deviations of sample groups to determine whether differences in means are statistically significant. As you can see in Figure A.8, the farther apart group means are, the more likely it is that they are statistically significant. In other words, if the men are on average 5 inches taller than the women, it is more likely that the difference is statistically significant than if the men are only one-quarter of an inch taller on average. *Principle 1: Everything else being equal, the greater the difference between means, the greater the probability that the difference is statistically significant.* This makes sense. After all, if you were told that your neighbor's car had gotten one-tenth of a mile more per gallon of gas than your car in the past year, you would probably attribute the difference to chance fluctuation. But if the difference were greater, say 14 miles per gallon, you would probably assume that the difference reflected an actual difference in driving habits or the efficiency of the automobile.

As you can see in Figure A.9, the smaller the standard deviations (a measure of variability) of the groups, the more likely it is that the difference between means is statistically significant. Consider the extreme example in which there is *no* variability within each group.

FIGURE A.8 | Decreasing and Increasing the Mean Group Difference in Heights

Everything else being equal, the greater the difference in group means, the greater the probability that the difference is statistically significant. The distribution on the right shows a greater difference in group means; therefore, there is a greater probability that the difference is statistically significant.

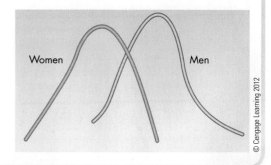

© Cengage Learning 2012

That is, imagine that every woman in the randomly selected sample of 1,000 women is exactly 5'5" tall. Similarly, imagine that every man in the randomly selected sample of 1,000 men is exactly 5'10" tall. In such a case the heights of the men and women would not overlap at all, and it would appear that the differences were statistically significant. Consider the other extreme—one with unnaturally large variability. Imagine that the heights of the women vary from 2' to 14' and that the heights of the men vary from 2'1" to 14'3". In such a case we might be more likely to assume that the difference in group means of 5" was a chance fluctuation. *Principle 2: Everything else being equal, the smaller the variability of the distributions of scores, the greater the probability that the difference in group means is statistically significant.*

Therefore, we cannot conclude that men are taller than women unless we know the average heights of men and women and how much the heights within each group vary. We must know both the central tendencies (means) and variability of the two distributions of heights to infer that the mean heights are statistically significantly different.

We have been "eyeballing" the data and making assumptions. We have been relying on what one professor of mine called the "Wow!" effect. As noted, psychologists and other researchers actually use mathematical techniques that take group means and standard deviations into account to determine whether group differences are statistically significant. It is often the case that eyeballing real data does not yield clear results or even good guesses.

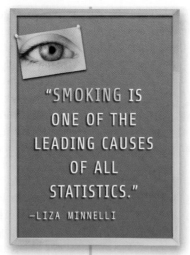

"SMOKING IS ONE OF THE LEADING CAUSES OF ALL STATISTICS."
—LIZA MINNELLI

App-5b SAMPLES AND POPULATIONS

Inferential statistics are mathematical tools that psychologists apply to samples of scores to determine whether they can generalize or extend their findings to populations of scores. They must, therefore, be quite certain that the samples involved actually represent the populations from which they were drawn. Sampling techniques are crucial. Random sampling is the best method, and sampling is random only if every member of the target population has an equal chance of being selected.

It matters little how sophisticated our statistical methods are if the samples studied do not represent the target populations. We could use a variety of sophisticated statistical techniques to analyze the heights

"Statistics show that of those who contract the habit of eating, very few survive."
—GEORGE BERNARD SHAW

of the New York Big Apples and the California Quakes, but none of these methods would tell us much about the height of the general population. Or about the height of women. (Or about the height of people who can't pass the ball, shoot, or play defense.)

FIGURE A.9 | Decreasing and Increasing the Variability of the Distributions of Scores

Everything else being equal, the smaller the variability in group scores, the greater the probability that the difference in group means is statistically significant. The distribution on the right shows a greater difference in the variability of the groups; therefore, there is a *lower* probability that the difference in group means is statistically significant.

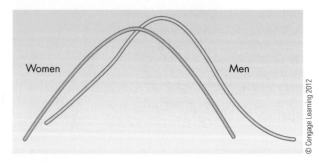

© Cengage Learning 2012

WHY CHOOSE?

Every 4LTR Press solution comes complete with a visually engaging textbook in addition to an interactive eBook. Go to CourseMate for PSYCH3 to begin using the eBook. Access at **www.cengagebrain.com**

Complete the Speak Up survey in CourseMate at **www.cengagebrain.com**

 Follow us at **www.facebook.com/4ltrpress**

ANSWERS TO STUDY TOOLS QUESTIONS

Chapter 1

FILL-INS
1. behavior
2. Clinical
3. Wilhelm Wundt
4. Gestalt
5. Evolutionary
6. Clark
7. population
8. survey
9. control
10. ethical

MULTIPLE CHOICE
1. A
2. B
3. C
4. A
5. D
6. D
7. A
8. A
9. C
10. C

Chapter 2

FILL-INS
1. neurotransmitters
2. axon
3. myelin
4. schizophrenia
5. autonomic
6. cerebellum
7. existence
8. instincts
9. Down
10. monozygotic (identical)

MULTIPLE CHOICE
1. C
2. B
3. A
4. B
5. A
6. D
7. D
8. A
9. A
10. D

Chapter 3

FILL-INS
1. Perception
2. absolute
3. rods; cones
4. optic
5. retina
6. olfactory
7. taste
8. position
9. semicircular
10. file-drawer

MULTIPLE CHOICE
1. C
2. B
3. A
4. D
5. C
6. C
7. A
8. D
9. A
10. B

Chapter 4

FILL-INS
1. awareness
2. paradoxical
3. five
4. activation
5. trance
6. mantra
7. abuse
8. abstinence
9. Cocaine
10. Hallucinogenic

MULTIPLE CHOICE
1. D
2. C
3. B
4. A
5. C
6. B
7. D
8. A
9. B
10. A

Chapter 5

FILL-INS
1. unconditioned
2. conditioned
3. extinguish
4. spontaneous
5. Albert
6. flooding
7. Negative
8. fixed-interval
9. Programmed
10. contingency

MULTIPLE CHOICE
1. B
2. D
3. C
4. C
5. A
6. C
7. D
8. D
9. C
10. A

Chapter 6

FILL-INS
1. episodic
2. Semantic
3. maintenance
4. elaborative
5. sensory; short-term; long-term
6. eidetic
7. flashbulb
8. retroactive
9. proactive
10. synapses

MULTIPLE CHOICE
1. B
2. C
3. D
4. A
5. A
6. D
7. C
8. D
9. B
10. C

Chapter 7

FILL-INS
1. Concepts
2. algorithm
3. Heuristic
4. mental
5. linguistic
6. overregularization
7. *g*
8. multiple
9. practical
10. intelligence quotient

MULTIPLE CHOICE
1. D
2. D
3. B
4. B
5. C
6. D
7. C
8. D
9. B
10. C

Chapter 8

FILL-INS
1. Motives
2. incentive
3. homeostasis
4. self-actualization
5. Anorexia
6. excitement
7. organizing
8. Apperception
9. performance
10. action

MULTIPLE CHOICE
1. C
2. A
3. A
4. B
5. C
6. D
7. C
8. D
9. D
10. A

Chapter 9

FILL-INS
1. reflexes
2. concrete
3. zone
4. initial-preattachment
5. secondary
6. formal
7. imaginary
8. diffusion
9. fluid
10. do not

MULTIPLE CHOICE
1. B
2. A
3. C
4. D
5. B
6. C
7. D
8. B
9. C
10. B

Chapter 10

FILL-INS
1. id
2. superego
3. anal
4. collective
5. inferiority
6. antisocial
7. actualization
8. reference
9. collectivists
10. ambiguous

MULTIPLE CHOICE
1. B
2. A
3. C
4. C
5. B
6. D
7. A
8. D
9. C
10. B

Chapter 11

FILL-INS
1. hassles
2. conflict
3. Ellis
4. higher
5. commitment
6. alarm
7. fight; flight
8. befriend
9. immune
10. cholesterol

MULTIPLE CHOICE
1. B
2. D
3. C
4. B
5. A
6. C
7. D
8. C
9. A
10. B

Chapter 12

FILL-INS
1. perception
2. phobia
3. obsessive-compulsive
4. amnesia
5. identity
6. somatoform
7. flight
8. internal
9. Catatonic
10. Personality

MULTIPLE CHOICE
1. B
2. B
3. A
4. A
5. D
6. C
7. B
8. A
9. D
10. A

Chapter 13

FILL-INS
1. psychological
2. unconscious
3. Operant
4. free
5. Humanistic
6. Client-centered
7. Cognitive
8. desensitization
9. irrational
10. Minor

MULTIPLE CHOICE
1. C
2. B
3. B
4. B
5. A
6. B
7. B
8. D
9. A
10. C

Chapter 14

FILL-INS
1. cognitive
2. dissonance
3. categorization
4. attraction-similarity
5. passion
6. primacy
7. social
8. facilitation
9. deindividualization
10. bystander

MULTIPLE CHOICE
1. D
2. B
3. A
4. B
5. C
6. B
7. B
8. A
9. B
10. C

REFERENCES

A

Abele, S., & Diehl, M. (2008). Finding teammates who are not prone to sucker and free-rider effects: The Protestant work ethic as a moderator of motivation losses in group performance. *Group Processes and Intergroup Relations, 11*(1), 39–54.

Aboa-Éboulé, C., Brisson, C., Maunsell, E., Mâsse, B., Bourbonnais, R., Vézina, M., ... Dagenais, G. R. (2007). Job strain and risk of acute recurrent coronary heart disease events. *Journal of the American Medical Association, 298,* 1652–1660.

Ackard, D. M., Fulkerson, J. A., & Neumark-Sztainer, D. (2007). Prevalence and utility of *DSM-IV* eating disorder diagnostic criteria among youth. *International Journal of Eating Disorders, 40*(5), 409–417.

Adams, A. L., Doucette, T. A., James, R., & Ryan, C. L. (2009). Persistent changes in learning and memory in rats following neonatal treatment with domoic acid. *Physiology and Behavior, 96*(4–5), 505–512.

Agras, W. S., Walsh, T., Fairburn, C. G., Wilson, G. T., & Kraemer, H. C. (2000). A multicenter comparison of cognitive-behavioral therapy and interpersonal psychotherapy for bulimia nervosa. *Archives of General Psychiatry, 57*(5), 459–466.

Agrawal, A., Silberg, J. L., Lynskey, M. T., Maes, H. H., & Eaves, L. J. (2010). Mechanisms underlying the lifetime co-occurrence of tobacco and cannabis use in adolescent and young adult twins. *Drug and Alcohol Dependence, 108* (1–2), 49–55.

Ahs, F., Pissiota, A., Michelgård, A., Frans, O., Furmark, T., Appel, L., & Fredrikson, M. (2009). Disentangling the web of fear: Amygdala reactivity and functional connectivity in spider and snake phobia. *Psychiatry Research, 172*(2), 103–108.

Ainsworth, M. D. S., Blehar, M. C., Waters, E., & Wall, S. (1978). *Patterns of attachment: A psychological study of the strange situation.* Hillsdale, NJ: Erlbaum.

Ainsworth, M. D. S., & Bowlby, J. (1991). An ethological approach to personality development. *American Psychologist, 46,* 333–341.

Alarcón, R. D., Becker, A. E., Lewis-Fernández, R., Like, R. C., Desai, P., Foulks, E., ... Primm, A. (2009). Issues for *DSM-V*: The role of culture in psychiatric diagnosis. *Journal of Nervous and Mental Disease, 197*(8), 559–660.

Alberts, A., Elkind, D., & Ginsberg, S. (2007). The personal fable and risk-taking in early adolescence. *Journal of Youth and Adolescence, 36*(1), 71–76.

Alexander, G. M., Wilcox, T., & Woods, R. (2009). Sex differences in infants' visual interest in toys. *Archives of Sexual Behavior, 38*(3), 427–433.

Allen, J. P., & Antonishak, J. (2008). Adolescent peer influences: Beyond the dark side. In M. J. Prinstein & K. A. Dodge (Eds.), *Understanding peer influence in children and adolescents* (pp. 141–160). New York: Guilford.

Allport, G. W., & Odbert, H. S. (1936). Traitnames: A psycho-lexical study. *Psychological Monographs, 47,* 211.

Amanatullah, E. T., & Morris, M. W. (2010). Negotiating gender roles: Gender differences in assertive negotiating are mediated by women's fear of backlash and attenuated when negotiating on behalf of others. *Journal of Personality and Social Psychology, 98*(2), 256–267.

Ambrosius, U., Lietzenmaier, S., Wehrle, R., Wichniak, A., Kalus, S., Winkelman, J., ... E. Friess. (2008). Heritability of sleep electroencephalogram. *Biological Psychiatry, 64*(4), 344–348.

American Cancer Society. (2010). Retrieved from http://www.cancer.org/

American Lung Association. (2010). Smoking. Retrieved from http://www.lungusa.org/stop-smoking/about-smoking/health-effects/smoking.html

American Psychiatric Association. (2000). *Diagnostic and statistical manual of mental disorders, DSM–IV–TR* (4th ed., text revision). Washington, DC: Author.

American Psychological Association. (2002). Ethical principles of psychologists and code of conduct. *American Psychologist, 57*(12), 1060–1073.

American Psychological Association. (2008). Award for distinguished scientific contributions: Michael S. Gazzaniga. *American Psychologist, 63*(8), 636–638.

American Psychological Association, Center for Workforce Studies. (2009). *Doctoral psychology workforce fast facts. Health service provider subfields.* Retrieved from http://research.apa.org/fastfacts-09.pdf

American Psychological Assoication. (2012). Stress in America 2009: Executive summary. Retrieved from www.apa.org/news/press/releases/stress/2011/final-2011.pdf

The anatomy of anxiety. (2002). *Time, 159,* 50.

Anchin, J. C., & Pincus, A. L. (2010). Evidence-based interpersonal psychotherapy with personality disorders: Theory, components, and strategies. In J. J. Magnavita (Ed.), *Evidence-based treatment of personality dysfunction: Principles, methods, and processes* (pp. 113–166). Washington, DC: American Psychological Association.

Andersen, A. E., & Ryan, G. L. (2009). Eating disorders in the obstetric and gynecologic patient population. *Obstetrics and Gynecology, 114*(6), 1353–1367.

Anderson, C. A., Sakamoto, A., Gentile, D. A., Ihori, N., & Shibuya, A. (2008). Longitudinal effects of violent video games on aggression in Japan and the United States. *Pediatrics, 122*(5), e1067–e1072.

Anderson, C. A., Shibuya, A., Ihori, N., Swing, E. L., Bushman, B. J., Sakamoto, A., ... Bartlett, C. P. (2010). Violent video game effects on aggression, empathy, and prosocial behavior in Eastern and Western countries: A meta-analytic review. *Psychological Bulletin, 136*(2), 151–173.

Anderson, O. (1995). The buzz on exercise. *Men's Health, 10,* 88–89.

Andreano, J. M., & Cahill, L. (2009). Sex influences on the neurobiology of learning and memory. *Learning and Memory, 16,* 248–266.

Ansburg, P.I. (2000). Individual differences in problem solving via insight. *Current Psychology, 19,* 143.

Antoni, M. H., & Lutgendorf, S. (2007). Psychosocial factors and disease progression in cancer. *Current Directions in Psychological Science, 16*(1), 42–46.

Apovian, C. M. (2010). The causes, prevalence, and treatment of obesity revisited in 2009: What have we learned so far? *American Journal of Clinical Nutrition, 91*(1), 277S–279S.

Archer, J. (2009). The nature of human aggression. *International Journal of Law and Psychiatry, 32*(4), 202–208.

Archer, R. P., Buffington-Vollum, J. K., Stredny, R. V., & Handel, R. W. (2006). A survey of psychological test use patterns among forensic psychologists. *Journal of Personality Assessment, 87*(1), 84–94.

Arden, G. (2003, February 21). Test for color vision;-and save sight. *Optician,* p. 2.

Arendt, J. (2009). Managing jet lag: Some of the problems and possible new solutions. *Sleep Medicine Reviews, 13*(4), 249–256.

Arias, E., Rostron, B. L., & Tejada-Vera, B. (2010). United States life tables, 2005. *National Vital Statistics Report, 58*(10). National Center for Health Statistics. Retrieved from http://198.246.98.21/nchs/data/nvsr/nvsr58/nvsr58_10.pdf

Arnett, J. J. (1999). Adolescent storm and stress, reconsidered. *American Psychologist, 54*(5), 317–326.

Arnett, J. J. (2000). Emerging adulthood. *American Psychologist, 55*(5), 469–480.

Arnett, J. J. (2012). New horizons in research on emerging and young adulthood. *National Symposium on Family Issues, 2*(5), 231–244.

Arthritis Foundation. (2000, April 6). Pain in America: Highlights from a Gallup survey. Retrieved from http://www.arthritis.org/answers/sop_factsheet.asp

Artigas, F. (2008). Serotonin receptors: Role in depression. *Actas Españolas de Psiquiatría, 36*(Suppl. 1), 28–30.

Asch, S. E. (1952). *Social psychology.* Englewood Cliffs, NJ: Prentice Hall.

Ashtari, M., Cervellione, K., Cottone, J. Ardekani, B. A., Serge Sevy, S., & Kumra, S. (2009). Diffusion abnormalities in adolescents and young adults with a history of heavy cannabis use. *Journal of Psychiatric Research, 43*(3), 189–204.

Atkins, M. S., McKay, M. M., Frazier, S. L., Jakobsons, L. J., Arvanitis, P., Cunningham, T., … Lambrecht, L. (2002). Suspensions and detention in an urban, low-income school: Punishment or reward? *Journal of Abnormal Child Psychology, 30*(4), 361–371.

Atkinson, R. C., & Shiffrin, R. M. (1968). Human memory: A proposed system and its control processes. In K. Spence (Ed.), *The psychology of learning and motivation* (Vol. 2). New York: Academic Press.

Auyeung, B., Baron-Cohen, S., Ashwin, E., Knickmeyer, R., Taylor, K., Hackett, G., & Hines, M. (2009). Fetal testosterone predicts sexually differentiated behavior in girls and in boys. *Psychological Science, 20*(2), 144–148.

B

Back, S. E., Brady, K. T., Waldrop, A. E., Yeatts, S. D., McRae, A. L., & Spratt, E. (2008). Early life trauma and sensitivity to current life stressors in individuals with and without cocaine dependence. *American Journal of Drug and Alcohol Abuse, 34*(4), 389–396.

Baddeley, A. (1982). *Your memory: A user's guide.* New York: Macmillan.

Bae, S., Holloway, S. D., Li, J., & Bempechat, J. (2008). Mexican-American students' perceptions of teachers' expectations: Do perceptions differ depending on student achievement levels? *Urban Review, 40*(2), 210–225.

Bagchi, D., & Preuss, H. G. (2007). *Obesity: Epidemiology, pathophysiology, and prevention.* Boca Raton, FL: CRC Press.

Bahrick, H. P., Bahrick, P. O., & Wittlinger, R. P. (1975). Fifty years of memory for names and faces. *Journal of Experimental Psychology: General, 104,* 54–75.

Bahrick, H. P., Hall, L. K., & Da Costa, L. A. (2008). Fifty years of memory of college grades: Accuracy and distortions. *Emotion, 8*(1), 13–22.

Baker, L. A., DeFries, J. C., & Fulker, D. W. (1983). Longitudinal stability of cognitive ability in the Colorado adoption project. *Child Development, 54,* 290–297.

Bakst, S., Rabinowitz, J., & Bromet, E. (2009). Is premorbid functioning a risk factor for suicide attempts in first-admission psychosis? *Schizophrenia Research, 116*(2), 210–216.

Baltes, P. B., & Staudinger, U. M. (2000). Wisdom: A metaheuristic (pragmatic) to orchestrate mind and virtue toward excellence. *American Psychologist, 55,* 122–136.

Banaji, M. R., & Heiphetz, L. (2008). Attitudes. In S. T. Fiske, D. T. Gilbert, & G. Lindzey (Eds.), *Handbook of social psychology* (5th ed., Vol. 1., pp. 353–393). Hoboken, NJ: Wiley.

Bandelow, B., Wedekind, D., Pauls, J., Broocks, A., Hajak, G., & Ruther, E. (2000). Salivary cortisol in panic attacks. *American Journal of Psychiatry, 157,* 454–456.

Bandura, A. (1986). *Social foundations of thought and action: Associal-cognitive theory.* Englewood Cliffs, NJ: Prentice Hall.

Bandura, A. (1999). Social cognitive theory: An agentic perspective. *Asian Journal of Social Psychology, 2*(1), 21–41.

Bandura, A. (2008). An agentic perspective on positive psychology. In S. J. Lopez (Ed.), *Positive psychology: Discovering human strengths* (pp. 167–214). Santa Barbara, CA: ABC-CLIO.

Bandura, A., Blanchard, E. B., & Ritter, B. (1969). The relative efficacy of desensitization and modeling approaches for inducing behavioral, affective, and cognitive changes. *Journal of Personality and Social Psychology, 13,* 173–199.

Bandura, A., & Locke, E. A. (2003). Negative self-efficacy and goal effects revisited. *Journal of Applied Psychology, 88*(1), 87–99.

Bandura, A., Ross, S. A., & Ross, D. (1963). Imitation of film-mediated aggressive models. *Journal of Abnormal and Social Psychology, 66,* 3–11.

Bandura, A., Taylor, C. B., Williams, S. L., Medford, I. N., & Barchas, J. D. (1985). Catecholamine secretion as a function of perceived coping self-efficacy. *Journal of Consulting and Clinical Psychology, 53,* 406–414.

Barber, J. G. (2001). Relative misery and youth suicide. *Australian and New Zealand Journal of Psychiatry, 35*(1), 49–57.

Barbey, A. K., & Barsalou, L. W. (2009). Reasoning and problem solving: Models. *Encyclopedia of Neuroscience, 8,* 35–43.

Barbor, C. (2001). The science of meditation. *Psychology Today, 34,* 54.

Bard, P. (1934). The neurohumoral basis of emotional reactions. In C. A. Murchison (Ed.), *Handbook of general experimental psychology.* Worcester, MA: Clark University Press.

Barelli, C., Heistermann, M., Boesch, C., & Reichard, U. H. (2008). Mating patterns and sexual swellings in pair-living and multiple groups of wild white-handed gibbons, *Hylobates lar. Animal Behaviour, 75*(3), 991–1001.

Baron, R. A., Branscombe, N. R., & Byrne, D. R. (2009). *Social psychology* (12th ed.). Boston: Allyn & Bacon.

Bartone, P. T., Roland, R. R., Picano, J. J., & Williams, T. J. (2008). Psychological hardiness predicts success in U.S. Army special forces candidates. *International Journal of Selection and Assessment, 16*(1), 78–81.

Bartoshuk, L. M. (2000). Psychophysical advances aid the study of genetic variation in taste. *Appetite, 34*(1), 105.

Basic Behavioral Science Task Force of the National Advisory Mental Health Council. (1996c). Basic behavioral science research for mental health: Sociocultural and environmental practices. *American Psychologist, 51,* 722–731.

Bassok, M., & Novick, L. R. (2012). Problem solving. In K. J. Holyoak & R. G. Morrison (Eds.), *The Oxford handbook of thinking and reasoning* (pp. 413–432). New York: Oxford University Press.

Bates, E. (2001) Plasticity, localization and language development. In S. T. Parker, J. Langer, & C. Milbrath (Eds.), *Biology and knowledge revisited* (pp. 205–254). London: Routledge.

Batson, C. D., Qian, Z., & Lichter, D. T. (2006). Interracial and intraracial patterns of mate selection among America's diverse Black populations. *Journal of Marriage and the Family, 68,* 658–672.

Baucom, D. H., Epstein, N. B., LaTaillade, J. J., & Kirby, J. S. (2002). Cognitive-behavioral couple therapy. In A. S. Gurman (Ed.), *Handbook of couple therapy* (pp. 31–72). New York: Guilford Press.

Baumeister, R. F. (1996). *Evil: Inside human cruelty and violence.* New York: W. H. Freeman /Times Books/ Henry Holt & Co.

Baumrind, D. (1989). Rearing competent children. In W. Damon (Ed.), *Child development today and tomorrow.* San Francisco: Jossey-Bass.

Baumrind, D. (2005). Taking a stand in a morally pluralistic society: Constructive obedience and responsible dissent in moral/character education. In L. Nucci (Ed.), *Conflict, contradiction, and contrarian elements in moral development and education* (pp. 21–50). Mahwah, NJ: Erlbaum.

Bear, R. E., Fitzgerald, P., Rosenfeld, J. V., & Bittar, R. G. (2010). Neurosurgery for obsessive–compulsive disorder: Contemporary approaches. *Journal of Clinical Neuroscience, 17*(1), 1–5.

Beck, A. T., Butler, A. C., Brown, G. K., Dahlsgaard, K. K., Newman, C. F., & Beck, J. S. (2001). Dysfunctional beliefs discriminate personality disorders. *Behaviour Research and Therapy, 39*(10), 1213–1225.

Beesdo, K., Pine, D. S., Lieb, R., & Wittchen, H.-U. (2010). Incidence and risk patterns of anxiety and depressive disorders and categorization of generalized anxiety disorder. *Archives of General Psychiatry, 67*(1), 47–57.

Behar, E., Dobrow DiMarco, I., Hekler, E. B., Mohlman, J., & Staples, A. M. (2009). Current theoretical models of generalized anxiety disorder (GAD): Conceptual review and treatment implications. *Journal of Anxiety Disorders, 23*(8), 1011–1023.

Belsky, J. (2006). Determinants and consequences of infant–parent attachment. In L. Baker & C. S. Tamis-LeMonda (Eds.), *Child psychology: A handbook of contemporary issues* (2nd ed.) (pp. 53–57). New York: Psychology Press.

Belsky, J., & Pluess, M. (2009). Beyond diathesis stress: Differential susceptibility to environmental influences. *Psychological Bulletin, 135*(6), 885–908.

Belsky, J., Weinraub, M., Owen, M., & Kelly, J. (2001, April). Quantity of child care and problem behavior. In J. Belsky (Chair), *Early childcare and children's development prior to school entry.* Symposium conducted at the 2001 biennial meetings of the Society for Research in Child Development, Minneapolis, MN.

Bem, D. J. (2011). Feeling the future: Experimental evidence for anomalous retroactive influences on cognition and affect. *Journal of Personality and Social Psychology, 100*(3), 407–425.

Bender, H. L., Allen, J. P., Boykin McElhaney, K. J., Antonishak, C. M., Moore, H., O'Beirne K., & Davis, S. M. (2007). Use of harsh physical discipline and developmental outcomes in adolescence. *Development and Psychopathology, 19*(1) 227–242.

Benke, K., & Fallin, M. (2010). Methods: Genetic epidemiology. *Psychiatric Clinics of North America, 33*(1), 15–34.

Benson, H. (1975). *The relaxation response.* New York: Morrow.

Ben-Zur, H. (2002). Associations of Type A behavior with the emotional traits of anger and curiosity. *Anxiety, Stress and Coping: An International Journal, 15*(1), 95–104.

Berk, M. S., Henriques, G. R., Warman, D. M., Brown, G. K., & Beck, A. T. (2004). A cognitive therapy intervention for suicide attempters: An overview. *Cognitive and Behavioral Practice. 11*(3), 265–277.

Berkowitz, L. (2004). Two views of evil: Evil is not only banal. *PsycCRITIQUES.*

Bermudez, P., Lerch, J. P., Evans, A. C., & Zatorre, R. J. (2009). Neuroanatomical correlates of musicianship as revealed by cortical thickness and voxel-based morphometry. *Cerebral Cortex, 19*(7), 1583–1596.

Bernardin, H. J., Cooke, D. K., & Villanova, P. (2000). Conscientiousness and agreeableness as predictors of rating leniency. *Journal of Applied Psychology, 85*(2) 232–236.

Bernstein, D. M., & Loftus, E. F. (2009). How to tell if a particular memory is true or false. *Perspectives on Psychological Science, 4*(4), 370–374.

Berscheid, E. (2009). Love in the fourth dimension. *Annual Review of Psychology, 61,* 1–25.

Berten, H., & Rossem, R. V. (2009). Doing worse but knowing better: An exploration of the relationship between HIV/AIDS knowledge and sexual behavior among adolescents in Flemish secondary schools. *Journal of Adolescence, 32*(5), 1303–1319.

Bexton, W. H., Heron, W., & Scott, T. H. (1954). Effects of decreased variation in the sensory environment. *Canadian Journal of Psychology, 8,* 70–76.

Bidell, M. P., Turner, J. A., & Casas, J. M. (2002). First impressions count: Ethnic/racial and lesbian/gay/bisexual content of professional psychology application materials. *Professional Psychology: Research and Practice, 33*(1), 97–103.

Bienvenu, O. J., et al. (2005). Anxiety and depressive disorders and the five-factor model of personality: A higher- and lower-order personality trait investigation in a community sample. *Depression & Anxiety, 20*(2), 92–97.

Bierman, K. L., Domitrovich, C. E., Nix, R. L., Gest, S. D., & Welsh, J. A. (2008). flynn Promoting academic and social-emotional school readiness: The Head Start REDI program. *Child Development, 79*(6), 1802–1817.

Binder, E. B., & Nemeroff, C. B. (2009). The CRF system, stress, depression, and anxiety—Insights from human genetic studies. *Molecular Psychiatry, 15*(6), 574–588.

Bishop, D. V. M. (2009). Genes, cognition, and communication. *Annals of the New York Academy of Sciences, 1156,* 1–18.

Bizer, G. Y., et al. (2004). The impact of personality on cognitive, behavioral, and affective political processes: The effects of need to evaluate. *Journal of Personality, 72*(5), 995–1027.

Bjorklund, D. F. (2000). *Children's thinking* (3rd ed.). Pacific Grove, CA: Brooks/Cole.

Blake, P., Fry, R., & Pesjack, M. (1984). *Self-assessment and behavior change manual.* New York: Random House.

Blass, T. (2009). From New Haven to Santa Clara: A historical perspective on the Milgram obedience experiments. *American Psychologist, 64*(1), 37–45.

Blechert, J., Wilhelm, F. H., Meuret, A. E., Wilhelm, E. M., & Roth, W. T. (2010). Respiratory, autonomic, and experiential responses to repeated inhalations of 20% CO_2 enriched air in panic disorder, social phobia, and healthy controls. *Biological Psychology, 84*(1), 104–111.

Block, N. (2009). The mind as the software of the brain. In S. Schneider (Ed.), *Science fiction and philosophy: From time travel to superintelligence* (pp. 170–185). Hoboken, NJ: Wiley.

Blum, K., Chen, A. L. C., Chen, T. J. H., Bowirrat, A., Downs, B. W., Waite, R. L., ... Comings, D. E. (2009). Genes and happiness. *Gene Therapy and Molecular Biology, 13,* 91–129.

Bogen, J. E. (1969). The other side of the brain II: An appositional mind. *Bulletin of the Los Angeles Neurological Society, 34,* 135–162.

Bogen, J. E. (2000). Split-brain basics: Relevance for the concept of one's other mind. *Journal of the American Academy of Psychoanalysis, 28*(2), 341–369.

Bohner, G., & Dickel, N. (2011). Attitudes and attitude change. *Annual Review of Psychology, 62,* 391–417.

Bolinskey, K. P., & Gottesman, I. I. (2010). Premorbid personality indicators of schizophrenia-related psychosis in a hypothetically psychosis-prone college sample. *Scandinavian Journal of Psychology, 51*(1), 68–74.

Bonds-Raacke, J.M., Fryer, L.S., Nicks, S.D., and Durr, R.T. (2001). Hindsight bias demonstrated in the prediction of a sporting event. *The Journal of Social Psychology, 141,* 349.

Bonn-Miller, M. O., Zvolensky, M. J., & Bernstein, A. (2007). Marijuana use motives: Concurrent relations to frequency of past 30-day use and anxiety sensitivity among young adult marijuana smokers. *Addictive Behaviors, 32*(1), 49–62.

Boom, J., Wouters, H., & Keller, M. (2007). A cross cultural validation of stage development. A Rasch re-analysis of longitudinal socio-moral reasoning data. *Cognitive Development, 22*(2), 213–229.

Bouchard, C. (2010). Defining the genetic architecture of the predisposition to obesity: A challenging but not insurmountable task. *American Journal of Clinical Nutrition, 91*(1), 5–6.

Bouton, M. E. (2010). The multiple forms of "context" in associative learning theory. In B. Mesquita, L. F. Barrett, & E. R. Smith (Eds.), *The mind in context* (pp. 233–258). New York: Guilford Press.

Bower, B. (1997). Forbidden flavors: Scientists consider how disgusting tastes can linger surreptitiously in memory. *Science News, 151,* 198–199.

Bower, B. (1991). Oedipus Wrecked: Freud's Theory of Frustrated Incest Goes on the Defensive. *Science News, 140,* 248–250.

Bowlby, J. (1988). *A secure base.* New York: Basic Books.

Boyatzis, R. E. (1974). The effect of alcohol consumption on the aggressive behavior of men. *Quarterly Journal for the Study of Alcohol, 35,* 959–972.

Braarud, H. C., & Stormark, K. M. (2008). EJ814142—Prosodic modification and vocal adjustments in mothers' speech during face-to-face interaction with their two- to four-month-old infants: A double video study. *Social Development, 17*(4), 1074–1084.

Brackett, M. A., Rivers, S. E., & Salovey, P. (2011). Emotional intelligence: Implication for personal, social, academic, and workplace success. *Social and Personality Psychology, 5*(1), 88–103.

Bradley, R. H., et al. (1989). Home environment and cognitive development in the first 3 years of life. *Developmental Psychology, 25,* 217–235.

Bradley, R. H. (2006). The home environment. In N. F. Watt, C. Ayoub, R. H.

Bradley, J. E. Puma, & W. A. Lebeouf (Eds.), *The crisis in youth mental health: Critical issues and effective programs: Vol. 4. Early intervention programs and policies: Child psychology and mental health* (pp. 89–120). Westport, CT: Praeger/Greenwood.

Brand, J. (2000). Cited in McFarling, U. L. (2000, August 27). Sniffing out genes' role in our senses of taste and smell. *The Los Angeles Times online.*

Brand, J. S., & van der Schouw, Y. T. (2010). Testosterone, SHBG and cardiovascular health in postmenopausal women. *International Journal of Impotence Research, 22,* 91–104.

Braun, B. G. (1988). *Treatment of multiple personality disorder.* Washington, DC: American Psychiatric Press.

Bravender, T., Bryant-Waugh, R., Herzog, D., Katzman, D., Kriepe, R. D., Lask, B., … Zucker, N. (2010). Classification of eating disturbance in children and adolescents: Proposed changes for the *DSM-V. European Eating Disorders Review, 18*(2), 79–89.

Brewer, M.B. (1999). The psychology of prejudice: Ingroup love or outgroup hate? *Journal of Social Issues, 55,* 429.

Brewer, M. B., & Chen, Y-R. (2007). Where (who) are collectives in collectivism? Toward conceptual clarification of individualism and collectivism. *Psychological Review, 114*(1), 133–151.

Briñol, P., Petty, R., & Barden, J. (2007). Happiness versus sadness as a determinant of thought confidence in persuasion: A self-validation analysis. *Journal of Personality and Social Psychology, 93*(5), 711–727.

Brody, J. E. (2000, April 25). Memories of things that never were. *The New York Times,* p. F8.

Brook, J. S., Zheng, L., Whiteman, M., & Brook, D. W. (2001). Aggression in toddlers: Associations with parenting and marital relations. *Journal of Genetic Psychology, 162*(2), 228–241.

Brown, A. S. (2007). Identifying risks using a new assessment tool: The missing piece of the jigsaw in medical device risk assessment. *Clinical Risk, 13,* 56–59.

Brown, A. S., & Derkits, E. J. (2010). Prenatal infection and schizophrenia: A review of epidemiologic and translational studies. *American Journal of Psychiatry, 167,* 261–280.

Brown, G. R. (2009). Evolutionary perspectives on sexual coercion in human beings and other primates: The future of the rape debate. *Journal of Evolutionary Psychology, 7*(4), 347–350.

Brown, R. J., Schrag, A., Krishnamoorthy, E., & Trimble, M. R. (2007). Are patients with somatization disorder highly suggestible? *Acta Psychiatrica Scandinavica, 117*(3), 232–235.

Brown, R., & McNeill, D. (1966). The tip-of-the-tongue phenomenon. *Journal of Verbal Learning and Verbal Behavior, 5,* 325–337.

Brown, W. H., Pfeiffer, K. A., McIver, K. L., Dowda, M., Addy, C. L., & Pate, R. R. (2009). Social and environmental factors associated with preschoolers' nonsedentary physical activity. *Child Development, 80*(1), 45–58.

Brownlee, S. (1997). The senses: They delight, heal, define the boundaries of our world. And they are helping unlock the brain's secrets. *U.S. News & World Report, 122,* 50–57.

Brownstein, A. L. (2003). Biased predecision processing. *Psychological Bulletin, 129*(4), 545–568.

Bruce, T. J., & Sanderson, W. C. (2004). Evidence-based psychosocial practices: The past, present, and future. In C. Stout & R. Hayes (Eds.), *Evidence-based practice: Methods, models and tolls for mental health professionals* (pp. 220–243). New York: Wiley.

Bruene, M., & Ribbert, H. (2002). Grundsaetzliches zur Konzeption einer evolutionaeren Psychiatrie. *Schweizer Archiv für Neurologie und Psychiatrie, 153*(1), 4–11.

Brun, C. C., Lepore, N., Luders, E., Chou, Y.-Y., Madsen, S. K., Toga, A. W., & Thompson, P. M. (2009). Sex differences in brain structure in auditory and cingulate regions. *NeuroReport: For Rapid Communication of Neuroscience Research, 20*(10), 930.

Bryant, J., & Davies, J. (2006). Selective exposure processes. In J. Bryant & P. Vorderer (Eds.), *Psychology of entertainment* (pp. 19–34). London: Routledge.

Bryant, R. (2006). Acute stress disorder. *Psychiatry, 5*(7), 238–239.

Buchanan, T. W., Driscoll, D., Mowrer, S. M., Sollers, J. J., Thayer, J. F., Kirschbaum, C., & Tranel, D. (2010). Medial prefrontal cortex damage affects physiological and psychological stress responses differently in men and women. *Psychoneuroendocrinology, 35*(1), 56–66.

Buckley, P. F., Buchanan, R. W., Tamminga, C. A., & Schulz, S. C. (2000). Schizophrenia research. *Schizophrenia Bulletin, 26*(2), 411–419.

Budney, A. J., Vandrey, R. G., Hughes, J. R., Moore, B. A., & Bahrenburg, B. (2007). Oral delta-9-tetrahydrocannabinol suppresses cannabis withdrawal symptoms. *Drug and Alcohol Dependence, 86*(1), 22–29.

Bull, N. J., Hunter, M., & Finlay, D. C. (2003). Cue gradient and cue density interact in the detection and recognition of objects defined by motion, contrast, or texture. *Perception, 32*(1), 29–39.

Bullough, V.L. (1998). Alfred Kinsey and the Kinsey Report: Historical overview and lasting contributions. *The Journal of Sex Research, 35,* 127–131.

Burger, J. M. (2009). Replicating Milgram: Would people still obey today? *American Psychologist, 64*(1), 1–11.

Burghardt, G. M. (2009). Darwin's legacy to comparative psychology and ethology. *American Psychologist, 64*(2), 102–110.

Bushman, B. J., & Anderson, C. A. (2007). Measuring the strength of the effect of violent media on aggression. *American Psychologist, 62*(3), 253–254.

Buss, D. M. (2009a). The great struggles of life: Darwin and the emergence of evolutionary psychology. *American Psychologist, 64*(2), 140–148.

Buss, D. M. (2009b). How can evolutionary psychology successfully explain personality and individual differences? *Perspectives on Psychological Science, 4*(4), 359–366.

Buss, D. M., & Schmitt, D. P. (2011). Evolutionary psychology and feminism. *Sex Roles, 64*(9–10), 768–787.

Butler, A. C., Chapman, J. E., Forman, E. M., & Beck, A. T. (2006). The empirical status of cognitive-behavioral therapy: A review of meta-analyses. *Clinical Psychology Review, 26*(1), 17–31.

C

Cailhol, S., & Mormede, P. (2002). Conditioned taste aversion and alcohol drinking: Strain and gender differences. *Journal of Studies on Alcohol, 63,* 91–99.

Calcagni, E., & Elenkov, I. (2006). Stress system activity, innate and T helper cytokines, and susceptibility to immune-related diseases. *Annals of the New York Academy of Sciences, 1069,* 62–76.

Callahan, J. J. (2007). Sandwich anyone? *Gerontologist, 47*(4), 569–571.

Campbell, R. A., Machlus, K. R., & Wolberg, A. S. (2010). Smoking out the cause of thrombosis. *Arteriosclerosis, Thrombosis, and Vascular Biology, 30*(7), 75–79.

Campos, J. J. (2000). Cited in Azar, B. (2000). What's in a face? *Monitor on Psychology, 31*(1), 44–45.

Campos, J. J., Hiatt, S., Ramsey, D., Henderson, C., & Svejda, M. (1978). The emergence of fear on the visual cliff. In M. Lewis & L. Rosenblum (Eds.), *The origins of affect.* New York: Plenum Press.

Cannon, W. B. (1927). The James–Lange theory of emotions: A critical examination and an alternative theory. *American Journal of Psychology, 39,* 106–124.

Cannon, W. B. (1932). *The wisdom of the body.* New York: Norton.

Cannon, W. B., & Washburn, A. (1912). An explanation of hunger. *American Journal of Physiology, 29,* 441–454.

Cantalupo, C., & Hopkins, W. D. (2001). Asymmetric Broca's area in great apes: A region of the ape brain is uncannily similar to one linked with speech in humans. *Nature, 414*(6863), 505.

Carey, B. (2009, November 27). Psychosurgery for mental ills offers both hope and risk. *The New York Times,* p. A1.

Carmichael, L. L., Hogan, H. P., & Walter, A. A. (1932). An experimental study of the effect of language on the reproduction of visually perceived form. *Journal of Experimental Psychology, 15,* 73–86.

Carpenter, S. (2001, March). Everyday fantasia: The world of synesthesia. *Monitor on Psychology, 32.* Retrieved May 22, 2003, http://www.apa.org/monitor.mar01/synesthesia.html

Carré, J. M., & Putnam, S. K. (2010). Watching a previous victory produces an increase in testosterone among elite hockey players. *Psychoneuroendocrinology, 35*(3), 475–479.

Carré, J. M., Putnam, S. K., & McCormick, C. M. (2009). Testosterone responses to competition predict future aggressive behaviour at a cost to reward in men. *Psychoneuroendocrinology, 34*(4), 561–570.

Carver, C. S., & Harmon-Jones, E. (2009). Anger is an approach-related affect: Evidence and implications. *Psychological Bulletin, 135*(2), 183–204.

Carver, L. J., & Cluver, A. (2009). Stress effects on the brain system underlying explicit memory. In J. A. Quas & R. Fivush (Eds.), *Emotion and memory in development: Biological, cognitive, and social considerations* (pp. 278–311). New York: Oxford University Press.

Castelli, L., Zogmaister, C., & Tomelleri, S. (2009). The transmission of racial attitudes within the family. *Developmental Psychology, 45*(2), 586–591.

Castor, D., Pilowsky, D. J., Hadden, B., Fuller, C., Ompad, D. C., de Leon, C. L., ... Hoover, D. R. (2010). Sexual risk reduction among non-injection drug users: Report of a randomized controlled trial. *AIDS Care, 22*(1), 62–70.

Cattell, R. B. (1949). *The culture-free intelligence test.* Champaign, IL: Institute for Personality and Ability Testing.

Catts, V. S., & Catts, S. V. (2009). Psychotomimetic effects of PCP, LSD, and Ecstasy: Pharmacological models of schizophrenia? In P. S. Sachdev & M. S. Keshavan (Eds.), *Secondary schizophrenia* (pp. 141–168). Cambridge, England: Cambridge University Press.

Cavallaro, F. I., Cacace, I., Del Testa, M., Andre, P., Carli, G., De Pascalis, V., ... Santarcangelo, E. L. (2010). Hypnotizability-related EEG alpha and theta activities during visual and somesthetic imageries. *Neuroscience Letters, 470*(1), 13–18.

Ceci, S. J., Kulkofsky, S., Klemfuss, J. Z., Sweeney, C. D., & Bruck, M. (2007). Unwarranted assumptions about children's testimonial accuracy. *Annual Review of Clinical Psychology, 3,* 311–328.

Cellar, D. F., Nelson, Z. C., & Yorke, C. M. (2000). The five-factor model and driving behavior: Personality and involvements in vehicular accidents. *Psychological Reports, 86*(2) 454–456.

Cellard, C., Lefèbvre, A.-A., Maziade, M., Roy, M.-A., & Tremblay, S. (2010). An examination of the relative contribution of saturation and selective attention to memory deficits in patients with recent-onset schizophrenia and their unaffected parents. *Journal of Abnormal Psychology, 119*(1), 60–70.

Centers for Disease Control and Prevention. (2009). FastStats: Suicide and self-inflicted injury. Retrieved from http://www.cdc.gov/nchs/fastats/suicide.htm

Cervantes, J. M., & Parham, T. A. (2005). Toward a meaningful spirituality for people of color: Lessons for the counseling practitioner. *Cultural Diversity & Ethnic Minority Psychology, 11*(1), 69–81.

Chadwick, P. D. J., & Lowe, C. F. (1990). Measurement and modification of delusional beliefs. *Journal of Consulting and Clinical Psychology, 58,* 225–232.

Chafee, M. V., & Goldman-Rakic, P. S. (2000). Inactivation of parietal and prefrontal cortex reveals interdependence of neural activity during memory-guided saccades. *Journal of Neurophysiology, 83*(3), 1550–1566.

Champagne, F. A., Curley, J. P., Swaney, W. T., Hasen, N. S., & Keverne, E. B. (2009). Epigenetic mechanisms mediating the long-term effects of maternal care on development. *Behavioral Neuroscience, 123*(3), 469–480.

Chance, W. T., Xiao, C., Dayal, R., & Sheriff, S. (2007). Alteration of NPY and Y1 receptor in dorsomedial and ventromedial areas of hypothalamus in anorectic tumor-bearing rats. *Peptides, 28*(2), 295–301.

Chard, K. M., Schumm, J. A., Owens, G. P., & Cottingham, S. M. (2010). A comparison of OEF and OIF veterans and Vietnam veterans receiving cognitive processing therapy. *Journal of Traumatic Stress, 23*(1), 25–32.

Chen, J., & Rizzo, J. (2010). Racial and ethnic disparities in use of psychotherapy: Evidence from U.S. national survey data. *Psychiatric Services, 61,* 364–372.

Cherniak, C. (2009). Brain wiring optimization and non-genomic nativism. In M. Piatelli-Palmarini, P. Salaburu, & J. Uriagereka (Eds.), *Of minds and language: A dialogue with Noam Chomsky in the Basque country* (pp. 108–122). New York: Oxford University Press.

Cheung, C-K., & Leung, K-K. (2008). Ways by which comparable income affects life satisfaction in Hong Kong. *Social Indicators Research, 87*(1), 169–187.

Chida, Y., & Steptoe, A. (2009). The association of anger and hostility with future coronary heart disease: A meta-analytic review of prospective evidence. *Journal of the American College of Cardiology, 53*(11), 936–946.

Chiu, C., & Chao, M. M. (2009). Society, culture, and the person. In R. S. Wyer, C. Chiu, & Y. Hong (Eds.), *Understanding culture: Theory, research, and application* (pp. 457–468). Boca Raton, FL: CRC Press.

Christ, S. E., Van Essen, D. C., Watson, J. M., Brubaker, L. E., & McDermott, K. B. (2009). The contributions of prefrontal cortex and executive control to deception: Evidence from activation likelihood estimate meta-analyses. *Cerebral Cortex, 19*(7), 1557–1566.

Cialdini, R. B., Brown, S. L., Lewis, B. P., Luce, C., & Neuberg, S. L. (1997). Reinterpreting the empathy-altruism relationship: When one into one equals oneness. *Journal of Personality and Social Psychology, 73*(3), 481–494.

Cifani, C., Polidori, C., Melotto, S., Ciccocioppo, R., & Massi, M. (2009). A preclinical model of binge eating elicited by yo-yo dieting and stressful exposure to food: Effect of sibutramine, fluoxetine, topiramate, and midazolam. *Psychopharmacology, 204*(1), 113–225.

Cirelli, C. (2009). The genetic and molecular regulation of sleep: From fruit flies to humans. *Nature Reviews Neuroscience, 10,* 548–560.

Clancy, S. A. (2008). How do people come to believe they were abducted by aliens? In E. Goode & D. A. Vail (Eds.), *Extreme deviance* (pp. 54–63). Thousand Oaks, CA: Pine Forge Press.

Clancy, S. A., McNally, R. J., Schacter, D. L., Lenzenweger, M. F., & Pitman, R. (2002). Memory distortion in people reporting abduction by aliens. *Journal of Abnormal Psychology, 111*(3), 455–461.

Clark, A., & Misyak, J. B. (2009). Language, innateness, and universals. In *Language universals* (pp. 253–261). *Oxford Scholarship* Online Monographs.

Clark, D. A., & Beck, A. T. (2011). Cognitive therapy for the anxiety disorders. New York: Guilford.

Clark, E. V., & Nikitina, T. V. (2009). One vs. more than one: Antecedents to plural marking in early language acquisition. *Linguistics, 47*(1), 103–140.

Clark, S. (2009). Sleep deprivation: Implications for obstetric practice in the United States. *American Journal of Obstetrics and Gynecology, 201*(2), 136.e1–136.e4.

Clark, S. E., & Loftus, E. F. (1996). Space alien memories and scientific scrutiny. *PsycCRITIQUES, 41*(3), 294.

Clark, T. T. (2010). Reviewing the connection between paradigms and theories to understand adolescent drug use. *Journal of Child and Adolescent Substance Abuse, 19*(1), 16–32.

Cocking, C., Drury, J., & Reicher, S. (2009). The psychology of crowd behaviour in emergency evacuations. *Irish Journal of Psychology, 30*(1–2), 59–73.

Cohen, A., Young, R., Velazquez, M., Groysman, M., Noorbehesht, K., Ben-Shahar, O., Ettenberg, A. (2009). Anxiolytic effects of nicotine in a rodent test of approach–avoidance conflict. *Psychopharmacology, 204*(3), 541–549.

Cohen, S., Doyle, W. J., Turner, R., Alper, C. M., & Skoner, D. P. (2003). Sociability and susceptibility to the common cold. *Psychological Science, 14*(5), 389–395.

Cohen, S., Janicki-Deverts, D., Doyle, W. J., Miller, G. E., Frank, E., Rabin, B. S., & Turner, R. B. (2012). Chronic stress, glucocorticoid receptor resistance, inflammation, and disease risk. *Proceedings of the National Academy of Sciences, 109*(16), 5995–5999.

Collaer, M. L., & Hill, E. M. (2006). Large sex difference in adolescents on a timed line judgment task: Attentional contributors and task relationship to mathematics. *Perception, 35*(4), 561–572.

Collins, R. L., Taylor, S. L., Elliott, M. N., Ringel, J. S., Kanouse, D. E., & Beckman, R. (2010). Off-premise alcohol sales policies, drinking, and sexual risk among people living with HIV. *American Journal of Public Health, 100*(10), 1890–1892.

Collins, W. A., & Laursen, B. (2006). Parent–adolescent relationships. In P. Noller & J. A. Feeney (Eds.), *Close relationships: Functions, forms and processes* (pp. 111–125). Hove, England: Psychology Press/Taylor & Francis.

Comas-Diaz, L. (2008). Latino psychospirituality. In K. J. Schneider (Ed.), *Existential-integrative psychotherapy: Guideposts to the core of practice* (pp. 100–109). New York: Routledge/Taylor & Francis Group.

Comaty, J. E., Stasio, M., & Advokat, C. (2001). Analysis of outcome variables of a token economy system in a state psychiatric hospital: A program evaluation. *Research in Developmental Disabilities, 22*(3), 233–253.

Confer, J. C., Easton, J. A., Fleischman, D. S., Goetz, C. D., Lewis, D. M. G., Perilloux, C., & Buss, D. M. (2010). Evolutionary psychology: Controversies, questions, prospects, and limitations. *American Psychologist, 65*(2), 110–126.

Consortium of Social Science Associations. (2003). McQuery testifies to Homeland Security Science Subcommittee. *Washington Update, 22*(10), 1–7.

Cooke, B. (2008). The right to be human and human rights: Maslow, McCarthyism and the death of humanist theories of management. *Management and Organizational History, 3*(1), 27–47.

Cooper, M., Galbraith, M., & Drinkwater, J. (2001). Assumptions and beliefs in adolescents with anorexia nervosa and their mothers. *Eating Disorders: Journal of Treatment and Prevention, 9*(3), 217–223.

Corballis, M. C. (2009). The evolution and genetics of cerebral asymmetry. *Philosophical Transactions of the Royal Society, 364*(1519), 867–879.

Cornoldi, C. (2006). The contribution of cognitive psychology to the study of human intelligence. *European Journal of Cognitive Psychology, 18*(1), 1–17.

Coskun, O., Sener, K., Kilic, S., Erdem, H., Yaman, H., Besirbellioglu, A. B., & Eyigun, C. P. (2010). Stress-related Epstein-Barr virus reactivation. *Clinical and Experimental Medicine, 10*(1), 15–20.

Costigan, C. L., Cauce, A. M., & Etchison, K. (2007). Changes in African American mother–daughter relationships during adolescence: Conflict, autonomy, and warmth. In B. J. R. Leadbeater & N. Way (Eds.), *Urban girls revisited: Building strengths* (pp. 177–201). New York: New York University Press.

Cotton, S. M., & Richdale, A. L. (2010). Sleep patterns and behaviour in typically developing children and children with autism, Down syndrome, Prader-Willi syndrome and intellectual disability. *Research in Autism Spectrum Disorders, 4*(3), 490–500.

Cowen, P. J. (2002). Cortisol, serotonin and depression: All stressed out? *British Journal of Psychiatry, 180*(2), 99–100.

Cox, W. M., & Alm, R. (2005, February 28). Scientists are made, not born. *The New York Times* online.

Craig, J.C., & Rollman, G.B. (1999, Annual). Somesthesis. *Annual Review of Psychology,* p. 305.

Craik, F. I. M., & Bialystok, E. (2006). Cognition through the lifespan: Mechanisms of change. *Trends in Cognitive Sciences, 10*(3), 131–138.

Craik, F. I. M., & Lockhart, R. S. (2008). Levels of processing and Zinchenko's approach to memory research. *Journal of Russian and East European Psychology, 46*(6), 52–60.

Crighton, D. A., & Towl, G. J. (Eds.). (2010). *Forensic psychology.* Hoboken, NJ: Wiley.

Crisp, R. J., & Nicel, J. K. (2004). Disconfirming intergroup evaluations: Asymmetric effects for ingroups and out-groups. *Journal of Social Psychology, 144*(3), 247–271.

Crittenden, P. M., & Dallos, R. (2009). All in the family: Integrating attachment and family systems theories. *Clinical Child Psychology and Psychiatry, 14*(3), 389–409.

Crofoot, M. C., & Wrangham, R. W. (2010). Intergroup aggression in primates and humans: The case for a unified theory. In P. M. Kappeler & J. B. Silk (Eds.), *Mind the gap: Tracing the origins of human universals* (pp. 171–195). New York: Springer.

Cuijpers, P., van Straten, A., Warmerdam, L., & Andersson, G. (2009). Psychotherapy versus the combination of psychotherapy and pharmacotherapy in the treatment of depression: Asmeta-analysis. *Depression and Anxiety, 26*(3), 279–288.

Cummins, R. A., & Nistico, H. (2002). Maintaining life satisfaction: The role of positive cognitive bias. *Journal of Happiness Studies, 3*(1), 37–69.

Cunningham, G. B. (2008). Importance of friendship potential in reducing the negative effects of dissimilarity. *Journal of Social Psychology, 148*(5), 595–608.

Cunningham, M. G., Connor, C. M., Carlezon, W. A., & Meloni, E. (2009). Amygdalar GABAergic-rich neural grafts attenuate anxiety-like behavior in rats. *Behavioural Brain Research, 205*(1), 146–153.

Curry, K. (1993, October 22). Male menopause: Is it myth, or a reality of aging? *Knight Ridder/Tribune News Service.*

Curtis, A. (2001). Reward and punishment: In this regular feature examiners and teachers will explore baffling or taken for granted concepts and topics to give you clarity and insight into their meaning and their significance. *Psychology Review, 8,* 8–9.

Cutler, B. L., & Kovera, M. B. (2010). *Evaluating eyewitness identification.* New York: Oxford University Press.

D

Dabbs, J. M., Jr., Hargrove, M. F., & Heusel, C. (1996). Testosterone differences among college fraternities: Well-behaved vs. rambunctious. *Personality and Individual Differences, 20*(2), 157–161.

Dagyte, G., Den Boer, J. A., & Trentani, A. (2010). The cholinergic system and depression. *Behavioural Brain Research, 221*(2), 574–582.

Dai, S. R., Racette, N. M., Laird, J., Kagan, N, & Snidman, D. (2003). Association of a genetic marker at the corticotropin-releasing hormone locus with behavioral inhibition. *Biological Psychiatry, 54*(12), 1376–1381.

Damasio, A. R. (2000). A neural basis for sociopathy. *Archives of General Psychiatry online, 57*(2).

Dana, R. H. (2002). Mental health services for African Americans: A cultural/racial perspective. *Cultural Diversity and Ethnic Minority Psychology, 8*(1), 3–18.

Danhauer, J. L. (2009). Survey of college students on iPod use and hearing health. *Journal of the American Academy of Audiology, 20*(1), 5–27.

Darley, J. M., & Latané, B. (1968). Bystander intervention in emergencies: Diffusion of responsibility. *Journal of Personality and Social Psychology, 8,* 377–383.

Darwin, C. A. (1872). *The expression of the emotions in man and animals.* London: J. Murray.

Daud, M. K. M., Mohd Noor, R., Abd Rahman, N., Suhaimi Sidek, D., & Mohamad, A. (2010). The effect of mild hearing loss on academic performance in primary school children. *International Journal of Pediatric Otorhinolaryngology, 74*(1), 67–70.

David, D., Lynn, S. J., & Ellis, A. (Eds.). (2010). *Rational and irrational beliefs: Research, theory, and clinical practice.* New York: Oxford University Press.

David, E. J. R., Okazaki, S., & Saw, A. (2009). Bicultural self-efficacy among college students: Initial scale development and mental health correlates. *Journal of Counseling Psychology, 56*(2), 211–226.

Davidoff, J., Fonteneau, E., & Goldstein, J. (2008). Cultural differences in perception: Observations from a remote culture. *Journal of Cognition and Culture, 8*(3–4), 189–209.

Davies, M. F. (2008). Irrational beliefs and unconditional self-acceptance. III: The relative importance of different types of irrational belief. *Journal of Rational-Emotive and Cognitive-Behavior Therapy, 26*(2), 102–118.

Davis, J. I., Senghas, A., & Ochsner, K. N. (2009). How does facial feedback modulate emotional experience? *Journal of Research in Personality, 43*(5), 822–829.

Dawood, K., Bailey, J. M., & Martin, N. G. (2009). Genetic and environmental influences on sexual orientation. In Y.-K. Kim (Ed.), *Handbook of behavior genetics* (pp. 269–279). New York: Springer.

Dawson, T. L. (2002). New tools, new insights: Kohlberg's moral judgement stages revisited. *International Journal of Behavioral Development, 26*(2), 154–166.

de Hoog, N., Stroebe, W., & de Wit, J. B. F. (2007). The impact of vulnerability to and severity of a health risk on processing and acceptance of fear-arousing communications: A meta-analysis. *Review of General Psychology, 11*(3), 258–285.

De Houwer, J., Thomas, S., & Baeyens, F. (2001). Associative learning of likes and dislikes: A review of 25 years of research on human evaluative conditioning. *Psychological Bulletin, 127*(6), 853–869.

De Michele, P. E., Gansneder, B., & Solomon, G. B. (1998). Success and failure attributions of wrestlers: Further evidence of the self-serving bias. *Journal of Sport Behavior, 21*(3), 242–255.

De Rooij, S. R., Painter, R. C., Swaab, D. F., & Roseboom, T. J. (2009). Sexual orientation and gender identity after prenatal exposure to the Dutch famine. *Archives of Sexual Behavior, 38*(3), 411–416.

DeCasper, A. J., & Prescott, P. A. (1984). Human newborns' perception of male voices. *Developmental Psychobiology, 17*, 481–491.

Decety, J., & Batson, C. D. (2009). Empathy and morality: Integrating social and neuroscience approaches. In J. Verplaetse et al. (Eds.). *The moral brain.* (pp. 109-127). New York: Springer.

Deecher, D., Andree, T. H., Sloan, D., & Schechter, L. E. (2008). From menarche to menopause: Exploring the underlying biology of depression in women experiencing hormonal changes. *Psychoneuroendocrinology, 33*(1), 3–17.

Deep, A. L., Lilenfeld, L. R., Plotnicov, K. H., Pollice, C., & Kaye, W. H. (1999). Sexual abuse in eating disorder subtypes and control women: The role of comorbid substance dependence in bulimia nervosa. *International Journal of Eating Disorders, 25*(1), 1–10.

Del Giudice, M. J. (2010). What might this be? Rediscovering the Rorschach as a tool for personnel selection in organizations. *Journal of Personality Assessment, 92*(1), 78–89.

Delgado, J. M. R. (1969). *Physical control of the mind.* New York: Harper & Row.

DeMarree, K. G., Petty, R. E., & Briñol, P. (2007). Self and attitude strength parallels: Focus on accessibility. *Social and Personality Psychology Compass, 1*(1), 441–468.

Demeyer, M., De Graef, P., Wagemans, J., & Verfaillie, K. (2009). Transsaccadic identification of highly similar artificial shapes. *Journal of Vision, 9*(4), 1–14.

Demir, M., & Weitekamp, L. A. (2007). I am so happy 'cause today I found my friend: Friendship and personality as predictors of happiness. *Journal of Happiness Studies, 8*(2), 181–211.

Dennis, J., Markey, M., Johnston, K., Vander Wal, J., & Artinian, N. (2008). The role of stress and social support in predicting depression among a hypertensive African American sample. *Heart and Lung: Journal of Acute Critical Care, 37*(2), 105–112.

DeRubeis, R. J., & Crits-Christoph, P. (1998). Empirically supported individual and group psychological treatments for adult mental disorders. *Journal of Consulting and Clinical Psychology, 66*, 37–52.

DeSteno, D., Petty, R. E., Rucker, D. D., Wegener, D. T., & Braverman, J. (2004). Discrete emotions and persuasion: The role of emotion induced expectancies. *Journal of Personality & Social Psychology, 86*(1), 43–56.

Devilly, G. J. (2002). Eye movement desensitization and reprocessing: A chronology of its development and scientific standing. *Scientific Review of Mental Health Practice, 1*(2), 113–138.

Dhabhar, F. S. (2009). A hassle a day may keep the pathogens away: The fight-or-flight stress response and the augmentation of immune function. *Integrative and Comparative Biology, 49* (3), 215-236.

Dick, D. M., Prescott, C., & McGue, M. (2009). The genetics of substance use and substance use disorders. In Y.-K. Kim (Ed.), *Handbook of behavior genetics* (pp. 433–453). New York: Springer.

Dickerson, B. C., & Eichenbaum, H. (2009). The episodic memory system: Neurocircuitry and disorders. *Neuropsychopharmacology Reviews, 35*, 86–104.

Dickerson, F. D., Tenhula, W. N., & Green-Paden, L. (2005). The token economy for schizophrenia: Review of the literature and recommendations for future research. *Schizophrenia Research, 75*(2–3), 405–416.

Dienes, Z., Brown, E., Hutton, S., Kirsch, I., Mazzoni, G., & Wright, D. B. (2009). Hypnotic suggestibility, cognitive inhibition, and dissociation. *Consciousness and Cognition, 18*(4), 837–847.

Difede, J. (2005). In Lake, M. (2005, May 2). Virtual reality heals 9/11 wounds. *CNN*. Retrieved from http://www.cnn.com/2005/TECH/04/29/spark.virtual/index.html

DiGiuseppe, R. A. (2009). Rational-emotive behavior therapy. In N. Kazantzis, M. A. Reinecke, F. M. Dattilio, & A. Freeman (Eds.), *Cognitive and behavioral theories in clinical practice* (pp. 115–147). New York: Guilford Press.

Dodge, K. A. (2006). Translational science in action: Hostile attributional style and the development of aggressive behavior problems. *Development and Psychopathology, 18*(3), 791–814.

Dollard, J., Doob, L. W., Miller, N. E., Mowrer, O. H., & Sears, R. R. (1939). *Frustration and aggression.* New Haven, CT: Yale University Press.

Donovan, C.A., & Smolkin, L.B. (2002). Children's genre knowledge: An examination of K-5 student's performance on multiple tasks providing differing levels of scaffolding. *Reading Research Quarterly, 37*, 428–466.

Dotson, V. M., Kitner-Triolo, M. H., Evans, M. K., & Zonderman, A. B. (2009). Effects of race and socioeconomic status on the relative influence of education and literacy on cognitive functioning. *Journal of the International Neuropsychological Society, 15*, 580–589.

Downey, J. I. (2009). What women want: Psychodynamics of women's sexuality in 2008. *Journal of the American Academy of Psychoanalysis and Dynamic Psychiatry, 37*(2), 253–268.

Driessen, E., Cuijpers, P., de Maat, S. C., Abbass, A. A., de Jonghe, F., & Dekker, J. J (2010). The efficacy of short-term psychodynamic psychotherapy for depression: A meta-analysis. *Clinical Psychology Review, 30*(1), 25–36.

Drury, L. J. (2003). Community care for people who are homeless and mentally ill. *Journal of Health Care for the Poor and Underserved, 14*(2), 194–207.

Dube, S. R., Asman, K., Malarcher, A., & Carabollo, R. (2009). Cigarette smoking among adults and trends in smoking cessation—United States, 2008. *Morbidity and Mortality Weekly Report, 58*(44), 1227–1232.

Dubiela, F. P., Menezes De Oliveira, M. G., Di Monteiro Moreira, K., Nobrega, J. N., Tufik, S., & Hipólide, D. C. (2010). Inverse benzodiazepine agonist β-CCM does not reverse learning deficit induced by sleep deprivation. *Neuroscience Letters, 469*(1), 169–173.

Dubow, E. F., Boxer, P., Huesmann, L. R., Shikaki, K., Landau, S., Dvir Gvirsman, S., & Ginges, J. (2010). Exposure to conflict and violence across contexts: Relations to adjustment among Palestinian children. *Journal of Clinical Child and Adolescent Psychology, 39*(1), 103–116.

Duckworth, A. L., & Seligman, M. E. P. (2005). Self-discipline outdoes IQ in predicting academic performance of adolescents. *Psychological Science, 16*(12), 939–944.

Dufresne, A., Dugas, M.-A., Samson, Y., Barré, P., Turcot, L., & Marc, I. (2009). Do children undergoing cancer procedures under pharmacological sedation still report pain and anxiety? A preliminary study. *Pain Medicine, 11*(2), 215–223.

Duke, N. N., Pettingell, S. L., McMorris, B. J., & Borowsky, I. W. (2010). Adolescent violence perpetration: Associations with multiple types of adverse childhood experiences. *Pediatrics, 125*(4), e778–e786.

Dunkley, D. M., Sanislowc, C. A., Griloc, C. M., & McGlashan, T. H. (2009). Self-criticism versus neuroticism in predicting depression and psychosocial impairment for 4 years in a clinical sample. *Comprehensive Psychiatry, 50*(4), 335–346.

Dunn, J. R. (2008). Effects of housing circumstances on health, quality of life and healthcare use for people with severe mental illness: A review. *Health and Social Care in the Community, 16*(1), 1–15.

Durlez, B. (2011). Adolescent ethnic prejudice: Understanding the effects of parental extrinsic versus intrinsic goal promotion. *The Journal of Social Psychology, 151*(4), 441–454.

Dweck, C. S. (2006). *Mindset: The new psychology of success.* New York: Random House.

Dweck, C. S. (2009). Self-theories and lessons for giftedness: A reflective conversation. In T. Balchin, B. Hymer, & D. J. Matthews (Eds.), *The Routledge international companion to gifted education* (pp. 308–316). New York: Routledge/Taylor & Francis.

Dweck, C. S., & Master, A. (2008). Self-theories motivate self-regulated learning. In D. H. Schunk & B. J. Zimmerman (Eds.), *Motivation and self-regulated learning: Theory, research, and applications* (pp. 31–51). Mahwah, NJ: Erlbaum.

Dwivedi, Y. (2010). Brain-derived neurotrophic factor and suicide pathogenesis. *Annals of Medicine, 42*(2), 87–96.

Dworzynski, K., Happe, F., Bolton, P., & Ronald, A. (2009). Relationship between symptom domains in autism spectrum disorders: A population based twin study. *Journal of Autism and Developmental Disorders, 39*(8), 1197–1210.

E

Eagle, M. (2000). Repression, part I of II. *Psychoanalytic Review, 87*(1), 1–38.

Ebbinghaus, H. (1913). *Memory: A contribution to experimental psychology* (H. A. Roger & C. E. Bussenius, Trans.). New York: Columbia University Press. (Original work published 1885.)

Ebeling, M. (2008). Neuronal periodicity detection as a basis for the perception of consonance: A mathematical model of tonal fusion. *Journal of the Acoustical Society of America, 124*(4), 2320–2329.

Eberhart, N. K., & Hammen, C. L. (2010). Interpersonal style, stress, and depression: An examination of transactional and diathesis–stress models. *Journal of Social and Clinical Psychology, 29*(1), 23–38.

Ebstein, R., Israel, S., Chew, S., Zhong, S., & Knafo, A. (2010). Genetics of human social behavior. *Neuron, 65*(6), 831–844.

Egawa, T., Mishima, K., Egashira, N., Fukuzawa, M., Abe, K., Yae, T., ... Fujiwara, M. (2002). Impairment of spatial memory in kaolin-induced hydrocephalic rats is associated with changes in the hippocampal cholinergic and noradrenergic contents. *Behavioural Brain Research, 129*(1–2), 31–39.

Egerton, A., Allison, C., Brett, R. R., & Pratt, J. A. (2006). Cannabinoids and prefrontal cortical function: Insights from preclinical studies. *Neuroscience and Biobehavioral Reviews, 30*(5), 680–695.

Eichenbaum, H., & Fortin, N. (2003). Episodic memory and the hippocampus: It's about time. *Current Directions in Psychological Science, 12*(2), 53–57.

Eisend, M. (2007). Understanding two-sided persuasion: An empirical assessment of theoretical approaches. *Psychology and Marketing, 24*(7), 615–640.

Ekman, P. (1980). *The face of man.* New York: Garland Press.

Ekman, P. (1993). Facial expression and emotion. *American Psychologist, 48,* 384–392.

Ekman, P. (2003). Cited in Foreman, J. (2003, August 5). A conversation with Paul Ekman: The 43 facial muscles that reveal even the most fleeting emotions. *The New York Times online.*

Ekman, P., Friesen, W. V., O'Sullivan, M., Chan, A., Diacoyanni-Tarlatzis, I., Heider, K., ... Tzavaras, A. (1987). Universals and cultural differences in the judgments of facial expressions of emotion. *Journal of Personality and Social Psychology, 53,* 712–717.

Elkind, D. (1967). Egocentrism in adolescence. *Child Development, 38,* 1025–1034.

Elkind, D. (1985). Egocentrism redux. *Developmental Review, 5,* 218–226.

Elkind, D., & Bowen, R. (1979). Imaginary audience behavior in children and adolescents. *Developmental Psychology, 15*(1), 38–44.

Elkins, D. N. (2009). Why humanistic psychology lost its power and influence in American psychology. *Journal of Humanistic Psychology, 49*(3), 267–291.

Ellickson, P. L., Tucker, J. S., Klein, D. J., & McGuigan, K. A. (2001). Prospective risk factors for alcohol misuse in late adolescence. *Journal of Studies on Alcohol, 62*(6), 773–782.

Elliot, A. J., Kayser, D. N., Greitemeyer, T., Lichtenfeld, S., Gramzow, R. H., Maier, M. A., & Liu, H. (2010). Red, rank, and romance in women viewing men. *Journal of Experimental Psychology: General, 139*(3), 399–417.

Elliot, A. J., Maier, M. A., Moller, A. C., Friedman, R., & Meinhardt, J. (2007). Color and psychological functioning: The effect of red on performance attainment. *Journal of Experimental Psychology: General, 136,* 154–168.

Elliot, A. J., & Mapes, R. R. (2005). Approach–avoidance motivation and self-concept evaluation. In A. Teaser, J. V. Wood, & D. A. Stapel (Eds.), *On building, defending, and regulating the self: A psychological perspective* (pp. 171–196). New York: Psychology Press.

Elliot, A. J., & Niesta, D. (2008). Romantic red: Red enhances men's attraction to women. *Journal of Personality and Social Psychology, 95*(5), 1150–1164.

Ellis, A. (2005). *How to stubbornly refuse to make yourself miserable about anything—yes, anything.* New York: Kensington.

Ellis, M. A., Weiss, B., & Lochman, J. E. (2009). Executive functions in children: Associations with aggressive behavior and appraisal processing. *Journal of Abnormal Child Psychology, 37*(7), 945–956.

Else-Quest, N. M., & Grabe, S. (2012). The political is personal: Measurement and application of nation-level indicators of gender equity in psychological research. *Psychology of Women Quarterly.* doi: 10.1177/0361684312441592

Else-Quest, N. M., Hyde, J. S., & Linn, M. C. (2010). Cross-national patterns of gender differences in mathematics: A meta-analysis. *Psychological Bulletin, 136*(1), 103–127.

Emmons, R. A., & King, L. A. (1988). Conflict among personal strivings: Immediate and long-term implications for psychological and physical well-being. *Journal of Personality and Social Psychology, 54*(6), 1040–1048.

Engelhard, I. M., van den Hout, M. A., Janssen, W. C., & van der Beek, J. (2010). Eye movements reduce vividness and emotionality of "flashforwards." *Behaviour Research and Therapy, 48*(5), 442–447.

Epp, J., Keith, J. R., Spanswick, S. C., Stone, J. C., Prusky, G. T., & Sutherland, R. J. (2008). Retrograde amnesia for visual memories after hippocampal damage in rats. *Learning and Memory, 15,* 214–221.

Erikson, E. H. (1963). *Childhood and society.* New York: Norton.

Eriksson, C. J. P. (2008). Role of alcohol and sex hormones on human aggressive behavior. In D. W. Pfaff, C. Kordon, P. Chanson, & Y. Christen (Eds.), *Hormones and social behavior* (pp. 177–185). Berlin: Springer-Verlag.

Erixon, E., Högstorp, H., Wadin, K., & Rask-Andersen, H. (2009). Variational anatomy of the human cochlea: Implications for cochlear implantation. *Otology and Neurotology, 30*(1), 14–22.

Eron, L. D. (1982). Parent–child interaction, television violence, and aggression of children. *American Psychologist, 37,* 197–211.

Eron, L. D. (1993). Cited in DeAngelis, T. (1993). It's baaack: TV violence, concern for kid viewers. *APA Monitor, 24*(8), 16.

Escorial, S., Rebollo, I., Garcia, L. F., Colom, R., Abad, F. J., & Juan-Espinosa, M. (2003). Abilities that explain the intelligence decline: Evidence from the WAIS-III. *Psicothema, 15*(1), 19–22.

Esser, J. K., & Lindoerfer, J. S. (2006). Groupthink and the space shuttle *Challenger* accident: Toward a quantitative case analysis. *Journal of Behavioral Decision Making, 2*(3), 167–177.

Etaugh, C. A., & Bridges, J. S. (2006). Midlife transitions. In J. Worell & C. D. Goodheart (Eds.), *Handbook of girls'* and women's psychological health: Gender and well-being across the lifespan (pp. 359–367). Oxford series in clinical psychology. New York: Oxford University Press.

Eysenck, H. J., & Eysenck, M. W. (1985). Personality and individual differences. New York: Plenum Press.

F

Fairburn, C.G., & Harrison, P.J. (2003). Eating disorders. The Lancet, 361, 407.

Fanti, K. A., Vanman, E., Henrich, C. C., & Avraamides, M. N. (2009). Desensitization to media violence over a short period of time. Aggressive Behavior, 35(2), 179–187.

Fantz, R. L. (1961). The origin of form perception. Scientific American, 204(5), 66–72.

Farber, B. A., Brink, D. C., & Raskin, P. M. (1996). The psychotherapy of Carl Rogers: Cases and commentary. New York: Guilford Press.

Farmer, A., Elkin, A., & McGuffin, P. (2007). The genetics of bipolar affective disorder. Current Opinion in Psychiatry, 20(1), 8–12.

Farrer, L. A., Kranzler, H. R., Yu, Y., Weiss, R. D., Brady, K. T., Anton, R., ... Gelernter, J. (2009). Association of variants in MANEA with cocaine-related behaviors. Archives of General Psychiatry, 66(3), 267–274.

Farzan, F., Barr, M. S., Levinson, A. J., Chen, R., Wong, W., Fitzgerald, P. B., & Daskalakis, Z. J. (2010). Evidence for gamma inhibition deficits in the dorsolateral prefrontal cortex of patients with schizophrenia. Brain, 133(5), 1505–1514.

Fasmer, O., Akiskal, H., Hugdahl, K., & Oedegaard, K. (2008). Non-right-handedness is associated with migraine and soft polarity in patients with mood disorders. Journal of Affective Disorders, 108(3), 217–224.

Fatemi, S. H., & Folsom, T. D. (2009). The neurodevelopmental hypothesis of schizophrenia, revisited. Schizophrenia Bulletin, 35(3), 528–548.

Feeney, B. C. (2004). A secure base: Responsive support of goal strivings and exploration in adult intimate relationships. Journal of Personality & Social Psychology, 87(5), 631–648.

Fehr, B. (2008). Friendship formation. In S. Sprecher, A. Wenzel, & J. H. Harvey (Eds.), Handbook of relationship initiation (pp. 29–54). New York: CRC Press.

Feinstein, J. S., Adolphs, R., Damasio, A., & Tranel, D. (2010). The human amygdala and the induction and experience of fear. Current Biology, 22(1), 34–38.

Felsted, J. A., Ren, X., Chouinard-Decorte, F., & Small, D. M. (2010). Genetically determined differences in brain response to a primary food reward. Journal of Neuroscience, 30(7), 2428–2432.

Fenton, B. W. (2010). Measuring quality of life in chronic pelvic pain syndrome.

Expert Review of Obstetrics and Gynecology, 5(1), 115–124.

Ferrario, M. M., Veronesi, G., Chambless, L. E., Sega, R., Fornari, C., Bonzini, M., & Cesana, G. (2011). The contribution of major risk factors and job strain to occupational class differences in coronary heart disease. Occupational and Environmental Medicine, 68, 717–722.

Festinger, L., & Carlsmith, J. M. (1959). Cognitive consequences of forced compliance. Journal of Abnormal and Social Psychology, 58, 203–210.

Festinger, L., Riecken, H. W., Jr., & Schachter, S. (1956). When prophecy fails. Minneapolis: University of Minnesota Press.

Fetissov, S. O., & Meguid, M. M. (2010). Serotonin delivery into the ventromedial nucleus of the hypothalamus affects differently feeding pattern and body weight in obese and lean Zucker rats. Appetite, 54(2), 346–353.

Fields, R. D. (2005, February). Making memories stick. Scientific American, 75–81.

Fifer, W. P., & Moon, C. (2003). Prenatal development. In A. Slater & G. Bremner (Eds.), An introduction to developmental psychology (pp. 95–114). Malden, MA: Blackwell Publishers.

Finkelstein, E. A., Brown, D. S., Wrage, L. A., Allaire, B. T., & Hoerger, T. J. (2010). Individual and aggregate years-of-life-lost associated with overweight and obesity. Obesity, 18(2), 333–339.

Fisher, B. S., Daigle, L. E., & Cullen, F. T. (2008). Rape against women. Journal of Contemporary Criminal Justice, 24(2), 163–177.

Fisher, C. B. (2009). Decoding the ethics code: A practical guide for psychologists (2nd ed.). Thousand Oaks, CA: Sage.

Fisher, T. D., Moore, Z. T., & Pittenger, M. (2012). Sex on the brain? An examination of frequency of sexual cognitions as a function of gender, erotophilia, and social desirability. Journal of Sex Research, 49(1), 69–77.

Flavell, J. H. (2000). Development of children's knowledge about the mental world. International Journal of Behavioral Development, 24(1), 15–23.

Flavell, J. H., Miller, P. H., & Miller, S. A. (2002). Cognitive development (4th ed.). Upper Saddle River, NJ: Prentice Hall.

Flegal, K. M., Carroll, M. D., Ogden, C. L., & Curtin, L. R. (2010). Prevalence and trends in obesity among U.S. adults, 1999–2008. Journal of the American Medical Association, 303(3), 235–241.

Flett, G. L., Besser, A., Hewitt, P. L., & Davis, R. A. (2007). Perfectionism, silencing the self, and depression. Personality and Individual Differences, 43(5), 1211–1222.

Fligor, B. J., & Cox, L. C. (2004). Output levels of commercially available portable compact disc players and the potential risk to hearing. Ear and Hearing, 25, 513–527.

Flouri, E., & Buchanan, A. (2003). The role of father involvement and mother involvement in adolescents' psychological well-being. British Journal of Social Work, 33(3), 399–406.

Folkman, S. (Ed.). (2011). The Oxford handbook of stress, health and coping. New York: Oxford University Press.

Folkman, S., & Moskowitz, T. (2000a). Positive affect and the other side of coping. American Psychologist, 55(6), 647–654.

Folkman, S., & Moskowitz, J. T. (2000b). The context matters. Personality and Social Psychology Bulletin, 26(2), 150–151.

Fontaine, R. G., Tanha, M., Yang, C., Dodge, K. A., Bates, J. E., & Pettit, G. S. (2010). Does response evaluation and decision (RED) mediate the relation between hostile attributional style and antisocial behavior in adolescence? Journal of Abnormal Child Psychology, 38(5), 615–626.

Foote, B., Smolin, Y., Kaplan, M., Legatt, M. E., & Lipschitz, D. (2006). Prevalence of dissociative disorders in psychiatric outpatients. American Journal of Psychiatry, 163(4), 623–629.

Forcehimes, A. A., & Tonigan, J. S. (2008). Self-efficacy as a factor in abstinence from alcohol/other drug abuse: A meta-analysis. Alcoholism Treatment Quarterly, 26(4), 480–489.

Forrest, D. V. (2008). Alien abduction: A medical hypothesis. Journal of the American Academy of Psychoanalysis and Dynamic Psychiatry, 36(3), 431–442.

Förster, J. (2009). Cognitive consequences of novelty and familiarity: How mere exposure influences level of construal. Journal of Experimental Social Psychology, 45(2), 444–447.

Fortin, S., Godbout, L., & Braun, C. M. J. (2002). Strategic sequence planning and prospective memory impairments in frontally lesioned head trauma patients performing activities of daily living. Brain & Cognition, 48(2–3), 361–365.

Franco, K., Mancilla, J. M., Alvarez, G., Vazquez, R., Lopez, X., & Diaz, F. (2009). The role of perfectionism in eating behaviors among women with eating disorder. Appetite, 52(3), 832.

Franklin, T. R., Harper, D., Kampman, K., Kildea-McCrea, S., Jens, W., Lynch, K. G., ... Childress, A. R. (2009). The GABA B agonist baclofen reduces cigarette consumption in a preliminary double-blind placebo-controlled smoking reduction study. Drug and Alcohol Dependence, 103(1–2), 30–36.

Frasure-Smith, N., & Lespérance, F. (2008). Depression and anxiety as predictors of 2-year cardiac events in patients with stable coronary artery disease. Archives of General Psychiatry, 65(1), 62–71.

Freeman, D., Pugh, K, Vorontsova, N., Antley, A., & Slater, M. (2010). Testing the continuum of delusional beliefs: An experimental study using virtual reality.

Journal of Abnormal Psychology, 119(1), 83–92.

Freeman, M. S., Spence, M. J., & Oliphant, C. M. (1993, June). *Newborns prefer their mothers' low-pass filtered voices over other female filtered voices.* Paper presented at the annual convention of the American Psychological Society, Chicago, IL.

Freitas, A. L., Clark, S. L., Kim, J. Y., & Levy, S. R. (2009). Action-construal levels and perceived conflict among ongoing goals: Implications for positive affect. *Journal of Research in Personality, 43*(5), 938–941.

Freud, S. (1964). A religious experience. In *Standard edition of the complete psychological works of Sigmund Freud* (Vol. 21). London: Hogarth Press. (Original work published 1927.)

Freud, S. (1998). The baby and the bathwater: Some thoughts on Freud as a postmodernist. *Families in Society: The Journal of Contemporary Human Services, 79,* 455–464.

Freund, M. (2009). On the notion of concept: II. *Artificial Intelligence, 173*(1), 167–179.

Friedrich, C. K., Schild, U., & Roder, B. (2009). Electrophysiological indices of word fragment priming allow characterizing neural stages of speech recognition. *Biological Psychology, 80*(1), 105–113.

Frisby, B. N., Dillow, M. R., Gaughan, S., & Nordlund, J. (2010). Flirtatious communication: An experimental examination of social-sexual communication motivated by evolutionary forces. *Sex Roles, 64*(9–10), 682–694.

Frisch, R. (1997). Cited in Angier, N. (1997). Chemical tied to fat control could help trigger puberty. *The New York Times,* pp. C1, C3.

Fritsch, G., & Hitzig, E. (1960). On the electrical excitability of the cerebrum. In G. von Bonin (Ed.), *Some papers on the cerebral cortex.* Springfield, IL: Thomas. (Original work published 1870.)

Froeliger, B., Gilbert, D. G., & McClernon, F. J. (2009). Effects of nicotine on novelty detection and memory recognition performance: Double-blind, placebo-controlled studies of smokers and nonsmokers. *Psychopharmacology, 205*(4), 625–633.

Fuentes, R., Petersson, P., Siesser, W. B., Caron, M. G., & Nicolelis, M. A. L. (2009). Spinal cord stimulation restores locomotion in animal models of Parkinson's disease. *Science, 323*(5921), 1578–1582.

Fukushima, M., Sharp, S., & Kobayashi, E. (2009). Born to bond, collectivism, and conformity: A comparative study of Japanese and American college students. *Deviant Behavior, 30*(5), 434–466.

Furnham, A., Petrides, K. V., Sisterson, G., & Baluch, B. (2003). Repressive coping style and positive self-presentation. *British Journal of Health Psychology, 8*(2), 223–249.

G

Galdo-Alvarez, S., Lindín, M., & Díaz, F. (2009). Age-related prefrontal over-recruitment in semantic memory retrieval: Evidence from successful face naming and the tip-of-the-tongue state. *Biological Psychology, 82*(1), 89–96.

Gallese, V., Fadiga, L., Fogassi, L., & Rizzolatti, G. (1996). Action recognition in the premotor cortex. *Brain, 119*(2), 593–609.

Gans, D., & Silverstein, M. (2006). Norms of filial responsibility for aging parents across time and generations. *Journal of Marriage and Family, 68*(4), 961–976.

Gao, Y., Raine, A., Venables, P. H., Dawson, M. E., & Mednick, S. A. (2010a). Association of poor childhood fear conditioning and adult crime. *American Journal of Psychiatry, 167,* 56–60.

Gao, Y., Raine, A., Venables, P. H., Dawson, M. E., & Mednick, S. A. (2010b). Reduced electrodermal fear conditioning from ages 3 to 8 years is associated with aggressive behavior at age 8 years. *Journal of Child Psychology and Psychiatry, 51*(5), 550–558.

Garb, H. N., Wood, J. M., Lilienfeld, S. O., & Nezworski, M. T. (2005). Roots of the Rorschach controversy. *Clinical Psychology Review, 25*(1), 97–118.

Garcia, J., & Koelling, R. A. (1966). Relation of cue to consequences in avoidance learning. *Psychonomic Science 4,* 123–124.

Garcia-Falgueras, A., & Swaab, D. F. (2010). Sex hormones and the brain: An essential alliance for sexual identity and sexual orientation. In S. Loche, M. Cappa, L. Ghizzoni, M. Maghnie, & M. O. Savage (Eds.), *Pediatric neuroendocrinology* (Vol. 17, pp. 22–35). Basel, Switzerland: Karger.

Gardini Gardenghi, G., Boni, E., Todisco, P., Manara, F., Borghesi, A., & Tantucci, C. (2009). Respiratory function in patients with stable anorexia nervosa. *Chest, 136*(5), 1356–1363.

Gardner, H. (1983/1993). *Frames of mind.* New York: Basic Books.

Gardner, H. (2001, April 5). Multiple intelligence. *The New York Times,* p. A20.

Gardner, H. (2009). Birth and the spreading of a "meme." In J.-Q. Chen, S. Moran, & H. Gardner (Eds.), *Multiple intelligences around the world* (pp. 3–16). Hoboken, NJ: Wiley.

Garrett, R. K. (2009). Politically motivated reinforcement seeking: Reframing the selective exposure debate. *Journal of Communication, 59*(4), 676–699.

Garza, Y., & Watts, R. E. (2010). Filial therapy and Hispanic values: Common ground for culturally sensitive helping. *Journal of Counseling and Development, 88*(1), 108–113.

Gatchel, R. J., Haggard, R., Thomas, C., & Howard, K. J. (2012). Biopsychosocial approaches to understanding chronic pain. *Handbook of pain and palliative care,* 1–16. doi: 10.1007/978-1-4419-1651-8_1

Gatchel, R. J., & Kishino, N. D. (2010). Managing pain. In J. C. Thomas & M. Hersen (Eds.), *Handbook of clinical psychology competencies* (pp. 1181–1192). New York: Springer.

Gay, P. (1999). Psychoanalyst: Sigmund Freud. *Time, 153,* 66.

Gegenfurtner, K. R., & Kiper, D. C. (2003). Color vision. *Annual Review of Neuroscience, 26,* 181–206.

Geher, G., Bauman, K.P., Hubbard, S.E.K., & Legare, J.R. (2002). Self and other obedience estimates: Biases and moderators. *The Journal of Social Psychology, 142,* 677–689.

Gerdes, A. B. M., Uhl, G., & Alpers, G. W. (2009). Spiders are special: Fear and disgust evoked by pictures of arthropods. *Evolution and Human Behavior, 30*(1), 66–73.

Gershoff, E. T. (2002). Corporal punishment by parents and associated child behaviors and experiences: A meta-analytic and theoretical review. *Psychological Bulletin, 128*(4), 539–579.

Getzels, J. W., & Jackson, P. W. (1962). *Creativity and intelligence.* New York: Wiley.

Gigerenzer, G. (2010). Personal reflections on theory and psychology. *Theory & Psychology, 20*(6), 733–743.

Gigerenzer, G., Hoffrage, U., & Goldstein, D. G. (2008). Postscript: Fast and frugal heuristics. *Psychological Review, 115*(1), 238–239.

Gilbert, P. (2009). Biopsychosocial approaches and evolutionary theory as aids to integration in clinical psychology and psychotherapy. *Clinical Psychology and Psychotherapy.* doi:10.1002/cpp.5640020302

Gilbert, S. J., Bird, G., Brindley, R., Frith, C. D., & Burgess, P. W. (2008). Atypical recruitment of medial prefrontal cortex in autism spectrum disorders: An fMRI study of two executive function tasks. *Neuropsychologia, 46*(9), 2281–2291.

Gilovich, T., & Eibach, R. (2001). The fundamental attribution error where it really counts. *Psychological Inquiry, 12*(1), 23–26.

Giuliano, P. (2007). Living arrangements in Western Europe: Does cultural origin matter? *Journal of the European Economic Association, 5*(5), 927–952.

Glantz L. A., et al. (2010). Pro-apoptotic Par-4 and dopamine D2 receptor in temporal cortex in schizophrenia, bipolar disorder and major depression. *Schizophr Research 118*(1-3): 292–299.

Glaser, R., Pearson, G. R., Bonneau, R. H., Esterling, B. A., Atkinson, C., & Kiecolt-Glaser, J. K. (1993). Stress and the memory T-cell response to the Epstein-Barr virus. *Health Psychology, 12,* 435–442.

Glass, D. C., Krakoff, L. R., Contrada, R., Hiltn, W. F., Kehoe, K., Mannucci, E. G., … Elting, E. (2007). Effects of harassment and competition upon cardiovascular and plasma catecholamine responses in Type A and Type B individuals. *Psychophysiology, 17*(5), 453–463.

Glasser, C. L., Robnett, B., & Feliciano, C. (2009). Internet daters' body type preferences: Race–ethnic and gender differences. *Sex Roles, 61*(1–2), 14–33.

Glynn, R. J. (2010). The USPSTF recommendation statement on coronary heart disease risk assessment. *Annals of Internal Medicine, 152,* 403–404.

Goez, H., & Zelnik, N. (2008). Handedness in patients with developmental coordination disorder. *Journal of Child Neurology, 23*(2), 151–154.

Goldman-Rakic, P. S. (1995). Cited in Goleman, D. (1995, May 2). Biologists find site of working memory. *The New York Times,* pp. C1, C9.

Goldston, D. B., & Compton, J. S. (2010). Adolescent suicidal and nonsuicidal self-harm behaviors and risk. In E. J. Marsh & R. A. Barkley (Eds.), *Assessment of childhood disorders* (pp. 305–346). New York: Guilford Press.

Goleman, D. J. (1995). *Emotional intelligence.* New York: Bantam Books.

Golombok, S., Rust, J., Zervoulis, K., Croudace, T., Golding, J., & Hines, M. (2008). Developmental trajectories of sex-typed behavior in boys and girls: A longitudinal general population study of children aged 2.5–8 years. *Child Development, 79*(5), 1583–1593.

González, H. M., Vega, W. A., Williams, D. R., Tarraf, W., West, B. T., & Neighbors, H. W. (2010). Depression care in the United States: Too little for too few. *Archives of General Psychiatry, 67,* 37–46.

González, Y. S., Moreno, D. S., & Schneider, B. H. (2004). Friendship expectations of early adolescents in Cuba and Canada. *Journal of Cross-Cultural Psychology, 35*(4), 436–445.

Goodenough, F. (1926). *Measurement of intelligence by drawings.* Yonkers, NY: World Book.

Gotlib, I. H., & Joormann, J. (2010). Cognition and depression: Current status and future directions. *Annual Review of Clinical Psychology, 6,* 285–312.

Gottesman, I. I. (1991). *Schizophrenia genesis.* New York: Freeman.

Gottfredson, G. D. (2009). John Holland (1919–2008). *American Psychologist, 64*(6), 561.

Gould, S. J. (2002). *The structure of evolutionary theory.* Cambridge, MA: Belknap Press /Harvard University Press.

Grace, D. M., David, B. J., & Ryan, M. K. (2008). Investigating preschoolers' categorical thinking about gender through imitation, attention, and the use of self-categories. *Child Development, 79*(6), 1928–1941.

Greenberg, J. (1985) Family size tied to SAT, IQ scores. *Science News.* Science Service, Inc.

Greenberger, E., Chen, C., Tally, S. R., & Dong, Q. (2000). Family, peer, and individual correlates of depressive symptomology among U.S. and Chinese adolescents. *Journal of Consulting and Clinical Psychology, 68,* 209–219.

Greenhalgh, J., Dickson, R., & Dundar, Y. (2010). Biofeedback for hypertension: A systematic review. *Journal of Hypertension, 28*(4), 644–652.

Greenwood, P. M., Sundararajan, R., Lin, M.-K., Kumar, R., Fryxell, K. J., & Parasuraman, R. (2009). Both a nicotinic single nucleotide polymorphism (SNP) and a noradrenergic SNP modulate working memory performance when attention is manipulated. *Journal of Cognitive Neuroscience, 21*(11), 2139–2153.

Gregory, V. L., Jr. (2010). Cognitive-behavioral therapy for schizophrenia: Applications to social work practice. *Social Work in Mental Health, 8*(2), 140–159.

Greidanus, E., & Everall, R. D. (2010). Helper therapy in an online suicide prevention community. *British Journal of Guidance and Counselling, 38*(2), 191–204.

Griffin, C. (2001). Imagining new narratives of youth: Youth research, the "new Europe" and global youth culture. *Childhood: Global Journal of Child Research, 8*(2), 147–166.

Griffin, K.W., Botvin, G. J., Nichols, T. R., & Scheier, L. M. (2004). Low perceived chances for success in life and binge drinking among inner-city minority youth. *Journal of Adolescent Health, 34*(6), 501–507.

Grillon, M.-L., Krebs, M.-O., Gourevitch, R., Giersch, A., & Huron, C. (2010). Episodic memory and impairment of an early encoding process in schizophrenia. *Neuropsychology, 24*(1), 101–108.

Gross, A. L., Gallo, J. J., & Eaton, W. W. (2010). Depression and cancer risk: 24 years of follow-up of the Baltimore Epidemiologic Catchment Area. *Cancer Causes and Control, 21*(2), 191–199.

Gross, R. (2002). The prison simulation experiment. *Psychology Review, 8,* 15–17.

Grundy, E., & Henretta, J. C. (2006). Between elderly parents and adult children: A new look at the intergenerational care provided by the "sandwich generation." *Ageing & Society, 26*(5), 707–722.

Grusec, J. E. (2006). The development of moral behavior and conscience from a socialization perspective. In M. Killen & J. G. Smetana (Eds.), *Handbook of moral development* (pp. 243–265). Mahwah, NJ: Erlbaum.

Gupta, V. B., Nwosa, N. M., Nadel, T. A., & Inamdar, S. (2001). Externalizing behaviors and television viewing in children of low-income minority parents. *Clinical Pediatrics, 40*(6), 337–341.

Guzzetti, B. J. (2010). Feminist perspectives on the new literacies. In E. A. Baker & D. J. Leu (Eds.), *The new literacies* (pp. 242–264). New York: Guilford Press.

H

Haenen, J. (2001). Outlining the teaching–learning process: Piotr Gal'perin's contribution. *Learning and Instruction, 11*(2), 157–170.

Hafemeister, L., Gaussier, P., Maillard, M., Boucenna, S., & Giovannangeli, C. (2010). Perception: Insights from the sensori-motor approach. *European Workshop of Visual Information Processing.* Retrieved from http://hal.archives-ouvertes.fr/hal-00520433/

Hall, J. A., Park, N., Song, H., & Cody, M. J. (2010). Strategic misrepresentation in online dating: The effects of gender, self-monitoring, and personality traits. *Journal of Social and Personal Relationships, 27*(1), 117–135.

Halpern, D. F. (2003). Sex differences in cognitive abilities. *Applied Cognitive Psychology, 17*(3), 375–376.

Halpern, D. F., Benbow, C. P., Geary, D. C., Gur, R. C., Shibley Hyde, J., & Gernsbacher, M. A. (2007). The science of sex differences in science and mathematics. *Psychological Science in the Public Interest, 8*(1), 1–51.

Halpern, D. F., & LaMay, M. L. (2000). The smarter sex: A critical review of sex differences in intelligence. *Educational Psychology Review, 12*(2), 229–246.

Halpern, R. (2005). [Review of the book *Examining adolescent leisure time across cultures: New directions for child and adolescent development, No. 99* by S. Verma and R. Larson, eds.]. *Journal of Adolescent Research, 20*(4), 524–525.

Hancock, J. (2007). Digital deception: When, where, and how people lie online. In K. McKenna, T. Postmes, U. Reips, & A. Joinson (Eds.), *Oxford handbook of Internet psychology* (pp. 287–301). Oxford, England: Oxford University Press.

Harlow, H. F. (1959). Love in infant monkeys. *Scientific American, 200,* 68–86.

Harlow, J. M. (1868). Recovery from the passage of an iron bar through the head. *Publication of the Massachusetts Medical Society, 2,* 327.

Harris, J. L., Bargh, J. A., & Brownell, K. D. (2009). Priming effects of television food advertising on eating behavior. *Health Psychology, 28*(4), 404–413.

Hasin, D. S., Goodwin, R. D., Stinson, F. S., & Grant, B. F. (2005). Epidemiology of major depressive disorder. *Archives of General Psychiatry, 62,* 1097–1106.

Haustein, K.-O., & Groneberg, D. (2009). Pharmacology and pharmakinetics of nicotine. In K.-O. Haustein & D. Groneberg (Eds.), *Tobacco or health?* (pp. 61–86). New York: Springer.

Haworth, C. M. A., Dale, P. S., & Plomin, R. (2009a). Sex differences and science: The etiology of science excellence. *Journal of Child Psychology and Psychiatry, 50*(9), 1113–1120.

Haworth, C. M. A., Wright, M. J., Martin, N. W., Martin, N. G., Boomsma, D. I.,

Bartels, M., ... Plomin, R. (2009b). A twin study of the genetics of high cognitive ability selected from 11,000 twin pairs in six studies from four countries. *Behavior Genetics, 39*(4), 359–370.

Health, United States (2002). http:/www.cdc.gov/ nchs (National Center for Health Statistics).

Heber, D. (2010). An integrative view of obesity. *American Journal of Clinical Nutrition, 91*(1), 280S–283S.

Heidenreich, T., & Michalak, J. (2003). Mindfulness as a treatment principle in behavior therapy. *Verhaltenstherapie, 13*(4), 264–274.

Heimpel, S. A., Wood, J. V., Marshall, M. A., & Brown, J. D. (2002). Do people with low self-esteem really want to feel better? Self-esteem differences in motivation to repair negative moods. *Journal of Personality & Social Psychology, 82*(1), 128–147.

Helms, J. E. (2006). Fairness is not validity or cultural bias in racial-group assessment: A quantitative perspective. *American Psychologist, 61*(8), 845–859.

Henderson, A. S. (2009). Alzheimer's disease in its epidemiological context. *Acta Neurologica Scandinavica, 88*(S149), 1–3.

Henderson, T. L., Roberto, K. A., & Kamo, Y. (2010). Older adults' responses to Hurricane Katrina. *Journal of Applied Gerontology, 29*(1), 48–69.

Heng, M. A. (2000). Scrutinizing common sense: The role of practical intelligence in intellectual giftedness. *Gifted Child Quarterly, 44*(3), 171–182.

Henley, C. L., Nunez, A. A., & Clemens, L. G. (2010). Exogenous androgen during development alters adult partner preference and mating behavior in gonadally intact male rats. *Hormones and Behavior, 57*(4–5), 488–495.

Henry, D. B. (2008). Changing classroom social settings through attention to norms. In M. Shinn & H. Yoshikawa (Eds.), *Toward positive youth development* (pp. 40–57). New York: Oxford University Press.

Henry, J. D., MacLeod, M. S., Phillips, L. H., & Crawford, J. R. (2004). A meta-analytic review of prospective memory and aging. *Psychology and Aging, 19*(1), 27–39.

Herbenick, D., Reece, M., Sanders, S. A., Schick, V., Dodge, B., & Fortenberry, J. D. (2010a). Sexual behavior in the United States: Results from a national probability sample of males and females ages 14 to 94. *Journal of Sexual Medicine, 7*(Suppl. 5), 255–265.

Herbenick, D., Reece, M., Schick, V., Sanders, S. A., Dodge, B., & Fortenberry, J. D. (2010b). Sexual behaviors, relationships, and perceived health among adult women in the United States: Results from a national probability sample. *Journal of Sexual Medicine, 7*(Suppl. 5), 277–290.

Herbenick, D., Reece, M., Schick, V., Sanders, S. A., Dodge, B., & Fortenberry, J. D. (2010c). An event-level analysis of the sexual characteristics and composition among adults ages 18 to 59: Results from a national probability sample in the United States. *Journal of Sexual Medicine, 7*(Suppl. 5), 346–361.

Hergenhahn, B. R. (2009). *An introduction to the history of psychology* (6th ed.). Belmont, CA: Cengage.

Heron, M., & Tejada-Vera, B. (2009). Deaths: Leading causes. *National Vital Statistics Reports, 58*(8). Retrieved from http://www.cdc.gov/nchs/data/nvsr/nvsr58/nvsr58_08.pdf

Higgs, S., & Woodward, M. (2009). Television watching during lunch increases afternoon snack intake of young women. *Appetite, 52*(1), 39–43.

Hill, S. Y., et al. (2007). Cerebellar volume in offspring from multiplex alcohol dependence families. *Biological Psychiatry, 61*(1), 41–47.

Hingson, R., Zha, W., & Weitzman, E. R. (2002). *A call to action: Changing the culture of drinking at U.S. colleges.* Washington, DC: National Institutes of Health: National Institute of Alcohol Abuse and Alcoholism.

Hirst, W., Phelps, E. A., Buckner, R. L., Budson, A. E., Gabrieli, J. D. E., Johnson, M. K., ... Vaidya, C. J. (2009). Long-term memory for the terrorist attack of September 11: Flashbulb memories, event memories, and the factors that influence their retention. *Journal of Experimental Psychology: General, 138*(2), 161–176.

Ho, M. Y., Cheung, F. M., & Cheung, S. F. (2010). The role of meaning in life and optimism in promoting well-being. *Personality and Individual Differences, 48*(5), 658–663.

Hobson, J. A. (2003). *Dreaming: An introduction to the science of sleep.* New York: Oxford University Press.

Hobson, J. A. (2009). REM sleep and dreaming. *Nature Reviews Neuroscience, 10,* 803–813.

Hoff, E. (2005). *Language development* (3rd ed.). Belmont, CA: Wadsworth.

Hoffman, H. G. (2004). Virtual reality therapy. *Scientific American, 291*(2), 58–65.

Hoge, C. W., et al. (2004). Combat duty in Iraq and Afghanistan, mental health problems, and barriers to care. *New England Journal of Medicine, 351*(1), 13–22.

Hojnoski, R. L., Morrison, R., Brown, M., & Matthews, W. J. (2006). Projective test use among school psychologists. *Journal of Psychoeducational Assessment, 24*(2), 145–159.

Hollingshead, A. B., & Redlich, F. C. (1958). *Social class and mental illness.* New York: Wiley.

Hollon, S. D., & Shelton, R. C. (2001). Treatment guidelines for major depressive disorder. *Behavior Therapy, 32*(2), 235–258.

Holmes, T. H., & Rahe, R. H. (1967). The social readjustment rating scale. *Journal of Psychosomatic Research, 11,* 213–218.

Honorton, C. (1985). Meta-analysis of psi Ganzfeld research. *Journal of Parapsychology, 49,* 51–91.

Honts, C. R., & Handler, M. (2011, January). *Interrogations, false confessions and the polygraph: Issues and concerns from psychological science.* Invited address at the Annual Meeting, American Association of Police Polygraphists, Boston, MA.

Hoover, R. N. (2000). Cancer—Nature, nurture, or both? *New England Journal of Medicine online, 343*(2).

Hopkins, R. A., & Powers, T. L. (2009). Development and test of new dimensions of altruistic buying behavior. *Journal of Consumer Marketing, 26*(3), 185–199.

Horan, W. P., Wynn, J. K., Kring, A. M., Simons, R. F., & Green, M. F. (2010). Electrophysiological correlates of emotional responding in schizophrenia. *Journal of Abnormal Psychology, 119*(1), 18–30.

Horn, J. M. (1983). The Texas adoption project. *Child Development, 54,* 268–275.

Hornstein, E. P., Verweij, J., & Schnapf, J. L. (2004). Electrical coupling between red and green cones in primate retina. *Nature Neuroscience, 7*(7), 745–750.

Howard, G., Lau, M. Y., Maxwell, S. E., Venter, A., Lundy, R., & Sweeny, R. M. (2009). Do research literatures give correct answers? *Review of General Psychology, 13*(2), 116–121.

Howard, K. J., Ellis, H. B., & Khaleel, M. A. (2010). Psychological factors that may influence outcome after joint replacement surgery. *Current Orthopaedic Practice, 21*(2), 144–148.

Hrabosky, J. I., Cash, T. F., Veale, D., Neziroglu, F., Soll, E. A., Garner, D. M., ... Phillips, K. A. (2009). Multidimensional body image comparisons among patients with eating disorders, body dysmorphic disorder, and clinical controls: A multisite study. *Body Image, 6*(3), 155–163.

Hu, X., Yang, Y., Liu, L., Liu, X., & Tong, Y. (2010). Early psychological intervention following a natural disaster. *Social Behavior and Personality, 38*(1), 71–74.

Hubel, D. H., & Wiesel, T. N. (1979). Brain mechanisms of vision. *Scientific American, 241,* 150–162.

Huesmann, L. R., Moise-Titus, J., Podolski, C., & Eron, L. D. (2003). Longitudinal relations between children's exposure to TV violence and their aggressive and violent behavior in young adulthood: 1977–1992. *Developmental Psychology, 39*(2), 201–221.

Hughes, T. F., Andel, R., Small, B. J., Borenstein, A. R., & Mortimer, J. A. (2008). The association between social resources and cognitive change in older adults. *Journals of Gerontology Series B: Psychological Sciences and Social Sciences, 63,* P241–P244.

Hunter, B.T. (2002). How food communicates with your taste buds: The chemistry of perception. *Consumers' Research Magazine, 85,* 26–28.

Hunter, D. J. (2005). Gene–environment interactions in human diseases. *Nature Reviews Genetics, 6,* 287–298.

Huntjens, R. J. C., Postma, A., Peters, M. L., Woertman, L., & van der Hart, O. (2003). Interidentity amnesia for neutral, episodic information in dissociative identity disorder. *Journal of Abnormal Psychology, 112*(2), 290–297.

Hurka, T. (2010). Morality and political violence. *Philosophical Review, 119*(1), 115–117.

Hustad, J. T. P., Barnett, N. P., Borsari, B., & Jackson, K. M. (2010). Web-based alcohol prevention for incoming college students: A randomized controlled trial. *Addictive Behaviors, 35*(3), 183–189.

Hwang, C. H., Guo, D., Harris, M. A., Howard, O., Mishina, Y., Gan, L., ... Wu, D. K. (2010). Role of bone morphogenetic proteins on cochlear hair cell formation. *Developmental Dynamics, 239*(2), 505–513.

Hyde, J. S., Lindberg, S. M., Linn, M. C., Ellis, A. B., & Williams, C. C. (2008). Gender similarities characterize math performance. *Science, 321,* 494–495.

Hyde, J. S., & Mertz, J. E. (2009). Gender, culture, and mathematics performance. *Proceedings of the National Academy of Sciences, 106*(22), 8801–8807.

Hyman, R. (2011). Cited in B. Carey. (2011, January 5). Journal's paper on ESP expected to prompt outrage. *The New York Times online.*

I

Iacono, W. G. (2008). Accuracy of polygraph techniques: Problems using confessions to determine ground truth. *Physiology and Behavior, 95*(1–2), 24–26.

Inaba, M., Maruyamab, T., Yoshimurab, Y., Hosoia, H., & Komatsu, Y. (2009). Facilitation of low-frequency stimulation-induced long-term potentiation by endogenous noradrenaline and serotonin in developing rat visual cortex. *Neuroscience Research, 64*(2), 191–198.

Inhelder, B., & Piaget, J. (1958). *The growth of logical thinking.* New York: Basic Books.

International Human Genome Sequencing Consortium. (2006). Finishing the euchromatic sequence of the human genome. *Nature, 431,* 931–945.

Isarida, T., & Isarida, T. K. (2006). Influences of environmental context on the recency effect in free recall. *Memory and Cognition, 34*(4), 787–794.

Isen, J., Raine, A., Baker, L., Dawson, M., Bezdjian, S., & Lozano, D. I. (2010). Sex-specific association between psychopathic traits and electrodermal reactivity in children. *Journal of Abnormal Psychology, 119*(1), 216–225.

Ismail, S. A., & Mowafi, H. A. (2009). Melatonin provides anxiolysis, enhances analgesia, decreases intraocular pressure, and promotes better operating conditions during cataract surgery under topical anesthesia. *Anesthesia and Analgesia, 108,* 1146–1151.

Ito, H., Yamauchi, H., Kaneko, H., Yoshikawa, T., Nomura, K., & Honjo, S. (2011). Prefrontal overactivation, autonomic arousal, and task performance under evaluative pressure. *Psychophysiology, 48*(11), 1563–1571.

Iverson, P., Kuhl, P. K., Akahane-Yamada, R., Diesch, E., Tohkura, Y., Kettermann, A., & Siebert, C. (2003). A perceptual interference account of acquisition difficulties for non-native phonemes. *Cognition, 87*(1), B47–B57.

Iwasaki, A., & Medzhitov, R. (2010). Regulation of adaptive immunity by the innate immune system. *Science, 327*(5963), 291–295.

J

Jackson, E. C. (2009). Nocturnal enuresis: Giving the child a "lift." *Journal of Pediatrics, 154*(5), 636–637.

Jackson, H., & Nuttall, R. L. (2001). Risk for preadolescent suicidal behavior: An ecological model. *Child and Adolescent Social Work Journal, 18*(3), 189–203.

Jackson, L. C., & Greene, B. (2000). *Psychotherapy with African American women: Innovations in psychodynamic perspectives and practice.* New York: Guilford Press.

Jackson, M. L. (2009). *The effects of sleep deprivation on simulated driving, neurocognitive functioning and brain activity in professional drivers.* Retrieved from http://researchbank. swinburne .edu.au/vital/access/manager/ Repository/swin:14257

James, W. (1890). *The principles of psychology.* New York: Henry Holt.

Jamison, K. R. (2000). Suicide and bipolar disorder. *Journal of Clinical Psychiatry, 61*(Suppl. 9), 47–51.

Jang, K. L., Livesley, W. J., Vernon, P. A., & Jackson, D. N. (2007). Heritability of personality disorder traits: A twin study. *Acta Psychiatrica Scandinavica, 94*(6), 438–444.

Janis, I. L. (1982). *Groupthink* (2nd ed.). Boston: Houghton Mifflin.

Janowitz, H. D., & Grossman, M. I. (1949). Effects of variations in nutritive density on intake of food in dogs and cats. *American Journal of Physiology, 158,* 184–193.

Jemal, A., Siegel, R., Ward, E., Hao, Y., Xu, J., & Thun, M. J. (2009). Cancer statistics, 2009. *CA: Cancer Journal for Clinicians, 59,* 225–249.

Jennings, M., Heitner, K., & Heravi, N. (2009). Identification of factors associated with academic success and persistence to graduation in online learning environments. *Proceedings of World Conference on Educational Multimedia, Hypermedia and Telecommunications 2009* (pp. 4216–4219). Chesapeake, VA: AACE.

Jensen, M. P., Barber, J., Romano, J. M., Hanley, M. A., Raichle, K. A., Molton, I. R., ... Patterson, D. R. (2009). Effects of self-hypnosis training and EMG biofeedback relaxation training on chronic pain in persons with spinal-cord injury. *International Journal of Clinical and Experimental Hypnosis, 57*(3), 239–268.

Jetten, J., & Hornsey, M. J. (2011). *Rebels in groups.* Hoboken, NJ: Wiley.

Johnson, S. B., Sudhinaraset, M., & Blum, R. W. (2010). Neuromaturation and adolescent risk taking: Why development is not determinism. *Journal of Adolescent Research, 25*(1), 4–23.

Johnson, W., Jung, R. E., Colom, R., & Haier, R. J. (2008). Cognitive abilities independent of IQ correlate with regional brain structure. *Intelligence, 36*(1), 18–28.

Johnson, W., & Krueger, R. F. (2006). How money buys happiness: Genetic and environmental processes linking finances and life satisfaction. *Journal of Personality and Social Psychology, 90*(4), 680–691.

Johnston, L. D., O'Malley, P. M., Bachman, J. G., & Schulenberg, J. E. (2010). *Monitoring the future national results on adolescent drug use: Overview of key findings, 2008* (NIH Publication No. 09-7401). Bethesda, MD: National Institute on Drug Abuse.

K

Kagan, J., & Saudino, K. J. (2001). Behavioral inhibition and related temperaments. In R. N. Emde & J. K. Hewitt (Eds.), *Infancy to early childhood: Genetic and environmental influences on developmental change* (pp. 111–122). New York: Oxford University Press.

Kahana, E., Kahana, B., Wykle, M., & Kulle, D. (2009). Marshalling social support: A care-getting model for persons living with cancer. *Journal of Family Social Work, 12*(2), 168–193.

Kalavana, T. V., Maes, S., & De Gucht, V. (2010). Interpersonal and self-regulation determinants of healthy and unhealthy eating behavior in adolescents. *Journal of Health Psychology, 15*(1), 44–52.

Kamalanabhan, T. J., Sunder, D. L., & Vasanthi, M. (2000). An evaluation of the Choice Dilemma Questionnaire as a measure of risk-taking propensity. *Social Behavior and Personality, 28*(2), 149–156.

Kamphaus, R. W., Petoskey, M. D., & Rowe, E. W. (2000). Current trends in psychological testing of children. *Professional Psychology: Research and Practice, 31*(2), 155–164.

Kandel, E. R. (2006). *In search of memory: The emergence of a new science of mind.* New York: Norton.

Kaplan, R. M., & Saccuzzo, D. P. (2008). *Psychological testing: Principles, applications, and issues.* Belmont, CA: Cengage.

Karolewicz, B., Maciag, D., O'Dwyer, G., Stockmeier, C. A., Feyissa, A. M., &

Rajkowska, G. (2009). Reduced level of glutamic acid decarboxylase-67 kDa in the prefrontal cortex in major depression. *International Journal of Neuropsychopharmacology. 13*(4), 411–420.

Karremans, J., Stroebe, W., & Claus, J. (2006). Beyond Vicary's fantasies: The impact of subliminal priming and brand choice. *Journal of Experimental Social Psychology, 42*, 792–798.

Katigbak, M. S., Church, A. T., Guanzon-Lapeña, M. A., Carlota, A. J., & del Pilar, G. H. (2002). Are indigenous personality dimensions culture specific? Philippine inventories and the five-factor model. *Journal of Personality and Social Psychology, 82*(1), 89–101.

Kawano, Y. (2010). Physio-pathological effects of alcohol on the cardiovascular system: Its role in hypertension and cardiovascular disease. *Hypertension Research, 33*, 181–191.

Kazdin, A. E. (2008). Evidence-based treatment and practice: New opportunities to bridge clinical research and practice, enhance the knowledge base, and improve patient care. *American Psychologist, 63*(3), 146–159.

Kazim, S. F., Aly, Z., Bangash, H. K., Harchandani, B. P., Bin Irfan, A., Javed, S. M., ... Moosa Khan, M. (2008). Attitudes toward suicide bombing in Pakistan. *Crisis: Journal of Crisis Intervention and Suicide Prevention, 29*(2), 81–85.

Kegeles, L. S., Abi-Dargham, A., Frankle, W. G., Gil, R., Cooper, T. B., Slifstein, M., ... Laruelle, M. (2010). Increased synaptic dopamine function in associative regions of the striatum in schizophrenia. *Archives of General Psychiatry, 67*(3), 231–239.

Keller, S. S., Roberts, N., & Hopkins, W. (2009). A comparative magnetic resonance imaging study of the anatomy, variability, and asymmetry of Broca's area in the human and chimpanzee brain. *Journal of Neuroscience, 29*(46), 14607–14616.

Kelly, J. F., Stout, R. L., Magill, M., Tonigan, J. S., & Pagano, M. E. (2010). Mechanisms of behavior change in Alcoholics Anonymous: Does AA lead to better alcohol use outcomes by reducing depression symptoms? *Addiction, 105*(4), 626–636.

Kemeny, M. E. (2009). Psychobiological responses to social threat: Evolution of a psychological model in psychoneuroimmunology. *Brain, Behavior, and Immunity, 23*(1), 1–9.

Kendler, K. S., et al. (2000a). Illicit psychoactive substance use, heavy use, abuse, and dependence in a U.S. population-based sample of male twins. *Archives of General Psychiatry, 57*, 261–269.

Kendler, K. S., Myers, J., Prescott, C. A., & Neale, M. C. (2001). The genetic epidemiology of irrational fears and phobias in men. *Archives of General Psychiatry, 58*(3), 257–265.

Kerlin, J. R., Shahin, A. J., & Miller, L. M. (2010). Attentional gain control of ongoing cortical speech representations in a "cocktail party." *Journal of Neuroscience, 30*(2), 620–628.

Kessler, R. C., Berglund, P., Demler, O., Jin, R., Koretz, D., Merikangas, K. R., ... Wang, P. S. (2003). The epidemiology of major depressive disorder: Results from the National Comorbidity Survey Replication (NCS-R). *Journal of the American Medical Association, 289*(23), 3095–3105.

Kessler, R. C., Berglund, P., Demler, O., Jin, R., Merikangas, K. R., & Walters, E. E. (2005a). Lifetime prevalence and age-of-onset distributions of DSM-IV disorders in the National Comorbidity Survey Replication. *Archives of General Psychiatry, 62*(6), 593–602.

Kessler, R. C., Berglund, P., Borges, G., Nock, M., & Wang, P. S. (2005b). Trends in suicide ideation, plans, gestures, and attempts in the United States, 1990–1992 to 2001–2003. *Journal of the American Medical Association, 293*, 2487–2495.

Keyes, C. L. M., & Goodman, S. H. (Eds.). (2006). *Women and depression: A handbook for the social, behavioral, and biomedical sciences.* New York: Cambridge University Press.

Kiecolt-Glaser, J. K., Marucha, P. T., Atkinson, C., & Glaser, R. (2001). Hypnosis as a modulator of cellular immune dysregulation during acute stress. *Journal of Consulting and Clinical Psychology, 69*(4), 674–682.

Kiecolt-Glaser, J. K. et al. (2002a). Psychoneuroimmunology and psychosomatic medicine: Back to the future. *Psychosomatic Medicine, 64*(1),15–28.

Kiecolt-Glaser, J. K., McGuire, L., Robles, T. F., & Glaser, R. (2002b). Emotions, morbidity, and mortality: New perspectives from psychoneuroimmunology. *Annual Review of Psychology, 53*(1), 83–107.

Kihlstrom, J. F. (2002). No need for repression. *Trends in Cognitive Sciences, 6*(12), 502.

Kikuchi, H., Fujii, T., Abe, N., Suzuki, M., Takagi, M., Mugikura, S., ... Mori, E. (2010). Memory repression: Brain mechanisms underlying dissociative amnesia. *Journal of Cognitive Neuroscience, 22*(3), 602–613.

Kilpatrick, D. G., Amstadter, A. B., Resnick, H. S., & Ruggiero, K. J. (2007). Rape-related PTSD: Issues and interventions. *Psychiatric Times, 24*(7). Retrieved from http://www.psychiatrictimes.com/ptsd/content/article/10168/53921?pageNumber=3

Kim, B. S. K., & Omizo, M. M. (2003). Asian cultural values, attitudes toward seeking professional psychological help, and willingness to see a counselor. *Counseling Psychologist, 31*(3), 343–361.

King, B. J. (2008). ME...ME...WASHOE: An appreciation. *Sign Language Studies, 8*(3), 315–323.

King, S. (2005). Virtual reality heals 9/11 wounds. Cited in M. Lake (2005). Retrieved from http://www.cnn.com/2005/TECH/04/29/spark.virtual/index.html

Kingsbury, S.J. (1997). What is solution-focused therapy? *Harvard Mental Health Letter, 13*, 8.

Kinsey, A. C., Pomeroy, W. B., & Martin, C. E. (1948). *Sexual behavior in the human male.* Philadelphia: Saunders.

Kinsey, A. C., Pomeroy, W. B., Martin, C. E., & Gebhard, P. H. (1953). *Sexual behavior in the human female.* Philadelphia: Saunders.

Kirke, D. M. (2009). Gender clustering in friendship networks. *Methodological Innovations Online, 4*, 23–36.

Kiviniemi, M. T., & Rothman, A. J. (2010). Specifying the determinants of people's health beliefs and health behavior. In J. M. Suls, K. W. Davidson, & R. M. Kaplan (Eds.), *Handbook of health psychology and behavioral medicine.* (pp. 64–83). New York: Guilford Press.

Kleinmuntz, B., & Szucko, J. J. (1984). Lie detection in ancient and modern times. *American Psychologist, 39*, 766–776.

Klüver, H., & Bucy, P. C. (1939). Preliminary analysis of functions of the temporal lobe in monkeys. *Archives of Neurology and Psychiatry, 42*, 979–1000.

Knapp, L.G., Kelly-Reid, J. E., & Ginder, S. A. (2011). *Enrollment in Postsecondary Institutions, Fall 2009; Graduation Rates, 2003 & 2006 Cohorts; and Financial Statistics, Fiscal Year 2009* (NCES 2011-230). U.S. Department of Education. Washington, DC: National Center for Education Statistics. Retrieved from http://nces.ed.gov/pubsearch

Knaus, L. K., & Knaus, J. W. (2012). Ethical issues in multiperson therapy. In S. J. Knapp et al. (Eds.). *APA handbook of ethics in psychology, Vol 2: Practice, teaching, and research. APA handbooks in psychology* (pp. 29–43). Washington, DC, US: American Psychological Association.

Knickmeyer, R., Wheelwright, S., Hackett, G., Taylor, K., Raggatt, P., & Baron-Cohen. S. (2005). Gender-typed play and amniotic testosterone. *Developmental Psychology, 41*, 517–528.

Knight, R. G., & Titov, N. (2009). Use of virtual reality tasks to assess prospective memory: Applicability and evidence. *Brain Impairment, 10*(1), 3–13.

Koenig, P., Smith, E. E, Troiani, V., Anderson, C., Moore, P., & Grossman, M. (2008). Medial temporal lobe involvement in an implicit memory task: Evidence of collaborating implicit and explicit memory systems from fMRI and Alzheimer's disease. *Cerebral Cortex, 18*(12), 2831–2843.

Koerber, A., Graumlich, S., Punwani, I. C., Berbaum, M. L., Burns, J. L., Levy, S. R., ... Flay, B. R. (2006). Covariates of tooth-brushing frequency in low-income African Americans from grades 5 to 8. *Pediatric Dentistry, 28*(6), 524–530.

Kohlberg, L. (1969). *Stages in the development of moral thought and action*. New York: Holt, Rinehart and Winston.

Kohlberg, L. (1981). *The philosophy of moral development*. San Francisco: Harper & Row.

Kohn, N., & Smith, S. M. (2009). Partly versus completely out of your mind: Effects of incubation and distraction on resolving fixation. *Journal of Creative Behavior, 43*(2), 102–118.

Kolb, B., Halliwell, C., & Gibb, R. (2009). Factors influencing neocortical development in the normal and injured brain. In M. S. Blumberg, J. H. Freeman, & S. R. Robinson (Eds.), *Oxford Handbook of Developmental Behavioral Neuroscience* (pp. 375–387). New York: Oxford University Press.

Kong, L. L., Allen, J. B., & Glisky, E. L. (2008). Interidentity memory transfer in dissociative identity disorder. *Journal of Abnormal Psychology, 117*(3), 686–692.

Koss, M. P., Figueredo, A. J., & Prince, R. J. (2002). Cognitive mediation of rape's mental, physical and social health impact: Tests of four models in cross-sectional data. *Journal of Consulting and Clinical Psychology, 70*(4), 926–941.

Koster, E. H. W., Fox, E., & MacLeod, C. (2009). Introduction to the special section on cognitive bias modification in emotional disorders. *Journal of Abnormal Psychology, 118*(1), 1–4.

Kotagal, S. (2009). Parasomnias in childhood. *Sleep Medicine Reviews, 13*(2), 157–168.

Kownacki, R. J., & Shadish, W. R. (1999). Does Alcoholics Anonymous work? The results from a meta-analysis of controlled experiments. *Substance Use and Misuse, 34*, 1897–1916.

Krähenbühl, S., Blades, M., & Eiser, C. (2009). The effect of repeated questioning on children's accuracy and consistency in eyewitness testimony. *Legal and Criminological Psychology, 14*(2), 263–278.

Kramer, M. D., Krueger, R. F., & Hicks, B. M. (2008). The role of internalizing and externalizing liability factors in accounting for gender differences in the prevalence of common psychopathological syndromes. *Psychological Medicine, 38*, 51–61.

Kramer, P. D. (2003, June 22). Your Zoloft might prevent a heart attack. *The New York Times,* p. WK3.

Krueger, F., Spampinato, M. V., Pardini, M., Pajevic, S., Wood, J. N., Weiss, G. H., Landgraf, S., & Grafman, J. (2009). Integral calculus problem solving: An fMRI investigation. *Neuroreport, 19*(11), 1095–1099.

Kuczmarski, R. J., Ogden, C. L., Grummer-Strawn, L. M., Flegal, K. M., Guo, S. S., Wei, R., ... Johnson, C. L. (2000, December 4). CDC growth charts: United States. *Advance data from vital and health statistics* (No. 314). Hyattsville, MD: National Center for Health Statistics.

Kumari, V., Das, M., Taylor, P. J., Barkataki, I., Andrew, C., Sumich, A., ... Ffytchef, D. H. (2009). Neural and behavioural responses to threat in men with a history of serious violence and schizophrenia or antisocial personality disorder. *Schizophrenia Research, 110*(1), 47–58.

Kuntzman, G. (2007). Stop "iPod oblivion." Retrieved from http://www.brooklynpaper.com/stories/30/6/30_06ipods.html

Kuo, P.-H., Neale, M. C., Walsh, D., Patterson, D. G., Riley, B., Prescott, C. A., & Kendler, K. S. (2010). Genome-wide linkage scans for major depression in individuals with alcohol dependence. *Journal of Psychiatric Research, 44*(9), 616–619.

Kvavilashvili, L., Mirani, J., Schlagman, S., Foley, K., & Kornbrot, D. E. (2009). Consistency of flashbulb memories of September 11 over long delays: Implications for consolidation and wrong time slice hypotheses. *Journal of Memory and Language, 61*(4), 556–572.

L

Lam, M. P., Nurmi, H., Rouvinen, N., Kiianmaa, K., & Gianoulakis, C. (2009). Effects of acute ethanol on beta-endorphin release in the nucleus accumbens of selectively bred lines of alcohol-preferring AA and alcohol-avoiding ANA rats. *Psychopharmacology, 208*(1), 121–130.

Lan, Y.-J., & Zuo, B. (2009). An introduction to social identity model of deindividuation effects. *Advances in Psychological Science, 17*(2), 467–472.

Lander, K., & Pritchett, J. (2009). When to care: The economic rationale of slavery health care provision. *Social Science History, 33*(2), 155–182.

Lane, R. D., McRae, K., Reiman, E. M., Chen, K., Ahern, G. L., & Thayer, J. F. (2009). Neural correlates of heart rate variability during emotion. *NeuroImage, 44*(1), 213–222.

Laney, C., & Loftus, E. F. (2009). Eyewitness memory. In R. N. Kocsis (Ed.), *Applied criminal psychology: A guide to forensic behavioral sciences* (pp. 121–145). Springfield, IL: Thomas.

Lang, A. R., Goeckner, D. J., Adesso, V. J., & Marlatt, G. A. (1975). Effects of alcohol on aggression in male social drinkers. *Journal of Abnormal Psychology, 84*, 508–518.

Lang, E. V., Benotsch, E. G., Fick, L. J., Lutgendorf, S., Berbaum, M. L., Berbaum, K. S., Logan, H., & Spiegel, D. (2000). Adjunctive non-pharmacological analgesia for invasive medical procedures: A randomised trial. *Lancet, 355*, 1486–1490.

Lange, R. A., & Hillis, L. D. (2010). Sudden death in cocaine abusers. *European Heart Journal, 31*(3), 271–273.

Langer, S. (1997). Break the chain-control stress with optimal nutrition. *Better Nutrition, 59*, 24–28.

Langlois, J. H., Kalakanis, L., Rubenstein, A. J., Larson, A., Hallam, M., & Smoot, M. (2000). Maxims or myths of beauty? A meta-analytic and theoretical review. *Psychological Bulletin, 126*(3), 390–423.

Larsen, J. T., Berntson, G. G., Poehlmann, K. M., Ito, T. A., & Cacioppo, J. T. (2008). The psychophysiology of emotion. In M. Lewis, J. M. Haviland-Jones, & L. F. Barrett (Eds.), *Handbook of emotions* (pp. 180–195). New York: Guilford Press.

Lashley, K. S. (1950). In search of the engram. In *Symposium of the Society for Experimental Biology* (Vol. 4). New York: Cambridge University Press.

Lau, A. S., Litrownik, A. J., Newton, R. R., Black, M. M., & Everson, M. D. (2006). Factors affecting the link between physical discipline and child externalizing problems in Black and White families. *Journal of Community Psychology, 34*(1), 89–103.

Lawless, H. T., & Heymann, H. (2010). Measurement of sensory thresholds. In H. T. Lawless & H. Heymann (Eds.). *Sensory evaluation of food* (2nd ed.) (pp. 125–147). New York: Springer.

Lawson, T.J., & Reardon, M. (1997). A humorous demonstration of in vivo systematic desensitization: The case of eraser phobia. *Teaching of Psychology, 24*, 270–271.

Lazarus, R. S., DeLongis, A., Folkman, S., & Gruen, R. (1985). Stress and adaptational outcomes. *American Psychologist, 40*, 770–779.

Leach, K. P. (2008). Serotonin transporter and depression: From the emotional to the social brain. *Actas Españolas de Psiquiatríia, 36*(Suppl. 1), 21–24.

LeDoux, J. E., & Phelps, E. A. (2008). Emotional networks in the brain. In M. Lewis, J. M. Haviland-Jones, & L. F. Barrett (Eds.), *Handbook of emotions* (pp. 159–179). New York: Guilford Press.

Lee, A., & Hankin, B. L. (2009). Insecure attachment, dysfunctional attitudes, and low self-esteem predicting prospective symptoms of depression and anxiety during adolescence. *Journal of Clinical Child and Adolescent Psychology, 38*(2), 219–231.

Lee, S. A. S., & Davis, B. L. (2010). Segmental distribution patterns of English infant- and adult-directed speech. *Journal of Child Language, 37*, 767–791.

Lee, S. J., Bellamy, J. L., & Guterman, N. B. (2009). Fathers, physical child abuse, and neglect. *Child Maltreatment, 14*(3), 227–231.

Lefcourt, H. M. (1997). Cited in Clay, R. A. (1997). Researchers harness the power of humor. *APA Monitor, 28*(9), 1, 18.

Lengen, C., Regard, M., Joller, H., Landis, T., & Lalive, P. (2008). Anomalous brain dominance and the immune system: Do left-handers have specific immunological patterns? *Brain and Cognition, 69*(1), 188–193.

Leonard, B. E. (2005). Mind over matter: Regulation of peripheral inflammation by the CNS. *Human Psychopharmacology: Clinical & Experimental, 20*(1), 71–72.

Leonard, B. E. (2008). Current antidepressant drugs. *Actas Españolas de Psiquiatriía, 36*(Suppl. 1), 31–34.

Leonardo, E. D., & Hen, R. (2006). Genetics of affective and anxiety disorders. *Annual Review of Psychology, 57,* 117–137.

Leppel, K. (2002). Similarities and differences in the college persistence of men and women. *Review of Higher Education: Journal of the Association for the Study of Higher Education, 25*(4), 433–450.

Leung, P., Curtis, R. L., Jr., & Mapp, S. C. (2010). Incidences of sexual contacts of children: Impacts of family characteristics and family structure from a national sample. *Children and Youth Services Review, 32*(5), 650–656.

Levine, E. S., & Schmelkin, L.-P. (2006). The move to prescribe: Aschange in paradigm? *Professional Psychology: Research and Practice, 37*(2), 205–209.

Levinson, D. J. (1996). *The seasons of a woman's life.* New York: Knopf.

Levinson, D. J., Darrow, C. N., Klein, E. B., Levinson, M. H., & McKee, B. (1978). *The seasons of a man's life.* New York: Knopf.

Levy, R. A., & Ablon, J. S. (Eds.). (2009). *Handbook of evidence-based psychodynamic psychotherapy: Bridging the gap between science and practice.* New York: Humana Press.

Li, M., & Chapman, G. B. (2009). "100% of anything looks good": The appeal of one hundred percent. *Psychonomic Bulletin and Review, 16,* 156–162.

Li, S. X., Wing, Y. K., Lam, S. P., Zhang, J., Yu, M. W. M., Ho, C. K. W., ... Mok, V. (2009). Validation of a new REM sleep behavior disorder questionnaire (RBDQ-HK). *Sleep Medicine, 11*(1), 43–48.

Liebman, B., & Schardt, D. (2002). Tangled memories: Alzheimer's disease: The story so far. *Nutrition Action Healthletter, 29,* 1–8.

Lincoln, T. M., Ziegler, M., Mehl, S., & Rief, W. (2010). The jumping to conclusions bias in delusions: Specificity and changeability. *Journal of Abnormal Psychology, 119*(1), 40–49.

Lindgren, A. P., Mullins, P. M., Neighbors, C., & Blayney, J. A. (2010). Curiosity killed the cocktail? Curiosity, sensation seeking, and alcohol-related problems in college women. *Addictive Behaviors, 35*(5), 513–516.

Lippa, R. A. (2010). Sex differences in personality traits and gender-related occupational preferences across 53 nations: Testing evolutionary and social-environmental theories. *Archives of Sexual Behavior, 39*(3), 619–636.

Liu, A. (2009). Critical race theory, Asian Americans, and higher education: A review of research. *InterActions: UCLA Journal of Education and Information Studies, 5*(2). Retrieved from http://www.escholarship.org/uc/item/98h4n45j

Livesley, W. J., & Jang, K. L. (2008). The behavioral genetics of personality disorder. *Annual Review of Clinical Psychology, 4,* 247–274.

Lochman, J. E., Powell, N. P., Boxmeyer, C. L., & Jiminez-Camargo, L. (2011). Cognitive-behavioral therapy for externalizing disorders in children and adolescents. *Child and Adolescent Psychiatric Clinics of North America, 20*(2), 305–318.

Loftus, E. F., & Davis, D. (2006). Recovered memories. *Annual Review of Clinical Psychology, 2,* 469–498.

Loftus, E. F., & Palmer, J. C. (1974). Reconstruction of automobile destruction. *Journal of Verbal Learning and Verbal Behavior, 13,* 585–589.

Lohman, D. F., & Lakin, J. M. (2009). Consistencies in sex differences on the Cognitive Abilities Test across countries, grades, test forms, and cohorts. *British Journal of Educational Psychology, 79*(2), 389–407.

Loop, M. S., Shows, J. F., Mangel, S. C., & Kuyk, T. K. (2003). Colour thresholds in dichromats and normals. *Vision Research, 43*(9), 983–992.

Lopez, S. R., & Guarnaccia, P. J. J. (2000). Cultural psychopathology: Uncovering the social world of mental illness. *Annual Review of Psychology, 51,* 571–598.

Lorenz, K. Z. (1981). *The foundations of ethology.* New York: Springer-Verlag.

Louie, K., & Wilson, M. A. (2001). Temporally structured replay of awake hippocampal ensemble activity during rapid eye movement sleep. *Neuron, 29*(1), 145–156.

Loving, T. J., & Agnew, C. R. (2001). Socially desirable responding in close relationships: A dual-component approach and measure. *Journal of Social and Personal Relationships, 18*(4), 551–573.

Low, N. C. P., Cui, L., & Merikangas, K. R. (2008). Specificity of familial transmission of anxiety and comorbid disorders. *Journal of Psychiatric Research. 42*(7), 596-604.

Lu, L. (2001). Understanding happiness: A look into the Chinese folk psychology. *Journal of Happiness Studies, 2*(4), 407–432.

Lubinski, D., & Benbow, C. P. (2006). Study of mathematically precocious youth after 35 years: Uncovering antecedents for the development of math-science expertise. *Perspectives on Psychological Science, 1*(4), 316–345.

Luchins, A. S. (1957). Primacy-recency in impression formation. In C. I. Hovland (Ed.), *The order of presentation in persuasion* (pp. 33–61). New Haven, CT: Yale University Press.

Ludescher, B. et al. (2009) Correlation of fat distribution in whole body MRI with generally used anthropometric data. *Investigative Radiology, 44*(11), 712–719.

Ludwick-Rosenthal, R., & Neufeld, R. W. J. (1993). Preparation for undergoing an invasive medical procedure. *Journal of Consulting and Clinical Psychology, 61,* 156–164.

Lukaszewski, A. W., & Roney, J. R. (2009). Estimated hormones predict women's mate preferences for dominant personality traits. *Personality and Individual Differences, 47*(3), 191–196.

Luo, L., & Craik, F. I. M. (2009). Age differences in recollection: Specificity effects at retrieval. *Journal of Memory and Language, 60*(4), 421–436.

Lupien, S. J., McEwen, B. S., Gunnar, M. R., & Heim, C. (2009). Effects of stress throughout the lifespan on the brain, behaviour and cognition. *Nature Reviews Neuroscience, 10,* 434–445.

Lupton, D. (2002). Road rage: Driver's understandings and experiences. *Journal of Sociology, 38,* 275–291.

Luszczynska, A., Benight, C. C., Cieslak, R., Kissinger, P., Reilly, K. H., & Clark, R. A. (2009). Self-efficacy mediates effects of exposure, loss of resources, and life stress on posttraumatic distress among trauma survivors. *Applied Psychology: Health and Well-Being, 1*(1), 73–90.

Lykken, D. T. (2007). A more accurate estimate of heritability. *Twin Research and Human Genetics, 10*(1), 168–173.

Lykken, D. T., & Csikszentmihalyi, M. (2001). Happiness—Stuck with what you've got? *Psychologist, 14*(9), 470–472.

Lynn, B. M., McCord, J. L., & Halliwell, J. R. (2007). Effects of menstrual cycle and sex on progesterone hemodynamics. *American Journal of Physiology: Regulatory, Integrative, and Comparative Physiology, 292,* R1260–R1270.

Lynn, S. J., Kirsch, I., & Hallquist, M. N. (2008a). Social cognitive theories of hypnosis. In M. R. Nash & A. J. Barnier (Eds.), *The Oxford handbook of hypnosis: Theory, research, and practice* (pp. 111–139). New York: Oxford University Press.

Lynn, S. J., Matthews, A., & Barnes, S. (2008b). Hypnosis and memory: From Bernheim to the present. In K. D. Markham, W. M. P. Klein, & J. A. Suhr (Eds.), *Handbook of imagination and mental stimulation* (pp. 103–118). Danvers, MA: CRC Press.

M

MacGeorge, E.L. (2003, February). Gender differences in attributions and emotions in helping contexts. *Sex Roles: A Journal of Research,* 175–182.

Machery, E. (2009). Three fundamental kinds of concept: Prototypes, exemplars, theories. In E. Machery (Ed.), *Doing Without Concepts* (pp. 76–121). Oxford Scholarship Online Monographs.

Machery, O., & Carlyon, R. P. (2010). Temporal pitch percepts elicited by dual-channel stimulation of a cochlear implant. *Journal of the Acoustical Society of America, 127*(1), 339–349.

MacNeill, I. (2003). Stressed: Warning signs that you could be hitting the danger zone. *BC Business, 31,* 60–63.

Maddi, S. R. (2008). The courage and strategies of hardiness as helpful in growing despite major, disruptive stresses. *American Psychologist, 63*(6), 563–564.

Maddi, S. R., Harvey, R. H., Khoshaba, D. M., Fazel, M., & Resurreccion, N. (2009). The personality construct of hardiness, IV. *Journal of Humanistic Psychology, 49*(3), 292–305.

Magno, C. (2010). Looking at Filipino pre-service teachers' values for education through epistemological beliefs about learning and Asian values. *Asia-Pacific Education Researcher, 19*(1), 61–78.

Maiden, B., & Perry, B. (2010). Dealing with free riders in assessed group work: Results from a study at a UK university. *Assessment and Evaluation in Higher Education.* doi:10.1080/02602930903429302

Maier, N. R. F., & Schneirla, T. C. (1935). *Principles of animal psychology.* New York: McGraw-Hill.

Mair, C., Martincova, M., & Shepperd, M. (2009). A literature review of expert problem solving using analogy. *EASE—Evaluation and Assessment in Software Engineering.* Retrieved from http://www.bcs.org/upload/pdf/ewic_ea09_s5paper1.pdf

Malgady, R. G., Rogler, L. H., & Costantino, G. (1990). Hero/heroine modeling for Puerto Rican adolescents. *Journal of Consulting and Clinical Psychology, 58,* 469–474.

Maltby, J., & Day, L. (2001). The relationship between exercise motives and psychological well-being. *The Journal of Psychology, 135,* 651–660.

Mamelak, M. (2009). Narcolepsy and depression and the neurobiology of gammahydroxybutyrate. *Progress in Neurobiology, 89*(2), 193–219.

Maniglio, R. (2009). The impact of child sexual abuse on health: A systematic review of reviews. *Clinical Psychology Review, 29*(7), 647–657.

Manning, R., Levine, M., & Collins, A. (2007). The Kitty Genovese murder and the social psychology of helping: The parable of the 38 witnesses. *American Psychologist, 62*(6), 555–562.

Mantovani, A., & Sica, A. (2010). Macrophages, innate immunity and cancer: Balance, tolerance, and diversity. *Current Opinion in Immunology, 22*(2), 231–237.

Manuck, S. B., Craft, S., & Gold, K. J. (2007). Coronary-prone behavior pattern and cardiovascular response. *Psychophysiology, 15*(5), 403–411.

Marcus, D., Hughes, K., & Arnau, R. (2008). Health anxiety, rumination, and negative affect: A meditational analysis. *Journal of Psychosomatic Research, 64*(5), 495–501.

Marian, V., & Neisser, U. (2000). Language-dependent recall of autobiographical memories. *Journal of Experimental Psychology: General, 129*(3), 361–368.

Markham, B. (2006). Older women and security. In J. Worell & C. D. Goodheart (Eds.), *Handbook of girls' and women's psychological health: Gender and well-being across the lifespan* (pp. 388–396). Oxford series in clinical psychology. New York: Oxford University Press.

Markus, H. & Kitayama, S. (1991). Culture and the self. *Psychological Review, 98*(2), 224–253.

Marlatt, G. A. (2010). Update on harm-reduction policy and intervention research. *Annual Review of Clinical Psychology, 6,* 591–606.

Marsh, R. L., Hicks, J. L., & Cook, G. I. (2005). On the relationship between effort toward an ongoing task and cue detection in event-based prospective memory. *Journal of Experimental Psychology: Learning, Memory, and Cognition, 31*(1):68–75.

Martin, C. L., & Ruble, D. (2004). Children's search for gender cues: Cognitive perspectives on gender development. *Current Directions in Psychological Science, 13*(2), 67–70.

Martin, R. A., & Lefcourt, H. M. (1983). Sense of humor as a moderator of the relation between stressors and moods. *Journal of Personality and Social Psychology, 45,* 1313–1324.

Martin, S. (2002). Easing migraine pain. *Monitor on Psychology, 33*(4), 71.

Martinez, E., Tatum, K. L., Glass, M., Bernath, A., Ferris, D., Reynolds, P., & Schnoll, R. A. (2010). Correlates of smoking cessation self-efficacy in a community sample of smokers. *Addictive Behaviors, 35*(2), 175–178.

Martinez, G., Copen, C. E., & Abma, J. C. (2011). Teenagers in the United States: Sexual activity, contraceptive use, and childbearing, 2006–2010. *National Survey of Family Growth. National Center for Health Statistics. Vital Health Statistics, 23*(31).

Marziali, E., McDonald, L., & Donahue, P. (2008). The role of coping humor in the physical and mental health of older adults. *Aging and Mental Health, 12*(6), 713–718.

Maslow, A. H. (1970). *Motivation and personality* (2nd ed.). New York: Harper & Row.

Mason, V., Andrews, H., & Upton, D. (2010). The psychological impact of exposure to floods. *Psychology, Health and Medicine, 15*(1), 61–73.

Masters, W. H., & Johnson, V. E. (1966). *Human sexual response.* Boston: Little, Brown.

Mathews, J. R., & Barch, D. M. (2010). Emotion responsivity, social cognition, and functional outcome in schizophrenia. *Journal of Abnormal Psychology, 119*(1), 50–59.

Matsuda, Y.-T., Ueno, K., Waggoner, R. A., Erickson, D., Shimura, Y., Tanaka, K., … Mazuka, R. (2011). Processing of infant-directed speech by adults. *NeuroImage, 54*(1), 611–621.

Matsumoto, D., Keltner, D., Shiota, M. N., O'Sullivan, M., & Frank, M. (2008). Facial expressions of emotion. In M. Lewis, J. M. Haviland-Jones, & L. F. Barrett (Eds.), *Handbook of emotions* (pp. 211–234). New York: Guilford Press.

Maxwell, J. P., Visek, A. J., & Moores, E. (2009). Anger and perceived legitimacy of aggression in male Hong Kong Chinese athletes: Effects of type of sport and level of competition. *Psychology of Sport and Exercise, 10*(2), 289–296.

May, D. E., & Kratochvil, C. J. (2010). Attention-deficit hyperactivity disorder: Recent advances in paediatric pharmacotherapy. *Drugs, 70*(1), 15–40.

May, R. (2005). How do we know what works? *Journal of College Student Psychotherapy, 19*(3), 69–73.

Mayer, J. D., Salovey, P., & Caruso, D. R. (2008). Emotional intelligence: New ability or eclectic traits? *American Psychologist, 63*(6), 503–517.

Mayers, A. G., Grabau, E. A. S., Campbell, C., & Baldwin, D. S. (2009). Subjective sleep, depression, and anxiety. *Human Psychopharmacology, 24*(6), 495–501.

Mazure, C. M., Bruce, M. L., Maciejewski, P. K., & Jacobs, S. C. (2000). Adverse life events and cognitive personality characteristics in the prediction of major depression and antidepressant response. *American Journal of Psychiatry, 157,* 896–903.

Mbwana, J., Berl, M. M., Ritz, E. K., Rosenberger, L., Mayo, J., Weinstein, S., … Gaillard, W. D. (2008). Limitations to plasticity of language network reorganization in localization-related epilepsy. *Brain, 132*(2), 347–356.

McCardle, P., Colombo, J., & Freud, L. (2009). Measuring language in infancy. In J. Colombo, P. McCardle, & L. Freud (Eds.), *Infant pathways to language: Methods, models, and research disorders* (pp. 1–12). New York: Psychology Press.

McCartney, K., Owen, M. T., Booth, C. L., Clarke-Stewart, K. A., & Vandell, D. L. (2004). Testing a maternal attachment model of behavior problems in early childhood. *Journal of Child Psychology and Psychiatry, 45*(4), 765–778.

McCauley, J. L., Ruggiero, K. L., Resnick, H. S., & Kilpatrick, D. G. (2010). Incapacitated, forcible, and drug/alcohol-facilitated rape in relation to binge drinking, marijuana use, and illicit drug use: A national survey. *Journal of Traumatic Stress, 23*(1), 132–140.

McClelland, D. C. (1958). Methods of measuring human motivation. In J. W. Atkinson (Ed.), *Motives in fantasy, action, and society.* Princeton, NJ: Van Nostrand.

McClelland, D. C. (1965). Achievement and entrepreneurship. *Journal of Personality and Social Psychology, 1,* 389–392.

McCormick, B., Blum, N., Hansel, R., Franklin, J. A., St. John, D., Pfohl, B., … Black, D. W. (2007). Relationship of sex to symptom severity, psychiatric comorbidity, and health care utilization in 163 subjects with borderline personality disorder. *Comprehensive Psychiatry, 48*(5), 406–412.

McCormick, M.J. (2001). Self-efficacy and leadership effectiveness: Applying social cognitive theory to leadership. *Journal of Leadership Studies, 8*, 22–33.

McCrae, R. R., & Costa, P. T., Jr. (1997). Personality trait structure as a human universal. *American Psychologist, 52*(5), 509–516.

McCrae, R. R., Costa, P. T., Ostendorf, F., Angleitner, A., Hrebíčková, M., Avia, M. D., … Smith, P. B. (2000). Nature over nurture: Temperament, personality, and life span development. *Journal of Personality and Social Psychology, 78*(1), 173–186.

McDevitt-Murphy, M. E., Williams, J. L., Bracken, K. L., Fields, J. A., Monahan, C. J., & Murphy, J. G. (2010). PTSD symptoms, hazardous drinking, and health functioning among U.S. OEF and OIF veterans presenting to primary care. *Journal of Traumatic Stress, 23*(1), 108–111.

McDonald, M. G. (2008). The nature of epiphanic experience. *Journal of Humanistic Psychology, 48*(1), 89–115.

McDougall, W. (1904). The sensations excited by a single momentary stimulation of the eye. *British Journal of Psychology, 1*, 78–113.

McDougall, W. (1908). *An introduction to social psychology.* London: Methuen.

McGovern, C.M. (1993). Asylum: The complex and controversial story of mental institutions in the U.S.A. *Journal of Social History, 26*, 668–669.

McGue, M., Bouchard, T. J., Jr., Iacono, W. G., & Lykken, D. T. (1993). Behavioral genetics of cognitive ability: A life-span perspective. In R. Plomin & G. E. McClearn (Eds.), *Nature, nurture & psychology* (pp. 59–76). Washington, DC: American Psychological Association.

McKenzie, C. R. M., Lee, S. M., & Chen, K. K. (2002). When negative evidence increases confidence: Changes in belief after hearing two sides of a dispute. *Journal of Behavioral Decision Making, 15*(1), 1–18.

McLachlan, N., & Wilson, S. (2010). The central role of recognition in auditory perception: A neurobiological model. *Psychological Review, 117*(1), 175–196.

McLaughlin, K. A., Conron, K. J., Koenen, K. C., & Gilman, S. E. (2010). Childhood adversity, adult stressful life events, and risk of past-year psychiatric disorder: A test of the stress sensitization hypothesis in a population-based sample of adults. *Psychological Medicine, 40,* 1647–1658.

McMurran, M., Blair, M., & Egan, V. (2002). An investigation of the correlations between aggression, impulsiveness, social problem-solving, and alcohol use. *Aggressive Behavior, 28,* 439–445.

Mechner, F. (2009). Analyzing variable behavioural contingencies. *Behavioural Processes, 81*(2), 316–321.

Medland, S. E., Duffy, D. L., Wright, M. J., Geffen, G. M., Hay, D. A., Levy, F., …

Boomsma, D. I. (2008). Genetic influences on handedness: Data from 25,732 Australian and Dutch twin families. *Neuropsychologia, 47*(2), 330–337.

Mehta, P. H., & Gosling, S. D. (2008). Bridging human and animal research: A comparative approach to studies of personality and health. *Brain, Behavior, and Immunity, 22*(5), 651–661.

Meijer, J., & Elshout, J. J. (2001). The predictive and discriminant validity of the zone of proximal development. *British Journal of Educational Psychology, 71*(1), 93–113.

Meijer, W. M., Faber, A., van den Ban, E., & Tobi, H. (2009). Current issues around the pharmacotherapy of ADHD in children and adults. *Pharmacy World and Science, 31*(5), 509–516.

Meltzoff, A. N., & Brooks, R. (2009). Social cognition and language: The role of gaze following in early word learning. In J. Colombo, P. McCardle, & L. Freund (Eds.), *Infant pathways to language: Methods, models, and research disorders.* (pp. 169–194). New York: Psychology Press.

Meltzoff, A. N., & Gopnik, A. (1997). *Words, thoughts, and theories.* Cambridge, MA: MIT Press.

Meltzoff, A. N., & Prinz, W. (2002). *The imitative mind: Development, evolution, and brain bases.* Cambridge, England: Cambridge University Press.

Melzack, R., & Katz, J. (2006). Pain in the 21st century: The neuromatrix and beyond. In G. Young, A. W. Kane, & K, Nicholson (Eds.), *Psychological knowledge in court* (pp. 129–148). New York: Springer.

Mendelsohn, F., & Warren, M. (2010). Anorexia, bulimia, and the female athlete triad: Evaluation and management. *Endocrinology and Metabolism Clinics of North America, 39*(1), 155–167.

Merari, A., Diamant, I., Bibi, A., Broshi, Y., & Zakin, G. (2010). Personality characteristics of "self martyrs"/"suicide bombers" and organizers of suicide attacks. *Terrorism and Political Violence, 22*(1), 87–101.

Mercado, E. (2008). Neural and cognitive plasticity: From maps to minds. *Psychological Bulletin, 134*(1), 109–137.

Mesoudi, A. (2009). How cultural evolutionary theory can inform social psychology and vice versa. *Psychological Review, 116*(4), 929–952.

Metcalfe, J. (1986). Premonitions of insight predict impending error. *Journal of Experimental Psychology: Learning, Memory, and Cognition, 12,* 623–634.

Metz, R. (2005, March 10). Think of a number… Come on, think! *The New York Times online.*

Metzger, K. L., et al. (2007). Effects of nicotine vary across two auditory evoked potentials in the mouse. *Biological Psychiatry, 61*(1), 23–30.

Meyer-Lindenberg, A., Poline, J.-B., Kohn, P. D., Holt, J. L., Egan, M. F., Weinberger, D. R., & Berman, K. F. (2001). Evidence for abnormal cortical functional connectivity during working memory in

schizophrenia. *American Journal of Psychiatry, 158,* 1809–1817.

Meyersburg, C. A., Bogdan, R., Gallo, D. A., & McNally, R. J. (2009). False memory propensity in people reporting recovered memories of past lives. *Journal of Abnormal Psychology, 118*(2), 399–404.

Milgram, S. (1963). Behavioral study of obedience. *Journal of Abnormal and Social Psychology, 67,* 371–378.

Milgram, S. (1974). *Obedience to authority.* New York: Harper & Row.

Miller, A. L., Rathus, J. H., DuBose, A. P., Dexter-Mazza, E. T., & Goldklang, A. R. (2007). Dialectical behavior therapy for adolescents. In L. A. Dimeff & K. Koerner (Eds.), *Dialectical behavior therapy in clinical practice* (pp. 245–297). New York: Guilford Press.

Miller, G. A. (1956). The magical number seven, plus or minus two: Some limits on our capacity for processing information. *Psychological Review, 63,* 81–97.

Miller, M. A., Weafer, J., & Fillmore, M. T. (2009). Gender differences in alcohol impairment of simulated driving performance and driving-related skills. *Alcohol and Alcoholism, 44*(6), 586–593.

Miller, N. E. (1944). Experimental studies of conflict. In J. McVicker Hunt (Ed.), *Personality and the behavior disorders* (Vol. 1, pp. 431–465). Oxford, England: Ronald Press.

Miller, N. E. (1969). Learning of visceral and glandular responses. *Science, 163,* 434–445.

Miller, N. E. (1995). Clinical-experimental interactions in the development of neuroscience. *American Psychologist, 50,* 901–911.

Milne, R. D., Syngeniotis, A., Jackson, G., & Corballis, M. C. (2002). Mixed lateralization of phonological assembly in developmental dyslexia. *Neurocase, 8*(3), 205–209.

Milner, B. R. (1966). Amnesia following operation on temporal lobes. In C. W. M. Whitty & O. L. Zangwill. London: Butterworths, pp. 109–133.

Milstead, M., Lapsley, D., & Hale, C. (1993, March). *A new look at imaginary audience and personal fable.* Paper presented at the meeting of the Society for Research in Child Development, New Orleans, LA.

The mind and the immune system-part I. (2002). *Harvard Mental Health Letter, 18,* NA.

Mineka, S., & Oehlberg, K. (2008). The relevance of recent developments in classical conditioning to understanding the etiology and maintenance of anxiety disorders. *Acta Psychologica, 127*(3), 567–580.

Miniño A. M. (2010). *Mortality among teenagers aged 12–19 years: United States, 1999–2006* (NCHS Data Brief No. 37). Hyattsville, MD: National Center for Health Statistics.

MIT researchers ID gene involved in memory retrieval. (2002, June 21). *Genomics & Genetics Weekly,* p. 4.

Miyake, Y., Okamoto, Y., Onoda, K., Shirao, N., Okamoto, Y., Otagaki, Y., & Yamawaki, S. (2010). Neural processing of negative word stimuli concerning body image in patients with eating disorders: An fMRI study. *NeuroImage, 50*(3), 1333–1339.

Mohr, D. C., Ho, J., Duffecy, J., Baron, K. G., Lehman, K. A., Jin, L., & and Reifler, D. (2010). Perceived barriers to psychological treatments and their relationship to depression. *Journal of Clinical Psychology, 66*(4), 394–409.

Molfese, V. J., DiLalla, L. F., & Bunce, D. (1997). Prediction of the intelligence test scores of 3- to 8-year-old children by home environment, socioeconomic status, and biomedical risks. *Merrill-Palmer Quarterly, 43*(2), 219–234.

Montero, I., & De Dios, M. J. (2006). Vygotsky was right. An experimental approach to the relationship between private speech and task performance. *Estudios de Psicología, 27*(2), 175–189.

Montoya, R. M., Horton, R. S., & Kirchner, J. (2008). Is actual similarity necessary for attraction? A meta-analysis of actual and perceived similarity. *Journal of Social and Personal Relationships, 25*(6), 889–922.

Moore, C. C., Romney, A. K., & Hsia, T. (2002). Cultural, gender, and individual differences in perceptual and semantic structures of basic colors in Chinese and English. *Journal of Cognition and Culture, 2*(1), 1–28.

Moos, R. H., & Moos, B. S. (2006). Participation in treatment and Alcoholics Anonymous: A 16-year follow-up of initially untreated individuals. *Journal of Clinical Psychology, 62*(6), 735–750.

Morewedge, C. K., & Norton, M. I. (2009). When dreaming is believing: The (motivated) interpretation of dreams. *Journal of Personality and Social Psychology, 96*(2), 249–264.

Moruzzi, G., & Magoun, H. W. (1949). Brain stem reticular formation and activation of the EEG. *Electroencephalography and Clinical Neurophysiology, 1*, 455–473.

Most, S. B., Sorber, A. V., & Cunningham, J. G. (2007). Auditory Stroop reveals implicit gender association in adults and children. *Journal of Experimental Social Psychology, 43*(2), 287–294.

Moyà-Solà, S., Köhler, M., Alba, D. M., Casanovas-Vilar, I., & Galindo, J. (2004). Pierolapithecus catalaunicus, a new middle Miocene great ape from Spain. *Science, 19*, 1339–1344.

Muraleedharan, K., & Jones, T. H. (2010). Testosterone replacement may be beneficial in hypogonadal men with cardiovascular disease. *Endocrine Abstracts, 21*, 176.

Murata, A., & Fuson, K. (2006). Teaching as assisting individual constructive paths within an interdependent class learning zone: Japanese first graders learning to add using 10. *Journal for Research in Mathematics Education, 37*(5), 421–456.

Murray, L., Creswell, C., & Cooper, P. J. (2009). The development of anxiety disorders in childhood: An integrative review. *Psychological Medicine, 39*, 1413–1423.

Myers, L. B., & Brewin, C. R. (1994). Recall of early experience and the repressive coping style. *Journal of Abnormal Psychology, 103*, 288–292.

Mystkowski, J. L., & Mineka, S. (2007). Behavior therapy for specific fears and phobias: Context specificity of fear extinction. In T. A. Treat, R. R. Bootzin, & T. B. Baker (Eds.), *Psychological clinical science: Papers in honor of Richard M. McFall* (pp. 197–222). London: Routledge.

N

Nader, K., Schafe, G. E., & Le Doux, J. E. (2000). Fear memories require protein synthesis in the amygdala for reconsolidation after retrieval. *Nature, 406*, 722–726.

Nampiaparampil, D. E. (2008). Prevalence of chronic pain after traumatic brain injury: A systematic review. *Journal of the American Medical Association, 300*(6), 711–719.

Naragon-Gainey, K. (2010). Meta-analysis of the relations of anxiety sensitivity to the depressive and anxiety disorders. *Psychological Bulletin, 136*(1), 128–150.

Narayan, V. M., Narr, K. L., Kumari, V., Woods, R. P., Thompson, P. M., Toga, A. W., & Sharma, T. (2007). Regional cortical thinning in subjects with violent antisocial personality disorder or schizophrenia. *American Journal of Psychiatry, 164*, 1418–1427.

National Center for Health Statistics. (2010). *Health, United States, 2009: With special feature on medical technology.* Hyattsville, MD: Author. Retrieved from http://www.cdc.gov/nchs/data/hus/hus09.pdf#032

National Center for Injury Prevention and Control. (2005, June 19). Suicide: Fact sheet. Retrieved from http://www.cdc.gov/ncipc /factsheets /suifacts .htm

National Eating Disorders Association. (2010). Retrieved from http://www.nationaleatingdisorders.org/information-resources/general-information.php

National Institute on Alcohol Abuse and Alcoholism (NIAAA). (2005). Cage questionnaire. Retrieved from http://pubs.niaaa .nih.gov/publications/inscage.htm

National Sleep Foundation. (2001, November 19). Events of 9-11 took their toll on Americans' sleep, particularly for women, according to new National Sleep Foundation poll. Retrieved from http://www.sleepfoundation.org/whatsnew/crisis_poll.html

National Sleep Foundation. (2009). Sleep apnea and sleep. Retrieved from http://www.sleepfoundation.org/article/sleep-related-problems/obstructive-sleep-apnea-and-sleep

Neisser, U. (1997). Cited in Sleek, S. (1997). Can "emotional intelligence" be taught in today's schools? *APA Monitor, 28*(6), 25.

Neisser, U., Boodoo, G., Bouchard, Jr., T. J., Boykin, A. W., Brody, N., Ceci, S. J., ... Urbina, S. (1996). Intelligence: Knowns and unknowns. *American Psychologist, 51*, 77–101.

Nestoriuc, Y., Rief, W., & Martin, A. (2008). Meta-analysis of biofeedback for tension-type headache: Efficacy, specificity, and treatment moderators. *Journal of Consulting and Clinical Psychology, 76*(3), 379–396.

Neve, K. A. (2009). *The dopamine receptors* (2nd ed.). New York: Springer.

Newman, S. D., Greco, J. A., & Lee, D. (2009). An fMRI study of the Tower of London: A look at problem structure differences. *Brain Research, 1286*, 123–132.

Nicholson, A. (2008). Socio-economic status over the life-course and depressive symptoms in men and women in Eastern Europe. *Journal of Affective Disorders, 105*(1-3), 125–136.

Nickell, J. (2001). Exorcism! Driving out the nonsense. *Skeptical Inquirer, 25*, 20.

Nilsson, H., Juslin, P., & Olsson, H. (2008). Exemplars in the mist: The cognitive substrate of the representativeness heuristic. *Scandinavian Journal of Psychology, 49*(3), 201–212.

Nir, Y., & Tononi, G. (2010). Dreaming and the brain: From phenomenology to neurophysiology. *Trends in Cognitive Sciences, 14*(2), 88–100.

Nisbett, R. E. (2009). *Intelligence and how to get it: Why schools and cultures count.* New York: Norton.

Nock, M. K., & Kazdin, A. E. (2002). Examination of affective, cognitive, and behavioral factors and suicide-related outcomes in children and young adolescents. *Journal of Community Psychology, 31*(1), 48–58.

Nokes, T. J., & VanLehn, K. (2008). Bridging principles and examples through analogy and explanation. In *Proceedings of the eighth International Conference for the Learning Sciences* (Vol. 3, pp. 100–102). Utrecht, Netherlands: International Conference on Learning Sciences.

Nolan, J. M., Schultz, P. W., Cialdini, R. B., Goldstein, N. J., & Griskevicius, V. (2008). Normative social influence is underdetected. *Personality and Social Psychology Bulletin, 34*(7), 913–923.

Nolen-Hoeksema, S., Wisco, B. E., & Lyubomirsky, S. (2008). Rethinking rumination. *Perspectives on Psychological Science, 3*(5), 400–424.

Nonaka, A. M. (2004). The forgotten endangered languages: Lessons on the importance of remembering from Thailand's Ban Khor Sign Language. *Language in Society. 33*(5), 737–767.

Norton, A., & D'Ambrosio, B. S. (2008). ZPC and ZPD: Zones of teaching and learning. *Journal for Research in Mathematics Education, 39*(3), 220–246.

Novick, L. R., & Coté, N. (1992). The nature of expertise in anagram solution. In *Proceedings of the 14th annual conference of the Cognitive Science Society*. Hillsdale, NJ: Erlbaum.

Nyberg, L., et al. (2000). Large scale neurocognitive networks underlying episodic memory. *Journal of Cognitive Neuroscience, 12*(1), 163–173.

O

O'Driscoll, M. P., & Brough, P. (2010). Work organization and health. In S. Leka & J. Houdmont (Eds.), *Occupational health psychology* (pp. 57–87). Hoboken, NJ: Wiley.

Oertelt-Prigione, S., & Regitz-Zagrosek, V. (2009). Gender aspects in cardiovascular pharmacology. *Journal of Cardiovascular Translational Research, 2*(3), 258–266.

Ohayon, M., & Schatzberg, A. (2010). Social phobia and depression: Prevalence and comorbidity. *Journal of Psychosomatic Research, 68*(3), 235–243.

Ohayon, M. M., Guilleminault, C., & Priest, R. G. (1999). Night terrors, sleepwalking, and confusional arousals in the general population: Their frequency and relationship to other sleep and mental disorders. *Journal of Clinical Psychiatry, 60*(4), 268–276.

Öhman, A., & Mineka, S. (2001). Fears, phobias, and preparedness: Toward an evolved module of fear and fear learning. *Psychological Review, 108*(3), 483–522.

Öhman, A., & Mineka, S. (2003). The malicious serpent: Snakes as a prototypical stimulus for an evolved module of fear. *Current Directions in Psychological Science, 12*(1), 5–9.

Olatunji, B. O., & Wolitzky-Taylor, K. B. (2009). Anxiety sensitivity and the anxiety disorders: A meta-analytic review and synthesis. *Psychological Bulletin, 135*(6), 974–999.

Old, S. R., & Naveh-Benjamin, M. (2008). Memory for people and their actions: Further evidence for an age-related associative deficit. *Psychology and Aging, 23*(2), 467–472.

Olds, J. (1969). The central nervous system and the reinforcement of behavior. *American Psychologist, 24*, 114–132.

Olds, J., & Milner, P. (1954). Positive reinforcement produced by electrical stimulation of the septal area and other regions of the rat brain. *Journal of Comparative and Physiological Psychology, 47*, 419–427.

Oliver, B. R., & Plomin, R. (2007). Twins' Early Development Study (TEDS): A multivariate, longitudinal genetic investigation of language, cognition and behavior problems from childhood through adolescence. *Twin Research and Human Genetics, 10*(1), 96–105.

Olson, M. J. (2003). Counselor understanding of Native American spiritual loss. *Counseling and Values, 47*(2), 109–117.

Orsi, J. M., Margellos-Anast, H., & Whitman, S. (2010). Black–White health disparities in the United States and Chicago: A 15-year progress analysis. *American Journal of Public Health, 100*(2), 349–356.

Osborn, K. A., Irwin, B. C., Skogsberg, N. J., & Feitz, D. L. (2012). The Kohler Effect: Motivation gains and losses in real sports groups. *Sport, Exercise, and Performance Psychology*. doi: 10.1037/a0026887

P

Packard, M. G. (2009). Exhumed from thought: Basal ganglia and response learning in the plus-maze. *Behavioural Brain Research, 199*(1), 24–31.

Packer, D. J. (2009). Avoiding groupthink. *Psychological Science, 20*(5), 546–548.

Pang, J.-J., Gao, F., Lem, J., Bramblett, D. E., Paul, D. L., & Wu, S. M. (2010). Direct rod input to cone BCs and direct cone input to rod BCs challenge the traditional view of mammalian BC circuitry. *Proceedings of the National Academy of Sciences, 107*(1), 395–400.

Pani, P. P., Maremmanib, I., Trogua, E., Gessae, G. L., Ruizf, P., & Akiskalg, H. S. (2010). Delineating the psychic structure of substance abuse and addictions: Should anxiety, mood and impulse-control dysregulation be included? *Journal of Affective Disorders, 122*(3), 185–197.

Papadopoulos, F. C., Ekbom, A., Brandt, L., & Ekselius, L. (2009). Excess mortality, causes of death and prognostic factors in anorexia nervosa. *British Journal of Psychiatry, 194*, 10–17.

Park, B., & Judd, C. M. (2005). Rethinking the link between categorization and prejudice within the social cognition perspective. *Personality and Social Psychology Review, 9*(2), 108–130.

Parr, L. A., Winslow, J. T., Hopkins, W. D., & de Waal, F. B. M. (2000). Recognizing facial cues: Individual discrimination by chimpanzees (*Pan troglodytes*) and rhesus monkeys (*Macaca mulatta*). *Journal of Comparative Psychology, 114*(1), 47–60.

Patterson, G. R., Dishion, T. J., & Yoerger, K. (2000). Adolescent growth in new forms of problem behavior: Macro- and micro-peer dynamics. *Prev Sci, 1*(1), 3–13.

Paulussen-Hoogeboom, M. C., Stams, G. J. J. M., Hermanns, J. M. A., & Peetsma, T. T. D. (2007). Child negative emotionality and parenting from infancy to preschool: A meta-analytic review. *Developmental Psychology, 43*(2), 438–453.

Pavlov, I. (1927). *Conditioned reflexes*. London: Oxford University Press.

Penfield, W. (1969). Consciousness, memory, and man's conditioned reflexes. In K. H. Pribram (Ed.), *On the biology of learning*. New York: Harcourt Brace Jovanovich.

Perna, F. M., Antoni, M. H., Baum, A., Gordon, P., & Schneiderman, N. (2003). Cognitive behavioral stress management effects on injury and illness among competitive athletes: A randomized clinical trial. *Annals of Behavioral Medicine, 25*(1), 66–73.

Perrett, D. I., May, K. A., & Yoshikawa, S. (1994). Facial shape and judgments of female attractiveness, *Nature, 368*, 239–242.

Peterson, C., & Seligman, M. E. P. (2004). *Character strengths and virtues: A handbook and classification*. Washington, DC: American Psychological Association.

Peterson, D. (2006). *Jane Goodall: The woman who redefined man*. Boston: Houghton Mifflin.

Peterson, L. R., & Peterson, M. J. (1959). Short-term retention of individual verbal items. *Journal of Experimental Psychology, 58*, 193–198.

Petrill, S. A., Hart, S. A., Harlaar, N., Logan, J., Justice, L. M., Schatschneider, C., ... Cutting, L. (2010). Genetic and environmental influences on the growth of early reading skills. *Journal of Child Psychology and Psychiatry, 51*(6), 660–667.

Petry, N. M., Martin, B., Cooney, J. L., & Kranzler, H. R. (2000). Give them prizes and they will come: Contingency management for treatment of alcohol dependence. *Journal of Consulting and Clinical Psychology, 68*, 250–257.

Petty, R. E., Briñol, P., & Priester, J. R. (2009a). Mass media attitude change: Implications of the elaboration likelihood model of persuasion. In J. Bryant & M. B. Oliver (Eds.), *Media effects: Advances in theory and research* (pp. 125–164). Oxford, England: Taylor & Francis.

Petty, R. E., Fazio, R. H., & Briñol, P. (Eds.). (2009b). *Attitudes: Insights from the new implicit measures*. New York: Psychology Press.

Phalet, K., & Schoenpflug, U. (2001). Intergenerational transmission of collectivism and achievement values in two acculturation contexts: The case of Turkish families in Germany and Turkish and Moroccan families in the Netherlands. *Journal of Cross-Cultural Psychology, 32*(2), 186–201.

Phinney, J. S. (2006). Acculturation is not an independent variable: Approaches to studying acculturation as a complex process. In M. H. Bornstein & L. R. Cote (Eds.), *Acculturation and parent–child relationships: Measurement and development* (pp. 79–96). London: Routledge.

Phinney, J. S., & Baledelomar, O. A. (2011). Identity development in multiple cultural contexts. In L. A. Jensen (Ed.), *Bridging cultural and developmental approaches to psychology* (pp. 161–187). New York: Oxford University Press.

Phinney, J. S., & Ong, A. D. (2007). Ethnic identity in immigrant families. In J. E. Lansford, K. Deater-Deckard, & M. H. Bornstein (Eds.), *Immigrant families in* contemporary society. *Duke series in child development and public policy* (pp. 51–68). New York: Guilford Press.

Phoenix, C. H. (2009). Organizing action of prenatally administered testosterone propionate on the tissues mediating mating behavior in the female guinea pig. *Hormones and Behavior, 55*(5), 566.

Piaget, J. (1963). *The origins of intelligence in children.* New York: Norton.

Piaget, J., & Smith, L. (Trans.). (2000). Commentary on Vygotsky's criticisms of language and thought of the child and judgment and reasoning in the child. *New Ideas in Psychology, 18* (2–3), 241–259.

Piccinni, A., Del Debbioa, A., Meddaa, P., Bianchia, C., Roncagliaa, I., Veltria, A., ... Dell'Osso, L. (2009). Plasma brain-derived neurotrophic factor in treatment-resistant depressed patients receiving electroconvulsive therapy. *European Neuropsychopharmacology, 19*(5), 349–355.

Pickens, C. L., & Holland, P. C. (2004). Conditioning and cognition. *Neuroscience & Biobehavioral Reviews, 28*(7), 651–661.

Pietrzak, R. H., Johnson, D. C., Goldstein, M. B., Malley, J. C., Rivers, A. J., Morgan, C, A., & Southwick, S. M. (2010). Psychosocial buffers of traumatic stress, depressive symptoms, and psychosocial difficulties in veterans of Operations Enduring Freedom and Iraqi Freedom: The role of resilience, unit support, and postdeployment social support. *Journal of Affective Disorders, 120*(1), 188–192.

Piffer, R. C., Garcia, P. C., & Pereira, O. C. M. (2009). Adult partner preference and sexual behavior of male rats exposed prenatally to betamethasone. *Physiology and Behavior, 98*(1–2), 163–167.

Pihl, R. O., Peterson, J. B., & Finn, P. (1990). Inherited predisposition to alcoholism. *Journal of Abnormal Psychology, 99*, 291–301.

Piliavin, J. A. (2009). Altruism and helping: The evolution of a field. *Social Psychology Quarterly, 72*(3), 209–225.

Pinker, S. (1994a, June 19). Building a better brain. *The New York Times Book Review,* pp. 13–14.

Pinker, S. (2007). *The stuff of thought: Language as a window into human nature.* New York: Penguin Books.

Pinker, S. (2011). *Words and rules.* New York: HarperCollins Publishers.

Piolino, P., Desgranges, B., & Eustache, F. (2009). Episodic autobiographical memories over the course of time: Cognitive, neuropsychological and neuroimaging findings. *Neuropsychologia, 47*(11), 2314–2329.

Plaisier, I., et al. (2008). Work and family roles and the association with depressive and anxiety disorders: Differences between men and women. *Journal of Affective Disorders, 105*(1-3), 63–72.

Plomin, R. (2000). Behavioural genetics in the 21st century. *International Journal of Behavioral Development, 24*(1), 30–34.

Plomin, R., & Asbury, K. (2005). Nature and nurture: Genetic and environmental influences on behavior. *The Annals of the American Academy of Political and Social Science, 600*(1), 86–98.

Plomin, R., DeFries, J. C., McClearn, G. E., & McGuffin, P. (2008). *Behavioral genetics.* New York: Worth Publishers.

Plomin, R., & Haworth, C. M. A. (2009). Genetics of high cognitive abilities. *Behavior Genetics, 39*(4), 347–349.

Plomin, R., & Schalkwyk, L. C. (2007). Microarrays. *Developmental Science, 10*(1), 19–23.

Plomin, R., & Spinath, F. M. (2004). Intelligence: Genetics, genes, and genomics. *Journal of Personality and Social Psychology, 86*(1), 112–129.

Pluess, M., Conrad, A., & Wilhelm, F. H. (2009). Muscle tension in generalized anxiety disorder: A critical review of the literature. *Journal of Anxiety Disorders, 23*(1), 1–11.

Polanczyk, G., Moffitt, T. E., Arseneault, L., Cannon, M., Ambler, A., Keefe, R. S. E., ... Caspi, A. (2010). Etiological and clinical features of childhood psychotic symptoms. *Archives of General Psychiatry, 67*(4), 328–338.

Polina, E. R., Contini, V., Hutz, M. H., & Bau, C. H. D. (2009). Thesserotonin 2A receptor gene in alcohol dependence and tobacco smoking. *Drug and Alcohol Dependence, 101*(1–2), 128–131.

Pollatos, O., Schandry, R., Auer, D. P., & Kaufmann, C. (2007). Brain structures mediating cardiovascular arousal and interoceptive awareness. *Brain Research, 1141*, 178–187.

Popma, A., Vermeiren, R., Geluk, C. A. M. L., Rinne, T., van den Brink, W., Knol, D. L., ... Doreleijers, T. A. H. (2007). Cortisol moderates the relationship between testosterone and aggression in delinquent male adolescents. *Biological Psychiatry, 61*(3), 405–411.

Porsolt, R. D., Moser, P. C., & Castagne, V. (2010). Behavioral indices in antipsychotic drug discovery. *Journal of Pharmacology and Experimental Therapeutics, 333*(3), 632–638.

Porter, R. (1997). Bethlem/Bedlam: Methods of madness? *History Today, 47*, 41–46.

Porter, S., & ten Brinke, L. (2008). Reading between the lies: Identifying concealed and falsified emotions in universal facial expressions. *Psychological Science, 19*(5), 508–514.

Posada, G., Jacobs, A., Richmond, M. K., Carbonell, O. A., Alzate, G., Bustamante, M. R., & Quiceno, J. (2002). Maternal caregiving and infant security in two cultures. *Developmental Psychology, 38*(1), 67–78.

Postmes, T., & Spears, R. (1998). Deindividuation and antinormative behavior: A meta-analysis. *Psychological Bulletin, 123*(3), 238–259.

Potter, W. J. (2008). Adolescents and television violence. In P. E. Jamieson &

D. Romer (Eds.), *The changing portrayal of adolescents in the media since 1950* (pp. 221–249). New York: Oxford University Press.

Power, T. G., Stewart, C. D., Hughes, S. O., & Arbona, C. (2005). Predicting patterns of adolescent alcohol use: A longitudinal study. *Journal of Studies on Alcohol, 66*(1), 74–81.

Pradhan, D. S., Newman, A., Wacker, D. W., Wingfield, J. C., Schlinger, B. A., & Soma, K. K. (2010). Aggressive interactions rapidly increase androgen synthesis in the brain during the non-breeding season. *Hormones and Behavior, 57*(4-5), 381–389.

Prato-Previde, E., Fallani, G., & Valsecchi, P. (2006). Gender differences in owners interacting with pet dogs: An observational study. *Ethology, 112*(1), 64–73.

Pressman, S. D., & Cohen, S. (2005). Does positive affect influence health? *Psychological Bulletin, 131*(6), 925–971.

Preti, A., & Vellante, M. (2007). Creativity and psychopathology: Higher rates of psychosis proneness and nonright-handedness among creative artists compared to same age and gender peers. *Journal of Nervous and Mental Disease, 195*(10), 837–845.

Principe, C. P., & Langlois, J. H. (2011). Faces differing in attractiveness elicit corresponding affective responses. *Cognition & Emotion, 25*(1), 140–148.

Prochaska, J. O., & Norcross, J. C. (2010). *Systems of psychotherapy* (7th ed.). Belmont, CA: Wadsworth.

Proverbio, A. M., Riva, F., & Zani, A. (2010). When neurons do not mirror the agent's intentions: Sex differences in neural coding of goal-directed actions. *Neuropsychologia, 48*(5), 1454–1463.

Psychodynamic perspective. (1999). *Psychology Review, 6*, 32.

Pulley, B. (1998, June 16). Those seductive snake eyes: Tales of growing up gambling. *The New York Times,* pp. A1, A28.

Pusey, A., Murray, C., Wallauer, W., Wilson, M., Wroblewski, E., & Goodall, J. (2008). Severe aggression among female *Pan troglodytes schweinfurthii* at Gombe National Park, Tanzania. *International Journal of Primatology, 29*(4), 949–973.

Q

Qi, Z., & Gold, P. E. (2009). Intrahippocampal infusions of anisomycin produce amnesia: Contribution of increased release of norepinephrine, dopamine, and acetylcholine. *Learning and Memory, 16*, 308–314.

R

Rachman, S. (2000). Joseph Wolpe (1915–1997): Obituary. *American Psychologist, 55*(4), 431–432.

Radcliffe, R. A., Erwin, V. G., Bludeau, P., Deng, X.-S., Fay, T., Floyd, K. L., &

Deitrich, R. A. (2009). A major QTL for acute alcohol sensitivity in the alcohol tolerant and non-tolerant rat lines. *Genes, Brain, and Behavior, 8*(6), 611–625.

Raine, A. (2008). From genes to brain to antisocial behavior. *Current Directions in Psychological Science, 17*(5), 323–328.

Rainville, P., et al. (2002). Hypnosis modulates activity in brain structures involved in the regulation of consciousness. *Journal of Cognitive Neuroscience, 14*(6), 887–901.

Ramagopalan, S. V., Dyment, D. A., Handunnetthi, L., Rice, G. P., & Ebers, G. C. (2010). A genome-wide scan of male sexual orientation. *Journal of Human Genetics, 55,* 131–132.

Ramel, W., Goldin, P. R., Carmona, P. E., & McQuaid, J. R. (2004). The effects of mindfulness meditation on cognitive processes and affect in patients with past depression. *Cognitive Therapy & Research, 28*(4), 433–455.

Randolph, M. E., Torres, H., Gore-Felton, C., Lloyd, B., & McGarvey, E. L. (2009). Alcohol use and sexual risk behavior among college students. *American Journal of Drug and Alcohol Abuse, 35*(2), 80–84.

Rathus, J. H., & Sanderson, W. C. (1999). *Marital distress: Cognitive behavioral interventions for couples.* Northvale, NJ: Jason Aronson.

Rathus, S.A. (2009-2010). *HDEV.* Mason, OH: 4LTR Press/Cengage Learning.

Rathus, S. A., Nevid, J. S., & Fichner-Rathus, L. (2011). *Human sexuality in a world of diversity* (8th ed.). Boston: Allyn & Bacon.

Rawley, J. B., & Constantinidis, C. (2008). Neural correlates of learning and working memory in the primary posterior parietal cortex. *Neurobiology of Learning and Memory, 91*(2), 129–138.

Rayner, L., Kershaw, K., Hanna, D., & Chaplin, R. (2009). The patient perspective of the consent process and side effects of electroconvulsive therapy. *Journal of Mental Health, 18*(5), 379–388.

Redrobe, J. P., & Bourin, M. (2009). The effect of lithium administration in animal models of depression. *Fundamental and Clinical Pharmacology, 13*(3), 293–299.

Reece, M., Herbenick, D., Schick, V., Sanders, S. A., Dodge, B., & Fortenberry, J. D. (2010). Sexual behaviors, relationships, and perceived health among adult men in the United States: Results from a national probability sample. *Journal of Sexual Medicine, 7*(Suppl. 5), 291–304.

Reeder, G. D. (2001). On perceiving multiple causes and inferring multiple internal attributes. *Psychological Inquiry, 12*(1), 34–36.

Reeder, G. D. (2009). Mindreading: Judgments about intentionality and motives in dispositional inference. *Psychological Inquiry, 20*(1), 1–18.

Rees, T., Ingledew, D. K., & Hardy, L. (2005). Attribution in sports psychology: Seeking congruence between theory, research and practice. *Psychology of Sport and Exercise, 6*(2), 189–204.

Reeve, C.L. (2002). Race and intelligence: Separating science from myth. (Book Review). *Personnel Psychology, 55,* 778–781.

Reeve, J. (2002). Discussing prejudice with your child. *The Brown University Child and Adolescent Behavior Letter, 18,* S1.

Regier, T. (2005). The emergence of words: Attentional learning in form and meaning. *Cognitive Science: A Multidisciplinary Journal, 29*(6), 819–865.

Reid, L. W. (2008). Disaggregating the effects of racial and economic equality on early twentieth-century execution rates. *Sociological Spectrum, 28*(2), 160–174.

Reinecke, M. A., DuBois, D. L., & Schultz, T. M. (2001). Social problem solving, mood, and suicidality among inpatient adolescents. *Cognitive Therapy and Research, 25*(6), 743–756.

Reis, H. T., Maniaci, M. R., Caprariello, P. A., Eastwick, P. W., Finkel, E. J. (2011). Familiarity does indeed promote attraction in live interaction. *Journal of Personality and Social Psychology, 101*(3), 557–570.

Reis, O., & Youniss, J. (2004). Patterns in identity change and development in relationships with mothers and friends. *Journal of Adolescent Research, 19*(1), 31–44.

The relation of child care to cognitive and language development. (2000). *Child Development, 71,* 960.

Rescorla, R. A. (1967). Inhibition of delay in Pavlovian fear conditioning. *Journal of Comparative and Physiological Psychology, 64*(1), 114–120.

Rescorla, R. A. (1988). Pavlovian conditioning: It's not what you think it is. *American Psychologist, 43,* 151–160.

Rescorla, R. A. (1999). Partial reinforcement reduces the associative change produced by nonreinforcement. *Journal of Experimental Psychology: Animal Behavior Processes, 25*(4), 403–414.

Rhee, S. H., & Waldman, I. D. (2002). Genetic and environmental influences on antisocial behavior: A meta-analysis of twin and adoption studies. *Psychological Bulletin, 128*(3), 490–529.

Ricca, V., Castellini, G., Sauro, C. L., Ravaldi, C., Lapi, F., Mannucci, E., ... Faravelli, C. (2009). Correlations between binge eating and emotional eating in a sample of overweight subjects. *Appetite, 53*(3), 418–421.

Ricciardelli, L.A., & McCabe, M.P. (2001, February). Self-esteem and negative affect as moderators of sociocultural influences on body dissatisfaction, strategies to decrease weight, and strategies to increase muscles among adolescent boys and girls. *Sex Roles: A Journal of Research, 189.*

Ringach, D. L., & Jentsch, J. D. (2009). We must face the threats. *Journal of Neuroscience, 29*(37), 11417–11418.

Riniolo, T.C., Koledin, M., Drakulic, G.M., & Payne, R.A. (2003). An archival study of eyewitness memory of the Titanic's final plunge. *The Journal of General Psychology, 130,* 89–95.

Risch, N., Herrell, R., Lehner, T., Liang, K.-Y., Eaves, L., Hoh, J., ... Merikangas, J. R. (2009). Interaction between the serotonin transporter gene (*5-HTTLPR*), stressful life events, and risk of depression. *Journal of the American Medical Association, 301*(23), 2462–2471.

Robbins, J. (2000, July 4). Virtual reality finds a real place as a medical aid. *The New York Times online.*

Roberson, D., Davidoff, J., & Shapiro, L. (2002). Squaring the circle: The cultural relativity of good shape. *Journal of Cognition and Culture, 2*(1), 29–51.

Roberts, J., Lennings, C. J., & Heard, R. (2009). Nightmares, life stress, and anxiety. *Dreaming, 19*(1), 17–29.

Robins, R. W., Gosling, S. D., & Craik, K. H. (1999). An empirical analysis of trends in psychology. *American Psychologist, 54*(2), 117–128.

Robinson, E. (2011). *Disintegration: The splintering of black America.* New York: Simon & Schuster.

Rodin, G., Lo, C., Mikulincer, M., Donner, A., Gagliese, L., & Zimmermann, C. (2009). Pathways to distress: The multiple determinants of depression, hopelessness, and the desire for hastened death in metastatic cancer patients. *Social Science and Medicine, 68*(3), 562–569.

Rodriguez, C. J., Burg, M. M., Meng, J., Pickering, T. G., Jin, Z., Sacco, R. L.,... Di Tullio, M. R. (2008). Effect of social support on nocturnal blood pressure dipping. *Psychosomatic Medicine, 70,* 7–12.

Roediger, H. L., & McCabe, D. P. (2007). Evaluating experimental research. In R. J. Sternberg, H. L. Roediger, & D. F. Halpern (Eds.), *Critical thinking in psychology* (pp. 15–36). New York: Cambridge University Press.

Roelofs, K., Hoogduin K. A., Keijsers G. P., Näring G. W., Moene F. C., Sandijck P. (2002). Hypnotic susceptibility in patients with conversion disorder. *Journal of Abnormal Psychology, 111*(2), 390–395.

Roepke, S., Schröder-Abé, M., Schütz, A., Jacob, G., Dams, A., Vater, A., ... Lammers, C.-H. (2011). Dialectic behavioural therapy has an impact on self-concept clarity and facets of self-esteem in women with borderline personality disorder. *Clinical Psychology and Psychotherapy, 18*(2), 148–158.

Rogers, C. R. (1951). *Client-centered therapy.* Boston: Houghton Mifflin.

Rogers, D. (2009). The other philosophy club: America's first academic women philosophers. *Hypatia, 24*(2), 164–185.

Roid, G. H., & Tippin, S. M. (2009). Assessment of intellectual strengths and weaknesses with the Stanford–Binet Intelligence Scales—5th edition. In J. A. Naglieri & S. Goldstein (Eds.), *Practitioner's guide to assessing intelligence* and achievement (pp. 127–152). Hoboken, NJ: Wiley.

Rolls, E. T. (2009). Functional neuroimaging of *umami* taste: What makes *umami* pleasant? *American Journal of Clinical Nutrition, 90*(3), 804S–813S.

Romero, E., Luengo, M. A., & Sobral, J. (2001). Personality and antisocial behaviour: Study of temperamental dimensions. *Personality and Individual Differences, 31*(3), 329–348.

Rosekind, M. R., Gregory, K. B., Mallis, M. M., Brandt, S. L., Seal, B., & Lerner, D. (2010). The cost of poor sleep: Workplace productivity loss and associated costs. *Journal of Occupational and Environmental Medicine, 52*(1), 91–98.

Rosenberg, M. J. (2009). The conditions and consequences of evaluation apprehension. In R. Rosenthal & R. L. Rosnow (Eds.), *Artifacts in behavioral research* (pp. 211–263). New York: Oxford University Press.

Ross, C. A. (2006). Dissociative identity disorder. *Current Psychosis and Therapeutics Reports, 4*(3), 112–116.

Ross, S.E., Niebling, B.C., & Heckert, T.M. (1999). Sources of stress among college students. *College Student Journal, 33,* 312.

Roth, G. (2000). The evolution and ontogeny of consciousness. *Neural correlates of consciousness: Empirical and conceptual questions.* Cambridge, MA: MIT Press.

Roth, T. L., Lubin, F. D., Sodhi, M., & Kleinman, J. E. (2009). Epigenetic mechanisms in schizophrenia. *Biochimica et Biophysica Acta, 1790*(9), 869–877.

Rothbaum, F., Rosen, K., Ujiie, T., & Uchida, N. (2002). Family systems theory, attachment theory, and culture. *Family Process, 41,* 328–350.

Rotter, J. B. (1990). Internal versus external control of reinforcement. *American Psychologist, 45,* 489–493.

Rouder, J. N., & Morey, R. D. (2009). The nature of psychological thresholds. *Psychological Review, 116*(3), 655–660.

Rubia, K. (2009). The neurobiology of meditation and its clinical effectiveness in psychiatric disorders. *Biological Psychology, 82*(1), 1–11.

Rude, S. S., Hertel, P. T., Jarrold, W., Covich, J., & Hedlund, S. (1999). Depression-related impairments in prospective memory. *Cognition & Emotion, 13*(3), 267–276.

Rudy, D., & Grusec, J. E. (2006). Authoritarian parenting in individualist and collectivist groups: Associations with maternal emotion and cognition and children's self-esteem. *Journal of Family Psychology, 20*(1), 68–78.

Ruiter, R. A. C., Abraham, C., & Kok, G. (2001). Scary warnings and rational precautions: A review of the psychology of fear appeals. *Psychology and Health, 16*(6), 613–630.

Rushton, J. P., Skuy, M., & Fridjhon, P. (2003). Performance on Raven's Advanced Progressive Matrices by African, East Indian, and White engineering students in South Africa. *Intelligence, 31*(2), 123–137.

S

Safford, S., Alloy, L., Abramson, L., & Crossfield, A. (2007). Negative cognitive style as a predictor of negative life events in depression-prone individuals: A test of the stress-generation hypothesis. *Journal of Affective Disorders, 99*(1), 147–154.

Saffran, J. R. (2009). Acquiring grammatical patterns: Constraints on learning. In J. Colombo, P. McCardle, & L. Freud (Eds.), *Infant pathways to language: Methods, models, and research disorders* (pp. 31–47). New York: Psychology Press.

Salmon, P., et al. (2004). Mindfulness meditation in clinical practice. *Cognitive & Behavioral Practice, 11*(4), 434–446.

Salovey, P., Detweiler-Bedell, B. T., Detweiler-Bedell, J. B., & Mayer, J. D. (2008). Emotional intelligence. In M. Lewis, A. M. Haviland-Jones, & L. F. Barrett (Eds.), *Handbook of emotions* (3rd ed.) (pp. 533–545). New York: Guilford Press.

Salovey, P., Rothman, A. J., Detweiler, J. B., & Steward, W. T. (2000). Emotional states and physical health. *American Psychologist, 55,* 110–121.

Salthouse, T. A. (2001). Structural models of the relations between age and measures of cognitive functioning. *Intelligence, 29*(2), 93–115.

Sanchez, D. T., Shih, M., & Garcia, J. A. (2009). Juggling multiple racial identities: Malleable racial identification and psychological well-being. *Cultural Diversity and Ethnic Minority Psychology, 15*(3), 243–254.

Sanders, G. S. (1984). Effects of context cues on eyewitness identification responses. *Journal of Applied Social Psychology, 14,* 386–397.

Sanna, L. J., & Meier, S. (2000). Looking for clouds in a silver lining: Self-esteem, mental simulations, and temporal confidence changes. *Journal of Research in Personality, 34*(2), 236–251.

Santarius, T., Shipley, J., Brewer, D., Stratton, M. R., & Cooper, C. S. (2010). Epigenetics and genetics: A census of amplified and overexpressed human cancer genes. *Nature Reviews Cancer, 10*(1), 59–64.

Sarbin, T. R., & Coe, W. C. (1972). *Hypnosis.* New York: Holt, Rinehart and Winston.

Sava, S., & Yurgelun-Todd, D. A. (2008). Functional magnetic resonance in psychiatry. *Topics in Magnetic Resonance Imaging, 19*(2), 71–79.

Savin-Williams, R. C., & Cohen, K. M. (2007). Development of same-sex attracted youth. In I. H. Meyer & M. E. Northridge (Eds.), *The health of sexual minorities: Public health perspectives on lesbian, gay, bisexual, and transgender populations* (pp. 27–47). New York: Springer Science + Business Media.

Sawa, A., & Snyder, S. H. (2002). Schizophrenia: Diverse approaches to a complex disease. *Science,* pp. 692–695.

Sayette, M. A., Reichle, E. D., & Schooler, J. W. (2009). Lost in the sauce: The effects of alcohol on mind wandering? *Psychological Science, 20*(6), 747–752.

Scarr, S., & Weinberg, R. A. (1983). The Minnesota adoption studies: Genetic differences and malleability. *Child Development, 54,* 260–267.

Schacter, D. L. (1992). Understanding implicit memory: A cognitive neuroscience approach. *American Psychologist, 47*(4), 559–569.

Schacter, D. L., Cooper, L. A., & Treadwell, J. (1993). Preserved priming of novel objects across size transformation in amnesic patients. *Psychological Science, 4*(5), 331–335.

Schacter, D. L., Gallo, D. A., & Kensinger, E. A. (2007). The cognitive neuroscience of implicit and false memories: Perspectives on processing specificity. In H. L. Roediger & J. S. Nairne (Eds.), *The foundations of remembering: Essays in honor of Henry L. Roediger III* (pp. 355–379). New York: Psychology Press.

Schachter, S., & Singer, J. E. (1962). Cognitive, social, and physiological determinants of emotional state. *Psychological Review, 69,* 379–399.

Schmidt, N. B., Keough, M. E., Mitchell, M. A., Reynolds, E. K., MacPherson, L., Zvolensky, M. J., & Lejuez, C. W. (2010). Anxiety sensitivity: Prospective prediction of anxiety among early adolescents. *Journal of Anxiety Disorders, 24*(5), 503–508.

Schmitt, D. P. (2003). Universal sex differences in the desire for sexual variety: Tests from 52 nations, 6 continents, and 13 islands. *Journal of Personality and Social Psychology, 85*(1), 85–104.

Schmitt, D. P. (2008). An evolutionary perspective on mate choice and relationship initiation. In S. Sprecher, A. Wenzel, & J. H. Harvey (Eds.), *Handbook of relationship initiation* (pp. 55–74). New York: CRC Press.

Schmitt, D. P., Jonason, P. K., Byerley, G. J., Flores, S. D., Illbeck, B. E., O'Leary, K. N., & Qudrat, A. (2012). A reexamination of sex differences in sexuality: New studies reveal old truths. *Current Directions in Psychological Science, 21*(2), 135–139.

Schnall, S., Roper, J., & Fessler, D. M. T. (2010). Elevation leads to altruistic behavior. *Psychological Science, 21*(3), 315–320.

Schneider-Garces, N. J., Gordon, B. A., Brumback-Peltz, C. R., Shin, E., Lee, Y., Sutton, B. P., ... Fabiani, M. (2010). Span, CRUNCH, and beyond: Working memory capacity and the aging brain. *Journal of Cognitive Neuroscience, 22*(4), 655–669.

Schneiderman, N., Ironson, G., & Siegel, S. D. (2005). Stress and health: Psychological, behavioral, and biological determinants. *Annual Review of Clinical Psychology, 1*(1), 607–628.

Schubert, S., & Lee, C. W. (2009). Adult PTSD and its treatment with EMDR: A review of controversies, evidence, and theoretical knowledge. *Journal of EMDR Practice and Research, 3*(3), 117–132.

Schulte, M. T., Ramo, D., & Brown, S. A. (2009). Gender differences in factors influencing alcohol use and drinking progression among adolescents. *Clinical Psychology Review, 29*(6), 535–547.

Schwartz, B. L. (2008). Working memory load differentially affects tip-of-the-tongue states and feeling-of-knowing judgments. *Memory and Cognition, 36*(1), 9–19.

Schwartz, N. (2007) Evaluating surveys and questionnaires. In R. J. Sternberg, H. L. Roediger, & D. F. Halpern (Eds.), *Critical thinking in psychology* (pp. 54–74). New York: Cambridge University Press.

Schwartz, R. M., & Gottman, J. M. (1976). Toward a task analysis of assertive behavior. *Journal of Consulting and Clinical Psychology, 44*, 910–920.

Schwartz, S. J., Unger, J. B., Zamboanga, B. L., & Szapocznik, J. (2010). Rethinking the concept of acculturation: Implications for theory and research. *American Psychologist, 65*(4), 237–251.

Scott, J. (1994, May 9). Multiple personality cases perplex legal system. *The New York Times*, pp. A1, B10, B11.

Sebe, N., Lew, M. S., Sun Y., Cohen, I., Gevers, T., & Huang, T. S. (2007). Authentic facial expression analysis. *Image and Vision Computing, 25*(12), 1856–1863.

Second thoughts. (1989). *The Economist, 313*, 69.

Segerdahl, P., Fields, W., & Savage-Rumbaugh, S. (2006). *Kanzi's primal language: The cultural initiation of primates into language.* New York: Palgrave Macmillan.

Sekizuka, H., Kida, K., Akashi, Y. J., Yoneyama, K., Osada, N., Omiya, K., & Miyake, F. (2010). Relationship between sleep apnea syndrome and sleep blood pressure in patients without hypertension. *Journal of Cardiology, 55*(1), 92–98.

Seligman, M. (1975). *Helplessness: On depression, development, and death.* New York: Freeman.

Seligman, M. E. P. (1996, August). *Predicting and preventing depression.* Master lecture presented at the meeting of the American Psychological Association, Toronto, Canada.

Selye, H. (1976). *The stress of life* (Rev. ed.). New York: McGraw-Hill.

Shah, C., Trivedi, R. S., Diwan, J., Dixit, R., & Anand, A. K. (2009). Common stressors and coping with stress by medical students. *Journal of Clinical and Diagnostic Research, 3,* 1621–1626.

Shapiro, F. (1989). Efficacy of the eye movement desensitization procedure in the treatment of traumatic memories. *Journal of Traumatic Stress, 2,* 199–223.

Shedler, J. (2010). The efficacy of psychodynamic psychotherapy. *American Psychologist, 65*(2), 98–109.

Sheeber, L. B., Davis, B., Leve, C., Hops, H., & Tildesley, E. (2007). Adolescents' relationships with their mothers and fathers: Associations with depressive disorder and subdiagnostic symptomatology. *Journal of Abnormal Psychology, 116*(1), 144–154.

Sheldon, K. M. (2009). Providing the scientific backbone for positive psychology: A multi-level conception of human thriving. *Psychological Topics, 18*(2), 267–284.

Sherman, D. K., Bunyan, D. P., Creswell, J. D., & Jaremka, L. M. (2009). Psychological vulnerability and stress: The effects of self-affirmation on sympathetic nervous system responses to naturalistic stressors. *Health Psychology, 28*(5), 554–562.

Sherrington, J. M., Hawton, K. E., Fagg, J., Andrews, B., & Smith, D. (2001). Outcome of women admitted to hospital for depressive illness: Factors in the prognosis of severe depression. *Psychological Medicine, 31*(1), 115–125.

Sherwood, C. C., Rilling, J. K., Holloway, R. L., & Hof, P. R. (2008). Evolution of the brain: In humans—Specializations in a comparative perspective. In M. D. Binder, N. Hirokawa, U. Windhorst, & M. C. Hirsch (Eds.), *Encyclopedia of neuroscience* (pp. 1–5). New York: Springer-Verlag.

Shi, W., & Jia, F.-X. (2011). A review on the psychology of suicide terrorism. *Advances in Psychological Science.* Retrieved from http://en.cnki.com.cn/Article_en/CJFDTOTAL-XLXD201109017.htm

Shirayamaa, Y., Obatab, T., Matsuzawaa, D., Nonakab, H., Kanazawab, Y., Yoshitomeb, E., … Iyo, M. (2010). Specific metabolites in the medial prefrontal cortex are associated with the neurocognitive deficits in schizophrenia: A preliminary study. *NeuroImage, 49*(3), 2783–2790.

Shneidman, E. S. (2001). *Comprehending suicide.* Washington, DC: American Psychological Association.

Short, S. J., Lubach, G. R., Karasin, A. I., Olsen, C. W., Styner, M., Knickmeyer, R. C., … Coe, C. L. (2010). Maternal influenza infection during pregnancy impacts postnatal brain development in the rhesus monkey. *Biological Psychiatry, 67*(10), 965–973.

Shrager, Y., Kirwan, C., & Squire, L. R. (2008). Activity in both hippocampus and perirhinal cortex predicts the memory strength of subsequently remembered information. *Neuron, 59*(4), 547–553.

Shreeve, J. (1995). What happened to Phineas? *Discover, 16,* 78–79.

Shuper, P. A., Neuman, M., Kanteres, F., Baliunas, D., Joharchi, N., & Rehm, J. (2010). Causal considerations on alcohol and HIV/AIDS—A systematic review. *Alcohol and Alcoholism, 45*(2), 159–166.

Shyrack, J., Steger, M. F., Krueger, R. F., & Kallie, C. S. (2010). The structure of virtue: An empirical investigation of the dimensionality of the virtues in action inventory of strengths. *Personality and Individual Differences, 48*(6), 714–719.

Siegel, J. M. (2009). Sleep viewed as a state of adaptive inactivity. *Nature Reviews Neuroscience, 10,* 747–753.

Siesta time; Power napping. (2002, June 1). *The Economist.*

Sileo, C. C. (1993). Multiple personalities: The experts are split. *Insight on the News, 43,* 18–22.

Silver, E. (1994). Cited in DeAngelis, T. (1994). Experts see little impact from insanity plea ruling. *APA Monitor, 25*(6), 28.

Silver, S. M., Rogers, S., Knipe, J, & Colelli, G. (2005). EMDR therapy following the 9/11 terrorist attacks: A community-based intervention project in New York City. *International Journal of Stress Management, 12*(1), 29–42.

Simeon, D., Knutelska, M., Yehuda, R., Putnam, F., Schmeidler, J., & Smith, L. M. (2007). Hypothalamic-pituitary-adrenal axis function in dissociative disorders, post-traumatic stress disorder, and healthy volunteers. *Biological Psychiatry, 61*(8), 966–973.

Simon, T. R., Ikeda, R. M., Smith, E. P., Reese, L. E., Rabiner, D. L., Miller, S., … Allison, K. W. (2009). The ecological effects of universal and selective violence prevention programs for middle school students: A randomized trial. *Journal of Consulting and Clinical Psychology, 77*(3), 526–542.

Simons, A. D., Gordon, J. S., Monroe, S. M., & Thase, M. E. (1995). Toward an integration of psychologic, social, and biologic factors in depression. *Journal of Consulting and Clinical Psychology, 63,* 369–377.

Simonton, D. K. (2009). *Genius 101.* New York: Springer.

Singareddy, R. K., & Balon, R. (2002). Sleep in posttraumatic stress disorder. *Annals of Clinical Psychiatry, 14*(3), 183–190.

Singh, D., & Singh, D. (2011). Shape and significance of feminine beauty: An evolutionary perspective. *Sex Roles, 64*(9–10), 723–731.

Singh, L., Nestor, S., Parikh, C., & Yull, A. (2009). Influences of infant-directed speech on early word recognition. *Infancy, 14*(6), 654–666.

Sio, U. N., & Ormerod, T. C. (2009). Does incubation enhance problem solving? *Psychological Bulletin, 135*(1), 94–120.

Sixsmith, R., & Furnham, A. (2010). A content analysis of British food advertisements aimed at children and adults. *Health Promotion International, 25*(1), 24–32.

Skinner, B. F. (1938). *The behavior of organisms: An experimental analysis.* New York: Appleton.

Skinner, B. F. (1948). *Walden Two.* New York: Macmillan.

Sleep and dreams. (2002). *Science Weekly, 19,* 1–12.

Slobin, D. I. (1983). *Crosslinguistic evidence for basic child grammar.* Paper presented at the biennial meeting of the Society for Research in Child Development, Detroit, MI.

Sloman, S. A., Harrison, M. C., & Malt, B. C. (2002). Recent exposure affects artifact naming. *Memory and Cognition, 30*(5), 687–695.

Small, E., Shah, H. P., Davenport, J. J., Geier, J. E., Yavarovich, K. R., Yamada, H., ... Bruijnzeel, A. W. (2010). Tobacco smoke exposure induces nicotine dependence in rats. *Psychopharmacology, 208*(1), 143–158.

Smetana, J. G., Daddis, C., & Chuang, S. S. (2003). "Clean your room!" A longitudinal investigation of adolescent–parent conflict and conflict resolution in middle-class African American families. *Journal of Adolescent Research, 18*(6), 631–650.

Smetana, J. G., Campione-Barr, N., & Metzger, A. (2006). Adolescent development in interpersonal and societal contexts. *Annual Review of Psychology, 57,* 255–284.

Smillie, L. D., Cooper, A. J., Proitsi, P., Powell, J. F., Pickering, A. D. (2009). Variation in DRD2 dopamine gene predicts extraverted personality. *Neuroscience Letters, 468*(3), 234–237.

Smith, J. F. (2001). Biological evidence for evolution. *Journal of the Idaho Academy of Science, 37,* 102–104.

Smith, K. L. (2009). Humor. In M. Snyder & R. Lindquist (Eds.), *Complementary and alternative therapies in nursing* (pp. 107–122). New York: Springer.

Smith, M. L., & Glass, G. V. (1977). Meta-analysis of psychotherapy outcome studies. *American Psychologist, 32,* 752–760.

Smith, N. A., & Trainor, L. J. (2008). Infant-directed speech is modulated by infant feedback. *Infancy, 13*(4), 410–420.

Smith, R. A., & Weber, A. L. (2005). Applying social psychology in everyday life. In F. W. Schneider, et al. (Eds.), *Applied social psychology: Understanding and addressing social and practical problems* (pp. 75–99). Thousand Oaks, CA: Sage Publications.

Snijders, T. A. B., Steglich, C. E. G., & Schweinberger, M. (2007). Modeling the coevolution of networks and behavior. In K. van Montfort, J. Oud, & A. Satorra (Eds.), *Longitudinal models in the behavioral and related sciences* (pp. 41–71). London: Routledge.

Snyder, C. R., Lopez, S. J., & Pedrotti, J. T. (2010). *Positive psychology* (2nd ed.). Newbury Park, CA: Sage Publications.

Snyder, D. J., & Bartoshuk, L. M. (2009). Epidemiological studies of taste function: Discussion and perspectives. *Annals of the New York Academy of Sciences, 1170,* 574–580.

Solomon, R. C. (2008). The philosophy of emotions. In M. Lewis, J. M. Haviland-Jones, & L. F. Barrett (Eds.), *Handbook of emotions* (pp. 3–16). New York: Guilford Press.

Sorensen, S. B., & Rutter, C. M. (1991). Transgenerational patterns of suicide attempt. *Journal of Consulting and Clinical Psychology, 59,* 861–866.

Souren, N. Y., Paulussen, A. D. C., Loos, R. J. F., Gielen, M., Beunen, G., Fagard, R., ... Zeegers, M. P. (2007). Anthropometry, carbohydrate and lipid metabolism in the East Flanders Prospective Twin Survey: Heritabilities. *Diabetologia, 50*(10), 2107–2116.

Soussignan, R. (2002). Duchenne smile, emotional experience, and autonomic reactivity: A test of the facial feedback hypotheses. *Emotion, 2*(1), 52–74.

Spelts, K., & Gaynor, J. (2010). Pain management strategies. In S. Bryant (Ed.), *Anesthesia for veterinary technicians* (pp. 345–356). Hoboken, NJ: Wiley.

Spencer, M. D., Moorhead, T. W. J., Gibson, R. J., McIntosh, A. M., Sussmann, J. E. D., Owens, D. G. C., ... Johnstone, E. C. (2008). Low birthweight and preterm birth in young people with special educational needs: A magnetic resonance imaging analysis. *BMC Medicine, 6*(1). doi:10.1186/1741-7015-6-1

Spencer, M. S., Chen, J., Gee, G. C., Fabian, C. G., & Takeuchi, D. T. (2010). Discrimination and mental health–related service use in a national study of Asian Americans. *American Journal of Public Health, 100*(12), 2410–2417.

Spencer, T. J., Montaldi, D., Gong, Q.-Y., Roberts, N., & Mayes, A. R. (2009). Object priming and recognition memory: Dissociable effects in left frontal cortex at encoding. *Neuropsychologia, 47*(13), 2942–2947.

Sperling, G. (1960). The information available in brief visual presentations. *Psychological Monographs, 74,* 1–29.

Spinhoven, P., Elzinga, B. M., Hovens, J., Roelofs, K., Zitman, F. G., van Oppen, P., & Penninx, B. (2010). The specificity of childhood adversities and negative life events across the life span to anxiety and depressive disorders. *Journal of Affective Disorders, 126*(1), 103–112.

Spittle, A. J., Boyd, R. N., Inder, T. E., & Doyle, L. W. (2009). Predicting motor development in very preterm infants at 12 months' corrected age. *Pediatrics, 123*(2), 512–517.

Sporer, S. L., & Goodman-Delahunty, J. (2009). Disparities in sentencing decisions. In M. E. Oswald, S. Bieneck, & J. Hupfeld-Heinemann (Eds.), *Social psychology of punishment of crime* (pp. 379–401). Hoboken, NJ: Wiley.

Sprecher, S., & Felmlee, D. (2008). Insider perspectives on attraction. In S. Sprecher, A. Wenzel, & J. H. Harvey (Eds.),

Handbook of relationship initiation (pp. 297–314). New York: CRC Press.

Sprecher, S., Sullivan, Q., & Hatfield, E. (1994). Mate selection preferences. *Journal of Personality and Social Psychology, 66*(6), 1074–1080.

Sprecher, S., Wenzel, A., & Harvey, J. H. (Eds.). (2008). *Handbook of relationship initiation.* New York: CRC Press.

Squire, L. R. (2004). Memory systems of the brain: A brief history and current perspective. *Neurobiology of Learning and Memory, 82*(3), 171–177.

Squire, L. R. (2009). The legacy of patient H. M. for neuroscience. *Neuron, 61*(1), 6.

Squire, L. R., & Kandel, E. R. (2008). *Memory: From mind to molecules.* Greenwood Village, CO: Roberts.

Sroufe, L. A. (1998). Cited in S. Blakeslee (1998, August 4), Re-evaluating significance of baby's bond with mother, *New York Times,* pp. F1, F2.

Staff, J., Mortimer, J. T., & Uggen, C. (2004). Work and leisure in adolescence. In R. M. Lerner & L. Steinberg (Eds.), *Handbook of adolescent psychology* (2nd ed.) (pp. 429–450). Hoboken, NJ: Wiley.

Stanley, B., & Siever, L. J. (2010). The interpersonal dimension of borderline personality disorder: Toward a neuropeptide model. *American Journal of Psychiatry, 167,* 24–39.

Starratt, V. G., & Shackelford, T. K. (2010). The basic components of the human mind were solidified during the Pleistocene epoch. In F. J. Ayala & R. Arp (Eds.), *Contemporary debates in philosophy of biology* (pp. 243–252). Hoboken, NJ: Wiley.

Stasser, G. (1999). A primer of social decision scheme theory: Models of group influence, competitive model-testing, and prospective modeling. *Organizational Behavior and Human Decision Processes, 80*(1), 3–20.

Steele, H. (2005). Editorial. *Attachment & Human Development, 7*(4), 345.

Steenari, R., Vuontela, V., Paavonen, E. J., Carlson, S., Fjallberg, M., & Aronen, E. T. (2003). Working memory and sleep in 6 to 13-year old schoolchildren. *Journal of the American Academy of Child and Adolescent Psychiatry, 42,* 85–92.

Stein, A. D., Pierik, F. H., Verrips, G. H. W., Susser, E. S., & Lumey, L H. (2009). Maternal exposure to the Dutch famine before conception and during pregnancy. *Epidemiology, 20*(6), 909–915.

Stereotypes can affect memory when identifying criminal suspects. (2002, December 20). *Ascribe Higher Education News Service.*

Sternberg, R. J. (1988). Triangulating love. In R. J. Sternberg & M. J. Barnes (Eds.), *The psychology of love* (pp. 119–138). New Haven, CT: Yale University Press.

Sternberg, R. J. (2000). In search of the zipperump-a-zoo. *Psychologist, 13*(5), 250–255.

Sternberg, R. J. (2006). Creating a vision of creativity: The first 25 years. *Psychol-*

ogy of Aesthetics, Creativity, and the Arts, S(1), 2–12.

Sternberg, R. J. (2007). Intelligence and culture. In S. Kitayama & D. Cohen (Eds.), Handbook of cultural psychology (pp. 547–568). New York: Guilford Press.

Sternberg, R. J. (2009). The assessment of creativity. Creativity Research Journal, 24(1),3–12.

Sternberg, R. J., Gabora, L., & Bonney, C. R. (2012). Introduction to the special issue on college and university admissions. Educational Psychologist, 47(1), 1–4.

Sternberg, R. J., Grigorenko, E. L., & Kidd, K. K. (2005). Intelligence, race, and genetics. American Psychologist, 60(1), 46–59.

Stewart, A. J., & Ostrove, J. M. (1998). Women's personality in middle age: Gender, history, and midcourse corrections. American Psychologist, 53(11), 1185–1194.

Stocco, A., & Anderson, J. A. (2008). Endogenous control and task representation: An fMRI study in algebraic problem-solving. Journal of Cognitive Neuroscience, 20(7), 1300–1314.

Stocker, S. (1994). Stop a headache in 5 minutes. Prevention, 46, 65–72.

Stone, J., & Fernandez, N. C. (2008). How behavior shapes attitudes: Cognitive dissonance processes. In W. D. Crano & R. Prislin (Eds.), Attitudes and attitude change (pp. 313–336). Boca Raton, FL: CRC Press.

Story, P. A., Hart, J. W., Stasson, M. F., & Mahoney, J. M. (2009). Using a two-factor theory of achievement motivation to examine performance-based outcomes on self-regulatory processes. Personality and Individual Differences, 46(4), 391–395.

Stuart, K., & Conduit, R. (2009). Auditory inhibition of rapid eye movements and dream recall from REM sleep. Sleep, 32(3), 399–408.

Stunkard, A. J., Harris, J. R., Pedersen, N. L., & McLearn, G. E. (1990). A separated twin study of the body mass index. New England Journal of Medicine, 322, 1483–1487.

Sue, S., Zane, N., Hall, G. C. N., & Berger, L. K. (2009). The case for cultural competency in psychotherapeutic interventions. Annual Review of Psychology, 60, 525–548.

Suinn, R. M. (2001). The terrible twos—anger and anxiety: Hazardous to your health. American Psychologist, 56(1), 27–36.

Suslow, T., Kugel, H., Reber, H., Bauer, J., Dannlowski, U., Kersting, A., ... Egloff, B. (2010). Automatic brain response to facial emotion as a function of implicitly and explicitly measured extraversion. Neuroscience, 167(1), 111–123.

Susser, E., St. Clair, D., & He, L. (2009). Latent effects of prenatal malnutrition on adult health: The example of schizophrenia. Annals of the New York Academy of Sciences, 1136, 185–192.

Swami, V., Furnham, A., Haubner, T., Stieger, S., & Voracek, M. (2009). The truth is out there: The structure of beliefs about extraterrestrial life among Austrian and British respondents. Journal of Social Psychology, 149(1), 29–43.

Swan, G. E., Jack, L. M., Valdes, A. M., Ring, H. Z., Ton, C. C., Curry, S. J., & McAfee, T. (2007). Joint effect of dominergic genes on likelihood of smoking following treatment with bupropion SR. Health Psychology, 26(3), 361–368.

Swartout, K. M., & White, J. W. (2010). The relationship between drug use and sexual aggression in men across time. Journal of Interpersonal Violence, 25(9), 1716–1735.

Szentirmai, E., Kapas, L., Sun, Y., Smith, R. G., & Krueger, J. M. (2010). Restricted feeding-induced sleep, activity, and body temperature changes in normal and preproghrelin-deficient mice. American Journal of Physiology—Regulatory, Integrative, and Comparative Physiology, 298, R467–R477.

T

Taber, C. S., Cann, D., & Kucsova, S. (2009). The motivated processing of political arguments. Political Behavior, 31(2), 137–155.

Tait, M., Nikolopoulos, T. P., De Raeve, L., Johnson, S., Datta, G., Karltorp, E., ... Frijns, J. H. M. (2010). Bilateral versus unilateral cochlear implantation in young children. International Journal of Pediatric Otorhinolaryngology, 74(2), 206–211.

Takahaski, T., Wood, S. J., Yung, A. R., Soulsby, B., McGorry, P. D., Suzuki, M., ... Kawasaki, Y. (2009). Progressive gray matter reduction of the superior temporal gyrus during transition to psychosis. Archives of General Psychiatry, 66(4), 366–376.

Takemura, K. (1994). Influence of Elaboration on the Framing of Decision. The Journal of Psychology, 128, 33–39.

Tamis-LeMonda, C. S., Cristofaro, T. N., Rodriguez, E. T., & Bornstein, M. H. (2006). Early language development: Social influences in the first years of life. In L. Balter & C. S. Tamis-LeMonda (Eds.), Child psychology: A handbook of contemporary issues (2nd ed.) (pp. 79–108). New York: Psychology Press.

Tanner, J. L., & Arnett, J. J. (2011). Presenting "emerging adulthood": What makes it developmentally distinctive? In J. J. Arnett, M. Kloep, L. B. Hendry, & J. L. Tanner. Debating emerging adulthood: Stage or process? (pp. 13–30). New York: Oxford University Press.

Taylor, A., Goehler, L., Galper, D., Innes, K., & Bourguignon, C. (2010). Top-down and bottom-up mechanisms in mind–body medicine. EXPLORE: Journal of Science and Healing, 6(1), 29–41.

Taylor, S., Thordarson, D. S., Maxfield, L., Fedoroff, I. C., Lovell, K., & Ogrodniczuk, J. (2003). Comparative efficacy, speed, and adverse effects of three PTSD treatments: Exposure therapy, EMDR, and relaxation training. Journal of Consulting and Clinical Psychology, 71, 330–338.

Taylor, S. E. (2006). Tend and befriend: Biobehavioral bases of affiliation under stress. Current Directions in Psychological Science, 15(6), 273–277.

Taylor, S. E., Klein, L. C., Lewis, B. P., Gruenewald, T. L., Gurung, R. A. R., & Updegraff J. A. (2000). Biobehavioral responses to stress in females: Tend-and-befriend, not fight-or-flight. Psychological Review, 107(3), 411–429.

Teachout, T. (2000, April 2). For more artists, a fine old age. The New York Times online.

Tenenbaum, H. R., Hill, D. B., Joseph, N., & Roche, E. (2010). "It's a boy because he's painting a picture": Age differences in children's conventional and unconventional gender schemas. British Journal of Psychology, 101(1), 137–154.

Terrace, H. S., & Metcalfe, J. A. (2005). The missing link in cognition: Origins of self-reflective consciousness. New York: Oxford University Press.

Tetlock, P. E., & McGraw, A. P. (2005). Theoretically framing relational framing. Journal of Consumer Psychology, 15(1), 35–37.

Thomas, A. K., & Loftus, E. F. (2002). Creating bizarre false memories through imagination. Memory and Cognition, 30(3), 423–431.

Thomas, K. R. (2008). An exploratory study of factors that relate to academic success among high-achieving African American males. Dissertation Abstracts International, 69 (12). (UMI No. 3340955)

Thomas, S. L., Skitka, L. J., Christen, S., & Jurgena, M. (2002). Social facilitation and impression formation. Basic and Applied Social Psychology, 24(1), 67–70.

Thompson, B. R., & Thornton, H. J. (2002). The transition from extrinsic to intrinsic motivation in the college classroom: A first year experience. Education, 122, 785–782.

Thompson, L. E., Barnett, J. R., & Pearce, J. R. (2009). Scared straight? Fear-appeal anti-smoking campaigns, risk, self-efficacy and addiction. Health, Risk, and Society, 11, 181–196.

Thompson, P. M., et al. (2001). Mapping adolescent brain change reveals dynamic wave of accelerated gray matter loss in very early-onset schizophrenia. Proceedings of the National Academy of Sciences USA. 98(20):11650–11665.

Thompson, S. C. (2009). The role of personal control in adaptive functioning. In I. C. R. Snyder & S. J. Lopez (Eds.), Oxford handbook of positive psychology (pp. 271–278). New York: Oxford University Press.

Thurstone, L. L. (1938). Primary mental abilities. Psychometric Monographs, 1.

Tigner, R. B., & Tigner, S. S. (2000). Triarchic theories of intelligence: Aristotle and Sternberg. *History of Psychology, 3*(2), 168–176.

Tohidian, I. (2009). Examining linguistic relativity hypothesis as one of the main views on the relationship between language and thought. *Journal of Psycholinguistic Research, 38*(1), 65–74.

Tolman, E. C., & Honzik, C. H. (1930). Introduction and removal of reward, and maze performance in rats. *University of California Publications in Psychology, 4,* 257–275.

Toma, C. L., Hancock, J. T., & Ellison, N. B. (2008). Separating fact from fiction: An examination of deceptive self-presentation in online dating profiles. *Personality and Social Psychology Bulletin, 34*(8), 1023–1036.

Tong, H. (2001). Loneliness, depression, anxiety, and the locus of control. *Chinese Journal of Clinical Psychology, 9*(3), 196–197.

Tønnesen, P. (2009). Smoking cessation: How compelling is the evidence? A review. *Health Policy, 91,* S15–S25.

Tost, H., Alam, T., & Meyer-Lindenberg, A. (2009). Dopamine and psychosis: Theory, pathomechanisms and intermediate phenotypes. *Neuroscience and Biobehavioral Reviews, 34*(5), 689–700.

Townsend, E., Hawton, K., Altman, D. G., Arensman, E., Gunnell, D., Hazell, P., ... Van Heeringen, K. (2001). The efficacy of problem-solving treatments after deliberate self-harm: Meta-analysis of randomized controlled trials with respect to depression, hopelessness and improvement in problems. *Psychological Medicine, 31*(6), 979–988.

Travis, S. G., Sparks, F. T., Arnold, T., Lehmann, H., Sutherland, R. J., & Whishaw, I. Q. (2010). Hippocampal damage produces retrograde but not anterograde amnesia for a cued location in a spontaneous exploratory task in rats. *Hippocampus, 20*(9), 1095–1104.

Triandis, H. C. (2001). Individualism–collectivism and personality. *Journal of Personality, 69*(6), 907–924.

Triandis, H. C. (2005). Issues in individualism and collectivism research. In R. M. Sorrentino, et al. (Eds.). *Cultural and social behavior: The Ontario Symposium, 10.* (pp. 207–225). Mahwah, NJ: Erlbaum.

Triandis, H. C. (2006). Cultural aspects of globalization. *Journal of International Management, 12*(2), 208–217.

Triandis, H. C., & Suh, E. M. (2002). Cultural influences on personality. *Annual Review of Psychology, 53*(1), 133–160.

Truchot, D., Maure, G., & Patte, S. (2003). Do attributions change over time when the actor's behavior is hedonically relevant to the perceiver? *The Journal of Social Psychology, 143,* 202–208.

Trull, T. J., Stepp, S. D., & Durrett, C. A. (2003). Research on borderline personality disorder: An update. *Current Opinion in Psychiatry, 16*(1), 77–82.

Tsang, Y. C. (1938). Hunger motivation in gastrectomized rats. *Journal of Comparative Psychology, 26,* 1–17.

Tulving, E. (1985). How many memory systems are there? *American Psychologist, 40,* 385–398.

Turner, E. A., Chandler, M., & Heffer, R. W. (2009). Influence of parenting styles, achievement motivation, and self-efficacy on academic performance in college students. *Journal of College Student Development, 50*(3), 337–346.

Tversky, A., & Kahneman, D. (1982). Judgment under uncertainty. In D. Kahneman, P. Slovic, & A. Tversky (Eds.), *Judgment under uncertainty: Heuristics and biases* (pp. 3–22). New York: Cambridge University Press.

Tversky, A., & Kahneman, D. (2003). Emotional versus intuitive reasoning: The conjunction fallacy in probability judgment. In E. Shafir (Ed.), *Amos Tversky: Preference, belief, and similarity: Selected writings* (pp. 221–256). Cambridge, MA: MIT Press.

Twenge, J. M. (2009). Change over time in obedience: The jury's still out, but it might be decreasing. *American Psychologist, 64*(1), 28–31.

Tyagi, H., Brummond, L. M., & Fineberg, N. A. (2010). Treatment for obsessive compulsive disorder. *Current Psychiatry Reviews, 6*(1), 46–55.

U

U.S. Bureau of the Census. (2008). *Statistical abstract of the United States* (128th ed.). Washington, DC: U.S. Government Printing Office.

U.S. Bureau of the Census. (2011). Families and living arrangements. Retrieved from http://www.census.gov/population/www/socdemo/hh-fam.html

Uhlhaas, P. J., Roux, F., Rodriguez, E., Rotarska-Jagiela, A., & Singer, W. (2010). Neural synchrony and the development of cortical networks. *Trends in Cognitive Sciences, 14*(2), 72–80.

Umek, L. M., Podlesek, A., & Fekonja, U. (2005). Assessing the home literacy environment: Relationships to child language comprehension and expression. *European Journal of Psychological Assessment, 21*(4), 271–281.

Underhill, J. B. (2008). The politics of crisis management: Public leadership under pressure and lessons on leadership by terror: Finding Shaka Zulu in the attic. *Political Psychology, 29*(1), 139–143.

Uzakov, S., Frey, J. U., & Korz, V. (2005). Reinforcement of rat hippocampus LTP by holeboard training. *Learning and Memory, 12,* 165–171.

V

van de Wetering, S., Bernstein, D. M., & Loftus, E. F. (2002). Public education against false memories: A modest proposal. *International Journal of Cognitive Technology, 7*(2), 4–7.

Van der Kolk, B. A., Spinazzola, J., Blaustein, M. E., Hopper, J. W., Hopper, E. K., Korn, D. L., & Simpson, W. B. (2007). A randomized clinical trial of eye movement desensitization and reprocessing (EMDR), fluoxetine, and pill placebo in the treatment of posttraumatic stress disorder. *Journal of Clinical Psychiatry, 68,* 1–10.

van Straaten, I., Engels, R. C. M. E., Finkenauer, C., & Holland, R. W. (2009). Meeting your match: How attractiveness similarity affects approach behavior in mixed-sex dyads. *Personality and Social Psychology Bulletin, 35*(6), 685–697.

Van Swol, L. M. (2008). Performance and process in collective and individual memory: The role of social decision schemes and memory bias in collective memory. *Memory, 16*(3), 274–287.

Vanhaudenhuyse, A., Boly, M., Balteau, E., Schnakers, C., Moonen, G., Luxen, A., ... Faymonville, M. E. (2009). Pain and non-pain processing during hypnosis: A thulium-YAG event-related fMRI study. *NeuroImage, 47,* 1047–1054.

Veenstra-Vanderweele, J., & Cook, E. H. (2003). Genetics of childhood disorders: XLVI. Autism, part 5: Genetics of autism. *Journal of the American Academy of Child and Adolescent Psychiatry, 42*(1), 116–118.

Velmans, M. (1999). When perception becomes conscious. *British Journal of Psychology, 90,* 543.

Verhagen, A. P., Damen, L., Berger, M. Y., Passchier, J., & Koes, B. W. (2009). Behavioral treatments of chronic tension-type headache in adults: Are they beneficial? *CNS Neuroscience and Therapeutics, 15*(2), 183–205.

Vernon, D., Egner, T., Cooper, N., Compton, T., Neilands, C., Sheri, A., & Gruzelier, J. (2003). The effect of training distinct neurofeedback protocols on aspects of cognitive performance. *International Journal of Psychophysiology, 47*(1), 75–85.

Veselka, L., Schermer, J. A., Petrides, K. V., & Vernon, P. A. (2009). Evidence for a heritable general factor of personality in two studies. *Twin Research and Human Genetics, 12*(3), 254–260.

Viets, V. L., Baca, C., Verney, S. P., Venner, K., Parker T., & Wallerstein, N. (2009). Reducing health disparities through a culturally centered mentorship program for minority faculty: The Southwest Addictions Research Group (SARG) experience. *Academic Medicine, 84*(8), 1118–1126.

Villa, K. K., & Abeles, N. (2000). Broad spectrum intervention and the remediation of prospective memory declines in the able elderly. *Aging & Mental Health, 4*(1), 21–29.

Viulli, W. F. (2008). On Joseph Banks Rhine. *Monitor on Psychology, 39*(6), 4.

Vodosek, M. (2009). The relationship between relational models and individualism and collectivism: Evidence from culturally diverse work groups. *International Journal of Psychology, 44*(2), 120–128.

von Békésy, G. (1957, August). The ear. *Scientific American*, pp. 66–78.

Voorspoels, W., Vanpaemel, W., & Storms, G. (2008). Exemplars and prototypes in natural language concepts: A typicality-based evaluation. *Psychonomic Bulletin and Review, 15*(3), 630–637.

Voss, J. L. (2009). Long-term associative memory capacity in man. *Psychonomic Bulletin and Review, 16*, 1076–1081.

Vygotsky, L. (1978). *Mind in society: The development of higher psychological processes.* Cambridge, MA: Harvard University Press.

W

Wacker, J., Chavanon, M.-L., & Stemmler, G. (2009). Resting EEG signatures of agentic extraversion: New results and meta-analytic integration. *Journal of Research in Personality, 44*(2), 167–179.

Wade, N. (1998, January 6). Was Freud wrong? Are dreams the brain's start-up test? *The New York Times online.*

Wagar, B. M., & Thagard, P. (2004). Spiking Phineas Gage: A neurocomputational theory of cognitive-affective integration in decision making. *Psychological Review, 111*(1), 67–79.

Wagstaff, G. S., Wheatcroft, J., Cole, J., Brunas-Wagstaff, J., Blackmore, V., & Pilkington, A. (2009). Some cognitive and neuropsychological aspects of social inhibition and facilitation. *European Journal of Cognitive Psychology, 20*(4), 828–846.

Wais, P. E., Wixted, J. T., Hopkins, R., & Squire, L. R. (2006). The hippocampus supports both the recollection and the familiarity components of recognition memory. *Neuron, 49*(3), 459–466.

Waite, L. J., Luo, Y., & Lewin, A. C. (2009). Marital happiness and marital stability: Consequences for psychological well-being. *Social Science Research, 38*(1), 201–212.

Waitt, C., Gerald, M. S., Little, A. C., & Krasielburd, E. (2006). Selective attention toward female secondary sexual characteristics. *American Journal of Primatology, 68*, 738–744.

Wallace, D. M., & Hinsz, V. B. (2009). Group members as actors and observers in attributions of responsibility for group performance. *Small Group Research, 40*(1), 52–71.

Walle, A. H. (2004). Native Americans and alcoholism therapy: The example of Handsome Lake as a tool of recovery. *Journal of Ethnicity in Substance Abuse, 3*(2), 55–79.

Walther, E., Nagengast, B., & Trasselli, C. (2005). Evaluative conditioning in social psychology: Facts and speculations. *Cognition & Emotion, 19*(2), 175–196.

Wanchoo, S. J., Lee, M. J., Swann, A. C., & Dafny, N. (2010). Bilateral six-hydroxydopamine administration to PFC prevents the expression of behavioral sensitization to methylphenidate. *Brain Research, 1312*(2), 89–100.

Wang, A-C., Hsieh, H.-H., Tsai, C.-Y., & Cheng, B.-S. (2011). Does value congruence lead to voice? Cooerative voice and cooperative silence under team and differentiated transformational leadership. *Management and Organization Review.* doi: 10.1111/j.1740-8784.2011.00255.x

Wang, L., LaBar, K. S., Smoski, M., Rosenthal, M. Z., Dolcos, F., Lynch, T. R., … McCarthy, G. (2008). Prefrontal mechanisms for executive control over emotional distraction are altered in major depression. *Psychiatry Research: Neuroimaging, 163*(2), 143–155.

Wang, Q. (2008). Emotion knowledge and autobiographical memory across the preschool years: A cross-cultural longitudinal investigation. *Cognition, 108*(1), 117–135.

Wang, X., Gao, L., Shinfuku, N., Zhang, H. B., Zhao, C. Z., & Shen, Y. C. (2000). Longitudinal study of earthquake-related PTSD in a randomly selected community sample in North China. *American Journal of Psychiatry, 157*, 1260–1266.

Wang, Y., Anderson, J. A., Chan, C., Kinsner, W., Latombe, J.-C., Patel, D., … Zhang, D. (2009). A doctrine of cognitive informics. *Fundamenta Informaticae, 90*(3), 203–228.

Wang, Y., & Chiew, V. (2010). On the cognitive process of human problem solving. *Cognitive Systems Research, 11*(1), 81–92.

Wann, D. L., Rogers, K., Dooley, K., & Foley, M. (2011a). Applying the team identification–social psychological health model to older sports fans. *The International Journal of Aging and Human Development, 72*(4), 303-315.

Wann, D. L., Waddill, P. J., Polk, J., & Weaver, S. (2011b). The team identification–social psychological health model: Sports fans gaining connections to others via sport team identification. *Group Dynamics: Theory, Research, and Practice, 15*(1), 75-89.

Ward, C. P., McCoy, J. G., McKenna, J. T., Connolly, N. P., McCarley, R. W., & Strecker, R. E. (2009). Spatial learning and memory deficits following exposure to 24 h of sleep fragmentation or intermittent hypoxia in a rat model of obstructive sleep apnea. *Brain Research, 1294*, 128–137.

Warman, D. M., & Beck, A. T. (2003). Cognitive behavioral therapy for schizophrenia: An overview of treatment. *Cognitive & Behavioral Practice, 10*(3), 248–254.

Warman, D. M., & Cohen, R. (2000). Stability of aggressive behaviors and children's peer relationships. *Aggressive Behavior, 26*(4), 277–290.

Warman, D. M., Grant, P., Sullivan, K., Caroff, S., & Beck, A. T. (2005). Individual and group cognitive-behavioral therapy for psychotic disorders: A pilot investigation. *Journal of Psychiatric Practice, 11*(1), 27–34.

Washburn, D. A., Gulledge, J. P., James, F., & Rumbaugh, D. M. (2007). A species

difference in visuospatial working memory: Does language link "what" with "where"? *International Journal of Comparative Psychology, 20*, 55–64.

Waters, M. (2000). Psychologists spotlight growing concern of higher suicide rates among adolescents. *Monitor on Psychology, 31*(6), 41.

Watson, H. J., Raykos, B. C., Street, H., Fursland, A., & Nathan, P. R. (2011). Mediators between perfectionism and eating disorder psychopathology: Shape and weight overvaluation and conditional goal-setting. *International Journal of Eating Disorders, 44*(2), 142–149.

Watson, J. B. (1913). Psychology as the behaviorist views it. *Psychological Review, 20*, 158–177.

Watson, J. B. (1924). *Behaviorism.* New York: Norton.

Webster, J. D. (2003). An exploratory analysis of a self-assessed wisdom scale. *Journal of Adult Development, 10*(1), 13–22.

Weems, C. F., Taylor, L. K., Cannon, M. F., Marino, R. C., Romano, D. M., Scott, B. G., … Triplett, V. (2010). Post traumatic stress, context, and the lingering effects of the Hurricane Katrina disaster among ethnic minority youth. *Journal of Abnormal Child Psychology, 38*(1), 49–56.

Weiner, B. (2006). *Social motivation, justice, and the moral emotions: An attributional approach.* Mahwah, NJ: Erlbaum.

Weiner, B. (2010). The development of an attribution-based theory of motivation: A history of ideas. *Educational Psychologist, 45*(1), 28–36.

Weiner, I. B. (2006). The Rorschach inkblot method. In R. P. Archer (Ed.), *Forensic uses of clinical instruments* (pp. 181–208). London: Routledge.

Weinmann, M., Bader, J., Endrass, J., & Hell, D. (2001). Sind Kompetenz- und Kontrollueberzeugungen depressionsabhaengig? Eine Verlaufsuntersuchung. *Zeitschrift fuer Klinische Psychologie und Psychotherapie, 30*(3), 153–158.

Weiss, A., et al. (2005). Cross-sectional age differences in personality among Medicare patients aged 65 to 100. *Psychology and Aging, 20*(1), 182–185.

Werner, L. A., & Bernstein, I. L. (2001). Development of the auditory, gustatory, olfactory, and somatosensory systems. In E. B. Goldstein (Ed.), *Blackwell handbook of perception, Handbook of experimental psychology series* (pp. 669–708). Boston: Blackwell.

Wessel, J., Moratorio, G., Rao, F., Mahata, M., Zhang, L., Greene, W., … O'Connor, D, T. (2007). C-reactive protein, an "intermediate phenotype" for inflammation: Human twin studies reveal heritability, association with blood pressure and the metabolic syndrome, and the influence of common polymorphism at catecholaminergic/β-adrenergic pathway loci. *Journal of Hypertension, 25*(2), 329–343.

Westen, D. I., Stirman, S. W., & DeRubeis, R. J. (2006). Are research patients and clinical trials representative of clinical practice? In J. C. Norcross, L. E. Beutler, & R. F. Levant (Eds.), *Evidence-based practices in mental health: Debate and dialogue on the fundamental questions* (pp. 161–189). Washington, DC: American Psychological Association.

Wetzler, S. E., & Sweeney, J. A. (1986). Childhood amnesia. In D. C. Rubin (Ed.), *Autobiographical memory* (pp. 191–201). New York: Cambridge University Press.

Wheeler, M. A., & McMillan, C. T. (2001). Focal retrograde amnesia and the episodic–semantic distinction. *Cognitive, Affective and Behavioral Neuroscience, 1*(1), 22–36.

Wheeler, M. E., & Treisman, A. M. (2002). Binding in short-term visual memory. *Journal of Experimental Psychology: General, 131*(1), 48–64.

White, M. A., Masheb, R. M., & Grilo, C. M. (2009). Regimented and lifestyle restraint in binge eating disorder. *International Journal of Eating Disorders, 42*(4), 326–331.

Whorf, B. (1956). *Language, thought, and reality.* New York: Wiley.

Widiger, T. A., & Simonsen, E. (2005). Alternative dimensional models of personality disorder: Finding a common ground. *Journal of Personality Disorders, 19*(2), 110–130.

Wiebe, R. E., & McCabe, S. B. (2002). Relationship perfectionism, dysphoria, and hostile interpersonal behaviors. *Journal of Social and Clinical Psychology, 21*(1), 67–91.

Wienke, C., & Hill, G. J. (2009). Does the "marriage benefit" extend to partners in gay and lesbian relationships? *Journal of Family Issues, 30*(2), 259–289.

Wilhelm, K., Wedgwood, L., Parker, G., Geerligs, L., Hadzi-Pavlovic, D. (2010). Predicting mental health and well-being in adulthood. *Journal of Nervous and Mental Disease, 198*(2), 85–90.

Willcutt, E., & McQueen, M. (2010). Genetic and environmental vulnerability to bipolar spectrum disorders. In D. J. Miklowitz & D. Cicchetti (Eds.), *Understanding bipolar disorder: A developmental psychopathology perspective* (pp. 225–258). New York: Guilford Press.

Williams, J. E., Paton, C. C., Siegler, I. C., Eigenbrodt, M. L., Nieto, F. J., & Tyroler, H. A. (2000). Anger proneness predicts coronary heart disease risk: Prospective analysis from the Atherosclerosis Risk In Communities (ARIC) study. *Circulation, 101*(17), 2034–2039.

Willmott, C., Ponsford, J., Hocking, C., & Schönberger, M. (2009). Factors contributing to attentional impairments after traumatic brain injury. *Neuropsychology, 23*(4), 424–432.

Wilner, P., Bergman, J., & Sanger, D. (2009). Behavioural pharmacology of impulse control. *Behavioural Pharmacology, 20*(5–6), 558–560.

Wilson, C. R. E., Baxter, M. G., Easton, A., & Gaffan, D. (2008). Addition of fornix transection to frontal-temporal disconnection increases the impairment in object-in-place memory in macaque monkeys. *European Journal of Neuroscience, 27*(7), 1814–1822.

Wilson, G. T., Wilfley, D. E., Agras, W. S., & Bryson, S. W. (2010). Psychological treatments of binge eating disorder. *Archives of General Psychiatry, 67*(1), 94–101.

Wilson, I. B., Carter, A. E., & Berg, K. M. (2009). Improving the self-report of HIV antiretroviral medication adherence: Is the glass half full or half empty? *Current HIV/AIDS Reports, 6*(4), 177–186.

Wilson, R. S. (1983). The Louisville twin study: Developmental synchronies in behavior. *Child Development, 54,* 298–316.

Winegard, B. (2010). The evolutionary significance of Red Sox nation: Sport fandom as a byproduct of coalitional psychology. *Evolutionary Psychology, 8*(3), 432–446.

Wisco, B. E., & Nolen-Hoeksema, S. (2009). The interaction of mood and rumination in depression: Effect on mood maintenance and mood-congruent autobiographical memory. *Journal of Rational-Emotive and Cognitive-Behavior Therapy, 27*(3), 144–159.

Wood, R. I., & Stanton, S. J. (2011). Testosterone and sport: Current perspectives. *Hormones and Behavior*, doi: 10.1016/j.yhbeh.2011.09.010

Wooten, P. (1996). Humor: An antidote for stress. *Holistic Nursing Practice, 10,* 49–56.

Wright, D. B., & Loftus, E. F. (2008). Eyewitness memory. In G. Cohen & M. A. Conway (Eds.), *Memory in the real world* (3rd ed.) (pp. 91–105). New York: Psychology Press.

Wu, A. H., Yu, M. C., Tseng, C.-C., Stanczyk, F. Z., & Pike, M. C. (2009). Dietary patterns and breast cancer risk in Asian American women. *American Journal of Clinical Nutrition, 89,* 1145–1154.

Wu, J., Kramer, G. L., Kram, M., Steciuk, M., Crawford, I. L., & Petty, F. (1999). Serotonin and learned helplessness: A regional study of 5-HT1A, 5-HT2A receptors and the serotonin transport site in rat brain. *Journal of Psychiatric Research, 33*(1), 17–22.

Wykes, T., Steel, C., Everitt, B., & Tarrier, N. (2008). Cognitive behavior therapy for schizophrenia: Effect sizes, clinical models, and methodological rigor. *Schizophrenia Bulletin, 34*(3), 523–537.

X

Xie, Y., & Goyette, K. (2003). Social mobility and the educational choices of Asian Americans. *Social Science Research, 32*(3), 467–498.

Y

Yamada, Y., Mizuno, M., Sugiura, M., Tanaka, S., Mizuno, Y., Yanagiya, T., & Hirosawa, M. (2008). Bus drivers' mental conditions and their relation to bus passengers' accidents with a focus on the psychological stress concept. *Journal of Human Ergology, 37,* 1–11.

Yamamoto, S., Tomoe, M., Toyama, K., Kawai, M., & Uneyama, H. (2009). Can dietary supplementation of monosodium glutamate improve the health of the elderly? *American Journal of Clinical Nutrition, 90*(3), 844S–849S.

Yamasue, H., Abe, O., Suga, M., Yamada, H., Rogers, M. A., Aoki, S., … Kasai, K. (2008). Sex-linked neuroanatomical basis of human altruistic cooperativeness. *Cerebral Cortex, 18*(10), 2331–2340.

Yang, L., Li, J., Yiping, Z., Wendong, Z., Fuqiang, D., Ren, Z., & Maycock, B. (2009). Reported reasons for initiating drug use among drug-dependent adolescents and youths in Yunnan, China. *American Journal of Drug and Alcohol Abuse, 35*(6), 445–453.

Yartz, A. R., Zvolensky, M. J., Bernstein, A., Bonn-Miller, M. O., & Lejuez, C. W. (2008). Panic-relevant predictability preferences: A laboratory test. *Journal of Abnormal Psychology, 117*(1), 242–246.

Yazzie, A. (2010). Visual-spatial thinking and academic achievement: A concurrent and predictive validity study. *Dissertation Abstracts International: Section A, Humanities and Social Sciences, 70*(8-A), 2897.

Yeh, C., & Chang, T. (2004). Understanding the multidimensionality and heterogeneity of the Asian-American experience. *PsycCRITIQUES, 49*(5), 583–586.

Yehuda, R. (2002). Post-traumatic stress disorder. *New England Journal of Medicine, 346*(2), 108–114.

Yin, L., Smith, R. G., Sterling, P., & Brainard, D. H. (2009). Physiology and morphology of color-opponent ganglion cells in a retina expressing a dual gradient of S and M opsins. *Journal of Neuroscience, 29*(9), 2706–2724.

Yokota, F., & Thompson, K. M. (2000). Violence in G-rated animated films. *Journal of the American Medical Association, 283,* 2716–2720.

Yurgelun-Todd, D. A. (2007). Emotional and cognitive changes during adolescence. *Current Opinion in Neurobiology, 17*(2), 251–257.

Z

Zagrosek, A., et al. (2010). Effect of binge drinking on the heart as assessed by cardiac MRI. *Journal of the American Medical Association, 304*(12),1328–1330.

Zaitsoff, S. L., & Grilo, C. M. (2010). Eating disorder psychopathology as a marker of psychosocial distress and suicide risk in female and male adolescent psychiatric patients. *Comprehensive Psychiatry, 51*(2), 142–150.

Zanarini, M. C., Frankenburg, F. R., Reich, D. B., & Fitzmaurice, G. (2010). Time to attainment of recovery from borderline personality disorder and stability of recovery: A 10-year prospective follow-up study. *American Journal of Psychiatry, 167,* 663–667.

Zapf, P. A., Zottoli, T. M., & Pirelli, G. (2009). Insanity in the courtroom: Issues of criminal responsibility and competency to stand trial. In J. D. Lieberman & D. A. Krauss, *Psychological expertise in court* (pp. 79–102). Farnham, Surrey, England: Ashgate.

Zayas, L., Gulbas, L. E., Fedoravicius, N., & Cabassa, L. J. (2010). Patterns of distress, precipitating events, and reflec-tions on suicide attempts by young Latinas. *Social Science and Medicine, 70*(11), 1773–1779.

Zimbardo, P. G. (2004). A situationist perspective on the psychology of evil: Understanding how good people are transformed into perpetrators. In A. G. Miller (Ed.), *The social psychology of good and evil* (pp. 21–50). New York: Guilford Press.

Zimbardo, P. G., LaBerge, S., & Butler, L. D. (1993). Psychophysiological consequences of unexplained arousal. *Journal of Abnormal Psychology, 102,* 466–473.

Zimmer, C. (2002, December–2003, January). Searching for your inner chimp. *Natural History, 112.*

Zohar, J., & Westenberg, H. G. M. (2007). Anxiety disorders: A review of tricyclic antidepressants and selective serotonin reuptake inhibitors. *Acta Psychiatrica Scandinavica, 101*(S403), 39–49.

Zosuls, K. M., Ruble, D. N., Tamis-Lemonda, C. S., Shrout, P. E., Bornstein, M. H., & Greulich, F. K. (2009). The acquisition of gender labels in infancy: Implications for gender-typed play. *Developmental Psychology, 45*(3), 688–701.

Zucker, A. N., Ostrove, J. M., & Stewart, A. J. (2002). College- educated women's personality development in adulthood: Perceptions and age differences. *Psychology and Aging, 17*(2), 236–244.

NAME INDEX

A

Abele, S., 348
Abeles, N., 138, 237
Ablon, J. S., 323
Aboa-Éboulé, C., 280
Ackard, D. M., 198
Adams, A. L., 154
Adler, A., 248
Agnew, C. R., 340
Agras, W. S., 323
Ahs, F., 41
Ainsworth, M. S., 12, 227, 229
Alberts, A., 233
Alexander, G. M., 255
Allen, J. P., 234
Allport, G. W., 250
Alm, R., 182
Amanatullah, E. T., 255
Ambrosius, U., 52
Anchin, J. C., 323
Andersen, A. E., 198
Anderson, C. A., 128, 130
Anderson, J. A., 38
Andreano, J. M., 181
Antoni, M. H., 280, 281
Antonishak, J., 234
Apovian, C. M., 197, 198
Archer, J., 346
Archer, R. P., 262
Arias, E., 280
Aristotle, 5
Arnett, J. J., 233, 234, 235
Artigas, F., 297
Asbury, K., 49
Asch, S., 345
Atkins, M. S., 122
Atkinson, R., 140
Auyeung, B., 255

B

Back, S. E., 269
Baddeley, A., 153
Bae, S., 181
Bagchi, D., 281
Bahrick, H., 149, 150
Bakst, S., 298
Baledelomar, O. A., 259, 260
Balon, R., 92
Baltes, P. B., 239
Banaji, M. R., 334
Bandelow, B., 289
Bandura, A., 128, 129, 254, 256, 273, 291, 316
Barber, T. X., 298
Barbey, A. K., 146
Barch, D. M., 300
Bard, P., 209
Barelli, C., 338
Baron, R. A., 341
Barsalou, L. W., 146
Bartoshuk, L. M., 77

Bassok, M., 164
Bates, E., 174
Batson, C. D., 339, 350
Baucom, D. H., 323
Baumrind, D., 229
Bear, R. E., 327
Beck, A. T., 319, 323
Beesdo, K., 292
Behar, E., 290
Belsky, J., 14, 228, 287
Bem, D., 80
Benbow, C. P., 174
Bender, H. L., 230
Benke, K., 278
Benoit, C., 46
Benoit, N., 46
Benson, H., 96
Ben-Zur, H., 272
Bermudez, P., 231
Bernardin, H. J., 252
Bernstein, D. M., 2, 15, 144
Bernstein, I. L., 220
Berscheid, E., 340
Berten, H., 231
Bexton, W. H., 193
Bidell, M. P., 340
Bienvenu, O. J., 252
Binder, E. B., 292
Binet, A., 177
Binswanger, L., 256
Bishop, D. V. M., 303
Bizer, G. Y., 333
Bjorklund, D. F., 224, 225
Blake, P., 269
Blass, T., 344
Blechert, J., 289
Block, N., 36
Blum, K., 49
Bohner, G., 332, 333, 334
Bolinskey, K. P., 301
Boom, J., 226
Boss, M., 256
Bouchard, C., 197
Bourin, M., 326
Bowen, R., 233
Bowlby, J., 228
Boyatzis, R. E., 19, 20
Braarud, H. C., 173
Bradley, R. H., 184
Brand, J., 77
Brand, J. S., 200
Bravender, T., 199
Brewer, M. B., 259
Brewin, C. R., 245
Bridges, J. S., 238
Briñol, P., 335
Brody, J. E., 152
Brook, J. S., 130
Brooks, R., 173
Brough, P., 269
Brown, A. S., 302
Brown, R., 148
Brown, R. J., 294
Brown, W., 219

Brownstein, A. L., 349
Bruce, T. J., 323
Bruene, M., 350
Brun, C. C., 181
Bryant, J., 334
Bryant, R., 291
Bryant, W. C., 239
Buchanan, T. W., 270
Buckley, P. F., 300
Bucy, P., 40
Burger, J. M., 344
Burghardt, G. M., 192
Bushman, B. J., 130
Buss, D. M., 48, 255, 337, 338, 346
Butler, A. C., 319, 323

C

Cahill, L., 181
Calcagni, E., 277
Calkins, M. W., 11–12
Callahan, J. J., 238
Campos, J. J., 207, 220
Cannon, W. B., 196, 209, 275
Cantalupo, C., 168
Carey, B., 327
Carlsmith, J. M., 335
Carlyon, R. P., 76
Carré, J. M., 346
Cartwright, J., 309
Carver, C. S., 206
Carver, L. J., 136
Castelli, L., 234
Castor, D., 121
Cattell, R. B., 181
Catts, S. V., 105
Catts, V. S., 105
Cavallaro, F. I., 95
Ceci, S. J., 155
Cellar, D. F., 252
Cellard, C., 299
Cervantes, J. M., 324
Chadwick, P. D. J., 327
Chafee, M. V., 155
Champagne, F. A., 45
Chance, W. T., 196
Chang, T., 180
Chao, M. M., 341
Chapman, G. B., 167
Chard, K. M., 290
Charles, Prince of Wales, 44
Chen, J., 324
Chen, Y-R., 259
Cheniak, C., 173
Cheung, C-k., 207
Chida, Y., 280
Chiew, V., 164
Chiu, C., 341
Chomsky, N., 173
Christ, S. E., 157
Cialdini, R. B., 350
Cifani, C., 199
Cirelli, C., 91

Clancy, S. A., 1, 2
Clark, A., 173
Clark, E. V., 172
Clark, K. B., 10
Clark, M. P., 10
Clark, S. E., 2, 91
Clark, T. T., 98
Cluver, A., 136
Cocking, C., 350
Coe, W. C., 95
Cohen, A., 103
Cohen, K. M., 204
Cohen, R., 126
Cohen, S., 274, 278
Collaer, M. L., 181
Collins, W. A., 99, 233, 234
Comas-Diaz, L., 11
Comaty, J. E., 318
Compton, J. S., 298
Conduit, R., 92
Confer, J. C., 192, 346
Constantinidis, C., 42
Cook, E. H., 52
Cooper, M., 199
Cornoldi, C., 174
Coskun, O., 278
Costa, P. T., Jr., 251, 252
Costigan, C. L., 233, 234
Coté, N., 164, 165
Cotton, S. M., 94
Cowen, P. J., 297
Cox, L. C., 73
Cox, W. M., 182
Craik, F. I. M., 146
Crick, F., 50
Crighton, D. A., 4
Crisp, R. J., 337
Crittenden, P. M., 199
Crofoot, M. C., 346
Csikszentmihalyi, M., 207
Cuijpers, P., 327
Cummins, R. A., 207
Cunningham, G. B., 336
Cunningham, M., 237
Cutler, B. L., 155

D

Dabbs, J., 346
Dagyte, G., 326
Dai, S. R., 252
Dallos, R., 199
Damasio, A. R., 28
D'Ambrosio, B. S., 226
Dana, R. H., 324
Danhauer, J. L., 73
Darwin, C., 6, 9, 47–48, 206
Daud, M. K. M., 76
David, D., 270, 272, 319, 323
David, E. J. R., 260
Davidoff, J., 162
Davies, J., 334
Davis, D., 152
Davis, J. I., 208

SUBJECT INDEX

Note: *Italic* page numbers indicate material in tables or figures. **Bold** page numbers indicate definitions.

A

A–B problem, **332**
absolute threshold, **58**
abstinence syndrome, **97**, 97
accommodation, **221**, 221
acculturation, **260**, 260
acetylcholine (ACh), **32**, 32
ACh. *See* acetylcholine
achievement motivation, 204–205
acrophobia, **289**
ACTH. *See* adrenocorticotrophic hormone
action potential, **30**, 30
activating effect, **200**
activation–synthesis model, **92**, 92–93
actor–observer effect, **341**, 341
acupuncture, 79
acute stress disorder, **291**, 291
additive process, 64, 65
adolescence, 230–234
    adolescents diagnosed schizophrenia, *301*
    cognitive development, 231–233
    defined, **230**
    egocentrism, 232–233
    physical development, 230–231
    social and emotional development, 233–234
    suicide, 298
adoption studies, 52
adrenal glands, 46
adrenocorticotrophic hormone (ACTH), 46
adulthood, 235–240
    cognitive development, 236
    physical development, 235–236
    social and emotional development, 237–240
afferent neurons, **29**, 29
African Americans
    coronary heart disease and, 280
    psychotherapy and, 324
afterimages, 65, 65
aggression, 128–131, 346–347
    biology, chemistry, and, 346
    psychological aspects of, 346–347
agoraphobia, **289**
alarm reaction, **275**, 275
alcohol, 99–100
algorithms, **163**, 163
all-or-none principle, **31**, 31
alpha waves, **89**, 89
altruism, **350**, 350
Alzheimer's disease, **237**, 237
ambivalent/resistant attachment, 228

American Psychiatric Association, 287
American Psychological Association, 269–270
amnesia
    anterograde, 153
    infantile, 152–153
    retrograde, 153
amniotic sac, **208**, 218
amphetamines, 100–101, **101**
amygdala, **40**, 40–41
anagrams, 163
anal stage, **246**, 246
analogies, 164
analytical psychology, **247**, 247
anchoring and adjustment heuristic, **167**, 167
anger, 206
anorexia nervosa, **198**, 198
anterograde amnesia, **153**, 153
antianxiety drugs, 325
antibodies, **277**, 277
antidepressants, **326**, 326
antidiuretic hormone, 45
antigens, **277**, 277
antipsychotic drugs, 325–326, 327
antisocial personality disorder, **304**, 304
anxiety disorders, 288–292
    biological views, 291–292
    biopsychosocial views, 292
    defined, **289**
    generalized anxiety disorder, 290
    obsessive–compulsive disorder, 290
    origins of, 291–292
    panic disorder, 289–290
    phobic disorders, 289
    psychological views, 291
    stress disorders, 290–291
aphagic, **197**, 197
aphasia, **42**, 42
applied research, **3**, 3
archetypes, 247
Asch study, *345*, 345–346
Asian Americans, 324
assimilation, **221**, 221
association areas, 42
asylums, **310**, 310
Ativan, 325
Atkinson–Shiffrin Model, *140*
attachment, **227**, 227–229
    in infant monkeys, *228*
    phases of, 228
    strange situation and patterns of, 227–228
    theoretical views of, 228–229
attitude-discrepant behavior, **335**, 335
attitudes
    changing means of cognitive dissonance, 335–336

changing through persuasion, 333–335
    defined, **332**
    formation, 333
    predicting behavior from, 332–333
attraction, **337**, 337–340
    color and, 338
    facial attractiveness, *337*
    gender differences in selection of a romantic partner, 338
    physical appearance, 337–338
attraction–similarity hypothesis, 338–339
attribution, **340**, 340
attribution theory, 340–342
    actor–observer effect, 341
    dispositional and situational attributions, 340
    fundamental attribution error, 341
    self-serving bias, 341–342
attributional style, **296**, 296
auditory nerve, **74**, 74
auditory stimulation, 73
authoritarian parents, **229**, 229
authoritative parents, **229**, 229
autonomic nervous system (ANS), **34**, 34–35, *35*, 205, 292
availability heuristic, **167**, 167
average, *355*, **356**
aversive conditioning, **317**, 317
avoidant attachment, 228
avoidant personality disorder, **304**, 304
awareness, 85
axon, **29**

B

barbiturates, **101**, 101
basilar membrane, **74**, 74
behavior
    attitude-discrepant, 335
    changing means of cognitive dissonance, 335–336
    patterns of, 48–49
    predicting from attitudes, 332–333
behavior modification, 126, 313
behavior therapy, 315–319
    aversive conditioning, 317
    defined, **315**
    fear-reduction methods, 316–317
    operant conditioning procedures, 317–319
behavioral genetics, 49
behaviorism, **6**, 6–7, 253–254

benzodiazepines, 325
BFT. *See* biofeedback training
bimodal, **359**, *359*, 359
binocular cues, **70**, 70–71
biofeedback, 96–97
biofeedback training (BFT), **96**, 96, 126, **318**, 318–319
biological perspective, **9**, 9, 296–297
biological preparedness, **118**, 118
biological therapies, 325–327
    drug therapy, 325–326
    effectiveness of, 327
    electroconvulsive therapy, 326
biology
    gender-typing and, 255
    traits and, 252
biopsychosocial perspective
    defined, **278**
    to health, 278
    on mood disorders, 297
    on schizophrenia, 303
bipolar cells, **63**, 63
bipolar disorder, **295**, 295–296
blind spot, **63**, 63
blind studies, **19**, 19–20
borderline personality disorder, **304**, 304
bottom-up processing, **68**, 68
brain, 36–45
    adolescents diagnosed schizophrenia, *301*
    cerebral cortex, 41–43
    experimenting with, 37–38
    feature detectors in, 60
    handedness and, 44
    imaging techniques, *38*
    left-brained/right-brained, 43
    overview of, 38–41
    parts of, *39*
    prefrontal cortex of, *156*
    split-brain experiments, 44–45
    structures, 155–156
brain development, 231
brightness constancy, **71**, 71
Broca's area, **42**, 43, *43*
bulimia nervosa, **199**, 199
bystander effect, **350**, 350

C

cancer, 280–281
cannabis sativa, 104
Cannon–Bard theory, 210
case studies, **15**, 15
CAT scan. *See* computerized axial tomography
catastrophize, 272
catatonic schizophrenia, **300**, 300
catharsis, **312**, 312

Cattell's Culture-Fair Intelligence Test, *181*
(CBT). *See* cognitive-behavioral therapy
cells, *50*
central nervous system, **34**, 34, *325*
cerebellum, 38, **39**, *39*
cerebral cortex, 41–43
  Broca's area, 42, *43*
  defined, **41**
  geography of, *41*
  language functions and, 42–43
  thinking, language and, 42
  Wernicke's area, 42, *43*
cerebrum, **41**, *41*
CHD. *See* coronary heart disease
childhood, 219–230
  cognitive development, 220–227
  motor development, 219
  perceptual development, 219–220
  physical development, 219–220
  reflexes, 219
  social and emotional development, 227–230
chimpanzees, 168
chromosomes, **49**, 49–51, *50*
chronic health problems, 278–281
chunking, 143
chunks, **143**
circadian rhythm, **88**, *88*
clairvoyance, 80
classical conditioning, **112**, 112–118
  applications of, 117–118
  explaining, 113
  extinction and spontaneous recovery in, 115–116
  generalization and discrimination, 116–117
  higher-order conditioning, 117
  schematic representation of, *113*
  stimuli and responses in, 113
  taste aversion, 114
claustrophobia, 289
client-centered therapy, 313–315
clinical psychologists, 3
closure, **67**, *67*, 67
clozapine, 325
Clozaril, 325
cocaine, *102*, 102–103
cochlea, **74**, *74*
cognition, **162**, *162*
cognitive appraisal, 333
cognitive appraisal theory, 210–211
cognitive-behavioral therapy (CBT), **320**, 320–321
cognitive development, 220–227
  adolescence, 231–233
  childhood, 220–227
  Kohlberg's theory of moral development, 226–227

Piaget's cognitive-development theory, 221–225
Piaget's stages of cognitive development, 221
sociocultural theory, 225–226
two-month-olds' preferences for visual stimuli, *221*
cognitive-dissonance theory, **335**, *335*
cognitive maps, **127**, 127, *165*
cognitive perspective, **9**, *9*
cognitive therapy, 319–321
  cognitive-behavioral therapy, 320–321
  rational emotive behavior therapy, 320
collective unconscious, **247**, 247
collectivist, **259**, 259
color, 338
color blindness, **66**, 66
color constancy, **71**, *71*
color vision, **64**
  complementary colors, 64–65
  theories of, 65–66
  warm and cool colors, 64
color wheel, *64*
commitment, **339**, *339*
common fate, **68**, *68*
community mental health movement, 311
complementary colors, **64**, 64–65
computerized axial tomography (CAT/CT scan), 37, *37*, *38*
concepts, **162**, *162*
concrete operational stage, **224**, *224*
conditional positive regard, **257**, *257*
conditional reflexes, 112
conditioned reinforcers, **122**
conditioned response (CR), 112, **113**, *113*
conditioned stimulus (CS), **113**, *113*, 127
conditioning, 333
conditions of worth, **257**, *257*
cones, **63**, 63–64
conflict, **270**, 270–271
conformity, 345–346
consciousness, 85–109
  altering through drugs, 97–106
  altering through hypnosis, meditation and biofeedback, 94–97
  as awareness, 85
  defined, **86**
  humanistic–existential perspective, 9
  as personal unity, 86
  as waking state, 87
conservation, **223**, 223, *224*
consumer psychologists, 4
consummate love, **340**, 340
contact comfort, **229**, *229*
contemporary psychological models, 287

context-dependent memory, **148**, *148*
contingency theory, **127**, 127–128
continuity, **68**, *68*
continuous reinforcement, **123**, *123*
control, 274
control groups, **18**, *18*
conventional level, **226**, 226
convergence, 70, **71**, *71*
convergent thinking, **177**, *177*
conversion disorder, **294**, 294
cool colors, 64
cornea, **62**, *62*
coronary heart disease (CHD), 280, *281*
coronary-prone behavior pattern, 272
corpus callosum, **41**, *41*
correlation, 17–18
  defined, **14**
  positive and negative, *17*, *363*
correlation coefficient, **17**, *363*, 363–364
correlational method, **17**
correlational relationships, cause and effect, *364*
corticosteroids, 46
counseling psychologists, 3
counterconditioning, **118**, *118*
couple therapy, 321
CR. *See* conditioned response
creative self, **248**, *248*
creativity, **177**, *177*
cretinism, 46
critical period, **229**, 229
critical thinking, **12**, 12–13
crystallized intelligence, **237**, 237
CS. *See* conditioned stimulus
CT scan. *See* Computerized axial tomography
culture, 170
curare, 32
current cognitions, 319

D

dark adaptation, **64**, 64
dB. *See* decibel
deafness, 76
debrief, **21**, *21*
decentration, **224**, *224*
decibel (dB), **73**, *73*, 74
decision making, 166–167
deindividuation, 349–350, **350**
delayed reinforcers, 121–122
delirium tremens (DTs), 98
delusions, **299**, 299
delusions of grandeur, 299
delusions of persecution, 299
demonological model, 286–287
dendrites, 29
deoxyribonucleic acid (DNA), **49**, 49–50, *50*
dependent variables, **18**, *18*
depolarize, **30**, 30
depressants, **97**, *97*, 99–101
depression, 206, 297

depth perception, 69–71
Descent of Man, The (Darwin), 47
descriptive statistics, **356**, 356–361
  frequency distribution, 357–358
  measures of central tendency, 358–360
  measures of variability, 360–361
desensitization, **60**, 60
developmental psychologists, 3
Diagnostic and Statistical Manual of Mental Disorders, 287
dichromats, **66**, 66
DID. *See* dissociative identity disorder
difference threshold, **59**, *59*
diffusion of responsibility, **348**, 348
direct inner awareness, **86**, *86*
discrimination, **116**, 116–117, **336**, 336–337
discriminative stimuli, **123**, 123
disgust, 206
disorganized schizophrenia, **300**, 300
displace, **144**, *144*
displacement, **169**, *169*
dispositional attributions, **340**, 340
dissociative amnesia, **152**, *152*, **292**, 292
dissociative disorders, 292–293
  defined, **292**
  dissociative amnesia, 292
  dissociative fugue, 292–293
  dissociative identity disorder, 293
  origins of, 293
dissociative fugue, **292**, 292–293
dissociative identity disorder (DID), **293**, 293
divergent thinking, **177**, *177*
dizygotic (DZ) twins, **52**, *52*, 291–292
DNA. *See* deoxyribonucleic acid
dopamine, **32**, *32*
double-blind studies, **19**, 19–20
Down syndrome, **50**, 51
dream analysis, 313
dreams, 91–93
drive-reduction theory, **193**, 193
drives, **192**
drug therapy, 325–326
  antianxiety drugs, 325
  antidepressants, 326
  antipsychotic drugs, 325–326
  mood stabilizers, 326
  psychosurgery, 326
drugs
  altering consciousness through, 97–106
  depressants, 99–101

primary reinforcers, **122**
primary sex characteristics, 47
priming, **137**, *137* ·
proactive interference, **152**, *152*
problem solving, 163–166
progesterone, 47
programmed learning, 126
Project Pigeon, 119, *120*
projective tests, **261**, *261–262*
prospective memory, **137**, *137*
proximity, **68**, *68*
psi communication, 80
psi phenomena, 80
psychoactive substances, **97**, *97*
psychoanalysis, **8**, *8*, **312**, *312*,
    312–313
psychodynamic perspective,
    9–10
psychodynamic theories, **244**,
    244–250
psychodynamic therapies,
    311–313
    defined, **311**
    dream analysis, 313
    traditional psychoanalysis,
        312–313
    transference, 312–313
psycholinguistic theory, **173**,
    173
psychological disorders,
    285–307
    anxiety disorders, 288–292
    characteristics of, 285–288
    classifying, 287
    contemporary psychologi-
        cal models, 287
    defined, **286**
    demonological model,
        286–287
    dissociative disorders,
        292–293
    medical model, 287
    mood disorders, 294–299
    past-year and lifetime prev-
        alences of, *288*
    personality disorders,
        303–305
    perspectives on, 286–287
    prevalence of, 287–288
    schizophrenia, 299–303
    somatoform disorders, 294
psychological hardiness, **273**,
    273
psychologists, types of, 3–4
psychology
    approaches, 8–12
    chronic health problems
        and, 278–281
    defined, **2**
    fields of, 3–4
    history, *5–8*
    new doctorates in, *4*
    as science, 2
    theories, 2
psychomotor retardation, **295**,
    295
psychosexual development,
    246, *246*
psychosocial development,
    249, *249*
psychosurgery, **327**, *327*
psychotherapy, **310**, *310*
    African Americans and, 324
    Asian Americans and, 324

effectiveness of, 322–325,
    327
ethnicity and, 324–325
evidence-based practices,
    323, *323*
Latin Americans and, 324
Native Americans and,
    324–325
PTSD. *See* posttraumatic stress
    disorder
puberty, **230**, *230*
punishments, 122–123, *123*
pupil, **62**, *62*
pure research, **3**, *3*

R

random samples, **15**, *15*
range, **360**, *360*
rapid eye movement (REM)
    sleep, **89**, *89*
rapid flight of ideas, **295**, *295*
ratio schedules, 124–125
rational emotive behavior
    therapy (REBT), **320**, *320*
rebound anxiety, **325**, *325*
(REBT). *See* rational emotive
    behavior therapy
recall, 149–150
recency effect, **340**, *340*
receptor sites, **32**, *32*
recognition, 149
reflex, **112**, *112*, **219**, *219*
reflex arc, *36*
refractory period, **31**, *31*, **201**,
    201
reinforce, **119**
reinforcement, **7**, *7*, **119–120**,
    123–125, 347
reinforcers, 122–123
relearning, 151
reliability, **260**, *260*
REM sleep. *See* rapid eye
    movement sleep
representativeness heuristic,
    166, *166*
repression, **87**, *87*, **144**, *144*,
    152
research
    ethical standards for ani-
        mal, 21
    ethical standards for hu-
        man, 20–21
    problems, 14–15
    pure and applied, 3
resistance, **312**, *312*
resistance stage, **276**, *276*
resolution phase, **201**, *201*
response set theory, **95**, *95*
resting potential, **30**, *30*
reticular formation, **39**, *39*, *40*
retina, **63**, *63*
retinal disparity, **70**, *70*
retrieval, **139**, *139–140*
retroactive interference, **151**,
    151
retrograde amnesia, **153**, *153*
retrospective memory, **137**, *137*
rewards, 122–123
right-brained, 43
risky shift, 348–349
rods, **63**, *63–64*
role diffusion, **234**, *234*

role theory, **95**, *95*
romantic love, **340**, *340*
rooting, **219**, *219*
Rorschach inkblot test, 262

S

saccadic eye movements, 142
sample, **355**, *356*
samples, **14**, *14*, 366
sandwich generation, **238**, *238*
satiety, **195**, *195*
saturation, 64
savings, **151**, *151*
SBIS. *See* Stanford-Binet
    Intelligence Scale
scaffolding, **225**, *225*
schema, **221**, *221*
schemas, **145**, *145*
schizoid personality disorder,
    303, *303–304*
schizophrenia, 32, 299–303
    adolescents, *301*
    antipsychotic drugs and,
        326
    biological views, 301–302
    biopsychosocial perspec-
        tive, 303, *303*
    contributing factors,
        300–303
    genetic vulnerability, *302*
    problems in actions, emo-
        tions, and social inter-
        action, 299–300
    problems in perception, 299
    problems in thinking and
        language, 299
    psychological views, 300
    sociocultural views,
        300–301
    symptoms of, 299–300
    types of, 300
schizotypal personality disor-
    der, **303**, *303–304*
school psychologists, 3
scientific method, **13**, *13–14*
secondary reinforcers, **122**
secondary sex characteristics,
    47, **230**, *230*
secondhand smoke, **104**, *104*
secure attachment, 228
selection factors, **14**
selective attention, **86**, *86*
selective avoidance, **334**, *334*
selective serotonin-reuptake
    inhibitors (SSRIs), **326**, *326*
self-actualization, **194**, *194*,
    256, *256–258*
self-concept, 257
self-efficacy expectations, 254,
    273, *273*
self-esteem, 257
self-help groups, 322
self-serving bias, **341**, *341–342*
self theory, 257–258
semantic memory, **136**, *136*
semanticity, **169**, *169*
sensation
    absolute threshold and,
        58–59
    defined, **58**
    difference threshold and, 59
    feature detectors and, 60

perception and, 57–60
sensory adaptation, 60
signal-detection theory and,
    59–60
sensitization, **60**, *60*
sensorimotor stage, **222**, *222*
sensory adaptation, **60**, *60*
sensory memory, **140**, *140–142*
serial-position effect, **143**, *143*
serotonin, **33**, *33*
sex chromosomes, **50**, *51*
sexual abuse, 297, 298
sexual behavior
    kinds of, *202*
    of teenagers, *202*
*Sexual Behavior in the Human
    Female* (Kinsey), 16
*Sexual Behavior in the Human
    Male* (Kinsey), 16
sexual motivation
    hormones and, 200
    sexual orientation and,
        203–204
    sexual response and sexual
        behavior, 200–201
    surveys of sexual behavior,
        201–202
sexual orientation, **203**,
    203–204
sexual response cycle, **200**, *200*
shape constancy, **72**, *72*, *72*
shaping, **125**, *125–126*
short-term memory, **142**,
    142–144, *144*
signal-detection theory, **59**,
    59–60
similarity, **68**, *68*
situational attributions, **340**,
    340
size constancy, **71**, *71*
skeletons, *47*
skin senses, 77–79
    pain, 78–79
    temperature, 77–78
    touch and pressure, 77
sleep
    biological and circadian
        rhythms, 88
    cycles, *90–91*
    disorders, 93–94
    dreams and, 91–93
    functions of, 90–91
    for mammals, *88*
    problems among
        Americans before/after
        September 11, 2001,
        291
    stages of, 88–90, *89*
sleep apnea, **93**, *93*
sleep terrors, **93**, *93–94*
smell, 76
smiling, *209*
smoking, *105*
social-cognitive theorists, 10
social-cognitive theory, **10**,
    254, *254*, 254–256
social decision schemes, **348**,
    348
social development
    adolescence, 233–234
    childhood, 227–230
    early adulthood, 237–238
    late adulthood, 239–240
    middle adulthood, 238

WHAT'S NEW?
WHAT'S CHANGED?

Colin Anderson/Getty Images

Chung Sung-Jun/Getty Images

Colin Anderson/Jupiter Images

Across-the-Board Changes

- We have added a two-page self-assessment to the end of each chapter, including fill-in-the-blank and multiple-choice questions
- Updated the references throughout
- Updated the figures and photos throughout

Chapter 1 Changes

- Revised the chapter-opening vignette
- Made small revisions to the section on Psychology as a Science
- Made small revisions to the section on Psychoanalysis
- Revised the section on Ethnicity
- Added *critical thinking* as a key term
- Added *scientific method* as a key term
- Added *correlation coefficient* as a key term

Chapter 2 Changes

- Mentioned the role of the interneuron in the section on the CNS
- Clarified the Truth or Fiction box on the size of the human brain
- Clarified and updated the section on MRI and fMRI
- Changed the reticular activating system to reticular formation
- Added new examples to the Handedness section
- Revised the "Steroids, Behavior, and Mental Processes" box
- Updated research on DZ and MZ twins

Chapter 3 Changes

- This chapter was Chapter 4 in the previous edition
- Added a brief section on subliminal stimulation
- Added *visible light* as a key term
- Added the box, "iPods on Campus: The Sounds of Oblivion"
- Revised the Perception of Loudness and Pitch section to include volley principle
- Condensed the section on ESP, also updating it to include the 2011 Bem article

Chapter 4 Changes

- This chapter was Chapter 5 in the previous edition
- Added a Truth or Fiction on heroin
- Added PET scan data to the Activation-Synthesis Model of Dreaming section

- Changed the apnea section and key term to *sleep apnea*
- Added the term "somnambulism" to the discussion of sleepwalking
- Updated the section on transcendental meditation with new research
- Included mention of binge drinking in the Substance Abuse section
- Removed the key term *withdrawal symptoms*; added the key term *abstinence syndrome*
- Added the box, "Do You Have a Problem with Alcohol?"

Chapter 5 Changes

- This chapter was Chapter 6 in the previous edition
- Added a new Learning Objective, Define learning
- Added a new chapter-opening vignette
- Added a brief section on biological preparedness
- Added a brief section on Thorndike and the Law of Effect
- Clarified the distinction between positive and negative punishments
- Condensed the section on biofeedback training
- Included a brief mention of mirror neurons

Chapter 6 Changes

- This chapter was Chapter 7 in the previous edition
- Made edits to the Kinds of Memory section to improve clarity
- Added the Bahrick et al., 2008 study on memory of college grades
- Added a revised/condensed box, "Can We Trust Eyewitness Testimony?"

Chapter 7 Changes

- This chapter was Chapter 8 in the previous edition
- Condensed the chapter-opening vignette
- Revised the Linguistic-Relativity Hypothesis section slightly
- Condensed the Prelinguistic Vocalizations section
- Added a box on Motherese
- Condensed The Nativist Approach to Language Development section
- Updated the Differences in Intellectual Functioning section

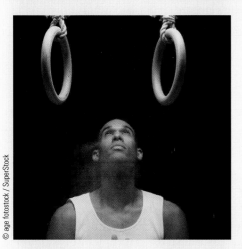

Chapter 8 Changes

- This chapter was Chapter 9 in the previous edition
- Small edits were made throughout for clarity of material, including the explanation of hypothalamus

- Changed the Obesity head to Overweight; updated the section related to factors in becoming overweight
- Replaced NHSLS with recent National Survey of Sexual Health and Behavior (NSSHB)
- Updated the Sexual Orientation section
- Condensed the Positive Psychology section

Chapter 9 Changes

- This chapter was Chapter 3 in the previous edition
- Added a Learning Objective on emerging adulthood
- Revised the section on Erik Erikson slightly
- Condensed the section on phases of attachment
- Added information on brain development in adolescence
- Revised the section on social and emotional development in adolescence
- Made edits throughout the adulthood section to update and improve content
- Included information on the empty-nest syndrome and sandwich generation

Chapter 10 Changes

- Made small edits throughout to make areas more concise
- Psychoanalytic perspective changed to psychodynamic perspective
- Added a brief section on biology and traits
- Changed the Social Cognitive Theory section into a box, updating it and calling it "Biology, Social Cognition, and Gender Typing"
- Included discussion of existentialism in humanist perspective
- Condensed the section on sociocultural perspective slightly
- Pared back coverage of MMPI

Chapter 11 Changes

- Made small edits throughout to update and clarify
- Added a new chapter-opening vignette
- Updated the Stress in America section

- Updated research on the value of social support
- Revised the box, "Are There Gender Differences in Response to Stress?"
- Added the box, "Stress Tip Sheet"
- Pared back the section on cancer

Chapter 12 Changes

- Reordered the discussion of disorders in the chapter
- Revised the Truth or Fiction questions
- Added a new chapter-opening vignette (previously an example in the dissociative disorders section)
- Revised the discussion on perspectives on psychological disorders to fall under its own head

Chapter 13 Changes

- Made small edits throughout to make areas more concise
- Added a new chapter-opening vignette (previously an example in the virtual therapy section)
- Changed psychoanalytic perspective to psychodynamic perspective
- Condensed the virtual therapy section
- Added a brief section on self-help and support groups
- Revised the "Does Psychotherapy Work?" section
- Created a new head, "Does Biological Therapy Work?," which pulls together parts of various sections

Chapter 14 Changes

- Revised the learning objectives
- Updated the chapter-opening vignette
- Added the box, "When It Comes to Sex, Red May Mean 'Go'"
- Deleted the section on body language
- Added a section on aggression
- Revised the section on groupthink

To help you succeed, we have designed a review card for each chapter.

KEY TERMS

1.1

psychology the science that studies behavior and mental processes

theory a set of hypothesized statements about the relationships among events

1.2

pure research research conducted without concern for immediate applications

applied research research conducted in an effort to find solutions to particular problems

1.3

introspection deliberate looking into one's own cognitive processes to examine one's thoughts and feelings

structuralism the school of psychology that argues that the mind consists of three basic elements—sensations, feelings, and images—that combine to form experience

functionalism th[e]...
sizes the uses or fu[...]
elements of experi[...]

> Here, you'll find the key terms and definitions in the order they appear in the chapter.

behaviorism the school of psychology that defines psychology as the study of observable behavior and studies relationships between stimuli and responses

reinforcement a stimulus that follows a response and increases the frequency of the response

Gestalt psychology the school of psychology that emphasizes the tendency to organize perceptions into wholes and to integrate separate stimuli into meaningful patterns

psychoanalysis the school of psychology that emphasizes the importance of unconscious motives and conflicts as determinants of human behavior

1.4

biological per[...]
ogy that seeks t[...]
between biolog[...]
the functioning [...]
and heredity, on[...]
tal processes, on[...]

cognitive havi[...]
as sensation an[...]
guage, thought, [...]

social-cogniti[...]
the behaviorist [...]
in the explanatio[...]
termed social lea[...]

sociocultural [...]
on the roles of e[...]
nomic status in [...]

> **How to Use the Card:**
>
> 1. Look over the card to preview the new concepts you'll be introduced to in the chapter.
>
> 2. Read your chapter to fully understand the material.
>
> 3. Go to class (and pay attention).
>
> 4. Review the card one more time to make sure you've registered the key concepts.
>
> 5. Don't forget, this card is only one of many PSYCH learning tools available to help you succeed in your psychology course.

SUMMARY

1.1

Define psychology. Psychology is the scientific study of behavior and mental processes. Topics of interest to psychologists include the nervous system, sensation and perception, learning and memory, intelligence, language, thought, growth and development, personality, stress and health, psychological disorders, ways of treating those disorders, sexual behavior, and the behavior of people in social settings such as groups and organizations. The goal of the psychologist, like other scientists, is to descri[be] the events he or she studies—in this case, behavior and men[tal]...

> In this column, you'll find summary points supported by exhibits from the chapters.

1.2

Describe the various fields of psychology. Psychologists are found in a number of different specialties:

[C]linical psychologists help people with psychological disorders adjust to the demands of life.

Counseling psychologists typically see clients with adjustment problems but not serious psychological disorders.

School psychologists help school systems identify and assist students who have problems that interfere with learning.

Educational psychologists research theoretical issues related to learning, measurement, and child development.

Developmental psychologists study the changes—physical, cognitive, social, and emotional—that occur throughout the life span.

Personality psychologists identify and measure human traits and determine influences on human thought processes, feelings, and behavior.

Social psychologists are concerned with the nature and causes of individuals' thoughts, feelings, and behavior in social situations.

Environmental psychologists study the ways that people and the environment influence one another.

Experimental psychologists specialize in basic processes such as the nervous system, sensation and perception, learning and memory, thought, motivation, and emotion.

Industrial psychologists focus on the relationships between people and work.

Organizational psychologists study the behavior of people in organizations such as businesses.

Human factors psychologists make technical systems more user-friendly.

Consumer psychologists study the behavior of shoppers in an effort to predict and influence their behavior.

Health psychologists study the effects of stress on health problems such as headaches, cardiovascular disease, and cancer

Forensic psychologists apply principles of psychology to the criminal justice system.

Sport psychologists help people improve their performance in sports.

1.3

Describe the origins of psychology and identify people who made significant contributions to the field. An ancient contributor to the modern field of psychology, Aristotle argued that human behavior, like the movements of the stars and the seas, is subject to rules and laws. Today, as then, the subject matter of the study of human behavior includes the study of personality, sensation and perception, thought, intelligence, needs and motives, feelings and emotion, and memory. The following is a list of the historic schools of psychology and the major proponent(s) of each: Structuralism: Wilhelm Wundt; Functionalism: William James; Behaviorism: John B. Watson and B. F. Skinner; Gestalt Psychology: Max Wertheimer, Kurt Koffka, and Wolfgang Köhler; and Psychoanalysis: Sigmund Freud, Carl Jung, Alfred Adler, Karen Horney, and Er[...]

> When it's time to prepare for exams, use the Card and the technique to the left to ensure successful study sessions.

PSYCH was designed for students just like you—busy people who want choices, flexibility, and multiple learning options.

PSYCH delivers concise, focused information in a fresh and contemporary way. In addition to your tear-out review cards, PSYCH offers a variety of learning materials designed with you in mind. Visit CourseMate for PSYCH at www.cengagebrain.com to access multiple PSYCH resources to help you succeed.

- *Learning Outcomes* Downloadable learning outcomes from PSYCH.
- *Interactive Flashcards* Key terms are also available as interactive flash cards that allow you to shuffle the deck, remove a card, view the term first, or view the definition first.
- *Printable Flash Cards* Our extensive research shows that almost all students use flash cards to reinforce their understanding of core psychology concepts. To help you prepare flash cards that fit your specific study needs, the website provides three varieties of downloadable flash cards: 1) term only, 2) definition only, or 3) term and definition. Each set of cards is formatted to fit the standard Avery business card template.
- *Glossary* Select a chapter to view glossary terms and definitions.
- *Quizzes* You can practice before chapter tests, midterms, and finals by taking these interactive quizzes.
- *Study Games* Games provide fun study practice.
- *Interactive Practice* Learning Modules and Drag-and-Drops help you learn more about concepts covered in PSYCH.
- *Videos* News and research video clips bring chapter concepts to life.

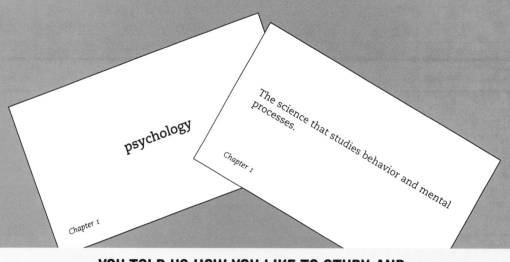

psychology

Chapter 1

The science that studies behavior and mental processes.

Chapter 1

YOU TOLD US HOW YOU LIKE TO STUDY, AND

WE LISTENED.

KEY TERMS

1.1

psychology the science that studies behavior and mental processes

theory a set of hypothesized statements about the relationships among events

1.2

pure research research conducted without concern for immediate applications

applied research research conducted in an effort to find solutions to particular problems

1.3

introspection deliberate looking into one's own cognitive processes to examine one's thoughts and feelings

structuralism the school of psychology that argues that the mind consists of three basic elements—sensations, feelings, and images—that combine to form experience

functionalism the school of psychology that emphasizes the uses or functions of the mind rather than the elements of experience

behaviorism the school of psychology that defines psychology as the study of observable behavior and studies relationships between stimuli and responses

reinforcement a stimulus that follows a response and increases the frequency of the response

Gestalt psychology the school of psychology that emphasizes the tendency to organize perceptions into wholes and to integrate separate stimuli into meaningful patterns

psychoanalysis the school of psychology that emphasizes the importance of unconscious motives and conflicts as determinants of human behavior

1.4

biological perspective the approach to psychology that seeks to understand the nature of the links between biological processes and structures such as the functioning of the brain, the endocrine system, and heredity, on the one hand, and behavior and mental processes, on the other

cognitive having to do with mental processes such as sensation and perception, memory, intelligence, language, thought, and problem solving

social-cognitive theory a school of psychology in the behaviorist tradition that includes cognitive factors in the explanation and prediction of behavior; formerly termed social learning theory

sociocultural perspective the view that focuses on the roles of ethnicity, gender, culture, and socioeconomic status in behavior and mental processes

SUMMARY

1.1

Define psychology. Psychology is the scientific study of behavior and mental processes. Topics of interest to psychologists include the nervous system, sensation and perception, learning and memory, intelligence, language, thought, growth and development, personality, stress and health, psychological disorders, ways of treating those disorders, sexual behavior, and the behavior of people in social settings such as groups and organizations. The goal of the psychologist, like other scientists, is to describe, explain, predict, and control the events he or she studies—in this case, behavior and mental processes.

1.2

Describe the various fields of psychology. Psychologists are found in a number of different specialties:

Clinical psychologists help people with psychological disorders adjust to the demands of life.

Counseling psychologists typically see clients with adjustment problems but not serious psychological disorders.

School psychologists help school systems identify and assist students who have problems that interfere with learning.

Educational psychologists research theoretical issues related to learning, measurement, and child development.

Developmental psychologists study the changes—physical, cognitive, social, and emotional—that occur throughout the life span.

Personality psychologists identify and measure human traits and determine influences on human thought processes, feelings, and behavior.

Social psychologists are concerned with the nature and causes of individuals' thoughts, feelings, and behavior in social situations.

Environmental psychologists study the ways that people and the environment influence one another.

Experimental psychologists specialize in basic processes such as the nervous system, sensation and perception, learning and memory, thought, motivation, and emotion.

Industrial psychologists focus on the relationships between people and work.

Organizational psychologists study the behavior of people in organizations such as businesses.

Human factors psychologists make technical systems more user-friendly.

Consumer psychologists study the behavior of shoppers in an effort to predict and influence their behavior.

Health psychologists study the effects of stress on health problems such as headaches, cardiovascular disease, and cancer

Forensic psychologists apply principles of psychology to the criminal justice system.

Sport psychologists help people improve their performance in sports.

1.3

Describe the origins of psychology and identify people who made significant contributions to the field. An ancient contributor to the modern field of psychology, Aristotle argued that human behavior, like the movements of the stars and the seas, is subject to rules and laws. Today, as then, the subject matter of the study of human behavior includes the study of personality, sensation and perception, thought, intelligence, needs and motives, feelings and emotion, and memory. The following is a list of the historic schools of psychology and the major proponent(s) of each: Structuralism: Wilhelm Wundt; Functionalism: William James; Behaviorism: John B. Watson and B. F. Skinner; Gestalt Psychology: Max Wertheimer, Kurt Koffka, and Wolfgang Köhler; and Psychoanalysis: Sigmund Freud, Carl Jung, Alfred Adler, Karen Horney, and Erik Erikson.

1 What Is Psychology?

gender the culturally defined concepts of masculinity and femininity

critical thinking a way of evaluating the claims and comments of other people that involves skepticism and examination of evidence

1.5

scientific method an organized way of using experience and testing ideas to expand and refine knowledge

hypothesis in psychology, a specific statement about behavior or mental processes that is tested through research

correlation an association or relationship among variables, as we might find between height and weight or between study habits and school grades

selection factor a source of bias that may occur in research findings when participants are allowed to choose for themselves a certain treatment in a scientific study

sample part of a population

population a complete group of interest to researchers, from which a sample is drawn

random sample a sample drawn so that each member of a population has an equal chance of being selected to participate

stratified sample a sample drawn so that identified subgroups in the population are represented proportionately in the sample

volunteer bias a source of bias or error in research reflecting the prospect that people who offer to participate in research studies differ systematically from people who do not

case study a carefully drawn biography that may be obtained through interviews, questionnaires, and psychological tests

survey a method of scientific investigation in which a large sample of people answer questions about their attitudes or behavior

naturalistic observation a scientific method in which organisms are observed in their natural environments

correlational method a mathematical method of determining whether one variable increases or decreases as another variable increases or decreases

correlation coefficient a number between +1.00 and −1.00 that expresses the strength and direction (positive or negative) of the relationship between two variables

experiment a scientific method that seeks to confirm cause-and-effect relationships by introducing independent variables and observing their effects on dependent variables

independent variable a condition in a scientific study that is manipulated so that its effects may be observed

dependent variable a measure of an assumed effect of an independent variable

1.4

Identify theoretical perspectives from which today's psychologists view behavior and mental processes. There are several influential perspectives in contemporary psychology: biological, cognitive, humanistic–existential, psychodynamic, learning, and sociocultural.

- Psychologists with a *biological perspective* seek to understand the relationships between the brain, hormones, heredity, and evolution, on the one hand, and behavior and mental processes, on the other.
- Psychologists with a *cognitive perspective* investigate how we perceive and mentally represent the world by learning, memory, planning, problem solving, decision making, and language.
- The *humanistic–existential perspective* is cognitive in flavor, yet emphasizes more the role of subjective (personal) experience.
- Neoanalysts with a *psychodynamic perspective* focus less on the unconscious—as was done in Freud's day—and more on conscious choice and self-direction.
- The first of two learning perspectives, *behaviorists* emphasize environmental influences and the learning of habits through repetition and reinforcement. *Social-cognitive theorists,* in contrast, suggest that people can modify and create their environments, and engage in intentional learning by observing others.
- A psychologist with a *sociocultural perspective* studies the influences of ethnicity, gender, culture, and socioeconomic status on behavior and mental processes.

1.5

Explain how psychologists study behavior and metal processes, focusing on critical thinking, research methods, and ethical considerations. Psychologists, like other scientists, must use careful means to observe and measure behavior and the factors that influence behavior. Psychologists use evidence and critical thinking—the process of thoughtfully analyzing and probing the questions, statements, and arguments of others. The scientific method is a systematic way of organizing and expanding scientific knowledge. Daily experiences, common beliefs, and scientific observations all contribute to the development of theories. Psychological theories explain observations and lead to hypotheses about behavior and mental processes. Observations can then confirm the theory or lead to its refinement or abandonment. Many factors—such as the nature of the research sample—must be considered in interpreting the accuracy of the results of scientific research. Psychologists must also adhere to a number of ethical standards that are intended to promote individual dignity, human welfare, and scientific integrity. The standards are also intended to ensure that psychologists do not engage in harmful research methods or treatments.

experimental groups in experiments, groups whose members obtain the treatment

control groups in experiments, groups whose members do not obtain the treatment, while other conditions are held constant

placebo a bogus treatment that has the appearance of being genuine

blind in experimental terminology, unaware of whether or not one has received a treatment

double-blind study a study in which neither the subjects nor the observers know who has received the treatment

informed consent a participant's agreement to participate in research after receiving information about the purposes of the study and the nature of the treatments

debrief to explain the purposes and methods of a completed procedure to a participant

KEY TERMS

computerized axial tomography (CAT scan or CT scan) a method of brain imaging that passes a narrow X-ray beam through the head and measures structures that reflect the rays from various angles, enabling a computer to generate a three-dimensional image

positron emission tomography (PET scan) a method of brain imaging that injects a radioactive tracer into the bloodstream and assesses activity of parts of the brain according to the amount of glucose they metabolize

magnetic resonance imaging (MRI) a method of brain imaging that places a person in a magnetic field and uses radio waves to cause the brain to emit signals that reveal shifts in the flow of blood which, in turn, indicate brain activity

functional MRI (fMRI) a form of MRI that enables researchers to observe the brain "while it works" by taking repeated scans

medulla a oblong area of the hindbrain involved in regulation of heartbeat and respiration

pons a structure of the hindbrain involved in respiration, attention, and sleep and dreaming

cerebellum a part of the hindbrain involved in muscle coordination and balance

reticular formation a part of the brain involved in attention, sleep, and arousal

thalamus an area near the center of the brain involved in the relay of sensory information to the cortex and in the functions of sleep and attention

hypothalamus a bundle of nuclei below the thalamus involved in body temperature, motivation, and emotion

limbic system a group of structures involved in memory, motivation, and emotion

amygdala a part of the limbic system that apparently facilitates stereotypical aggressive responses

cerebrum the large mass of the forebrain, which consists of two hemispheres

cerebral cortex the wrinkled surface area (gray matter) of the cerebrum

corpus callosum a thick fiber bundle that connects the hemispheres of the cortex

somatosensory cortex the section of cortex in which sensory stimulation is projected. It lies just behind the central fissure in the parietal lobe

motor cortex the section of cortex that lies in the frontal lobe, just across the central fissure from the sensory cortex. Neural impulses in the motor cortex are linked to muscular responses throughout the body

SUMMARY

The geography of the cerebral cortex. The cortex has four lobes: frontal, parietal, temporal, and occipital. The visual area of the cortex is in the occipital lobe. The hearing or auditory cortex lies in the temporal lobe. The motor and somatosensory areas—shown here—face each other across the central fissure. Note that the face and the hands are "super-sized" in the motor and somatosensory areas. Why do you think this is so?

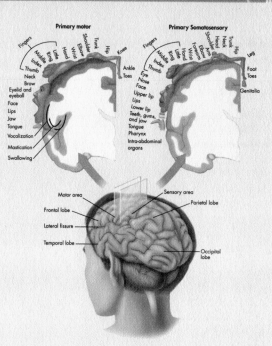

2.3

Explain the role of the endocrine system and list the endocrine glands. The glands of the endocrine system secrete hormones regulating development and activity. The pituitary gland secretes growth hormone, prolactin, and oxytocin. The pineal gland secretes the hormone melatonin, which helps regulate the sleep-wake cycle and may affect the onset of puberty. The thyroid regulates metabolism. The adrenal cortex produces steroids. The adrenal medulla secretes epinephrine, which increases the metabolic rate and stimulates general emotional arousal. The sex hormones are responsible for sexual differentiation and regulate the menstrual cycle in females.

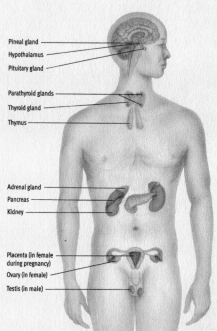

aphasia a disruption in the ability to understand or produce language

Wernicke's aphasia a language disorder characterized by difficulty comprehending the meaning of spoken language

Broca's aphasia a language disorder characterized by slow, laborious speech

epilepsy temporary disturbances of brain functions that involve sudden neural discharges

2.3

gland an organ that secretes one or more chemical substances such as hormones, saliva, or milk

endocrine system the body's system of ductless glands that secrete hormones and release them directly into the bloodstream

hormone a substance secreted by an endocrine gland that regulates various body functions

pituitary gland the gland that secretes growth hormone, prolactin, antidiuretic hormone, and other hormones

2.4

natural selection a core concept of the theory of evolution that holds that adaptive genetic variations among members of a species enable individuals with those variations to survive and reproduce

mutation a sudden variation in an inheritable characteristic, as distinguished from a variation that results from generations of gradual selection

evolutionary psychology the branch of psychology that studies the ways in which adaptation and natural selection are connected with mental processes and behavior

instinct a stereotyped pattern of behavior that is triggered by a particular stimulus and nearly identical among members of a species, even when they are reared in isolation

heredity the transmission of traits from parent to offspring by means of genes

genetics the area of biology that focuses on heredity

gene a basic unit of heredity, which is found at a specific point on a chromosome

chromosome a microscopic rod-shaped body in the cell nucleus carrying genes that transmit hereditary traits from generation to generation. Humans normally have 46 chromosomes

DNA acronym for deoxyribonucleic acid, the substance that forms the basic material of chromosomes. It takes the form of a double helix and contains the genetic code

polygenic referring to traits that are influenced by combinations of genes

genotype one's genetic makeup, based on the sequencing of the nucleotides we term A, C, G, and T

2.4

Describe evolutionary psychology and the connections between heredity, behavior, and mental processes. Evolutionary psychology studies the ways in which adaptation and natural selection are connected with mental processes and behavior. One of the concepts of evolutionary psychology is that not only physical traits but also many patterns of behavior, including social behavior, evolve and can be transmitted genetically from generation to generation. Behavior patterns that help an organism to survive and reproduce may be transmitted to the next generation. Such behaviors are believed to include aggression, strategies of mate selection, even altruism.

Heredity defines one's nature, which is based on biological structures and processes. Heredity refers to the biological transmission of traits that have evolved from generation to generation. The subfield of biology that studies heredity is called genetics.

Genes are the most basic building blocks of heredity. Genes regulate the development of specific traits and are segments of chromosomes. That is, chromosomes are made up of strings of genes. Each cell in the body contains 46 chromosomes arranged in 23 pairs. Chromosomes are large complex molecules of DNA (short for *deoxyribonucleic acid*), which has several chemical components.

Cell — Nucleus

Chromosomes

DNA

phenotype one's actual development and appearance, as based on one's genotype and environmental influences

nature the inborn, innate character of an organism

nurture the sum total of the environmental factors that affect an organism from conception onward

sex chromosomes the 23rd pair of chromosomes, whose genetic material determines the sex of the individual

Down syndrome a condition caused by an extra chromosome on the 21st pair and characterized by mental deficiency, a broad face, and slanting eyes

monozygotic (MZ) twins twins that develop from a single fertilized ovum that divides in two early in prenatal development. MZ twins thus share the same genetic code. Also called *identical twins*

dizygotic (DZ) twins twins that develop from two fertilized ova and who are thus as closely related as brothers and sisters in general. Also called *fraternal twins*

KEY TERMS

2.1

neuron a specialized cell of the nervous system that receives and transmits messages

glial cells cells that remove dead neurons and waste products from the nervous system nourish and insulate neurons, form myelin, and play a role in neural transmission of messages

dendrites rootlike structures, attached to the cell body of a neuron, that receive impulses from other neurons

axon a long, thin part of a neuron that transmits impulses to other neurons from branching structures called *axon terminals* or *terminal buttons*

myelin a fatty substance that encases and insulates axons, facilitating transmission of neural impulses

afferent neurons neurons that transmit messages from sensory receptors to the spinal cord and brain Also called *sensory neurons*

efferent neurons neurons that transmit messages from the brain or spinal cord to muscles and glands. Also called *motor neurons*

neural impulse the electrochemical discharge of a nerve cell, or neuron

polarize to ready a neuron for firing by creating an internal negative charge in relation to the body fluid outside the cell membrane

resting potential the electrical potential across the neural membrane when it is not responding to other neurons

depolarize to reduce the resting potential of a cell membrane from about 70 millivolts toward zero

action potential the electrical impulse that provides the basis for the conduction of a neural impulse along an axon of a neuron

all-or-none principle the fact that a neuron fires an impulse of the same strength whenever its action potential is triggered

refractory period a phase following firing during which a neuron is less sensitive to messages from other neurons and will not fire

synapse a junction between the axon terminals of one neuron and the dendrites or cell body of another neuron

neurotransmitters chemical substances involved in the transmission of neural impulses from one neuron to another

receptor site a location on a dendrite of a receiving neuron tailored to receive a neurotransmitter

acetylcholine (ACh) a neurotransmitter that controls muscle contractions

SUMMARY

2.1

Describe the nervous system, including neurons, neural impulses, and neurotransmitters. The nervous system regulates the body and is involved in thought processes, emotional responses, heartbeat, and motor activity. The central nervous system contains the brain and the spinal cord. The somatic nervous system transmits sensory information about skeletal muscles, skin, and joints and controls skeletal muscular activity. The autonomic nervous system regulates glands and activities like digestion. Neurons transmit information through electrochemical neural impulses. Their dendrites receive messages and their axons conduct messages, transmitting them to other cells via neurotransmitters. The autonomic nervous system also has two branches, or divisions: sympathetic and parasympathetic.

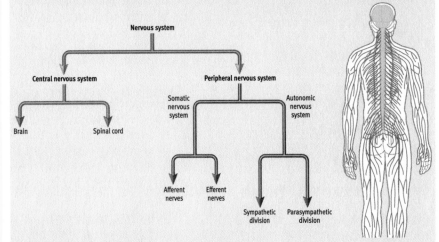

The Anatomy of a Neuron. "Messages" enter neurons through dendrites, are transmitted along the trunk-like axon, and then are sent from axon terminal buttons to muscles, glands, and other neurons. Axon terminal buttons contain sacs of chemicals called neurotransmitters. Neurotransmitters are released into the synaptic cleft, where many of them bind to receptor sites on the dendrites of the receiving neuron.

2 Biology and Psychology

hippocampus a structure of the brain that is involved in memory formation

dopamine a neurotransmitter that affects the ability to perceive pleasure, voluntary movement, and learning and memory; it is involved in Parkinson's disease and appears to play a role in schizophrenia

norepinephrine a neurotransmitter whose action is similar to that of the hormone epinephrine and that may play a role in depression

serotonin a neurotransmitter involved in emotional arousal and sleep; deficiencies of serotonin have been linked to eating disorders, alcoholism, depression, aggression, and insomnia

gamma-aminobutyric acid (GABA) an inhibitory neurotransmitter that apparently helps calm anxiety

endorphins inhibitory neurotransmitters that occur naturally in the brain and in the bloodstream and are similar to the narcotic morphine in their functions and effects

nerve a bundle of axons from many neurons

central nervous system the brain and spinal cord

peripheral nervous system the part of the nervous system consisting of the somatic nervous system and the autonomic nervous system

somatic nervous system the division of the peripheral nervous system that connects the central nervous system with sensory receptors, skeletal muscles, and the surface of the body

autonomic nervous system (ANS) the division of the peripheral nervous system that regulates glands and activities such as heartbeat, respiration, digestion, and dilation of the pupils

sympathetic division the branch of the ANS that is most active during emotional responses, such as fear and anxiety, that spend the body's reserves of energy

parasympathetic division the branch of the ANS that is most active during processes (such as digestion) that restore the body's reserves of energy

spinal cord a column of nerves within the spine that transmits messages from sensory receptors to the brain and from the brain to muscles and glands throughout the body

spinal reflex a simple, unlearned response to a stimulus that may involve only two neurons

gray matter the grayish neurons and neural segments that are involved in spinal reflexes

white matter axon bundles that carry messages from and to the brain

2.2

electroencephalograph (EEG) a method of detecting brain waves by means of measuring the current between electrodes placed on the scalp

The Parasympathetic and Sympathetic Branches of the Autonomic Nervous System (ANS). The parasympathetic branch of the ANS generally acts to replenish stores of energy in the body. The sympathetic branch is most active during activities that expend energy. The two branches of the ANS frequently have antagonistic effects on the organs they service.

2.2

List the structures of the brain and their functions.

The hindbrain includes the medulla, the pons, and the cerebellum. The reticular formation begins in the hindbrain but it ascends through the midbrain into the lower part of the forebrain.

Important structures of the forebrain include the thalamus, which serves as a relay station for sensory stimulation; the hypothalamus, which regulates body temperature and influences motivation and emotion; the limbic system, which is involved in memory, emotion, and motivation; and the cerebrum, which handles thinking and language. The outer fringe of the cerebrum is the cerebral cortex, which is divided into four lobes: frontal, parietal, temporal, and occipital.

The Parts of the Human Brain

The view of the brain, split top to bottom, shows some of the most important structures. The "valleys" in the cerebrum are called fissures.

3.1

sensation the stimulation of sensory receptors and the transmission of sensory information to the central nervous system

perception the process by which sensations are organized into an inner representation of the world

absolute threshold the minimal amount of energy that can produce a sensation

pitch the highness or lowness of a sound, as determined by the frequency of the sound waves

subliminal stimulation sensory stimulation below a person's absolute threshold for conscious perception

difference threshold the minimal difference in intensity required between two sources of energy so that they will be perceived as being different

Weber's constant the fraction of the intensity by which a source of physical energy must be increased or decreased so that a difference in intensity will be perceived

just noticeable difference (jnd) the minimal amount by which a source of energy must be increased or decreased so that a difference in intensity will be perceived

signal-detection theory the view that the perception of sensory stimuli involves the interaction of physical, biological, and psychological factors

feature detectors neurons in the sensory cortex that fire in response to specific features of sensory information such as lines or edges of objects

sensory adaptation the processes by which organisms become more sensitive to stimuli that are low in magnitude and less sensitive to stimuli that are constant or ongoing in magnitude

sensitization the type of sensory adaptation in which we become more sensitive to stimuli that are low in magnitude; also called *positive adaptation*

desensitization the type of sensory adaptation in which we become less sensitive to constant stimuli. Also called *negative adaptation*

3.2

visible light the part of the electromagnetic spectrum that stimulates the eye and produces visual sensations

hue the color of light, as determined by its wavelength

cornea transparent tissue forming the outer surface of the eyeball

iris a muscular membrane whose dilation regulates the amount of light that enters the eye

pupil the black-looking opening in the center of the iris, through which light enters the eye

lens a transparent body behind the iris that focuses an image on the retina

3.1

Define and differentiate between sensation and perception. Stimulation of the senses is an automatic process. It results from sources of energy, like light and sound, or from the presence of chemicals, as in smell and taste. Perception is an active process. Perception may begin with sensation, but it also reflects our experiences and expectations as it makes sense of sensory stimuli.

3.2

Identify the parts of the eye; explain the properties of light and the theories of color vision. It is visible light that triggers visual sensations. Yet visible light is just one small part of a spectrum of electromagnetic energy that surrounds us. All forms of electromagnetic energy move in waves, and different kinds of electromagnetic energy have signature wavelengths.

In both the eye and a camera, light enters through a narrow opening and is projected onto a sensitive surface. In the eye, the photosensitive surface is called the retina, and information concerning the changing images on the retina is transmitted to the brain.

3.3

Describe the organization of visual perception perceptions. Visual perception is the process by which we organize or make sense of the sensory impressions caused by the light that strikes our eyes. The attempt to identify the rules that govern these processes resulted in what are referred to as the laws of perceptual organization: figure-ground perception, and the laws of proximity, similarity, continuity, and common fate.

3.4

Identify the parts of the ear; describe the sense of hearing. Sound, or auditory stimulation, travels through the air like waves. A single cycle of compression and expansion is one wave of sound, which can occur many times in a second. The ear has three parts: the outer ear, middle ear, and inner ear. The outer ear funnels sound to the eardrum. Inside the eardrum, vibrations transmit sound to the inner ear. Vibrations in the cochlea transmit the sound to the auditory nerve.

3.5

Describe the chemical senses. In smell and taste, we sample molecules of substances. An odor is a sample of molecules of a substance in the air. Odors trigger firing of receptor neurons in the olfactory membrane high in each nostril. Taste is sensed through taste cells—receptor neurons located on taste buds.

3.6

Explain the properties of the skin senses and theoretical explanations for pain. The skin senses include touch, pressure, warmth, cold, and pain. Pain results when neurons called nociceptors in the skin are stimulated. The pain message to the brain is initiated by the release of chemicals such as prostaglandins, bradykinin, and P.

3.7

Describe the kinesthetic and vestibular senses. Kinesthesis and the vestibular sense alert us to our movements and body position without relying on vision. In kinesthesis, sensory information is fed back to the brain from sensory organs in the joints, tendons, and muscles. The vestibular sense makes use of sensory organs located in the semicircular canals and elsewhere in the ears to monitor the body's motion and position in relation to gravity.

3 Sensation and Perception

retina the area of the inner surface of the eye that contains rods and cones

photoreceptors cells that respond to light

bipolar cells neurons that conduct neural impulses from rods and cones to ganglion cells

ganglion cells neurons whose axons form the optic nerve

optic nerve the nerve that transmits sensory information from the eye to the brain

rods rod-shaped photoreceptors that are sensitive only to the intensity of light

cones cone-shaped photoreceptors that transmit sensations of color

fovea an area near the center of the retina that is dense with cones and where vision is consequently most acute

blind spot the area of the retina where axons from ganglion cells meet to form the optic nerve

visual acuity sharpness of vision

presbyopia a condition characterized by brittleness of the lens

dark adaptation the process of adjusting to conditions of lower lighting by increasing the sensitivity of rods and cones

complementary descriptive of colors of the spectrum that when combined produce white or nearly white light

afterimage the lingering visual impression made by a stimulus that has been removed

trichromatic theory the theory that color vision is made possible by three types of cones, some of which respond to red light, some to green, and some to blue

opponent-process theory the theory that color vision is made possible by three types of cones, some of which respond to red or green light, some to blue or yellow, and some to the intensity of light

trichromat a person with normal color vision

monochromat a person who is sensitive to black and white only and hence color-blind

dichromat a person who is sensitive to black–white and either red–green or blue–yellow and hence partially color-blind

3.3

closure the tendency to perceive a broken figure as being complete or whole

perceptual organization the tendency to integrate perceptual elements into meaningful patterns

proximity nearness; the perceptual tendency to group together objects that are near one another

similarity the perceptual tendency to group together objects that are similar in appearance

continuity the tendency to perceive a series of points or lines as having unity

common fate the tendency to perceive elements that move together as belonging together

3.8

Explain why psychologists are skeptical about extrasensory perception. Extrasensory perception (ESP)—also referred to as parapsychological or psi phenomena—refers to the perception of objects or events through means other than the known sensory organs. One method for studying *telepathy* (direct communication between minds) is the *ganzfeld procedure*. In all ESP studies, not one person has emerged who can reliably show ESP from one occasion to another and from one researcher to another.

top-down processing the use of contextual information or knowledge of a pattern in order to organize parts of the pattern

bottom-up processing the organization of the parts of a pattern to recognize, or form an image of, the pattern they compose

illusions sensations that give rise to misperceptions

stroboscopic motion a visual illusion in which the perception of motion is generated by a series of stationary images that are presented in rapid succession

monocular cues stimuli suggestive of depth that can be perceived with only one eye

perspective a monocular cue for depth based on the convergence (coming together) of parallel lines as they recede into the distance

texture gradient a monocular cue for depth based on the perception that closer objects appear to have rougher (more detailed) surfaces

motion parallax a monocular cue for depth based on the perception that nearby objects appear to move more rapidly in relation to our own motion

binocular cues stimuli suggestive of depth that involve simultaneous perception by both eyes

retinal disparity a binocular cue for depth based on the difference in the image cast by an object on the retinas of the eyes as the object moves closer or farther away

convergence a binocular cue for depth based on the inward movement of the eyes as they attempt to focus on an object that is drawing nearer

size constancy the tendency to perceive an object as being the same size even as the size of its retinal image changes according to the object's distance

color constancy the tendency to perceive an object as being the same color even though lighting conditions change its appearance

brightness constancy the tendency to perceive an object as being just as bright even though lighting conditions change its intensity

shape constancy the tendency to perceive an object as being the same shape although the retinal image varies in shape as it rotates

3.4

hertz (Hz) a unit expressing the frequency of sound waves; one hertz equals one cycle per second

decibel (dB) a unit expressing the loudness of a sound

cochlea the inner ear; the bony tube that contains the basilar membrane and the organ of Corti

basilar membrane a membrane that lies coiled within the cochlea

organ of Corti the receptor for hearing that lies on the basilar membrane in the cochlea

auditory nerve the axon bundle that transmits neural impulses from the organ of Corti to the brain

place theory the theory that the pitch of a sound is determined by the section of the basilar membrane that vibrates in response to the sound

frequency theory the theory that the pitch of a sound is reflected in the frequency of the neural impulses that are generated in response to the sound

3.5

flavor a complex quality of food and other substances that is based on their odor, texture, and temperature as well as their taste

olfactory nerve the nerve that transmits information concerning odors from olfactory receptors to the brain

taste cells receptor cells that are sensitive to taste

taste buds the sensory organs for taste. They contain taste cells and are located mostly on the tongue

3.7

kinesthesis the sense that informs us about the positions and motion of parts of our bodies

vestibular sense the sense of equilibrium that informs us about our bodies' positions relative to gravity

3.8

extrasensory perception (ESP) perception of objects or events through means other than the recognized sensory organs

KEY TERMS

4.1

consciousness a concept with many meanings, including sensory awareness of the world outside, direct inner awareness of one's thoughts and feelings, personal unity, and the waking state

selective attention the focus of one's consciousness on a particular stimulus

direct inner awareness knowledge of one's own thoughts, feelings, and memories without the use of sensory organs

preconscious in psychoanalytic theory, descriptive of material that is not in awareness but can be brought into awareness by focusing one's attention

unconscious in psychoanalytic theory, descriptive of ideas and feelings that are not available to awareness; also: without consciousness

repression in psychoanalytic theory, the automatic (unconscious) ejection of anxiety-evoking ideas, impulses, or images from awareness

suppression the deliberate, or conscious, placing of certain ideas, impulses, or images out of awareness

nonconscious descriptive of bodily processes such as growing hair, of which we cannot become conscious. We may "recognize" that our hair is growing, but we cannot directly experience the biological process

4.2

circadian rhythm a cycle that is connected with the 24-hour period of the earth's rotation

alpha waves rapid low-amplitude brain waves that have been linked to feelings of relaxation

nonrapid eye movement (NREM) sleep the first four stages of sleep

rapid eye movement (REM) sleep a stage of sleep characterized by rapid eye movements, which have been linked to dreaming

theta waves slow brain waves produced during the hypnagogic state

delta waves strong, slow brain waves usually emitted during stage 4 sleep

activation–synthesis model the view that dreams reflect activation of cognitive activity by the reticular formation and synthesis of this activity into a pattern

narcolepsy a "sleep attack" in which a person falls asleep suddenly and irresistibly

sleep apnea temporary absence or cessation of breathing while sleeping

sleep terrors frightening dreamlike experiences that occur during the deepest stage of NREM sleep; nightmares, in contrast, occur during REM sleep

SUMMARY

4.1

Define consciousness. The concept of consciousness has various meanings. One meaning is *sensory awareness* of the environment. Another aspect of consciousness is *selective attention*. Selective attention means focusing one's consciousness on a particular stimulus. We are conscious of—or have *direct inner awareness* of—thoughts, images, emotions, and memories. Sigmund Freud, the founder of psychoanalysis, differentiated between the thoughts and feelings of which we are *conscious*, or aware, and those that are preconscious and unconscious. *Preconscious* material is not currently in awareness but is readily available. Still other mental events are *unconscious*, or unavailable, to awareness under most circumstances. Some bodily processes, such as the firings of neurons, are *nonconscious*. They cannot be experienced through sensory awareness or direct inner awareness. In the sense that the *self* forms intentions and guides its own behavior, consciousness is *self*. The word conscious also refers to the *waking state* as opposed, for example, to sleep.

4.2

Explain the nature of sleep and various sleep disorders. When we sleep, we slip from consciousness to unconsciousness. When we are conscious, our brains emit waves characterized by certain frequencies (numbers of waves per second) and amplitudes (heights—an index of strength). Brain waves are rough indicators of the activity of neurons. The strength or energy of brain waves is expressed in volts (an electrical unit). When we sleep, our brains emit waves that differ from those emitted when we are conscious. Sleep disorders seriously interfere with daily functioning and include insomnia, narcolepsy, and sleep apnea. The less-common sleep disorders—sleep terrors, bedwetting, and sleepwalking—occur during deep (stage 3 or 4) sleep.

Awake — beta waves (low amplitude, high frequency)

Awake

Drowsy — alpha waves (higher amplitude, slower frequency)

Stage 1 sleep — theta waves (low frequency, low amplitude)

Sleep spindle   K complex

Stage 2 sleep — sleep spindles and the K complex

NREM Sleep

Stage 3 sleep — beginning of delta waves (low frequency, high amplitude)

Stage 4 sleep — delta waves continue to increase in amplitude

REM Sleep
Occurs when we re-enter Stage 1, about ninety minutes after falling asleep (frequently called *paradoxical sleep*)

REM sleep — brain-wave patterns are very similar to those of initial NREM stage 1

4 Consciousness

4.3

hypnosis an altered state of consciousness in which people are highly suggestible and behave as though they are in a trance

role theory a theory that explains hypnotic events in terms of the person's ability to act as though he or she were hypnotized

response set theory the view that response expectancies play a key role in the production of the experiences suggested by the hypnotist

transcendental meditation (TM) the simplified form of meditation brought to the United States by the Maharishi Mahesh Yogi and used as a method for coping with stress

mindfulness meditation (MM) a form of meditation that provides clients with techniques they can use to focus on the present moment rather than ruminate about problems

biofeedback training (BFT) the systematic feeding back to an organism information about a bodily function so that the organism can gain control of that function

electromyograph (EMG) an instrument that measures muscle tension

4.4

psychoactive substances drugs that have psychological effects such as stimulation or distortion of perceptions

depressant a drug that lowers the rate of activity of the nervous system

stimulant a drug that increases activity of the nervous system

substance abuse persistent use of a substance even though it is causing or compounding problems in meeting the demands of life

substance dependence loss of control over use of a substance; biologically speaking, dependence is typified by tolerance, withdrawal symptoms, or both

tolerance habituation to a drug, with the result that increasingly higher doses of the drug are needed to achieve similar effects

abstinence syndrome a characteristic cluster of withdrawal symptoms that result from sudden decrease in an addictive drug's level of usage

opiates a group of narcotics derived from the opium poppy that provide a euphoric rush and depress the nervous system

narcotics drugs used to relieve pain and induce sleep. The term is usually reserved for opiates

opioids chemicals that act on opiate receptors but are not derived from the opium poppy

barbiturate an addictive depressant used to relieve anxiety or induce sleep

amphetamines stimulants derived from alpha-methyl-beta-phenyl-ethylamine, a colorless liquid consisting of carbon, hydrogen, and nitrogen

4.3

Explain the natures and uses of hypnosis, meditation, and biofeedback in altering consciousness. Hypnosis—an altered state of consciousness in which people are highly suggestible and behave as though they are in a trance—is derived from the Greek word for sleep. Hypnotism can be used as an anesthetic in dentistry, childbirth, and medical procedures. Some psychologists use hypnosis to help clients reduce anxiety, overcome fears, or lessen the perception of chronic pain. One common form of meditation, transcendental meditation (TM), was brought to the United States by the Maharishi Mahesh Yogi in 1959. People practice TM by concentrating on mantras—words or sounds that are claimed to help the person achieve an altered state of consciousness. Mindfulness meditation (MM), as opposed to TM, makes no pretense of achieving spiritual goals. Instead, MM provides clients with mantra-like techniques they can use to focus on the present moment rather than ruminate about problems. Biofeedback is a system that provides, or "feeds back," information about a bodily function to an organism. Through biofeedback training, people have learned to gain voluntary control over a number of functions that are normally automatic, such as heart rate and blood pressure.

4.4

Define substance abuse and dependence, identify categories of psychoactive drugs, and explain their allures and dangers. Substance abuse and dependence usually begin with experimental use in adolescence. People experiment with drugs for various reasons, including curiosity, conformity to peer pressure, parental use, rebelliousness, escape from boredom or pressure, and excitement or pleasure. Use of a substance may be reinforced by peers or by the drug's positive effects on mood and its reduction of anxiety, fear, and stress. Many people use drugs as a form of self-medication for anxiety and depression, even low self-esteem. For people who are physiologically dependent, avoidance of withdrawal symptoms is also reinforcing. Psychoactive drugs include depressants (alcohol, opiates, and barbiturates), stimulants (amphetamines, cocaine, and nicotine), and hallucinogens (LSD, marijuana, PHP, and mescaline).

How Cocaine Produces Euphoria and Why People "Crash"

hydrocarbons chemical compounds consisting of hydrogen and carbon

second-hand smoke smoke from the tobacco products and exhalations of other people; also referred to as passive smoking

hallucinogen a substance that causes hallucinations

marijuana the dried vegetable matter of the Cannabis sativa plant

LSD lysergic acid diethylamide; a hallucinogen

flashbacks distorted perceptions or hallucinations that occur days or weeks after lsd usage but mimic the LSD experience

mescaline a hallucinogen derived from the mescal (peyote) cactus

phencyclidine (PCP) another hallucinogen whose name is an initialism for its chemical structure

CHAPTER REVIEW

KEY TERMS

5.1

learning (1) according to behaviorists, a relatively permanent change in behavior that results from experience (2) according to cognitive theorists, the process by which organisms make relatively permanent changes in the way they represent the environment because of experience

5.2

classical conditioning a simple form of learning in which a neutral stimulus comes to evoke the response usually evoked by another stimulus by being paired repeatedly with the other stimulus

reflex a simple unlearned response to a stimulus

stimulus an environmental condition that elicits a response

unconditioned stimulus (UCS) a stimulus that elicits a response from an organism prior to conditioning

unconditioned response (UCR) an unlearned response to an unconditioned stimulus

orienting reflex an unlearned response in which an organism attends to a stimulus

conditioned stimulus (CS) a previously neutral stimulus that elicits a conditioned response because it has been paired repeatedly with a stimulus that already elicited that response

conditioned response (CR) a learned response to a conditioned stimulus

extinction the process by which stimuli lose their ability to evoke learned responses because the events that had followed the stimuli no longer occur; the learned responses are said to be *extinguished*

spontaneous recovery the recurrence of an extinguished response as a function of the passage of time

generalization in conditioning, the tendency for a conditioned response to be evoked by stimuli that are similar to the stimulus to which the response was conditioned

discrimination in conditioning, the tendency for an organism to distinguish between a conditioned stimulus and similar stimuli that do not forecast an unconditioned stimulus

higher-order conditioning a classical conditioning procedure in which a previously neutral stimulus comes to elicit the response brought forth by a *conditioned* stimulus by being paired repeatedly with that conditioned stimulus

biological preparedness readiness to acquire a certain kind of conditioned response due to the biological makeup of the organism

SUMMARY

5.1

Define learning. From the strict behaviorist perspective, learning is a relatively permanent change in behavior that arises from practice or experience. The behaviorist perspective plays down the roles of cognition and choice. Cognitive psychologists define learning as the process by which organisms make relatively permanent changes in the way they represent the environment because of experience.

5.2

Describe principles and methods of classical conditioning. Classical conditioning is a simple form of associative learning in which organisms come to anticipate or associate events with one another. When a neutral stimulus (like a bell ringing) and one that evokes a response (like dog food) are paired together repeatedly, the conditioned neutral stimulus will begin to trigger a response (like salivation) on its own.

KIND OF LEARNING: Classical conditioning
Major theorists: Ivan Pavlov (known for basic research with dogs); John B. Watson (known as the originator of behaviorism)

WHAT IS LEARNED
Association of events; anticipations, signs, expectations; automatic responses to new stimuli

HOW IT IS LEARNED
A neutral stimulus is repeatedly paired with a stimulus (an unconditioned stimulus, or UCS) that elicits a response (an unconditioned response, or UCR) until the neutral stimulus produces a response (conditioned response, or CR) that anticipates and prepares for the unconditioned stimulus. At this point, the neutral stimulus has become a conditioned stimulus (CS).

5.3

Describe the principles and methods of operant conditioning. Operant conditioning is defined as a simple form of learning in which an organism learns to engage in certain behavior because of the effects of that behavior. Positive reinforcers increase the probability that a behavior will occur when they are applied. Food and approval usually serve as positive reinforcers. Negative reinforcers increase the probability that a behavior will occur when the reinforcers are removed.

KIND OF LEARNING: Operant conditioning
Major theorists: Edward Thorndike and B. F. Skinner

WHAT IS LEARNED
Behavior that operates on, or affects, the environment to produce consequences

HOW IT IS LEARNED
A response is rewarded or reinforced so that it occurs with greater frequency in similar situations.

counterconditioning a fear-reduction technique in which pleasant stimuli are associated with fear-evoking stimuli so that the fear-evoking stimuli lose their aversive qualities

flooding a behavioral fear-reduction technique based on principles of classical conditioning; fear-evoking stimuli (CSs) are presented continuously in the absence of actual harm so that fear responses (CRs) are extinguished

systematic desensitization a behavioral fear-reduction technique in which a hierarchy of fear-evoking stimuli is presented while the person remains relaxed

5.3

law of effect Thorndike's view that pleasant events stamp in responses, and unpleasant events stamp them out

reinforce to follow a response with a stimulus that increases the frequency of the response

operant behavior behavior that operates on, or manipulates, the environment

operant conditioning a simple form of learning in which an organism learns to engage in behavior because it is reinforced

operant the same as an operant behavior

positive reinforcer a reinforcer that when presented increases the frequency of an operant

negative reinforcer a reinforcer that when removed increases the frequency of an operant

primary reinforcer an unlearned reinforcer whose effectiveness is based on the biological makeup of the organism and not on learning

secondary reinforcer a stimulus that gains reinforcement value through association with established reinforcers

conditioned reinforcer another term for a secondary reinforcer

discriminative stimulus in operant conditioning, a stimulus that indicates that reinforcement is available

continuous reinforcement a schedule of reinforcement in which every correct response is reinforced

partial reinforcement one of several reinforcement schedules in which not every correct response is reinforced

fixed-interval schedule a schedule in which a fixed amount of time must elapse between the previous and subsequent times that reinforcement is available

variable-interval schedule a schedule in which a variable amount of time must elapse between the previous and subsequent times that reinforcement is available

fixed-ratio schedule a schedule in which reinforcement is provided after a fixed number of correct responses

variable-ratio schedule a schedule in which reinforcement is provided after a variable number of correct responses

Procedure	Behavior	Consequence	Change in behavior
Use of positive reinforcement	Behavior (Studying)	Positive reinforcer (Teacher approval) is *presented* when student studies	Frequency of behavior *increases* (Student studies more)
Use of negative reinforcement	Behavior (Studying)	Negative reinforcer (Teacher disapproval) is *removed* when student studies	Frequency of behavior *increases* (Student studies more)

5.4

Describe cognitive factors in learning. Learning is often more complex than association and reinforcement; it involves searching for information, weighing evidence, and making decisions. Cognitive psychologists study mental structures, schemas, templates, and information processing to prove that learning can occur without conditioning. Latent learning—like a cognitive map of a maze—may not be revealed without motivation. Contingency theory suggests that learning occurs when a conditioned stimulus provides information about the unconditioned stimulus. Finally, observational learning makes it possible to acquire skills and knowledge by watching others rather than through direct experience.

© Stockbyte/First Light

KIND OF LEARNING:
Observational learning
Major theorists: Albert Bandura; Julian Rotter; Walter Mischel

WHAT IS LEARNED
Expectations (if–then relationships), knowledge, and skills

HOW IT IS LEARNED
A person observes the behavior of another person (live or through media such as films, television, or books) and its effects

shaping a procedure for teaching complex behaviors that at first reinforces approximations of the target behavior

successive approximations behaviors that are progressively closer to a target behavior

5.4

cognitive map a mental representation of the layout of one's environment

latent learning learning that is hidden or concealed

contingency theory the view that learning occurs when stimuli provide information about the likelihood of the occurrence of other stimuli

observational learning the acquisition of knowledge and skills through the observation of others (who are called *models*) rather than by means of direct experience

model an organism that engages in a response that is then imitated by another organism

KEY TERMS

6.1

explicit memory memory that clearly and distinctly expresses (explicates) specific information

episodic memory memories of events experienced by a person or that take place in the person's presence

semantic memory general knowledge, as opposed to episodic memory

implicit memory memory that is suggested (implied) but not plainly expressed, as illustrated in the things that people do but do not state clearly

priming the activation of specific associations in memory, often as a result of repetition and without making a conscious effort to access the memory

retrospective memory memory for past events, activities, and learning experiences, as shown by explicit (episodic and semantic) and implicit memories

prospective memory memory to perform an act in the future, as at a certain time or when a certain event occurs

6.2

encoding modifying information so that it can be placed in memory; the first stage of information processing

storage the maintenance of information over time; the second stage of information processing

maintenance rehearsal mental repetition of information to keep it in memory

elaborative rehearsal the kind of coding in which new information is related to information that is already known

retrieval the location of stored information and its return to consciousness; the third stage of information processing

memory the processes by which information is encoded, stored, and retrieved

6.3

sensory memory the type or stage of memory first encountered by a stimulus; sensory memory holds impressions briefly, but long enough so that series of perceptions are psychologically continuous

memory trace an assumed change in the nervous system that reflects the impression made by a stimulus

icon a mental representation of a visual stimulus that is held briefly in sensory memory

iconic memory the sensory register that briefly holds mental representations of visual stimuli

eidetic imagery the maintenance of detailed visual memories over several minutes

echo a mental representation of an auditory stimulus (sound) that is held briefly in sensory memory

SUMMARY

6.1

Define memory and differentiate between types of memories. Memory is the processes by which information is encoded, stored, and retrieved. *Explicit memory*—also referred to as declarative memory—is memory for specific information. Two kinds of explicit memories are identified according to the type of information they hold: episodic memories are memories of the things that happen to us or take place in our presence ("I remember…") and semantic memory refers to general knowledge ("I know…") *Implicit memory*—also referred to as nondeclarative memory—is memory of how to perform a procedure or skill; it is the act itself, doing something, like riding a bike.

Retrospective memory is the recalling of information that has been previously learned. *Episodic, semantic,* and *implicit memories* involve remembering things that were learned. *Prospective memory* refers to remembering to do things in the future.

6.2

Explain the processes of memory. The first stage of information processing is changing information so that we can place it in memory: encoding. When we encode information, we transform it into psychological formats that can be represented mentally. To do so, we commonly use visual, auditory, and semantic codes. The second memory process is storage. Storage means maintaining information over time. The third memory process is retrieval. The retrieval of stored information means locating it and returning it to consciousness. The phrase below might be more easily recalled if you think of it as an acronym of the first two letters of the name of a nation (hint, hint).

THUNSTOFAM

6.3

Explain the stages of memory. The Atkinson–Shiffrin model proposes that there are three stages of memory: (a) sensory memory, (b) short-term memory, and (c) long-term

Three Stages of Memory: The Atkinson–Shiffrin Model

6 Memory: Remembrance of Things Past—and Future

echoic memory the sensory register that briefly holds mental representations of auditory stimuli

short-term memory the type or stage of memory that can hold information for up to a minute or so after the trace of the stimulus decays

working memory another term for short-term memory

serial-position effect the tendency to recall more accurately the first and last items in a series

chunk a stimulus or group of stimuli that are perceived as a discrete piece of information

displace in memory theory, to cause information to be lost from short-term memory by adding new information

long-term memory the type or stage of memory capable of relatively permanent storage

repression in Freud's psychodynamic theory, the ejection of anxiety-evoking ideas from conscious awareness

schema a way of mentally representing the world, such as a belief or an expectation, that can influence perception of persons, objects, and situations

tip-of-the-tongue (TOT) phenomenon the feeling that information is stored in memory although it cannot be readily retrieved

context-dependent memory information that is better retrieved in the context in which it was encoded and stored, or learned

state-dependent memory information that is better retrieved in the physiological or emotional state in which it was encoded and stored, or learned

6.4

nonsense syllables meaningless sets of two consonants, with a vowel sandwiched in between, that are used to study memory

paired associates nonsense syllables presented in pairs in experiments that measure recall

method of savings a measure of retention in which the difference between the number of repetitions originally required to learn a list and the number of repetitions required to relearn the list after a certain amount of time has elapsed is calculated

savings the difference between the number of repetitions originally required to learn a list and the number of repetitions required to relearn the list after a certain amount of time has elapsed

interference theory the view that we may forget stored material because other learning interferes with it

retroactive interference the interference of new learning with the ability to retrieve material learned previously

proactive interference the interference by old learning with the ability to retrieve material learned recently

dissociative amnesia loss of memory of personal information thought to stem from psychological conflict or trauma

infantile amnesia inability to recall events that occur prior to the age three or so; also termed childhood amnesia

hippocampus a structure in the limbic system that plays an important role in the formation of new memories

anterograde amnesia failure to remember events that occur after physical trauma because of the effects of the trauma

retrograde amnesia failure to remember events that occur prior to physical trauma because of the effects of the trauma

memory. Part a shows that sensory information impacts on the registers of sensory memory. Memory traces are held briefly in sensory memory before decaying. If we attend to the information, much of it can be transferred to short-term memory (STM). Part b: Information may be maintained in STM through maintenance rehearsal or elaborative rehearsal. Otherwise, it may decay or be displaced. Part c: Once information is transferred to long-term memory (LTM), it may be filed away indefinitely. However, if the information in LTM is organized poorly, or if we cannot find cues to retrieve it, it can be lost.

6.4

Identify contributors to forgetting. Recognition, recall, and relearning are three basic memory tasks that have been used by psychologists to measure forgetting. Nonsense syllables have been used in studying each of them. According to interference theory, we forget material in short-term and long-term memory because newly learned material interferes with it. The two basic types of interference are retroactive interference and proactive interference. According to Sigmund Freud, we are motivated to repress painful memories and unacceptable ideas because they produce anxiety, guilt, and shame. Freud also believed that young children repress memories of aggressive impulses and perverse lusts toward their parents, which would explain why people could not recall episodes in their early childhoods (infantile amnesia). Adults also experience amnesia, although usually for biological reasons, as in the cases of anterograde and retrograde amnesia.

6.5

Describe the biological aspects of memory. Psychologists assume that mental processes such as the encoding, storage, and retrieval of information—that is, memory—are accompanied by changes in the brain. Much research on the biology of memory focuses today on the roles of stimulants, neurons, neurotransmitters, hormones, and structures in the brain.

One Avenue to Long-Term Potentiation (LTP)

LTP can occur via the action of neurotransmitters such as serotonin and glutamate at synapses. Structurally, LTP can also occur as shown in Parts A and B, when dendrites sprout new branches that connect with transmitting axons, increasing the amount of stimulation they receive.

Part A

Part B

6.5

engram (1) an assumed electrical circuit in the brain that corresponds to a memory trace (2) an assumed chemical change in the brain that accompanies learning (from the greek en-, meaning "in," and gramma, meaning "something that is written or recorded")

long-term potentiation (LTP) enhanced efficiency in synaptic transmission that follows brief, rapid stimulation

misinformation effect the shaping of bogus or slanted memories by providing inaccurate information as, for example, in the form of "leading questions"

KEY TERMS

7.1

cognition mental activity involved in understanding, processing, and communicating information

thinking paying attention to information, mentally representing it, reasoning about it, and making decisions about it

concept a mental category that is used to class together objects, relations, events, abstractions, ideas, or qualities that have common properties

prototype a concept of a category of objects or events that serves as a good example of the category

exemplar a specific example

algorithm a systematic procedure for solving a problem that works invariably when it is correctly applied

systematic random search an algorithm for solving problems in which each possible solution is tested according to a particular set of rules

heuristics rules of thumb that help us simplify and solve problems

means–end analysis a heuristic device in which we try to solve a problem by evaluating the difference between the current situation and the goal

mental set the tendency to respond to a new problem with an approach that was successfully used with similar problems

insight in Gestalt psychology, a sudden perception of relationships among elements of the mentally represented elements of a problem that permits its solution

incubation in problem solving, a process that sometimes occurs when we stand back from a frustrating problem for a while and the solution "suddenly" appears

functional fixedness tendency to view an object in terms of its name or familiar usage

representativeness heuristic a decision-making heuristic in which people make judgments about samples according to the populations they appear to represent

availability heuristic a decision-making heuristic in which our estimates of frequency or probability of events are based on how easy it is to find examples

anchoring and adjustment heuristic a decision-making heuristic in which a presumption or first estimate serves as a cognitive anchor; as we receive additional information, we make adjustments but tend to remain in the proximity of the anchor

framing effect the influence of wording, or the context in which information is presented, on decision making

SUMMARY

7.1

Define thinking and the various concepts involved in thinking. Thinking entails attending to information, representing it mentally, reasoning about it, and making judgments and decisions about it; thinking means making conscious, planned attempts to make sense of our world, as well as categorizing new concepts and manipulating relationships among concepts. Factors that affect problem solving include: level of expertise; whether you fall prey to a mental set; whether you develop insight into the problem; whether you engage in incubation; and whether you experience functional fixedness.

7.2

Describe how language develops. Language is the communication of thoughts and feelings by means of symbols that are arranged according to rules of grammar. True language is distinguished from the communication systems of lower animals by properties such as semanticity, infinite creativity, and displacement. Language development reflects the interactions between the influences of heredity (nature) and the environment (nurture). Learning theorists see language developing according to imitation and reinforcement, where parents serve as models.

7.3

Identify the concept of intelligence and the techniques used to measure intelligence. Intelligence is broadly thought of as the underlying ability to understand the world and cope with its challenges. Intelligence allows people to think, understand complex ideas, reason, solve problems, learn from experience, and adapt to the environment. Two intelligence tests are the Stanford-Binet intelligence scale and the Wechsler scales.

Analytical intelligence
(Academic ability)
Abilities to solve problems, compare and contrast, judge, evaluate, and criticize

Creative intelligence
(Creativity and insight)
Abilities to invent, discover, suppose, or theorize

Practical intelligence
("Street smarts")
Abilities to adapt to the demands of one's environment and apply knowledge in practical situations

Approximate Distribution of IQ Scores

7.2

language the communication of information by means of symbols arranged according to rules of grammar

semanticity meaning; the quality of language in which words are used as symbols for objects, events, or ideas

infinite creativity the capacity to combine words into original sentences

displacement the quality of language that permits one to communicate information about objects and events in another time and place

linguistic-relativity hypothesis the view that language structures the way we view the world

holophrase a single word used to express complex meanings

overregularization the application of regular grammatical rules for forming inflections (e.g., past tense and plurals) to irregular verbs and nouns

psycholinguistic theory the view that language learning involves an interaction between environmental factors and an inborn tendency to acquire language

language acquisition device (LAD) in psycholinguistic theory, neural "prewiring" that facilitates the child's learning of grammar

7.3

intelligence a general mental capability that involves the ability to reason, plan, solve problems, think abstractly, comprehend complex ideas, learn quickly, and learn from experience

g Spearman's symbol for general intelligence, which he believed underlay more specific abilities

s Spearman's symbol for specific factors, or s factors, which he believed accounted for individual abilities

primary mental abilities according to Thurstone, the basic abilities that make up intelligence

creativity the ability to generate novel and useful solutions to problems

convergent thinking a thought process that narrows in on the single best solution to a problem

divergent thinking a thought process that attempts to generate multiple solutions to problems

mental age (MA) the accumulated months of credit that a person earns on the Stanford–Binet intelligence scale

intelligence quotient (IQ) (1) originally, a ratio obtained by dividing a child's score (or mental age) on an intelligence test by chronological age (2) generally, a score on an intelligence test

7.4

heritability the degree to which the variations in a trait from one person to another can be attributed to, or explained by, genetic factors

7.4

Describe the controversy surrounding intelligence testing. The role that nature and nurture play in intellectual functioning is a controversial topic in psychology. Education contributes to intelligence. For example, Head Start programs enhance IQ scores, achievement scores, and academic skills of disadvantaged children. Adoptee studies suggest a genetic influence on intelligence. But they also suggest a role for environmental influence. All in all, studies generally suggest that the heritability of intelligence is between 40% and 60%. Intellectual functioning would appear to reflect the interaction of genetic, physical, personal, and sociocultural factors.

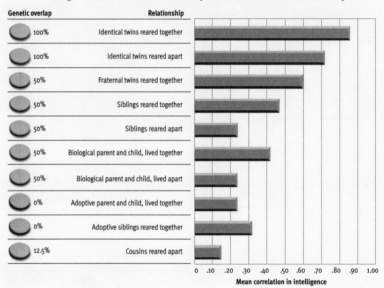

Findings of Studies of the Relationship Between IQ Scores and Heredity

The Complex Web of Factors That Affect Intellectual Functioning

Genetic factors

A stimulating environment in the home and in the schools

Health
Socioeconomic status
Flexibility
Achievement motivation
Academic/educational adjustment
Belief that education and
    achievement are keys to
    self-development and
    fulfillment

8.1

motivation the state in which an organism experiences an inducement or incentive to do something

motive a hypothetical state within an organism that propels the organism toward a goal

need a state of deprivation

drive a condition of arousal in an organism that is associated with a need

incentive an object, person, or situation perceived as being capable of satisfying a need

8.2

instinct an inherited disposition to activate specific behavior patterns that are designed to reach certain goals

drive-reduction theory the view that organisms learn to engage in behaviors that have the effect of reducing drives

homeostasis the tendency of the body to maintain a steady state

self-actualization according to Maslow and other humanistic psychologists, self-initiated striving to become what one is capable of being

hierarchy of needs Maslow's ordering of needs from most basic (physiological needs such as hunger and thirst) to most elaborate and sophisticated (self-actualization)

8.3

satiety the state of being satisfied; fullness

ventromedial nucleus (VMN) a central area on the underside of the hypothalamus that appears to function as a stop-eating center

hyperphagic characterized by excessive eating

lateral hypothalamus an area at the side of the hypothalamus that appears to function as a start-eating center

aphagic characterized by under-eating

anorexia nervosa a life-threatening eating disorder characterized by dramatic weight loss and a distorted body image

bulimia nervosa an eating disorder characterized by repeated cycles of binge eating and purging

activating effect the arousal-producing effects of sex hormones that increase the likelihood of sexual behavior

estrus the periodic sexual excitement of many female mammals, as governed by levels of sex hormones

8.4

sexual response cycle Masters and Johnson's model of sexual response, which consists of four stages or phases: excitement, plateau, orgasm, and resolution

8.1

Define motivation including needs, drives, and incentives. The psychology of motivation concerns the whys of behavior. Motives are hypothetical states that activate behavior toward goals and may take the form of needs, drives, and/or incentives. Needs come in two types: physiological (needs necessary for survival) and psychological (needs for achievement, power, self-esteem, etc.). Physiological and psychological needs differ in two ways: psychological needs are not necessarily based on deprivation; psychological needs may be acquired through experience. Needs give rise to drives that arouse us to action. Incentives are objects, persons, or situations viewed as capable of satisfying a need or as desirable for their own sake.

8.2

Identify the theories of motivation. Psychologists do not agree about the precise nature of motivation. The evolutionary perspective holds that animals are naturally prewired to respond to certain stimuli in certain ways. The drive reductionism and homeostasis perspective holds that primary drives trigger arousal (tension) and activate behavior. Organisms engage in behaviors that reduce tension and are motivated to maintain a steady state (homeostasis). Other theorists hold with the stimulus motivation perspective—that an organism is motivated to increase stimulation, not reduce a drive. Stimulus motivation provides an evolutionary advantage: Animals that are active and motivated to learn about their environment are more likely to survive. A humanistic theorist, Abraham Maslow believed that people are motivated by the conscious desire for personal growth. Maslow's hierarchy of needs ranges from physiological needs such as hunger and thirst through self-actualization (self-initiated striving to become whatever we believe we are capable of being). Critics argue that there is too much individual variation for the hierarchy of motives to apply to everyone.

Hierarchy of Needs

(pyramid labels from top to bottom: Self-actualization; Esteem needs; Love and belongingness; Safety needs; Physiological needs)

8.3

Describe the biological and psychological contributions to hunger.
Biological mechanisms that regulate hunger include stomach pangs associated with stomach contractions, the functions of the hypothalamus, blood sugar level, and receptors in the liver. The ventromedial nucleus of the hypothalamus is the "stop-eating" center of the brain; the lateral hypothalamus is the "start-eating" center of the brain. Psychological factors also influence hunger.

Problems associated with unhealthy weight are on the upswing. The origins of eating disorders aren't entirely clear. Exposure to cultural standards and role models that emphasize excessive slenderness plays a major role. Eating disorders are also more common when the family environment is negative—possibly a history of child abuse or exposure to high parental expectations.

8 Motivation and Emotion

vasocongestion engorgement of blood vessels with blood, which swells the genitals and breasts during sexual arousal

myotonia muscle tension

excitement phase the first phase of the sexual response cycle, which is characterized by muscle tension, increases in the heart rate, and erection in the male and vaginal lubrication in the female

plateau phase the second phase of the sexual response cycle, which is characterized by increases in vasocongestion, muscle tension, heart rate, and blood pressure in preparation for orgasm

ejaculation the process of propelling seminal fluid (semen) from the penis

orgasm the height or climax of sexual excitement, involving involuntary muscle contractions, release of sexual tensions and usually, subjective feelings of pleasure

resolution phase the fourth phase of the sexual response cycle, during which the body gradually returns to its prearoused state

refractory period in the sexual response cycle, a period of time following orgasm during which an individual is not responsive to sexual stimulation

organizing effect the directional effect of sex hormones—for example, along typical male or female patterns of mating

sexual orientation the directionality of one's sexual and romantic interests; that is, whether one is sexually attracted to and desires to form a romantic relationship with, members of the other gender or of one's own gender

heterosexual referring to people who are sexually aroused by, and interested in forming romantic relationships with, people of the other gender

homosexual referring to people who are sexually aroused by, and interested in forming romantic relationships with people of the same gender

8.6

emotion a state of feeling that has cognitive, physiological, and behavioral components

autonomic nervous system (ANS) the division of the peripheral nervous system that regulates glands and activities such as heartbeat, respiration, digestion, and dilation of the pupils

sympathetic nervous system the branch of the autonomic nervous system that is most active during processes that spend body energy from stored reserves, such as in a fight-or-flight reaction to a predator or when you are anxious about a big test

parasympathetic nervous system the branch of the autonomic nervous system that is most active during processes that restore reserves of energy to the body, such as relaxing and eating

8.4

Explain the role of sex hormones and the sexual response cycle in human sexuality. Sexual motivation, although natural, is also strongly influenced by religious and moral beliefs, cultural tradition, folklore, and superstition. What is considered "normal" depends on the society in which one lives. Level of education is connected with sexual behavior. Much about the development of sexual orientation remains speculative. Sex hormones have activating effects: they affect the sex drive and promote sexual response. Sex hormones also have organizing effects: they motivate lower animals toward masculine or feminine mating patterns. The *sexual response cycle* describes the four phases (*excitement, plateau, orgasm,* and *resolution*) that occur in the body as men and women become sexually aroused.

8.5

Describe achievement motivation. Henry Murray developed the Thematic Apperception Test (TAT) in an attempt to assess motivation. The TAT contains cards with pictures and drawings that are subject to various interpretations. Subjects are to construct stories about the picture.

Performance goals are usually met through extrinsic rewards. Examples of extrinsic rewards include praise and income. Learning goals usually lead to *intrinsic rewards.* Self-satisfaction is an example of an intrinsic reward. Extrinsic, or tangible, rewards can serve as an incentive for maintaining good grades. An intrinsic goal—e.g., feeling capable and intelligent—tends to have more long-lasting effects.

8.6

Identify the theoretical explanations of emotions. Emotions are feeling states with physiological, cognitive, and behavioral components. A physiological reaction can involve the sympathetic nervous system and result in rapid heartbeat, breathing, sweating, or muscle tension. Behavioral tendencies occur with emotions. For example, fear leads to avoidance or escape, and anger may lead to "pay-back" behaviors. Parasympathetic nervous system arousal can also occur. Joy, grief, jealousy, disgust, and so on all have cognitive, physiological, and behavioral components.

Various perspectives hold that cognitive processes—or a combination of arousal and thoughts—may determine the emotional response (see graphic below). All three theories have aspects of correctness but none fully explain emotions.

Theories of Emotion

A. James–Lange   B. Cannon–Bard   C. Cognitive appraisal

positive psychology the field of psychology that is about personal well-being and satisfaction; joy, sensual pleasure, and happiness; and optimism and hope for the future

facial-feedback hypothesis the view that stereotypical facial expressions can contribute to stereotypical emotions

KEY TERMS

9.1

zygote a fertilized ovum (egg cell)

germinal stage the first stage of prenatal development, during which the dividing mass of cells has not become implanted in the uterine wall

amniotic sac a sac within the uterus that contains the embryo or fetus

placenta a membrane that permits the exchange of nutrients and waste products between the mother and her developing child but does not allow the maternal and fetal bloodstreams to mix

umbilical cord a tube between the mother and her developing child through which nutrients and waste products *are* conducted

9.2

reflex a simple unlearned response to a stimulus

rooting the turning of an infant's head toward a touch, such as by the mother's nipple

fixation time the amount of time spent looking at a visual stimulus

assimilation according to Piaget, the inclusion of a new event into an existing schema

schema according to Piaget, a hypothetical mental structure that permits the classification and organization of new information

accommodation according to Piaget, the modification of schemas so that information inconsistent with existing schemas can be integrated or understood

object permanence recognition that objects removed from sight still exist, as demonstrated in young children by continued pursuit

sensorimotor stage the first of Piaget's stages of cognitive development, characterized by coordination of sensory information and motor activity, early exploration of the environment, and lack of language

preoperational stage the second of Piaget's stages, characterized by illogical use of words and symbols, spotty logic, and egocentrism

egocentrism according to Piaget, the assumption that others view the world as one does oneself

conservation according to Piaget, recognition that basic properties of substances such as weight and mass remain the same when superficial features change

objective responsibility according to Piaget, the assignment of blame according to the amount of damage done rather than the motives of the actor

concrete operational stage Piaget's third stage, characterized by logical thought concerning tangible objects, conservation, and subjective morality

SUMMARY

9.1

Explain prenatal development and the role that sex hormones play.
The fetal stage lasts from the beginning of the third month until birth. By the end of the third month, the major organ systems and the fingers and toes have formed. In the middle of the fourth month, the mother usually detects the first fetal movements. By the end of the sixth month, the fetus moves its limbs so vigorously that mothers often feel that they are being kicked. The fetus opens and shuts its eyes, sucks its thumb, alternates between periods of being awake and sleeping, and responds to light. It also turns somersaults, which can be perceived by the mother. During the three months prior to birth, the organ systems of the fetus continue to mature. The heart and lungs become increasingly capable of sustaining independent life. The fetus gains about $5\frac{1}{2}$ pounds and doubles in length. Newborn boys average about $7\frac{1}{2}$ pounds and newborn girls about 7 pounds.

9.2

Explain the physical, cognitive, moral, social, and emotional development of children. Childhood begins with birth. During infancy—the first two years of childhood—dramatic gains in height and weight continue. Babies usually double their birth weight in about five months and triple it by their first birthday. Their height increases by about 10 inches in the first year. Children grow another four to six inches during the second year and gain some four to seven pounds. After that, they gain about two to three inches a year until they reach the adolescent growth spurt. Other aspects of physical development in childhood include reflexes and perceptual development. Theories in cognitive development include Piaget's stage theory, Vygotsky's sociocultural theory, and Kohlberg's theory of moral development. Erikson's theory of psychosocial development and Ainsworth's attachment studies explore critical aspects of social and emotional development in childhood.

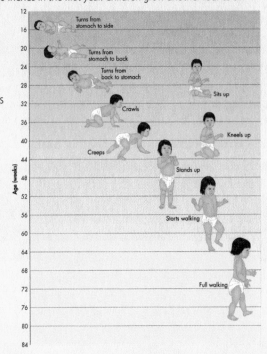

9.3

Explain the physical, cognitive, moral, social, and emotional development of adolescents. Adolescence is bounded by the onset of puberty—the period during which the body becomes sexually mature—and the assumption of adult responsibilities. Except for infancy, more changes occur during adolescence than during any other time. One of the most noticeable physical developments of adolescence is a growth spurt that lasts two to three years and ends the gradual changes in height and weight that characterize most of childhood. Within this short span of years,

decentration simultaneous focusing on more than one dimension of a problem, so that flexible, reversible thought becomes possible

subjective moral judgment according to Piaget, moral judgment that is based on the motives of the perpetrator

zone of proximal development (ZPD) Vygotsky's term for the situation in which a child carries out tasks with the help of someone who is more skilled, frequently an adult who represents the culture in which the child develops

scaffolding Vygotsky's term for temporary cognitive structures or methods of solving problems that help the child as he or she learns to function independently

preconventional level according to Kohlberg, a period during which moral judgments are based largely on expectation of rewards or punishments

conventional level according to Kohlberg, a period during which moral judgments largely reflect social conventions; a "law and order" approach to morality

attachment the enduring affectional tie that binds one person to another

contact comfort a hypothesized primary drive to seek physical comfort through contact with another

ethologist a scientist who studies the characteristic behavior patterns of species of animals

critical period a period of time when an instinctive response can be elicited by a particular stimulus

imprinting a process occurring during a critical period in the development of an organism, in which that organism responds to a stimulus in a manner that will afterward be difficult to modify

authoritative parents parents who are strict and warm; authoritative parents demand mature behavior but use reason rather than force in discipline

authoritarian parents parents who are rigid in their rules and who demand obedience for the sake of obedience

permissive parents parents who impose few, if any, rules and who do not supervise their children closely

uninvolved parents parents who generally leave their children to themselves

9.3

adolescence the period of life bounded by puberty and the assumption of adult responsibilities

puberty the period of physical development during which sexual reproduction first becomes possible

secondary sex characteristics characteristics that distinguish the sexes, such as distribution of body hair and depth of voice, but that are not directly involved in reproduction

menarche the beginning of menstruation

formal operational stage Piaget's fourth stage, characterized by abstract logical thought and deduction from principles

adolescents grow some 8 to 12 inches. According to Piaget, children undergo three stages of cognitive development prior to adolescence: sensorimotor, preoperational, and concrete operational. The stage of formal operations is the final stage in Piaget's theory, and it represents cognitive maturity. Formal operational thought generally begins at about the beginning of adolescence. The major achievements of the stage of formal operations involve classification, logical thought, and the ability to hypothesize. Central features are the ability to think about ideas as well as objects and to group and classify ideas, such as symbols and statements. Kohlberg's research around the levels of moral reasoning found postconventional moral judgments were absent until about age 16, when stage 5 reasoning is shown by about 20% of adolescents. According to Erik Erikson's eight stages of psychosocial development, the fifth stage—ego identity versus role diffusion—occurs in adolescence.

9.4

Explain the features of emerging adulthood. In earlier days, adolescents made a transition directly into adulthood. Now many of them in affluent nations spend time in what some theorists consider a new period of development, roughly spanning the ages of 18 to 25; emerging adulthood. During this time, many young people attend college and graduate school, sort out identity issues, and create meaningful life plans.

9.5

Explain the physical, cognitive, moral, social, and emotional development of adults. A number of physical changes occur during the later years. The reasons for aging, however, are not yet completely understood. People can also affect the pace of their aging by eating properly, exercising, maintaining a positive outlook, and finding and meeting challenges that are consistent with their abilities. People are at the height of their cognitive powers during early adulthood. Cognitive development in adulthood has many aspects—creativity, memory functioning, and intelligence. Changes in social and emotional development during adulthood are probably the most "elastic" or fluid. According to Erik Erikson, young adulthood is characterized by the task of developing abiding intimate relationships; middle adulthood involves being productive and contributing to younger generations; the challenge for late adulthood is to maintain one's sense of identity despite physical deterioration.

imaginary audience an aspect of adolescent egocentrism; the belief that other people are as concerned with our thoughts and behaviors as we are

personal fable another aspect of adolescent egocentrism; the belief that our feelings and ideas are special and unique and that we are invulnerable

postconventional level according to Kohlberg, a period during which moral judgments are derived from moral principles and people look to themselves to set moral standards

ego identity Erikson's term for a firm sense of who one is and what one stands for

role diffusion Erikson's term for lack of clarity in one's life roles (due to failure to develop ego identity)

9.4

emerging adulthood period of development, roughly spanning the ages of 18 to 25, during which time many young people in affluent na-

tions attend college and graduate school, sort out identity issues, and create life plans

9.5

menopause the cessation of menstruation

crystallized intelligence one's lifetime of intellectual achievement, as shown largely through vocabulary and knowledge of world affairs

fluid intelligence mental flexibility as shown in learning rapidly to solve new kinds of problems

Alzheimer's disease a progressive form of mental deterioration characterized by loss of memory, language, problem solving, and other cognitive functions

empty-nest syndrome a sense of depression and loss of purpose felt by some parents when the youngest child leaves home

sandwich generation people in middle adulthood who are responsible for meeting the needs of their children yet also responsible for aging parents

10.1

personality the reasonably stable patterns of emotions, motives, and behavior that distinguish one person from another

psychodynamic theory Sigmund Freud's perspective, which emphasizes the importance of unconscious motives and conflicts as forces that determine behavior

id the psychic structure, present at birth, that represents physiological drives and is fully unconscious

ego the second psychic structure to develop, characterized by self-awareness, planning, and delay of gratification

superego the third psychic structure, which functions as a moral guardian and sets forth high standards for behavior

psychosexual development in psychoanalytic theory, the process by which libidinal energy is expressed through different erogenous zones during different stages of development

oral stage the first stage of psychosexual development, during which gratification is hypothesized to be attained primarily through oral activities

anal stage the second stage of psychosexual development, when gratification is attained through anal activities

phallic stage the third stage of psychosexual development, characterized by a shift of libido to the phallic region

Oedipus complex a conflict of the phallic stage in which the boy wishes to possess his mother sexually and perceives his father as a rival in love

Electra complex a conflict of the phallic stage in which the girl longs for her father and resents her mother

latency a phase of psychosexual development characterized by repression of sexual impulses

genital stage the mature stage of psychosexual development, characterized by preferred expression of libido through intercourse with an adult of the other gender

analytical psychology Jung's psychoanalytic theory, which emphasizes the collective unconscious and archetypes

collective unconscious Jung's hypothesized store of vague memories that represent the history of humankind

inferiority complex feelings of inferiority hypothesized by Adler to serve as a central motivating force

creative self according to Adler, the self-aware aspect of personality that strives to achieve its full potential

10.1

Describe the psychoanalytical perspective and how it contributed to the study of personality.

Focus of Research
- Unconscious conflict
- Drives such as sex, aggression, and the need for superiority come into conflict with law, social rules, and moral codes

View of Personality
- Three structures of personality—id, ego, superego
- Five stages of psychosexual development— oral, anal, phallic, latency, genital

10.2

Explain the trait perspective and the "Big Five" trait model.

Focus of Research
- Rely on the mathematical technique of *factor analysis* to catalog and organize basic human personality traits

View of Personality
- Based on theory of Hippocrates and work of Gordon Allport
- Eysenck's two-dimensional model: introversion– extraversion and emotional stability–instability
- Current emphasis on the five-factor model (the "Big Five")— extraversion, agreeableness, conscientiousness, neuroticism, openness to experience

10.3

Identify the contributions of learning theory to understand personality.

Focus of Research
- Behaviorists focus on situational factors that determine behavior
- Social cognitive emphasis on observational learning and person variables—competencies subjective values and self-efficacy expectations

View of Personality
- Watson saw personality as plastic and determined by external, situational variables
- Skinner believed that society conditions individuals into wanting certain things
- Bandura developed social cognitive theory, which focuses on learning by observation and on the cognitive processes that underlie personal differences

10 Personality: Theory and Measurement

individual psychology Adler's psychoanalytic theory, which emphasizes feelings of inferiority and the creative self

psychosocial development Erikson's theory of personality and development, which emphasizes social relationships and eight stages of growth

ego identity a firm sense of who one is and what one stands for

10.2

trait a relatively stable aspect of personality that is inferred from behavior and assumed to give rise to consistent behavior

introversion a trait characterized by intense imagination and the tendency to inhibit impulses

extraversion a trait characterized by tendencies to be socially outgoing and to express feelings and impulses freely

10.3

social cognitive theory a cognitively oriented learning theory in which observational learning and person variables such as values and expectancies play major roles in individual differences

gender-typing the process by which males and females come to display behavior patterns consistent with stereotypical masculine and feminine gender roles

gender-schema theory a cognitive view of gender-typing that proposes that once girls and boys become aware of their anatomic sex, they begin to blend their self-expectations and self-esteem with the ways in which they fit the gender roles prescribed in a given culture

10.4

humanism the view that people are capable of free choice, self-fulfillment, and ethical behavior

existentialism the view that people are completely free and responsible for their own behavior

self-actualization in humanistic theory, the innate tendency to strive to realize one's potential

unconditional positive regard a persistent expression of esteem for the value of a person, but not necessarily an unqualified acceptance of all of the person's behaviors

conditional positive regard judgment of another person's value on the basis of the acceptability of that person's behaviors

conditions of worth standards by which the value of a person is judged

10.5

sociocultural perspective the view that focuses on the roles of ethnicity, gender, culture, and socioeconomic status in personality formation, behavior, and mental processes

10.4

Describe the humanistic-existential perspective on personality.

Focus of Research
- The experience of being human and developing one's unique potential within an often hostile environment

View of Personality
- People have inborn drives to become what they are capable of being
- Carl Rogers' unconditional positive regard leads to self-esteem, which facilitates individual growth and development

10.5

Describe the sociocultural perspective on personality.

Focus of Research
- The roles of ethnicity, gender, culture, and socioeconomic status in personality formation and behavior

View of Personality
- Development differs in individualistic and collectivist societies
- Discrimination, poverty, and acculturation affect self-concept and self-esteem

A. Independent view of the self   B. Interdependent view of the self

10.6

Describe the different kinds of tests psychologists use to measure personality.
The two most widely used types of personality tests are objective tests and projective tests. Objective tests present respondents with a standardized group of test items in the form of a questionnaire. Responses are limited to a specific range of answers. The MMPI is the most widely used objective test.

In projective tests, people are shown ambiguous stimuli such as inkblots or drawings and asked to say what they look like. People project their own personalities into their responses. The Rorschach inkblot test and the Thematic Apperception Test (TAT) are examples of projective tests.

individualist a person who defines herself or himself in terms of personal traits and gives priority to his or her own goals

collectivist a person who defines herself or himself in terms of relationships to other people and groups and gives priority to group goals

acculturation the process of adaptation in which immigrants and native groups identify with a new, dominant culture by learning about that culture and making behavioral and attitudinal changes

10.6

reliability in psychological testing, the consistency or stability of test scores from one testing to another

validity in psychological testing, the degree to which a test measures what it is supposed to measure

standardization in psychological testing, the process by which one obtains and organizes test scores from various population groups, so that the results of a person's completing a test can be compared to those of others of his or her sex, in his or her age group, and so on

objective tests tests whose items must be answered in a specified, limited manner; tests whose items have concrete answers that are considered correct

projective test a psychological test that presents ambiguous stimuli onto which the test taker projects his or her own personality in making a response

CHAPTER REVIEW

11

11.1

stress the demand that is made on an organism to adapt

eustress (YOU-stress) stress that is healthful

health psychology the field of psychology that studies the relationships between psychological factors (e.g., attitudes, beliefs, situational influences, and behavior patterns) and the prevention and treatment of physical illness

pathogen a microscopic organism (e.g., bacterium or virus) that can cause disease

conflict being torn in different directions by opposing motives; feelings produced by being in conflict

catastrophize to interpret negative events as being disastrous; to "blow out of proportion"

type A behavior behavior characterized by a sense of time urgency, competitiveness, and hostility

11.2

self-efficacy expectations our beliefs that we can bring about desired changes through our own efforts

psychological hardiness a cluster of traits that buffer stress and are characterized by commitment, challenge, and control

locus of control the place (locus) to which an individual attributes control over the receiving of reinforcers—either inside or outside the self

internals people who perceive the ability to attain reinforcements as being largely within themselves

externals people who perceive the ability to attain reinforcements as being largely outside themselves

11.1

Define stress and identify various sources of stress. Psychological factors such as stress, behavior patterns, and attitudes can lead to or aggravate illness. People can cope with stress, and in fact there is such a thing as healthful stress (eustress). Small stressors, such as daily hassles, can threaten or harm our well-being and lead to nervousness, worrying, inability to get started, feelings of sadness, and feelings of loneliness. Hassles can predict health problems such as heart disease, cancer, and athletic injuries.

Conflict is the feeling of being pulled in two or more directions by opposing motives and can be frustrating and stressful. There are four types of conflict as illustrated in the figure below: Approach-approach conflict (A) is the least stressful type. Each of two goals is desirable and both are within reach. Avoidance-avoidance conflict (B) is more stressful. A person is motivated (M) to avoid each of two negative goals. Avoiding one of them requires approaching the other. In approach-avoidance conflict, (C), the same goal produces both approach and avoidance motives. Multiple approach-avoidance conflict (D) occurs when each of several alternative courses of action has pluses and minuses. Decision-making can be stressful—especially when there is no clear correct choice.

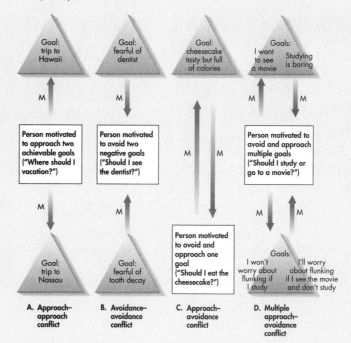

11.2

Identify the psychological moderators of stress. Psychological factors can influence, or moderate, the effects of stress. For example, self-efficacy expectations affect our ability to withstand stress (high self-efficacy expectations are accompanied by relatively lower levels of adrenaline and noradrenaline in the bloodstream). People who are self-confident are less prone to be disturbed by adverse events. Humor, laughter, and feelings of happiness may have beneficial effects on the immune system. On the other hand, there is a significant relationship between negative life events and stress scores, although the ability to predict a stressor apparently moderates its impact. Control and even the illusion of control can also moderate impact. Social support also seems to act as a buffer against the effects of stress. Sources of social support include: emotional concern, instrumental aid, information, appraisal, and socializing.

11.3

general adaptation syndrome (GAS) Selye's term for a hypothesized three-stage response to stress

alarm reaction the first stage of the GAS, which is triggered by the impact of a stressor and characterized by sympathetic activity

fight-or-flight reaction an innate adaptive response to the perception of danger

resistance stage the second stage of the GAS, characterized by prolonged sympathetic activity in an effort to restore lost energy and repair damage; also called the adaptation stage

exhaustion stage the third stage of the GAS, characterized by weakened resistance and possible deterioration

immune system the system of the body that recognizes and destroys foreign agents (antigens) that invade the body

leukocytes white blood cells (derived from the Greek words leukos, meaning "white," and kytos, literally meaning "a hollow" but used to refer to cells)

antigen a substance that stimulates the body to mount an immune system response to it (for antibody generator)

antibodies substances formed by white blood cells that recognize and destroy antigens

inflammation increased blood flow to an injured area of the body, resulting in redness, warmth, and an increased supply of white blood cells

11.4

biopsychosocial having to do with the interactions of biological, psychological, and sociocultural factors

11.3

Describe the impact of stress on the body. The General Adaptation Syndrome, proposed by Selye, is a cluster of bodily changes that occur in three stages—alarm, resistance, and exhaustion. The alarm reaction is triggered by perception of a stressor. The reaction mobilizes or arouses the body. This mobilization is the basis for the instinctive fight-or-flight reaction. The alarm reaction involves bodily changes that are initiated by the brain and regulated by the endocrine system and the sympathetic division of the autonomic nervous system (ANS). If the stressor isn't removed, we enter the adaptation or resistance stage, in which the body attempts to restore lost energy and repair bodily damage. If the stressor isn't dealt with, we may enter the exhaustion stage—the body is depleted of the resources required for combating stress.

Stress suppresses the immune system. Feelings of control and social support can moderate these effects. The immune system has several functions that combat disease. One function is production of white blood cells (leukocytes). These cells recognize and eradicate foreign agents and unhealthy cells. Foreign substances are called antigens. The body generates specialized proteins or antibodies to fight antigens. Inflammation is another function of the immune system. This is increased blood supply, which floods the region with white blood cells. One of the reasons stress exhausts us is that it stimulates the production of steroids. Steroids suppress the functioning of the immune system. Persistent secretion of steroids decreases inflammation and interferes with the formation of antibodies. We become more vulnerable to various illnesses.

Hypothalamus

Pituitary

The hypothalamus secretes corticotrophin-releasing hormone (CRH)

CRH causes the pituitary gland to secrete adrenocorticotrophic hormone (ACTH)

Stressor

ACTH then causes the adrenal cortex to secrete corticosteroids

Adrenal glands

Kidneys

The adrenal medulla releases a mixture of adrenaline and noradrenaline

11.4

Explain the relationships between psychology and health. The biopsychosocial approach to health recognizes that there are complex factors (biological, psychological, and sociocultural factors) that contribute to health and illness and that there is no single, simple answer. Biological factors such as pathogens, inoculations, injuries, age, gender, and a family history of disease may be the most obvious cause of disease, although genetics certainly plays a role. Coronary heart disease (CHD) is the leading cause of death in the United States. Risks for CHD include family history, physiological conditions, patterns of consumption, Type A behavior, hostility and holding in feelings of anger, job strain, chronic fatigue and chronic emotional strain, sudden stressors, and a physically inactive lifestyle. Cancer is the second-leading cause of death in the United States. Cancer is characterized by the development of abnormal, or mutant, cells that may take root anywhere in the body. If not controlled early, the cancerous cells may metastasize—establish colonies elsewhere in the body. Risk factors for cancer include heredity and behaviors such as smoking, drinking alcohol, eating animal fats, sunbathing, and prolonged psychological conditions such as depression.

KEY TERMS

insanity a legal term descriptive of a person judged to be incapable of recognizing right from wrong or of conforming his or her behavior to the law

12.1

psychological disorders patterns of behavior or mental processes that are connected with emotional distress or significant impairment in functioning

hallucination a perception in the absence of sensory stimulation that is confused with reality

ideas of persecution erroneous beliefs that one is being victimized or persecuted

12.2

anxiety disorders disorders characterized by excessive worrying, fear of losing control, nervousness, and inability to relax

specific phobia persistent fear of a specific object or situation

claustrophobia fear of tight, small places

acrophobia fear of high places

social phobia an irrational, excessive fear of public scrutiny

agoraphobia fear of open, crowded places

panic disorder recurrent experiencing of attacks of extreme anxiety in the absence of external stimuli that usually elicit anxiety

generalized anxiety disorder feelings of dread and foreboding and sympathetic arousal of at least six months' duration

obsessive–compulsive disorder (OCD) an anxiety disorder defined by recurrent, anxiety-provoking thoughts or images that seem irrational and beyond control (obsessions) and seemingly irresistible urges to engage in thoughts or behaviors that tend to reduce the anxiety (compulsions)

post-traumatic stress disorder (PTSD) a disorder that follows a distressing event outside the range of normal human experience and that is characterized by features such as intense fear, avoidance

acute stress disorder a disorder, like PTSD, that is characterized by feelings of anxiety and helplessness and caused by a traumatic event; acute stress disorder occurs within a month of the event and lasts from two days to four weeks

12.3

dissociative disorders disorders in which there are sudden, temporary changes in consciousness or self-identity

dissociative amnesia a dissociative disorder marked by loss of memory or self-identity; skills and general knowledge are usually retained

SUMMARY

12.1

Define psychological disorders and describe their prevalence. Psychological disorders are characterized by unusual behavior, faulty perception of reality, personal distress, self-defeating behavior, dangerous behavior, and socially unacceptable behavior. The American Psychiatric Association groups disorders on the basis of clinical syndromes and factors related to adjustment. About half of us will experience a psychological disorder at one time or another.

The Granger Collection, New York

12.2

Describe the symptoms and possible origins of anxiety disorders. Anxiety disorders are characterized by feelings of dread and sympathetic arousal. They include phobias, panic disorder, generalized anxiety, obsessive-compulsive disorder, and stress disorders. Some people may be genetically predisposed to acquire certain fears. Cognitive theorists focus on ways in which people interpret threats.

12.3

Describe the symptoms and possible origins of dissociative disorders. Dissociative disorders are characterized by sudden, temporary changes in consciousness or self-identity. They include dissociative amnesia, dissociative fugue, and dissociative identity disorder (multiple personality). Dissociative disorders may help people keep disturbing memories or ideas out of mind, especially memories of child abuse.

12.4

Describe the symptoms and possible origins of somatoform disorders. People with somatoform disorders display or complain of physical problems, although no medical evidence for them can be found. They include conversion disorder and hypochondriasis. Somatoform disorders may reflect the relative benefits of focusing on physical symptoms or features rather than life problems that most people would consider to be more important.

12.5

Describe the symptoms and possible origins of mood disorders. Mood disorders involve disturbances in expressed emotions. Major depression is characterized by persistent feelings of sadness, loss of interest, feelings of worthlessness or guilt, and inability to concentrate. Bipolar disorder is characterized by mood swings between elation and depression. Genetic factors may be involved in mood disorders. Research emphasizes possible roles for learned helplessness, attributional styles, and underutilization of serotonin in depression. People who are depressed are more likely than other people to make internal, stable, and global attributions for failures. Most people who commit suicide do so because of depression.

Michael Blann/Stone/Getty Images

12 Psychological Disorders

dissociative fugue a dissociative disorder in which one experiences amnesia and then flees to a new location

dissociative identity disorder (DID) (formerly termed multiple personality disorder) a disorder in which a person appears to have two or more distinct identities or personalities that may alternately emerge

12.4

somatoform disorders disorders in which people complain of physical (somatic) problems even though no physical abnormality can be found

conversion disorder a disorder in which anxiety or unconscious conflicts are "converted" into physical symptoms that often have the effect of helping the person cope with anxiety or conflict

la belle indifférence a French term descriptive of the lack of concern for their (imagined) medical problem sometimes shown by people with conversion disorders

hypochondriasis a somatoform disorder characterized by persistent belief that one is ill despite lack of medical findings

12.5

mood disorders a disturbance in expressed emotions, generally involving excessive or inappropriate sadness or elation

major depressive disorder a serious to severe depressive disorder in which the person may show loss of appetite, psychomotor retardation, and impaired reality testing

psychomotor retardation slowness in motor activity and (apparently) in thought

bipolar disorder a disorder in which the mood alternates between two extreme poles (elation and depression); also referred to as manic depression

manic elated, showing excessive excitement

rapid flight of ideas rapid speech and topic changes, characteristic of manic behavior

learned helplessness a possible explanation for some depressive behavior, based on findings that organisms in aversive situations learn to show inactivity when their behavior is not reinforced

attributional style the tendency to attribute one's behavior to internal or external factors, stable or unstable factors, and global or specific factors

neuroticism a personality trait characterized largely by persistent anxiety

12.6

Describe the symptoms, types, and possible origins of schizophrenia. Schizophrenia is characterized by disturbances in thought and language, perception and attention, motor activity, mood, and social interaction. Schizophrenia is connected with smaller brains in some people, especially fewer synapses in the prefrontal region, and larger ventricles. A genetic vulnerability to schizophrenia may interact with other factors, such as stress, complications during pregnancy and childbirth, and quality of parenting, to cause the disorder to develop. People with schizophrenia may also use more dopamine than other people do.

12.7

Describe the symptoms and possible origins of personality disorders. Personality disorders are inflexible, maladaptive behavior patterns that impair personal or social functioning. Genetic factors may be involved in personality disorders. Antisocial personality disorder may develop from some combination of genetic vulnerability (less gray matter in the prefrontal cortex of the brain, which may provide lower-than-normal levels of arousal), inconsistent discipline, and a cynical worldview.

12.6

positive symptoms those symptoms of schizophrenia that indicate the presence of inappropriate behavior, such as hallucinations, delusions, agitation, and inappropriate giggling

negative symptoms those symptoms of schizophrenia that reflect the absence of appropriate behavior, such as blank faces, monotonic voices, and motionless bodies

mutism refusal to talk

delusions false, persistent beliefs that are unsubstantiated by sensory or objective evidence

stupor a condition in which the senses, thought, and movement are dulled

paranoid schizophrenia a type of schizophrenia characterized primarily by delusions—commonly of persecution—and by vivid hallucinations

disorganized schizophrenia a type of schizophrenia characterized by disorganized delusions and vivid hallucinations

catatonic schizophrenia a type of schizophrenia characterized by striking motor impairment

waxy flexibility a feature of catatonic schizophrenia in which people can be molded into postures that they maintain for quite some time

12.7

personality disorders enduring patterns of maladaptive behavior that are sources of distress to the individual or others

paranoid personality disorder a personality disorder characterized by persistent suspiciousness but not involving the disorganization of paranoid schizophrenia

schizotypal personality disorder a personality disorder characterized by oddities of thought and behavior but not involving bizarre psychotic behaviors

schizoid personality disorder a personality disorder characterized by social withdrawal

borderline personality disorder a personality disorder characterized by instability in relationships, self-image, mood, and lack of impulse control

antisocial personality disorder the diagnosis given a person who is in frequent conflict with society, yet who is undeterred by punishment and experiences little or no guilt and anxiety

avoidant personality disorder a personality disorder in which the person is unwilling to enter relationships without assurance of acceptance because of fears of rejection and criticism

13.1

psychotherapy a systematic interaction between a therapist and a client that brings psychological principles to bear on influencing the client's thoughts, feelings, or behavior to help the client overcome abnormal behavior or adjust to problems in living

asylum an institution for the care of the mentally ill

13.2

psychodynamic therapy a type of psychotherapy that is based on Freud's thinking and that assumes that psychological problems reflect early childhood experiences and internal conflicts

psychoanalysis Freud's method of psychotherapy

catharsis in psychoanalysis, the expression of repressed feelings and impulses to allow the release of the psychic energy associated with them

free association in psychoanalysis, the uncensored uttering of all thoughts that come to mind

resistance the tendency to block the free expression of impulses and primitive ideas—a reflection of the defense mechanism of repression

transference responding to one person (such as a psychoanalyst) in a way that is similar to the way one responded to another person (such as a parent) in childhood

wish fulfillment in dreams, the acting out of ideas and impulses that are repressed when one is conscious

ego analyst a psychodynamically oriented therapist who focuses on the conscious, coping behavior of the ego instead of the hypothesized, unconscious functioning of the id

13.3

humanistic therapy a form of psychotherapy that focuses on the client's subjective, conscious experience in the "here and now"

client-centered therapy Carl Rogers's method of psychotherapy, which emphasizes the creation of a warm, therapeutic atmosphere that frees clients to engage in self-exploration and self-expression

Gestalt therapy Fritz Perls' form of psychotherapy, which attempts to integrate conflicting parts of the personality through directive methods designed to help clients perceive their whole selves

13.4

behavior therapy systematic application of the principles of learning to the direct modification of a client's problem behaviors

systematic desensitization Wolpe's method for reducing fears by associating a hierarchy of images of fear-evoking stimuli with deep muscle relaxation

13.1

Define psychotherapy and describe the history of treatment of psychological disorders. Psychotherapy uses psychological principles to help clients overcome psychological disorders or problems. Throughout most of history, it has been generally assumed that psychological disorders represent possession, and cruel "treatment" methods such as exorcism have been used. Asylums, mental hospitals, and community treatment are relatively recent innovations.

13.2

Describe traditional psychoanalysis and short-term psychodynamic therapies. The main method of a Freudian psychoanalysis is free association, but dream analysis and interpretations are also used. Modern approaches are briefer and more directive, and the therapist and client usually sit face to face.

13.3

Define humanistic therapy and contrast its two main approaches.
Rogers' client-centered therapy uses nondirective methods: The therapist shows unconditional positive regard, empathy, and genuineness. Perls' directive method of Gestalt Therapy provides exercises aimed at helping people integrate conflicting parts of their personality.

13.4

Define behavior therapy and identify various behavioral approaches to therapy. Behavior therapy relies on principles of learning to help clients develop adaptive behavior patterns and discontinue maladaptive ones. These include systematic desensitization, modeling, and aversive conditioning. Virtual therapy is a new method for desensitizing patients to fears. Operant conditioning methods include token economies, successive approximation, social skills training, and biofeedback training.

David Buffington/Digital Vision/Getty Images

13 Methods of Therapy

modeling a behavior-therapy technique in which a client observes and imitates a person who approaches and copes with feared objects or situations

token economy a controlled environment in which people are reinforced for desired behaviors with tokens (such as poker chips) that may be exchanged for privileges

successive approximations in operant conditioning, a series of behaviors that gradually become more similar to a target behavior

social skills training a behavior-therapy method for helping people in their interpersonal relations that uses self-monitoring, behavior rehearsal, and feedback

biofeedback training (BFT) the systematic feeding back to an organism of information about a bodily function so that the organism can gain control of that function

cognitive therapy a form of therapy that focuses on how clients' cognitions (e.g., expectations, attitudes, beliefs) lead to distress and may be modified to relieve distress and promote adaptive behavior

rational emotive behavior therapy (REBT) Albert Ellis's form of therapy that encourages clients to challenge and correct irrational expectations and maladaptive behaviors

cognitive-behavior therapy (CBT) an approach to therapy that uses cognitive and behavioral techniques that have been validated by research

13.8

rebound anxiety anxiety that can occur when one discontinues use of a tranquilizer

antidepressant acting to relieve depression

selective serotonin-reuptake inhibitors (SSRIs) antidepressant drugs that work by blocking the reuptake of serotonin by presynaptic neurons, thus increasing the amount of serotonin available to the brain

electroconvulsive therapy (ECT) treatment of disorders like major depression by passing an electric current (that causes a convulsion) through the head

psychosurgery surgery intended to promote psychological changes or to relieve disordered behavior

prefrontal lobotomy the severing or destruction of a section of the frontal lobe of the brain

13.5

Define cognitive therapy and describe Beck's approach and REBT. Cognitive therapy aims to give clients insight into irrational beliefs and cognitive distortions and replace them with rational beliefs and accurate perceptions. Beck notes that clients may develop depression because they minimize accomplishments and catastrophize failures. Ellis originated rational emotive behavior therapy (REBT), which holds that people's irrational beliefs about events shape their responses to them.

13.6

Identify various types of group therapy and discuss their advantages and disadvantages. Group therapy is more economical than individual therapy. Moreover, group members benefit from the social support and experiences of other members. However, some clients cannot disclose their problems to a group or risk group disapproval. Specialized methods include couple therapy and family therapy.

13.7

Explain whether psychotherapy works and who benefits from it. Statistical analyses such as meta-analysis show that people who obtained psychodynamic therapy showed greater well-being, on average, than 70% to 75% of those who did not obtain treatment. Similarly, nearly 75% of the clients who obtained client-centered therapy were better off than people who did not obtain treatment. Psychoanalytic and client-centered approaches are most helpful with highly verbal and motivated individuals. Behavioral and cognitive therapies have provided strategies for treating anxiety disorders, social skills deficits, and problems in self-control. People from various cultural backgrounds may profit from different kinds of treatment.

13.8

Describe methods of biological therapy, their benefits and side effects. Antipsychotic drugs help many people with schizophrenia by blocking the action of dopamine. Antidepressants help many people by increasing the action of serotonin. Lithium often helps people with bipolar disorder. The use of antianxiety drugs for daily tensions is controversial because people build tolerance and do not learn to solve their problems. ECT, another controversial treatment, induces a seizure and frequently relieves severe depression. The prefrontal lobotomy is a form of psychosurgery that attempts to alleviate agitation by severing nerve pathways in the brain but has been largely discontinued because of side effects.

PhotoLink/Photodisc/Getty Images

KEY TERMS

social psychology the field of psychology that studies the nature and causes of people's thoughts and behavior in social situations

14.1

attitude an enduring mental representation of a person, place, or thing that evokes an emotional response and related behavior

A–B problem the issue of how well we can predict behavior on the basis of attitudes

elaboration likelihood model the view that persuasive messages are evaluated (elaborated) on the basis of central and peripheral cues

fear appeal a type of persuasive communication that influences behavior on the basis of arousing fear instead of rational analysis of the issues

selective avoidance diverting one's attention from information that is inconsistent with one's attitudes

selective exposure deliberately seeking and attending to information that is consistent with one's attitudes

cognitive-dissonance theory the view that we are motivated to make our cognitions or beliefs consistent with each other and with our behavior

attitude-discrepant behavior behavior inconsistent with an attitude that may have the effect of modifying an attitude

effort justification in cognitive-dissonance theory, the tendency to seek justification (acceptable reasons) for strenuous efforts

14.2

prejudice an attitude toward a group that leads people to evaluate members of that group negatively

discrimination hostile behavior that results is directed against groups toward whom one is prejudiced

stereotyping erroneous assumptions that all members of a group share the same traits or characteristics

14.3

attraction in social psychology, an attitude of liking or disliking (negative attraction)

triangular model of love Sternberg's view that love involves combinations of three components: intimacy, passion, and commitment

intimacy close acquaintance and familiarity; a characteristic of a relationship in which partners share their inmost feelings

passion strong romantic and sexual feelings

commitment the decision to maintain a relationship

consummate love the ideal form of love within Sternberg's model, which combines passion, intimacy, and commitment

SUMMARY

Social psychology studies the nature and causes of behavior and mental processes in social situations.

14.1

Define attitude and discuss factors that shape it. Attitudes are comprised of cognitive evaluations, feelings, and behavioral tendencies. A number of factors influence the likelihood that we can predict behavior from attitudes: specificity, strength of attitudes, vested interest, and accessibility. Attitudes with a strong emotional impact are more accessible. People attempt to change other people's attitudes and behavior by means of persuasion. According to the elaboration likelihood model, persuasion occurs through central and peripheral routes. Repeated messages generally "sell" better than messages delivered once. People tend to respond more to fear appeals than the purely factual presentation. Persuasive communicators tend to show expertise, trustworthiness, attractiveness, or similarity to the audience.

14.2

Define prejudice and discrimination. *Prejudice* is an attitude toward a group that leads people to evaluate members of that group negatively—even though they have never met them. In behavioral terms, prejudice is connected with avoidance, aggression, and discrimination. *Discrimination* refers to behavior that results from prejudice. Prejudice involves *stereotyping*—that is, erroneous assumptions that all members of a group share the same traits or characteristics.

14.3

Discuss factors that contribute to interpersonal attraction and love. Attitudes of liking and loving can lead to important, lasting relationships. They are the flip side of the coin of prejudice—positive attitudes that are associated with interpersonal attraction rather than avoidance. Among the factors contributing to attraction are physical appearance, similarity, and reciprocity. The *attraction similarity hypothesis* holds that people tend to develop romantic relationships with people who are similar to themselves in physical attractiveness and other traits. There are a number of theories about romantic love. One theory is Robert Sternberg's triangular model of love (see figure below).

14 Social Psychology

romantic love an intense, positive emotion that involves sexual attraction, feelings of caring, and the belief that one is in love

14.4

social perception a subfield of social psychology that studies the ways in which we form and modify impressions of others

primacy effect the tendency to evaluate others in terms of first impressions

recency effect the tendency to evaluate others in terms of the most recent impression

attribution a belief concerning why people behave in a certain way

dispositional attribution an assumption that a person's behavior is determined by internal causes such as personal attitudes or goals

situational attribution an assumption that a person's behavior is determined by external circumstances such as the social pressure found in a situation

fundamental attribution error the assumption that others act predominantly on the basis of their dispositions, even when there is evidence suggesting the importance of their situations

actor–observer effect the tendency to attribute our own behavior to situational factors but to attribute the behavior of others to dispositional factors

self-serving bias the tendency to view one's successes as stemming from internal factors and one's failures as stemming from external factors

14.5

social influence the area of social psychology that studies the ways in which people influence the thoughts, feelings, and behavior of others

foot-in-the-door technique a method for including compliance in which a small request is followed by a larger request

14.6

social facilitation the process by which a person's performance is increased when other members of a group engage in similar behavior

evaluation apprehension concern that others are evaluating our behavior

diffusion of responsibility the spreading or sharing of responsibility for a decision or behavior within a group

social decision schemes rules for predicting the final outcome of group decision making on the basis of the members' initial positions

groupthink a process in which group members are influenced by cohesiveness and a dynamic leader to ignore external realities as they make decisions

deindividuation the process by which group members may discontinue self-evaluation and adopt group norms and attitudes

altruism unselfish concern for the welfare of others

bystander effect the tendency to avoid helping other people in emergencies when other people are also present and apparently capable of helping

14.4

Define social perception and describe factors that influence it. The primacy effect refers to the fact that we often judge people in terms of our first impressions. The recency effect appears to be based on the fact that recently learned information is easier to remember. The attribution process is the tendency to infer the motives and traits of others through observation of their behavior. In dispositional attributions, we attribute people's behavior to internal factors. In situational attributions, we attribute people's behavior to external forces. According to the actor–observer effect, we tend to attribute the behavior of others to internal, dispositional factors, but we tend to attribute our own behavior to external, situational factors. The fundamental attribution error is the tendency to attribute too much of other people's behavior to dispositional factors.

14.5

Explain why people obey authority figures and conform to social norms. Other people and groups can exert enormous pressure on us to behave according to their norms. In fact, classic experiments have demonstrated that people influence others to engage in destructive obedience or conform to social norms. For example, the majority of subjects in the Milgram studies complied with the demands of authority figures, even when the demands required that they hurt innocent people by means of electric shock. Factors contributing to obedience include socialization, lack of social comparison, perception of legitimate authority figures, the foot-in-the-door technique, inaccessibility of values, and buffers between perpetrator and victim. Asch's research in which subjects judged the lengths of lines suggests that most people will follow the crowd, even when the crowd is wrong. Personal factors such as desire to be liked by group members, low self-esteem, high self-consciousness, and shyness contribute to conformity. Group size also contributes.

14.6

Discuss factors that contribute to aggression. Numerous biological structures are involved in aggression. Chemistry is also involved in aggression, especially in the form of the male sex hormone testosterone. Cognitive psychologists assert that our behavior is influenced by our values, by how we interpret situations, and by choice. People who believe that aggression is sometimes necessary and justified—as during wartime— are likely to act aggressively. From the behavioral perspective, organisms that are reinforced for aggressive behavior are more likely to behave aggressively in situations similar to those in which reinforcement occurs.

14.7

Describe differences between the ways in which people behave as individuals and as members of a group. The concept of social facilitation refers to the effects on performance that result from the presence of other people. The presence of others may facilitate performance for reasons such as increased arousal and evaluation apprehension. Anonymous group members, however, may experience diffusion of responsibility and performance may fall off, as in social loafing. Social psychologists have identified several decision-making schemes, including the majority-wins scheme, the truth-wins scheme, the two-thirds majority scheme, and the first-shift rule. Group decisions tend to be more polarized and riskier than individual decisions, largely because groups diffuse responsibility. Group decisions may be highly productive when group members are knowledgeable, there is an explicit procedure for arriving at decisions, and there is a process of give and take.